Volume 1

BIOTERRORISM: THE HISTORY OF A CRISIS IN AMERICAN SOCIETY

BIOTERRORISM: THE HISTORY OF A CRISIS IN AMERICAN SOCIETY

Epidemics, Bioweapons, and Policy History

Edited by
DAVID McBRIDE

Routledge
Taylor & Francis Group
LONDON AND NEW YORK

First published in 2003 by Routledge

This edition first published in 2021
by Routledge
2 Park Square, Milton Park, Abingdon, Oxon OX14 4RN

and by Routledge
52 Vanderbilt Avenue, New York, NY 10017

Routledge is an imprint of the Taylor & Francis Group, an informa business

British Library Cataloguing in Publication Data
A catalogue record for this book is available from the British Library

ISBN: 978-0-367-64259-4 (Set)
ISBN: 978-1-00-312845-8 (Set) (ebk)
ISBN: 978-0-367-64231-0 (Volume 1) (hbk)
ISBN: 978-0-367-64246-4 (Volume 1) (pbk)
ISBN: 978-1-00-312364-4 (Volume 1) (ebk)

Publisher's Note
The publisher has gone to great lengths to ensure the quality of this reprint but points out that some imperfections in the original copies may be apparent.

Disclaimer
The publisher has made every effort to trace copyright holders and would welcome correspondence from those they have been unable to trace.

Bioterrorism
The History of a Crisis in American Society

Edited with introductions by

David McBride
Penn State University

A ROUTLEDGE SERIES

Contents of the Collection

Volume 1
Epidemics, Bioweapons, and Policy History

Volume 2
Public Health, Law Enforcement,
and Minority Issues

Bioterrorism

Volume 1

Epidemics, Bioweapons, and Policy History

Edited with introductions by

David McBride

Penn State University

ROUTLEDGE

New York/London

Published in 2003 by
Routledge
29 West 35th Street
New York, NY 10001
www.routledge-ny.com

Published in Great Britain by
Routledge
11 New Fetter Lane
London EC4P 4EE
www.routledge.co.uk

Routledge is an imprint of the Taylor & Francis Group.

Printed in the United States of America on acid-free paper.

10 9 8 7 6 5 4 3 2 1

Library of Congress Cataloging-in-Publication Data

Bioterrorism: history of a crisis in American society / edited with introductions by David McBride

p. cm.

Contents: v. 1. History, documents, analysis — v. 2. Public health, public policy, and social perspectives.

ISBN 0-415-94277-2 (set)

1. Bioterrorism—United States. 2. Bioterrorism—United States—Prevention—History. 3. Biological warfare. 4. Biological weapons. 5. Public health—United States. 6. Emergency management—United States. I. McBride, David.

HV6432 .B56 2002

363.3'2—dc21 2002031833

ISBN 0-415-94278-0 (v. 1: alk. paper)

ISBN 0-415-94279-9 (v. 2: alk. paper)

Summary of Contents

Volume One—Epidemics, Bioweapons, and Policy History

Part A. Epidemics and Early Biological Warfare
Part B. National Defense, Bioweapons, and International Agreements: World War One through The Cold War
Part C. A New National Threat
Part D. Anti-Bioterrorism Laws and Policy
D. 1 Domestic Issues
D. 2 Protecting the Public and Legal Order
D. 3 International Issues

Volume Two—Public Health, Law Enforcement, and Minority Issues

Part A. Responding to Bioterrorism Attacks
A. 1. Public Health and Medical Preparedness
A. 2. Federal Agencies and the CDC
A. 3. State and Municipal Responses
Part B. Courts, Constitutional Guarantees, and the Accused
Part C. Civic and Community Responses
Part D. Critical Perspectives on Bioterrorism and the Future

Contents

xi Volume Introduction

PART A. EPIDEMICS AND EARLY BIOLOGICAL WARFARE

2 Smallpox and the Indians in the American Colonies
John Duffy

20 Biological Warfare: A Historical Perspective
George W. Christopher, Theodore J. Cieslak, Julie A. Pavlin and Edward M. Eitzen Jr.

27 Preemptive Biopreparedness: Can We Learn Anything from History?
Elizabeth Fee and Theodore M. Brown

33 Implications of Pandemic Influenza for Bioterrorism Response
Monica Schoch-Spana

PART B. NATIONAL DEFENSE, BIOWEAPONS, AND INTERNATIONAL AGREEMENTS: WORLD WAR ONE THROUGH THE COLD WAR

39 United States Use of Biological Warfare
William H. Neinast

54 The Birth of the U. S. Biological-Warfare Program
Barton J. Bernstein

61 Medicine in Defense Against Biological Warfare
David L. Huxsoll, Cheryl D. Parrot and William C. Patrick III

64 Gene Wars
Jonathan B. Tucker

75 The Second Review Conference of the Biological Weapons Convention: One Step Forward, Many More to Go
Eric J. McFadden

PART C. A NEW NATIONAL THREAT

100 The Specter of Biological Weapons
Leonard A. Cole

107 Confronting a Biological Armageddon: Experts Tackle Prospect of Bioterrorism
Joan Stephenson

110 Bioterrorism in our Midst?

111 Chemical/Biological Terrorism: Coping with a New Threat
Jonathan B. Tucker

128 Stalking the Next Epidemic: ProMED Tracks Emerging Diseases
Jack Woodall

133 Anthrax as a Potential Biological Warfare Agent
James C. Pile, John D. Malone, Edward M. Eitzen and Arthur M. Friedlander

139 Bioterrorism
Peter Pringle

144 Bioterrorism: Thinking the Unthinkable
Richard Wise

PART D. ANTI-BIOTERRORISM LAWS AND POLICY

D. 1 Domestic Issues

145 The Biological Weapons Anti-Terrorism Act of 1989

148 Statement on Signing the Biological Weapons Anti-Terrorism Act of 1989
George H. W. Bush

149 Terrorism: The Problem and the Solution—The Comprehensive Prevention Act of 1995
Melissa A. O'Loughlin

167 Provisions of the Anti-Terrorism Bill
Elizabeth A. Palmer and Keith Perine

171 Biological Weapons and U.S. Law
James R. Ferguson

175 Biological Terrorism: Legal Measures for Preventing Catastrophe
Barry Kellman

209 The Defense Threat Reduction Agency: A Note on the United States' Approach to the Threat of Chemical and Biological Warfare
Matthew Linkie

243 Bioterrorism: Perfectly Legal
Heather E. Dagen

283 A Precarious 'Hot Zone:' The President's Plan to Control Bioterrorism
Victoria V. Sutton

303 Summary of *U.S.A. Patriot Act*

307 U.S.A. Patriot Act Boosts Government Powers While Cutting Back on Traditional Checks and Balances

D. 2 Protecting the Public and Legal Order

311 U. S. Preparations for Biological Terrorism: Legal Limitations and the Need for Planning
Juliette N. Kayyem

338 The Malevolent Use of Microbes and the Rule of Law: Legal Challenges Presented by Bioterrorism
David P. Fidler

D. 3 International Issues

343 Clear and Present Danger: Enforcing the International Ban on Biological and Chemical Weapons Through Sanctions, Use of Force, and Criminalization
Michael P. Scharf

389 The Regime to Prevent Biological Weapons: Opportunities for a Safer, Healthier, More Prosperous World
Graham S. Pearson

405 Bioterrorism, Public Health, and International Law
David P. Fidler

425 Acknowledgments

Volume Introduction

The purpose of these volumes is to provide a collection of sources that trace the growing issue of bioterrorism in American society. These political, legal, and public-health materials offer the reader a wide body of facts and perspectives relating to the tortuous path the United State has been treading to confront the national and international threat of bioterrorism. Compared to other forms of terrorism, bioterrorism has been a little-studied subject. By contrast, political terrorism involving conventional weapons has been widely explored throughout Western scholarship and international law.

Throughout the twentieth century, following each major war or pogrom, leading scholars and legalists wrestled with the description of political terrorism. They asked: How is political terrorism different from other forms of political and social violence? What makes terror for political purposes an especially pernicious action in all societies throughout the world? What are the political and judicial means for preventing and curtailing terrorism?

According Hannah Arendt, one of the greatest political thinkers of the twentieth century, terrorism was the process that defined totalitarian systems. In her analysis of the rise of modern society, the Nazi concentration camps and Stalin's labor prisons epitomized political terror. For Arendt, terror and totalitarianism together comprised the "radical evil" that scorched through the undemocratic societies of the modern age.[1]

Jean-Paul Sartre widened the description of political terror; to him, it was integral to more than just totalitarian states and institutions. He viewed political terror as inherent in nations generally. According to his political analysis, various forms of terror rest precariously in the hands of all modern nation-states. It is the means by which the modern state wields its absolute authority and sovereignty—deterring incessant violent conflicts between the individuals and groups that make up a society, as well as conflicts between nations. Thus, for Sartre the sad reality for modern society is that political terror is the "violence that negates violence."[2] No wonder, as Maurice Cranston has shown, Sartre has a character in his play *Huis-clos* remark, "Hell is other people."[3]

Unlike political terrorism, biological terrorism (or bioterrorism for short) has elicited relatively little sustained historical, theoretical, or philosophical analysis in the social sciences. Moreover, relatively small coverage of this issue has emerged directly from the U. S. federal courts. Instead, the public-health and legal ideas regarding defining and responding to bioterrorism have been developing practically—bit by bit inside institutions and, more recently, by federal legislation. This collection provides key studies and essays that illuminate this gradual construction of the bioterrorism problem. It reveals the wide range of debates and initiatives that institutions have generated to grind forward and meet the challenge of bioterrorism. These institutions include government, military defense agencies, health-care and legal organizations, and community groups. Learning about these divergent initiatives is vital for developing broader scholarly and legal perspectives on this critical issue in the future.

One of the most important traditional functions of American government is to guard and preserve the public's health. Indeed, throughout its history, the nation's public-health and political institutions have wrestled with biological dangers to public safety. These biological crises have occurred in a variety of shapes—from epidemics to toxic chemical accidents and pollution. However, bioterrorism is a unique form of public-health danger—one that involves disease agents intentionally introduced to a locale for terrorist purposes by malevolent individuals, groups, or foreign militaries. Using poisoned weapons against one's enemy is a tactic of war that extends back to ancient history,[4] but using knowledge and techniques of the biological sciences to make weapons capable of killing civilians on a massive scale is largely a twentieth-century phenomenon.

Terrorist events create intense disorder for society's government agencies and civic institutions. The psychological fear they trigger in individuals and communities not caught in the actual attack can also be harrowing. This disorder and fear is magnified manyfold throughout the tens of thousands of communities that make up our society by the speed and vividness with which national media transmit the gruesome factuality of these events. As historian Walter Laqueur has stated, bioterrorism is part of our new age of "postmodern terrorism." Terrorists no longer target military or political officials, but innocent individuals and communities. They use or plot to use "the weapons of mass destruction [that] include biological and chemical agents and man-made chemical compounds that attack the nervous system, skin, or blood."[5]

This compilation includes sources from both political and legal institutions, on the one hand, and public-health and medical institutions on the other. Although they derive largely from specialized journals and institutions, these materials reflect in common the growing sense of urgency gripping institutions as a result of recent terrorist events. These incidents include the Oklahoma City bombing in 1995, the Aum Shinrikyo cult bioterror attack in Tokyo, the World Trade Center attack in 1993, the

World Trade Center and Pentagon attacks of September 11, 2001, and the anthrax mailings that followed. Materials in these volumes allow us to place shifts in current institutions and policy discourse in broader historical context. This history includes subjects such as national defense programs to deter biological weapons, civil rights and liberties doctrines, and international initiatives to prohibit biological and chemical weapons.

Terrorist violence tests the political, legal, and social foundations of any society in which it strikes. The materials in this collection show that bioterrorism can be even more disconcerting to government, law enforcement, and health authorities. Infectious diseases disseminated by terrorists can lie dormant for long periods of time. Thus, the occurrence of a bioterrorism attack is not always immediately known. Sophisticated epidemiological, medical, and laboratory expertise is necessary to assess the extent of contamination of a population, or to establish that a bioterrorism attack has occurred in the first place. The pressures on a locale's emergency services and medical institutions could easily exceed those required for accidents or attacks involving explosives or chemical releases.[6] For these reasons, compared to terrorism involving firearms and explosives, bioterrorism has proven to be a more insidious form of violence for legal and public health institutions to constrain.

The items in this compilation are arranged to cover the history of bioterrorism and American society (Volume One), and specific policy and practical responses to the current bioterrorism crisis (Volume Two). Volume One traces the emergence of the bioterrorism issue in the United States through four stages. The first stage (covered in Part A) involved the social and political impact of epidemics in the early history of the North American colonies and United States. The second stage (Part B) centered on the development of military biological warfare during and following the two world wars. After World War II, the United States took a leading role conducting military research on biological and chemical weapons.[7] This initiative was part of the country's overall military defense strategy for the Cold War. The goal was to develop means to counter the extensive biochemical weaponry and research programs of the Soviet Union. International agreements were made as increasing numbers of nations around the world attempted to prohibit the spread and use of biological and chemical weapons.

The third stage in the emergence of the bioterrorism issue involved the emergence of a growing public awareness of the potential for biological-weapon attacks occurring inside the United States. This public awareness was fueled by the rise of a "bioweapons" arms race during the 1970s and 1980s (Part C). The intense distrust between the superpower nations led some to explore using advances in biotechnology and genetics for their biological warfare arsenals. By 1990, a leading authority on biological warfare wrote, "[t]he legal prohibitions of chemical and biological warefare seems today considerably less solid than it did in the 1970s."[8] The fourth phase in the evolution of the current bioterrorism crisis dealt with the implementation of laws and policy to curtail the threat, apprehend bioterrorists, and strengthen international agreements banning biological weapons (Part D).

Volume Two shifts away from the broad historical and policy aspects of the bioterrorism issue to specific governmental, institutional, and intellectual responses to this problem. Materials cover the approaches of federal, state, and local public-health agencies and medical institutions for preparing for and minimizing a bioterrorism attack (Part A). Issues involving the arrest, detention, and prosecution and/or deportation of suspected terrorists and groups are covered (Part B). Most of these items deal with constitutional questions that have surfaced in legislation and the courts involving terrorism in general, as well as in the implementation of laws prohibiting chemical weapons. Although these items do not address bioterrorism directly, they are instructive of what types of issues might arise if and when suspected bioterrorists are apprehended in future scenarios. As government agencies and legal institutions increased their anti-terrorism measures, new concerns emerged regarding the discriminatory effects of these policies on disadvantaged communities. (Part C) Finally, a set of essays giving the views of leading intellectuals on the future of terrorism and the bioterrorism threat to American society are covered (Part D).

The items in these volumes show that legal measures to apprehend and incarcerate those planning to commit bioterrorism have been growing in quantity and complexity. This collection also makes clear that legal and public-health advocates have been concerned that state institutions preserve traditional constitutional and civil rights' standards and practices when dealing with those suspected of terrorist activities. This is especially true with law enforcement involving surveillance and detention of members of socially disadvantaged segments, or with non-citizens lacking access to counsel and other resources necessary for their fair legal defense. Also, rights advocates in medical fields have raised concerns that the civil liberties of medical personnel and the public not be trammeled by quarantine measures enacted by public authorities during a bioterrorism incident.

Overall, these volumes are intended to provide a factual reference base for general readers and specialists alike wishing to learn more about the historical roots and institutional responses to bioterrorism. We acknowledge and commend the work of the scores of authors who wrote the materials herein, as well as the hundreds of editors of the individual publications in which these materials originally appeared. Also, we thank the organizations and publishers who granted permission to use their materials. Communities, professionals, and civic activists can now gain broader knowledge about bioterrorism from such materials; without these materials, it would be all the more difficult for them to change their institutions to prevent the bioterrorism danger from continually unfolding.

Notes

1. D. R. Villa, *Politics, Philosophy, Terror: Essays on the Thought of Hannah Arendt* (Princeton: Princeton University Press, 1999).
2. Maurice Cranston, "Jean-Paul Sartre: Solitary Man in a Hostile Universe," in *Contemporary Political Philosophers*, ed. A. de Crespigny and K. Minogue (New York: Dodd, Mead & Co., 1975), 221.
3. Sartre's play *Huis-clos* as quoted in Cranston, "Jean-Paul Sartre," 221–222. The exact quote is: "l'Enfer, c'est les autres."
4. R. M. Price, *The Chemical Weapons Taboo* (Ithaca, N. Y.: Cornell University Press, 1997), 22–21.
5. Walter Laqueur, "Postmodern Terrorism," *Foreign Affairs* 75 (September/October, 1996), 28.
6. J. D. Simon, *The Terrorist Trap: America's Experience with Terrorism* (Bloomington: Indiana University Press, 1994), 358–360.
7. For a groundbreaking, interdisciplinary study of this development, see Susan Wright, ed., *Preventing a Biological Arms Race* (Cambridge, Mass.: MIT Press, 1990).
8. Wright, *Preventing a Biological Arms Race*, 3.

Additional Sources

Alexander, Yonah and Milton Hoenig. *Super Terrorism: Biological, Chemical, and Nuclear.* Ardsley, NY: Transnational, 2001.

Crenshaw, Martha, ed. *Terrorism in Context.* University Park: Pennsylvania State University Press, 1995.

Derskowitz, A. M. *Shouting Fire: Civil Liberties in a Turbulent Age.* Boston: Little, Brown, 2002.

Dowling, H. F. *Fighting Infection: Conquests of the Twentieth Century.* Cambridge: Commonwealth Fund/Harvard University Press, 1978.

Drell, S. D., Sofaer, A. D., and G. D. Wilson, eds. *The New Terror: Facing the Threat of Biological and Chemical Weapons.* Stanford, Calif.: Hoover Institution Press/Stanford University, 1999.

Endicott, S. and E Hagerman. *The United States and Biological Warfare: Secrets from the Early Cold War and Korea.* Bloomington: Indiana University Press, 1998.

Garrett, L. *The Coming Plague: Newly Emerging Diseases in a World Out of Balance.* New York: Penguin, 1994.

Han, H. H., ed. *Terrorism & Political Violence: Limits & Possibilities of Legal Control.* New York: Oceana, 1993.

Heymann, P. B. *Terrorism and America: A Commonsense Strategy for a Democratic Society* Cambridge: MIT Press, 1998.

Mangold, T. and J. Goldberg. *Plague Wars: A True Story of Biological Warfare.* New York: St. Martin's Press, 1999.

McBride, D. *From TB to AIDS: Epidemics among Urban Blacks Since 1900.* Albany: SUNY Press, 1991.

McNeill, W. H. *Plagues and People.* Garden City, N. Y.: Anchor Press, 1971.

Mullins, W. C. *A Sourcebook on Domestic and International Terrorism: An Analysis of Issues, Organizations, Tactics and Responses.* 2nd ed. Springfield, Il.: Charles C. Thomas, 1997.

Osterholm, M. T. and J. Scwartz. *Living Terrors: What America Needs to Know to Survive the Coming Bio-terrorist Catastrophe.* New York: Delacorte Press, 2000.

Piller, C., and K. R. Yamamoto. *Gene Wars: Military Control Over the New Genetic Technologies.* New York: Beech Tree/William Morrow, 1988.

Price, R. M. *The Chemical Weapons Taboo.* Ithaca, N. Y.: Cornell University Press, 1997.

Regis, E. *The Biology of Doom: The History of America's Secret Germ Warfare Project.* New York: Henry Holt Co., 1999.

Schulhofer, S. J. *Combating Terrorism: Intelligence Gathering, Law Enforcement, and Civil Liberties in the Wake of September 11.* New York: Century Foundation Press, 2002.

Siegrist, D. W. and M. Graham. *Countering Bioterrorism in the United States: An Understanding of Issues and Strategies.* Dobbs Ferry, N. Y.: Oceana, 1999.

Simon, J. D. *The Terrorist Trap: America's Experience with Terrorism.* Bloomington: Indiana University Press, 1994.

Sims, N. A. *The Evolution of Biological Disarmament.* Stockholm International Peace Research Institute; Oxford: Oxford University Press, 2001.

Tucker, J. B. *Toxic Terrors: Terrorist Use of Chemical and Biological Weapons.* Cambridge: MIT Press, 2000.

Wright, Susan, ed. *Preventing a Biological Arms Race.* Cambridge: MIT Press, 1990.

Introduction to the 2020 Edition

Bioterrorism: The History of a Crisis in American Society (Volumes 1 and 2) contains a wide range of studies, documents, and reports by science leaders, legal professionals, scholars, and public health experts. These materials cover the historical growth of bioterrorism as a major issue in American society. In these volumes, bioterrorism means the intentional infliction of harm to humans and their living environments by terrorists or state actors using destructive biological materials and techniques. Specifically, these volumes cover bioterrorism emerging as an urgent concern within the nation's political, security, public health, and civil institutions.

Prior to, 1990 America's preoccupation with bioterrorism developed in three phases, all connected with the bioweapon threats associated with international political conflict. First, during World War I, U.S. political and military leaders observed firsthand the horrific effects of chemical warfare. As a result, America assisted in developing international treaties and policies to restrict the making and use of biological weapons. Second, the nation began its own biological weapon research during World War II. During the second half of the twentieth century, U.S. political, military and public health authorities broadened their participation in international anti-bioterror policies. However, the nation also increased its scientific and public health research on defense against biological weapons.

As the United States moved through the Gulf War of 1991, the 9/11 terror attacks, and the anthrax-letter mailing incident of 2001, bioterrorism moved to the top of America's domestic security agenda. Furthermore, in the wake of the AIDS epidemic, global flu outbreaks, and the SARS outbreaks, epidemics of infectious diseases also rose high among the national security and public health concerns in the U.S. and, indeed, the world. The materials in these volumes show that as these specific incidents and public health threats occurred, U.S. security, scientific, and civil agencies sought to upgrade military, public health, and civilian ways to detect and counter bioterrorism. Also, these ever-shifting anti-bioterror measures sometimes resulted in harmful impacts on the constitutional liberties and health conditions for the nation's minority groups – the subject addressed especially in Volume 2.

Since the original appearance of these volumes, national security and public health specialists have been assessing new emergent threats of bioterrorism on the American horizon. Noted security studies expert G. D. Koblentz points out that over recent decades the use of biological materials by terrorist groups has actually been few in number. However, he emphasizes that policymakers and the lay public must recognize that the future threat from bioterrorism remains serious. Several trends are behind this growing possibility. First, the expansion of globalization is increasing the spread of information, expertise, and physical materials that could be utilized by terrorists to devise and deploy a biological weapon. Secondly, the increased knowledge base in the life sciences is enabling more persons with little specialized expertise to master shortcuts to utilize biological materials for destructive purposes. Finally, Koblentz suggests a current terrorist using hazardous biological materials likely will be a state actor such as a dictator. Thus, the scale of destruction that a biological terrorist could unleash will be much larger than that of the individual bioterrorist of the pre-2003 period.

Other future bioterrorism challenges have been identified by the arms control expert Jonathan Tucker. These bioterrorism threats stem from what he terms the "dual-use dilemma." Cutting edge technologies such as nanotechnology and neuropharmacology are producing new products and procedures that can improve human health. But these specialties also pose the risk of being intentionally misused to produce dangerous viral agents. Tucker emphasizes authorities in government, science, and medicine need new "decision frameworks" to anticipate and control this risk.

The final area of new concerns with biological harm caused by human or nature-driven bio-crises pertains to biological pathogens that develop into epidemics or global pandemics. Whether they are deliberately engineered or the result of human error, large-scale infectious disease outbreaks can crush a nation's public health infrastructure and, in turn, threaten national security and economic order. Investigators such as Andrew Price-Smith and Laurie Garrett have highlighted in their works the destabilizing effects of epidemic diseases like HIV/AIDS, influenza, SARS, and coronaviruses.

As the opening studies in Volume 2 will clearly illustrate, scientific, public health, and security specialists began emphasizing the seriousness of the bioterrorism threat in 2000 .They all implored the national public health sector be fundamentally redesigned and then expanded. In the last two decades, these professionals and civil leaders along with their public constituencies have set about building new anti-bioterror policies, technologies, and resources interconnecting government, public health, and research science—a so-called biodefense. (See studies listed on the Additional Readings.) However, the current response by U.S. health, civil, and military authorities to the COVID-19 pandemic has proven these efforts fundamentally incomplete. As much as the nation attempted to build an effective biodefense against epidemic disease or biological weapon scenarios, gapping weaknesses nonetheless were and remain evident throughout both the national and global public health infrastructures. Throughout modern history, nations have fought to curtail deadly pathogens—viruses, bacteria, and toxins—and now must include genetically engineered viruses and other superbugs on this list biological dangers. It will take every layer of a new 21st-century biodefense, framed on genuine domestic and international partnerships, to meet the coming challenges of bioterrorism.

David McBride
July 2020

ADDITIONAL READINGS

Beamish, T. D. *Community at Risk: Biodefense and the Collective Search for Security.* Stanford, Calif.: Stanford University Press, 2015.

Clunan, A. L., P. R. Lavoy, and S B. Martin. *Terrorism, War, or Disease? Unraveling the Use of Biological Weapons.* Stanford, Calif.: Stanford University Press, 2008.

Garrett, Laurie. *Betrayal of Trust: The Collapse of Global Public Health.* New York: Hyperion, 2003.

Guillemin, Jeanne. *Biological Weapons: From the Invention of State-Sponsored Programs to Contemporary Bioterrorism.* New York: Columbia University Press, 2005.

Koblentz, G. D. *Living Weapons: Biological Warfare and International Security.* Ithaca, N.Y.: Cornell University Press, 2009.

Osterholm, Michael T. and Mark Olshaker. *Deadliest Enemy: Our War Against Killer Germs.* New York: Hatchett Books, 2020 edition.

Ouagrham-Gormely, Sonia Ben. *Barriers to Bioweapons: The Challenges of Expertise and Organization for Weapons Development.* Ithaca, N. Y.: Cornell University Press, 2014. Price-Smith, Andrew T. *The Health of Nations: Infectious Disease, Environmental Change, and Their Effects on National Security and Development.* Cambridge: MIT Press, 2002.

Price-Smith, A. T. *Contagion and Chaos: Disease, Ecology, and National Security in the Era of Globalization.* Cambridge, MA: MIT Press, 2009.

Smith, Frank. *American Biodefense: How Dangerous Ideas about Biological Weapons Shape National Security.* Ithaca, NY: Cornell University Press, 2014.

Smith III, Frank L. "A Casualty of Kinetic Warfare: Military Research, Development, and Acquisition for Biodefense," *Security Studies* 20, n. 4 (2011): 663– 96.

Trust for America's Health. *Ready or Not: Protecting the Public's Health from Diseases, Disasters, and Bioterrorism—Reports for 2017* and *2020.* N.pl.: Trust for America's Health, access online at: https://www.tfah.org/reports/.

Tucker, J. B., (ed.) *Innovation, Dual Use, and Security: Managing the Risks of Emerging Biological and Chemical Technologies.* Cambridge: MIT Press, 2012.

Tucker, J. B. *Scourge: The Once and Future Threat of Smallpox.* New York: Atlantic Monthly Press, 2001.

Tucker, J. B. *War of Nerves: Chemical Warfare from World War I to Al Qaeda*. New York: Anchor Books, 2007.

Wheelis, Mark, Rozsa, Lajos and Malcolm Dando, eds. *Deadly Cultures: Biological Weapons Since 1945*. Cambridge: Harvard University Press, 2006.

Zubay, Geoffrey. *Agents of Bioterrorism: Pathogens & Their Weaponization*. New York: Columbia University Press, 2005.

Bioterrorism

Volume 1

Epidemics, Bioweapons, and Policy History

SMALLPOX AND THE INDIANS IN THE AMERICAN COLONIES

JOHN DUFFY

Romanticized versions of the conquest of North America—for conquest it was—emphasize the heroic battles and perennial warfare of the frontier. The picture of pioneers in their log cabins warding off Indian attacks, or of small garrisons grimly defending themselves from hordes of savages is a familiar one to all Americans. And certainly such scenes were characteristic of the frontier. Yet the extirpation of the Indians was far more the result of the white man's diseases than his weapons. Once the Europeans gained a foothold, their advance guards of disease bore the brunt of the attack and carried death and devastation on an unprecedented scale far into the Indian territory. Historians of the Indian frontier have long been aware that smallpox and other contagions played a significant role in white-Indian relations in North America, but other than noting the fact, little has been written about it.[1]

Prior to the advent of the whites, North America was little troubled with contagious infections. In contrast to the many complaints of sickness and death which characterized the later seventeenth and eighteenth centuries, early explorers and traders universally commented on the salubrity of the climate and the good health of the Indians. For example, Captain Bartholomew Gosnold, who explored the New England coast in 1602 and named Martha's Vineyard, found "the people of a perfect constitution of body, active, strong healthful, and very witty. . . . For ourselves, we found ourselves rather increased in health and strength than otherwise; for all our toyle, bad dyet and lodging; yet no one of us was touched with any sickness."[2] The absence of diseases was also noticed by the early settlers in New England, one of whom wrote in 1633: "Heare I find three great blessings, peace, plenty and health in a Comfortable measure the place well agreeth with our English bodies that they were never so healthy in their native Contrey generally all heare, as never could

[1] William C. Macleod in his *American Indian Frontier* (New York, 1928) briefly mentions smallpox, but devotes much of his attention to venereal disorders. P. M. Ashburn, *The Ranks of Death* (New York, 1947), a first-rate work, deals only cursorily with smallpox. The best short general study of the subject is *The Effect of Smallpox on the Destiny of the Amerindian* (Boston, 1945) by E. W. and Allen E. Stearn which surveys the period from 1492 to the end of the nineteenth century.

[2] P. M. Ashburn, *The Ranks of Death* (New York, 1947), p. 16.

be rid of the head ach, tooth ach, Cough and the like are now better and freer (?) heare and those that were weake are now well long since and I can heare of but two weake in all the plantation Gods name be praised." [3] Little doubt exists that the Indians were relatively free from most of the contagions prevalent in Europe. Smallpox and measles, for example, were certainly absent, and in all likelihood, malaria, yellow fever, typhoid, typhus, and the venereal diseases were among those introduced from the Old World. These infections exacted a heavy toll even among Europeans who had acquired some tolerance to them, but their impact upon the Indians was a major tragedy.

Lest the foregoing present too cheerful a view of health conditions among the early settlers, it must be remembered that in the seventeenth and eighteenth centuries life was short, and sickness and death were omnipresent. Major epidemics swept through Europe with fearful regularity, and endemic disorders steadily winnowed the population. Removal to the New World brought no relief, for contagious sicknesses migrated with the first settlers. And as the wealth and resources of America offered unlimited opportunity for the whites, so their infections found a virgin field in the native population. By way of retribution, the disorders, after ravaging the Indian tribes, occasionally returned with renewed virulence to plague the settlers. However, this danger was relatively minor in relation to the other problems besetting those emigrating to the New World. In the first place, the passage to the colonies, which was made in small overcrowded vessels, ordinarily took from eight to fourteen weeks. Food, on the long voyage, was both scant and dietetically unsound, and sanitation was either neglected or rudimentary. On arrival in the colonies, at least during the first years of colonization, the settlers found a continuation of poor food and inadequate housing. It was small wonder that sickness and disease were a more serious threat to the colonists than the Indians. However, epidemic sicknesses were a familiar evil to Europeans, who looked upon them as the inexplicable instruments of a Divine Providence, whereas for the Indians, they were a new and terrifying experience.

The Spaniards in the sixteenth century were the first to benefit from the services of contagious infections which they, unwittingly, turned loose upon the Indian tribes. Their chroniclers were amazed and, in the case of the Jesuits, shocked at the tremendous casualties which these epidemic diseases inflicted upon the Indians. Certainly such an attitude was justi-

[3] Master Wells to Family, New England, 1633, Sloane MSS (Library of Congress Transcript), vol. 922, no. 90.

fied since the estimates of smallpox deaths alone in Spanish-America during the colonial period run into the millions. Meanwhile other disorders, too, were exacting a heavy tribute. The courage and determination of the small bands of Spaniards who pushed on into vast, unknown, and populous lands cannot be gainsaid, but the glorious victories attributed to Spanish arms would not have been possible without the devastation wrought by Spanish diseases. Spanish arms performed a notable feat; but it was their most potent weapon, sickness, which made the Spanish-American Empire, and later, as an ally of the English and French, was to subdue the Indians in North America.

In contrast to the Spanish missionaries, who worried over the fact that conversion to Christianity so often proved a death warrant to the natives, and that sickness and death were too frequently the result of missionary endeavors, the English in North America during the seventeenth century openly rejoiced when the Lord sent his " Avenging Angels " to destroy the heathen. The American frontier conception that the only good Indian was a dead one characterized relations between the whites and Indians in British North America from the beginning of colonial times. Increase Mather records that when the colonists prayed the Lord to destroy the Indians, an answer was prompt in forthcoming, " For it is known that the Indians were distressed with famine, multitudes of them perishing for want of bread; and the Lord sent Sicknesses amongst them, that Travellers have seen many dead Indians up and down in the woods that were by famine and sickness brought unto that untimely end. Yea the Indians themselves have testified, that more amongst them have been cut off by the sword of the Lord in these respects than by the sword of the English."[4] A missionary to New York wrote home in 1705, ". . . the English here are a very thriving growing people, and ye Indians quite otherwise, they wast away & have done ever since our first arrival amongst them (as they themselves say) like Snow agt. ye Sun, So that very probably forty years hence there will scarce be an Indian seen in our America, God's Providence in this matter seems very wonderful, & no cause of their Decrease visible unless their drinking Rum, with some new Distempers we have brought amongst them."[5]

[4] Increase Mather, "An Historical Discourse Concerning the Prevalency of Prayer," in *A Relation of the Troubles Which Have Happened in New-England by Reason of the Indians there, from the Year 1614 to the Year 1675, etc.* (Boston, John Foster, 1677), p. 6.

[5] Mr. Moor to the Secretary, New York, November 13, 1705, in the Society for the Propagation of the Gospel in Foreign Parts MSS (Library of Congress Photo.), London Letters, A 2, fpp. 272-78 (hereinafter cited as S. P. G.).

Of the many contagious sicknesses which the Europeans brought to plague the Indians, smallpox was far the most deadly. Although the disease is now largely a thing of the past in the more advanced countries, it was one of the leading causes of death in seventeenth and eighteenth century Europe. For example, the London Bills of Mortality from 1731 to 1765 attribute nine per cent of all fatalities to this infection.[6] In the American colonies, too, smallpox was a major threat, but here it more than compensated for any damages inflicted upon the settlers by its ravages among the Indians. A loathsome and exceedingly fatal sickness, smallpox found in the vulnerable Red Men a fertile field for conquest. Unable to comprehend the nature of this unseen foe, the Indians first died in droves huddled in their camps. Later, when bitter experience had made them wiser, they fled in terror at its approach. The infection menaced both whites and Indians throughout the colonial period; it played a part in all colonial wars, fighting sometimes for the French, sometimes for the British, but in all cases warring against the Indians.

The Pilgrims, who first settled New England, entered that region in the wake of a major epidemic which, some three years earlier, had devastated the New England tribes to such an extent that they were unable to make even a token resistance to white occupation. The disorder which smoothed the path for these settlers was undoubtedly of European origin, but its exact nature is still in dispute among medical historians. Smallpox or bubonic plague are the two most likely suspects, but the evidence is inconclusive.[7] No doubt exists, however, about the smallpox outbreak which occurred in New England in 1633. Increase Mather explains that "the Indians began to be quarrelsome touching the Bounds of the Land which they had sold to the English, but God ended the Controversy by sending the Smallpox amongst the Indians of Saugust who were before that time exceeding numerous. Whole Towns of them were swept away, in some not so much as one soul escaping the Destruction." [8] Another colonial writer declares: "This contagious Disease was so noisome & terrible to these naked Indians, that they in many Places, left their Dead

[6] *Gentlemen's Magazine*, 1731-1765, volumes 1 to 35. See also John Duffy, *A History of Epidemics in the American Colonies*, doctoral dissertation, University of California at Los Angeles.

[7] The best study of this outbreak is Herbert U. Williams, "Epidemic among Indians, 1616-1620," *Johns Hopkins Hospital Bulletin*, XX, no. 224 (1909), pp. 340-49. Williams believes the infection was bubonic plague, but there is no agreement among the medical historians.

[8] Increase Mather, *A Relation of the Troubles*, etc., p. 23.

unburied, as appeared by the multitude of the bones up & down the countries where had been the greatest Numbers of them." [9]

By 1634 the infection had spread to the Narragansetts and the Connecticuts with similarly disastrous results. William Bradford asserts that in this year the Indians near the Connecticut River " fell sick of the small poxe, and dyed most miserably; for a sorer disease cannot befall them; they fear it worse than the plague; for usually they that have this disease have them in abundance . . . they dye like rotten sheep. . . . But by the marvelous goodness and providens of God not one of the English was so much as sicke, or in the least measure tainted with this disease." [10] In all likelihood previous exposure had made the English immune to the sickness, but to contemporary observers it seemed a miraculous preservation.

It is more than a coincidence that the Jesuits in Canada reported outbreaks of smallpox among the Indians in the same year that the infection was plaguing the tribes in the Connecticut valley. The river provided one of the easier routes to the St. Lawrence and the series of epidemics which flared up in the Great Lakes and St. Lawrence region from 1634 to 1641 were undoubtedly a continuation of the New England epidemic. The Montagnais around the St. Lawrence were infected in 1634, and the disorder soon was passed on to the other tribes.[11]

The Hurons, who lived north of Lake Ontario, were particularly hard hit in 1636 as indicated by the following graphic description:

> Terror was universal. The contagion increased as autumn advanced; and when winter came, far from ceasing as the priests had hoped, its ravages were appalling. The season of the Huron festivity was turned to a season of mourning; and such was the despondency and dismay, that suicides became frequent. The Jesuits singly or in pairs, journeyed in the depth of winter from village to village, ministering to the sick, and seeking to commend their religious teaching by their efforts to relieve bodily distress. . . . No house was left unvisited. As the missionary, physician at once to body and soul, entered one of these smoky dens, he saw the inmates, their heads muffled in their robes of skins, seated around the fires in silent dejection. Everywhere was heard the wail of the sick and dying children; and on or under the platforms at the sides of the house crouched squalid men and women, in all stages of the distemper.[12]

[9] *Notebook*, Ebenezer Hazard MSS, Library of Congress.

[10] J. Franklin Jameson, ed., *Bradford's History of Plymouth Plantation, 1606-1646, Original Narratives of Early American History*, American Historical Association (New York, 1908), pp. 312-313.

[11] John J. Heagerty, *Four Centuries of Medical History in Canada* (Toronto, 1928), I, 20.

[12] Francis Parkman, *The Jesuits in North America in the Seventeenth Century* (Boston, 1888), p. 87.

Despite their ardent labors on behalf of the sick, the Jesuits found themselves objects of suspicion to the natives. Father Le Jeune reported " They (the Indians) observed with some sort of reason that since our arrival in these lands those who had been the nearest to us had happened to be the most ruined by the disease, and that whole villages of those who had received us now appeared utterly exterminated." [13] Further along in his journal he noted sorrowfully that " it has happened very often and has been remarked more than a hundred times, that where we were most welcome, where we baptized most people, there it was in fact where they died the most." [14] Le Jeune, like the other missionaries of his time, did not realize that although the Europeans had acquired some immunity to the infection, their ministrations to the sick and dying served to make them carriers of the disease.

Smallpox again returned to New England in 1638 and inflicted some casualties upon the English.[15] The following year a group of the Indians contracted the disease while trading with the Abenakis tribe of Maine who had probably acquired it from the New England settlers.[16] Subsequently a major outbreak developed which lasted well into 1640.

Little further is heard of the disease until the 1660's, when it exacted a heavy toll.[17] It struck the Iroquois in 1662-63 and evoked the following notation: " The small-pox, which is the American's pest, has wrought sad havoc in their villages and has carried off many men, besides great numbers of women and children; and as a result their villages are nearly deserted, and their fields are only half-tilled." [18] The disorder soon spread to the Indians in Canada, where it remained for several years.[19] A particularly virulent form of the contagion inflicted heavy casualties among the colonists in New England in 1666. According to one medical writer,

[13] Heagerty, *op. cit.*, I, 22.

[14] *Ibid.*, p. 23.

[15] Noah Webster, *A Brief History of Epidemic and Pestilential Diseases, etc.* (Hartford, Connecticut, 1799), I, 185.

[16] Reuben G. Thwaites, ed., *Jesuit Relations and Allied Documents* (Cleveland, 1896-1901), XVI, 101 (hereinafter cited as *Jesuit Relations*).

[17] The Stearns list an epidemic in Quebec in 1649 following an attack by an English expeditionary force. Their source is Chevalier de Callieres' report to M. de Seignelay, dated 1649, in E. B. O'Callaghan, ed., *Documents Relative to the Colonial History of the State of New York Procured in Holland, England, and France* (Albany, New York, 1856-1861), IX, 492 (hereinafter cited as *Doc. Rel. to Col. Hist. of N. Y.*). However, since the date 1689 appears in the content and reference is made to Count de Frontenac, this outbreak is undoubtedly the one which occurred in 1690. The date 1649 is probably a typographical transposition of 1694.

[18] Heagerty, *op. cit.*, I, 27.

[19] *Ibid.*

the infection was imported by sea,[20] but the prevalence of the sickness among the French and Indians during the preceding years makes the Indians a more likely source. As has been pointed out earlier, a mild type of the infection among the whites often gained in virulence when passed on to the Indians, and was then returned to the colonists in a more malignant form.

During the early years of the seventeenth century, nearly all evidence of smallpox among the Indian tribes relates to the northern regions. The first recorded epidemic in the southern colonies occurred in 1667, when a sailor, infected with the disease, landed in what is now Northampton County, Virginia, and conveyed the disease to some of the local Indians. The usual fatal results ensued, and it was reported that " they died by the hundred . . . in this way practically every tribe fell into the hands of the grim reaper and disappeared, the only exception being the Gengaskins." [21] Little more is heard of smallpox in the southern colonies until the end of the century when the disease once again made a destructive path through the various tribes.

In 1669-70, a severe outbreak affected the Indians in eastern Canada, New England, and upper New York. The Algonquins suffered most, but the Hurons, too, were affected.[22] Seven years later another major epidemic broke out on a wide front. William Hubbard in his narration of the Indian troubles states that " sundry diseases " weakened the Red Men in 1676 at a time when the whites were gradually gaining the upper hand in the bloody Indian struggle known as King Philip's War (1675-77).[23] Whether smallpox was one of these diseases is not known, but the infection did ravage all of New England, affecting both whites and Indians, in the following two years. Incidentally, this outbreak led to the publication of the first medical work in America, a broadside by Thomas Thacher entitled, *A Brief Rule to Guide the Common People of New England how to order themselves and theirs in the Small Pocks, or Measles.*

In addition to ravaging New England, smallpox caused a few deaths

[20] Francis R. Packard, *History of Medicine in the United States* (New York, 1931), I, 75.

[21] Thomas B. Robertson, " An Indian King's Will," *Virginia Magazine of History and Biography*, XXXVI (1928), 192-93.

[22] *Jesuit Relations*, LIII, 59 ff.

[23] William Hubbard, *A Narrative of the Troubles with the Indians in New-England, from the First Planting thereof in the Year 1607, to This Present Year 1677, etc.* (Boston, John Foster, 1677), p. 95.

among the Indians in the Great Lakes area,[24] and, according to the diary of Increase Mather, "destroyed a great part of the Indians of Delaware Bay." [25]

Next year, 1679, the Iroquois were decimated by the pestilence. Count de Frontenac declared of the Iroquois "that the Small Pox, which is the Indian Plague, desolates them to such a degree that they think no longer of Meeting nor of Wars, but only of bewailing the dead, of whom there is already an immense number." [26] Three years later the disease struck the Indians at the Jesuit mission of Sillery near Quebec.[27] However, the outbreak was localized, and the disease apparently subsided in North America for a brief period.

The years 1688 to 1691 saw smallpox prevailing extensively among both Indians and whites, French and British. Whether the disease originated in the French or English settlements is not clear; possibly both regions may have been infected independently. In any case, the hostilities of King William's War broadcast the smallpox virus far and wide. Both sides suffered heavy casualties from the contagion since smallpox showed no partiality when Europeans fought each other. In fact, on more than one occasion well-planned military campaigns were thwarted by this unseen enemy. In 1690, the English, allied with the Mohegans and Iroquois, planned an assault on Quebec, but were foiled by an outbreak of smallpox. When British and Mohegan emissaries, still bearing the marks of the pestilence, were sent to the Iroquois, they were accused of bringing the plague. Subsequently the Iroquois became contaminated, about 300 died, and the rest refused to join the expedition.[28] Father Michael DeCourvert reported to Count de Frontenac from Quebec in 1690, "A malady which was prevalent among the English having communicated itself to the Loups, and some of them having died, the Loups laid the blame upon the English." [29] As a result the English abandoned the campaign. The next year, 1691, Father Millet, another Jesuit, stated specifically that the

[24] *Jesuit Relations*, LXIII, 205.

[25] Samuel A. Green, ed., *Diary by Increase Mather, March, 1675—December, 1676, Together with Extracts from Another Diary by Him, 1674-1687* (Cambridge, Massachusetts, 1900), pp. 20-21.

[26] Count de Frontenac to the King, Quebec, November 6, 1679, in *Doc. Rel. to Col. Hist. of N. Y.*, IX, 129.

[27] *Jesuit Relations*, LXII, 145.

[28] Count de Frontenac to Minister, December 12, 1690, in *Doc. Rel. to Col. Hist. of N. Y.*, IX, 460-61.

[29] Father Michael DeCourvert to Count de Frontenac, Quebec, 1690, in *Jesuit Relations*, LXIV, 47.

British had sent two armies against Quebec, adding that "smallpox stopped the first completely, and also scattered the second." [30]

Meanwhile the disease continued to rage among the Indians and whites in New York province. Major General Winthrop, in his journal of marches in the vicinity of Albany, New York, during these years often mentions the presence of smallpox among the troops and in the towns through which they passed.[31] As usual, the Indians were the chief sufferers. Robert Livingston reported the deaths of an entire group of Dovaganhae Indians who had come to Albany to trade in 1691.[32] In short, whether engaged in trade or in warfare, the Indian susceptibility to smallpox steadily reduced their numbers.

The southern provinces were the next to bear the brunt of smallpox attacks. An outbreak began in Jamestown, Virginia, in 1696 and gradually spread into the Carolinas, where it brought many fatalities to the whites, and even more to the Indians. One tribe, probably the Pemlico Indians, was almost completely destroyed. A correspondent from South Carolina reported in 1699 that smallpox was "said to have swept away a whole neighboring (Indian) nation, all to 5 or 6 which ran away and left their dead unburied, lying upon the ground for the vultures to devour." [33] The extermination of this tribe was described in 1707 by John Archdale, whose account subsequently was copied by John Oldmixon and many other eighteenth century writers.[34] The infection probably spread as far west as the Lower Mississippi valley for the tribes here were attacked at this time.[35]

The eighteenth century saw the decimation of the American Indian continue at an accelerated speed. Smallpox, which first became a serious problem in England and on the Continent around the time of the Stuart

[30] "Letter of Father Millet," 1691, in *Jesuit Relations*, LXIV, 97-99. Millet probably had in mind the two expeditions sent against Quebec in 1690: The New England and New York troops based at Albany attacked by land, and a naval force under the direction of Sir William Phips by sea.

[31] "Journal of Major General Winthrop's March from Albany to Wood Creek, July to September, 1690," *Doc. Rel. to Col. Hist. of N. Y.*, IV, 193-96.

[32] Letter from Robert Livingston, Albany, New York, June 4, 1691, in *ibid.*, III, 778.

[33] Mrs. Afra Coming to sister, March 6, 1699, quoted in Edward McCrady, *The History of South Carolina under the Proprietary Government*, 1670-1719 (New York, 1897), p. 308.

[34] John Archdale, *A New Description of that Fertile and Pleasant Province of Carolina* (London, 1707), in Bartholomew R. Carroll, *Historical Collections of South Carolina* (New York, 1836), II, 462-535. The account by John Oldmixon in his *British Empire in America* is identical with Archdale's.

[35] Stearn and Stearn, *op. cit.*, p. 33.

Restoration, grew steadily worse during the eighteenth century, tapering off only slightly during the last twenty years. The same held true in the American colonies although here the widespread use of variolation, or inoculation with smallpox, among the settlers greatly reduced the smallpox hazard by the 1760's.[36] For the Indians, however, there was no relief, and the higher incidence of the disease among the whites during the first half of the eighteenth century brought only further suffering and death to the Red Men.

In 1702 a mild form of smallpox was prevalent among the colonists in New York province. Governor Cornbury reported that the infection had been carried to the River Indians.[37] As so often happened, the disease spread north via the Indians and soon reached the town of Quebec which endured one of its most severe epidemics in the winter of 1702-1703. Heagerty estimates about 3,000 deaths from the contagion in Quebec alone.[38] Quite possibly the disease, which was relatively mild in New York, gained virulence as it progressed through the Indian tribes. Little evidence exists of its effect upon the Indians, but it doubtless took a heavy toll.

From 1703 to 1715 the English colonies gained relief from smallpox; but in the latter year it broke out anew and was to ravage all sections during the next seven years. The first reports of the sickness came from New Jersey in 1715.[39] By the following year, it was general throughout New York province. A missionary for the Society for the Propagation of the Gospel, a Church of England missionary society, wrote in October, 1716, " The Small Pox has been much among ye Indians here this last Summer & swept off a great many of ym & now it is got among ye other Nations beyond us, & Die as many there with it." [40] The disease continued to plague the Indians throughout 1716 and 1717, with few of the tribes in the Northwest escaping it.

In June, 1717, Governor Hunter of New York held a conference with the representatives of the Five Nations at Albany. In his opening address, he expressed sympathy " for the loss that has happened by the Small Pox

[36] Duffy, *op. cit.*; see chapter on variolation.

[37] Lord Cornbury to the Lords of Trade, New York, June 30, 1703, in *Doc. Rel. to Col. Hist. of N. Y.*, IV, 996-97.

[38] Heagerty, *op. cit.*, I, 67-68.

[39] Rowland Ellis to the Secretary, New Jersey, 1715, in S. P. G. MSS (L. C. Photo.), New York Letters, A 12, fp. 165.

[40] William Andrews to the Secretary, Fort by Mohawk Castle, October 11, 1716, in S. P. G. MSS (L. C. Photo.), London Letters, A 12, fp, 136.

to the bretheren, or any of your friends and allies." He pointed out, ". . . but we Christians look upon that disease and others of that kind as punishments for our misdeeds and sin, such as breaking of covenants & promises, murders, and robbery, and the like." [41] The Indians were not overly impressed and replied that they intended to dispatch someone to "Canistoge, Virginy, or Maryland" to find out who had been sending the contagion and to prevent them from so doing.[42] A French official who recorded the results of a meeting between the French and the Indians in October mentioned that the Iroquois were afflicted with the disease.[43]

The culmination of this widespread outbreak was an attack on Boston in 1721, which brought sickness to 60 per cent of the population and caused almost 900 deaths.[44] Following the Boston epidemic, the disease subsided for about nine years. In 1730, this city was again the scene of a major epidemic. On this occasion, some 4,000 cases developed and the death toll was approximately 500.[45] Neighboring towns such as Medfield and Cambridge reported additional cases, and a correspondent from Chatham noted that the disease was among the Indians, of whom, he said, "not so much as one has yet escaped." [46] The following spring the infection was reported among the Dutch around Albany and Schenectady, from whence it soon spread to the Indians in Eastern Canada.[47] By fall, the Senecas and other Iroquois tribes were victimized.[48] The infection continued to rage among the Indians in Canada throughout the winter, inflicting severe casualties. One tribe, the "Sounontonans," lost half their number.[49] Fear of the disorder in Canada drove many of the Indians into British territory, where they alarmed the frontier settlements.[50]

Meanwhile the tribes to the south of the Great Lakes-St. Lawrence

[41] Governor Hunter's Reply to the Five Nations at the Conference at Albany, New York, June 13, 1717, reported by Robert Livingston, Secretary of Indian Affairs, in *Doc. Rel. to Col. Hist. of N. Y.*, V, 485-86.

[42] Indian Reply to Governor Hunter, New York, June 13, 1717, in *ibid.*, p. 487.

[43] M. de Vaudreuil's Conference with Indians, October 24, 1717, in *Doc. Rel. to Col. Hist. of N. Y.*, IX, 877.

[44] See Duffy, *op. cit.*, p. 48 *passim*.

[45] William Douglass, *A Summary, Historical and Political, of the First Planting, Progressive Improvements, and Present State of the British Settlements in North America* (London, 1760), II, 396-397.

[46] Boston *Weekly Newsletter* (L. C. Photo), no. 1400, November 19-26, 1730.

[47] New York *Gazette* (L. C. Photo.), no. 248, March 26—April 5, 1731.

[48] M. de Beauharnois to Count de Maurepas, October 15, 1732, in *Doc. Rel. to Col. Hist. of N. Y.*, IX, 1035-1037.

[49] Heagerty, *op. cit.*, p. 35.

[50] *Belcher Papers*, Massachusetts Historical Society *Collections*, ser. 6, VI, 367.

region, too, paid toll to this grim pestilence. In September, Governor William Cosby of New York offered condolences to the Five Nations for the "great mortality among you by the small pox." [51] No statistics are available as to the number of cases or deaths in the various tribes, but the Indian susceptibility to the infection coupled with its widespread distribution must have produced some grim results.

The year, 1738, saw Charleston the victim of a major smallpox outbreak which sickened almost half the population. The neighboring Cherokee Indians, to whom the disease was carried, were devastated, losing fifty per cent of their members. Unable to explain this catastrophe, the Indians accused the English of poisoning them and threatened to trade with the French; this latter contingency was avoided only by careful diplomacy.[52] The Cherokees were estimated to have about 6,000 warriors prior to 1738 when the number was cut in half. Alexander Hewat, an eighteenth-century South Carolina historian, blamed smallpox for much of the decline in Indian population and asserted that by 1765 the Cherokees were reduced to less than 2,000 warriors.[53] In this same year, 1738, smallpox was transmitted to the Indians in the Hudson Bay region and spread widely in northern Canada.[54]

During the winter of 1746-47 the infection was again present in New York province and spread both north and south in the ensuing year. The governor of Canada was obliged to dispatch a message of condolence to the Onondagas for their sufferings from smallpox during the preceding winter.[55] In the American colonies, Maryland and Delaware were infected with the disease, but there is little evidence of it among the Indians. However, John Brainerd, a missionary in New Jersey, later spoke of a "Mortal Sickness," which may have been smallpox, carrying off many Indians in 1747.[56]

[51] *Doc. Rel. to Col. Hist. of N. Y.*, V, 963.

[52] "A Treaty Between Virginia and the Catawbas and Cherokees, 1756," *Virginia Magazine of History and Biography*, XIII (January, 1906), 227 fn.; see also Newton D. Mereness, *Travels in the American Colonies* (New York, 1916), p. 239. Captain James Oglethorpe met a delegation of Indians in September, 1739, and managed to allay their suspicions of the English.

[53] Alexander Hewat, *An Historical Account of the Rise and Progress of the Colonies of South Carolina and Georgia* (London, 1779), II, 279-80.

[54] Heagerty, *op. cit.*, I, 36-37.

[55] Colonel William Johnson to Governor Clinton, May 7, 1747, *Doc. Rel. to Col. Hist. of N. Y.*, VI, 362.

[56] John Brainerd to Mrs. Smith, Brotherton, New Jersey, August 24, 1761, in Simon Gratz Collection, Pennsylvania Historical Society MSS, American Clergymen.

The next smallpox epidemic among the Indians occurred in the Great Lakes region in 1752. The Miami tribe, to whom the French were looking for help, was completely routed by the infection. The French post at Detroit was attacked also, and one contemporary observer asserted that the sickness was "ravaging the whole of that Continent." [57] However, the Ohio valley and the areas to the East remained unaffected. Boston suffered a large scale outbreak in 1751, but the disease was sea-borne and does not seem to have spread beyond the city.

Three years later, 1755, the sickness reappeared. This time, contrary to its usual course, it began in Canada and then moved south into New York. Heagerty asserts that Canadians for years afterwards referred to 1755 as the year of the great smallpox epidemic, and that all activities, even the perennial warfare, ceased.[58] This disastrous plague in Canada did not wear itself out until late in 1757 after having swept through both French and Indian settlements. The epidemic first ravaged the French settlers and then spread to the Indian tribes. The Senecas were attacked in 1755 [59] and by the following spring nearly all of the Indians in Eastern Canada and the New England region were affected. In June, 1756, a French dispatch from Canada stated that the Indians on the borders of Acadia and New England were still hostile to the English, adding, however, ". . . unfortunately, they have not as yet been able to go on the war path, having been afflicted by the smallpox in all their villages." [60] Two months later a French official wrote of his difficulty in marshalling the Indians against the English because of their fears of the infection "at Niagara, Prequ'Isle and Fort Duquesne." [61]

The English settlements and the Indians to the south also were victimized in 1756. A report from Virginia stated that the contagion was raging among the Delawares who had caught the infection "in some Scalps they carried off from a place 20 miles above Bethlehem." [62] Meanwhile the infection manifested itself in the British armies, occasioning much alarm. The appearance of the disease in Albany, according to one writer, frightened the provincial troops more than the presence of Montcalm himself could have done, and made it necessary to garrison the town

[57] M. de Longueil to M. de Rouille, April 21, 1752, in *Doc. Rel. to Col. Hist. of N. Y.*, X, 246-50.

[58] Heagerty, *op. cit.*, I, 39-40.

[59] *Doc. Rel. to Col. Hist. of N. Y.*, X, 345.

[60] *Ibid.*, X, 408.

[61] *Ibid.*, X, 435-38; VII, 240.

[62] Boston *Weekly News-Letter* (L. C. Photo.), no. 2815, June 17, 1756.

entirely with British troops and to discharge all colonial soldiers there except one regiment raised in New York.[63]

Smallpox continued to flare up sporadically in most of the Middle colonies during 1757, and, as was usually the case, among the adjacent Indian tribes. A report to the French government in July asserted that the disorder was plaguing the English at Forts George and Lidius [Edward].[64] A month or two earlier a conference between the Indians and the English at Philadelphia had been disrupted when a number of the Indian representatives fell victim to smallpox. Soon the infection spread to the other Indians, who decided to return home immediately.[65] Subsequently the Governor's Council in Pennsylvania granted presents and extended condolences to the Indians for their heavy losses from the disease.[66]

In April, 1758, General Montcalm reported that a number of the Upper Country Indians were dying from smallpox " caught from the English on the expedition against Fort William Henry." [67] On this occasion, the garrison, hit hard by smallpox, surrendered to the French and their Indian allies. As was often the case, the Indians got out of control, murdered the sick, and in their quest for scalps, even dug up the bodies of those who had died.[68] Retribution was swift and severe for the Pandora's box, once opened, brought them far more death and suffering than they had inflicted upon the whites. In the long struggle between the Red Men and the colonists, the Indians, unfortunately, won far too many of these Pyrrhic victories.

The year 1758 again saw smallpox widespread in the provinces of New York and New Jersey. In December an S. P. G. minister wrote that the disease had " made dreadful havock . . . among thousands of white people and Indians when taken in the natural way." [69] His reference to " taken in the natural way " was to differentiate from smallpox inoculation which was then coming into general use. As a matter of fact, it was the indis-

[63] John Marshall, *A History of the Colonies Planted by the English on the Continent of North America* (Philadelphia, 1824), pp. 303-304.

[64] M. de Vaudreuil to M. de Moras, Montreal, July 12, 1757, in *Doc. Rel to Col. Hist. of N. Y.*, X, 579-580.

[65] Report of the Conferences with the Indians at Philadelphia, April 4, 1757, in *Minutes of the Provincial Council for Pennsylvania, Colonial Records*, VII, 517.

[66] " Minutes of the Council at Lancaster," May 21, 1757, in *ibid.*, p. 546.

[67] M. de Montcalm to M. de Paulmy, Montreal, April 18, 1758, in *Doc. Rel. to Col. Hist. of N. Y.*, X, 698-700.

[68] Francis Parkman, *Montcalm and Wolfe* (Boston, 1886), 11, 5.

[69] Colin Campbell to the Secretary, Burlington, New Jersey, December 20, 1759, in S. P. G. MSS (L. C. Photo.), London Letters, B 24, fpp. 151-153.

criminate use of variolation which not infrequently served to disseminate the infection among the settlers. The next section to feel the weight of smallpox was the southern colonies where the Indians in Georgia and South Carolina were devastated by the infection in 1759-60. The first notice of the outbreak occurred in a report from Georgia published in August, 1759, which stated that Savannah was exercising all precautions against the introduction of the disease; that Augusta was free of it; and that it had almost disappeared from among the Chickasaws [70] On December 15, the *South Carolina Gazette* commented editorially: " It is pretty certain that the Smallpox has lately raged with great Violence among the Catawba Indians, and that it has carried off near one-half of that nation, *by throwing themselves into the River*, as soon as they found themselves ill—This Distemper has since appeared amongst the Inhabitants of the *Charraws* and *Waterees*, where Many Families are down; so that unless special care is taken, it must soon [spread] thro' the whole country." [71] Over a month later a correspondent in Augusta wrote: " The late Accounts from Keowee are, that the Small-Pox has destroyed a great many of the Indians there; that those who remained alive, and have not yet had that Distemper, were gone into the Woods, where many of them must perish as the Catawbas did." [72] During the ensuing months smallpox continued its inexorable progress through the Indian tribes. On August 13, 1760, a *Pennsylvania Gazette's* correspondent reported from Augusta: " We learn from the Cherokee country, that the People of the Lower Towns have carried smallpox into the Middle Settlement and Valley, where that disease rages with great violence, and that the People of the Upper Towns are in such Dread of the Infection, that they will not allow a single Person from the above named Places to come amongst them." [73] In October the Gazette noted that the " Cherokees had brought the Small-Pox into the Upper Creek Nation." [74]

To add to the Indian troubles, Governor Henry Lyttleton of South Carolina led an expedition against the Cherokees in 1759 which resulted in the Treaty of Fort St. George late in the fall. As the treaty was signed, smallpox, which had been raging in a nearby Indian village, broke out in the Governor's camp. The effect produced by the appearance of this dreaded plague among the colonial expeditionary force has been vividly

[70] Boston *News-Letter* (L. C. Photo.), no. 3021, August 2, 1759.
[71] *South Carolina Gazette*, no. 1321, December 15, 1759.
[72] *Pennsylvania Gazette*, no. 1625, February 14, 1760.
[73] *Ibid.*, no. 1654, September 4, 1760.
[74] *Ibid.*, no. 1662, October 30, 1760.

described by Dr. Alexander Hewat, a contemporary historian: " As few of his little army had ever gone through that distemper, and as the surgeons were totally unprovided for such an accident, his men were struck with terror, and in great haste returned to the settlements, cautiously avoiding all intercourse with one another, and suffering much from hunger and fatigue by the way." [75] Despite all precautions, returning troops carried the infection into Charleston and the other towns.

Ordinarily the Indians were the chief victims of smallpox, but the South Carolina outbreak was an exception to the general rule. The renewed virulence which often characterized smallpox after it had circulated among the Indian tribes held true of the virus which the Indians communicated to the troops in 1759. During the winter that followed about 75 per cent of Charleston's inhabitants sickened with the infection and the ensuing deaths totaled well over 700.[76] However, many of the smallpox cases resulted from the practice of inoculation, to which the people of Charleston resorted. Augusta and Savannah, too, were infected, and like Charleston, bore heavy casualties. The destruction among the whites was small consolation to the Indians whose already thin ranks were decimated, and who could ill afford such a depletion of manpower in the face of the steadily increasing European settlements. The seriousness of the loss to the Indians is indicated in an article describing the Catawba Indians published in one of the colonial newspapers. The account, written in 1760, declared that seventy years ago the Catawbas were a strong nation with four thousand members, but had been reduced since by " Rum, War and Small-Pox " to less than " 100 gunmen." [77] Simultaneously with the major outbreak in South Carolina and Georgia, scattered epidemics occurred all the way to Canada. Hostilities between the English and French widely disseminated the contagion, which seems to have been endemic among the troops. The journals and diaries of soldiers in the field speak constantly of the omnipresent threat from smallpox. And the Indians, either as allies or enemies, were even more susceptible to the disease than the colonial troops. For example, a group of Dakotas, who journeyed to Quebec after its capture by the English, became infected, and the Menominee tribe in Wisconsin was greatly reduced by the ravages

[75] Bartholomew R. Carroll, *Historical Collections of South Carolina* (New York, 1836), I, 452.

[76] *Pennsylvania Gazette*, no. 1633, April 10, 1760; *South Carolina Gazette*, no. 1340, April 19, 1760.

[77] Boston *News-Letter* (L. C. Photo.), no. 2615, June 5, 1760.

of war and smallpox.[78] Sporadic outbreaks continued to develop throughout the war and few sections of British-controlled North America escaped.

The colonists were well aware of the potency of smallpox as a weapon against the Indians, and on several occasions deliberate efforts were made to infect the Red Men. One of these instances occurred during the Pontiac conspiracy in 1763. The British commander, Sir Jeffrey Amherst, added the following postscript to a letter to Colonel Henry Bouquet, "Could it not be contrived to send the small-pox among these disaffected tribes of Indians? We must on this occasion use every strategem in our power to reduce them." Bouquet replied on July 13, 1763, "I will try to inoculate the ----- with some blankets that may fall in their hands, and take care not to get the disease myself." [79] Just how successful Bouquet's experiment was is not known.

In the years 1764-65 smallpox flared up among the Indians in a number of widely separated regions. On July 30, 1764, the New York *Mercury* stated that "Smallpox has gone among the Creek Indians & carried off great Nos. of them." [80] The following spring the *Pennsylvania Gazette* reported that "1,500 Choctaws and 300 Chicksaws had died from the infection." [81] Later in the summer, Cornelius Bennett, an S. P. G. missionary among the Indians in the vicinity of Mohawk Castle, explained to the Society that the danger from smallpox had compelled him to return to Boston.[82] The notorious lack of enthusiasm among these missionaries for working with the Indians may have caused Bennett to overrate the danger; however, he did write the following year that he was ready to return to the mission field, which indicates that his concern over smallpox may have been justified.[83] Meanwhile the contagion was reported to be menacing the "Shawnese." [84] The settlers in Maryland were plagued with the infection in 1765, and Quebec suffered a major outbreak, but apparently these epidemics had little effect upon the Indians.

Smallpox subsided during the rest of the colonial period and did not constitute a serious threat to either the colonists or the Indians until the

[78] Francis Parkman, *History of the Conspiracy of Pontiac and the War of the North American Tribes against the English Colonies after the Conquest of Canada* (Boston, 1851), pp. 318 ff.

[79] Heagerty, *op. cit.*, I, 43.

[80] New York *Mercury* (L. C. Photo.), no. 666, July 30, 1764.

[81] *Pennsylvania Gazette*, no. 1901, May 30, 1765.

[82] Cornelius Bennett to Secretary, Boston, September 12, 1765, in S. P. G. MSS (L. C. Photo.), London Letters, B 22, fpp. 130-131.

[83] *Ibid.*

[84] Heagerty, *op. cit.*, I, 43.

opening hostilities of the Revolutionary War. As in previous wars, the troops carried the virus into all areas, infecting both civilians and Indians alike. By this time smallpox had already contributed much to the reduction of the Indian threat, but its task was still undone. Well into the nineteenth century smallpox continued its grim work of decimating the Indian tribes. In fact, it was not until the beginning of the present century that the infection was finally controlled.

The exact role played by smallpox in the settlement of North America is not easily determined. Certain tribes were literally wiped out, yet others survived many attacks, and were even, in the intervals between outbreaks, able to recoup their losses through a natural population increase. However, by eliminating a number of Indian tribes, smallpox cleared the way for white occupation in some areas with only a minimum of friction. Major epidemics among the surviving Red Men permitted easier advances into Indian territory, and often by the time the tribes had recovered enough to make an effective resistance, the whites were too well entrenched to be driven back. In times of war, smallpox, although a dangerous ally, was frequently a decisive factor in the victories of the Europeans over the Indians. The task of settling the New World was a difficult one at best. The enormous physical job of clearing forests and preparing land for cultivation combined with the constant menace of the Indians, always numerous, shrewd, and skillful adversaries, makes it apparent that the determination and courage of the early settlers has not been exaggerated.

Biological Warfare

A Historical Perspective

LTC George W. Christopher, USAF, MC; LTC Theodore J. Cieslak, MC, USA;
MAJ Julie A. Pavlin, MC, USA; COL Edward M. Eitzen, Jr, MC, USA

The deliberate use of microorganisms and toxins as weapons has been attempted throughout history. Biological warfare has evolved from the crude use of cadavers to contaminate water supplies to the development of specialized munitions for battlefield and covert use. The modern development of biological agents as weapons has paralleled advances in basic and applied microbiology. These include the identification of virulent pathogens suitable for aerosol delivery and industrial-scale fermentation processes to produce large quantities of pathogens and toxins. The history of biological warfare is difficult to assess because of a number of confounding factors. These include difficulties in verification of alleged or attempted biological attacks, the use of allegations of biological attacks for propaganda purposes, the paucity of pertinent microbiological or epidemiologic data, and the incidence of naturally occurring endemic or epidemic diseases during hostilities. Biological warfare has been renounced by 140 nations, primarily for strategic and other pragmatic reasons. International diplomatic efforts, including the 1972 Biological Weapons Convention, have not been entirely effective in preventing the enhancement and proliferation of offensive biological warfare programs. The threats posed by biological weapons are likely to continue into the future.

JAMA. 1997;278:412-417

HUMANS, regrettably, have used available technologies for destructive as well as for beneficial purposes throughout history. Modern attempts to "weaponize" biological toxins such as botulinum and ricin were anticipated by the use of curare and amphibian-derived toxins as arrow poisons by aboriginal South Americans using neolithic technology. Fomites (ie, objects that harbor and can transmit disease agents) have been used to deliberately transmit infectious diseases since antiquity. The study of the history of biological warfare is confounded by several factors. These include difficulties confirming allegations of biological attack, the lack of reliable microbiological and epidemiologic data regarding alleged or attempted attacks, the use of allegations of biological attack for propaganda, and the secrecy surrounding biological weapons programs. However, a review of historical sources demonstrates that interest in developing biological weapons has persisted throughout history and is likely to continue into the future.

From the Operational Medicine Division, US Army Medical Research Institute of Infectious Diseases, Fort Detrick, Md.

The opinions expressed in this article are those of the authors and do not reflect the positions or policies of the US Department of the Air Force, the US Department of the Army, the US Department of Defense, or the US government.

Reprints: LTC George W. Christopher, USAF, MC, US Army Medical Research Institute of Infectious Diseases, Attn: MCMR-UIZ-T/LTC Christopher, 1425 Porter St, Fort Detrick, MD 21702-5011 (e-mail: george_christopher@detrick.army.mil).

EARLY ATTEMPTS

Recognition of the potential impact of infectious diseases on armies resulted in the crude use of filth, cadavers, animal carcasses, and contagion as weapons. These have been used to contaminate wells, reservoirs, and other water sources of armies and civilian populations under attack since antiquity, through the Napoleonic era, and into the 20th century.[1] The use of fomites directly against humans has continued, as evidenced by the smearing of pungi sticks with excrement by the Viet Cong in the early 1960s.[2]

One of the earliest recorded attempts of using fomites against a population illustrates the complex epidemiologic issues raised by biological warfare. During the 14th-century siege of Kaffa (now Feodosia, Ukraine), the attacking Tatar force experienced an epidemic of plague. The Tatars attempted to convert their misfortune into an opportunity by catapulting the cadavers of their deceased into the city to initiate a plague epidemic. An outbreak of plague was followed by the retreat of defending forces and the conquest of Kaffa. Ships carrying plague-infected refugees (and possibly rats) sailed to Constantinople, Genoa, Venice, and other Mediterranean ports and are thought to have contributed to the second plague pandemic.[3] However, given the complex ecology and epidemiology of plague, it may be an oversimplification to implicate the biological attack as the sole cause of the plague epidemic in Kaffa. Plague may have been imported into Kaffa by a natural cycle involving sylvatic and urban rodents and their fleas,[4,5] and the population under siege may have been at increased risk of epidemics because of deteriorating sanitation and hygiene. Since plague-transmitting fleas leave cadavers to parasitize living hosts, we would suggest that the corpses catapulted over the walls of Kaffa may not have been carrying competent plague vectors.

> ... it may be an oversimpification to implicate the biological attack as the sole cause of the plague epidemic in Kaffa.

Smallpox was used as a biological weapon against Native Americans in the 18th century. During the French and Indian War (1754-1767), Sir Jeffrey Amherst, commander of British forces in North America, suggested the deliberate use of smallpox to "reduce" Native American tribes hostile to the British.[6] An outbreak of smallpox at Fort Pitt resulted in the generation of fomites and an opportunity to execute Amherst's plan. On June 24, 1763, Captain Ecuyer, one of Amherst's subordinates, gave blankets and a handkerchief from the smallpox hospital to the Native Americans and recorded in his journal, "I hope it will have the desired effect."[7] While this adaptation of the Trojan horse ruse was followed by epidemic smallpox among Native American tribes in the Ohio River valley,[8] other contacts between colonists and Native Americans may have contributed to these epidemics.[9] Smallpox epidemics among immunologically naive tribes of Native Americans following initial contacts with Europeans had been occurring for more than 200 years. In addition, the transmission of smallpox by fomites was inefficient compared with respiratory droplet transmission.[9]

Both of these early attempts at biological warfare illustrate the difficulty of differentiating naturally occurring epidemics from alleged or attempted biological attack. This problem has had continued relevance because naturally occurring endemic diseases have been ascribed to alleged biological attacks for propaganda purposes.

THE ERA OF MODERN MICROBIOLOGY AND THE USE OF BIOLOGICAL WEAPONS DURING THE WORLD WARS

The formulation of Koch's postulates and the development of modern microbiology during the 19th century afforded the capability to isolate and produce stocks of specific pathogens. Substantial evidence suggests that Germany developed an ambitious biological warfare program during World War I, featuring covert operations in neutral trading partners of the Allies to infect livestock and contaminate animal feed to be exported to Allied forces.[10] *Bacillus anthracis* and *Burkholderia (Pseudomonas) mallei*, the etiologic agents of anthrax and glanders, were to be used to infect Romanian sheep for export to Russia. Cultures confiscated from the German Legation in Romania in 1916 were identified as *B anthracis* and *B mallei* at the Bucharest Institute of Bacteriology and Pathology.[4,5] *Burkholderia mallei* was allegedly used by German saboteurs operating in Mesopotamia to inoculate 4500 mules and in France to infect horses of the French cavalry.[4] Argentinian livestock intended for export to Allied forces were infected with *B anthracis* and *B mallei*, resulting in the deaths of more than 200 mules from 1917 to 1918.[4] Operations in the United States included attempts to contaminate animal feed and to infect horses intended for export during World War I.[11]

In response to the horror of chemical warfare during World War I, international diplomatic efforts were directed toward limiting the proliferation and use of weapons of mass destruction. The first diplomatic attempt at limiting biological warfare was the 1925 Geneva Protocol for the Prohibition of the Use in War of Asphyxiating, Poisonous or Other Gases, and of Bacteriological Methods of Warfare.[12] This treaty prohibited the use of biological weapons. However, the treaty did not proscribe basic research, production, or possession of biological weapons, and many countries ratified the protocol while stipulating a right of retaliation.[12] There were no provisions for inspection. Parties to the Geneva Protocol that began basic research programs to develop biological weapons after World War I included Belgium, Canada, France, Great Britain, Italy, the Netherlands, Poland, and the Soviet Union.[13] The United States did not ratify the Geneva Protocol until 1975.

Japan conducted biological weapons research in occupied Manchuria from 1932 until the end of World War II under the direction of Shiro Ishii (1932-1942) and Kitano Misaji (1942-1945). Unit 731, a biological warfare research facility located near the town of Pingfan, was the center of the Japanese biological weapons development program and contained 150 buildings, 5 satellite camps, and a staff of more than 3000 scientists and technicians. Additional units were located at Mukden, Changchun, and Nanking. Prisoners were infected with pathogens including *B anthracis*, *Neisseria meningitidis*, *Shigella* spp, *Vibrio cholerae*, and *Yersinia pestis*.[13,14] At least 10 000 prisoners died as a result of experimental infection or execution following experimentation during the Japanese program between 1932 and 1945.[14]

> As many as 15 million fleas were released per attack to initiate epidemics of plague.

Participants in the Japanese program who had been captured by the Soviet Union during World War II admitted to 12 large-scale field trials of biological weapons in testimony obtained during war crimes prosecution.[15,16] At least 11 Chinese cities were attacked with biological agents. Attacks featured contaminating water supplies and food items with pure cultures of *B anthracis*, *V cholerae*, *Shigella* spp, *Salmonella* spp, and *Y pestis*. Cultures were also tossed directly into homes and sprayed from aircraft.[13-15] Plague was allegedly developed as a biological weapon by allowing laboratory-bred fleas to feed on plague-infected rats. These potentially infected fleas were then harvested and released from aircraft over Chinese cities. As many as 15 million fleas were released per attack to initiate epidemics of plague. Dr P. Z. King, director general of the Chinese National Health Administration, attributed epidemic plague to these attacks; however, rigorous epidemiologic and bacteriologic data are not available.[17] In addition, the Japanese had not adequately prepared, trained, or equipped their own troops for the hazards of biological weapons. An attack on Changteh in 1941 reportedly led to approximately 10 000 biological casualties and 1700 deaths among Japanese troops, with most cases due to cholera.[16] Field trials were terminated by Misaji in 1942, although basic research continued until the end of the war.[14]

Hitler reportedly issued orders prohibiting biological weapons development in Germany. However, with the support of high-ranking Nazi party officials, German scientists began biological weapons research, although their results lagged far behind those of other countries. A German offensive biological weapons threat never materialized.[18] Prisoners in Nazi concentration camps were forcibly infected with *Rickettsia prowazekii*, *Rickettsia mooseri*, hepatitis A virus, and *Plasmodia* spp and treated with investigational vaccines and drugs. These inhumane experiments were done to study pathogenesis, to develop vaccines against rickettsiae, and to develop sulfonamides rather than to develop biological weapons.[18] The only known German tactical use of biological warfare was the pollution of a large reservoir in northwestern Bohemia with sewage in May 1945.[1] Ironically, the combination of a vaccine and a serologic test was used as a biological defense against the Nazis. The German army avoided areas with epidemic typhus by using the Weil-Felix reaction for diagnosis. Consequently, physicians used formalin-killed *Proteus* OX-19 as a vaccine to induce biological false-positive tests for typhus in an area of occupied Poland, and residents were protected from deportation to concentration camps.[19]

The Allies developed biological weapons for potential retaliatory use in response to German biological attack. Bomb experiments of weaponized spores of *B anthracis* were conducted on Gruinard Island near the coast of Scotland and resulted in heavy contamination. Viable anthrax spores persisted until the island was decontaminated with formaldehyde and seawater during 1986.[20]

THE US PROGRAM

In the United States, an offensive biological program was begun in 1942 under the direction of a civilian agency, the War Reserve Service. The program included a research and development facility at Camp Detrick, Md (renamed Fort Detrick in 1956), testing sites in Mississippi and Utah, and a production facility in Terre Haute, Ind. Experiments were conducted using pathogens, including *B anthracis* and *Brucella suis*. However, the production facility lacked adequate engineering safety measures. For example, tests of the fermentation and storage processes using nonpathogenic *Bacillus subtilis* var *globigii* as a *B anthracis* simulant disclosed contamination of the plant and environs. These findings precluded large-scale production of biological weapons during World War II, although 5000 bombs filled with *B anthracis* spores were produced at a pilot plant at Camp Detrick.[21] After the war, the production facility was leased and converted to commercial pharmaceutical production.[21] Basic research and development activities were continued at Camp Detrick. Ishii, Misaji, and other Japanese scientists in American custody who had participated in the Unit 731 program were granted immunity from war crimes prosecution on the condition that they would disclose information obtained during their program. Secret debriefings were conducted during the postwar era.[13,16]

The US program was expanded during the Korean War (1950-1953). A new production facility incorporating adequate biosafety measures was constructed at Pine Bluff, Ark. Technical advances allowed large-scale fermentation, concentration, storage, and weaponization of microorganisms; production was begun in 1954. In addition, a program to develop countermeasures, including vaccines, antisera, and therapeutic agents to protect troops from possible biological attack, was begun in 1953.

Cities were surreptitiously used as laboratories to test aerosolization and dispersal methods . . .

Animal studies were performed at Fort Detrick, at remote desert sites, and on barges in the Pacific Ocean. Human experimentation using military and civilian volunteers was initiated in 1955. Biological munitions were detonated inside a 1-million-liter, hollow, metallic, spherical aerosolization chamber at Fort Detrick known as the "eight ball." Volunteers inside the chamber were exposed to *Francisella tularensis* and *Coxiella burnetii*. These and other challenge studies were done to determine vulnerability to aerosolized pathogens and the efficacy of vaccines, prophylaxis, and therapies under development. Additional studies were done using simulants. *Aspergillus fumigatus*, *B subtilis* var *globigii*, and *Serratia marcescens* were selected for use as simulants; these organisms were thought to be nonpathogenic and were used to study production and storage techniques as well as aerosolization methods, the behavior of aerosols over large geographic areas, and the effects of solar irradiation and climatic conditions on the viability of aerosolized organisms. Cities were surreptitiously used as laboratories to test aerosolization and dispersal methods when simulants were released during covert experiments in New York City, San Francisco, and other sites between 1949 and 1968.[21,22,23]

Concerns regarding potential public health hazards of simulant studies were raised after an outbreak of urinary tract infections caused by nosocomial *S marcescens* (formerly *Chromobacterium prodigiosum*) occurred at Stanford University Hospital between September 1950 and February 1951.[24] The outbreak followed covert experiments using *S marcescens* as a simulant in San Francisco.[23] The outbreak involved 11 cases, resulting in 1 transient bacteremia and 1 death from endocarditis. All patients had undergone urinary tract catheterization, and 5 had undergone cystoscopy for urologic indications. Exposure to multiple antibiotics was cited as a contributing factor to the outbreak.[24] No similar outbreaks were reported by other hospitals in the San Francisco area. This outbreak is thought to represent an early example of nosocomial epidemics caused by opportunists of low virulence, related to antibiotic use, new medical devices, and surgical procedures.[25]

In view of the temporal relationship of the outbreak with the simulant studies, the army convened an investigative panel in 1952, including members from the Communicable Disease Center, the National Institutes of Health, the City of New York Health Department, and Ohio State University. The panel did not comment directly on the possible association of the nosocomial outbreak and the simulant studies. The panel recommended continued use of *S marcescens* in view of its low virulence, but added that a search for better simulants to replace *S marcescens* should be pursued.[23] However, simulant studies using *S marcescens* continued until 1968. Public interest in these covert experiments was aroused in 1976 when the *Washington Post* reported them[26] and implied that the endocarditis death was a direct result of the simulant testing. It was further implied that sudden increases in the incidence of pneumonia in Calhoun County, Alabama, and Key West, Fla, were related to simulant studies at those locales. As a result of the ensuing public outcry, Senate hearings were held in 1977, and the army was severely criticized for the continued use of *S marcescens* following awareness of the Stanford outbreak.[22]

Nonetheless, several facts cast doubt on an etiologic relationship between military use of *S marcescens* and outbreaks of human disease. The Centers for Disease Control reported that in 100 outbreaks of *S marcescens* infection, none was caused by the 8UK strain used by the army (biotype A6, serotype O8:H3, phage type 678).[27] Numerous reports during the 1970s postulated a link between the army experiments and cases of *S marcescens* endocarditis, septic arthritis, and osteomyelitis in California heroin addicts; where strains were available for testing, they were likewise shown to differ antigenically from the army test strain.[27] A review of the role of *S marcescens* in the army biological program was published in 1979.[25]

Table 1.—Biological Agents Weaponized and Stockpiled by the US Military (Destroyed 1971-1973)

Lethal agents*
Bacillus anthracis
Botulinum toxin
Francisella tularensis
Incapacitating agents*
Brucella suis
Coxiella burnetii
Staphylococcal enterotoxin B
Venezuelan equine encephalitis virus
Anticrop agents†
Rice blast
Rye stem rust
Wheat stem rust

*Weaponized.
†Stockpiled, but not weaponized.

There were 456 cases of occupational infections acquired at Fort Detrick during the offensive biological program (1943-1969), at a rate of less than 10 infections per 1 million hours worked. The rate of occupational infection was well within the contemporary standards of the National Safety Council and below the rates reported from other laboratories. There were 3 fatalities due to occupationally acquired infections—2 cases of anthrax in 1951 and 1958 and a case of viral encephalitis in 1964. The mortality rate was lower than those of other contemporary surveys of laboratory-acquired infections. There were 48 occupational infections and no fatalities reported from production and testing sites. The safety program included the development and use of new vaccines as well as engineering safety measures.[23]

By the late 1960s, the US military had developed a biological arsenal that included numerous bacterial pathogens, toxins, and fungal plant pathogens that could be directed against crops to induce crop failure and famine (Table 1).[23] In addition, weapons for covert use using cobra venom, saxitoxin, and other toxins were developed for use by the Central Intelligence Agency; all records regarding their development and use were destroyed during 1972.[28]

KOREAN WAR AND COLD WAR ALLEGATIONS

The Soviet Union, China, and North Korea accused the United States of using biological warfare against North Korea and China during the Korean War. These accusations were supported by a series of investigations conducted by the International Scientific Commission, a group of scientists, and other organizations not part of the commission. Although these investigations were described as impartial, they were carefully controlled by the North Korean and Chinese governments.[29] The United States admitted to having biological warfare capabilities, but denied using biological weapons. The United States requested impartial investigations. The International Committee of the Red Cross suggested the formation of a special commission to investigate, and the World Health Organization offered to intervene. Neither China nor North Korea responded to the International Committee of the Red Cross, and the World Health Organization's offer was rebuffed as a disguised attempt at espionage. Consequently, the United States and 15 other nations submitted a resolution to the United Nations (UN) requesting the formation of a neutral commission to investigate the allegations; however, implementation of the resolution was prevented by the Soviet Union. The credibility of the United States was undermined by its failure to ratify the 1925 Geneva Protocol, by knowledge of its offensive biological warfare program, and the suspected covert collaboration with the Unit 731 scientists.[29] Although unsubstantiated, the accusations of US use of biological weapons attracted wide attention and resulted in a loss of international goodwill toward the United States. This episode demonstrated the propaganda value of biological warfare allegations, regardless of veracity.[29,30]

Numerous unsubstantiated allegations were made during the cold war era. These included Soviet accusations of US biological weapons testing against Canadian Eskimos resulting in a plague epidemic[31] and of a US and Columbian biological attack on Columbian and Bolivian peasants.[32] The United States also was accused of planning to initiate an epidemic of cholera in southeastern China[33] and of the covert release of dengue in Cuba.[34]

Similarly, the US allegations that Soviet armed forces and their proxies had used aerosolized trichothecene mycotoxins ("yellow rain"), potent inhibitors of DNA and protein synthesis derived from fungi of the genus *Fusarium*, in Laos (1975-1981), Kampuchea (1979-1981), and Afghanistan (1979-1981) are widely regarded as erroneous. The remote locations of the alleged attacks made intelligence investigations extremely difficult. Attacks were never witnessed by Western intelligence operatives, and samples of the aerosols were not recovered. Confounding factors included the following: contradictory testimonies from survivors of the alleged attack, discrepancies in reported symptoms, low disease rates in the allegedly exposed populations, the recovery of mycotoxin in less than 10% of the clinical and environmental samples submitted, the presence of *Fusarium* organisms as environmental commensals, the possible decay of toxin under prevailing environmental conditions, conflicting results of toxin assays from different laboratories, the similarity of alleged yellow rain deposits recovered from environmental surfaces to bee feces in ultrastructural appearance and pollen and mold content, and the natural occurrence of showers of bee feces from swarms of honey bees in the rain forests of southeast Asia.[35]

DISARMAMENT EFFORTS

During the late 1960s, there was increasing international concern regarding the indiscriminate nature, unpredictability, epidemiologic risks, and lack of epidemiologic control measures for biological weapons, as well as the ineffectiveness of the 1925 Geneva Protocol for preventing biological weapons proliferation. In July 1969, Great Britain submitted a proposal to the Committee on Disarmament of the UN prohibiting the development, production, and stockpiling of biological weapons and providing for inspections in response to alleged violations. During the following September, the Warsaw Pact nations submitted a biological disarmament proposal similar to the British proposal, but without provisions for inspections. Two months later, the World Health Organization issued a report regarding the potential consequences of biological warfare.[36] Estimates of the casualty figures that could result from biological attacks were staggering (Table 2).[36]

Table 2.—Estimates of Casualties Produced by Hypothetical Biological Attack*

Agent	Downwind Reach, km	No. Dead	No. Incapacitated
Rift Valley fever	1	400	35 000
Tick-borne encephalitis	1	9500	35 000
Typhus	5	19 000	85 000
Brucellosis	10	500	125 000
Q fever	>20	150	125 000
Tularemia	>20	30 000	125 000
Anthrax	>20	95 000	125 000

*Release of 50 kg of agent by aircraft along a 2-km line upwind of a population center of 500 000.[36]

Subsequently, the 1972 Convention on the Prohibition of the Development, Production, and Stockpiling of Bacteriological (Biological) and Toxin Weapons and on Their Destruction (BWC) was developed.[37] The treaty prohibits the development, possession, and stockpiling of pathogens or toxins in "quantities that have no justification for prophylactic, protective or other peaceful purposes." The BWC also prohibits the development of delivery systems intended to disperse biological agents and requires parties to destroy stocks of biological agents, delivery systems, and equipment within 9 months of ratifying the treaty. Transferring biological warfare technology or expertise to other countries is also prohibited. Signatories that have not yet ratified the BWC are obliged to refrain from activities that would defeat the purpose of the treaty until they explicitly communicate their intention not to ratify. However, there are unresolved controversies regarding the quantities of pathogens required for benevolent research and the definition of "defensive" research. Allegations of infractions may be lodged with the UN Security Council, which may in turn initiate inspections of accused parties; however, this provision is undermined by the right of Security Council members to veto proposed inspections.

The treaty was ratified in April 1972 and went into effect in March 1975. There were more than 100 signatory nations, including Iraq and the members of the Security Council (which included the United States and the Soviet Union). Review conferences were held in 1981, 1986, 1991, and 1996. Annual reports regarding biological research facilities, scientific conferences held at specified facilities, scientific exchanges, and epidemics are submitted to the UN as an additional confidence-building measure.[37]

President Nixon terminated the US offensive biological weapons program by executive order in 1969 and 1970. The United States adopted a policy never to use biological weapons, including toxins, under any circumstances whatsoever. National Security Decisions 35 and 44, issued during November 1969 (microorganisms) and February 1970 (toxins), mandated the cessation of offensive biological research and production and the destruction of the biological arsenal. Research efforts were directed exclusively to the development of defensive measures such as diagnostic tests, vaccines, and therapies for potential biological weapons threats. Stocks of pathogens and the entire biological arsenal were destroyed between May 1971 and February 1973 under the auspices of the US Department of Agriculture, the US Department of Health, Education, and Welfare, and the Departments of Natural Resources of Arkansas, Colorado, and Maryland. Small quantities of pathogens were retained at Fort Detrick to test the efficacy of investigational preventive measures and therapies. The Central Intelligence Agency was admonished during a 1975 congressional hearing for illegally retaining samples of toxins after presidential orders mandating their destruction.[23]

While many welcomed the termination of the US offensive program for moral and ethical reasons, the decision to terminate the offensive biological program was motivated by pragmatic considerations. Given the available conventional, chemical, and nuclear weapons, biological weapons were not considered essential for national security. The potential effects of biological weapons on military and civilian populations were still conjectural, and for obvious ethical and public health reasons could not be empirically studied. Biological weapons were considered untried, unpredictable, and potentially hazardous for the users as well as for those under attack. Field commanders and troops were unfamiliar with their use. In addition, the United States and allied countries had a strategic interest in outlawing biological weapons programs to prevent the proliferation of relatively low-cost weapons of mass destruction. By outlawing biological weapons, the arms race for weapons of mass destruction would be prohibitively expensive, given the expense of nuclear programs.[38]

After the termination of the offensive biological program, the US Army Medical Research Institute of Infectious Diseases (USAMRIID) was established to continue the development of medical defenses for the US military against potential biological attack. The mission of USAMRIID is to conduct research to develop strategies, products, information, and training programs for medical defense against potential biological weapons. Endemic or epidemic infectious diseases due to highly virulent pathogens requiring high-level containment for laboratory safety are also studied. The USAMRIID is an open research institution; no research is classified. The in-house programs are complemented by contract programs with universities and other research institutions.

FOLLOWING THE 1972 BWC

Several signatory nations of the 1972 BWC, including Iraq and the former Soviet Union, have participated in activities outlawed by the convention. These events demonstrate the ineffectiveness of the convention as the sole means for eradicating biological weapons and preventing further proliferation.

Biological weapons were used for covert assassination during the 1970s. Ricin, a lethal toxin derived from castor beans, was weaponized by the secret service of the Soviet Union and deployed by the Bulgarian secret service. Metallic pellets that were 1.7 mm in diameter were cross drilled, filled with ricin, and sealed with wax intended to melt at body temperature. The pellets were discharged from spring-powered weapons disguised as umbrellas. These weapons were used to assassinate Georgi Markov, a Bulgarian defector living in London, and during an unsuccessful assassination attempt against another defector, Vladamir Kostov, in 1978. Similar weapons may have been used for at least 6 other assassinations.[39]

An epidemic of anthrax occurred during April 1979 among people who lived or worked within a distance of 4 km in a narrow zone downwind of a Soviet military microbiology facility in Sverdlovsk (now Ekaterinburg, Russia). In addition, livestock died of anthrax along the extended axis of the epidemic zone out to a distance of 50 km.[40] The facility was suspected by Western intelligence of being a biological warfare research facility, and the epidemic was attributed by Western analysts to the accidental airborne release of anthrax spores.

The Soviets maintained that the epidemic was caused by ingestion of contaminated meat purchased on the black market. In 1992, Boris Yeltsin, the president of Russia, admitted that the facility had been part of an offensive biological weapons program and that the epidemic had been caused by a nonintentional release of anthrax spores.[41] It was determined that air filters had not been activated early on the morning of April 3.[42] Inhalation anthrax was identified at autopsy as the cause of death in victims.[43] At least 77 cases and 66 deaths occurred, constituting the largest documented epidemic of inhalation anthrax in history.[42] The Soviets continued an offensive biological warfare program after the BWC of 1972 under the aegis of Biopreparat, an organization under the Ministry of Defense.[44] During the 1970s and 1980s, Biopreparat operated at least 6 research laboratories and 5 production facilities and employed up to 55 000 scientists and technicians.[45] The extensive program of the former Soviet Union is now controlled largely by Russia. Yeltsin stated in 1992 that he would end further offensive biological research and production[41]; however, the degree to which the program has been reduced is not known. A 1995 report estimated that the Russian program continues to employ 25 000 to 30 000 people.[45]

Before the Persian Gulf War, intelligence reports suggested that the Iraqi regime had sponsored an ambitious biological warfare program. Coalition forces prepared for potential biological warfare by training in protective masks and equipment, reviewing decontamination procedures, and immunizing troops against potential biological warfare threats. Approximately 150 000 US troops received a Food and Drug Administration–licensed toxoid vaccine against anthrax, and 8000 received a botulinum toxoid vaccine approved by the Food and Drug Administration as an Investigational New Drug. In addition, 30 million 500-mg oral doses of ciprofloxacin were stockpiled in the theater of operations to provide a 1-month course of chemoprophylaxis for the 500 000 US troops in the event that anthrax spores were used as a biological weapon.

Information regarding the Iraqi offensive biological program was obtained after the Persian Gulf War during UN weapons inspections. Iraqi officials admitted to having had an offensive biological weapons program that included basic research on *B anthracis*, rotavirus, camel pox virus, aflatoxin, botulinum toxins, mycotoxins, and an anticrop agent (wheat cover rust).[46,47] Fortunately, biological weapons were not used during the Persian Gulf War. The Iraqi government claims to have destroyed its biological arsenal after the war. Research and production facilities that had escaped destruction during the war were demolished by the UN Special Commission on Iraq (UNSCOM) in 1996. The Persian Gulf War and postwar findings have lead to a recent decision by the US military to develop a plan to immunize troops against anthrax.[48]

The biological threat posed by non-state-sponsored terrorists was demonstrated by the intentional contamination of salad bars in Oregon restaurants with *Salmonella* Typhimurium by the Rajneeshee cult during late September 1984. This incident resulted in 751 cases of enteritis and 45 hospitalizations. Although the Rajneeshees were suspected, and despite rigorous epidemiologic analyses by the Wasco-Sherman Public Health Department, the Oregon State Health Division, and the Centers for Disease Control,[49,50] the origin of the epidemic as a deliberate biological attack was not confirmed until a cult member admitted to the attack in 1985.[51,52]

The threat of biological terrorism resurfaced following the Aum Shinrikyo sarin attack of the Tokyo subway system in March 1995. Police raids and investigations of the cult's facilities disclosed evidence of a rudimentary biological weapons program. The cult was allegedly conducting research of *B anthracis*, *Clostridium botulinum*, and *C burnetii*. The cult's arsenal seized by police allegedly contained botulinum toxin and drone aircraft equipped with spray tanks.[53] The cult had allegedly launched 3 unsuccessful biological attacks in Japan using *B anthracis* and botulinum toxin and had sent members to the former Zaire during 1992 to obtain Ebola virus for weapons development.[54]

CONCLUSIONS

Allegations of biological attacks have been made since World War I. However, most of these have not been confirmed in the absence of compelling microbiological or epidemiologic data supporting a biological attack. Furthermore, the Rajneeshee incident in Oregon demonstrated that biological attacks may be easy to conceal despite state-of-the-art microbiological and epidemiologic analysis. These incidents underscore the difficulty of differentiating biological attacks from naturally occurring epidemics or endemic disease and emphasize the increased risk of epidemics during hostilities because of deteriorating hygiene, sanitation, and public health infrastructure. The practice of ascribing naturally occurring epidemic or endemic diseases to alleged biological attacks for propaganda purposes demonstrates the perception of psychological vulnerability to the threat of biological warfare.

Confirmed incidents involving biological weapons since World War II include the Sverdlovsk accident, the ricin assassination attempts, the Rajneeshee incident, and the discovery of the Aum Shinrikyo biological weapons effort. The most immediate threat of biological warfare to date was posed by Iraq during the Persian Gulf War. The reasons behind Saddam Hussein's decision not to use his biological arsenal are unknown. The most frequently proposed hypothesis forwarded by Western military analysts and intelligence sources has been possible Iraqi concern regarding the risk of provoking massive retaliation. Alternatively, other considerations may have included the possible ineffectiveness of Hussein's biological weapons and hazards to his own forces because of deficiencies in Iraqi training and equipment.[55]

International agreements to limit biological weapons proliferation have not been completely effective, as evidenced by events in the former Soviet Union and Iraq, both of which demonstrated activities prohibited by the BWC of 1972. Efforts to formulate legally binding measures to verify compliance with the BWC have been undertaken but, as of the Fourth Review Conference in December 1996 in Geneva, Switzerland, such efforts have not been successful. Disagreements continue regarding the utility of routine inspections at biological research facilities and the political, economic, commercial, and security consequences of such inspections. The Ad Hoc Group of Government Experts on Verification will continue to negotiate measures to verify compliance and is charged to complete its work "as soon as possible," and no later than 2001. A Fifth Review Conference is to be held in 2001.[56,57]

Concern continues regarding the possibility of proliferation or enhancement of state-sponsored, offensive biological weapons programs and the possible use of biological weapons by terrorist organizations. Following the termination of the US offensive program from 1969-1970, biological defense in the US military has focused on the development of countermeasures including detection capabilities, personal protective equipment, vaccines, diagnostics, and therapies to protect our military members.

This article is dedicated to the late Jay P. Sanford, MD, in appreciation for his invaluable contributions to the fields of infectious diseases, military medicine, and medical education.

References

1. Stockholm International Peace Research Institute (SPIRI). *The Rise of CB Weapons: The Problem of Chemical and Biological Warfare.* New York, NY: Humanities Press; 1971;1.
2. Stubbs M. Has the West an Achilles heel: possibilities of biological weapons. *NATO's Fifteen Nations.* June/July 1962;7:94-99.
3. Derbes VJ. De Mussis and the great plague of 1348: a forgotten episode of bacteriological war. *JAMA.* 1966;196:59-62.
4. Robertson AG, Robertson LJ. From aspe to allegations: biological warfare in history. *Mil Med.* 1995;160:369-373.
5. Berdal BP, Omland T. *Biologiske vapen-konvensjoner og historikk. Tidsskr Nor Laegeforen.* 1990;110:736-741.
6. Parkman F. *The Conspiracy of Pontiac and the Indian War After the Conquest of Canada.* Boston, Mass: Little Brown & Co Inc; 1901;2.
7. Sipe CH. *The Indian Wars of Pennsylvania.* Harrisburg, Pa: Telegraph Press; 1929.
8. Stearn EW, Stearn AE. *The Effect of Smallpox on the Destiny of the Amerindian.* Boston, Mass: Bruce Humphries; 1945.
9. Fenner F, Henderson DA, Arita I, Jezek Z, Ladnyi ID. *Smallpox and Its Eradication.* Geneva, Switzerland: World Health Organization; 1988.
10. Hugh-Jones M. Wickham Steed and German biological warfare research. *Intell Natl Secur.* 1992;7:379-402.
11. Witcover J. *Sabotage at Black Tom: Imperial Germany's Secret War in America, 1914-1917.* Chapel Hill, NC: Algonquin Books of Chapel Hill; 1989.
12. Geissler E. *Biological and Toxin Weapons Today.* New York, NY: Oxford University Press Inc; 1986.
13. Harris SH. *Factories of Death.* New York, NY: Routledge; 1994.
14. Harris S. Japanese biological warfare research on humans: a case study of microbiology and ethics. *Ann N Y Acad Sci.* 1992;666:21-52.
15. Tomlin VV, Berezhnai RV. Exposure of criminal activity of the Japanese military authorities regarding preparation for biological warfare. *Voen Med Zh.* 1985;8:26-29.
16. Williams P, Wallace D. *Unit 731: Japan's Secret Biological Warfare in World War II.* New York, NY: Free Press; 1989.
17. King PZ. Bacteriological warfare. *Chin Med J.* 1943;61:259-263.
18. Mitscherlich A, Mielke F. *Medizin ohne Menschlichkeit: Dokumente des Nurnberger Arzteprozesses.* Frankfurt am Main, Germany: Fischer Taschenbuchverlag; 1983.
19. Lazowski ES, Matulewicz S. Serendipitous discovery of artificial Weil-Felix reaction used in 'private immunological war.' *ASM News.* 1977;43:300-302.
20. Manchee RJ, Stewart R. The decontamination of Gruinard Island. *Chem Br.* 1988;24:690-691.
21. Harris R, Paxman JA. *A Higher Form of Killing.* New York, NY: Hill & Wang; 1982.
22. US Congress. *Biological Testing Involving Human Subjects by the Department of Defense, 1977: Hearings before the Subcommittee on Health and Science Research of the US Senate,* 95th Cong, 1st Sess. Washington, DC: US Congress; March 8 and May 23, 1977.
23. US Dept of the Army. *US Army Activity in the US Biological Warfare Programs.* Washington, DC: US Dept of the Army; February 24, 1977;2. Publication DTIC B193427 L.
24. Wheat RP, Zuckerman A, Rantz LA. Infection due to chromobacteria. *Arch Intern Med.* 1951;88:461-466.
25. Yu VL. *Serratia marcescens:* historical perspective and clinical review. *N Engl J Med.* 1979;300:887-893.
26. *Washington Post.* December 22, 1976.
27. Farmer JJ III, Davis BR, Grimont PAD, Grimont F. Source of American *Serratia. Lancet.* 1977;2:459-460.
28. US Senate. *Unauthorized Storage of Toxic Agents: Hearings before US Senate Intelligence Committee,* 94th Cong, 1st Sess. Washington, DC: US Senate; September 16-18, 1975.
29. Van Courtland Moon JE. The Korean War case. *Ann N Y Acad Sci.* 1992;666:53-83.
30. Rolicka M. New studies disputing allegations of bacteriological warfare during the Korean War. *Mil Med.* 1995;160:97-100.
31. Soviet organ sees confusion in US. *New York Times.* April 13, 1951:6.
32. *Pravda.* July 11, 1964:3.
33. Chinese reds blame US in cholera rise. *New York Times.* August 23, 1961:7.
34. Schaap B. US biological warfare: the 1981 Cuban dengue epidemic. *Covert Action.* 1982;17:28-31.
35. Seeley TD, Nowicke JW, Meselson M, Guillemin J, Akratanakkul P. Yellow rain. *Sci Am.* 1985;253(3):128-137.
36. WHO Group of Consultants. *Health Aspects of Chemical and Biological Weapons.* Geneva, Switzerland: World Health Organization; 1970.
37. Sims NA. *The Diplomacy of Biological Disarmament.* New York, NY: Plenum Press; 1983.
38. Becket B. *Weapons of Tomorrow.* New York, NY: Plenum Press; 1983.
39. Livingstone NC, Douglass DJD. *CBW: The Poor Man's Atom Bomb.* Cambridge, Mass: Institute for Foreign Policy Analysis Inc; 1984.
40. Meselson M, Guillemin J, Hugh-Jones M, et al. The Sverdlovsk anthrax outbreak of 1979. *Science.* 1994;266:1202-1208.
41. Smith RJ. Yeltsin blames '79 anthrax on germ warfare efforts. *Washington Post.* June 16, 1992:A1.
42. Rich V. Russia: anthrax in the Urals. *Lancet.* 1992;339:419-420.
43. Abramova FA, Grinberg LM, Yamposkaya OV, et al. Pathology of inhalation anthrax in 42 cases from the Sverdlovsk outbreak of 1979. *Proc Natl Acad Sci U S A.* 1993;90:2291-2294.
44. Leitenberg M. The biological weapons program of the former Soviet Union. *Biologicals.* 1993;21:187-191.
45. McCall S. A higher form of killing. *Proc US Naval Inst.* 1995;121:40-45.
46. United Nations, Security Council. *Report of the Secretary General on the Status of the Implementation of the Special Commission's Plan for the Ongoing Monitoring and Verification of Iraq's Compliance With Relevant Parts of Section C of Security Council Resolution 687 (1991).* New York, NY: United Nations; October 11, 1995. Publication S/1995/864.
47. Zilinskas RA. Iraq's biological weapons: the past as future? *JAMA.* 1997;278:418-424.
48. Graham B. Military chiefs back anthrax inoculations; initiative would affect all of nation's forces. *Washington Post.* October 2, 1996:A1.
49. Weaver J. The town that was poisoned. *Congressional Record.* February 28, 1985;131:H901-H905.
50. Oregon Health Division. Salmonellosis in The Dalles. *Commun Dis Summ.* 1984;33:20.
51. Lon J. Rajneesh dies in Indian commune. *Oregonian.* January 20, 1990:A1.
52. Török TJ. A large community outbreak of salmonellosis caused by intentional contamination of restaurant salad bars. *JAMA.* 1997;278:389-395.
53. Smith RJ. Japanese cult had network of front companies, investigators say. *Washington Post.* November 1, 1995:A8.
54. Daplan DE, Marshall A. *The Cult at the End of the World.* New York, NY: Crown Publishing Group; 1996.
55. Goldstein L. Saddam's biological warfare card. *Washington Post.* October 11, 1996:A24.
56. United Nations. *Fourth Review Conference of the Parties to the Convention on the Prohibition of the Development, Production, and Stockpiling of Bacteriological (Biological) and Toxin Weapons and on Their Destruction.* 1996; Geneva, Switzerland. Publication BW/CONF IV/9.
57. Chemical and Biological Arms Control Institute. *The Fourth Review Conference of the Biological and Toxin Weapons Convention: Doing No Harm;* February 1997; Alexandria, Va. Unpublished manuscript.

Preemptive Biopreparedness: Can We Learn Anything From History?

Elizabeth Fee, PhD, and Theodore M. Brown, PhD

ABSTRACT

The threat of bioterrorism is in the public eye again, and major public health agencies are urging preparedness efforts and special federal funding. In a sense, we have seen this all before.

The Centers for Disease Control and Prevention grew substantially during the Cold War era in large part because Alexander Langmuir, Chief Epidemiologist of the CDC, used an earlier generation's anxieties to revitalize the CDC, create an Epidemic Intelligence Service, and promote epidemiologic "surveillance" as part of the nation's defense. Retrospective investigation suggests that, while Langmuir contributed to efforts promoted by the Department of Defense and the Federal Civil Defense Administration, the United States did not have real cause to fear Communist biological warfare aggression.

Given clear historical parallels, it is appropriate to ask, What was gained and what was lost by Langmuir's central role in that first instance of American biopreparedness? Among the conclusions drawn is that biopreparedness efforts fed the Cold War climate, narrowed the scope of public health activities, and failed to achieve sustained benefits for public health programs across the country. (*Am J Public Health*. 2001;91:721–726)

Bioterrorism seems to be the topic of the hour. Our medical and public health journals are full of articles, like one in this issue of the Journal, that raise questions about our state of readiness to deal with bioterrorist attacks, sound alarms about our lack of preparedness, or point to shortcomings in our institutional infrastructure. We are cautioned that most local health departments lack plans to address bioterrorist events and that few public health agency staff members have received comprehensive bioterrorism training.[1] We are warned that we are "perilously vulnerable" and that a bioterrorism event, possibly one of catastrophic proportions, is likely to occur within the next several years.[2,3] Major public health organizations and institutions, such as the Centers for Disease Control and Prevention (CDC) and the Association of State and Territorial Health Officers, are centrally involved in urging the importance of the bioterrorist threat.[4–6] So are public health leaders formerly known for their success in global immunization campaigns. Most notably, D. A. Henderson, former dean of the Johns Hopkins School of Public Health and director of the World Health Organization campaign to eradicate smallpox, now serves as director of the Hopkins Center for Civilian Biodefense Studies. His group publishes the *Biodefense Quarterly*, which provides up-to-date news about "the myriad issues related to biodefense" and helps "establish ties among the diverse members of the biodefense community."[7]

Whereas the Departments of Defense, Justice, and Energy now receive most of the funds for biological terrorism control, public health agencies and departments have urged that they be given a larger share of available funds. In fiscal year 2000, the Department of Health and Human Services devoted $277 million to "anti-terrorism funding," of which the largest single amount ($90 million) went to the CDC for surveillance, developing epidemiologic expertise, and improving laboratory facilities for detecting bioterrorism agents.[8] In June 2000, senators Bill Frist and Edward Kennedy introduced a bill in the US Senate that they have named the "Public Health Threats and Emergencies Act." This legislation would encourage funding for a coordinated national network of training programs to prepare personnel to protect civilians against bioterrorism, and would support research on microbial resistance on the grounds that such research is needed as a counterterrorist measure.[9] In another recent news item, the Food and Drug Administration approved ciprofloxacin as the nation's first medication specifically designated for use after a bioterrorist event.[10]

The First Wave of Biopreparedness

In a very real sense, we have seen all of this before. As Elizabeth Etheridge and others have documented, the CDC (then called the Communicable Disease Center) played a central role in America's response to the threat of "biological warfare" during the Cold War era.[11] The effort was led by Alexander D. Langmuir, a major public health leader from the 1940s through the 1970s, who served for many years as chief epidemiologist at the CDC. Langmuir brilliantly exploited an earlier generation's fear of biological warfare to revitalize the CDC in the postwar period, design a system of disease reporting, and create the Epidemic Intelligence Service (EIS), a practical training program for young epidemiologists. The EIS in turn served as educational preparation for many national and international public health leaders who would spread the Langmuir philosophy of surveillance and disease control.[12]

Langmuir studied medicine at Cornell and public health at Johns Hopkins, earning his master of public health degree in 1940. Even before the United States entered World War II, he served as a consultant to the Armed Forces Epidemiological Board, and in 1942 he accepted a post as epidemiologist for the Commission on Respiratory Diseases at Fort Bragg, NC. There, he worked on the transmission and spread of acute respiratory diseases, including airborne infections—a topic soon to be of central interest to the biological warfare establishment. After the war, Langmuir returned to the Johns Hopkins School of Hygiene and Public Health as associate professor of epidemiology. There, he became close to Kenneth

Elizabeth Fee is with the National Library of Medicine, History of Medicine Division, Bethesda, Md. Theodore M. Brown is with the University of Rochester, Rochester, NY. Elizabeth Fee and Theodore M. Brown contributed equally to this essay.

Requests for reprints should be sent to Elizabeth Fee, PhD, National Library of Medicine, History of Medicine Division, 8600 Rockville Pike, Bethesda, MD 20894.

This article was accepted December 20, 2000.

Maxcy, who was then professor of bacteriology and epidemiology and a member of the Department of Defense's Committee on Biological Warfare. This committee, which met for the first time in 1941, was responsible for developing the United States' program and policy on biological warfare. Langmuir served first as Maxcy's alternate and later, when Maxcy was incapacitated by Parkinson's disease, as his full-time replacement on the biological warfare committee. Langmuir later recalled that although he was initially "over his head" on this highly classified committee that "used up a great deal of time," he had learned much from the experience.[13] Beginning in 1949, he also served on the Army Chemical Corps' Administrative Council, the entity responsible for overseeing biological warfare research. Etheridge notes that Langmuir knew more about biological warfare than anyone else in the Public Health Service. He had a high-level security clearance, higher even than that of the surgeon general.[11(pp41–42)]

Langmuir was recruited to the CDC in June 1949. Within a few months of his arrival there, in October 1949, he raised the question of biological warfare defense in a meeting with state health officers. He argued that sabotage of food and water supplies was the most likely mode of attack and that epidemiologists must form the first line of national defense. Two months later, the National Security Resources Board declared that the nation must develop ways of responding to bacteriological warfare. The CDC ordered planning reports from each of its divisions and called in consultants from 20 states to gauge the adequacy of responses to a potential biological assault. Historically, this was a tense moment, as the nation was rocked with waves of anticommunist anxiety. In September, the Soviet Union had exploded an atomic bomb and in October, the victorious Chinese Communist army had declared a People's Republic. Senator Joseph McCarthy was beginning his campaign to root out suspected or supposed communists from the State Department and the federal government; the Hiss trials were in progress; the news media were reflecting and in some cases cultivating a general atmosphere of fear and suspicion. In his inaugural address of January 1949, President Truman had spoken only of foreign policy and denounced communism as a false doctrine of deceit and violence.[14] By June 1950, the nation was at war in Korea. President Truman ordered all nondefense budgets to be scaled down so that maximum resources could be devoted to the wartime emergency.

At the CDC, "epidemiologic intelligence" was listed as a defense expenditure. Apparently, it was Joseph W. Mountin, the man who secured congressional approval to found the CDC, who first coined the phrase "epidemic intelligence service," with its overtones of covert activity.[15] The phrase was a clever encapsulation of Langmuir's general concept of a nationwide team of epidemiologists ready at any moment to respond to the threat of biological attack. Langmuir also popularized, if he did not invent, the term "surveillance" to describe the general practice of gathering epidemiologic intelligence.[16] "Surveillance" had overtones of military or intelligence activities, and the term suggested more excitement than the traditional public health process of disease reporting, with its associations of dull bureaucratic paperwork. Langmuir became known for the concept of surveillance as well as for the energy with which it was implemented.

In December 1950, the Executive Office of the President published the government's official position on biological warfare, *Health Services and Special Weapons Defense*, a report to which Langmuir contributed. This manual stated baldly that a determined and resourceful enemy could effectively employ agents of biological warfare and that such agents could well be used either in covert actions or in open warfare. Many different agents could be used and might be transmitted by air, food, or water. The Federal Civil Defense Administration was charged with organizing a national system of defense against atomic, biological, and chemical warfare and planning "to treat simultaneously the great numbers of living casualties resulting from each attack."[17]

The Federal Civil Defense Administration and the US Army published popular pamphlets, such as *What You Should Know About Biological Warfare*, to explain the threat of biological warfare to the general public.[18] The pamphlets stated that the main danger of biological warfare came from aerosol sprays that could be carried aboard airplanes or submarines, "blown into the air intake of a factory ventilating system," or loaded into specially designed bombs. Secret agents might try to poison food and water supplies; plant and animal diseases could be unleashed to destroy food supplies. The many possible biological agents included plague, typhus, cholera, smallpox, anthrax, glanders, plant blights, and botulinum toxins. The pamphlets offered some very specific advice: when an alarm sounded, people should get into a shelter and stay there until an all-clear signal sounded. Afterward, polluted clothing should be washed and boiled or dry-cleaned. People should be careful what they eat; preferably, they should consume canned or bottled goods with unbroken seals. To play it safe, people could boil all foodstuffs for 10 minutes and use a service gas mask to protect against airborne pathogens.

These official pamphlets communicated a curious mix of anxiety, information, and reassurance. They discounted some dramatic rumors about biological toxins that could wipe out whole cities in an instant, but they also fed popular apprehensions through authoritative assertions that an invisible biological warfare attack could come at any time, without warning. A similar impression was provided by a popular television program, *What You Should Know About Biological Warfare*, aired by the Department of Defense and leaders of the Federal Civil Defense Administration in early 1951 as part of the weekly Johns Hopkins University science program.[19] Starring a youthful and intensely serious Alexander Langmuir, the program presented a compelling case for both the threat of biological warfare and the importance of the public health system as the country's best defense.

At one point in the program, Langmuir turned on a Waring blender filled with dry ice for a vivid demonstration of how clouds of aerosol mist could contaminate a whole studio and infect everyone inside. He then used a familiar can of insecticide to demonstrate the working of an aerosol spray. Employing much the same principles, he said, an enemy could mount aerosols on airplanes and cover a city with a vast cloud of infectious material. Langmuir also injected colored liquid into a model of the water supply of a city to show how easily a biological warfare agent could spread. How could anyone protect or defend against such an attack? The only real answer, said Langmuir, was to build a complete biological warfare defense program. This would be based on the existing public health system, but it would use more effective sampling methods to detect biological warfare agents and employ faster reporting of disease incidence, upgraded

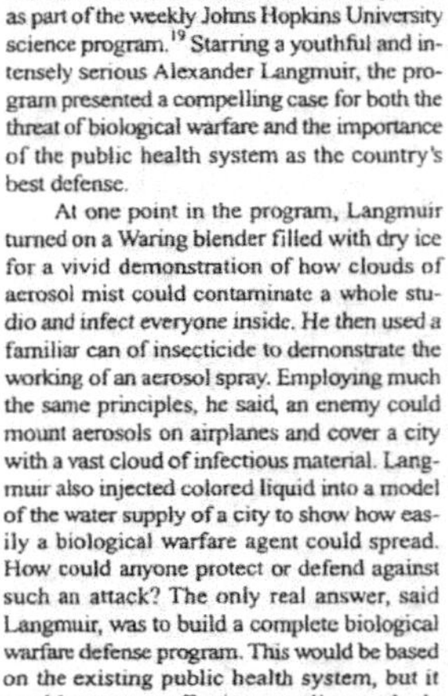

1951 pamphlet "What You Should Know About Biological Warfare," shown on the TV program with the same name. (Courtesy of the National Library of Medicine.)

Alexander D. Langmuir explaining how an insecticide spray works, from the TV program "What You Should Know About Biological Warfare," 1951. (Courtesy of the National Library of Medicine.)

laboratory facilities, more extensive immunization programs, and better investigations of all outbreaks of disease. In short, he said, the country needed an epidemic intelligence service. The program Langmuir outlined was not only a blueprint for the creation of the EIS but also in many ways a plan for the future development of the CDC.

The Epidemic Intelligence Service

Langmuir had already raised the idea of, and received approval for, an epidemic intelligence service in July 1950 at a meeting in Washington called to discuss biological warfare. Funding for the EIS was included in the budget for civil defense activities presented in Congress. Langmuir started with a training team of 6 members; by September 1950, once doctors knew they would soon be subject to the military draft, applications to the new EIS began pouring in. The first class of 23 recruits arrived in July 1951. After a rapid and very challenging training, they were ready to be sent out across the country to assist official health agencies in investigating infectious disease outbreaks. The entire EIS training course was managed with Langmuir's characteristic flair for the dramatic; at all times, trainees had to have a bag packed and be ready and willing to respond to an official alert within hours of a request for assistance. The challenge appealed to the bright young doctors Langmuir recruited for the program.

Three faculty members from Johns Hopkins—John Hume, Phillip Sartwell, and Abraham Lillienfeld—offered the first year's curriculum. The course was based on the Johns Hopkins case study method as originally developed by Wade Hampton Frost, Hopkins' first professor of epidemiology. It added something that the Hopkins course often lacked: an immediacy and relevance created by reports from officers in the field who discussed the problems with which they were dealing. Some of the reports came in by radio; all were timely and up-to-the-minute "breaking news."

By all accounts, however, Langmuir put his personal stamp on the entire program. He dominated the training of EIS officers and insisted that the experience be made "as exciting as we knew how." During his years as chief epidemiologist at the CDC (1949–1970), Langmuir was responsible for training some 672 officers of the EIS, many of whom considered the experience a highlight of their careers.[20]

The EIS provides a direct connection between Langmuir's era and our own through the relationship of Langmuir to D. A. Henderson. Henderson was one of those bright young recruits to the EIS; he arrived in 1955, trained under Langmuir, and later became one of Langmuir's deputies at the CDC. Langmuir gave each of his most talented trainees a specially challenging assignment; he nominated Henderson to be chief of the surveillance section of the CDC. When Langmuir was becoming interested in the global problem of smallpox, he made Henderson chief of the CDC Smallpox Eradication Program. Starting on this foundation, Henderson would go on to lead the extraordinarily successful World Health Organization smallpox eradication program.

Henderson gave Langmuir's insistence on accurate disease surveillance much credit for the success of the global smallpox eradication program. In the course of his career, Henderson had worked for 12 years with Langmuir and had absorbed Langmuir's insistence that surveillance was the key to infectious disease control. "One does not spend 12 months, let alone 12 years, with Langmuir without obtaining a point of view," said Henderson.[21] His close identification with Langmuir's career, approach, and ideas is evident in the videotaped oral history interview he conducted with Langmuir for the Alpha Omega Alpha series *Leaders in American Medicine*.[13] More recently, Henderson has taken on his mentor's concern with and interest in biological warfare—now reconceptualized as defense against bioterrorism.[22]

The Threat of Biological Warfare

The connections between an earlier era of biological warfare defense and the contemporary concern about bioterrorism invite us to look more closely at that earlier historical experience for some cautionary guidance. One central question about the earlier episode is, How good was the available information about the clear and present threat of biological aggression against the United States? On the basis of our reading, we found it very difficult, if not impossible, to discover much evidence for any real threat of biological aggression against the United States around the time of the Korean War. The strongest arguments presented in official government documents are based not on facts but on speculative constructs and hypothetical scenarios. These documents contend that since a biological warfare attack was *technically feasible*, the threat required every possible preparation.

As we have noted, Langmuir was himself recognized as a leading national expert on the threat of biological warfare. A close reading of his papers of that period reveals that his primary case for American preparedness was based on theoretical explorations and hypothetical projections rather than on any clear documentation of imminent enemy threat. He laid out the epidemiologic possibility of biological warfare by airborne infection or food and water contamination, but he freely admitted that he was modeling potential rather than empirically established threats.[23] His projections were typically phrased in such terms as "Let us now visualize the problems that might be encountered in surreptitious attacks," and "To visualize more clearly the need for epidemiologists in the civil defense organization, let us outline the events which might follow a biological warfare attack."[24] Even in retrospect, Langmuir recollected in his oral history interview that his argument for the EIS depended on biological warfare being "even a slight probability."[13]

The best recent historical research, in fact, suggests that, whatever may have been the case in more recent decades, the one nation in the early Cold War period with the most fully developed commitment to investigating the possibilities of biological warfare was the United States.[25] If a biological warfare attack was technically feasible, it was the Americans, the British, and the Canadians who proved it so. According to recent research based on previously classified documents, the British had done the key research to prove the possibility of using biological weapons; the Americans had demonstrated the feasibility of their mass production.[26]

Biological warfare research had started during World War II in the Army Chemical Warfare Service with about 4000 workers and a budget of $60 million.[27] Oversight of the secret program was then moved into the civilian Federal Security Agency under the newly named War Research Service headed by George W. Merck, president of the pharmaceutical firm Merck and Co, Inc. In the early period, work focused on anthrax and botulism. Research was, however, conducted on a series of biological agents for use against people and plants. One specific plan to drop ammonium thiocyanate on rice-producing areas near major Japanese cities was preempted by the dropping of atomic bombs on Hiroshima and Nagasaki.

Japanese occupying troops in China had carried out their own biological warfare experiments. A biological weapons development program under the direction of Shiro Ishii employed 3000 scientists and technicians to carry out experimental infections in large-scale field trials in which at least 10 000 prisoners are said to have died. The Japanese also attacked Chinese cities with biological agents, although the results of these attacks are uncertain or disputed. After the war, the United States offered immunity from war crimes prosecution to some of the leading Japanese scientists responsible for biological warfare experiments in China, on condition that they disclose information about these experiments in secret debriefings. Much later, the Americans decided that the Japanese data were poor and of little use in developing biological weapons capacity.[26]

After the war, the United States continued to develop its own biological warfare research. Science historian Susan Wright has traced the development of biological warfare capacity by the United States and the buildup of biological weaponry intended by the US military as deterrence.[28] The military tended to regard each type of weapon of mass destruction as needing to be deterred with a similar weapon: nuclear with nuclear, chemical with chemical, biological with biological. As support for basic research and development of biological weapons rose throughout the 1950s and 1960s, the Army built a 500-acre research and development facility at Camp Detrick, Md (renamed Fort Detrick in 1956), created huge testing sites in Mississippi and Utah, and obtained 6100 acres for a manufacturing plant near Terre Haute, Ind.[29] The research and development network centered in Fort Detrick expanded to include some 300 universities, research institutions, and corporations.

Alexander D. Langmuir and D. A. Henderson, from the 1979 videotaped interview for "Leaders in American Medicine," the Alpha Omega Alpha series. (Courtesy of National Library of Medicine.)

Ed Regis and other writers have recounted the history of extensive field tests using "simulants" and pathogens at Dugway Proving Ground, Utah, and other locations; research on human subjects; and aerosol spray tests carried out over major cities.[25–30] Alistair Hay has also used documents released under the Freedom of Information Act to elaborate details of this biological warfare research. One project, "Big Buzz," tested the feasibility of mass-producing mosquitoes and disseminating them from aircraft, with the idea that munitions loaded with mosquitoes carrying yellow fever virus could be targeted at the southern regions of the Soviet Union.[30] Such activities were justified by the need to defend against a Soviet threat or to stay well ahead of a future Soviet threat, arguments that followed the generally familiar and self-sustaining logic of the Cold War arms race.

During the Korean War, there were allegations that the United States had used biological weapons. These allegations were hotly debated at the time and continue to be matters of dispute. A recent book by Stephen Endicott and Edward Hagerman, *The United States and Biological Warfare*, which draws on extensive research in US and Chinese archives, has reopened the debate.[31] It shows beyond reasonable doubt that biological weapons were being intensively developed before and during the Korean War and that there was, for a period of several years, no clear constraint against their first use by the United States. Much of the evidence from this period, which could be relevant for settling these questions definitively, is still classified.

Learning From History

Given a brief historical review of this highly contentious area, we can ask what was gained and what was lost to public health by Langmuir's central role in the first episode of American biopreparedness. Certainly, resources were made available to build up the EIS and the CDC; these are important long-term achievements. Perhaps it is perfectly reasonable to build up public health activities, personnel, and institutions no matter what the source or overt purpose of the funding. This certainly seems to be the reasoning of many public health officials today, who are quite eager to use bioterrorism or health-alert funds to, as some would put it, "grow the public health infrastructure." And it is certainly true that some resources, such as better telecommunications for the public health workforce, clearer standards for communicating information, and more training for public health personnel, should have broad applicability for other, perhaps more pressing, public health issues. But there are also choices to be made. Funding turned toward one set of problems can be—and in our experience often is—diverted from others. Biological warfare funding in postwar Britain and America was devoted especially to the study of diseases such as anthrax that were not of any real threat to their populations outside of their presumptive use as biological weapons. Great attention was given to the experimental infection, with such organisms, of laboratory animals and to methods of delivery by air.

At the same time that funding for biological warfare research was increasing in the United States, funds for local health departments were cut sharply. Jobs in public health departments went unfilled for long periods of time because salaries offered were too low. In the 1950s, enrollments in schools of public health declined so dramatically that the Johns Hopkins School of Hygiene and Public Health considered eliminating entirely the master of public health degree—the main training program for public health personnel. Had it done so, arguably the oldest, largest, and most prominent public health education program would have been closed down, with the faculty and doctoral students left to focus their entire attention on funded research, freed from major teaching obligations. By 1955, the state of public health was so bad that the annual conference of the American Public Health Association offered a major symposium on the theme "Where Are We Going in Public Health?" During the generally gloomy assessments, Henry Vaughan suggested that if public health were dead, it should have a decent burial, and Hugh Leavell proposed "to apply a stethoscope to the chest and perhaps a mirror to the mouth to see if there is any breath left in it . . . before ordering the coffin."[32(p408)] It seems, then, that the funds made available for biological warfare research failed to have a notably beneficial effect on public health programs across the country.

Looking back, we can see that a brief period of enthusiasm and idealism within public health in the immediate postwar years was all but eliminated by the generally repressive ideologic atmosphere of the McCarthy period. At a time of declining health department budgets, one of the most important and clearly cost-effective public health measures, fluoridation of the water supplies, became bogged down in many localities in endless ideologic squabbles and fear-mongering. Why were many communities so afraid that the Communists were about to poison their water supplies that they refused to listen to the supposedly authoritative voices of scientists, physicians, and public health professionals? Perhaps publicity about the plausibility of a biological warfare attack did much to fan such fears.

Many of the more progressive voices in public health were silenced or muted in these years, and those who continued to speak out were subject to political suspicion. Such leading lights as Thomas Parran, the surgeon general, and Martha May Eliot, leader of the Children's Bureau, were publicly censured, as were medical care activists Fred Mott and Milton Roemer, who had sustained the innovative and important rural medical care programs of the Farm Security Administration.[33] There are many indications of the chilling effect of the Cold War era on particular areas of public health, such as health insurance and medical care organizations,[34] the compilation of mortality statistics by occupation and socioeconomic classification,[35] and the development of epidemiologic theory and methods that avoided dangerous speculation about the social determinants of health.[36] These issues have yet to be thoroughly explored.

Neither Langmuir nor the biological warfare establishment can be held responsible for all that was lost to public health in the late 1940s and early 1950s, but they were part of the same seismic shift rightward. First, by emphasizing the need for biopreparedness—however prudent that emphasis may have been from one perspective—Langmuir contributed, even if unintentionally, to the biological arms race. Merely by being involved so visibly, centrally, and convincingly in the debate, he added legitimacy to one dimension of the fear-driven mentality of the Cold War era. Most current viewers of the television programs or readers of the popular pamphlets on biological warfare are likely to agree that they tended to reinforce the anxieties of the Cold War rather than lead the nation toward a cool rationality and circumspect evaluation of its options and possibilities.

Within public health, and despite Langmuir's broad vision and wide range of interests, his involvement in preparedness efforts and his emphasis around the time of the Korean War on intelligence and surveillance both channeled the energy and narrowed the scope of epidemiologic research to an infectious disease focus. Most public health people agreed in the late 1930s and the immediate postwar period that the country's leading causes of mortality, morbidity, and disability were the chronic diseases, yet relatively little was done to address these issues in the 1950s. It was not until the 1960s and 1970s, for example, that the CDC began to develop programs in chronic diseases, occupational and environmental health, toxic hazards, birth defects, family planning, famines and disasters, and drug use. The fact that the institution grew in opportunistic response to anxieties about biological warfare with infectious agents was not the only reason that the CDC limited its initial focus, but the centrality accorded to the threat of biological warfare certainly did not help to widen its vision.

What are the risks we face today? Will the interest in bioterrorism—justified by a few incidents causing alarm (usually cited are the sarin attack on the Tokyo subway, airborne anthrax in the Soviet Union, and salmonella in salad bars in Oregon)—help or hinder the public health? Are the resources becoming available for defense against the threat of bioterrorism out of proportion to the seriousness of the threat? Does that possibly disproportionate allocation drain resources from other pressing public health needs? Will we "grow infrastructure"—not a bad outcome in itself—but limit the scope of public health in the process? Will present funding trends and policies seriously skew the system of health promotion and protection toward a few exotic threats rather than the sources of existing social inequalities in health? Some voices in public health argue that the new fascination with bioterrorism weapons bodes ill for the future of public health and may damage both domestic politics and international relations.[37,38]

We cannot say for sure, of course, what the future will bring, but we feel there may be lessons to be learned from our earlier encounters with the threat of biological warfare and its consequent less than stellar results for the development of public health. These questions deserve our attention. Perhaps we ought to pay heed to Yogi Berra's penetrating and uniquely stated wisdom: "It's like *déjà vu* all over again."[39] □

Acknowledgments

We are especially grateful to Susan Wright and Hillel Cohen for their comments.

References

1. Wetter DC, Daniell WE, Treser CD. Hospital preparedness for victims of chemical or biological terrorism. *Am J Public Health.* 2001;91: 710–716.
2. Fraser RF, Brown DL. Bioterrorism preparedness and local public health agencies: building

response capacity. *Public Health Rep.* 2000;115: 326–330.
3. Henderson DA. A new strategy for biological terrorism. *The Scientist.* 2000;14(16):6.
4. Osterholm MT. Bioterrorism: media hype or real potential nightmare? *Am J Infect Control.* 1999; 27:461–462.
5. Lillibridge SR, Bell AJ, Roman RS. Centers for Disease Control and Prevention bioterrorism preparedness and response. *Am J Infect Control.* 1999:27:463–464.
6. Bryan JL, Fields HF. An ounce of prevention is worth a pound of cure—shoring up the public health infrastructure to respond to bioterrorist attacks. *Am J Infect Control.* 1999;27:465–467.
7. Henderson DA. Greetings from the director. *Biodefense Q* [serial on-line]. June 1999;1(1). Available at: http://www.hopkins-biodefense.org/pages/news/quarter.html. Accessed March 6, 2001.
8. Department of Health and Human Services FY2000 anti-terrorism funding: $277,553,000. Available at: http://www.hopkins-biodefense.org/pages/news/tables/dhhs.html. Accessed February 13, 2001.
9. Grossman R. Biodefense bill introduced to Senate. *Biodefense Q* [serial on-line]. June 2000;2(1). Available at: http://www.hopkins-biodefense.org/pages/news/quarter.html. Accessed March 6, 2001.
10. Neergaard L. FDA picks drug to fight bioterrorism. *Philadelphia Inquirer.* September 1, 2000:A12.
11. Etheridge EW. *Sentinel for Health: A History of the Centers for Disease Control.* Berkeley: University of California Press; 1992.
12. Schaffner W, LaForce FM. Training field epidemiologists: Alexander D. Langmuir and the Epidemic Intelligence Service. *Am J Epidemiol.* 1996;144(suppl):S16–S22.
13. *The Alpha Omega Alpha Interview with Alexander D. Langmuir, MD, MPH, by D.A. Henderson* [videotape]. Bethesda, Md.: National Library of Medicine; 1979. Leaders in American Medicine Series.
14. McCullough D. *Truman.* New York, NY: Simon & Schuster; 1992:730.
15. Langmuir AD. The Epidemic Intelligence Service of the Center for Disease Control. *Public Health Rep.* 1980;95:470–477.
16. Langmuir AD. Evolution of the concept of surveillance in the United States. *Proc Royal Soc Med.* 1971;64:681–684.
17. *United States Civil Defense: Health Services and Special Weapons Defense.* Washington, DC: Executive Office of the President, Federal Civil Defense Administration; 1950:4.
18. Department of the Army. *What You Should Know About Biological Warfare.* Washington, DC: US Army; 1951.
19. What you should know about biological warfare [transcript]. "The Johns Hopkins Science Review." WAAM, Baltimore, Md. April 3, 1951.
20. Foster SO, Gangarosa E. Passing the epidemiologic torch from Farr to the world: the legacy of Alexander D. Langmuir. *Am J Epidemiol.* 1996; 144(suppl):S65–S73.
21. Henderson DA. Smallpox eradication. *Public Health Rep.* 1980;95:425.
22. Henderson DA. Weapons for the future. *Lancet.* 2000;354(suppl):SIV64.
23. Langmuir AD. The potentialities of biological warfare against man—an epidemiological appraisal. *Public Health Rep.* 1951;66:387–399.
24. Langmuir AD, Andrews JM. Biological warfare defense, II: the Epidemic Intelligence Service of the Communicable Disease Center. *Am J Public Health.* 1952;42:235–238.
25. Hay A. Simulants, stimulants and diseases: the evolution of the United States biological warfare programme, 1945–60. *Med Confl Surv.* 1999;15:198–214.
26. Regis E. *The Biology of Doom: The History of America's Secret Germ Warfare Project.* New York, NY: Henry Holt; 1999.
27. Bernstein BJ. The birth of the US biological-warfare program. *Sci Am.* 1987;256:116–121.
28. Wright S. Evolution of biological warfare policy, 1945–1990. In: Wright S, ed. *Preventing a Biological Arms Race.* Cambridge, Mass: MIT Press; 1990:26–68.
29. Christopher GW, Cieslak TJ, Paulin JA, Eitzin EM. Biological warfare: a historical perspective. *JAMA.* 1997;278:412–417.
30. Hay A. A magic sword or a big itch: An historical look at the United States biological weapons programme. *Med Confl Surv.* 1999:15:215–234.
31. Endicott S, Hagerman E. *The United States and Biological Warfare: Secrets From the Early Cold War and Korea.* Bloomington: Indiana University Press; 1998.
32. APHA Symposium. Where are we going in public health? *Am J Public Health.* 1956;46:408–426.
33. Grey MR. *New Deal Medicine: The Rural Health Programs of the Farm Security Administration.* Baltimore, Md: Johns Hopkins University Press; 1999.
34. Derickson A. The house of Falk: the paranoid style in American health politics. *Am J Public Health.* 1997;87:1836–1843.
35. Krieger N, Fee E. Measuring social inequalities in health in the United States: a historical review, 1900–1950. *Int J Health Serv.* 1996;26:391–418.
36. Krieger N. Epidemiology and the web of causation: has anyone seen the spider? *Soc Sci Med.* 1994;39:887–903.
37. Cohen HW, Gould RM, Sidel VW. Bioterrorism initiatives: public health in reverse? *Am J Public Health.* 1999;89:1629–1631.
38. Levy BS, Sidel VW, eds. *War and Public Health.* New York, NY: Oxford University Press and American Public Health Association; 1997.
39. Berra Y. *The Yogi Book.* New York, NY: Workman Publishing Co; 1998:30.

SPECIAL SECTION: CONFRONTING BIOLOGICAL WEAPONS

Donald A. Henderson, Thomas V. Inglesby, Jr., and Tara O'Toole, Section Editors

Implications of Pandemic Influenza for Bioterrorism Response

Monica Schoch-Spana

Center for Civilian Biodefense Studies, Johns Hopkins University School of Public Health, Baltimore, Maryland

The 1918–1919 influenza pandemic (Spanish flu) had catastrophic effects upon urban populations in the United States. Large numbers of frightened, critically ill people overwhelmed health care providers. Mortuaries and cemeteries were severely strained by rapid accumulation of corpses of flu victims. Understanding of the outbreak's extent and effectiveness of containment measures was obscured by the swiftness of the disease and an inadequate health reporting system. Epidemic controls such as closing public gathering places elicited both community support and resistance, and fear of contagion incited social and ethnic tensions. Review of this infamous outbreak is intended to advance discussions among health professionals and policymakers about an effective medical and public health response to bioterrorism, an infectious disease crisis of increasing likelihood. Elements of an adequate response include building capacity to care for mass casualties, providing emergency burials that respect social mores, properly characterizing the outbreak, earning public confidence in epidemic containment measures, protecting against social discrimination, and fairly allocating health resources.

At its peak, the 1918–1919 influenza pandemic (Spanish flu) incapacitated American cities and paralyzed the health care system. A 20th century outbreak of disease with calamitous effects in this country, Spanish flu is an apt case to influence current bioterrorism planning efforts. This article presents a set of principles meant to assist medical, public health, and government leaders as they construct a response to the potential mass casualties and social turmoil initiated by a bioterrorist attack.

Influenza: Evolving Pathogens and Profound Health Burden

Throughout human history, global influenza outbreaks have sickened large numbers of people, claimed many lives, and dramatically disrupted social and economic relations [1, 2]. The most infamous episode is the 1918–1919 influenza pandemic, which altered World War I battle plans and peace talks and made almost 1 billion people (one-half the world's population) ill, killing from 21 to 40 million [3, 4]. In interpandemic years, flu still exacts a harsh toll: excess deaths, in the aggregate, approach pandemic levels [2, 5, 6]. Influenza's destructive capacity resides in the pace and unpredictability of the evolution of the virus, which can subvert the body's immune response and outstrip society's efforts at containment [7, 8].

Influenza viruses infect human host cells (typically, epithelial cells that line the respiratory tract) and reproduce [9, 10]. Flu's characteristic structure is a sphere that contains RNA material and is studded with protein surface antigens: hemagglutinin that binds the virus to the host cell, initiating replication, and neuraminidase that frees up newly manufactured virions from the host cell, facilitating virus spread. Three types of influenza virus exist: type A, isolated from humans, birds, pigs, horses, and sea mammals; and types B and C, found only in humans. Influenza A viruses are subtyped according to the unique surface antigens that they manifest (e.g., H1N1 and H3N2). Fifteen different types of hemagglutinin and 9 types of neuraminidase have been observed.

Influenza A and B viruses are genetically and structurally more similar to each other than either are to influenza C viruses, and they contribute to a greater proportion of human disease than does influenza C virus [10, 11]. Epidemics of influenza A tend to affect all age groups but especially children and the elderly, spread widely across regions and continents, and exhibit significant excess mortality rates. About 1% of all US deaths from 1972 through 1992 could be attributed to influenza (9.1 deaths per 100,000 population per season), most occurring when influenza A (H3N2) viruses were prevalent [5]. Charac-

Received 17 July 2000; revised 7 August 2000; electronically published 17 November 2000.

Reprints or correspondence: Dr. Monica Schoch-Spana, Johns Hopkins Center for Civilian Biodefense Studies, Candler Building, Ste. 850, 111 Market Pl., Baltimore, MD 21202 (mschoch@jhsph.edu).

Clinical Infectious Diseases 2000;31:1409–13

1058-4838/2000/3106-0015$03.00

teristic of influenza B outbreaks are mild respiratory disease that tends to target children, potentially high attack rates among concentrated groups (e.g., schools), regional distribution of cases, and limited excess mortality despite high incidence. Influenza C infrequently causes mild respiratory disease, mainly in young children.

Recurrent human influenza virus infection and potential for severe outbreaks are a result of the virus' penchant for change [9–11]. In antigenic "drift," simple genetic mutations gradually transform the surface proteins (primarily hemagglutinin) to which the host produces antibodies. Vulnerability to infection arises with the increasing "mismatch" between antibodies and surface antigens: immunity developed during one flu season to a particular strain may have no or limited future value. In antigenic "shift," a profound change in surface proteins occurs, rendering the virus unrecognizable to the circulating antibodies in most people. Influenza B viruses evolve slowly through antigenic drift. Influenza A viruses transform more quickly, through both antigenic drift and shift.

A new influenza A virus subtype, produced through antigenic shift, sets the stage for a possible pandemic. Two forms of genetic reassortment have been hypothesized to generate pandemic virus. First, a commingling of gene segments from the prevailing human influenza virus and an avian influenza virus may occur, as is thought to have produced the 1957 Asian flu and the 1968 Hong Kong flu [10]. In some parts of Asia, pigs serve as animal intermediaries facilitating the exchange of viruses between bird and human hosts [10, 12]. A second mechanism involves reassortment of subtypes from prior human outbreaks within a human host [10, 13]. An alternate theory of emergence is that an avian or mammalian virus becomes infectious for humans and capable of person-to-person transmission, a possible scenario for Spanish flu [10].

A typical case of influenza causes high-grade fever, cough, sore throat, rhinitis, muscle ache, headache, and extreme fatigue with a 2-week recovery unless pneumonia or a secondary medical condition develops; complications are potentially fatal [14]. The collective burden of influenza in a community can be substantial, depending upon seasonal prevalence of infections, proportions and virulence of circulating strains, and population resistance [15]. Excess hospitalizations averaged 50 per 100,000 Americans per season in the early 1970s to mid-1990s [5, 16]. The number of deaths beyond what is typically expected during an outbreak of influenza-like illness (i.e., "excess death") have been substantial during pandemics: 1918 Spanish flu, 218.4 deaths per 100,000 Americans; 1957 Asian flu, 22 deaths per 100,000 population; 1968 Hong Kong flu, 13.9 deaths per 100,000 population [2]. Flu's direct costs (hospitalizations, medical fees, drugs, tests, and equipment) were estimated in 1986 at $1 billion annually; indirect costs were estimated from $2 to $4 billion (lost productivity and wages) [17]. Without a mass vaccination campaign, the cost of the next pandemic is projected at $71.3 to $166.5 billion in 1995 US dollars (inpatient and outpatient care, self-treatment, and lost work days and wages) [18].

Spanish Flu: Unparalleled Lethality and Social Distress

In early spring 1918, an influenza A (H1N1) virus began a global campaign, producing a moderate outbreak among US military recruits in the Midwest and Southeast before moving into the civilian population and then by troopships to Europe and beyond [3, 4, 19, 20]. By summer's end, this first wave had circled the world and earned the name Spanish flu after receiving much publicity in Spain, a neutral country without news censorship. This outbreak caused disproportionately high mortality rates among young adults, presaging the disastrous autumn when a related, more virulent form of the virus began to circulate. By late August, epidemics of unprecedented lethality had broken out in ports in France (Brest), the United States (Boston), and Sierra Leone (Freetown), after which the pathogen blanketed the globe, aided by ship, railroad, and by war-induced migrations of civilians and military personnel. Dispersed episodic outbreaks during winter and spring (1918–1919) comprised a third wave.

The course of disease during fall 1918 was often swift. Convalescence in survivors was protracted, with fatigue, weakness, and depression frequently lasting for weeks [3, 20–23]. Symptoms presented suddenly: high-grade fever and rigors, severe headache and myalgias, cough, pharyngitis, coryza, and in some cases epistaxis. Some patients had mild illness and recuperated without incident. Other patients were stricken quickly and severely, with symptoms and signs consistent with hemorrhagic pneumonia, and died within days and sometimes hours. Autopsies revealed inflamed hemorrhagic lungs. Still other patients with more typical flu developed severe superinfection with bacterial pneumonia, resulting in death or a laborious recovery. Unusually lethal, Spanish flu was also distinct in killing what was typically the cohort least vulnerable to influenza, 20- to 40-year-olds.

The disease's incidence, severity, and pattern of spread baffled laypeople and experts alike [3, 4, 20, 21]. Doctors debated possible pathogens, with no final consensus: Pfeiffer's bacillus (presumed cause of influenza since the 1889–1990 pandemic but rarely isolated from 1918 victims); *Yersinia pestis* (because of migrating laborers from China, the site of pneumonic plague outbreaks in 1910–1917); *Streptococcus* species, *Streptococcus pneumoniae*, and *Staphylococcus* species (cultured from specimens from patients with Spanish flu); and a hypothesized "filtrable virus" (based on experiments that produced an infectious filtrate after removing known microorganisms) were all suggested as possible etiologies. Popular explanations included the foul atmosphere conjured by the war's rotting corpses, mustard gas, and explosions; a covert German biological weapon; spiritual malaise due to the sins of war and materialism; and conditions fostered by the European conflict and overall impoverishment.

During the fall, the disease moved swiftly through US cities. Acute absenteeism among critical personnel strained industrial production, government services (e.g., sanitation, law enforcement, fire fighting, postal delivery), and maintenance of basic infrastructure (e.g., transportation, communications, health care, food supply) [3, 22, 24]. Given the incomplete disease reporting, inaccurate diagnoses, and circumscribed census practices of the day, morbidity and mortality figures are conservative estimates [3, 19]. Twenty-eight percent of Americans became ill, and there were 550,000 deaths in excess of what is normally expected during influenza season [3]. The case-fatality rate associated with Spanish flu has been estimated at 2.5% [20], but this rate more likely represents the experience of the developed world. Africa and Asia had fall death rates an order of magnitude higher than those of Europe and North America (e.g., India, 4200–6700 deaths per 100,000 population; England, 490 deaths per 100,000 population) [19].

Bioterrorism Response: Lessons from the 1918–1919 Influenza Pandemic

A catastrophic epidemic that would severely tax society's ability to care for the sick and dying and to contain disease is the scenario of greatest concern to medical, public health, and political leaders charged with developing a response to bioterrorism [25]. Surveying the prominent issues that arose during Spanish flu's fall peak in 1918 provides a number of lessons on how the suffering and social disruption caused by a large-scale lethal epidemic might be reduced. The following recommendations are meant to advance conversations among health professionals and policymakers about what constitutes an effective medical and public health reaction to a bioterrorist act and to inform planning for any large-scale infectious disease emergency (e.g., pandemic flu).

Build capacity to care for mass casualties. US cities sustained most influenza cases and deaths over 3–4 weeks in autumn 1918, crippling the health care system. Baltimore incurred 2 of every 3 pandemic-related deaths (3110 people or 0.5% of its population) in October alone [3]. Acute demand for medical, nursing, hospital, and pharmacy services exceeded supply. Over one-third of physicians and even more nurses were serving overseas [4], and hospitals found it difficult to fill every position (e.g., orderlies, custodians, and cooks) [3]. Influenza further reduced the pool of health care workers by infecting caregivers, pharmacists, and laboratory workers and other personnel [3, 21, 24] and by creating fear of contagion among some [23]. Community doctors faced tremendous caseloads, and public health nurses were frequently surrounded by throngs of tenement dwellers requesting help [22, 26]. Druggists struggled to fill demands for prescription medications, and customers, desperate for protection or relief, emptied pharmacy shelves of over-the-counter remedies (author's unpublished data).

Few in number, nurses were critical in alleviating the distress of Spanish flu: they provided comfort measures and reassurance, instructed families in basic care, and assisted with daily needs (e.g., laundry and cooking) [3, 22, 26]. Appealing to retired, private, and student nurses and women with any nursing experience, the Red Cross readied a network of professionals and volunteers for deployment in collaboration with the US Public Health Service and state health chiefs [3, 27]. To ameliorate the physician shortage, the US Public Health Service dispatched its Volunteer Medical Service Corps, a reserve of civilian doctors unable to serve overseas [3, 27]. States compensated for the lack of doctors by authorizing dentists as physicians, graduating medical students early, and expediting medical board examinations [4]. Without antibiotics or medical treatments for flu, however, physicians had very little to offer patients [3, 4], and conflicting reports about the effectiveness of different vaccines made most practitioners hesitant to use them [28].

Already inundated with patients, hospitals frequently turned people away for want of space and personnel. Facing extraordinary demand, hospitals lengthened staff hours, tasked student doctors and nurses with professional duties, discharged the least ill, accepted only urgent admissions, and prepared makeshift accommodations in halls, offices, porches, and tents [3, 26]. Basic supplies (e.g., linens, mattresses, bedpans, and gowns) were sometimes difficult to obtain [23]. Gymnasiums, state armories, parish halls, and other spaces served as emergency hospitals [3, 4, 26]. Many people languished at home, having neither strength nor opportunity to go to the hospital; social workers, visiting nurses, and Red Cross volunteers provided home health care as well as food, child care, and burial assistance to these patients and their families [26, 29].

Extrapolating from 1918, we can identify several elements that are likely to be critical to the capacity to handle mass casualties from a bioweapon among civilians. Health care workers, from least to most technically expert, would be a critical asset that should be protected, at minimum, by preventing secondary infection and by educating and reassuring them about the infectious disease outbreak. Hospitals, actual and symbolic loci of care, should have contingency plans in place and receive government support to endure a period of crisis as people converge on them. Decentralized delivery of aid (e.g., home care) would be indispensable in the context of overburdened health facilities or a contagious disease whose management dictates home isolation. In the context of a disease outbreak for which limited or no curative or preventive therapies were available, compassionate supportive care of the sick would be one of the few and most essential measures provided by the health care system.

Respect social mores relating to burial practices. At the climax of the Spanish flu pandemic, the numerous and rapid deaths overwhelmed undertakers and gravediggers (many of whom were ill) and exhausted supplies of caskets and burial plots (author's unpublished data; [3, 4, 23]). Corpses remained unburied at home as relatives searched for the virtually unobtainable: a willing mortician, an affordable yet "decent" coffin, and a prepared grave. Some funeral homes and cemeteries were accused of price gouging, and local leaders were accused of not doing enough to help the bereaved. With body disposal interrupted, city and hospital morgues exceeded capacity, in some cases 10-fold, prompting a search for auxiliary space. Cities took desperate measures: Philadelphia commissioned coffins from local woodworkers, Buffalo produced its own, and Washington, DC, seized railroad cars with coffins en route to Pittsburgh, where the demand was equally desperate. Emergency internment measures such as mass graves and families digging graves themselves undermined the prevailing sense of propriety. Bodies stranded at home and coffins accumulating at cemeteries provided powerful symbols of the country's inability to function normally during the fall of 1918. Proper treatment of the dead during an infectious disease emergency would require expeditious handling of corpses to prevent public health threats while avoiding mortuary practices seen to be dehumanizing.

Characterize outbreak accurately and promptly. Poor disease reporting systems seriously hampered the ability of public health officials to keep the public informed and to manage the outbreak. Influenza was not a reportable condition before the outbreak, and no well-developed system existed through which federal, state, and local health entities could sketch the course of the disease [3]. With a crisis evident, the US Surgeon General urged weekly reports from state and municipal health departments [27]. Preoccupied with vast patient loads, doctors did not register cases quickly [3, 19], and public health officers recognized their own inability to evaluate efforts to prevent influenza's spread (author's unpublished data). Death certificates poorly reflected flu's impact: physicians frequently cited preexisting conditions (e.g., heart disease) as the cause of death [3, 19], and overworked health departments could not analyze the multitude of death reports at the outbreak's peak (author's unpublished data). Despite the uncertainty of official counts, some newspapers relentlessly reported new cases and deaths, fueling public speculation as to whether the epidemic was retreating or advancing (author's unpublished data).

Faced with the uncertainties that accompany an epidemic (e.g., whom will it claim and when and how will it end), people need a way to measure and describe it. Health officials and clinicians need the means to judge the efficacy of interventions. Communities must have a way to make sense of individual and collective losses. An effective medical and public health response to bioterrorism would include the capacity to count cases and deaths accurately and promptly, measure the success of epidemic controls, and communicate with the public as the epidemic unfolds.

Earn public confidence in emergency measures. Some community members embraced public health measures to control Spanish flu; others resisted orders seen as inconsistent, burdensome, or contrary to common sense or deeply held values. At the US Surgeon General's October behest, state and local health officials suspended public gatherings: entertainment centers, schools, and churches were closed, meetings were postponed, funerals were banned, and retail hours were curtailed [3, 4, 27]. Gauze masks and sanitation ordinances (e.g., hosing of walkways and prohibition of spitting) complemented closures [4, 27]. Health department directives evoked strong criticism in Baltimore. The public argued that the order to keep streetcar windows open in the cold fall weather was promoting disease and not preventing it. Closed churches and open saloons revealed the arbitrariness of closures. Lay and religious observers loudly protested church closures, arguing that an exclusively medical perspective of human suffering ignored a more spiritual one, depriving residents of solace (author's unpublished data). Most San Franciscans ignored a mandate to redon masks during the winter/spring wave: civil libertarians railed against the tyranny of compulsory behavior; business owners, about a veiled public afraid to shop; and Christian Scientists, about trampled personal liberties [3].

Neither support nor resistance to public health recommendations by the community, a critical ally, should be taken for granted. A successful plan for managing an epidemic would convey consistent and meaningful messages, serve audiences with diverse beliefs and languages, and acknowledge citizen concerns and grievances.

Guard against discrimination and allocate resources fairly. Spanish flu fostered both social cohesion and distance. Through a common enemy and shared sacrifices of war, many Americans had a well-developed sense of fellowship when the epidemic struck [3]. At risk to themselves, neighbors nursed one another, fed the sick, helped with daily tasks, and joined the volunteer ranks [4]. Nonetheless, fear of contagion interrupted normal displays of intimacy (e.g., kissing, shaking hands, and huddling to gossip) [4] and pitted groups against one another in an effort to assign blame or to protect access to limited resources. Rumors circulated in the United States that German spies, some disguised as doctors and nurses, were spreading flu and that Bayer aspirin, a German product, was infected with flu germs [3, 27]. Baltimore hospitals, during Jim Crow segregation, were closed to blacks at their moment of dire need, and once the epidemic passed, an official defended the city's poor public health record by attributing high mortality rates to the number of black residents (author's unpublished data).

As evident during Spanish flu and other historic outbreaks, explanations of disease often convey prejudice and serve to reinforce existing social schisms and inequalities. In a bioterrorist scenario, medical, public health, and political leaders should protect against social discrimination and assure fair allocation of resources.

Conclusion: Signs of Unpreparedness in 2000

Influenza's lessons for bioterrorism planners do not end with an 80-year-old crisis. The 1999–2000 flu season, which the Centers for Disease Control and Prevention did not consider unusually severe, stymied US hospitals in ways that parallel 1918. At the season's peak, hospitals faced acute shortages of staff, beds, and equipment; patients confronted long delays in care. The disruption was the result, not of an especially virulent virus, but a health care system unable to cope with a nominal upswing in demand [30]. Hospitals have had to employ strategies (e.g., fewer staffed acute beds) to assure survival in a harsh fiscal climate (e.g., slim profit margins, managed care demands for cost reduction, and mandated yet uncompensated care for the uninsured), leaving the country ill-prepared to deal with a mass casualty scenario [31, 32].

Research and development needs in the control of influenza virus, a familiar if elusive pathogen, are substantial (e.g., accelerated manufacturing processes and development of alternate vaccines and antivirals) [6, 8], raising the question as to the vast research and development challenges posed by the more unusual pathogens identified as likely bioterrorist agents [33]. The logistics and time frame for manufacture and administration of the conventional killed influenza virus vaccine (6 months from identification of a strain to vaccine production and distribution and 1–2 months for delivery en masse) would inhibit the availability of vaccine before the first wave of a pandemic [2, 6, 8]. A comparably long production timetable characterizes the new live attenuated virus vaccines, which nonetheless promise broader immune response as well as easier administration and social acceptance through intranasal delivery [9]. Antiviral compounds may have limited value amidst pandemic conditions due to costs associated with prolonged use, the potential for drug resistance, and the short time in which demand would exceed supply [6, 8].

Medical, public health, and policy communities should attend to the warnings of influenza, in its pandemic form and during interpandemic years, about the potential frailty of populations and institutions in the face of an infectious disease emergency, particularly one initiated by a deliberately released pathogen.

References

1. Ghendon Y. Introduction to pandemic influenza through history. Eur J Epidemiol 1994:10:451–3.
2. Glezen WP. Emerging infections: pandemic influenza. Epidemiol Rev 1996; 18:64–76.
3. Crosby A. America's forgotten pandemic: the influenza of 1918. New York: Cambridge University Press, 1989.
4. Iezzoni I. Influenza 1918: the worst epidemic in American history. New York: TV Books, 1999.
5. Simonsen L. The global impact of influenza on morbidity and mortality. Vaccine 1999;17(Suppl 1):3–10.
6. Gross PA. Preparing for the next influenza pandemic: a re-emerging infection. Ann Intern Med 1996;124:682–5.
7. Cox NJ. Prevention and control of influenza. Lancet 1999;354:30.
8. Patriarca PA, Cox NJ. Influenza pandemic preparedness plan for the United States. J Infect Dis 1997;176(Suppl 1):4–7.
9. Laver WG, Bischofberger N, Webster RG. Disarming flu viruses. Sci Am 1999;280:78–87.
10. Webster RG, Bean WJ, Gorman OT, et al. Evolution and ecology of influenza A viruses. Microbiol Rev 1992:56:152–79.
11. Langmuir AD, Schoenbaum SC. The epidemiology of influenza. Hosp Pract 1976;11:49–56.
12. Webster RG. Predictions for future human influenza pandemics. J Infect Dis 1997;176(Suppl 1):14–9.
13. Oxford JS. Influenza A pandemics of the 20th century with special reference to 1918: virology, pathology and epidemiology. Rev Med Virol 2000;10: 119–33.
14. Centers for Disease Control and Prevention. Influenza fact sheet. Available at: www.cdc.gov/ncidod/diseases/flu/fluinfo.htm. Accessed 14 January 2000.
15. Izurieta HS, Thompson WW, Kramarz P, et al. Influenza and the rates of hospitalization for respiratory disease among infants and young children. N Engl J Med 2000;342:232–9.
16. Simonsen L, Fukuda K, Schonberger LB, et al. The impact of influenza epidemics on hospitalizations. J Infect Dis 2000;181:831–7.
17. Schoenbaum SC. Economic impact of influenza: the individual's perspective. Am J Med 1987;82:26–30.
18. Meltzer MI, Cox NJ, Fukuda K. The economic impact of pandemic influenza in the United States: priorities for intervention. Emerg Infect Dis 1999; 5:659–71.
19. Patterson KD, Pyle GF. The geography and mortality of the 1918 influenza pandemic. Bull Hist Med 1991;65:4–21.
20. Kolata G. Flu: the story of the great influenza pandemic of 1918 and the search for the virus that caused it. New York: Farrar, Straus, & Giroux, 1999.
21. Nuzum JW, Pilot I, Stangl FH, et al. 1918 pandemic influenza and pneumonia in a large civil hospital. IMJ Ill Med J 1976;150:612–6.
22. Keen-Payne R. We must have nurses: Spanish influenza in America 1918–1919. Nurs Hist Rev 2000;8:143–56.
23. McCord CP. The purple death: some things remembered about the influenza epidemic of 1918 at one army camp. J Occup Med 1966;8:593–8.
24. Straight WM. Florida and the Spanish flu. J Fla Med Assoc 1981;68:644 –54.
25. Inglesby TV, O'Toole T, Henderson, DA. Addressing the challenge of biological weapons. Clin Infect Dis 2000;30:926–9.
26. Robinson KR. The role of nursing in the influenza epidemic of 1918–1919. Nurs Forum 1990;25:19–26.
27. Gernhart G. A forgotten enemy: PHS's fight against the 1918 influenza pandemic. Public Health Rep 1999:114:559–61.
28. Heagerty JJ. Influenza and vaccination. CMAJ 1991;145:481–2.
29. Kerson TS. Sixty years ago: hospital social work in 1918. Soc Work Health Care 1979;4:331–43.
30. Schoch-Spana M. Hospitals buckle during normal flu season: implications for bioterrorism response. Biodefense Quarterly 2000;1:1–2, 8.
31. Espinal D. California health care 1999–2005: view of the future, the turn of the millennium. Sacramento, CA: California Healthcare Association, 1999.
32. Moore Jr JD. Understaffed in California: state report urges added ER capacity for flu season. Mod Healthc 1998;28:64, 6.
33. Committee on R&D Needs for Improving Civilian Medical Response to Chemical and Biological Terrorism Incidents, Health Science Policy Program, Institute of Medicine, and Board on Environmental Studies and Toxicology, Commission on Life Sciences, National Research Council. Chemical and biological terrorism: research and development to improve civilian medical response. Washington, DC: National Academy Press, 1999.

BIOLOGICAL WARFARE—TWO VIEWS

The possibility of the use of biological warfare in any future war raises important questions about its legality. Presented herein are two divergent views as to the legality of biological warfare under present international law and as to what that legality ought to be. While The Judge Advocate General's School does not adopt or endorse either position, they are presented here with a view toward stimulating legal research and analysis in this field and with the hope that additional inquiry into the subject may be made by international lawyers, both military and civilian. The importance of the questions discussed here cannot be overstated.

UNITED STATES USE OF BIOLOGICAL WARFARE*

By Major William H. Neinast**

I. INTRODUCTION

The ability to engage in biological warfare is, today, a reality.[1] Discussions on biological warfare are available in the United States in both technical and non-technical materials. The ethical, the legal, and the practical aspects are favorite topics of discussion.

These topics are approached in one of three ways.

* This article was adapted from a thesis presented to The Judge Advocate General's School, U.S. Army, Charlottesville, Virginia, while the author was a member of the Eleventh Career Course. The opinions and conclusions presented herein are those of the author and do not necessarily represent the views of The Judge Advocate General's School or any other governmental agency.

** JAGC, U.S. Army; Office of the Staff Judge Advocate, Headquarters, III U.S. Army Corps and Fort Hood, Fort Hood, Texas; A.B., 1950, University of Texas; LL.B., 1952, University of Texas; admitted to practice in the State of Texas, and before the United States Supreme Court and United States Court of Military Appeals.

[1] See, *e.g.*, U.S. Dep't of Army Field Manual No. 3-5, Tactics and Techniques of Chemical, Biological and Radiological (CBR) Warfare (1958) [hereafter cited as FM 3-5], para. 116; U.S. Dep't of Army, Technical Manual No. 3-216, Military Biology Warfare Agents (1956) [hereafter cited as TM 3-216], paras. 3, 7. "Biological warfare" is used in this article in preference to "bacteriological warfare." The latter, or "germ warfare," would be limited to the use of bacteria. Biological warfare, however, includes the use of bacteria, other micro-organisms, higher forms of life, such as insects and other pests, and the toxic products of these agents.

First, some consider biological warfare so horrible, so terrifying, that it should not be allowed under any circumstances.[2]

Secondly, others think that biological warfare has been grossly overrated. It is argued that biological warfare is directed toward temporary incapacitation rather than the permanent disability or death which results from more conventional weapons, and thus the arguments on the legality or morality of this type of warfare are regarded as exaggerated.[3] This second position is also maintained by those who argue that the means of waging biological warfare are ineffective weapons against which there are effective defenses, and therefore biological warfare has no military utility.[4]

---

[2] "Any country which really desires peace would limit rather than enlarge the means of human slaughter. This applies with special force to a destructive force which has such frightful possibilities." So spoke Rep. Burton of Ohio before the House of Rep. of the U.S. on Jan. 19, 1927 (68 CONG. REC. 1969). He was speaking in behalf of his proposed amendment to a War Dep't appropriations bill to reduce the amount of money being appropriated for the Chemical Warfare Service to "produce, manufacture, and test chemical warfare gases or other toxic substances." The remarks were directed primarily at the U.S.'s failure to ratify the Geneva Gas Protocol of June 17, 1925.

"But the surest clue to the state of world morality is to be found in the attitude toward the horror-weapons, and in the failure to take any effective measures against their spread. . . . But we do know that there has been much talk of . . . disease germs to bring the terrors of pestilence to entire populations. . . . [T]he fact remains that they . . . are mentioned as if they represent no more than new methods of exterminating houseflies . . . there appears to be little realization that they are as antihuman, as diabolical as the Satan of old demonlore could ever have conceived. COBLENTZ, FROM ARROW TO ATOM BOMB 460 (1953). The same author in 1927 predicted the use of 'pestilence breeders of bacteriology' in the 'next war.'" COBLENTZ, MARCHING MEN 450, 454 (1927).

[3] "[CBR chemical, biological, radiological warfare] is not a monstrosity born of the devil. CBR need not be a killer. In fact, much emphasis is laid upon temporary incapacitation from which the victim recovers completely." 106 CONG. REC. 2117–2118 (1960) (Remarks of Rep. Sikes). "To me there is something inconsistent in singling out gases, chemicals, bacteria and atoms and putting them outside the pale of international law, while other means of destruction accounted for some 40,000,000 dead and wounded in 1939–45 . . . ." ENOCK, THIS WAR BUSINESS 96 (1951).

[4] "Preventive disease knowledge has never been more advanced. And so the present time is the least propitious of all in history for any nation to attempt germ warfare. . . .

"All manner of germs and germ agents occur in abundance permanently in Korea; that is, the diseases which they cause are endemic. No more serious health hazards than already exist could have been created had germ warfare been waged against our troops. . . . Our methods of disease control . . . may be counted on to be successful against either neighborly or belligerent germs.

"Neither new diseases nor germs for new diseases can be produced at will. They are not manufacturable like airplanes or bombs, nor can they be trained like bloodhounds. Even if new forms of infective agents are experimentally developed, measures for their defense, both individual and populationwise, will simultaneously advance." Raymond W. Bliss, Maj. Gen. USA (Ret.), former Surgeon General of the Army, *Germ Warfare*, Atlantic Monthly, Nov. 1952, pp. 55–57.

The third approach requires that each means of biological warfare be considered as a separate weapon. This approach considers biological warfare to have a wide range. Horrible and ineffective weapons are at one extreme. Through the spectrum at the other end are found weapons which produce acceptable amounts of suffering and disability in relation or proportion to the desired military objective. Thus, separate conclusions may be required for each means of biological warfare.[5] This third approach represents the most objective opinion.

From the available discussion, it may be assumed that biological warfare is a distinct possibility in any war pitting the United States against the Soviet Union. Both of these giants, however, would consider several factors before resorting to such warfare: What military advantages can be gained by a use of biological warfare? What political advantages or disadvantages are possible through such means? What are the moral or humanitarian aspects of biological warfare? Is biological warfare legal?

This article will attempt to answer the last question, exploring specifically the legality of use by the United States of biological warfare in any future conflict.

One word of caution must be added before starting the formal inquiry. Any practical person approaching this subject should keep foremost in his mind the following common sense approach:

> ... [I]f it should ever come to an all-out contest by force between the super-Powers of our age, it would be sheer day-dreaming to expect that in their fight for survival, and so necessarily world hegemony, they would refrain from the use of any weapon in their arsenal.
>
> ... At this point, the first, and most self-denying, duty of the international lawyer is to warn against the dangerous illusion that his findings on the legality or illegality of nuclear weapons are likely to influence one way or the other, the decision on the use of these devices of mechanized barbarism.[6]

Although this admonition was originally written in relation to nuclear weapons, it applies with equal validity to biological warfare. The legality of biological warfare may be one of the considerations affecting the decision to employ such tactics, but it will not be the controlling factor.

II. THE HISTORY AND POSSIBLE FUTURE OF BIOLOGICAL WARFARE

A. *HISTORY*

Hand-to-hand fighting is the oldest surviving means of combat.

[5] See O'Brien, *Biological/Chemical Warfare and the International Law of War*, 51 GEO. L. J. 1 (1962).

[6] SCHWARZENBERGER, THE LEGALITY OF NUCLEAR WEAPONS 58–59 (1958).

As guns using black powder were not invented until early in the 14th Century,[7] biological warfare may be the second oldest means. Primitive forms of biological warfare are recorded as facts of that century. Bodies of plague victims thrown over the walls of a fortress in Crimea during the 14th Century by the Tartars forced the defending Italians to abandon their stronghold. The latter learned a lesson from this experience and included instructions in a manual of the 16th Century for constructing artillery shells for the delivery of disease to the enemy.[8]

Biological warfare is not a stranger to the American continent. European traders reportedly gave the blankets of smallpox victims to the Indians in North America during the colonial days in an effort to reduce their fighting strength. More than a century later, during World War I, German agents in the United States sent disease to Europe by infecting animals shipped there.[9]

Germany's biological warfare during World War I was not confined to the United States. It is alleged that the Germans and the Austrians dropped garlic and sweets infected with cholera bacilli in Rumania and Italy during the war,[10] that they infected Rumanian cavalry horses with glanders,[11] and that they infected wells with disease in the South-West African campaign of 1915.[12]

Research into the means of waging biological warfare was conducted in Germany, Russia, and Japan during the 1930's.[13] The United States got a belated start in such research, but did carry it on during World War II.[14]

Since World War II the United States has had a continuing program of research in biological warfare. Chemical-biological warfare research resulted in the death of three Americans in the ten years before 1960. This research was costing from 35 to 40 million dollars a year, or about one-tenth of one percent of the then current defense budget.[15]

---

7 11 ENCYC. BRITANNICA, *Gunpowder* 7 (1962).

8 H.R. REP. NO. 815, 86th Cong., 1st Sess. 5 (1959).

9 *Ibid.*

10 See SPAIGHT, AIR POWER AND WAR RIGHTS 191 (3d ed. 1947).

11 See H.R. REP. No. 815, 86th Cong., 1st Sess. 5 (1959).

12 See HALL, INTERNATIONAL LAW 636 n. 1 (8th ed., Higgins ed. 1924).

13 See H.R. REP. No. 815, 86th Cong., 1st Sess. 5 (1959).

14 See BROPHY, MILES & COCHRANE, U.S. ARMY IN WORLD WAR II—THE TECHNICAL SERVICES—THE CHEMICAL SERVICE: FROM LABORATORY TO FIELD 101–121 (1959). See generally BROPHY & FISCHER, U.S. ARMY IN WORLD WAR II—THE TECHNICAL SERVICES—THE CHEMICAL WARFARE SERVICE—ORGANIZING FOR WAR (1959).

15 H.R. REP. No. 815, 86th Cong., 1st Sess. 14 (1959).

The Soviet Union is among the other great powers preparing for biological warfare.[16] A Russian Army officer stated:

> It is true that a future war will to a significant degree be an atomic-hydrogen war, and perhaps a chemical and bacteriological one, too. It is true that a contemporary war is a war of the physical, chemical and biological sciences, of the technical sciences, of science in general.[17]

This statement was made in the only country that has conducted a war-crimes trial on charges of engaging in biological warfare.[18] The label "war crime" resulting from the Russian trial of the Japanese has had no apparent effect on developing means of conducting biological warfare.

In conflicts subsequent to World War II there were charges of, and actual use of, biological warfare. For instance, the Korean Conflict gave rise to charges that the United Nations Forces, to which the United States made the greatest contribution, were engaging in biological warfare. These charges, however, were successfully refuted.[19] There can be no such refutation or denial in Viet Nam. The United States is employing a method of warfare there that is described in its own military manuals on biological warfare. Guerrillas conduct the war in that country. Small bands of armed men raid Vietnamese points, then easily lose themselves in trails hidden by heavy jungle foliage. American technicians exposed these trails by spraying the areas with a chemical that defoliates the vegetation, but refused the urgings of the Republic of Viet Nam to use similar methods against the mainos

---

16 A biological warfare capability is not limited to States in one of the two blocs of the East-West bipolarization. The United Arab Republic reputedly is developing missiles with "bacteriological and poison gas warheads." This has led to charges that "the Egyptians are experimenting with genocidal weapons." *A-Threat to Israel Began in 1954 When Germans Arrived in Egypt*, Washington Post, March 24, 1963, p. A17, col. 1; *Rockets in Egypt*, Newsweek, April 15, 1963, p. 50.

17 Col. I Baz, *The Military Herald* (*Voennyi Vestnk*)—the principal Soviet Army journal—No. 6, June 1958, as translated and reprinted in GARTHOF, THE SOVIET IMAGE OF FUTURE WAR, Appendix A, 100 (1959).

18 Following World War II, 12 former members of the Japanese Army were convicted (*inter alia*) of preparing and using bacteriological weapons between 1939 and 1942. The weapons included those of typhoid, paratyphoid, cholera, anthrax, and plague. The accused were convicted although Japan did not ratify the Geneva Gas Protocol of 1925. GREENSPAN, THE MODERN WAR OF LAND WARFARE 358 n. 184 (1959).

19 These charges and their refutation are discussed *infra*, at pages 33–35. For a brief history, see BECHHOEFER, POSTWAR NEGOTIATIONS FOR ARMS CONTROL 194–201 (1961). For the official U.S. position, see Vols. 26, 27, & 28, DEP'T OF STATE BULL. (1951, 1952, & 1953).

and rice crops of the Communist guerrillas.[20] Attacking the crops would have been "chemical" warfare in its strictest sense, but it could also be referred to as biological warfare[21] and is treated as such as a matter of convenience in publications of the United States Army.[22] Moreover, the Viet Cong or Communist guerrillas are currently using the crudest form of biological warfare. A primary means of protecting their defensive positions is the *panji*. These are camouflaged pits with needle-sharp bamboo stalks imbedded in their bottoms. The traps are mined with hand grenades, and the defenders "usually urinate or defecate on the tips of the panji's slivers in hopes of inducing fatal infection or tetanus in victims." [23]

B. *THE FUTURE OF BIOLOGICAL WARFARE*

After this brief history of, biological warfare, one can but wonder what will be the next use of biological warfare. Its future, so far as the United States is concerned, is problematical.

1. *Non-adherence of the United States to the Geneva Gas Protocol.*

The so-called Geneva Gas Protocol[24] which prohibits "bacteriological" warfare is binding on a reciprocal basis among parties to the convention only. The United States, which ranks high among states in the preparation for biological warfare, has not ratified the Geneva Gas Protocol, but will most likely be engaged in any

[20] Bigart, *U.S. Shuns Harm to Vietnam Food*, N.Y. Times, Jan. 26, 1962, p. 2, col. 7. The Chinese and Russians have made similar charges more recently. Tuckman, *Reds Trumpet New Charges of Viet "Germ War,"* Washington Post, March 10, 1963, p. A10, col. 3. Excerpts from the latest charges are:

> "A broadcast dispatch from Hanoi charged that chemicals were sprayed in the Vietnamese war 'to poison innocent South Vietnamese people and devastate crops.' . . .
>
> "The Moscow article said 'American interventionists have again used poison substances in South Viet-Nam. Hundreds of people perished, great quantities of cattle were poisoned. . . .'
>
> "The article said the United States 'noticeably raised' its production of chemical and bacteriological materials in 1962. . . ."

[21] See H.R. REP. NO. 815, 86th Cong., 1st Sess. 7 (1959).

[22] See TM 3-216, at 2, 6, 33, 34.

[23] See Bashore, *Soldier of the Future*, SPECIAL WARFARE—U.S. ARMY 32 (1962) (a booklet prepared by the Office, Chief of Information, U.S. Dep't of Army):

"During one action a South Vietnam infantry battalion lost one man by a poisoned arrow, 10 wounded by panji traps. During this two-day fight no casualties were inflicted by bullet or bayonets."

[24] Protocol Prohibiting the Use in War of Asphyxiating, Poisonous or Other Gases, and of Bacteriological Methods of Warfare signed on June 17, 1925, 94 L.N.T.S. 65 [hereafter cited as the Geneva Gas Protocol].

major war of the future. This is one thing that makes the future use of biological weapons by the United States problematical.[25]

2. *Alliances of the United States.*

The United States' alliances with other states that are adherents to the Geneva Gas Protocol add another problematical element.[26] That protocol, as will be discussed more fully later,[27] is basically a contractual agreement that the adherents will not be the first to use chemical or "bacteriological" warfare in conflicts among themselves. Generally, the major adherents to the Protocol cease to be bound by its prohibitions if biological warfare is waged against them.[28]

The dilemma thus presented to the United States *vis-a-vis* some of her allies is reflected in the publications of two of its military departments. Both the Army's and the Navy's manuals on the laws of war simply state that the United States is not bound by a conventional prohibition against biological warfare.[29] Both manuals acknowledge the existence of the Geneva Gas Protocol, and the Navy manual refers to the nature and effect of the reservations by Great Britain, France, and Russia. But neither manual discusses whether the United States can or will use biological weapons as part of an operation by the North Atlantic Treaty Organization.[30] Moreover, as has been noted in relation to the

---

25 STONE, LEGAL CONTROLS OF INTERNATIONAL CONFLICT 557 (1954).

26 There are 46 adherents. See Brungs, *The Status of Biological Warfare in International Law*, *infra* at 47, 50 n. 73. The U.S. is involved in some type of defensive alliance or arrangement with at least 23 of these adherents.

27 See pages 28–30 *infra*.

28 See, for example, Russia's reservation to the Protocol which reads:

"(1) The said Protocol only binds the Government of the Union of Soviet Socialist Republics in relation to the States which have signed and ratified or which have definitely acceded to the Protocol.

"(2) The said Protocol shall cease to be binding on the Government of the Union of Soviet Socialist Republics in regard to all enemy States whose forces or whose allies *de jure* or in fact do not respect the restrictions which are the object of this Protocol." 94 L.N.T.S. 67 (1929). Of the 25 ratifications or adherences listed in that volume, France, Belgium, Rumania, Great Britain, India, Canada, South Africa, Australia, and New Zealand filed similar reservations. The others, with the exception of Spain, acceded without reservation. Spain's unique reservation provides:

"Declares as compulsory *ipso facto* and without special agreement in relation to any other member or State accepting and executing the same obligation, that is to say, on the basis of reciprocity, the [Protocol] . . . ."

29 See U.S. DEP'T OF ARMY, FIELD MANUAL 27-10, LAW OF LAND WARFARE [hereafter cited as FM 27-10], para. 38 (1956); U.S. DEP'T OF NAVY, LAW OF NAVAL WARFARE [hereafter cited as LAW OF NAVAL WARFARE], para. 612 (1959).

30 For a view which regards this as a problem of eminent importance, see Moritz, *The Common Application of the Laws of War Within the NATO Forces*, 13 MIL. L. REV. 1, 21–22 (1961).

Army's manual,[31] both manuals are careful not to assert a right on the part of the United States to use biological weapons. If such a right exists, will it, or should it, be asserted by the United States? The answer is not easy. It is basically a political decision which, depending on the circumstances existing when the decision is made, may or may not be influenced by the legality of biological warfare. Therefore, the inquiry "will" or "should" biological warfare be used by the United States will not be pursued. Instead, the inquiry will be simply: Can the United States legally engage in biological warfare?

3. *The Untested Nature of Biological Warfare.*

The untested nature of biological warfare adds a third problematical element. Notwithstanding the long history of biological warfare, it has not been used as an effective strategic or tactical means of waging war. A similar uncertainty about the use of gas in war was the basis of the United States' opposition to the Hague Gas Declaration of 1899.[32] The United States' delegation to the conference which produced that declaration stated that since no gas-emitting shell was in practical use, "a vote taken would be taken in ignorance of the facts." [33] This is a sound position from the viewpoint of lawyers trained by the nature of their profession to "get the facts" before acting.

Have not the facts concerning the devastation wrought by bacteria long been known? As a matter of medical practice, the answer must be "Yes!" We are concerned here, however, with the controlled use of bacteria as weapons of war. The facts in that regard are not known. Thus it behooves all concerned to make haste slowly. A decision to outlaw biological warfare *in toto* or to recognize no prohibitions on its use could have undesirable consequences later.[34]

---

[31] GREENSPAN, *op. cit. supra* note 18, at 357. See also, Fratcher, *New Law of Land Warfare*, 22 MO. L. REV. 143, 149 (1957).

[32] See HAGUE CONVENTIONS AND DECLARATIONS OF 1899 AND 1907, at 225 (2d ed., Scott ed., 1915).

[33] INSTRUCTIONS TO THE AMERICAN DELEGATES TO THE HAGUE PEACE CONFERENCE AND THEIR OFFICIAL REPORTS 36–37 (Scott ed. 1916).

[34] "Advancing technology . . . has given the advantage alternately to offensive and to defensive weapons. A great danger illustrated many times is for a nation once powerful to continue to rely on outmoded concepts. It is thus that many great states have been toppled in the past." H.R. REP. No. 815, 86th Cong., 1st Sess. 1 (1959).

III. DESCRIPTION OF BIOLOGICAL WARFARE[35]

A. *BIOLOGICAL WARFARE AND CHEMICAL WARFARE DISTINGUISHED*

Biological warfare is not chemical warfare. This truism should be constantly stressed. Unfortunately, however, the tendency has been to blur the distinction between the two means of warfare rather than to clarify it and make it a permanent division.

There are certain similarities in the two systems that are the cause of this blurring. For example, in the United States Army one service, the Chemical Corps, is responsible for developing chemical and biological weapons. Gas, one of the principal forms of chemical warfare, kills or incapacitates without destroying property.[36] Biological agents act in the same manner. Both chemical and biological agents are search weapons. They penetrate ordinary positions of strength and conventional shelters to act on conveniently grouped victims.[37]

There are certain basic differences between chemical and biological agents, however, which require that the two be treated separately for the purpose of legal analysis.

Notwithstanding their initial potency, chemical weapons are generally limited to battlefields of a few hundred square miles, whereas biological weapons can cover thousands of square miles in an attack. Within this much larger affected area, biological weapons could bring everything to a standstill by incapacitating—but not necessarily killing—10 to 20 per cent of the population. The effects would be quite different from a normal epidemic, because the biological agents would strike the entire population at precisely the same time. Hence doctors, nurses, transportation workers, and so on would be incapacitated at the same time.[38]

Related to the foregoing is the fact that biological agents multiply after dissemination.[39] This permits biological agents to have

---

35 Compare *The Ultimate Weapon?*, Newsweek, March 4, 1963, p. 56. Those with access to classified material on this subject may consider the following description woefully inadequate. Nevertheless, the purpose of this section is to give as full a description as possible from unclassified sources, in order to enable all readers to understand clearly the nature of biological warfare.

36 Kelly, *Gas Warfare in International Law*, 9 MIL. L. REV. 1, 18 (1960).

37 H.R. REP. No. 815, 86th Cong., 1st Sess. 11 (1959).

38 O'Brien, *supra* note 5, at 10 n. 17; J. H. Rothschild, Brig. Gen. USA (Ret.) [former Commanding General of the Chemical Corps' Research and Development Command] *Germs and Gas*, Harper's, June 1959, p. 32–33. According to another comparison, only 450 pounds of a concentrated biological agent would blanket 34,000 square miles while a 20-megaton nuclear device would cause severe burns within a mere 2,800 square miles. See *The Ultimate Weapon?*, Newsweek, March 4, 1963, p. 56.

39 TM 3–216, para. 41.

wider coverage than chemical agents, as mentioned above, and, under circumstances, it makes them more persistent agents than chemical agents.

Field detection of biological agents is not currently possible, but the presence of chemical agents can be detected on a battlefield.[40]

Not only is there a problem of detection of biological agents in the field, but it is harder to defend against them than to defend against chemical agents. It has been stated in this regard that the protective mask for biological warfare had to be 1,000,000 times more efficient than the standard service gas mask issued by the United States Army during World War II.[41]

While there may be other distinctions, these four are of primary concern in this article. These distinctions have both legal and military significance. Their legal significance will be discussed later.

Militarily, biological agents have peculiar characteristics which favor them in comparison with other types of weapons. Relatively minute amounts of them are required, as they are living and can multiply in the victim. Due to the difficulty in detecting and recognizing them, there is a slowness in the identification of them as a war weapon in the area. They have a delayed action and a spread or epidemic potential. Finally, they are suitable for subversion and sabotage.[42]

The characteristics of biological weapons that make them unique instruments of war are obvious. Yet lawyers and laymen, military personnel and civilians continue to treat biological warfare and chemical warfare in the same breath. This is difficult to understand. But to make matters worse, a third element—radiological warfare—is usually thrown in. CBR—Chemical/Biological/Radiological Warfare—is the *accepted* term. This is the same as referring consistently to tame chickens, domesticated pheasant, and wild ducks as "fowl" without any hint of the vast differences between those three members of the same animal family.

V. THE NECESSITY FOR PREPARATION

Related to the question of legality of biological warfare is the question: Should the United States prepare for biological warfare? As was noted in the discussion above of the United States' position concerning the charges of biological warfare in Korea, it is dangerous to overestimate the effectiveness of internationally imposed restraints or means of warfare such as the Geneva Gas Protocol. The value of such restraints is reduced by the history and legality of reprisals.[182]

The principle of reprisals is a two-edged sword. One edge is restraint; the other is justification. The threat or possibility of reprisal can effectively prevent belligerents from breaking the rules of war. It is possible that a belligerent who first uses an illegal means will find his enemy better equipped to use the same illegal means and thus be defeated at his own game.[183] It is this characteristic of reprisals that hones the other side of the sword. One of the best defenses against being the victim of illegal means of warfare is the ability to retaliate in kind. This, so the argument goes, "justifies" States in arming themselves with prohibited weapons of war. Later, if the need arises, reprisal will also "justify" the use of the weapons. As will be discussed below, biological

[182] SCHWARZENBERGER, *op. cit. supra* note 6, at 41, 58–59; O'Brien, *supra* note 5, at 8, 43–49.

[183] Stone suggests this as one reason for the non-use of biological agents in World War II. STONE, *op. cit. supra* note 25, at 354, 556.

Fear of retaliation in kind also played a part in the German decision not to use gas in World War II. This was brought out in the following testimony during the war crimes trials:

"In military circles there was certainly no one in favor of gas warfare. All sensible Army people turned gas warfare down as being utterly insane since, in view of your superiority in the air, it would not be long before it would bring the most terrible catastrophe upon German cities, which were completely unprotected." XVI Trial of the Major War Criminals 527 (1946).

warfare lends itself readily, but not necessarily practically, to the justification argument of reprisals.

There are also other reasons why biological agents are well qualified candidates for incorporation into arsenals without regard to the legality of their use. The agents must be identified and understood if there is to be a defense against them, "[S]erums for diseases yield only to research begun long in advance." [184] This characteristic would not justify manufacturing and storing biological agents after research had yielded the means of preventing or curing the disease concerned. It does, however, relate directly to two other characteristics which argue for manufacturing and storage. Although requiring considerable research, biological weapons are attainable at moderate cost. This makes them available to any nation on earth. They are not in the exclusive class of nuclear weapons.[185] A third characteristic is that the research into, and stockpiling of, biological agents can be clandestine. An old brewery or a drug house could be the cover for a considerable biological effort, carried on not only in the country planning their use, but in a free enterprise country which was the intended victim.[186] Finally, research involving biological agents can seldom be identified as related either to offensive or defensive systems. Research to develop a defensive system is dependent on a known offensive system, and the development of a new offensive agent automatically calls for the development of its antibody or serum to defend against its use by the enemy.[187]

The course of the United States, therefore, is clear. It must be prepared to wage and to defend against biological warfare.[188] Military commanders are aware of the potentials available to them in this field. Reference has been made to some of the unclassified manuals issued by the military departments. These manuals, by their factual treatment of types of biological weapons and their methods of employment, indicate that the United States is prepared to wage and to defend against biological warfare.

VI. SUMMARY

Of the three sources of international law considered, only two, international conventions and custom, offered guidance.[189]

The general principles of consequence, proportionality and re-

---

[184] H.R. REP. NO. 815, 86th Cong., 1st Sess. 12 (1959).
[185] *Id.* at 14; TM 3-216, para. 6*a*.
[186] H.R. REP. NO. 815, 86th Cong., 1st Sess. 14 (1959).
[187] BROPHY, MILES & COCHRANE, *op. cit. supra* note 14, at 110.
[188] H.R. REP. NO. 815, 86th Cong., 1st Sess. 12, 14 (1959).
[189] As noted in note 89, *supra*, FM 27-10, para. 4, provides that the two principal sources of the law of war are lawmaking treaties and custom.

prisals, have efficacy only after a determination is made as to the legality of biological warfare. If biological warfare is legal, the principle of proportionality will limit its use as it limits the use of all weapons. If biological warfare is considered illegal, the principle of proportionality will limit its use as it limits the use stances.

A weapon which is not prohibited by a treaty provision or by a customary rule of law may be used in war. The only treaty to which the United States is a party that might prohibit biological warfare is the Hague Regulations. Article 23*a* of those Regulations prohibits the use of poison and poisoned weapons. Biological weapons are poisons and seemingly would be subject to this prohibition. Events since 1907, however, indicate otherwise. The necessity for a number of major powers to agree in 1925 to ban biological warfare in wars between parties to the agreement, the wording of the agreement itself, and the reservations thereto evidenced a belief that as of that time biological warfare was not prohibited. This belief would extend to custom, to specific prohibitions such as Article 23*a* of the Hague Regulations, and to general prohibitions such as the St. Petersburg Declaration and Articles 22 and 23*e* of the Hague Regulations. The continued preparations for biological warfare since 1925 by both parties and non-adherents to the Geneva Gas Protocol, the tactics of the United States in 1951–1952 in treating the problem of biological warfare as one of disarmament rather than illegality in answering the charges of biological warfare in Korea, and the inability of the United Nations to secure a treaty absolutely prohibiting biological warfare are evidence of a widespread belief that biological warfare is not effectively banned.

VII. CONCLUSIONS AND RECOMMENDATIONS

The foregoing analysis leads to three conclusions. The first is that the distinction between biological warfare and chemical warfare is a vital one. The second conclusion that may be drawn is that the United States is not prohibited by treaty from engaging in biological warfare, and no nation is subject to customary prohibition of biological warfare. Finally, it may be concluded that the biological warfare policy of the United States will be influenced by the commitments and legal obligations of its allies.

A. *DISTINGUISHING BIOLOGICAL WARFARE*

As has been shown, biological warfare has unique characteristics which distinguish it from chemical warfare and other related systems; therefore, biological warfare is not subject to the same legal considerations as chemical warfare. Indeed, the United States, its agencies, and officials make serious mistakes in law, fact, and propaganda in treating biological warfare and chemical warfare as homogeneous.[190]

The United States should make an immediate, distinct, and permanent division of its doctrines and publications on biological warfare and chemical warfare. It should begin an active publicity campaign about biological warfare. The campaign should not only tell what biological warfare really is and what it can do, but further, indicate what the limitations of biological warfare are. Further, it should emphasize that the United States is not prohibited from engaging in biological warfare and that the use of biological warfare in the future, where needed, is a distinct possibility.[191]

B. *CONSIDERATIONS IN USE OF BIOLOGICAL WARFARE*

It has been demonstrated above that there are no customary rules in international law which prohibit the United States or any other nation from engaging in biological warfare, and further, that the United States is not a party to any international agreement which would deny her the use of biological agents in time of war. Nevertheless, the United States' use of biological agents in any war is subject to the policy consideration of the possible effect of such use on the treaty obligations of those among its allies who are parties to the Geneva Gas Protocol. Accordingly, the United States should amend its manuals for the military forces, such as *Field Manual 27–10,* and the *Rules of Naval Warfare* to remove the equivocation on the subject of biological warfare. It would be appropriate for the manuals to provide:

---

[190] For an excellent example of the propaganda against the United States resulting from its own unnatural mating of biological warfare and chemical warfare, see Tuckman, *supra* note 20. The 1963 Communist propaganda campaign was given sustenance by official U.S. publications. The activity in question was the use of exclusively chemical defoliants in Vietnam; yet FM 3–5 and TM 3–216 treat this as biological warfare "as a matter of convenience." If the United States is lax in its mixing of terms, it is no wonder that its enemies follow suit.

[191] There are indications that such a program is in progress. See, for example, the matter-of-fact statement that new missiles being supplied NATO forces by the U.S. have a biological capability in *Germany Spurns French Bid to Reject U.S. Missiles,* Daily Progress (Charlottesville, Va.), April 2, 1963, p. 8, col. 1; *Dugway's Top Secret CBR Course Is One for Top Service Planners,* Army Times, March 20, 1963, p. E4, col. 1.

The United States is not prohibited by a treaty obligation or by customary international law from engaging in biological warfare. Whether it will be used in war is a policy determination reserved for the national policy level. One reason for this reservation is the alliances between the United States and parties to the Geneva Gas Protocol. That Protocol prohibits parties to it from engaging in "bacteriological" warfare, but reservations to it by such countries as Russia, Great Britain, and France provide that the Protocol is not binding on a reserving Power who is at war with a nation who is not a party to the Protocol and ceases to be binding as to a reserving Power who is the victim of a biological attack by another Power to the Protocol or one of its allies. The United States is *not* a party to this Protocol.

The Birth of the U.S. Biological-Warfare Program

Recently declassified Government files reveal the events that led to research on biological weapons. Now a divisive public issue, the program started out as an obscure operation in World War II

by Barton J. Bernstein

"Why is it so confidential to destroy insect pests?" a perplexed Franklin D. Roosevelt asked his special assistant Wayne Coy on July 14, 1943, when the U.S. had been embroiled in World War II for a year and a half. The chief executive was looking over a Department of Agriculture request for $405,000 to support research on insect infestations and plant diseases. He knew only that his Bureau of the Budget was not informed about this project and that the War Department had instructed Agriculture to keep it secret.

Roosevelt asked Coy to investigate the mysterious enterprise. Two days later Coy told the president that details of the project were guarded for good reasons and suggested he ask a man named George W. Merck to tell him more about the work. Merck was in charge of a civilian adjunct to the War Department. Its mission was research on biological warfare.

Compared with the $2-billion Manhattan Project that gave rise to the atomic bomb, U.S. research on biological warfare during World War II was a small-scale venture: the project had a staff of about 4,000 workers, including scientists, and its total cost was about $60 million, including construction. Perhaps, then, it is not surprising that President Roosevelt did not remember that the Agriculture Department had joined the Army's Chemical Warfare Service in its efforts to develop biological weapons.

Neither Roosevelt nor Harry S Truman, his successor, ever confronted the decision to order a biological attack. The issue of biological warfare did not end, however, with World War II. The U.S. continued to develop its biological arsenal for many years after the war and American interest in funding such research has recently revived: appropriations for biological-weapons projects, which hit rock bottom during the Nixon, Ford and Carter administrations, climbed back to $60 million last year.

Last September a multinational congress met to review a 1972 convention that bans the development, production and possesion of biological weapons, including toxins, for offensive purposes. Both the U.S. and the U.S.S.R. are signatories of the convention, but the U.S. has charged the Soviets with several violations. Following up on informal contacts, scientific contingents from both countries gathered at Geneva in April to try to hammer out mutually acceptable measures for treaty verification. Given the controversial American allegations, Soviet reluctance at disclosure and disputes on each side about the other's activity, the 1972 agreement could be in trouble.

Under these circumstances it may be instructive to study the origins of the program and examine the decisions that stayed the use of biological weapons by the U.S. in World War II. About 100 key documents have helped me to piece together an account of the wartime deliberations. The documents were culled from thousands of American papers declassified on special request and from British files that were once secret.

In World War I chemical agents such as chlorine and mustard gas killed or injured more than a million soldiers and civilians. Outrage at these deaths prompted 40 nations in 1925 to sign the Geneva Protocol, which prohibited the first use of chemical and biological weapons but placed no constraints on research, production and stockpiling. In subsequent years most major industrial powers maintained active development programs. Although the U.S. signed the Geneva Protocol, it did not ratify the treaty until 1975.

The U.S. Army started conducting biological-warfare research in 1941 through its Chemical Warfare Service, but American efforts did not become substantial until 1942. In February of that year a special committee appointed by the National Academy of Sciences submitted a report to Secretary of War Henry L. Stimson containing recommendations for the future of the biological-warfare program. Stimson had requested the report a few months before the bombing of Pearl Harbor.

The committee, composed of eminent biologists such as Edwin B. Fred of the University of Wisconsin and Stanhope Bayne-Jones of Yale University, concluded that an enemy attacking with biological weapons could gravely harm human beings, crops and livestock. Although the report stressed defense and called for work on vaccines and protection of the water supply, the committee also recommended, rather vaguely, that the U.S. conduct research on the offensive potential of bacterial weapons.

Spurred by the scientists' warnings, Stimson sought presidential approval for a formal biological-warfare program that would include a small group of advisers to coordinate and direct all Government research. "We must be prepared," Stimson wrote to Roosevelt in an April 1942 memorandum. "And the matter must be handled with great secrecy as well as great vigor."

Stimson never mentioned that the Chemical Warfare Service had already begun research into biological weaponry, and the president probably did not know of the program. Still, the chemical service later received millions of dollars in appropriations through the Army's budget and became more instrumental in the biological-warfare program than the small advisory group that directed it. Why did Stimson press for the group?

Perhaps it was because, as he told Roosevelt, "biological warfare is dirty business." Stimson hoped to legitimize the research at the Chemical Warfare Service by naming civilians as monitors. Whereas some members of the National Academy of Sciences committee thought the program should be administered by the War Department, top Army officials preferred the establishment of a civilian agency with ties to the armed services. Stimson explained their reasoning to Roosevelt: "Entrusting the matter to a civilian agency would help in preventing the public from being unduly exercised over any ideas that the War Department might be contemplating the use of this weapon offensively."

Stimson suggested hiding the "germ warfare" advisory group in a New Deal welfare agency, called the Federal Security Agency, that oversaw the Public Health Service and Social Security. He wanted an academic luminary to direct the program, someone familiar with the university research system and skilled in administration. After a cabinet meeting on May 15 Roosevelt admitted he had not yet read the secretary's plan but told him to go ahead with it anyway. A week later Stimson discussed his ideas with Secretary of Agriculture Claude R. Wickard, whose agency would later take part in the research coordinated by the advisory group, and with Paul V. McNutt, who led the Federal Security Agency.

By midsummer three candidates had rejected an offer to head the new group: economist Walter W. Stewart, who chaired the Rockefeller Foundation, geographer Isaiah Bowman, president of Johns Hopkins University, and economist Edmund Ezra Day, president of Cornell University. Finally, in August, chemist George W. Merck, president of the pharmaceutical firm Merck & Co., Inc., accepted the position.

The innocuously named War Research Service (WRS) started out in mid-1942 with an initial allocation of $200,000. Wide contacts among major biologists and physicians enabled the eight-member directorate to initiate secret work in about 28 American universities, including Harvard University, Columbia University, Cornell University, the University of Chicago, Northwestern University, Ohio State University, the University of Notre Dame, the University of Wisconsin, Stanford University and the University of California. By January of 1943 the WRS had contracted with William A. Hagan of Cornell to explore offensive uses of botulism and with J. Howard Mueller of the Harvard Medical School to study anthrax.

Anthrax and botulism remained the foci of biological-warfare research during the war. Both deadly diseases are of bacterial origin, and the bacteria are hardy and prolific. Both have very short incubation periods, lasting for only a few days or even hours. The

TEAM OF SCIENTISTS inspects the facilities at Camp Detrick. In 1943 the camp was the center of the Chemical Warfare Service's biological-weapons program. Pictured are (*front, from left*) N. Paul Hudson of Ohio State University, Guilford B. Reed of Queen's University, Charles A. Mitchell of the Dominion Department of Agriculture, Everitt G. D. Murray of McGill University and Col. Oram C. Woolpert; behind them are James Craigie (*right*) of the University of Toronto and Col. Arvo T. Thompson.

The value of biological warfare will be a debatable question until it has been clearly proven or disproven by experience. Such experience may be forthcoming. The wise assumption is that any method which appears to offer advantages to a nation at war will be vigorously employed by that nation. There is but one logical course to pursue, namely to study the possibilities of such warfare from every angle, make every preparation for reducing its effectiveness and thereby reduce the likelihood of its use. In order to plan such preparation, it is advantageous to take the point of view of the aggressor and to give careful attention to the characteristics which a biologic offensive might have.

DECLASSIFIED
E.O. 12356, Sec. 3.3

~~SECRET~~

EXCERPT FROM RECOMMENDATIONS made in a 1942 National Academy of Sciences report stresses the feasibility of conducting research on biological weapons. The report probably persuaded President Roosevelt to create the War Research Service.

tough but virulent anthrax spores can be inhaled or absorbed through breaks in the skin; botulism results from ingestion of the bacterial poison botulin.

Reaching beyond college campuses, the WRS empowered the Chemical Warfare Service to expand greatly its own work on biological warfare. In 1942 and 1943 the chemical service received millions of dollars to build research facilities. The most notable one was Camp Detrick in Frederick, Md. (now Fort Detrick), which cost nearly $13 million. The service also hired many scientists to work there and elsewhere in the newly enlarged system.

The scientists, drawn largely from university faculties, put aside their repugnance at developing agents of death because the work seemed necessary in the exceptional situation of World War II. Theodor Rosebury, a Columbia microbiologist, argued in early 1942 that "the likelihood that bacterial warfare will be used against us will surely be increased if an enemy suspects that we are unprepared to meet it and return blow for blow." Soon afterward Rosebury entered the Chemical Warfare Service's laboratory and became a leader at Camp Detrick. "We were fighting a fire [the Axis]," he later wrote, "and it seemed necessary to risk getting dirty as well as burnt."

Stimson and McNutt might well have applauded these sentiments, but they would have been astonished at Rosebury's view of who held the reins. Rosebury believed the ethical concerns of the scientists in his laboratory governed the use of the weapons they were creating. He wrote years later: "Civilians, in or out of uniform, made all the important decisions; the professional military kept out of the way. We resolved the ethical question just as other equally good men resolved the same question at Oak Ridge and Hanford and Chicago and Los Alamos."

History tells a different story. Even though the president himself may not have set the course of the WRS, it seems clear that the key decisions were made in Washington, not in the laboratory.

In spite of Paul McNutt's primary concern with welfare and social services, he kept an eye on the secret biological-warfare program hidden in his agency. In February of 1943 McNutt informed President Roosevelt that the last of the WRS's $200,000 was being spent. The president, he said, would have to decide whether to "go more deeply into two or three...projects now under way." By April, with Stimson's approval, McNutt requested another $25,000 for the WRS fiscal 1943 budget and a total of $350,000 for fiscal 1944. Two days later Roosevelt endorsed McNutt's request with one laconic notation: "O.K. F.D.R." The WRS 1944 budget grew again several months later, when Roosevelt expanded it to $460,000.

In keeping with the tight security of the program, McNutt did not commit particular projects or details to writing, even in his correspondence with the president. Roosevelt's own files contain fewer than a dozen letters and memorandums on biological warfare. Of the handful pertaining to 1942 and 1943, most deal with the small appropriations and administrative arrangements for the War Research Service. Perhaps in discussions with McNutt and Stimson or in meetings with Gen. George C. Marshall, the trusted Army chief of staff, Roosevelt was kept informed of the additional millions of dollars in appropriations going to the biological-warfare work of the Chemical Warfare Service. Not one of the available records, however, shows that Roosevelt was receiving such reports.

Meanwhile the chemical service was enlarging its facilities for development, testing and production. In addition to the 500-acre Camp Detrick site, a 2,000-acre installation for field trials was established on Horn Island in Pascagoula, Miss. A 250-square-mile site near the Dugway Proving Ground in Utah was designated for bombing tests and 6,100 acres were secured for a manufacturing plant to be built near Terre Haute, Ind.

The technology was also advancing. With British technical assistance, the chemical service gained considerable ground in making biological bombs and in late 1943 began work on 500-pound anthrax bombs. These bombs held 106 four-pound "bomblets" that would disperse and break on impact. The bombs were untested, but it was known that pulmonary anthrax, which causes lesions on the lungs, was almost invariably fatal.

The chemical service also succeeded in producing botulin, one of the most potent of all gastrointestinal poisons. Merely tasting food infected with the toxin is usually sufficient to cause severe illness or death. In natural outbreaks the death rate ranges from 16 to 82 percent, but by varying the toxin and the delivery mechanism, the scientists at Camp Detrick hoped to produce a reliably lethal weapon.

Bolstered by its progress, the Chemical Warfare Service began lobbying early in 1944 for an additional $2.5 million to finance the manufacture of anthrax and botulin bombs. The service could produce either 275,000 botulin bombs or one million anthrax bombs every month with that allocation, but it would need time to build factories. Hence the weapons would not be available in quantity until 1945, by which time, military strategists predicted, only the war with Japan would remain.

The service got its funds. Although the vision of a biological arsenal with which to confront the Japanese was tempting, a more urgent threat may have underscored the significance of the service's research. Early in 1944 Allied intelligence experts were beginning to fear that Germany's powerful new V-1 "buzz bombs" might soon be directed against Britain or the troops in Normandy, and that the missiles' warheads might be loaded with germ-warfare agents. The German high command, the experts warned, was facing a strategic crisis; it was assembling all its resources and might resort to biological warfare to gain a permanent advantage.

The analyses were based on so-called worst-case assumptions. They were not comforting; by June, 1944, the U.S. had probably prepared only a few anthrax bombs for testing, if any. Certainly no bombs were available for use against an enemy.

To deter Germany from launching a biological strike, military leaders arranged to inoculate about 100,000 soldiers against botulin, hoping to convince the Germans that Allied troops were preparing for biological retaliation. If Germany had actually staged a biological attack, Anglo-American forces would probably have retaliated with gas.

Germany never called the bluff. Hitler used only conventional explosives in the V-1. As a matter of fact, for reasons that are still not known he had barred all research on offensive biological warfare. The American program—developed substantially to deal with a German threat that never existed—remained untried.

Work at Camp Detrick moved at a brisk pace. In May, 1944, Stimson and McNutt presented Roosevelt with a brief research summary that allotted only five lines to scientific developments. Much more could have been said. An anthrax plant received authorization through the Chemical Warfare Service to manufacture a million bombs and the service was making headway with short-range dispersal techniques for botulin in paste form. In November, Merck sent a report to Stimson and Marshall—but not to Roosevelt—that cryptically mentioned research on four additional "agents against men." Judging from other sources, these were probably brucellosis (undulant fever), psittacosis (parrot fever), tularemia (rabbit fever) and the respiratory disease glanders.

Merck said the Chemical Warfare Service was also developing "at least five agents for use against plants." (These agents are actually chemicals, but at the time they were defined as part of the biological program because they could kill crops.) A sixth compound, ammonium thiocyanate, was recommended for the decimation of "Japanese gardens."

These developments constituted 12 lines in Merck's short November report on biological warfare. The document is tucked away in Stimson's declassified Secretary of War records in Washington. There is no evidence that the secretary or the president devoted any attention to the scientific grist of the program.

Roosevelt neglected not only the science but also the politics of biological warfare. In spite of the considerable progress at Camp Detrick and fears of a German biological offensive, the president seems to have given the matter of biological warfare little thought. In 1942 and again in 1943 Roosevelt had promised publicly not to initiate gas warfare, but he threatened retaliation in kind if the Axis used gas. Apparently he never considered issuing a similar statement on germ warfare. Nor did any adviser propose such a warning to deter action by Germany or Japan.

In May, 1944, Roosevelt's ties to the biological-warfare program became even more tenuous when Stimson and McNutt urged him to abolish the War Research Service and make Merck a consultant to Stimson. The president readily acceded to this reorganization, which may have further distanced him from the secretive enterprise.

Then, in July, the president's military chief of staff Admiral William D. Leahy and several other advisers conducted in front of Roosevelt what Leahy later called "a spirited discussion of bacteriological warfare." The conversation focused on possible first use to destroy Japan's rice crop. Leahy wrote later that he recoiled from the idea; Roosevelt remained noncommittal. The president never indicated whether he would launch a biological-warfare

"BLACK MARIA," a somber tar-paper building, was constructed in 1944 to house biological-weapons experiments at Camp Detrick. A soldier armed with a submachine gun occupied the wood guard tower at the left. The building was razed soon after the war.

attack in retaliation against Axis first use or whether he would countenance first use against Japan. (At the time claims were circulating that Japan had used biological warfare against China.) In stark contrast to his public pledges that the U.S. would not initiate gas warfare, Roosevelt thus bequeathed to Truman an ambiguous legacy regarding biological weapons.

Two weeks after Truman entered the White House in April of 1945, and a day after the president had received a lengthy briefing on the atomic bomb, Secretary Stimson got a memo from his special assistant Harvey H. Bundy. Bundy wrote that Merck and several other members of the biological-warfare program were proposing the use of chemicals against Japanese food crops. "It is a pretty serious step," the assistant cautioned, "and you may want to speak to the President." Stimson sent a note to Marshall asking to confer with him at his convenience.

From that point until the war's conclusion, emphasis on biological warfare shifted from bacteriological agents to crop defoliants. American scientists certified that the chemicals were not poisonous to humans; the Judge Advocate's Office concluded that their use would be legal because they were nontoxic to people and because the U.S., as a warring nation, "is entitled to deprive the enemy of food and water, and to destroy the sources of supply in his fields."

Stimson, although deeply troubled by the mass killing of noncombatants that American bombing had already caused, seemed prepared to accept the poisoning of Japanese crops. Given that General Marshall wanted to use gas against Japanese troops, he too was probably not unnerved by the tactic of crop poisoning. In May and June an Army Air Force general drew up an elaborate plan for destroying Japan's rice crops by dropping ammonium thiocyanate on rice-producing areas near six major cities: Tokyo, Yokohama, Osaka, Nagoya, Kyoto and Kobe. The commander of the Air Force, Gen. Henry H. Arnold, rejected the plan on tactical rather than moral grounds. Bombing Japan's industry and cities, he judged, would have "earlier and more certain impact."

When other military planners discussed the use of crop poison against Japan, they, like Arnold and his staff, gave primacy to tactical problems. Some questioned whether the supply of chemicals was sufficient; some thought the destruction of the 1945 rice crop would not have any effect until 1946. By then, they believed, the war would have been won and American occupation forces would have the added burden of feeding a hungry civilian population.

On August 3, three days before the bombing of Hiroshima, Arnold's deputy, Lt. Gen. Ira C. Eaker, asked for a comprehensive report on crop destruction by air, including the capabilities of the Air Force, the best chemicals available and the best techniques for their application. He got the report on August 10, the day after the Nagasaki bombing. Four days later the war in the Pacific ended.

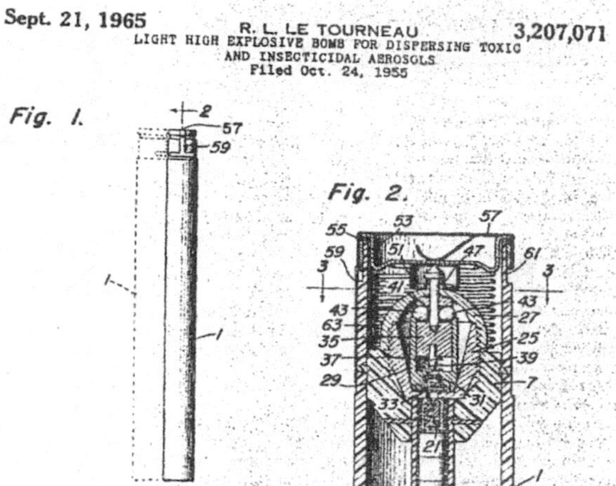

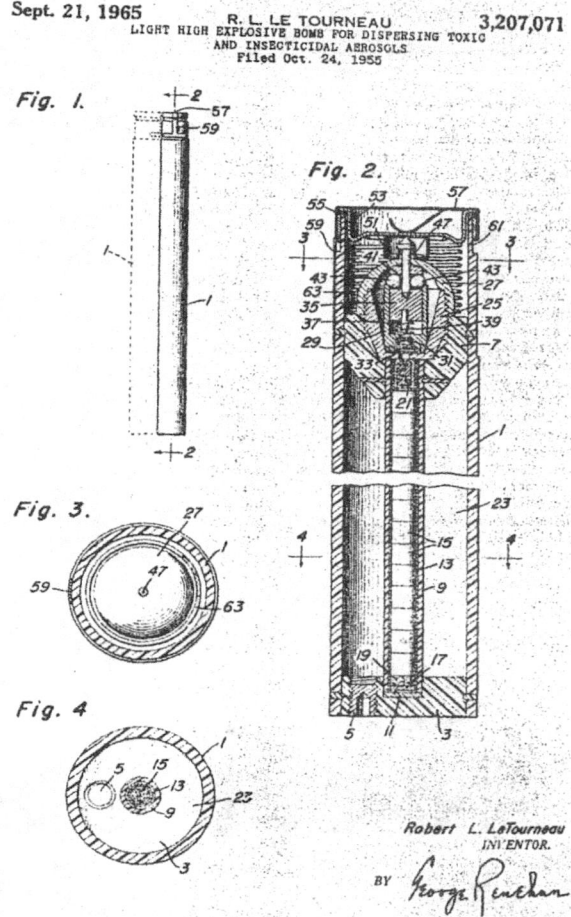

PATENT ILLUSTRATION accompanying a 1955 filing by Robert L. Le Tourneau shows an "explosive bomb for dispersing toxic and insecticidal aerosols." The design may be a descendant of those proposed for anthrax bombs during World War II, when Le Tourneau was involved in biological-warfare research. Details of the anthrax bomb are still secret.

ADVISERS FOR BIOLOGICAL WEAPONS gathered at Camp Detrick to consult technical experts. George W. Merck, president of Merck & Co., Inc., is in the middle. Other advisers, from the left, are scientific director Ira L. Baldwin, Capt. Nathaniel S. Prime, Brig. Gen. W. A. Borden, Rear Adm. Julius Zurer, Comdr. William B. Sarles, Colonel Woolpert and Lt. Col. Norman Pyle.

The nation's secretly developed U.S. germ-warfare arsenal was not forgotten in the final months of the war. One high-ranking Army general had commented earlier in the program's history that the Administration might consider a policy of first use against Japan. Later, strategists discussing retaliation concluded that if Japan broke the Geneva Protocol and resorted to gas agents, the U.S. should be prepared to respond with both gas and germ weapons. Adm. Donald B. Duncan, a staff member of the Joint Chiefs of Staff, pointed out that in some situations bacteriological attacks might be more effective than gas.

American beliefs about the morality of biological warfare, however, were never put to the test in World War II. The ultimate decision to use biological weapons would have fallen to Truman; he probably would have relied on the counsel of General Marshall, whom he greatly admired, and of Secretary Stimson, whom he regarded as a moral man. Having sanctioned the use of atomic bombs on Japanese cities, these key advisers might not have taken exception to poisoning rice fields to compel Japan's surrender.

Germ warfare, with its specters of epidemic and invisible poison, might have been harder to endorse. Years later, however, Truman implied in a letter to an associate that if the war in the Pacific had dragged on past mid-August, he would have employed both bacteriological and chemical agents—that, in effect, the atomic bombing he had approved was so much worse.

The U.S. continued the development and stockpiling of biological weapons until 1969, when, in response to the antiwar sentiments of the Vietnam era, President Nixon vowed to halt the programs and destroy the stores. Three years later the U.S. and more than 100 other nations signed the Biological and Toxin Weapons Convention, and many agreed to ban biological warfare outright.

At the beginning of this decade the U.S. began to suspect that the Soviet Union had an active biological-warfare program. The U.S. expanded its own program in response. Suspicions were prompted in part by a 1979 outbreak of anthrax that may or may not have escaped from a facility in Sverdlovsk that the U.S. asserts is a weapons laboratory.

The so-called yellow rain said to have fallen in Laos and Kampuchea has also fueled suspicions. The U.S. Government maintains it is a fungal toxin supplied by the Soviets to Vietnam, although some experts say it is only bee dung [see "Yellow Rain," by Thomas D. Seeley, Joan W. Nowicke, Matthew Meselson, Jeanne Guillemin and Pongthep Akratanakul; SCIENTIFIC AMERICAN, September, 1985].

The clandestine research that began in World War II has thus grown substantially to become an object worthy of international debate. How might peacetime decisions be made? If the past gives any indication, it is probable that the real decision makers are not in the laboratory. In World War II scientists provided the expertise to conceive and develop novel weapons, but historical evidence demonstrates that they lacked any authority to control deployment and use. Both wartime presidents, although decked with the formal authority of the commander-in-chief, knew very little about the biological arsenal over which they presided. Ironically, much of that arsenal had been developed primarily to deal with a country, namely Germany, that never intended to develop a capacity for offensive biological warfare.

American experience during World War II warns that weapons conceived for deterrence or retaliation may become attractive and may seem morally justifiable for offensive strikes. Once the war machine gears up for action, scientists may not be able to constrain use of the technology they have created, particularly in a conflict that is deemed a "just" war.

Medicine in Defense Against Biological Warfare

IT IS fitting in this issue of THE JOURNAL that we turn our attention to another means of mass destruction—biological warfare. This method of warfare, first used in the sixth century BC,[1] is widely available, easily obtained, silent, and invisible. Whether it be a fraction of a microgram of lethal toxin inhaled by one person or a drifting cloud that can kill or incapacitate tens of thousands, the potential threat of biological warfare is clear. In this commentary, we explain why research in medical defenses against this threat is needed as we answer yes to Orient's[2] question, "Should medical defenses against biological warfare be researched?"

See also pp 644 and 675.

We define *biological warfare* as the use of microorganisms or toxins derived from living organisms to produce death or disease in humans, animals, or plants. This definition is compatible with the National Security Decisions signed in 1969 and 1970, in which the United States renounced the use of biological agents and toxins as methods of warfare and stated its intention to confine US military biological programs to research for defensive purposes only. The definition is also consistent in terminology with the 1972 Convention on the Prohibition of the Development, Production, and Stockpiling of Bacteriological (Biological) and Toxin Weapons and on their Destruction (known as the Biological Weapons Convention), of which the United States is both a signatory and depositary nation. As Orient states, the convention permits research for defense against biological weapons. The convention also encourages exchange of equipment, materials, and scientific and technological information for the use in research of biological agents and toxins, which has broad applicability for the prevention and treatment of infectious diseases. Thus, research, development, storage, and use of medical countermeasures to threats of biological warfare both comply with and support the Biological Weapons Convention.

There are political reasons to support the convention and research against biological warfare. Absence of this support would not only break faith with our allies who have traditionally looked to the United States for leadership in medical defense, but it would also signal to the other signatory nations to the convention that we had lost confidence in the effectiveness and worth of the treaty. If the United States were to reverse national policy and halt research efforts on medical defense, our credibility and defense would be seriously weakened. After such a radical change of policy, might an adversary wonder whether the program had indeed continued, but in a classified mode? This would contribute nothing to international stability and trust among nations. Or if adversaries were convinced that the medical defense program no longer existed, might they begin to calculate US vulnerabilities and the potential success of a biological attack?

However, the moral reasons override the political and scientific reasons for our support of the Biological Weapons Convention. Our obligation is to protect, by every medical means available, those who have sworn to defend the United States. If we do not protect our armed forces against diseases that are endemic to regions of the world where they may be deployed and against potential biological warfare threats, we shirk this most basic responsibility.

The Biological Weapons Convention, however, is the fragile parchment of a gentleman's agreement. It requires enthusiastic adherence and obeisance to the spirit of the law, not the letter alone. To encourage such compliance with the convention, signatory nations have held review conferences in 1980 and 1986 in Geneva, Switzerland, and sought methods of strengthening the treaty. One such method is a series of "Confidence Building Measures." Each April, signatory nations are to submit to the United Nations reports on their national activities that promote openness and confidence in other signatory nations. These reports include (1) information regarding facilities where defense research against potential biological warfare threats is conducted; (2) updates on scientific conferences a declared laboratory facility may have hosted or sponsored; (3) descriptions of exchanges of scientific personnel and information; and (4) exchanges of information regarding disease outbreaks.

Potential Impact of the Threat

We agree with Orient that biological weapons development may be proliferating in other countries, especially among those in the Third World, and that controversy over allegations of biological weapons use continues to pose threats to the Biological Weapons Convention. We also concur that while many believe that world opinion and public censure will provide a deterrent influence to any country or group that contemplates the use of biological weapons, such thinking is at best naive. World opinion was not a deterrent when Iraq first employed chemical weapons in its war with Iran. The recent Iraq-Iran war experience clearly demonstrates that even today, if a nation's survival is at stake, it will use chemical or biological weapons to protect its citizens and its territory (*The Washington Post*. March 24, 1988;sect A:a37). These incidents emphasize the need not only for expanded efforts in medical defense, but also for increased participation by the world diplomatic community in mediating international disputes and for cooperation among nations to ensure that these banned weapons are not used.

From the US Army Medical Research Institute of Infectious Diseases, Fort Detrick, Frederick, Md.

The opinions or assertions contained herein are the private views of the authors and are not to be construed as official or as reflecting the views of the Department of the Army or the Department of Defense.

Reprint requests to the US Army Medical Research Institute of Infectious Diseases, Ft Detrick, Frederick, MD 21701-5011 (Dr Huxsoll).

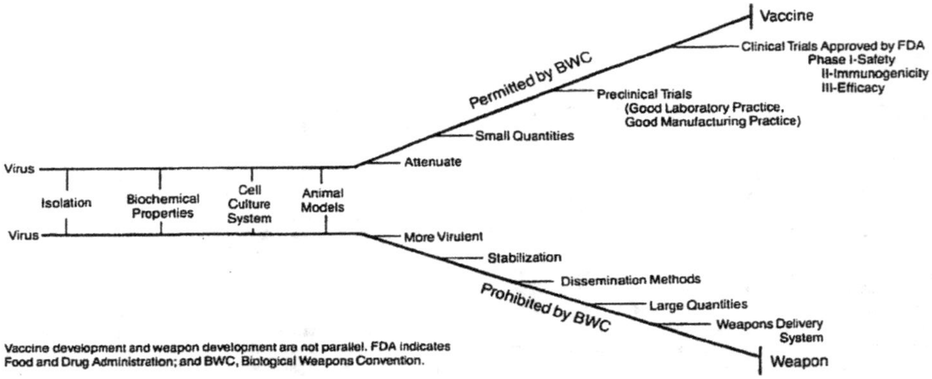

Vaccine development and weapon development are not parallel. FDA indicates Food and Drug Administration; and BWC, Biological Weapons Convention.

The United States remains highly vulnerable to strategic and tactical biological warfare attacks, as well as to state-supported and individual terrorism. Under the aegis of the now disestablished offensive program, the Chemical Corps' Biological Laboratories conducted broad-spectrum studies, many of which were recently reported by Cole,[4] that clearly demonstrated the vulnerability of the United States to biological warfare. Orient mentions one such study that was conducted to evaluate the impact of a covert attack on the subway system of New York City. Light bulbs filled with dry *Bacillus globigii* var *niger*, a harmless bacterial simulant, were dropped onto the subway roadbed from a rapidly moving train. This procedure proved to be an easy and effective method for the gross contamination of portions of the subway system. More specifically, the attacks were conducted in the three major lines within an approximately 5.2-km² area of mid-Manhattan. In 1965, approximately 1 million people used the subway system daily. Based on the levels of contamination measured with the simulant *Bacillus subtilis*, it is estimated by extrapolation that a lethal agent such as *Bacillus anthracis* would have caused 12 000 infections with a mortality rate of approximately 95%.

It is thought that the use of a more infectious agent, such as *Francisella tularensis*, would have caused 200 000 infections.[5] Without antibiotic therapy, pulmonary tularemia is estimated to cause a 40% mortality rate. A highly infectious and incapacitating agent such as *Coxiella burnetii* would produce more than 300 000 infections.[5] Regardless of whether the agent is lethal or incapacitating, the numbers of infections described herein would place an overwhelming burden on the medical systems of even a sophisticated city such as New York.

The following story of the introduction of smallpox into New York City in 1947 illustrates the magnitude of response by health authorities to a single primary case of an exotic disease. One can hardly comprehend the reaction should there be 100 000 cases that appear over a 24-hour period. An American tourist infected with smallpox virus arrived in New York City by bus from Mexico on March 1, 1947 (*The New York Times*. April 2, 1947;sect 1:21). He entered a hospital on March 5 and died on March 10. Smallpox infection spread to 3 other hospital patients, with tertiary spread to 12 other people. There were three deaths among the secondary and tertiary cases. The first positive diagnosis was not made until April 4, 1947. Following diagnosis, public health authorities immediately initiated mass immunization procedures, and some 6.35 million people were vaccinated within 30 days.

The Biological Defense Research Program

The United States addresses the biological warfare threat only in terms of defense; we have no biological weapons. This is in contrast to other weapons systems where defensive measures and retaliatory capabilities exist in kind. Development of biological warfare defense measures is directed primarily toward military personnel who are considered to be at highest risk. Such defense comprises many vital elements: gathering and analyzing of intelligence information, training of professional as well as lay personnel and the publication of appropriate technical manuals and field manuals for people at all levels, maintaining security of facilities and installations, and developing physical protective measures against chemical and biological agents.

In considering the biological threat, medical protection is an important reality in addition to physical defense. Therefore, to meet the needs, the Biological Defense Research Program of the US Army has a large medical component that develops strategies, products, information, procedures, and training for medical defense against biological warfare agents. The products include diagnostic reagents and procedures, drugs, vaccines, toxoids, and antitoxins. Emphasis is placed on protection of personnel before exposure to the biological agent. Thus, development of vaccines and pretreatment drugs receive priority. Approximately half of the basic scientific research of the medical biological defense program is accomplished through contracts or grants with universities, nonprofit research organizations, and other military and government laboratories. Products of the research include vaccines for tularemia, Rift Valley fever, chikungunya, Q fever, Argentine hemorrhagic fever, Venezuelan equine encephalitis, eastern equine encephalitis, and western equine encephalitis. The program has also developed an antiviral drug and a therapeutic agent for toxins. Development of vaccines for multiple toxins, more antiviral drugs effective against diverse viral families, and vaccines for the viral hemorrhagic fevers is under way.

Because aerosol attack is the most likely means of dissemination of a biological weapon, exposures are likely to be by the respiratory route.[5] Therefore, all protective and therapeutic regimens must counter the aerosol threat. Certain vaccines may be very effective against the natural means of exposure (eg, mosquito bite), but may not protect against an aerosol challenge. Thus, vaccine development strategy as applied to natural disease may not be effective against an aerosol attack. Conversely, vaccines developed to meet the more demanding challenge of an aerosol attack would protect against natural disease.

A "generic approach" in product development is used to eliminate the necessity to address every conceivable potential biological warfare agent. This approach may be in the form of the development of broad-spectrum antiviral drugs that are effective against multiple families of viruses. On the other hand, the approach might be generic but the product specific, as with the vaccinia-vectored vaccines.

The development process is composed of a series of scientific, clinical, and regulatory reviews to test the product's safety and efficacy. All research at the US Army Medical Research Institute of Infectious Diseases is performed in strict and full compliance with the guidelines and regulations of many government organizations, including the following: the Food and Drug Administration, the National Institutes of Health, the US Public Health Service, the Centers for Disease Control, the Nuclear Regulatory Commission, the US Department of Agriculture, and the Occupational Safety and Health Administration.

Although the Biological Defense Research Program is designed to provide defense and protection of military personnel, much medical information is shared with the Department of Health and Human Services as well as with the Department of Agriculture. For example, the livestock industry of the United States is highly susceptible to a number of exotic diseases that, if introduced, would not only destroy the industry, resulting in extreme financial loss, but would also remove US animal products from world markets. Research here has resulted in the development of vaccines for such zoonotic diseases as Venezuelan equine encephalitis, anthrax, and Rift Valley fever.

The US Army Medical Research Institute of Infectious Diseases also participates in the investigation and control of infectious disease outbreaks worldwide. In addition to the collaborative agreements with foreign countries, there are a number of individual scientists, American and foreign, who visit the US Army Medical Research Institute of Infectious Diseases for varying lengths of time to conduct their research. The institute also provides diagnostic services; diagnostic assays and reagents; monoclonal antibodies; DNA probes; and a variety of vaccines, toxoids, antitoxins, and antisera to federal, state, and local agencies, commercial organizations, and foreign governments.

The Controversy

Much of the controversy that surrounds research of medical defenses against biological weapons falls under the umbrella term "biotechnology." Technologies such as genetic engineering have opened new opportunities for development of effective defenses. At the same time, however, these techniques could be used by an adversary to develop biological weapons. Unfortunately, the army has borne the brunt of a disproportionate part of this controversy, so much so that the medical portion alone of the Biological Defense Research Program has been the subject of congressional hearings no fewer than four times since May 1988, and most recently before the Senate Government Affairs Committee on Biological Weapons Proliferation and the New Genetics on May 1, 1989. The distrust of the military has led many conscientious, concerned, and too often misinformed people to question military involvement in biomedical research. The controversy has focused on the intent and content of the Biological Defense Research Program. The intent of the program is defense: as previously stated, we have a moral, scientific, and political obligation to protect our soldiers from endemic disease and potential biological warfare threats. The content of the program is evidence of its defensive intent: development of vaccines, drugs, diagnostic systems, and methods for rapid detection; identification of disease agents; dissemination of procedures for casualty management; and training of personnel.

The only similarities between defensive and offensive research are that common laboratory techniques are used in each at the outset; but even at the outset, the experimental hypotheses are diametrically opposed. Thus, the data that are generated and compiled are different. There are many additional significant dissimilarities. An offensive program would include research programs on mass producing or storing large quantities of microorganisms, on stabilization in an aerosol, on improving virulence or persistence, or on methods for dissemination and weapon development. In contrast, defensive research comprises development of biological agent detection methods, treatment and protection, and decontamination capability. In the Figure, we have shown the divergent paths that lead to vaccines and weapons.

We believe the US program is a model of openness in its sharing of information, biologics, vaccines, drugs, and even scientists. Those of us who are committed to biomedical research for defense join with other concerned scientists in calling for increased openness in the biological defense research programs of all nations, not only those who are signatory nations to the Biological Weapons Convention, for therein lies freedom from biological warfare.

David L. Huxsoll, DVM, PhD
Cheryl D. Parrott
William C. Patrick III, MS

1. Ricaud P. La defense chimique. In: *Defense Nationale*. Nancy, France: l'Imprimerie Bialec; 1985.
2. Orient J. Chemical and biological warfare: should defenses be researched and deployed? *JAMA*. 1989;262:644-648.
3. United Nations document, reference DDA/16-88/BW, annex 3546/410, June 7, 1988.
4. Cole LH. *Clouds of Secrecy: The Army's Germ Warfare Tests Over Populated Areas*. Totowa, NJ: Rowman & Allenheld; 1988.
5. Calder KL. *Mathematical Models for Dosage and Casualty Coverage Resulting From Single Point and Line Source Releases of Aerosol Near Ground Level*. Technical study 1. Cameron Station, Alexandria, Va: Defense Technical Information Center; 1957. Publication AD 310-361.
6. Huxsoll DL, Patrick WC, Parrott CD. Veterinary services in biological disasters. *J Am Vet Med Assoc*. 1987:714-722.

GENE WARS

by Jonathan B. Tucker

Over the past decade, the development of recombinant-DNA technology has given mankind unprecedented control over the most fundamental processes of life. Scientists now routinely isolate from living cells long molecules of DNA (deoxyribonucleic acid), the genetic material, and manipulate them with remarkable precision. Thanks to enzymes, biological catalysts that cut and paste DNA molecules at specific sites, it has become possible to isolate genes—segments of DNA—that direct the production of useful biological proteins such as growth hormone and interferon. By splicing these pieces of foreign DNA into the DNA of ordinary bacteria, scientists can program the bacterial cells to churn out large quantities of previously rare substances.

The vast economic potential of this new technology has spawned an entire new industry capable of producing manifold benefits for humanity: more effective drugs, new materials and adhesives, highly productive crop strains that are resistant to drought and insect pests or that require no fertilizers, and recombinant bacteria capable of neutralizing toxic wastes.

But recombinant-DNA technology has a dark side as well. Ever since it became a reality, molecular biologists have feared the misuse of gene-splicing to develop new and more effective forms of biological warfare (BW) agents. Indeed, the rapid spread of biotechnology could foster suspicions of covert BW development, creating a political climate in which the logic of deterrence and counterdeterrence becomes hard to resist. Thus the potential for a renewed biological arms race seems present, despite the existence of a comprehensive arms control regime designed to foreclose such competition.

A treaty banning biological and toxin weapons has been in force ever since the early 1970s. Supplementing the 1925 Geneva Protocol, which prohibits the use of biological weapons in war, the 1972 Biological and Toxin Weapons Convention (BWC) outlaws the development, production, stockpiling, possession, or transfer to other countries of microbial or other biological agents and toxins, "whatever their origin or method of production." The only exceptions permitted are for small quantities that can be justified for "prophylactic, protective or other peaceful purposes." Also forbidden is development of BW munitions or delivery systems. The BWC has been ratified by more than 100 countries, including the United States and the Soviet Union. No retaliatory arsenals for deterrence are permitted.

Unfortunately, the BWC's credibility has been undermined in recent years by the lack of verification and enforcement mechanisms. The unresolved controversies that have flared over the outbreak of anthrax, a well-known BW agent, in the Soviet city of Sverdlovsk in 1979, and over alleged use by the Soviets and their allies of "yellow rain" in Indochina and Afghanistan, have been widely reported. But Cuba has charged that the CIA launched a series of covert BW attacks on Cuban agriculture in the early 1970s in an effort to destabilize the island's economy, and that the agency was also responsible for an epidemic of a highly infectious, hemorrhagic strain of dengue-2 fever that swept Cuba in 1979, causing as many as 300,000 cases and many deaths.

Concern over the BWC's viability has been heightened within the past year by a new U.S. allegation that the Soviets are violating the treaty by employing recombinant-DNA techniques to develop biological weapons. This complaint was made public in the 1984 edition of *Soviet Military Power*, an annual Defense Department survey. The Pentagon contends that the Soviet Union operates, under strict military control, at least seven top-security BW centers that are violating the BWC by actively investigating and evaluating the utility of biological weapons and their impact on the combat environment.

The Defense Department also contends that Moscow's recombinant-DNA research is linked

JONATHAN B. TUCKER *is a senior editor of* High Technology *magazine, where he covers biotechnology and other fields.*

to its biological warfare program, and observes that "normally harmless, non-disease producing organisms could be modified to become highly toxic or to produce diseases for which an opponent has no treatment or cure. Other agents, now considered to be too unstable for storage or biological warfare application, could be changed sufficiently to be an effective agent."

Shortly after the appearance of these allegations, the *Wall Street Journal* published an eight-part series of articles titled "Beyond Yellow Rain: The Threat of Soviet Genetic Engineering" on its editorial pages between April 23 and May 18, 1984. Interviews with Soviet scientists who had immigrated or defected to the United States convinced editorial writer William Kucewicz that three specialized laboratories near Leningrad, Moscow, and Novosibirsk are working on military applications of recombinant-DNA technology.

Kucewicz's April 23, 1984, article described one military project in which "Soviet scientists were attempting to recombine the venom-producing genes from cobra snakes with ordinary viruses and bacteria; such an organism would infect the body and surreptitiously produce paralytic cobra neurotoxin." The article went on to offer a chilling scenario in which the Soviet Union could immunize its own and allied populations against a potent recombinant organism—such as the hypothetical toxin-producing virus—and then release it throughout an enemy society. The target society would have great difficulty diagnosing and quickly counteracting this manmade plague.

But hard evidence for a Soviet gene warfare effort is scanty. Kucewicz does not reveal the number of his sources, and he identifies by name only one former Soviet scientist. Moreover, none of these former scientists worked on the research in question but rather learned of it through colleagues.

In an interview, Kucewicz admitted that he found no evidence to suggest that the Soviets have moved beyond basic research to develop or produce new biological weapons with recombinant-DNA technology. He contends that the Soviet system encourages scientists to

pursue military-related research, no matter how far-fetched. But, he adds, "Whether or not these lines of research would ever lead to a weapon is another question."

Similar doubts about the quality of intelligence behind the allegations in *Soviet Military Power* were raised during a symposium at the annual meeting of the American Association for the Advancement of Science (AAAS), held in New York in May 1984. John Birkner, a biologist who manages scientific and technical intelligence for the Defense Intelligence Agency, reiterated the administration's concerns about the military threat posed by Soviet recombinant-DNA research. But in response to a question, Birkner revealed that the Pentagon's allegations were no more than a "hypothesis" based solely on circumstantial evidence, including the importation of relevant equipment (which could also be used for peaceful research), the tight military grip maintained on several biological research centers, and the observation that some key Soviet molecular biologists have not published recently in the open scientific literature.

Nevertheless, the charges have raised tensions and further undermined the credibility of the arms control regime. Robert Mikulak, a chemist who specializes in chemical and biological warfare matters at the Arms Control and Disarmament Agency (ACDA), said at the AAAS symposium that, if left to fester, suspicions of Soviet military recombinant-DNA work can undermine not only the BWC but also efforts at arms control in other areas.

BW Dangers

The military utility of biological weapons has long been in doubt. In 1969, a National Security Council review concluded that U.S. biological warfare capabilities offered no compelling military advantages for either strategic or tactical threat or use. Existing BW agents were all slow-acting, unreliable, indiscriminate, unpredictable in their dispersal and effectiveness, capable of backfiring on the attacker, and likely to cause more damage to nearby civilian populations than to enemy forces, which would presumably be equipped with protective gear. These practical liabilities, as well as the repugnance with which BW agents are viewed by the international community—although they are inherently no more immoral than chemical or nuclear weapons—led the Nixon administration to renounce unilaterally the use and production of BW agents. But the United States demanded no quid pro quo from other countries.

Today, biotechnology's potential to alter the practical or political liabilities of BW is a matter of debate. Julian Perry Robinson, of the University of Sussex, England, points out that a whole constellation of genes must work together for a microorganism to be considered dangerous. Therefore, altering a few genes with recombinant-DNA methods is unlikely to yield a novel pathogen significantly more effective or usable than conventional disease agents. Responding to Kucewicz's scenario, Robinson says that a recombinant virus capable of producing cobra toxin would be no more deadly than the Venezuelan equine encephalitis virus, a standard BW agent.

Nevertheless, gene-splicing could remove a second major obstacle to the use of microbial BW agents: the current lack of effective vaccines. Using exotic viruses as weapons raises the risk that the agent will blow back and infect the attacker's own troops or population, unless they have been immunized. Conventional techniques for producing vaccines against the deadliest viruses require handling large quantities of dangerous, infectious material and hence must be performed in a high-containment facility. Moreover, these methods can result in impure or contaminated vaccines, as was demonstrated during the U.S. swine flu vaccination fiasco of 1976.

Yet recombinant-DNA technology makes it possible to mass-produce viral vaccines relatively safely. Unlike the more conventional methods, recombinant-DNA techniques permit the use of noninfectious material and yield a highly pure and safe product. The most powerful of these techniques is known as gene-cloning. Scientists isolate from a disease-causing bacterium or virus the gene coding for a protein on the outer coat of the microbe that induces the formation of protective antibodies. This piece of DNA is spliced into the DNA of

common bacterial cells, which are placed in a large fermentation chamber containing a nutrient medium and which rapidly reproduce themselves several million times over. The recombinant bacteria containing the foreign genes are then induced to manufacture large quantities of the immunity-inducing coat protein, yielding an effective vaccine. Another novel approach is the use of monoclonal antibodies—identical antibodies tailored to recognize a specific microbial protein or molecule—that will provide effective passive immunity against pathogens and toxins for up to 3 weeks.

In the not-too-distant future, countries throughout the world will learn how to produce an enormous variety of large ... molecules, including toxins, on a scale that was previously inconceivable.

These new techniques might enable a country to immunize its troops or population in preparation for a BW offensive. A mass vaccination campaign would be difficult to conceal, however, and might give an adversary enough intelligence to prepare its own defenses or to threaten retaliation.

Yet another potential military use of biotechnology is the cheap manufacture of toxin weapons. Residing in a gray area between bacteriological and chemical weapons, toxins are poisonous substances, usually produced by living organisms, that are inanimate and incapable of reproducing themselves. Toxins are more easily controlled and faster-acting than microbiological agents, and therefore are of potentially greater military utility.

An enormous number and variety of toxic substances exist in nature. Potent biological toxins are produced by bacteria (which create botulinum toxin), castor beans (ricin), fungi (aflatoxin and trichothecene mycotoxins), marine organisms (saxitoxin and tetrodotoxin), poisonous plants and mushrooms, and venomous insects, spiders, and snakes. Analogues or derivatives of toxins can also be produced in the test tube.

Until recently, many commercial chemicals and drugs were synthesized from petroleum-derived feedstocks. But since large protein molecules such as interferon and growth hormone are too complex to synthesize chemically, they had to be purified from large quantities of plant or animal tissue. This requirement made most biomolecules, including protein toxins, too costly to manufacture on a large scale.

Indeed, the enormous expense and effort needed to purify conventionally even small quantities of a natural toxin became clear during the 1975 hearings of the Senate Select Committee on Intelligence. The committee discovered that the CIA had processed, in an expensive and time-consuming operation, more than half a ton of shellfish to prepare a secret stockpile of 11 grams of a paralytic shellfish toxin. Today, however, gene-splicing technology has made it possible to manufacture virtually unlimited quantities of rare proteins, including protein toxins, under controlled laboratory conditions.

Renewed concern over the potential military use of toxins was aroused by the modification in 1982 of the U.S. federal guidelines on recombinant-DNA research, which are administered by the National Institutes of Health (NIH) in Bethesda, Maryland. Although the guidelines are binding only on researchers who receive NIH grants, the Defense Department and private industry comply voluntarily. The Recombinant-DNA Advisory Committee (RAC), an 18-member panel of leading biomedical scientists, evaluates the most hazardous proposed experiments and recommends to the NIH whether approval should be granted.

In April 1982, the RAC voted to revise the NIH guidelines on the cloning of toxin genes. Such experiments are no longer banned, but any work involving the cloning of highly lethal toxins must still receive specific approval from the RAC. To date, permission has been granted for several toxins with potential military value, including the Shiga and diphtheria toxins. On June 28, 1982, two RAC members, Richard Goldstein of Harvard Medical School

and Richard Novick of the Public Health Research Institute of New York, urged that the NIH guidelines be amended to prohibit "the construction of biological weapons by molecular cloning." But the committee voted down this proposal on the grounds that the BWC was sufficiently broad to prohibit military applications of recombinant-DNA research.

Nevertheless, the long-term implications of the spread of gene-cloning technology are troubling. As the world petroleum supply shrinks and the chemical and pharmaceutical industries convert gradually to biotechnological methods, the economics of production—and hence the types of products that are produced—will change dramatically. In the not-too-distant future, countries throughout the world will learn how to produce an enormous variety of large biological molecules, including toxins, on a scale that was previously inconceivable.

At present, no known toxins rival the military effectiveness of the chemical nerve gases, including sarin (GB), soman (GD), and VX. Nerve gases are considered effective weapons because they act rapidly and because minute quantities can decimate unprotected troops. Moreover, GD and VX can penetrate the skin as well as the lungs, forcing enemy soldiers to wear cumbersome protective suits and gas masks. In contrast, most toxins cannot penetrate the skin, tend to be unstable in air, and are nonvolatile, so that they cannot be disseminated as a wind-borne vapor. Thus trichothecene mycotoxin (T2), the alleged active ingredient of yellow rain, is less than one one-hundredth as potent as sarin.

But while only four major types of nerve gas are currently stockpiled, toxins abound naturally, and new types with bizarre properties continue to be discovered—thanks in part to the growing use of toxins for peaceful applications, such as anticancer therapy and biomedical research. Moreover, gene-splicing could be employed to engineer modified toxins that are more stable and that are also volatile, capable of penetrating the skin, or tailored to react with specific receptors (target molecules) in the body. Such modified toxins could be hundreds of times deadlier than nerve gas. These new supertoxins could also be mass-produced with recombinant-DNA techniques. Gene-cloned toxins would be more expensive than nerve gas, but this cost gap may narrow if petroleum prices rise and large-scale biotechnological processes become more efficient.

Gene-splicing's potential to facilitate the large-scale production of biological and toxin weapons raises another danger: proliferation. The recent use of mustard gas and nerve gas by Iraq in its war with Iran is one alarming example of the development, production, and use of chemical weapons in a major regional conflict. At least three types of BW proliferation can be envisioned. First, poor, non-nuclear countries could be driven to develop a BW capability by conditions such as a costly regional arms race, a protracted war that threatens national survival, or a heavily armed neighbor. Unlike the complex and expensive technological infrastructure required to design and produce nuclear weapons, a sophisticated recombinant-DNA facility can be set up without a large capital investment. And the necessary expertise is freely available in the scientific literature.

Second, biological and toxin weapons might be attractive to paramilitary organizations like the operations wings of the CIA, the KGB, and other intelligence services. Although the overt use of BW agents in wartime could pose major practical and political problems, such weapons might be more easily and clandestinely used in the Third World for covert operations like assassinations, counterinsurgency campaigns, and economic sabotage. Indeed, the fact that small quantities of BW agents can be easily concealed and transported makes them effective in situations where overt military action is not logistically or politically feasible.

Finally, international terrorist organizations might be drawn to biological weapons precisely because of the delayed and indiscriminate nature of their effects and the ease with which they could be employed covertly—for example, releasing them into a city's water supply. Identification of the attacker

and prompt retaliation would be exceedingly difficult.

None of these threats are new, nor are they specific to genetically engineered BW agents. But the misuse of gene-splicing for military ends, even if it failed to yield usable weapons, would be particularly dangerous. Although early fears about the hazards of peaceful recombinant-DNA research are now considered to have been exaggerated, the risks of military research that aimed to create large quantities of highly virulent microbial or toxin agents would obviously be much greater. In developed countries the most dangerous recombinant-DNA experiments, such as those involving the cloning of toxin genes, are restricted to specialized laboratories. But such carefully managed facilities would probably not be available in Third World countries, heightening the risk of accidental release of these deadly substances into the environment.

Unlike the complex and expensive technological infrastructure required to design and produce nuclear weapons, a sophisticated recombinant-DNA facility can be set up without a large capital investment.

The Reagan administration's major response to the renewed concern over biological warfare has been greater emphasis on defensive research and export controls. Although the BWC bans the development, possession, and stockpiling of BW agents or delivery systems, the prohibition applies only to types and to quantities of these substances "that have no justification for ... peaceful purposes." Both the United States and the Soviet Union have interpreted this phrase as permitting the maintenance of toxic seed stocks and the development of a variety of defensive systems, including vaccines, antidotes, diagnostic tests, detection and warning devices, protective masks and clothing, air and water filtration systems, and decontamination equipment.

After President Richard Nixon announced that the United States would unilaterally stop production of biological weapons and destroy existing stockpiles, the headquarters of the U.S. biological warfare program at Fort Detrick in Frederick, Maryland, was shut down. Some of the facility was turned over in 1970 to the NIH, which established a cancer research center on the site. The post was renamed. But a two-story army laboratory in a corner of the post, the U.S. Army Research Institute for Infectious Diseases (USAMRIID), was retained for research on BW defenses.

At that time, then national security adviser Henry Kissinger issued National Security Decision Memorandum 35, which articulated the new U.S. biological warfare policy. The November 25, 1969, memorandum declares: "The United States bacteriological/biological programs will be confined to research and development for defensive purposes (immunization, safety measures, et cetera). This does not preclude research into those offensive aspects of bacteriological/biological agents necessary to determine what defensive measures are required." A similar exemption for "peaceful" research was later incorporated into the BWC.

According to the Defense Department's fiscal 1983 obligation report to Congress, the purpose of the biological defense research program is "to provide and maintain the scientific base information necessary for the ... medical diagnosis, treatment and prevention of biological warfare (BW) casualties in order to meet the unique needs of the soldier fighting on a BW battlefield." "At least by having some defensive measures available and in place," says Colonel David Huxsoll, commander of USAMRIID, "one would hope that the options available to an adversary who might be inclined to use them would be reduced."

Spending on biological defense research declined slightly during the 4 years of the Carter administration, from more than $16.5 million in fiscal year 1978 to less than $15.1 million in fiscal 1981. But during the Reagan administration these expenditures jumped to almost $21.6 million in fiscal 1982 and more than $38.8 million in fiscal 1983. The fiscal 1984 appropriation for biological defense was $39.1 million, and the fiscal 1985 administration request is $50 million.

Today the U.S. biological defense research program, administered by the army, focuses on developing vaccines against endemic diseases that U.S. troops are likely to encounter abroad, like malaria, diarrheas, and dysenteries; against conventional BW agents such as anthrax, tularemia, dengue fever, Q fever, and Venezuelan equine encephalitis; against recently discovered pathogens, like acquired immune deficiency syndrome (AIDS); and against exotic viruses found only in remote parts of the world. Among the latter the emphasis is on deadly viral hemorrhagic fevers, including the Argentine, Bolivian, Ebola, Korean, Lassa, and Marburg varieties, that disrupt the body's blood-clotting mechanisms and cause death by massive internal bleeding. Other exotic viral agents under study include Rift Valley fever and the Chikungunya, O'nyong-nyong, Mayaro, and Ross River viruses.

Military-sponsored research is also under way to understand how potent toxins work and to develop antidotes. Finally, the army is funding research and development on broad-spectrum antiviral drugs and ultrasensitive systems for rapidly detecting and diagnosing biological and toxin agents in the field.

Since 1982, U.S. Army scientists have made increasing use of gene-splicing to study and prepare defenses against extremely hazardous biological and toxin agents. Between 1980 and 1984, the number of Pentagon-funded projects using recombinant-DNA technology grew from zero to more than 40, including 11 projects under way in army and navy laboratories (among them USAMRIID, the Walter Reed Army Institute of Research, and the Naval Medical Research Institute) and 32 others contracted to universities and private biotechnology firms in Israel, Scotland, and the United States.

This trend has been opposed by a number of leading scientists, including Robert Sinsheimer, a biophysicist and chancellor of the University of California at Santa Cruz, and Jonathan King, a molecular biologist at the Massachusetts Institute of Technology. The critics contend that developing medical defenses against potential BW agents would be futile, since it would be impossible to vaccinate troops or populations against every disease-causing agent in the world. Moreover, recombinant-DNA technology might enable an aggressor to create a virtually unlimited array of new recombinant pathogens against which vaccines could not be prepared in advance.

The critics also argue that defensive preparations are inherently provocative and destabilizing. After all, the capability to protect one's own troops or population through vaccination is a prerequisite for the offensive use of such weapons. Thus major defensive efforts could provoke fears of aggressive intent and touch off a renewed biological arms race.

Certain lines of biological research aimed ostensibly at defense could also be reoriented fairly easily to explore weapons potential. Studies on the genetic control of pathogenicity and virulence in microorganisms or on the workings of toxins, for example, could create an information base that would be useful for the eventual production of biological weapons.

One way to resolve the offensive-defensive dilemma is to prevent the classification of any military research involving recombinant-DNA methods or biological warfare materials and to make the results available to scientists of all countries. Says Robert Mikulak, "There is no justification for classified military research on recombinant DNA—in the United States, the Soviet Union, or anywhere else."

Today, however, Soviet recombinant-DNA research is shrouded in secrecy. Thomas Dashiell, a senior official in the Pentagon's Office of the Under Secretary for Research and Engineering, contends that the Defense Department "currently has no classified programs in the application of biotechnology. We see little need to classify such efforts [because] all work is in the basic science areas . . . and the possible application of such research is a number of years away." Nevertheless, some of the results of research on biological detection systems, sponsored by the U.S. Army Materiel Command, are secret.

In the spring of 1984, Defense and Com-

merce Department officials mapped out plans for tightened export controls on biotechnology equipment, materials, and expertise with potential military value. Certain types of bacteria, fungi, viruses, and protozoa are already controlled by the Pentagon munitions list and therefore cannot be shipped to Soviet-bloc countries. But the Defense Department seeks to add certain types of biotechnology equipment and methods to the Militarily Critical Technologies List (MCTL)—a classified document that serves as a guide to restricted exports. Biotechnologies that might be considered militarily sensitive include high-containment and decontamination equipment for production-scale facilities, large fermentation tanks and separators, systems for extracting solvents and drying biological products, and extremely small-bore spray nozzles capable of disseminating biological or toxin agents as a fine mist. The actual implementation of biotechnology export controls by the Commerce Department has been held up by the expiration of the Export Administration Act of 1979, which authorized Commerce to enforce the export regulations.

According to Henry Mitman, a senior official with the Office of Export Administration, passage of the revised version of the act—now in House-Senate conference committee—would empower the Commerce Department to establish a biotechnology technical advisory committee, made up of representatives from U.S. biotechnology, pharmaceutical, and scientific-equipment firms, to evaluate the national-security implications of biotechnology. This committee would advise Commerce on the military potential of individual biotechnologies, recommend controls on equipment and technical knowledge, such as unpublished data and licensing agreements, and determine which technologies are already available on the world market.

But although a monitoring system to keep track of which countries are importing sensitive biotechnologies makes sense, the effectiveness of export controls is questionable. In hearings before a subcommittee of the House Committee on Science and Technology on May 24, 1984, J. Leslie Glick, the head of

Genex Corporation, testified that the flourishing global trade in biotechnology would already render U.S. export controls ineffective and would "markedly harm our country's ability to compete in overseas markets."

The uncomfortable truth is that it is probably already too late to prevent the spread of gene-cloning technology. A toxin gene can be cloned into a bacterium with readily available microorganisms, enzymes, laboratory equipment, and widely published techniques. Moreover, large-capacity fermenters and other process equipment could be developed by any reasonably advanced country. Thus the only way to control such misuses of biotechnology is through a verifiable and enforceable arms control regime.

International Solutions

Although no reliable evidence exists to suggest that either superpower has begun to apply biotechnological techniques to develop new biological weapons, concern is growing worldwide that the continuing deterioration of U.S.-Soviet relations might spark BW rearmament. Thus diplomatic efforts are under way to strengthen the existing arms control regime.

During the First Review Conference of the BWC in 1980, signatories affirmed that the treaty is drafted broadly enough to cover not only existing but also any possible future means of biological and toxin warfare. This would undoubtedly clearly include the use of recombinant-DNA methods. Even assuming full coverage, however, some major loopholes in the convention remain.

The most serious loophole is in Article I, which qualifies the ban on biological and toxin weapons by permitting development, production, and stockpiling of small amounts that can be justified for "prophylactic, protective or other peaceful purposes." The quantity of seed stock allowed is not specified, nor is it clear who is to judge whether justification exists for the production of any given quantity.

The BWC should be amended to define permitted types of research in a more restrictive manner, specifying the precise quantities of toxic seed stocks that can be retained and

banning all classified military research involving BW agents or recombinant-DNA methods. A number of scientists have proposed internationalizing defensive BW research, using the legal precedent of Article X of the BWC, which obliges parties to the treaty to cooperate in the use of biological substances for peaceful purposes.

Until internationalization becomes politically feasible, unrestricted scientific exchange programs should be established so that scientists can visit infectious-disease laboratories in other countries and have full access to information. Moreover, administration of the U.S. biological defense research program should be transferred from the army to a civilian agency such as the U.S. Public Health Service or the Centers for Disease Control in Atlanta. Yet opening up defensive research alone would not prevent treaty violations. Because of the possibility of conducting prohibited research in secret laboratories, more intrusive verification methods will also be required.

A second major weakness of the BWC is its coverage of toxins. Toxins are not defined precisely, leaving much room for interpretation. According to Jozef Goldblat of the Stockholm International Peace Research Institute, the treaty's language is intended to ensure that the concept of toxin is interpreted broadly, covering both naturally occurring biological compounds and synthetically produced or modified analogues that could serve as warfare agents, "whatever their origin or method of production." But a country seeking to develop toxin weapons might rationalize its efforts by synthesizing analogues that are not only considerably smaller than the original toxin molecule but that have a markedly different chemical composition. These compounds might then be reclassified as chemical agents. Because a comprehensive chemical weapons ban does not exist, development of chemical agents remains unrestricted and can proceed in secret.

The legal distinction between chemical and toxin weapons is an artificial one, derived not from any clear-cut phenomenological difference but from the history of the negotiation process. In the Geneva Protocol of 1925, biological and chemical weapons are treated as a single entity. But the BWC negotiators decided to separate them on the grounds that a comprehensive ban on biological and toxin agents would be easier to achieve. At that time, biological disarmament was seen as a modest first step toward the more important goal of eliminating chemical weapons, to which all parties to the BWC were committed. Unfortunately, that goal has remained elusive. Until a chemical weapons treaty is negotiated, however, the term "toxin" in the BWC should be defined explicitly to include all fragments, modifications, and analogues of biological toxins, regardless of how they are produced.

Between 1980 and 1984, the number of Pentagon-funded projects using recombinant-DNA technology grew from zero to more than 40.

Now that recombinant-DNA technology has made the mass production of toxins technically and economically feasible, the need for a verifiable treaty banning all forms of chemical warfare has become all the more acute. If such a treaty were in force, no justification or incentive would exist for reclassifying modified toxins as chemical weapons.

Chemical weapons talks are now under way at the 40-nation Conference on Disarmament (CD) in Geneva—the principal forum for the negotiation of multilateral arms control and disarmament agreements. Progress has been slow, but one encouraging sign is the recent Soviet agreement in principle to the verification of a chemical weapons treaty by challenge inspections, although it has reserved the right to veto them. The U.S.-Soviet gap on verification was further narrowed in July 1984, when Washington agreed to open domestic, private-sector chemical plants to the same kind of unlimited on-site inspection it seeks to conduct of Soviet facilities. In order to achieve further progress, the United States should seek verification measures that are adequate

but not so stringent as to be politically infeasible. Worthy of U.S. support are efforts by the United Kingdom and other CD countries to create a more limited verification framework, such as an annual quota of on-site inspections.

The BWC's most serious flaw is the lack of effective verification and enforcement provisions. During the treaty negotiations few of the participating states saw much need for elaborate verification measures. Since the United States had already unilaterally renounced the production of BW agents, most countries concluded that such weapons had no military value. In addition, the strategic arms limitation talks were already getting under way, and the United States was seeking to ease tensions with the Soviet Union after a freeze in their relationship caused by the 1968 Soviet invasion of Czechoslovakia. Thus a quick settlement on a biological weapons ban was sought as a signal of good intentions.

As a result, the BWC's verification procedure is also weak. Substantive evidence of alleged violations may be lodged with the U.N. Security Council. And signatories are obliged to consult and to cooperate with any investigation that the council undertakes. In practice, however, this procedure may be easily circumvented. Since a violation of the BWC would probably be covert, legally obtaining sufficient evidence to substantiate a complaint would be extremely difficult. Indeed, the use of biological weapons could be hard to prove because bacterial or toxin agents break down or dissipate rapidly after use and because they are often indistinguishable from indigenous microorganisms or toxins.

Moreover, while the Security Council alone has the power to launch an investigation, council action can be blocked by a veto of one of the five permanent members—China, France, the Soviet Union, the United Kingdom, and the United States. The verification procedure is thus clearly unequal in its treatment of the parties. Besides, even if the Security Council does verify that a violation has occurred, it lacks reliable or effective enforcement mechanisms.

Governments and specialists disagree about the extent to which a strategically significant effort to develop or produce biological weapons could be detected with national means of verification, including surveillance satellites, ground monitoring stations, and human agents. "Unlike high energy physics experiments or the construction and testing of weapons delivery vehicles," says John Birkner, "new biotechnology research efforts devoted to military objectives would tend not to reveal themselves. Facilities, equipment, and personnel devoted ostensibly to food or drug production could easily be turned to military biotechnology R&D tasks." Consequently, both the Pentagon and the State Department have insisted on on-site inspections of suspect military facilities on very short notice.

The uncomfortable truth is that it is probably already too late to prevent the spread of gene-cloning technology.

It is difficult for anyone outside the intelligence community to know whether the U.S. position has a real technical basis or whether it is merely being used as an excuse to forestall negotiations. According to Matthew Meselson, a professor of biochemistry at Harvard University, a militarily significant strategic or tactical BW capability would require large-scale, high-containment facilities for the production of biological or toxin agents and munitions, and therefore could not be concealed for long from national means of verification. On the other hand, vaccine plants might be capable of secretly producing smaller quantities of BW agents for sabotage attacks, providing a compelling rationale for some form of on-site inspection regime.

Sweden, to its credit, was an early critic of the BWC's weak verification measures. At the 1982 session of the U.N. General Assembly, Sweden proposed convening a special conference to strengthen the BWC by establishing a "flexible, objective and non-discriminatory complaints procedure" for dealing with verification and compliance issues. But the Soviet Union voted against the proposal.

Sweden has since backed off from this proposal and plans instead to raise verification at the Second Review Conference of the BWC, scheduled to take place before the end of 1986. Sweden does not intend to amend the BWC but rather to interpret one of the articles in order to expand the verification provisions.

At the CD, Sweden is engaged in informal negotiations to try to find a verification formula that will be acceptable to the West without provoking Soviet fears of spying. "There are very definite limitations on how intrusive verification can be," says Ambassador Rolf Ekeus, head of the Swedish delegation in Geneva. "We must have full agreement among the major powers, not just the harmless, smaller countries."

Ekeus would not reveal any details of the Swedish proposals, but a number of approaches have been discussed elsewhere. In 1982 in the General Assembly, Sweden sought reassurances from the permanent members of the Security Council that they would not prevent council investigations of alleged BWC violations. Empowering the U.N. secretary general to request an investigation would also be a useful step.

In addition, Jozef Goldblat has suggested separating the complaints procedure into two phases: a fact-finding stage and an evaluation and judgment stage. The fact-finding stage would be the responsibility of a standing committee of internationally recognized biologists—not diplomats or military men—assembled from the Western bloc, the Soviet bloc, and the nonaligned countries, under the auspices of the World Health Organization. At the request of a quorum of BWC signatories, this expert body would be sent on short notice to investigate any apparent violation of the convention, according to procedures agreed upon in advance. No country would be permitted to refuse inspection of biological laboratories on the grounds of military secrecy. If this impartial scientific body obtained evidence of a violation, a complaint could then be lodged with the Security Council.

Such an impartial inspection mechanism would effectively deter possible use or secret development or possession of BW agents.

Moreover, a state that had been unjustly accused of BWC violations could dispel suspicions by inviting inspections. Further, parties to the convention might also agree to provide humanitarian and military assistance to any state attacked with biological or toxin weapons, and to implement comprehensive, mandatory economic sanctions or other collective punitive measures against the aggressor.

Since a financially ailing biotechnology firm could be pressured into accepting a secret military contract to develop new BW agents, the biotechnology industry should be included in any on-site inspection regime. Although the industry may claim that such inspections could reveal proprietary information to competitors, it should be willing to compromise on this point in the greater interest of U.S. national security.

In order to strengthen its hand with industry, the White House should push for legislation incorporating the BWC's provisions into the U.S. civil code, thereby making them binding on U.S. citizens and corporations. A bill to this effect (H.R. 7977) was unsuccessfully introduced in the House of Representatives by Peter Rodino (D.-New Jersey) on August 20, 1980.

Some ACDA officials support the creation of a U.S.-Soviet standing consultative committee, along the lines of the body set up by SALT I, which would meet regularly and privately to resolve compliance disputes relating to the BWC. In addition, as a confidence-building measure, the ACDA is officially seeking information exchanges on past and present activities related to biological warfare, including pre-BWC development programs, unusual or large-scale outbreaks of disease, and biological research facilities that handle particularly dangerous materials.

No matter what diplomats do to keep the new biology confined to peaceful applications, biologists themselves will have to shoulder much of the burden. The scientific community played a major role in lobbying for the eventual negotiation of the BWC when more than 5,000 scientists signed petitions urging the Johnson administration to ratify the Geneva Protocol. A similar effort is required today.

Scientific organizations such as the American Society for Microbiology, the National Academy of Sciences, the Soviet Academy of Sciences, and their counterparts in other countries, should amend their charters to forbid members to engage in classified biological research. And biologists should remain alert to possible abuses of recombinant-DNA technology by American or foreign scientists and should warn the public of any potential danger.

Like nuclear power, mankind's ability to manipulate the most fundamental processes of life cannot be "disinvented." And like the unlocking of the atom, biotechnology can bring enormous benefit or incalculable harm. Fortunately, there are grounds for cautious optimism. Biology remains one of the few areas of science that has not been mobilized on a large scale as a means of death and destruction. And although the BWC is under increasing political and technological pressure, there is still time to strengthen the legal, institutional, and sociocultural barriers to biological warfare.

The Second Review Conference of the Biological Weapons Convention: One Step Forward, Many More To Go

ERIC J. McFADDEN*

INTRODUCTION

The 1972 Biological Weapons Convention[1] has been hailed as "the most ambitious of all multinational arms treaties."[2] As one analyst notes:

> Nations that sign it undertake "never under any circumstances to develop, produce, stockpile, or otherwise acquire or retain microbiological or other biological agents, or toxins whatever their method of production, of types and in quantities that have no justification for prophylactic, protective, or other peaceful purposes." It also bans weapons and other delivery systems designed to use such agents and requires the destruction of any existing agents or weapons.[3]

The Convention entered into force on March 26, 1975, and now has one hundred thirteen signatories, representing two-thirds of the member states of the United Nations.[4] All of the

* Director, Midwest Office, Pacific Center for International Studies, Madison, Wisconsin. The author wishes to thank Robert Mikulak of the U.S. Arms Control and Disarmament Agency for supplying materials that proved invaluable in the preparation of this article.

[1] Convention on the Prohibition of the Development, Production and Stockpiling of Bacteriological (Biological) and Toxin Weapons and on Their Destruction, *opened for signature* Apr. 10, 1972, 26 U.S.T. 583, T.I.A.S. No. 8062, 11 I.L.M. 309, 310 (1972) (annex) [hereinafter Biological Weapons Convention].

[2] Heylin, *The Weapons Connection: Role of New Biology Uncertain*, CHEM. & ENG'G NEWS, Aug. 13, 1984, at 45, 46.

[3] *Id.* at 46.

[4] *Germ Warfare*, SCI. AM., Apr. 1987, at 62; Vaerno, *The Forthcoming Review Conference of the Parties To The Biological Weapons Convention*, 9 DISARMAMENT 211, 217, U.N. Sales No. E.86.IX.8 (1986).

permanent members of the U.N. Security Council are parties to the treaty.[5]

Unfortunately, several events in recent years have precipitated a crisis of confidence that threatens the continued viability of the treaty, and may portend a biological or toxin arms race. In the late 1970s and early 1980s, the United States accused the Soviet Union and its allies of deploying toxin agents[6] against resistance forces in Afghanistan[7] and Southeast Asia[8], although the validity of these allegations remains subject to serious question.[9]

[5] Vaerno, *supra* note 4, at 217.

[6] It is not entirely clear whether the United States was accusing the Soviet Union of illegally using biological or chemical weapons. As one commentator has noted, the United States government, journalists and scholars often use imprecise terms when discussing chemical and biological agents. Various reports of the Soviet Union's activities in Afghanistan and Southeast Asia have referred to the agents involved as "'fungus toxins,' 'chemical agents,' 'biochemical toxins,' 'biotoxins,' 'poisons,' 'biological warfare,' 'toxic chemicals' and 'toxin weapons.'" Note, *International Regulation Of Chemical And Biological Weapons: 'Yellow Rain' And Arms Control*, 1984 U. ILL. L. REV. 1011, 1019; *see also* 3 STOCKHOLM INT'L PEACE RESEARCH INST., THE PROBLEM OF CHEMICAL AND BIOLOGICAL WARFARE 13 n.1 (1979) (toxins are chemical weapons); A. THOMAS & A. THOMAS, JR., 2 DEVELOPMENT OF INTERNATIONAL LEGAL LIMITATIONS ON THE USE OF CHEMICAL AND BIOLOGICAL WEAPONS 2 (1968) (toxins are structurally closer to biological agents than chemical agents); Pringle, *Yellow Rain: The Cost of Chemical Arms Control*, 5 SAIS REV. 151, 153 (1984) (toxic agent identified by United States government actually both a biological and chemical agent). However, article I of the Biological Weapons Convention specifically proscribes the use or possession of toxins. Thus, it is certainly relevant to analyze United States charges within this framework.

[7] The United States alleged that the Soviet Union and the government of Afghanistan had used trichothecenes, a subclass of mycotoxins against Afghan resistance forces. *See* U.S. DEP'T OF STATE, SPECIAL REPORT NO. 98, CHEMICAL WARFARE IN SOUTHEAST ASIA AND AFGHANISTAN 4 (1982); *see also Chemical-Biological Warfare in Afghanistan*, Wall St. J., June 7, 1982, at 20, col. 3. Mycotoxins are produced by a mold or fungus that is highly toxic to humans and other animals. Exposure to mycotoxins may cause nausea, vomiting, dizziness, diarrhea with blood and internal hemorrhaging. Note, *supra* note 6, at 1020. More generally, toxins are highly poisonous substances produced by a large variety of living organisms, including bacteria, protozoa, fungi, amphibia and reptilia. Geissler & Lohs, *The Changing Status of Toxin Weapons*, in BIOLOGICAL AND TOXIN WEAPONS TODAY 36 (E. Geissler ed. 1986).

[8] In a speech on September 13, 1981 in Berlin, Secretary of State Alexander Haig announced that the United States had evidence that the Soviet Union and Vietnam had deployed trichothecene mycotoxins against resistance forces in Laos and Kampuchea. A. HAIG, THE DEMOCRATIC REVOLUTION AND ITS FUTURE 3 (Bureau of Public Affairs, U.S. Dep't of State, Current Policy No. 311, Sept. 13, 1981). The next day, the Department of State held a press conference in Washington and distributed a five-page fact sheet outlining the Government's evidence in support of these charges, including refugee testimony and leaf and stem samples from Kampuchea containing high levels of mycotoxins. *See* Bartley & Kucewicz, *'Yellow Rain' and the Future of Arms Agreements*, 61 FOREIGN AFF. 805, 812 (1983).

[9] The Reagan administration's charges have been widely assailed. Several teams of scientists, including a group led by Harvard biochemist Matthew Meselson and Yale entomologist Thomas Seeley, have concluded that the sticky yellow spots found on leaves collected by government researchers are not toxins, but rather bee feces. *See, e.g.*, See-

In the spring of 1979, a serious outbreak of anthrax occurred in the Soviet city of Sverdlovsk, killing anywhere from twenty to one thousand people. Relying largely on the reports of Soviet emigrants, the Carter administration in 1980 expressed its concern to the Soviets that the outbreak may have resulted from an accident at a suspected biological warfare facility in the vicinity.[10] In 1985, U.S. Defense Secretary Weinberger characterized the incident as an accident at a "biological warfare center" and cited the accident as proof of the Soviet Union's violation of the Biological Weapons Convention.[11] The Soviet Union has consistently denied the charges and has alleged that the epidemic was caused by the consumption of meat from animals that had contracted anthrax.[12] What really happened in Sverdlovsk remains

ley, Nowicke, Meselson, Guillemin & Akratanakul, *Yellow Rain*, SCI. AM., Sept. 1985, at 128; *Yellow Rain: Thai Bees' Faeces Found*, 308 NATURE 485 (1984). Perhaps the most convincing evidence for this theory is a palynological analysis of leaf samples of "yellow rain" conducted by Nowicke and Meselson in Southeast Asia which revealed that no two of the samples had the same pollen composition, a highly unlikely finding if the substances were disseminated by an artificial source such as toxin weapons. Nowicke & Meselson, *Yellow Rain: A Palynological Analysis*, 309 NATURE 205, 206 (1984). In another study, British and Canadian researchers examined biomedical and environmental samples taken from battlefields in Southeast Asia and were unable to find the high level of mycotoxins reported by the United States. While the Canadian research team did find toxin traces in the blood and urine of individuals in Thailand, these people had never been in battle zones, a fact which suggests that the toxins may have been present in their food. *Yellow Rain Evidence Slowly Whittled Away*, 233 SCIENCE 18 (1986); Salaff, "*Yellow Rain" In Southeast Asia: U.S. & Canadian Evaluations*, PEACE RES., May 1984, at 13, 14–15. The evidence of toxin deployment in Afghanistan is even weaker. The only physical evidence that the United States has presented is a single Soviet gas mask that was purchased from a refugee. Additionally, the trichothecenes found on the mask were on the outside of the mask, not in the filter, a detail suggesting that environmental sources of tricothecenes may have adhered to it after the wearer abandoned it. *See* Arms Control Ass'n, *The Biological and Toxin Weapons Convention and the Geneva Protocol*, ARMS CONTROL TODAY, April 1987, at 11A; Note, *supra* note 6, at 1022–23. For an excellent summary of the evidence against the Reagan administration's yellow rain allegations, see Robinson, Guillemin & Meselson, *Yellow Rain: The Story Collapses*, FOREIGN POL'Y, Fall 1987, at 100.

A number of commentators have accused the Reagan administration of attempting to score propaganda points by denouncing the Soviet Union for particular acts without providing adequate and convincing proof. Such unfounded allegations, it is argued, undermine America's credibility with its allies and poison arms control negotiations between the United States and the Soviet Union. *See, e.g.*, Smith, *Strengthening the Biological Weapons Convention During a Crisis of Confidence*, 1986 AM. A. FOR THE ADVANCEMENT OF SCI. 5–6.

10 *See generally* Arms Control Ass'n, *supra* note 9, at 12A; Gelb, *Keeping an Eye on Russia*, N.Y. Times, Nov. 29, 1981, § 6 (Magazine), at 31.

11 Wright, *The Military and the New Biology*, BULL. ATOM. SCIENTISTS, May 1985, at 10, 13.

12 Medvedev, *The Great Germ War Scare*, WORLD PRESS REV., Oct. 1980, at 65; Westing, *Chemical and Biological Weapons: Past and Present*, 3 PEACE & SCI. 25, 28 (1982). Anthrax is an extremely infectious disease produced by the bacterium *bacillus anthracis*. Inhalation of less than one microgram of spores can be a lethal dose for a human being.

unsettled. Initial reports from the accident indicated that the anthrax was a rare pulmonary form, strongly supporting the American hypothesis that the epidemic was caused by the accidental release of airborne spores.[13] However, more recent evidence of the prolonged time course of the epidemic suggests that the victims may have died of gastric anthrax, a conclusion consistent with the Soviet's tainted meat explanation.[14] Certainly, the Soviet Union's refusal to provide specific details about the incident has exacerbated the suspicions of many other nations that it may be developing a biological warfare capability.[15]

Less controverted evidence has emerged in recent years that both the Soviet Union and the United States are conducting substantial research on biological and toxin agents, threatening an arms race in these agents. A recent report by the U.S. National Security Council has identified at least two confirmed Soviet biological warfare centers and six suspected centers.[16] According to the report, much of the research is conducted in factories and laboratories otherwise "engaged in legitimate work on pharmaceuticals, medical science, agriculture and food processing."[17]

In the United States, military expenditures on biological and toxin research were virtually nonexistent for a decade after President Nixon renounced biological weapons in 1969. However, the Reagan administration has reversed this policy and increased the military's budget for biological weapons from less than $10 million under the Carter administration to more than $60 million

STOCKHOLM INT'L PEACE RESEARCH INST., WEAPONS OF MASS DESTRUCTION AND THE ENVIRONMENT 41–42 (1977).

13 Arms Control Ass'n, *supra* note 9, at 12A; Bartley & Kucewicz, *supra* note 8, at 819.

14 *See* Arms Control Ass'n, *supra* note 9, at 12A; Wyatt, *Anthrax: Recipe for a Blunt Weapon*, 87 NEW SCIENTIST 721, 722 (1980). Wyatt has also argued that the number of airborne spores that would have been required to kill one thousand or more people "would have to be astronomic." *Id.*; *see also Bottling Up Biological Warfare*, N.Y. Times, Sept. 20, 1986, at 26, col. 1; *Soviets Offer Account of '79 Anthrax Outbreak*, Wash. Post, Oct. 9, 1986, at A24, col. 1.

15 *See, e.g.*, Harris, *Sverdlovsk and Yellow Rain*, INT'L SECURITY, Spring 1987, at 41, 55; U.S. DEP'T OF STATE, CURRENT POLICY NO. 342, USE OF CHEMICAL WEAPONS IN ASIA 3 (Nov. 10, 1981).

16 Samuel, *Bio-War Plans*, DEF. WEEK, Aug. 26, 1985, at 14, 14; *see also Genetic Warfare*, Wall St. J., Aug. 25, 1986, at 20, col. 1.

17 Samuel, *supra* note 16, at 14. Reports from Soviet scientists who have defected to the United States indicate that Soviet biological research includes attempts to use genetic engineering to combine the venom-producing genes from cobra snakes with ordinary viruses. Such an organism would enter the body and produce paralytic cobra neurotoxins. *See Soviets Search for Eerie New Weapons*, Wall St. J., Apr. 23, 1984, at 30, col. 3.

in 1986.[18] A substantial portion of this funding has been devoted to research of chilling new biotechnologies, such as recombinant DNA and hybridoma technology.[19] The U.S. Department of Defense is currently seeking more than $300 million to expand its chemical and biological warfare facilities in Utah. These facilities would include a laboratory to test lethal biological and toxin agents, as well as aerosol delivery systems.[20] While both the superpowers assert that such research is purely for defensive or "prophylactic" purposes, permitted under article I(1) of the Biological Weapons Convention, the nature of much of this work makes such claims appear disingenuous.

Finally, there is increasing fear that Third World nations may seek to develop biological weapons in response to heavily-armed neighbors or a spiraling regional arms race, or out of desperation in a protracted war.[21] As one commentator noted:

> Unlike the complex and expensive technological infrastructure required to design and produce nuclear weapons, a sophisticated recombinant DNA facility can be set up without a large capital investment. And the necessary expertise is freely available in the scientific literature.[22]

Indeed, the Iraqi use of chemical weapons against Iran, in direct violation of the 1925 Geneva Protocol, is a chilling attestation to the willingness of nations to use the most horrible of weapons against opponents.[23]

18 *Germ Warfare*, *supra* note 4, at 62; *see also* Bernstein, *The Birth of the U.S. Biological-Warfare Program*, SCI. AM., June 1987, at 116; Wright, *supra* note 11, at 10; Sun, *Dugway Lab Plans Defended by Defense Department*, 233 SCIENCE 153 (1986); McCormick, *Open Questions In Military Biotech*, 2 BIO/TECH. 663 (1984); Wright & Sinsheimer, *Recombinant DNA and Biological Warfare*, BULL. ATOM. SCIENTISTS, Nov. 1983, at 20, 21–23. The Medical and Research Development Command of the United States Army has increased funding for biotechnology research tenfold since 1981. One of the projects funded by the Army is research work at the University of Kansas to clone the deadly toxin dengue. In all, the Army is funding projects at 24 universities and at many other commercial and military laboratories. *Controversy Grows Over Pentagon's Work on Biological Agents*, Wall St. J., Sept. 17, 1986, at 1, col. 1.

19 Wright, *supra* note 11, at 14.; *See generally* King, *The Threat of Biological Weapons*, TECH. REV., May–June 1982, at 10.

20 Smith, *Court Hears Suit on Biowarfare Laboratory*, 228 SCIENCE 827 (1985).

21 *See* Tucker, *Gene Wars*, FOREIGN POL'Y, Winter 1984–85, at 58, 66; Geissler, *Introduction*, in BIOLOGICAL AND TOXIN WEAPONS TODAY, *supra* note 7, at 1–2 (Geissler ominously notes that about 50% of the developing nations are not parties to the Biological Weapons Convention).

22 Tucker, *supra* note 21, at 66. Harvard biochemist Matthew Meselson has stated that biological weapons technology could "proliferate rather easily . . . you might say that biological weapons could become the poor man's hydrogen bomb." Meselson, *The Search For Yellow Rain*, ARMS CONTROL TODAY, Sept. 1986, at 31, 31.

23 *See* *UN's 'Big Five' Meet Behind Closed Doors on Iran-Iraq War*, CHRISTIAN SCIENCE MONITOR, June 10, 1987, at 13, col. 1; Terrill, *Chemical Weapons in the Gulf War*, STRATEGIC

In the face of these ominous developments, sixty-three parties to the Biological Weapons Convention, and four signatories who have not yet ratified the Convention, assembled in Geneva in September of 1986 for the Second Review Conference of the treaty. This article will analyze the Conferees' Final Declaration, which was adopted by consensus and signed by all of the nations present. Additionally, this article will discuss the actions taken at a follow-up ad hoc meeting of scientific and technical experts from forty-three Convention nations that took place from March 31 to April 15, 1987.

I. THE FINAL DECLARATION OF THE SECOND REVIEW CONFERENCE

At the Second Review Conference, the assembled parties reviewed each of the fifteen articles of the Biological Weapons Convention. This analysis will focus on the most important aspects of this review: those relating to articles I, IV, V and VI of the Convention.

A. *Article I: The Ban on Biological and Toxin Agents*

Article I of the Biological Weapons Convention precludes the development, production and stockpiling of biological and toxin agents "in quantities that have no justification for prophylactic, protective or other peaceful purposes." In the Final Declaration, the parties to the Second Review Conference reaffirmed that article I applies to "all natural or artificially created microbial or other biological agents or toxins whatever their origin or method of production." The parties held that this includes both proteinaceous and non-proteinaceous toxins, as well as synthetically produced analogues of natural toxins.[24]

Article I of the Convention prohibits possession of biological or toxin agents "whatever their origin or method of production." In recent years many parties to the Convention, including the Soviet Union and the United States, have reaffirmed the broad scope of the treaty's purview.[25] However, several commentators

REV., Spring 1986, at 51; *Iraq Using Gas, UN Leader Says*, Chicago Tribune, Mar. 15, 1986, at 7, col. 6; Ooms, *Chemical Weapons: Is Revulsion a Safeguard?*, 24 ATLANTIC COMMUNITY Q. 157, 165 (1986).

24 *Review Conference Held on Biological and Toxin Weapons Convention*, DEP'T OF STATE BULL., Dec. 1986, at 40, 42 [hereinafter *Review Conference*].

25 *See, e.g.*, Note, *supra* note 6, at 1045 n.222 (comprehensive scope of Convention accepted by parties at 1980 Convention Review Conference); Wright & Sinsheimer, *supra* note 18, at 20–21 (United States, Britain and Soviet Union's joint briefing paper

have speculated that agents produced through genetic engineering techniques might not be encompassed within this language because they are "artificially produced."[26]

One of the primary constraints in the past against research and production of biological agents on a large scale was the extreme hazard attendant to working with pathogens in the laboratory. Genetic engineering technology now enables scientists to replicate nucleic acids of animals and plants within bacterial cells. Thus, highly pathogenic viruses can be studied, manipulated and mass-produced within the protective "shell" of host bacteria, such as *Escherichia coli* K12.[27] For example, genetic engineering has enabled scientists safely to study and clone a genome of the deadly virus Lassa fever, frequently cited as a potential agent for biological warfare.[28]

Additionally, recombinant DNA technology can facilitate the production of biological agents orders of magnitudes more lethal than those extant only a decade ago. For example, gene splicing could be employed to produce toxins hundreds of times deadlier than nerve gases, one of the most lethal of all chemical weapons.[29] Biological components of several agents could also be

concluded that the Convention "fully covered" any agents that might be produced through the recombinant DNA process).

26 *See, e.g.*, Note, *supra* note 6, at 1044; Tucker, *supra* note 21, at 73. For an explanation of the genetic engineering process, see generally J. Donady, *What is DNA?*, in RECOMBINANT DNA RESEARCH AND THE HUMAN PROSPECT 9–25 (E. Hanson ed. 1982); Abelson, *Introduction to Recombinant DNA Research* in NAT'L ACAD. OF SCI., RESEARCH WITH RECOMBINANT DNA 4–13 (1977).

27 Geissler, *Implications of Genetic Engineering for Chemical and Biological Warfare*, in WORLD ARMAMENTS AND DISARMAMENT 1984 SIPRI Y.B. (Stockholm Int'l Peace Research Inst.) 421, 428. Gene splicing also now makes it possible to manufacture "virtually unlimited quantities" of lethal toxins, a process previously precluded by safety concerns and the costs of purifying natural toxins from animals or plants. Tucker, *supra* note 21, at 64.

28 *See* Gonzalez, Buchmeier, McCormick, Mitchell, Elliott & Kiley, *Comparative Analysis of Lassa and Lassa-like Arenavirus Isolates from Africa*, in SEGMENTED NEGATIVE STRAND VIRUSES 201 (R. Compans & D. Bishop eds. 1984); Clegg & Oram, *Molecular Cloning of Lassa Virus RNA: Nucleotide Sequence and Expression of the Nucleocapsid Protein Gene*, 144 VIROLOGY 363 (1985).

29 Tucker, *supra* note 21, at 65–66; Robinson, *Chemical and Biological Warfare*, 17 BULL. PEACE PROPOSALS 367, 372–73; Donnelly, *Winning the NBC War: Soviet Army Theory and Practice*, 8 INT'L DEF. REV. 989, 990 (1981). The median individual lethal dose for one of the nerve gas agents deployed by the United States or Soviet Union in their chemical weapons stockpiles is only between 0.4 and 1 milligram. Meselson & Robinson, *Chemical Warfare and Chemical Disarmament*, SCI. AM., Apr. 1980, at 38, 39. Use of such agents in a NATO-Warsaw Pact confrontation in Europe could result in millions of military and civilian casualties. *Id.* at 44–45. Yet the destructive capabilities of such agents pales in comparison to those of the genetically produced supertoxins that can now be created and mass produced. Tucker, *supra* note 21, at 64–65.

combined through genetic engineering to produce a virtually infinite number of new agents, obviating any realistic efforts by an opponent to produce a vaccine to protect its military and civilian populations against such weapons.[30] Conversely, the nation deploying such agents could simultaneously produce vaccines in order to immunize its troops and civilian population against these agents.[31] As Dr. Richard Goldstein of the Harvard Medical School concluded, "the key is vaccination . . . . [With recombinant DNA technology] you can make a vaccine against anything, and if you have a vaccine, it makes use of these weapons more feasible."[32]

Article I(1) only prohibits possession or production of such agents in "quantities that have no justification for prophylactic, protective or other peaceful purposes." This loophole fundamentally undermines the viability of the Convention. First, it does not establish a threshold above which the quantities of agents possessed by a nation can no longer be deemed to be for "prophylactic, protective or other peaceful purposes." Additionally, the language does not suggest how "defensive" research or production of biological and toxin agents can be distinguished from efforts to develop an offensive capability. Thus, the parties to the Convention are given carte blanche to develop and stockpile biological and toxin agents.

Both the United States and the Soviet Union have invoked article I(1) to justify substantial research and development of biological and toxin agents as purely "defensive" or "prophylactic" in nature.[33] For example, the United States has argued that the cloning, sequencing and expression of deadly viruses such as dengue, equine encephalomyelitis and lethal anthrax toxins, are necessary for the development of vaccines against such agents.[34] The Defense Department also has revealed plans to test aerosols

[30] *See, e.g.*, Hamm, *Deterrence, Chemical Warfare, and Arms Control*, 29 ORBIS 119, 133 (1985); King, *supra* note 19, at 11. Genetic engineering could also be used to alter slightly the antigenic structures of an infectious agent, overcoming natural and acquired immune defense mechanisms. Geissler, *A New Generation of Biological Weapons*, in BIOLOGICAL AND TOXIN WEAPONS TODAY, *supra* note 7, at 21, 29; *see also Biotechnology Development: Hearings Before The Subcomm. on Oversight and Investigations of the House Comm. on Energy and Commerce*, 99th Cong., 1st Sess. 83 (1985) [hereinafter *Biotechnology Development Hearings*].

[31] *See* King, *supra* note 19, at 11.

[32] Piller, *DNA—Key To Biological Warfare*, 237 NATION 585, 597–98 (1983).

[33] *See, e.g.*, Heylin, *supra* note 2, at 47–48; Budiansky, *U.S. Looks to Biological Weapons*, 297 NATURE 615 (1982); Humphrey, *Five Hundred Years of Plague*, SOUTH, June 1986, at 108, 109.

[34] *See* Heylin, *supra* note 2, at 47–48.

of lethal biological agents, maintaining that this research is essential for the development of an understanding of the agents and potential delivery systems.[35]

The claim of both superpowers that such biological research is purely "defensive" in nature is inherently suspect. As one analyst recently noted, because genetic engineering now facilitates the development of a virtually infinite number of biological and toxin agents, "the exact nature of a biological agent will in general only be available to a nation planning the *use* of the agent in an offensive mode."[36] Thus, it is unlikely that either the United States or the Soviet Union is engaged in efforts to develop vaccines against an unlimited variety of biological agents; any such efforts would almost certainly be futile. Even assuming, for the sake of argument, that a nation could develop a vaccine to protect against the exact agent that its opponent has deployed in battle, it has been estimated that even a superpower would take more than three months to produce enough vaccine to protect 8,000 troops or civilians, and over one year to produce enough to immunize 190,000. Additionally, several weeks or months would pass before vaccinated individuals would develop an adequate level of immunity; the delay would render such agents totally useless against fast-acting biological or toxin agents.[37] As a noted biologist recently averred:

> Even before the recombinant DNA era, it would have been a task of tremendous magnitude to develop and stockpile vaccines against all possible biological warfare agents sufficient for mass vaccination of the entire population. Even that, however, would have been of little use against an effective surprise attack, since a vaccine must be given well in advance of exposure to the organism.
>
> With the advent of recombinant DNA, the possibility of an effective vaccine defense has become even more remote. Since one could develop an infinite number of immunological variants by modifying and transplanting genes, there is no way to anticipate what a determined adversary might develop . . . . Any attempt to develop modi-

[35] *See* Wright, *New Designs for Biological Weapons*, BULL. ATOM. SCIENTISTS, Jan.–Feb. 1987, at 43; Piller, *supra* note 32, at 598.

[36] Strauss & King, *The Fallacy of Defensive Biological Weapon Programmes*, in BIOLOGICAL AND TOXIN WEAPONS TODAY, *supra* note 7, at 66, 70.

[37] Geissler, *A New Generation of Vaccines Against Biological and Toxin Weapons*, in BIOLOGICAL AND TOXIN WEAPONS TODAY, *supra* note 7, at 57, 64; *see also Biotechnology Development Hearings*, *supra* note 30, at 76 (statement of Richard P. Novick, Public Health Research Institute of the City of New York, Inc.).

> fied biological warfare agents in order to anticipate enemy action is an exercise in futility and simply cannot be justified on the grounds of defense.[38]

Ominously, it would be possible for a nation to develop both a heretofore unknown pathogen and a vaccine against it, and then immunize its troops and civilians in advance of an attack against another nation. This possibility may most accurately explain the interest of the superpowers in biological research.[39] Unfortunately, the parties to the Review Conference never addressed what Richard Falk has appropriately termed "a gigantic loophole capable of being reconciled with almost any desired path of research."[40]

B. *Article IV: Implementing the Convention within each State Party*

Article IV of the Convention provides that:

> Each State Party to this Convention shall, in accordance with its constitutional processes, take any necessary measures to prohibit and prevent the development, production, stockpiling, acquisition or retention of the agents, toxins, weapons, equipment and means of delivery specified in article I of the Convention, within the territory of such State, under its jurisdiction or under its control anywhere.

At the First Review Conference of the Convention in 1980, the parties agreed to provide the U.N. Department for Disarmament Affairs with information on national legislation or regulatory measures relevant to the Convention.[41] The parties at the Second Review Conference reaffirmed the desirability of this practice and emphasized the importance of three specific kinds of information: (1) national legislative and administrative measures designed to guarantee compliance with the Convention's mandates; (2) national legislation related to the protection of laboratories and other facilities to prevent unauthorized access to, or removal of, biological or toxin agents; and (3) inclusion of information about the mandates of the Convention in textbooks and the educational curriculum of students in the sciences, the mili-

38 *Biotechnology Development Hearings, supra* note 30, at 76 (statement of Richard P. Novick).

39 *See Genetic Warfare, supra* note 16 (testimony of Douglas J. Feith, Deputy Assistant Secretary of Defense For Negotiations Policy); Geissler, *supra* note 37, at 59.

40 Falk, *Inhibiting Reliance on Biological Weaponry: The Role And Relevance of International Law*, 1 AM. U.J. INT'L L. & POL'Y 17, 26 (1986).

41 *See Review Conference, supra* note 24, at 42.

tary and medicine.[42]

The provision of information about national legislation implementing the Convention, including information about the physical protection of laboratories, is an important component of the treaty. As is true with any arms control framework, disclosure of measures taken to comply with the Convention can serve as a means of building confidence among signatories by demonstrating their individual commitments to strengthening the treaty. Conversely, "[s]ecrecy generates the suspicions that produce escalating cycles of military response in the guise of defense."[43]

Unfortunately, Convention nations in recent years have pursued very few initiatives to strengthen national safeguards against illegal biological or toxin research. To the contrary, in several nations, most notably the United States, the activities of private research companies and universities, working under contract with government agencies, have given rise to allegations of covert research in violation of the Convention.[44]

C. *Articles V & VI: Consultation by Parties and Investigation of Suspected Violations*

Articles V and VI of the Convention provide mechanisms to investigate allegations of treaty violations and to resolve disputes that may arise between the signatories. Article V provides for consultation between the parties "in solving any problems which may arise in relation to the objective of, or in the application of the provisions of, the Convention." Article VI authorizes any party to the Convention that suspects a breach of the agreement by another party to lodge a complaint with the U.N. Security Council. The Convention further mandates that all parties shall cooperate in carrying out any investigation that the Security Council may choose to conduct in the matter.

At the First Review Conference of the Convention, the assembled parties agreed that any party should have the right to re-

42 *Id.*

43 Rosenberg, *Updating the Biological Weapons Ban,* BULL. ATOM. SCIENTISTS, Jan.–Feb. 1987, at 40, 41.

44 *See, e.g.,* Wright & Sinsheimer, *On Recombinant DNA Technology and Biological Warfare,* BULL. ATOM. SCIENTISTS, Feb. 1984, at 59, 60. In January 1987, the House Judiciary Committee introduced a bill that would make it a criminal offense for anyone in the United States, including Government personnel, to produce biological weapons. A conviction under the proposed statute would carry a sentence of life imprisonment. *Germ Warfare, supra* note 4, at 62.

quest a consultative meeting at the expert level. The final declaration of the Second Review Conference reflects the parties' effort to strengthen this mechanism. The parties agreed that consultative meetings should be promptly convened when requested by a party. Further, the conferees declared that the assistance of technical experts should be utilized to resolve ambiguities and disputes. The parties also emphasized that "appropriate international procedures within the framework of the United Nations" could be utilized to resolve disputes; however, the parties did not specify what those procedures were or the circumstances under which they could be invoked.[45] The conferees also briefly noted the importance of the provision in article VI for recourse to the U.N. Security Council when a party has been accused of breaching its obligations under the Convention. Finally, the parties declared that the Security Council could request the advice of the World Health Organization to carry out any investigation it chooses to conduct pursuant to article VI.[46]

1. *Past Failures of Investigation and Consultation*

While, in theory, consultative and investigatory procedures can help to resolve conflicts between Convention nations, articles V and VI can only operate effectively if the treaty's signatories are willing to cooperate when a crisis arises. Unfortunately, the historical evidence on compliance with such procedures in the context of biological and chemical weapons does not encourage optimism.

During the Korean war, North Korea accused the United States of attacking with biological weapons, including anti-personnel, anti-animal and anti-plant agents.[47] However, it was impossible to verify these allegations because North Korea refused to permit the International Committee of the Red Cross to conduct an on-site investigation.[48] The Soviet Union subsequently vetoed a U.N. Security Council resolution calling on the Interna-

45 *Review Conference*, *supra* note 24, at 42.

46 *Id.* at 43.

47 *See* 4 A. BOSERUP, J. ROBINSON, R. NEILD, & M. LEITENBERG, THE PROBLEM OF CHEMICAL AND BIOLOGICAL WARFARE: CB DISARMAMENT NEGOTIATIONS, 1920–1970, at 63 (1971); van Ginnekin, *Bacteriological Warfare*, 7 J. CONTEMP. ASIA 130, 135 (1977). The validity of these accusations has remained controversial and unresolved. *See, e.g.*, Westing, *The Threat of Biological Warfare*, 35 BIOSCI. 627, 629 (1985); Cowdrey, *'Germ Warfare' and Public Health in the Korean Conflict*, 7 ASIAN PERSP. 210 (1983); van Ginnekin, *supra*, at 142–49.

48 10 M. WHITEMAN, DIGEST OF INTERNATIONAL LAW 461, 462 (1968). The validity of these accusations has remained controversial and unresolved.

tional Committee of the Red Cross to investigate the charges and report back to the Security Council.[49] The North Koreans and the Chinese also refused to cooperate in a proposed investigation by a multistate commission under the auspices of the U.N. General Assembly.[50]

In 1980, the General Assembly adopted a resolution instructing the Secretary-General to investigate the allegations of several nations that chemical and biological weapons were being used in Southeast and Southwest Asia.[51] The four-man group of experts appointed by the Secretary-General was thwarted in its effort to conduct a meaningful investigation by the refusal of Afghanistan, Kampuchea and Laos to permit the group to conduct on-site testing. As a consequence, the group was forced to collect samples from refugees traveling to the contiguous nations of Thailand and Pakistan. The group's reports were generally recognized as inconclusive because it was impossible to monitor the sampling process and authenticate the samples.[52]

Finally, the Soviet Union's refusal to consult with other nations after the accident at Sverdlovsk is a telling example of how the Convention's commitments are often sacrificed when a nation deems it to be expedient. While the Soviets have been more forthcoming in the last year in discussing the accident,[53] their silence immediately after the incident and for the last seven years has exacerbated tensions between the superpowers and has probably fueled biological and toxin weapon research efforts in the United States and elsewhere.

49 *Id.* at 465.

50 *Id.* at 466.

51 G.A. Res. 144, 35 U.N. GAOR Supp. No.48 at 60–61, U.N. Doc. A/35/48 (1981); *see also Chemical and Bacteriological (Biological) Weapons: Report of the Secretary-General*, 36 U.N. GAOR Annex 1 (Agenda Item 42) at 5, 9, U.N. Doc. A/36/613 (1981) [hereinafter U.N. Report].

52 *Chemical and Bacteriological (Biological) Weapons: Report of the Secretary-General*, 37 U.N. GAOR Annex 1 (Agenda Item 54) at 26–41, U.N. Doc. A/37/259 (1982); *see also The U.N.'s Second Year with Yellow Rain*, Wall St. J., Nov. 22, 1982, at 30, col. 3. The U.N. Centre for Disarmament reported the results of a Finnish scientific report on the study concluding, "without on-site access possibilities for verification were very small, while early analysis of samples could lead to definite conclusions." 6 U.N. DISARM. Y.B. at 232, 312, U.N. Sales No. E.82.IX.6 (1981).

53 Dickson, *Gene Splicing Dominates Review of Weapons Pact*, 234 SCIENCE 144 (1986). On the first day of the Second Review Conference, Nikolai Antonov of the Soviet Ministry of Health offered Western delegates the opportunity to question him directly about the incident. Antonov subsequently presented an extensive report on the incident, once again alleging that the outbreak was caused by contaminated meat. While many Western delegates expressed skepticism about the Soviet explanation, even U.S. arms control officials admitted that they were surprised by the Soviet's willingness to open the subject up for discussion among scientific experts from both the East and West. *Id.* at 144.

If the conferees' proposals related to consultation and investigation are to be meaningful outside of the rarified atmosphere of the Review Conference, the parties must refrain from invoking the concepts of "sovereignty" and "national security" to deny on-site inspections by outside parties. Additionally, the consultation procedure contemplated by the parties can only be efficacious if a party under suspicion is willing to provide prompt explanations to other treaty parties of unusual incidents and submit to questioning by scientific experts from other nations.

2. *Exchange of Information*

The conferees also advocated an increased exchange of information between treaty parties, including the exchange of data about biological research facilities, promulgation of information about unusual outbreaks of infectious diseases caused by toxins, publication of results of biological research in scientific journals generally available to treaty parties and promotion of contacts between scientists conducting biological or toxin research.[54] Of course, the efficacy of such proposals is entirely contingent on the willingness of treaty parties to lift the veil of secrecy that has pervaded biological and toxin research for the last two decades.

The procedures established by scientific and technical experts from Convention nations at the Ad Hoc Meeting held in March and April 1987 provide some hope.[55] The experts established several "modalities for the exchange of information" about biological and toxin research activities in party nations.[56] The parties at the meeting agreed to provide data on all research centers or laboratories within their borders that have either maximum containment units or that specialize in research or development of biological or toxin agents for prophylactic or protective purposes.[57] These procedures may in fact result in more open and

54 *Review Conference, supra* note 24, at 43.

55 *Ad Hoc Meeting of Scientific and Technical Experts From States Parties to the Convention on the Prohibition of the Development, Production and Stockpiling of Bacteriological (Biological) and Toxin Weapons and on Their Destruction*, (Draft Report/Revision 3) BWC/CONF.II/EX/. . ., Apr. 15, 1987 [hereinafter *Ad Hoc Meeting*].

56 *Id.* at 4.

57 *Id.* In the interests of uniformity in reporting, the experts established a form to be used by Convention parties for exchanging data on such facilities. *Id.* at 4–5. The parties also discussed expanding the reporting requirements to include the exchange of information about facilities engaged in field aerosol experiments with biological and toxin agents, as well as facilities that did not use maximum containment facilities but which "in view of the type or scale of their activities involving highly pathogenic micro organisms and/or toxins, could be considered relevant . . . ." *Id.* at 13. Unfortunately, the parties did not agree to these more comprehensive reporting requirements and they

extensive exchange of information.

As indicated earlier in this article, the parties at the Second Review Conference, in response to the Sverdlovsk incident, agreed to exchange information on outbreaks of infectious diseases caused by biological or toxin agents that deviate from the normal patterns of disease in the area in which they occur. At the Ad Hoc Meeting, the experts formulated standards for determining when "an outbreak" of "infectious disease" has occurred and established a standardized procedure for reporting such occurrences to the international community.[58] In order to assuage any suspicions about the nature of an unusual outbreak of disease in any party nation, the experts also recommended that representatives from other state parties be allowed to "assist in the handling of an outbreak."[59] Finally, the parties assembled at the Ad Hoc Meeting called on all Convention parties to keep basic research in the biological sciences unclassified, especially research in areas directly related to the Convention.[60]

II. Strengthening the Biological Weapons Convention: Future Efforts

A. *The "Prophylactic" Production Exception*

The "prophylactic or defensive purposes" exception to the ban on biological and toxin agent production engenders insecurity among party states to the Biological Weapons Convention and threatens an uncontrollable arms race. As indicated earlier in this article, it is impossible to distinguish research and production of biological and toxin agents that is purely "defensive" in nature from efforts to create an offensive capability. As a consequence, nations may be developing the ability to wage war with such agents under the pretext of protecting themselves from aggressors. Additionally, as an expert panel appointed by the U.S. State Department to assess the impact of genetic engineering concluded, "an increased protection capability may be an inducement to use biological warfare, since the instigator has a de-

were listed in the final report of the experts only as proposals that had been "considered" by the experts. *Id.*

58 *Ad Hoc Meeting*, *supra* note 55, at 6–8.

59 *Id.* at 7. The Ad Hoc Meeting parties also established a form for reporting unusual outbreaks of infectious diseases and other similar events.

60 *Id.* at 9.

creased risk of being harmed by his own actions."[61] The study further argued that this danger would be particularly acute if the aggressor had the capability to use aerosol immunization to protect its military forces and civilian population.[62] Both the United States and the Soviet Union have conducted research on aerosol delivery systems in recent years under the rubric of "prophylactic or defensive research."[63] Finally, the article I prophylactic exception threatens to precipitate a biological or toxins arms race because no nation can be certain that other state actors are pursuing purely "defensive" research.

There is a clear and pressing need to amend article I of the Convention to address these concerns. Because genetic engineering makes it possible to produce an infinite number of new agents, obviating any realistic effort to develop a defense against such agents, the prophylactic exception to article I rests on shaky grounds. A number of possible amendments to article I have been suggested in recent years. One approach would be to simply strike the exception. Alternatively, several commentators have called for limiting the scope of the exception. For example, Falk has suggested that the wording "that have no justification" should be replaced by "unless they have an overwhelming and unambiguous justification."[64]

Both of these proposals are subject to criticism. Many nations might resist any proposal that would totally preclude defensive research related to biological and toxin agents with the claim that such research is essential to counter surreptitious efforts by others to develop offensive capabilities. Such an amendment might induce a number of important parties to withdraw from the treaty, a result necessarily vitiating efforts to strengthen the Convention framework.

The amendment proposed by Falk also has several shortcomings. First, Falk fails to specify who will determine if a nation's justification for conducting research on biological and toxin agents is "overwhelming and unambiguous." If a nation planning to conduct biological or toxin research is permitted to make this determination itself, the result will be a foregone conclusion.

[61] P. GIZEWSKI, BIOLOGICAL WEAPONS CONTROL 16 (Canadian Centre for Arms Control and Disarmament, Issue Brief No. 5, 1987).

[62] *Id.* at 2.

[63] *See* Geissler, *supra* note 37, at 64. *See generally Biological Testing Involving Human Subjects by the Department of Defense: Hearings Before the Subcomm. on Health and Scientific Research of the Senate Comm. on Human Resources*, 95th Cong., 1st Sess. (1977).

[64] Falk, *supra* note 40, at 31.

Placing this decision in the hands of other treaty parties would alleviate this problem, however many nations might balk at this diminution of sovereignty.

Additionally, Falk does not suggest the criteria that should be utilized to determine what would constitute an "overwhelming and unambiguous" justification for biological or toxin research or production. Would mere suspicion that another nation is developing biological or toxin weapons be sufficient to justify defensive research? Would more be required, such as documented evidence of weapons production by another nation? The language proposed by Falk would probably lead to disparate interpretations which could undermine the security of party states.

The optimal solution may lie not in amending the language of article I, but rather in mandating that all "prophylactic" research or production be internationalized.[65] An international panel of experts, comprised of representatives from all party nations, could be given the sole authority to conduct such research in facilities designated by Convention parties and accessible to observers. Results of the panel's research would be available to all Convention states. Article X of the Convention provides legal precedent for this proposal by requiring all parties to cooperate in "the fullest possible exchange of equipment, materials and scientific and technological information for the use of bacteriological (biological) agents and toxins for peaceful purposes."[66]

B. *Consultative and Investigative Procedures*

1. *Overview*

The importance of the Convention's provisions for consultation and investigation in articles V and VI cannot be overemphasized. An effective consultation mechanism can help resolve ambiguities and suspicions about the intentions of other parties, and thus potentially avert an arms race in biological and toxin weapons. The ability to investigate accusations that cannot be resolved at the consultative level may deter activities that contravene the Treaty and subject violators to the condemnation of the international community. Unfortunately, current procedures under articles V and VI of the Convention have proven wholly inadequate to achieve these objectives. In the face of serious al-

[65] *See, e.g.*, Tucker, *supra* note 21, at 73.

[66] *Biological Weapons Convention*, *supra* note 1, art. X; *see also* Tucker, *supra* note 21, at 73.

legations of illegal biological research at Sverdlovsk, the Soviet Union simply refused to consult with other Convention parties.[67] Efforts by Convention states to investigate charges of biological and toxin weapon deployment during the Korean war, and in Southeast Asia, were thwarted by Security Council vetoes.[68] The suggested policy options that follow may help to strengthen the investigative and consultative procedures of the Convention and thus ensure better security for party states.

2. *Consultative Procedures*

It should be noted at the outset that the efficacy of consultative procedures is wholly dependent on the political will of individual Convention states to cooperate in resolving ambiguous or suspicious situations. Assuming the existence of such cooperation, implementation of the following measures may strengthen the consultative mechanism of article V of the Convention:

a. *Immediate Consultation*

At the Second Review Conference, the parties to the Convention agreed that a consultative meeting should be "promptly convened" when requested by a State Party.[69] However, the parties failed to define precisely the term 'promptly,' a critical consideration because "evidence of chemical and biological warfare is particularly susceptible to rapid deterioration."[70] The parties to the Convention should agree to convene a consultative meeting no more than forty-eight hours after a party requests such a meeting. There is precedent for this requirement in the recently concluded Stockholm Agreement which prohibits the massing of military forces by party states without prior notification to other parties. Under the agreement, a party state may request an onsite ground or air inspection if it believes that another party is not complying with the agreement. Inspections are to begin within thirty-six hours of such a request.[71]

67 Note, *Establishing Violations of International Law: "Yellow Rain" and the Treaties Regulating Chemical and Biological Warfare*, 35 STAN. L. REV. 259, 273 n.60 (1981).

68 *Id.* at 274; Falk, *supra* note 40, at 18 n.1.

69 *Review Conference*, *supra* note 24, at 42.

70 Note, *supra* note 67, at 275; *see also Man With a Mission: Amos Townsend Scours Southeast Asia Seeking Proof of "Yellow Rain,"* Wall St. J., Feb. 25, 1983, at 1, col. 1, 13, col. 1.

71 *See* Borawski, *Accord at Stockholm*, BULL. ATOM. SCIENTISTS, Dec. 1986, at 34, 35; *see also* Borawski, Weeks & Thompson, *The Stockholm Agreement of September 1986*, 30 ORBIS 643, 657–58 (1987). The Stockholm agreement was reached on September 22, 1986 at the Conference on Confidence-and-Security-Building Measures and Disarmament in Europe, in which thirty-five nations participated. *Id.* at 643.

b. *On-site Consultation*

At the Ad Hoc Meeting of Experts, the parties to the Convention agreed to exchange information on outbreaks of infectious diseases or toxin agents. The conferees also "encouraged" Convention parties to invite experts from other state parties to assist in responding to such incidents.[72] State parties should agree to make this recommendation mandatory in any case where a consultative meeting is called to address an unusual outbreak of disease or sickness that may have been caused by biological or toxin agents. As the conferees at the Ad Hoc Meeting concluded, on-site consultation by other parties may "prevent or reduce the occurrence of ambiguities, doubts and suspicions."[73]

This proposal could meet substantial resistance from many party states that would consider on-site surveillance by other parties an encroachment on national sovereignty, as well as a threat to state and private sector proprietary secrets. Indeed, one of the primary sticking points in the ongoing negotiations to ban chemical weapons at the Conference on Disarmament has been Warsaw Pact opposition to on-site verification of chemical agent destruction and long-term surveillance of chemical production facilities.[74] However, in a dramatic breakthrough in February of 1987, the Soviet Union agreed to on-site inspection of chemical weapons stockpiles and other relevant facilities,[75] paving the way for the conclusion of an agreement to ban chemical weapons in 1988.[76] Additionally, as indicated in the immediately preceding section, Warsaw Pact and NATO nations have recently agreed to immediate on-site inspections of troop deployments. The United States and the Soviet Union recently agreed, at least in principle, to on-site monitoring of each other's nuclear testing facilities,[77] and to on-site inspection of manufacturing and storage facilities for intermediate nuclear missiles.[78] In October 1987, the Soviet

[72] *Ad Hoc Meeting supra* note 55, at 7.

[73] *Id.* at 7.

[74] *See, e.g.*, Goldblat, *Chemical Weapons Verification*, BULL. ATOM. SCIENTISTS, May 1985, at 19; E. SPIERS, CHEMICAL WARFARE 186–87 (1986).

[75] *Soviet Offers to Allow Chemical-Arms Inspections*, N.Y. Times, Feb. 18, 1987, at A10, col. 1. The Soviets have also acceded to demands by the United States that the proposed chemical weapons agreement include a provision for surprise inspections if violations of the agreement are suspected. *See* Lewis, *40 Nations Closer to a Pact Banning Chemical Weapons*, N.Y. Times, Apr. 30, 1987, at A1, col. 4.

[76] Lewis, *supra* note 75.

[77] *See Soviet Offers to Allow Some On-site Test Monitoring*, N.Y. Times, June 4, 1987, at A3, col. 3.

[78] *See The Real Test is at Hand*, N.Y. Times, Mar. 16, 1987, at 15.

Union opened a chemical warfare facility to inspection by a group of foreign experts and technical experts from forty-five nations.[79] The U.S. representative to the Geneva Disarmament Conference, Max L. Friedersdorf, stated that he believed that the Soviets had fully displayed its chemical weapons during the inspection.[80] The growing trend to include on-site verification procedures in superpower arms control agreements may be a favorable portent for the verification proposal outlined in this article.[81]

c. *Enhanced Scope of Information Exchange*

At the Second Review Conference, the parties to the Convention agreed that the article V consultation process should include the exchange of information about research centers and laboratory facilities that engage in biological research posing individual or community risks, or that specialize in research permitted under the Convention.[82] At the Ad Hoc Meeting of Experts in 1987, the assembled parties recommended that information should be provided on each research center or laboratory within a nation that either has a maximum containment unit(s), or has containment units and specializes in biological or toxin research for prophylactic or protective purposes.[83]

The increased exchange of information contemplated by these agreements may have the salutary effect of enhancing confidence in the Convention. However, the parties to the Convention should expand the scope of required information disclosure to include the following:

1) Data on all research centers or laboratories that engage in research related to biological or toxin weapons delivery systems, including aerosols.
2) Data on all research centers or laboratories that engage in research related to the physiological effects of biological or toxin agents, or their modes of transmission or absorption.
3) Exchange of information on outbreaks of infectious

[79] *See Russians Show Chemical-Arms Plant and Arsenal*, N.Y. Times, Oct. 5, 1987, at 8.

[80] *Id.*

[81] *But see* Yost, *Beyond MBFR: The Atlantic to the Urals Gambit*, 31 ORBIS 99, 104 (1987) (Warsaw Pact has balked at NATO proposals for on-site verification of troop reductions in Europe).

[82] *Review Conference*, *supra* note 24, at 43.

[83] *Ad Hoc Meeting*, *supra* note 55, at 4.

diseases, or similar occurrences caused by toxin agents, in plants and animals.
4) Registration of all activities related to the development and production of all toxins. The registration documents should include a description of the purposes and scope of these activities. A provision to protect proprietary information related to the project should also be incorporated into this requirement.[84]

Accurate and comprehensive information disclosure among Convention parties is extremely important. The adoption of the more expansive reporting requirements proposed here for biological and toxin research activities, and for accidents involving these agents, would aid in the deterrence of illegal activities and help to build confidence in the efficacy of the Convention's enforcement mechanisms.

3. *Investigation of Suspicious Activities*

a. *Overview*

As the discussion earlier in this article has indicated, the article VI provision for investigation of suspected breaches of Convention obligations has been thwarted by Security Council veto on at least one occasion.[85] Additionally, the refusal by several other nations, including North Korea, Kampuchea, Laos and Afghanistan, to cooperate in U.N. Security Council investigations has reduced article VI to little more than a theoretical enforcement mechanism.[86] Unfortunately, the Review Conference produced no specific proposals to address these concerns, the conferees being content to note "the need to further improve and strengthen this and other procedures to enhance greater confidence in the Convention."[87] In the future, Convention parties should consider the following policy options:

i. *Elimination of Security Council veto power over article VI investigations, or a shift of authority to the General Assembly.*

Allegations of biological or toxin weapon use in the past have usually implicated permanent Security Council members or their

[84] Several of these proposals were considered at the Ad Hoc Meeting but were not formally adopted in the final document. *Id.* at 13.
[85] *See supra* text accompanying notes 48–50.
[86] *See supra* text accompanying notes 50, 52.
[87] *Review Conference, supra* note 24, at 43.

allies.[88] Thus, the right of the five permanent Security Council members to veto investigations, and their proclivity to exercise this power, has figured largely in the moribund state of article VI.[89] To redefine article VI requests as procedural would obviate the use of the veto. However, the prospect for adoption of this proposal are dim because it would require the unanimous assent of the permanent members of the Security Council itself.[90]

A more viable option may be to amend article VI to vest the U.N. General Assembly with authority to investigate alleged treaty violations. Of course, the efficacy of this proposal is contingent on the cooperation of permanent member states of the Security Council in cases where their own activities are challenged, by no means a certain proposition.

ii. *Establishment of a permanent investigative organization for article VI investigations.*

Because evidence of biological or toxin warfare deteriorates quickly, prompt fact-finding is absolutely essential.[91] Under the current regime, however, an ad hoc investigatory team is only formed after an incident has been reported, necessarily resulting in substantial delay before an investigation can be initiated. A permanent organization to conduct article VI investigations should be established. The absence of an institutional mechanism to investigate ambiguous and suspicious activities "has allowed all manner of non-compliance allegations to acquire credibility, greatly undermining confidence in the treaty regime and, indeed, in arms control generally."[92]

The organization should be composed of experts from a wide cross section of nations and should be provided with the requi-

[88] As one commentator noted:

> Between 1948, the year in which the U.N. was established, and 1970 . . . all eleven allegations of biological warfare have been made against a permanent member of the Security Council. The allegations have either been direct accusations or have implicated the permanent members through a close ally. . . . Since 1971 . . . a disproportionate number of allegations have been lodged against permanent members of the Council.

Note, *supra* note 70, at 279 n.104.

[89] *See* Note, *supra* note 6, at 1045; *cf.* Tucker, *supra* note 21, at 77 (Sweden in 1982 sought assurances from Security Council members that they would not exercise veto power).

[90] *See* J. STOESSINGER, THE UNITED NATIONS AND THE SUPERPOWERS 5 (1977).

[91] *See supra* note 70 and accompanying text.

[92] Robinson, *Chemical and Biological Warfare: Developments in 1985*, in WORLD ARMAMENTS AND DISARMAMENT 1986 SIPRI Y.B. (Stockholm Int'l Peace Research Inst.) 159, 178.

site laboratory facilities and field equipment to conduct effective fact-finding. The organization should also be given the authority to seek assistance from other organizations, such as the Red Cross and the World Health Organization.[93] The preliminary duty of the organization upon receiving an article VI request for an investigation should be to determine whether the allegations are sufficiently plausible to warrant on-site investigation. If on-site fact-finding is deemed necessary, the organization should be provided with immediate access to the areas where illegal activities are purportedly occurring. The organization should be allowed to collect samples, interview witnesses and examine records that are relevant to the investigation.[94]

The framework suggested here would help create an effective mechanism for investigating allegations of biological warfare and subjecting violators to the censure of the international community. Additionally, the organization might serve as a model for other arms control efforts, such as the ongoing negotiations to ban chemical weapons or to reduce the strategic nuclear forces of the United States and the Soviet Union.

93 Several organizations, including the Red Cross, the World Health Organization and the Office of the United Nations High Commissioner for Refugees, refused to provide assistance to the United Nations inspection team that conducted an investigation of yellow rain allegations in Southeast Asia. *See, e.g.*, U.N. Report, *supra* note 51, at 37; *Foreign Policy and Arms Control Implications of Chemical Weapons: Hearings Before the Subcomms. on International Security and Scientific Affairs and on Asian and Pacific Affairs of the House Comm. on Foreign Affairs*, 97th Cong., 2d Sess. 71–76 (1982); *Refugees Camp Doctor Claims U.N. Team Misunderstood Yellow Rain Testimony*, Wall St. J., Oct. 15, 1982, at 38, col. 1. One commentator has suggested that these organizations felt that their involvement in a politically charged situation would jeopardize their image as neutral, humanitarian agencies. Note, *supra* note 70, at 281. However, such organizations might be willing to assist in the analysis of samples collected by the permanent organization, or might offer logistical support in the form of field investigation equipment or access to specialized laboratory facilities.

94 One analyst has observed that the United Nations had great difficulty assembling experts to conduct its investigation of "yellow rain" allegations in Southeast Asia, substantially delaying the beginning of the investigation. Note, *supra* note 67, at 275. Additionally, the paucity of qualified laboratories to process samples collected by the investigatory team resulted in the deterioration of many samples before they could be tested. *Id.* The establishment of a permanent investigative organization would obviate the problems attendant to assembling an ad hoc group of scientific experts each time an article VI investigation is required. Additionally, the establishment of permanent laboratories would facilitate the expeditious processing of samples, yielding more accurate test results. Finally, during those periods when the organization was not conducting investigations it could also organize and process data submitted by parties pursuant to the information disclosure requirements agreed to at the Second Review Conference and the Ad Hoc Conference Meeting of Experts. The organization could also aid in efforts to educate the public about biological and toxin weapons by giving presentations and publishing materials on the subject. *See infra* text accompanying notes 96–98.

C. *Educational Efforts*

In their review of article IV of the Convention, the parties at the Second Review Conference observed that inclusion of information about biological and toxin weapons in textbooks and educational curriculum would help strengthen the treaty.[95] Educational efforts in party states should be expanded beyond this narrow framework to reach the general public through techniques such as speakers' bureaus, educational forums, and the use of the media. The horrible ramifications of biological or toxin warfare should be conveyed to the citizens of party states to reinforce cultural norms against the use of such weapons. Historically, strongly held cultural norms have helped bolster the efficacy of legal constraints.[96] Falk emphasizes that society's aversion to disease may serve as the foundation for an educational campaign concerning biological weapons.

> [P]rohibitions on the use of biological weapons expressed in legal form can be powerfully reinforced, or not, by activating relevant cultural norms in an effective manner. The linkage between health and disease prevention is so deeply embedded in the public consciousness that the notion of deliberately spreading disease as a tactic of conflict seems abhorrent. Without implicitly validating other forms of warfare, it does seem useful to link the formal arrangement of the Biological Weapons Convention with this wider cultural orientation towards disease. In this regard, as governments increasingly locate terrorists associated with non-state actors outside the pale of civilization, it becomes a matter of credibility to designate certain forms of state behavior as similarly tainted.[97]

95 *Review Conference*, *supra* note 24, at 42.

96 *See, e.g.*, Falk, *Strengthening the Biological Weapons Convention of 1972*, in BIOLOGICAL AND TOXIN WEAPONS TODAY, *supra* note 7, 108, 118 (cultural norms played a role in U.S. decision not to use poisonous gas to flush out Pacific Island caves in World War II); McFadden, *Nuclear Weapons Free Zones: Toward An International Framework*, 16 CAL. W. INT'L L.J. 217, 249 (1986) (cultural norms and Geneva Protocol mutually reinforce constraints against use of chemical weapons).

97 Falk, *supra* note 96, at 118. Similarly, Westing observed:

> The general and persistent horror aroused by biological warfare may well stem from a long and intimate acquaintance with sickness and disease, which, in the past at least, was almost inevitably associated with pain, suffering, and tragedy. Diverse aspects of war—not to say war itself—although also dreadful, elicit no comparable feelings.

Westing, *supra* note 47, at 631.

Conclusion

In 1347, Tatar forces besieging the Genoese city of Caffa catapulted corpses infected with bubonic plague over the walls of the city. The plague spread quickly, killing thousands.[98] Fleeing inhabitants of the Black Sea city escaped by ship, carrying the plague to Italy, whence it spread to the rest of Europe. Ultimately, the "Black Death" killed an estimated twenty-five million Europeans, or about thirty percent of the continent's population at the time.[99]

Unchastened by the lessons of history, nations continue to experiment with biological and toxin agents which, if used in battle, could have implications no less horrible than a nuclear conflagration.[100]

As Nobel Laureate Joshua Lederberg averred:

> Molecular biology might be exploited for military purposes and result in a biological weapons race whose aim could well become the most efficient means for removing man from the planet. . . . [T]he potential undoubtedly exists for the design and development of infective agents against which no credible defense is possible, through the genetic and chemical manipulation of these agents.[101]

The agreements reached at the Second Review Conference of the Biological Weapons Convention embody the recognition of the party states that the world may be on the brink of a biological or toxin arms race of unprecedented proportions. Strengthening the Convention framework may be of paramount importance to the survival of life on this planet.

98 Derbes, *De Mussis and the Great Plague of 1348, A Forgotten Episode of Bacteriological Warfare*, 196 J. Am. Med. A. 179 (1966).

99 Geissler, *supra* note 21, at 7.

100 The World Health Organization has estimated that a single bomber could contaminate an area 30 km. long by 2 km. wide with anthrax organisms. WHO estimates that if anthrax were sprayed over a city of five million in a developed country, 100,000 would die and 150,000 would be incapacitated. S. Murphy, A. Hay & S. Rose, No Fire, No Thunder 72–73 (1984). Another study has suggested that a single aircraft could deliver enough anthrax spores to kill initially 75% of the population in an area of 4000 hectares. Westing, *supra* note 47, at 630.

Dissemination of the yellow fever virus through an aerosol delivery system could result in a fatality rate as high as 85% in an affected area. One aircraft could spray the virus over an area of 6000 hectares. World Health Organization, Health Aspects of Chemical and Biological Weapons 62–63, 98–99 (1970). Furthermore, it has been estimated that some biological agents could "remain viable in the soil and provide a continuing focus of infection for sixty years or more." Westing, *supra* note 47, at 630. Thus, there may be no true "end" to a war waged with biological and toxin weapons.

101 Lederberg, *Engineering Viruses for Health or Warfare*, Wash. Post, Aug. 16, 1970, at B2, col. 1; *see also* Lederberg, *Biological Warfare: A Global Threat*, 59 Am. Sci. 195 (1971).

The Specter of Biological Weapons

States and terrorists alike have shown a growing interest in germ warfare. More stringent arms-control efforts are needed to discourage attacks

by Leonard A. Cole

In 1995, on a whim, I asked a friend: Which would worry you more, being attacked with a biological weapon or a chemical weapon? He looked quizzical. "Frankly, I'm afraid of Alzheimer's," he replied, and we shared a laugh. He had elegantly dismissed my question as an irrelevancy. In civilized society, people do not think about such things.

The next day, on March 20, the nerve agent sarin was unleashed in the Tokyo subway system, killing 12 people and injuring 5,500. In Japan, no less, one of the safest countries in the world. I called my friend, and we lingered over the coincidental timing of my question. A seemingly frivolous speculation one day, a deadly serious matter the next.

That thousands did not die from the Tokyo attack was attributed to an impure mixture of the agent. A tiny drop of sarin, which was originally developed in Germany in the 1930s, can kill within minutes after skin contact or inhalation of its vapor. Like all other nerve agents, sarin blocks the action of acetylcholinesterase, an enzyme necessary for the transmission of nerve impulses.

The cult responsible for the sarin attack, Aum Shinrikyo ("Supreme Truth"), was developing biological agents as well. If a chemical attack is frightening, a biological weapon poses a worse nightmare. Chemical agents are inanimate, but bacteria, viruses and other live agents may be contagious and reproductive. If they become established in the environment, they may multiply. Unlike any other weapon, they can become more dangerous over time.

Certain biological agents incapacitate, whereas others kill. The Ebola virus, for example, kills as many as 90 percent of its victims in little more than a week. Connective tissue liquefies; every orifice bleeds. In the final stages, Ebola victims become convulsive, splashing contaminated blood around them as they twitch, shake and thrash to their deaths.

For Ebola, there is no cure, no treatment. Even the manner in which it spreads is unclear, by close contact with victims and their blood, bodily fluids or remains or by just breathing the surrounding air. Recent outbreaks in Zaire prompted the quarantine of sections of the country until the disease had run its course.

The horror is only magnified by the thought that individuals and nations would consider attacking others with such viruses. In October 1992 Shoko Asahara, head of the Aum Shinrikyo cult, and 40 followers traveled to Zaire, ostensibly to help treat Ebola victims. But the group's real intention, according to an October 31, 1995, report by the U.S. Senate's Permanent Subcommittee on Investigations, was probably to obtain virus samples, culture them and use them in biological attacks.

Interest in acquiring killer organisms for sinister purposes is not limited to groups outside the U.S. On May 5, 1995, six weeks after the Tokyo subway incident, Larry Harris, a laboratory technician in Ohio, ordered the bacterium that causes bubonic plague from a Maryland biomedical supply firm. The company, the American Type Culture Collection in Rockville, Md., mailed him three vials of *Yersinia pestis*.

Harris drew suspicion only when he called the firm four days after placing his order to find out why it had not arrived. Company officials wondered about his impatience and his apparent unfamiliar-

ity with laboratory techniques, so they contacted federal authorities. He was later found to be a member of a white supremacist organization. In November 1995 he pled guilty in federal court to mail fraud.

To get the plague bacteria, Harris needed no more than a credit card and a false letterhead. Partially in response to this incident, an antiterrorism law enacted this past April required the Centers for Disease Control and Prevention to monitor more closely shipments of infectious agents.

What would Harris have done with the bacteria? He claimed he wanted to conduct research to counteract Iraqi rats carrying "supergerms." But if he had cared to grow a biological arsenal, the task would have been frighteningly simple. By dividing every 20 minutes, a single bacterium gives rise to more than a billion copies in 10 hours. A small vial of microorganisms can yield a huge number in less than a week. For some diseases, such as anthrax, inhaling a few thousand bacteria—which would cover an area smaller than the period at the end of this sentence—can be fatal.

Kathleen C. Bailey, a former assistant director of the U.S. Arms Control and Disarmament Agency, has visited several biotechnology and pharmaceutical firms. She is "absolutely convinced" that a major biological arsenal could be built with $10,000 worth of equipment in a room 15 feet by 15. After all, one can cultivate trillions of bacteria at relatively little risk to one's self with gear no more sophisticated than a beer fermenter and a protein-based culture, a gas mask and a plastic overgarment.

Fortunately, biological terrorism has thus far been limited to very few cases. One incident occurred in September

FEARFUL of Iraqi biological and chemical weapons, travelers donned gas masks in Tel Aviv Airport during the 1991 Persian Gulf War.

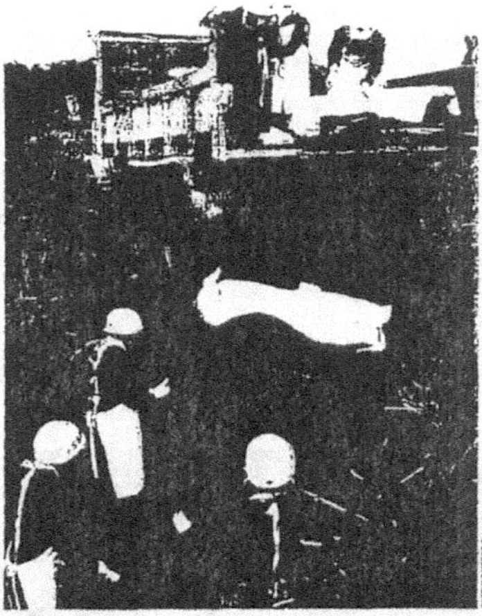

EBOLA VIRUS, victims of which were buried in a mass grave in Kikwit, Zaire, in 1995, was reportedly considered as a potential biological weapon by Japan's Aum Shinrikyo cult.

1984, when about 750 people became sick after eating in restaurants in an Oregon town called The Dalles. In 1986 Ma Anand Sheela confessed at a federal trial that she and other members of a nearby cult that had clashed with local Oregonians had spread salmonella bacteria on salad bars in four restaurants; the bacteria had been grown in laboratories on the cult's ranch. After serving two and a half years in prison, Sheela, who had been the chief of staff for the cult leader, Bhagwan Shree Rajneesh, was released and deported to Europe.

But as a 1992 report by the Office of Technology Assessment indicated, both biological and chemical terrorism have been rare. Also rare has been the use of biological agents as weapons of war. Perhaps the first recorded incident occurred in the 14th century, when an army besieging Kaffa, a seaport on the Black Sea in the Crimea in Russia, catapulted plague-infected cadavers over the city walls. In colonial America a British officer reportedly gave germ-infested blankets from a smallpox infirmary to Indians in order to start an epidemic among the tribes. The only confirmed instance in this century was Japan's use of plague and other bacteria against China in the 1930s and 1940s.

As the 20th century draws to a close, however, an unpleasant paradox has emerged. More states than ever are signing international agreements to eliminate chemical and biological arms. Yet more are also suspected of developing these weapons despite the treaties. In 1980 only one country, the Soviet Union, had been named by the U.S. for violating the 1972 Biological Weapons Convention, a treaty that prohibits the development or possession of biological weapons.

Since then, the number has ballooned. In 1989 Central Intelligence Agency director William Webster reported that "at least 10 countries" were developing biological weapons. By 1995, 17 countries had been named as biological weapons suspects, according to sources cited by the Office of Technology Assessment and at U.S. Senate committee hearings. They include Iran, Iraq, Libya, Syria, North Korea, Taiwan, Israel, Egypt, Vietnam, Laos, Cuba, Bulgaria, India, South Korea, South Africa, China and Russia. (Russian leaders insist that they have terminated their biological program, but U.S. officials doubt that claim.)

Grim Reality

The first five of these countries—Iran, Iraq, Libya, Syria and North Korea—are especially worrisome in view of their histories of militant behavior. Iraq, for example, has acknowledged the claims of U.N. inspectors that during the 1991 Persian Gulf War it possessed Scud missiles tipped with biological warheads. A 1994 Pentagon report to Congress cited instability in eastern Europe, the Middle East and Southwest Asia as likely to encourage even more nations to develop biological and chemical arms.

Reversing this trend should be of paramount concern to the community of nations. Indeed, the elimination of biological as well as chemical weaponry is a worthy, if difficult, goal. The failure of this effort may increase the likelihood of the development of a man-made plague from Ebola or some other gruesome agent.

Dedication to biological disarmament in particular should be enhanced by another grim truth: in many scenarios, a large population cannot be protected against a biological attack. Vaccines can prevent some diseases, but unless the causative agent is known in advance, such a safeguard may be worthless. Antibiotics are effective against specific bacteria or classes of biological agents, but not against all. Moreover, the incidence of infectious disease around the world has been rising from newly resistant strains of bacteria that defy treatment. In this era of biotechnology, especially, novel organisms can be engineered against which vaccines or antibiotics are useless.

Nor do physical barriers against infection offer great comfort. Fortunately, most biological agents have no effect on or through intact skin, so respiratory masks and clothing would provide adequate protection for most people. After a short while, the danger could recede as sunlight and ambient temperatures destroyed the agents. But certain microorganisms can persist indefinitely in an environment. Gruinard Island, off the coast of Scotland, remained infected with anthrax spores for 40 years after biological warfare tests were carried out there in the 1940s. And in 1981 Rex Watson, then head of Britain's Chemical and Biological Defense Establishment, asserted that if Berlin had been bombarded with anthrax bacteria during World War II, the city would still be contaminated.

Although many Israelis did become accustomed to wearing gas masks during the 1991 Persian Gulf War, it seems unrealistic to expect large populations of civilians to wear such gear for months or years, especially in warm regions. U.N. inspectors in Iraq report that in hot weather they can scarcely tolerate wearing a mask for more than 15 minutes at a time.

Calls for more robust biological defense programs have grown, particularly after the Persian Gulf War. Proponents of increased funding for biological defense research often imply that vaccines and special gear developed through such work can protect the public as well as troops. But the same truths hold for both the military and civilians: unless an attack organism is known in advance and is vulnerable to medical interventions, defense can be illusory.

Indeed, the Gulf War experience was in certain respects misleading. Iraq's biological weapons were understood to be anthrax bacilli and botulinum toxin. (Although toxins are inanimate products of microorganisms, they are treated as biological agents under the terms of the 1972 Biological Weapons Convention.) Both are susceptible to existing vaccines and treatments, and protection of military forces therefore seemed possible. Research that would lead to enhanced defense against these agents is thus generally warranted.

But the improbabilities of warding off attacks from less traditional agents deserve full appreciation. Anticipating that research can come up with defenses against attack organisms whose nature is not known in advance seems fanciful. Moreover, even with all its limitations, the cost of building a national civil defense system against biological and chemical weapons would be substantial. A 1969 United Nations report indicated that the expense of stockpiling gas masks, antibiotics, vaccines and other defensive measures for civilians could exceed $20 billion. That figure, when adjusted for inflation, would now be about $80 billion.

Vaccines and protective gear are not the only challenges to biological defense. Identifying an organism quickly in a battlefield situation, too, is problematic. Even determining whether a biological attack has been launched can be uncertain. Consequently, the Pentagon has begun to focus more on detection.

In May 1994 Deputy Secretary of Defense John Deutch produced an interagency report on counterproliferation activities concerning weapons of mass destruction. Biological agent detectors in particular, he wrote, were "not being pursued adequately." To the annual $110 million budgeted for the development of biological and chemical weapons detection, the report recommended adding $75 million. Already under way were Pentagon-sponsored programs involving such technologies as ion-trap mass spectrometry and laser-induced breakdown spectroscopy, approaches that look for characteristic chemical signatures of dangerous agents in the air. The army's hope, which its spokespersons admit is a long way from being realized, is to find a "generic" detector that can identify classes of pathogens.

Meanwhile the military is also advancing a more limited approach that identifies specific agents through antibody-antigen combinations. The Biological Integrated Detection System (BIDS) exposes suspected air samples to antibodies that react with a particular biological agent. A reaction of the antibody would signify the agent is present, a process that takes about 30 minutes.

BIDS can now identify four agents through antibody-antigen reactions: *Bacillus anthracis* (anthrax bacterium), *Y. pestis* (bubonic plague), botulinum toxin (the poison released by botulism organisms) and staphylococcus enterotoxin B (released by certain staph bacteria). Laboratory investigations to identify additional agents through antibody-antigen reactions are in progress. But scores of organisms and toxins are viewed as potential warfare agents. Whether the full range, or even most, will be detectable by BIDS remains uncertain.

The most effective safeguard against biological warfare and biological terrorism is, and will be, prevention. To this end, enhanced intelligence and regulation of commercial orders for pathogens are important. Both approaches have been strengthened by provisions in the antiterrorism bill enacted earlier this year. At the same time, attempts to identify and control emerging diseases are gaining attention. One such effort is ProMED (Program to Monitor Emerging Diseases), which was proposed in 1993 by the 3,000-member Federation of American Scientists.

Although focusing on disease outbreaks in general, supporters of ProMED are sensitive to the possibility of man-made epidemics. The ProMED surveillance system would include developing baseline data on endemic diseases throughout the world, rapid reporting of unusual outbreaks, and responses aimed at containing disease, such as providing advice on trade and travel. Such a program could probably distinguish disease outbreaks from hostile sources more effectively than is currently possible.

In addition, steps to strengthen the 1972 Biological Weapons Convention through verification arrangements—including on-site inspections—should be encouraged. The 139 countries that are parties to the convention are expected to discuss incorporating verification measures at a review conference in December of this year. After the last review conference, in 1991, a committee to explore such measures was established. VEREX, as the group was called, has listed various possibilities ranging from surveillance of the scientific literature to on-site inspections of potential production areas, such as laboratories, brew-

Potential Biological Agents

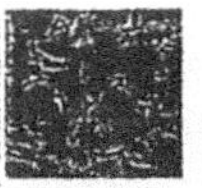

Bacillus anthracis. Causes anthrax. If bacteria are inhaled, symptoms may develop in two to three days. Initial symptoms resembling common respiratory infection are followed by high fever, vomiting, joint ache and labored breathing, and internal and external bleeding lesions. Exposure may be fatal. Vaccine and antibiotics provide protection unless exposure is very high.

Botulinum toxin. Cause of botulism, produced by *Clostridium botulinum* bacteria. Symptoms appear 12 to 72 hours after ingestion or inhalation. Initial symptoms are nausea and diarrhea, followed by weakness, dizziness and respiratory paralysis, often leading to death. Antitoxin can sometimes arrest the process.

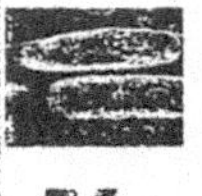

Yersinia pestis. Causes bubonic plague, the Black Death of the Middle Ages. If bacteria reach the lungs, symptoms—including fever and delirium—may appear in three or four days. Untreated cases are nearly always fatal. Vaccines can offer immunity, and antibiotics are usually effective if administered promptly.

Ebola virus. Highly contagious and lethal. May not be desirable as a biological agent because of uncertain stability outside of animal host. Symptoms, appearing two or three days after exposure, include high fever, delirium, severe joint pain, bleeding from body orifices, and convulsions, followed by death. No known treatment.

eries and pharmaceutical companies.

Given the ease with which bioweapons can be produced, individuals will always be able to circumvent international agreements. But the absence of such agents from national arsenals—and tightened regulations on the acquisition and transfer of pathogens—will make them more difficult to obtain for hostile purposes. Verification can never be foolproof, and therefore some critics argue that verification efforts are a waste of time. Proponents nonetheless assert that sanctions following a detected violation would provide at least some disincentive to cheaters and are thus preferable to no sanctions at all. Furthermore, a strengthened global treaty underscores a commitment by the nations of the world not to traffic in these weapons.

The infrequent use of biological weapons to date might be explained in many ways. Some potential users have probably lacked familiarity with how to develop pathogens as weapons; moreover, they may have been afraid of infecting themselves. Nations and terrorists alike might furthermore be disinclined to use bioagents because they are by nature unpredictable. Through mutations, a bacterium or virus can gain or lose virulence over time, which may be contrary to the strategic desires of the people who released it. And once introduced into the environment, a pathogen may pose a threat to anybody who goes there, making it difficult to occupy territory.

But beneath all these pragmatic concerns lies another dimension that deserves more emphasis than it generally receives: the moral repugnance of these weapons. Their ability to cause great suffering, coupled with their indiscriminate character, no doubt contributes to the deep-seated aversion most people have for them. And that aversion seems central to explaining why bioweapons have so rarely been used in the past. Contrary to analyses that commonly ignore or belittle the phenomenon, this natural antipathy should be appreciated and exploited. Even some terrorists could be reluctant to use a weapon so fearsome that it would permanently alienate the public from their cause.

The Poison Taboo

In recognition of these sentiments, the 1972 Biological Weapons Convention describes germ weaponry as "repugnant to the conscience of mankind." Such descriptions have roots that reach back thousands of years. (Not until the 19th century were microorganisms understood to be the cause of infection; before then, poison and disease were commonly seen as the same. Indeed, the Latin word for "poison" is "virus.")

Among prohibitions in many civilizations were the poisoning of food and wells and the use of poison weapons. The Greeks and Romans condemned the use of poison in war as a violation of *ius gentium*—the law of nations. Poisons and other weapons considered inhumane were forbidden by the Manu Law of India around 500 B.C. and among the Saracens 1,000 years later. The prohibitions were reiterated by Dutch statesman Hugo Grotius in his 1625 opus *The Law of War and Peace*, and they were, for the most part, maintained during the harsh European religious conflicts of the time.

Like the taboos against incest, cannibalism and other widely reviled acts, the taboo against poison weapons was sometimes violated. But the frequency of such violations may have been minimized because of their castigation as a "defalcation of proper principles," in the words of the 18th- and 19th-century English jurist Robert P. Ward. Under the law of nations, Ward wrote, "Nothing is more expressly forbidden than the use of *poisoned* arms" (emphasis in original).

Historian John Ellis van Courtland Moon, now professor emeritus at Fitchburg State College in Massachusetts, contends that growing nationalism in the 18th century weakened the disinclinations about poison weapons. As a result of what Moon calls "the nationalization of ethics," military necessity began to displace moral considerations in state policies; nations were more likely to employ any means possible to attain their aims in warfare.

In the mid-19th century, a few military leaders proposed that toxic weapons be employed, although none actually were. Nevertheless, gas was used in World War I. The experience of large-scale chemical warfare was so horrifying that it led to the 1925 Geneva Protocol, which forbids the use of chemical and bacteriological agents in war. Images of victims gasping, frothing and choking to death had a profound impact. The text of the protocol reflects the global sense of abhorrence. It affirmed that these weapons had been "justly condemned by the general opinion of the civilized world."

Chemical and biological weapons were used in almost none of the hundreds of wars and skirmishes in subsequent decades—until Iraq's extensive chemical attacks during the Iran-Iraq war. Regrettably, the international response to Iraqi behavior was muted or ineffective. From 1983 until the war ended in 1988, Iraq was permitted to get away with chemical murder. Fear of an Iranian victory stifled serious outcries against a form of weaponry that had been universally condemned.

The consequences of silence about Iraq's behavior, though unfortunate, were not surprising. Iraqi ability to use chemical weapons with impunity, and

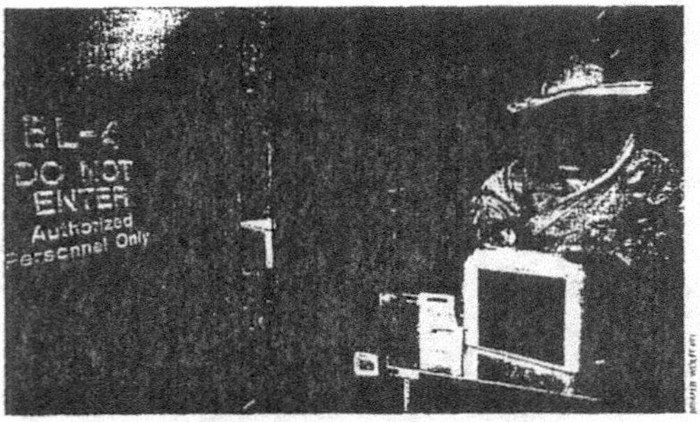

POTENTIAL GERM AGENTS and defenses are studied in a maximum-security laboratory at the U.S. Army Medical Research Institute of Infectious Diseases in Maryland.

their apparent effectiveness against Iran, prompted more countries to arm themselves with chemical and biological weapons. Ironically, in 1991 many of the countries that had been silent about the Iraqi chemical attacks had to face a chemically and biologically equipped Iraq on the battlefield.

To its credit, since the Persian Gulf War, much of the international community has pressed Iraq about its unconventional weapons programs by maintaining sanctions through the U.N. Security Council. Council resolutions require elimination of Iraq's biological weapons (and other weapons of mass destruction), as well as information about past programs to develop them. Iraq has been only partially forthcoming, and U.N. inspectors continue to seek full disclosure.

But even now, U.N. reports are commonly dry recitations. Expressions of outrage are rare. Any country or group that develops these weapons deserves forceful condemnation. We need continuing reminders that civilized people do not traffic in, or use, such weaponry. The agreement by the U.S. and Russia to destroy their chemical stockpiles within a decade should help.

Words of outrage alone, obviously, are not enough. Intelligence is important, as are controls over domestic and international shipments of pathogens and enhanced global surveillance of disease outbreaks. Moreover, institutions that reinforce positive behavior and values are essential.

The highest priority of the moment in this regard is implementation of the Chemical Weapons Convention, which outlaws the possession of chemical weapons. It lists chemicals that signatory nations must declare to have in their possession. Unlike the Biological Weapons Convention, the chemical treaty has extensive provisions to verify compliance, including short-notice inspections of suspected violations. It also provides added inducements to join through information exchanges and commercial privileges among the signatories.

In 1993 the chemical treaty was opened for signature. By October 1996, the pact had been signed by 160 countries and ratified by 64, one less than the number required for the agreement to enter into force. One disappointing holdout is the U.S. In part because of disagreements over the treaty's verification provisions, the U.S. Senate recently delayed a vote on the pact.

Implementing this chemical weapons treaty should add momentum to the current negotiations over strengthening the Biological Weapons Convention. Conversely, failure of the Chemical Weapons Convention to fulfill expectations will dampen prospects for a verification regime for the biological treaty. The most likely consequence would be the continued proliferation of chemical and biological arsenals around the world. The longer these weapons persist, the more their sense of illegitimacy erodes, and the more likely they will be used—by armies and by terrorists.

As analysts have noted, subnational groups commonly use the types of weapons that are in national arsenals. The absence of biological and chemical weapons from national military inventories may diminish their attractiveness to terrorists. According to terrorism expert Brian M. Jenkins, leaders of Aum Shinrikyo indicated that their interest in chemical weapons was inspired by Iraq's use of chemicals during its war with Iran.

Treaties, verification regimes, global surveillance, controlled exchanges of pathogens—all are the muscle of arms control. Their effectiveness ultimately depends on the moral backbone that supports them and the will to enforce them rigorously. By underscoring the moral sense behind the formal exclusion of biological weapons, sustaining their prohibition becomes more likely.

Defenses against Biological Weapons

Respirator or gas mask. Filters, usually made of activated charcoal, must block particles larger than one micron. Overgarments are also advisable to protect against contact with open wounds or otherwise broken skin.

Protective shelter. Best if a closed room, ideally insulated with plastic or some other nonpermeable material and ventilated with filtered air.

Decontamination. Such traditional disinfectants as formaldehyde are effective for sterilizing surfaces.

Vaccination. Must be for specific agent. Some agents require several inoculations over an extended period before immunity is conferred. For many agents, no vaccine is available.

Antibiotics. Effective against some but not all bacterial agents (and not effective against viruses). For some susceptible bacteria, antibiotic therapy must begin within a few hours of exposure—before symptoms appear.

Detection systems. Only rudimentary field units currently available for a few specific agents. Research is under way to expand the number of agents that can be detected in battlefield situations or elsewhere.

The Author

LEONARD A. COLE is an adjunct professor of political science and an associate in the program in science, technology and society at Rutgers University in Newark, N.J. He is an authority in the area of science and public policy, with special expertise in policy concerning biological and chemical warfare, radon and various health issues. He received a B.A. in political science from the University of California, Berkeley, in 1961 and a Ph.D. in political science from Columbia University in 1970.

Further Reading

CLOUDS OF SECRECY: THE ARMY'S GERM WARFARE TESTS OVER POPULATED AREAS. Leonard A. Cole. Rowman and Littlefield. 1990.

BIOLOGICAL WEAPONS: WEAPONS OF THE FUTURE? Edited by Brad Roberts. Center for Strategic and International Studies. 1993.

BIOLOGICAL WARFARE IN THE 21ST CENTURY. Malcolm Dando. Macmillan. 1994.

THE ELEVENTH PLAGUE: THE POLITICS OF BIOLOGICAL AND CHEMICAL WARFARE. Leonard A. Cole. W. H. Freeman and Company. 1996.

Confronting a Biological Armageddon: Experts Tackle Prospect of Bioterrorism

IT SOUNDS LIKE the plot of a Hollywood thriller du jour: Terrorists stealthily plant a cache of deadly anthrax spores in the air vents of the New York Stock Exchange. Hundreds die, plunging the global economy into turmoil.

Or consider another scenario: 2 dozen recently hospitalized people, stricken with what at first appears to be a particularly virulent strain of influenza, develop the alarming symptoms of a deadly hemorrhagic fever. By the time the source of the infection is identified as Ebola virus, introduced into blood products by a disgruntled blood bank supervisor whose spouse works at a government research lab, as many as 58 000 people have been significantly exposed to the infection. Some almost certainly carry the contagion with them as they flee the city in panic.

While screenwriters may well be cranking out a *Die Hard on Wall Street*, these scenarios were created by people who concern themselves with weapons of mass destruction rather than entertaining the masses. The stock exchange episode was used last year as the script for a war game to examine the US military's readiness to counter an attack featuring biological warfare; the Ebola scenario was presented at a recent conference on the medical consequences of terrorism.

Not surprisingly, given concerns about the possibility of terrorist attacks of any sort at the 1996 Summer Olympic Games in Atlanta, Ga, authorities were taking unprecedented precautions against the use of biological and chemical weapons. Preparations have included, for example, multiagency training exercises involving biological, chemical, and nuclear attacks, and plans by the Department of Defense (DoD) to deploy special chemical or biological weapons detection equipment around some of the sites of events.

Defense officials said that hundreds of military experts in both chemical and biological warfare, some of whom were to be moved temporarily close to Atlanta, would be on call to respond instantly in case of an attack. In addition, a new unit of 250 marines and navy personnel, part of a Camp Lejeune, NC–based chemical and biological incident response force, was training to be ready for the Olympics, should their presence be requested.

A Growing Concern

The increasing use of war games and exercises aimed at assessing how well military or civilian agencies respond to such threats reflects a growing concern about biological weapons. Many experts on terrorism and biological warfare believe that the probability of an attack by rogue nations, terrorist groups, or a Unabomber-type malcontent using infectious agents and biological toxins is greater than ever before.

"The odds are increasing, although how much is hard to quantify," says Michael L. Moodie, president of the Chemical and Biological Arms Control Institute, a nonprofit policy research organization in Alexandria, Va. "It's an issue that is probably more complex than people realize, and we have to walk a fine line between hyping the risk and being irresponsible and trying to convince people that [such an attack] is a possibility for which we need to invest resources."

Although biological weapons generally have received scant attention until recently, using microbes and toxins against one's enemies has a long history. In the 14th century, the Tartars reportedly cata-

US Army Medical Research Institute of Infectious Diseases (USAMRIID) personnel demonstrate the use of an isolator designed for transporting patients stricken with the most hazardous of infectious diseases (Photo © Brian R. Wolff/UPI 1996)

Centers for Disease Control and Prevention

Only 2 US laboratories, 1 at the Centers for Disease Control and Prevention (shown here) and 1 at USAMRIID, are designated as "BL-4" (Biosafety Level 4) facilities, which are equipped to handle the most dangerous pathogens.

pulted the bodies of plague victims into the city of Kaffa. During the French and Indian Wars in American colonial days, it is said the British deliberately gave Indians blankets contaminated with smallpox. During World War II, the Japanese tested biological weapons on prisoners of war in China, killing more than 1000.

A handful of events within the past few years, however, have made the prospect of biological warfare and terrorist attack seem less of a historical curiosity and more of a credible threat.

Despite signing the 1972 Biological and Toxins Weapons Convention, which prohibited the deliberate use of such agents, Soviet research on biological weapons continued. In 1994, US and Russian scientists reported that a 1979 anthrax outbreak in Sverdlovsk that killed at least 66 people was caused by spores accidentally released from a Soviet biological warfare plant, not by contaminated animal hides, as the Soviets had long maintained. In addition, defectors revealed in 1994 that the Russians were conducting research aimed at modifying *Yersenia pestis*, the plague bacterium, to make it more virulent and stable in the environment.

An April 1996 DoD report, *Proliferation and Response*, spotlights US concerns about Russia's current compliance with the Convention. "Russia may be retaining capacity for the production of biological warfare agents," the report warns, noting that Russia's biological warfare technology also "may be vulnerable to leakage to third parties" through theft or sale, an ongoing concern for nuclear materials.

Recent revelations about Iraq's substantial biological weapons program were "a wake-up call" for the intelligence community, US Navy Undersecretary Richard Danzig recently noted. The DoD report notes that the Iraqis claim to have manufactured 90 000 liters of botulinum toxin and 8300 liters of anthrax, as well as significant quantities of aflatoxin.

Iraqi officials also acknowledged to United Nations investigators that they produced roughly 200 missile warheads and aerial bombs containing these substances that were distributed to air bases and a missile site during the 1991 Persian Gulf War; they also admitted performing research on mycotoxins and a variety of infectious agents and other toxins, including *Clostridium perfringens* (the most common agent of gas gangrene) and ricin.

Investigators have learned that Aum Shinrikyo, the apocalyptic cult behind the March 1995 sarin gas attack on the Tokyo subway system that killed 11 people and injured more than 5000 others, had a large biological weapons program, involving such agents as anthrax and botulinum toxin. According to an expert, cult scientists had been trying to "weaponize" botulinum toxin—that is, formulate it so that it could be effectively dispersed in an aerosol form—as early as 1990.

The cult, which had amassed $1 billion in assets and recruited 40 000 members in Japan and Russia, including hundreds of scientists and engineers, also launched an expedition to Zaire to collect samples of Ebola virus. Another indication of the cult's future plans was noted in a recent report by a Senate panel: Aum Shinrikyo had acquired a Soviet-made helicopter for the purpose of spraying sarin, as well as 2 radio-controlled drones for disseminating biological agents.

A New Terrorism

The Tokyo subway attack brought home the potential of chemical and biological weapons as an escalated method of terrorism that few government and public safety agencies are currently prepared to cope with, notes Gary Eifried, of EAI Corporation, an Abingdon, Md–based group that performs chemical and biological agent studies and analysis.

There are a number of reasons why biological agents are likely to appeal to terrorist groups. One is the emergence of groups that lack the restraint of "traditional" terrorist organizations, which typically have a political agenda that they want to bring to the table without alienating the general public or eliciting a massive government crackdown, policy researcher Moodie recently testified to a Senate subcommittee. But as Aum Shinrikyo demonstrated, there are groups today that are willing to use weapons of mass destruction, including biological agents, "just to hurt society," Moodie noted.

Experts say the impact of biological weapons could be substantial. In a scenario presented in a 1993 report by the former Congressional Office of Technology Assessment, a small airplane equipped with a crop sprayer flying over Washington, DC, disseminating 100 kg of anthrax spores could deliver a fatal dose to as many as 3 million people.

Another reason biological weapons have piqued the interest of terrorist and fringe groups is that they don't require a large financial investment and the materials are relatively easy to acquire.

Recent news reports have underscored the alarming ease with which individuals associated with fringe groups and terrorist organizations have acquired pathogens and toxins. In April 1993, Canadian customs officials stopped an Arkansas man who had 4 guns and 20 000 rounds of ammunition, a supply of neo-Nazi literature, and enough ricin to kill at least 30 000 people. More recently, 2 members of a Minnesota right-wing group were convicted of plotting to use ricin to kill US marshals and Internal Revenue Service agents. And last year, an Ohio man was arrested for allegedly misrepresenting himself to order 3 vials of bubonic plague bacteria from a supplier in Maryland.

Biological weapons are also not detected by methods used for explosives and firearms, such as metal detectors and x-ray devices, notes Eifried. Moreover, because the first indication of an attack is likely to be hours to days after exposure—when people first begin to develop disease symptoms—the perpetrators can be long gone from the scene before health and law enforcement authorities are aware there is a problem.

Countering the Risk

How prepared is society to counter the risk of bioterrorism?

"We currently have little to no ability to anticipate a chemical or biological attack; little to no ability to detect one if it occurs, other than coping with the casualties; and a highly limited ability to manage the consequences of such an attack," says Brad Roberts, a specialist in international security policy.

But experts say that the recently heightened appreciation of the problem may lead to the kind of attention and resources needed to develop strategies to cope with bioterrorism.

One big push in the right direction may come from the US Congress, if the House passes legislation that received overwhelming approval in the Senate in June. The legislation allocates $35 million to develop strategies and train medical teams that will respond to chemical, biological, and nuclear attacks, $29 million for Pentagon and Department of Energy research into methods for detecting weapons of mass destruction, and $15 million to train local emergency response officials in how to meet attacks involving weapons of mass destruction.

Additional funds would target strengthening federal efforts to detect and intercept such weapons at US borders and programs aimed at improving the security or reducing the threat of weapon-related materials in the former Soviet Union.

Various government agencies, including the DoD, Department of Energy, Federal Emergency Management Agency (FEMA), Public Health Service, and others are formulating plans to clarify their respective responsibilities and the chain of command in coping with a bioterrorist attack and its medical consequences.

Some local governments are also trying to plan for such eventualities. After the Tokyo attack, New York City and Los Angeles conducted training exercises to identify problems in responding to such an event.

One promising effort involving a collaboration between the Arlington, Va, Fire Department, FBI, DoD, Public Health Service, and other federal agencies is the establishment of a Metropolitan Medical Strike Team intended to serve as a model for other cities. On call 24 hours a day, the 42-person team of volunteers with backgrounds in emergency preparedness, medicine, and law enforcement would mobilize to help limit contamination in an attack and minimize casualties.

Emerging Microbial Threats

Experts note that while biological weapons present a special challenge to law enforcement agencies and the military, the issues are familiar to medical researchers, clinicians, and public health experts concerned with the threat of emerging microbial infections resulting from "natural" causes rather than geopolitical or terrorist ones. The need to identify and contain the source of an epidemic as well as cope with the medical consequences is the same whatever its genesis.

Because it is likely that an act of biological terrorism will be detected by a physician or epidemiologist, medical personnel must be aware of symptoms and epidemiological patterns that might indicate a biological attack, notes Eifried. They also must know treatments for "exotic" diseases, such as anthrax and Rift Valley fever, that they are unlikely ever to have encountered.

Mindful of the intersection of emerging microbial infections and bioterrorism, the White House announced in June a new policy to track emerging infectious diseases through a worldwide infectious disease surveillance and response system. Noting that the United States is vulnerable to microbial diseases from a variety of sources, including an attack by rogue nations or terrorists, the policy is designed to address both the health and potential security challenges of deadly infectious agents.

Given the difficulty of predicting and preventing bioterrorist attacks, some experts say that more attention should be given to vaccine research and maintaining adequate supplies of vaccines, antitoxins, and antibiotics.

"We probably need vaccines against what is still a quite limited range of microbes that concern us the most," says Peter B. Jahrling, PhD, of the US Army Medical Research Institute of Infectious Diseases. But even if such vaccines were available, the issues of cost and determining who should be vaccinated would have to be dealt with.

Moreover, Jahrling notes, it would be impossible to develop vaccines for all the possible pathogens that could present a threat. What is really needed, he said, is to better understand the pathology of an illness and to treat its effect—like treating the dehydration of cholera victims.

Although the challenges of dealing with biowarfare and bioterrorism are daunting, experts say that the new visibility the problem is receiving is a good start to finding solutions.

"We've made more headway with this problem in the year or so since the Tokyo subway incident than ever before," says Roberts. But the big question, he adds, is "the durability of our will" to devote the money and the effort needed to see it through.

"The fact that people have woken up to the problem is the single most positive development with respect to this problem," agrees Moodie. "But there will be some turbulence ahead as we identify the tough questions and look for answers."

—by Joan Stephenson, PhD

Bioterrorism in Our Midst?

Perhaps nothing is more terrifying than the prospect of terrorists using a biological agent, but not all terrorist organizations are likely to unleash such a devastating weapon. At which groups should counterterrorism efforts be directed? That was one question before a panel of experts at the "Conference on Countering Biological Terrorism: Strategic Firepower in the Hands of Many?" held this summer by the Potomac Institute for Policy Studies.

According to Jerrold Post, M.D., professor of psychiatry, political psychology, and international affairs at The George Washington University and an expert in bioterrorism, two types of groups pose the highest threat of biological attack: religious fundamental terrorists and right wing fanatics such as survivalist, racist, and militia groups. Part of the reason fundamentalist groups are so dangerous, Post says, is that they, unlike terrorist groups looking to influence an audience, see no need to attain public acceptance of their acts.

"The audience for a religious terrorist is God," he says. The threat is particularly grave considering the likely growth of fanatical religious millennial groups, he adds.

> **Religious terrorism is likely to grow as fanatical groups become more prominent.**

According to Post, a look back at biological terrorism in recent decades can help predict tomorrow's attackers. Groups previously involved in bioterrorism such as Aum Shinrikyo, Aryan Nation, the Minnesota Patriots Council, and the Order of the Rising Sun all fit into the categories of likely users of biological weapons.

Commander Ken Campbell of the U.S. Navy, who has conducted extensive research on which groups might use weapons of mass destruction to cause mass casualties, says a first step is to examine the group's ideology to see whether a goal is to destroy an existing regime. Next, the group leader's personality, motivations, and intentions must be studied. Then experts should determine whether the intensity of the group's attacks is increasing.

Other factors in assessing the likelihood of using biological weapons include the group's sophistication of methods, membership demographics, financial resources, and availability of materials in their country.

For example, Aum Shinrikyo had an authoritarian, paranoid religious leader who recruited people with degrees in medicine and computers and with involvement in law enforcement.

Mick Donahue, president of Security Management International of Alexandria, Virginia, posits several factors that may lead to an increase in bioterrorism. These factors include heightened knowledge of microbiology and growing numbers of graduates with microbiology degrees, more availability of state sponsors and rogue suppliers of raw materials, and easier access to materials and assembly instructions, such as through the Internet.

Terrorists are becoming more experienced and professional, getting over their traditional preference of seeing an immediate impact such as an explosion, Donahue told attendees, realizing that an aerosol spray canister may be as effective as a truck bomb. Biological weapons are also attractive because they are difficult to detect, he says.

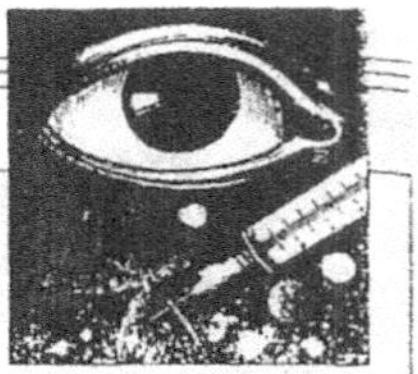

Drug Watch

Markets for heroin and marijuana are growing. The market for cocaine is stable, and hydrocodone, a narcotic pain reliever similar to codeine, may be the most widely diverted prescription drug in the United States, according to two recent overviews of national drug trends published by two federal government agencies.

The latest issue of "Pulse Check: National Trends in Drug Abuse," published by the Office of National Drug Control Policy (ONDCP), reports that young people are increasingly using heroin and marijuana, while most heroin and crack users are "a stable, older cohort of long-term users." The report adds that use of a mixture of hallucinogenic and hypnotic drugs such as ketamine and LSD is increasingly popular with youth.

According to the Drug Enforcement Administration's (DEA) "Diversion Quarterly Highlights," hydrocodone, oxycodone (another narcotic analgesic), and benzodiazepines (sedatives such as Valium) are the three most popular legal drugs for diversion. The report also discusses regional trends; for example, the DEA's Baltimore office reports increasing occurrences of ketamine (a hallucinatory anaesthetic) abuse; the Riverside, California, and Phoenix offices report rising concern over the diversion of precursor chemicals to manufacture methamphetamine; and the Chicago office reports that heroin is being taken in combination with a number of other compounds, such as diazepam.

Both reports can be read in their entirety on *SM Online*.

Illustration (top left) by **Andy Buttram**, illustration above by **John Pack**

PLS. 15(2), 167-183, Beech Tree Publishing, 10 Watford Close, Guildford, Surrey GU1 2EP, UK.

ROUNDTABLE ARTICLE

Chemical/Biological Terrorism: Coping with a New Threat

Jonathan B. Tucker Monterey Institute of International Studies, USA

Abstract. **In March 1995, Japanese terrorists released nerve gas on the Tokyo subway, causing eleven deaths and more than 5,000 injuries. Although terrorists have sought to acquire chemical/biological (C/B) agents in the past, and a few have employed them on a small scale, the Tokyo attack was the first large-scale terrorist use of a lethal chemical agent against unarmed civilians, weakening a long-standing psychological taboo. This tragic incident has therefore drawn worldwide attention to the emerging threat of chemical/biological terrorism. Despite significant technical hurdles associated with the production and delivery of C/B agents, such weapons are within the reach of terrorist groups that possess the necessary scientific know-how and financial resources. This article proposes a C/B counterterrorism strategy based on preemption and civil defense, and recommends several short-term and longer-term policy options for mitigating this emerging threat.**

Jonathan B. Tucker is Director for CBW Proliferation Issues, Center for Nonproliferation Studies, Monterey Institute of International Studies, 425 Van Buren Street, Monterey, CA 93940, USA. He holds a B.S. in biology from Yale University and a Ph.D. in political science from M.I.T., with a concentration in defense and arms control studies. Prior to joining the Monterey Institute in March of 1996, he served for five months as a senior policy analyst with the Presidential Advisory Committee on Gulf War Veterans' Illnesses. From 1993 to 1995, Dr. Tucker was a foreign affairs specialist in chemical and biological arms control at the U.S. Arms Control and Disarmament Agency (ACDA). He had previously served as a policy analyst with the congressional Office of Technology Assessment, where he contributed chapters on chemical and biological weapons to an OTA report on the proliferation of weapons of mass destruction. Dr. Tucker served as a biological-weapons inspector on the UNSCOM 112/BW 21 inspection team that visited Iraq in February 1995.

AT 8:05 A.M. ON MARCH 20, 1995, at the height of the morning rush hour in the Tokyo subway, members of a fanatical Buddhist sect called Aum Shinrikyo (Supreme Truth) staged a bizarre but deadly terrorist attack. Five two-person commando teams dressed in business suits placed plastic pouches concealed in morning newspapers on crowded subway cars, which were traveling on three major lines converging on Kasumigaseki Station between 8:09 and 8:13 a.m., just before the 8:30 start of the workday (Strasser, 1995). As the trains approached the targeted station, one terrorist in each team punctured the plastic pouch with a sharpened umbrella tip, releasing a puddle of clear liquid—the highly toxic chemical nerve agent sarin—while the other team-member kept lookout (Purver, 1995).

The liquid sarin evaporated slowly, giving most of the perpetrators time to escape, although one terrorist was overcome by the fumes. As the noxious vapors spread through the packed subway cars and into station platforms, pandemonium broke out as hundreds of commuters experienced troubled breathing, headache, chest pain, uncontrollable coughing, choking, vomiting, impairment of hand-eye coordination, and loss of voluntary control over body functions. Overcome passengers staggered off the trains at sixteen different stations along the three subway lines. Many of the victims lost consciousness, collapsed, and had to be revived in hospital. The final toll was eleven dead and more than 5,000 injured, with some seven hundred requiring hospitalization (Suzuki et al., 1995). Since Kasumigaseki Station is in the heart of Tokyo's government district, within walking distance to the major ministry buildings, the poison-gas attack was clearly intended to kill large numbers of government bureaucrats on their way to work. Had it not been for the poor quality of the sarin employed and the crude method of dissemination, the incident could have caused tens of thousands of casualties on the crowded Tokyo subway, which carries more than five million passengers per day.

0730/9384/96/020167-17 US$08.00 © Beech Tree Publishing 1996

The ability of a little-known religious cult to acquire the equipment, materials, and technical expertise needed to manufacture and deliver a deadly chemical warfare agent was a wake-up call for government policymakers. Aum Shinrikyo was a shadowy organization with about 50,000 members (including membership in Russia three times as large as the roughly 10,000 in Japan), assets worth more than $1 billion, and offices in Bonn, Sri Lanka, New York, and Moscow. An intensive police investigation later revealed that the cult had acquired more than 100 tons of chemical ingredients and had employed chemists working in a sophisticated clandestine production plant to manufacture sarin and other lethal nerve agents. Even more disturbing, the Aum cult was experimenting with the production of biological-warfare (BW) agents such as anthrax and botulinum toxin (Holley, 1995). Cult officials had also acquired a Russian military helicopter and two drone aircraft, which they planned to equip with sprayers to disseminate chemical and biological agents over major Japanese cities (U.S. Senate, 1995).

The Tokyo subway incident revealed the vulnerability of contemporary urban areas to terror attacks with chemical or biological weapons. As the first large-scale terrorist incident involving a lethal chemical agent, it weakened a long-standing psychological taboo and raised the spectre of more such incidents in the future. Lt. Gen. James Clapper, a former director of the Defense Intelligence Agency, has called the potential for terrorism involving mass-casualty weapons one of the "most nightmarish concerns" facing the United States and its allies (Starr, 1994). The Aum Shinrikyo incident has also raised a number of important policy issues about the emerging threat of chemical and biological (C/B) terrorism. How likely is another incident similar to that in the Tokyo subway, and how prepared are governments to deal with this contingency from the intelligence, law-enforcement, and public-health perspectives? What are the most immediate and least costly policy options for countering the emerging C/B terrorist threat? And what longer-term but potentially more effective steps should also be considered?

A New Type of Terrorist

Terrorist groups have generally sought to achieve their objectives with small arms and conventional explosives. This tendency may be changing, however, with the emergence of more deadly forms of terrorism. Most incidents in the 1960s and 1970s involved the highjacking of aircraft, the taking of hostages, and occasional shootings that resulted in relatively few casualties. Since the late 1980s, the number of international terrorist incidents has gradually declined—the total in 1994 was 321, down from 666 in 1987 (Nelan, 1995). At the same time, however, the average level of violence per incident has increased as terrorists have resorted to the indiscriminate use of high explosives to kill and injure large numbers of innocent civilians, in an apparent bid to win the attention of an increasingly desensitized public and news media. Examples of this trend include the bombing of a Pan Am jetliner over Lockerbie, Scotland, in December 1988, killing 259 passengers and 11 people on the ground; the bombing of the World Trade Center in New York in February 1993, killing 6 and injuring hundreds; and the bombing of the Federal Building in Oklahoma City in April 1995, killing 168 and injuring more than 500. The Tokyo subway incident was similarly indiscriminate, although the choice of weapon was particularly shocking.

Another troubling aspect of the Tokyo incident was the motive behind the crime. Shoko Asahara, the charismatic leader of the Aum Shinrikyo sect, preached that the contemporary social structure was beyond reform and had to be swept away by a vast cataclysm that Aum would help to bring about, allowing the cult to become the supreme power in Japan (U.S. Senate, 1995). To further this apocalyptic agenda, Aum members employed aggressive recruitment efforts (often involving the use of psychotropic drugs), acts of violence against opponents, and the systematic acquisition of materials and equipment for the production of C/B weapons through a network of front companies and agents overseas (Smith, 1995a). Aum Shinrikyo was thus a new type of terrorist organization, combining elements of a doomsday cult and a large-scale criminal enterprise.

Terrorists motivated by religious or racist fanaticism are particularly dangerous because, unlike politically motivated groups, they are not subject to rational constraints on the scope of their violent acts, nor are they easily deterrable by credible threats. Politically motivated groups such as the Irish Republican Army and the Basque, Kurdish, Tamil, Sikh, and Palestinian national liberation movements have used terrorist incidents as a form of "political theater" to draw public and media attention to their cause, to disrupt ongoing negotiations, or to obtain bargaining leverage with an adversary government by threatening similar attacks in the future if their demands are not met.

Despite the trend toward the indiscriminate use of explosives, politically motivated terrorists have not resorted to C/B weapons for a number of reasons. First, an attack that produced thousands of fatalities would be perceived as disproportionate to the political objective and would undermine the legitimacy of the terrorists' cause, alienating core supporters and potential sympathizers alike. This is particularly true with regard to chemical and biological weapons, which are widely viewed as abhorrent. A large-scale C/B attack would also provoke extreme countermeasures on the part of the state, possibly leading to the total annihilation of the group (Hurwitz, 1982; Rose, 1989).

Second, politically motivated terrorists may have been deterred from C/B agent use by the fact that the handling and dissemination of highly toxic or infectious agents involve hazards, technical problems, and uncertainties much greater than those associated with plastic explosives. In the case of open-air dispersal of C/B agents, the efficiency of dissemi-

Aum Shinrikyo did not use terror for political pressure or blackmail but rather in pursuit of a perceived moral imperative to destroy the existing social structure in Japan

nation depends on the prevailing meteorological conditions, making the effects of an attack fairly unpredictable and difficult to control. In an enclosed space like a subway car, the use of nerve agent would be no more devastating than a traditional pipe bomb—although the shock value would be arguably greater. Finally, unlike chemical weapons, biological weapons produce illness and death only after an incubation period lasting a few days, multiplying the uncertainties associated with their use. And because a BW agent exposure would have no immediate effects, it would not create the horrific images needed to attract media attention. For all of these reasons, politically motivated terrorists have generally been deterred from using C/B agents.

Despite these drawbacks, terrorist groups motivated by religious fanaticism or supremacist ideology might be drawn to C/B weapons if they

- possess the necessary technical know-how;
- are intent on inflicting mass casualties rather than attracting attention to a political cause;
- have no clearly defined base of popular support; and
- are willing to accept substantial physical risks.

All these conditions applied to Aum Shinrikyo, which did not use terror for political pressure or blackmail but rather in pursuit of a perceived moral imperative to destroy the existing social structure in Japan. Aum sought to discredit the Japanese government by demonstrating its lack of preparation and inability to respond. The sarin employed in the Tokyo subway was impure and ineffectively disseminated and thus caused relatively few deaths, but what mattered was the widespread public panic that the attack elicited. As arms control analyst Spurgeon Keeney, Jr. has pointed out,

> Political terrorists see themselves as fighters for a cause, seeking revenge, intimidation, or recognition. But because they serve a larger cause, their actions must be to some extent circumscribed, lest they invite retaliation that would endanger their goal or alienate political supporters. Now, we have the unconstrained terrorist, whose objective of unlimited destruction is a necessary first step to achieving his goal. (1995:2)

For such groups, C/B agents might be attractive because they are relatively cheap to produce and are deadly in small quantities, simplifying the problems of production and concealment. Indeed, the cultivation, transport, and delivery of BW agents could probably be carried out by a small number of people (Chevrier, 1993).

Other than the activities of Aum Shinrikyo in Japan, there have been relatively few cases of C/B terrorism over the past quarter-century, although the number has risen ominously in the past few years. Some major incidents reported by the news media are summarized below:

- In 1972, members of a U.S. fascist group called Order of the Rising Sun were found in possession of 30-40 kilograms of typhoid bacteria cultures, with which they planned to contaminate water supplies in Chicago, St. Louis, and other large Midwestern cities (U.S. Congress OTA, 1992).
- In 1984, two members of an Oregon cult headed by Bhagwan Shree Rajneesh cultivated *Salmonella* (food poisoning) bacteria and used them to contaminate restaurant salad bars in an attempt to affect the outcome of a local election. Although some 750 people became ill, and 45 were hospitalized, there were no fatalities (U.S. Congress OTA, 1992).
- In 1993, the Muslim terrorists who bombed the World Trade Center in New York allegedly packed their bomb with cyanide in order to spread the poison throughout the building. According to the judge who sentenced the defendants, the plot failed only because the cyanide burned in the explosion (Post, 1995).
- In March 1995, two members of the Minnesota Patriots Council—a right-wing militia organization advocating violent overthrow of the U.S. government—were convicted of conspiracy charges for planning to use ricin, a lethal biological toxin. The two men, Douglas Baker and Leroy Wheeler, allegedly conspired to assassinate Internal Revenue Service agents and a deputy U.S. marshall who had served papers on one of them for tax violations (Herbert, 1995).
- In April 1995, a month after the Tokyo subway incident, the *Baltimore Sun* reported that two Japanese citizens associated with Aum Shinrikyo had planned to launch a lethal sarin attack at Disneyland in California over the Easter weekend. According to the newspaper, FBI agents had been tipped off by the Tokyo police and had foiled the plot by arresting the two cult members at Los Angeles International Airport (Lait and Malnic, 1995). The U.S. Department of Justice later denied the story.
- In May 1995, Larry Wayne Harris, a member of the white supremicist organization Aryan Nation, was arrested on charges of forgery and receiving stolen property after allegedly misrepresenting himself when ordering three vials of freeze-dried bubonic plague bacteria from American Type Culture Collection, a Maryland biological supply house (Robinson, 1995).
- In December 1995, Thomas Lewis Lavy, an Arkansas man with survivalist group connections, was charged with having attempted to smuggle 130 grams of ricin

across the border from Alaska into Canada in 1993 and with intent to use the toxin as a weapon (Kifner, 1995). The next day, Lavy hanged himself in his jail cell (Associated Press, 1995).

The number of religious cults with a propensity to violence has also increased in recent years. Well-known examples are Jim Jones and members of the Peoples Temple, more than 900 of whom committed mass suicide in Guyana in November 1978; David Koresh and the Branch Davidians, more than 70 of whom died in a violent confrontation with U.S. federal agents near Waco, Texas, in April 1993; and Luc Jouret and the Order of the Solar Temple, more than 40 of whom committed mass suicide in October 1994 at sites in Switzerland and Quebec (Riding, 1994).

A wide variety of religious cults are now active, ranging from Christian white supremacists to messianic Jews, Islamic fundamentalists, Buddhists, and radical Sikhs. Some of these groups espouse a dangerous mixture of political paranoia, messianic fervor, and obsession with apocalyptic prophecy. As the year 2000 approaches, there may also be a growing number of "millennial" cults whose members believe that death in a cataclysmic battle against the forces of evil—that is, the federal government or anyone else who opposes their agenda—will guarantee them a place in paradise. According to Hal Mansfield, an expert on alternative religions, "We're in for a helluva ride with these millennial groups. Whatever technology is out there, they're going to use it" (Post, 1995:40).

A second potential danger is the emergence of a more virulent form of state-sponsored terrorism. The suspected pursuit of chemical and biological warfare capabilities by countries such as Iraq, Iran, Libya, Syria, and North Korea—all of which have supported terrorism in the past—raises the possibility that "rogue" governments might supply terrorist groups with C/B agents. Indeed, during the Persian Gulf War, U.S. intelligence services reportedly foiled a number of Iraqi-sponsored terrorist attacks against American targets, some of which may have involved C/B weapons. According to a partially declassified 1991 intelligence report, the East German State Security Service trained Iraqi agents in the use of chemical and biological agents against civilian targets at a special school near East Berlin and at training camps in the Middle East (GulfLINK, 1995). One possible scenario for state-sponsored terrorism is that a rogue government could ship small containers of C/B agents to its overseas embassies in diplomatic pouches—which are exempt from customs inspection—and distribute them to terrorists already in-country.

Technical Aspects of CB Terrorism

While both chemical and biological agents are capable of producing mass casualties, they differ significantly in their effects and production technology.

Chemical Warfare Agents

Chemical warfare (CW) agents are poisonous man-made gases, liquids or powders that have toxic effects on people and animals. "Blood" agents such as hydrogen cyanide interfere with cellular respiration, causing death by anoxia; "choking" agents such as phosgene cause severe lung damage; "blister" agents such as sulfur mustard and lewisite cause painful chemical burns of the skin, eyes, and lungs; and "nerve" agents such as tabun, sarin, soman, and VX disrupt the functioning of the nervous system. The various types of chemical agents differ in the rapidity of their effects: whereas hydrogen cyanide and some nerve agents produce incapacitating symptoms almost immediately, sulfur mustard does not give rise to pain and blistering until between three and eight hours after exposure.

The nerve agent sarin was discovered in 1939 by Gerhard Schrader of the German company IG Farben, during research on new organophosphorus pesticides. Throughout the Cold War, the United States and the Soviet Union produced and stockpiled chemical arsenals containing many thousands of tons of sarin and other nerve agents. These compounds exert their lethal effects by inactivating an enzyme called cholinesterase, which is essential for the normal transmission of nerve impulses. Absorption of a lethal dose of nerve agent disrupts the activity of the peripheral and central nervous systems, causing the victim to develop pinpoint pupils, a runny nose, and tremors, followed by loss of consciousness and convulsions. Death by respiratory arrest takes place in about five minutes. Although common pesticides such as malathion are also members of the organophosphate class, nerve agents are between 100 and 1,000 times more potent at inhibiting cholinesterase. The various nerve agents differ in volatility and persistence: whereas sarin is a volatile liquid that evaporates quickly and acts primarily through inhalation of vapors, VX is an oily liquid that persists in the environment for days or weeks, depending on ambient temperature, and can be absorbed both by inhalation and through the skin.

Terrorists intent on acquiring chemical weapons would have two options: buying or stealing them from existing national stockpiles, or manufacturing them independently. With respect to the first option, Russia has divulged that it possesses 40,000 metric tons of chemical-warfare agents, which are stored at seven declared storage sites. Recent visitors have found lax physical security at four of these sites, including unguarded doors, simple locks, and no alarms (Crossette, 1995; Smithson et al., 1995). The planned destruction of Russia's huge CW stockpile will eventually eliminate the risk of theft or purchase, but that task will take more than a decade once it begins. To date, the start of the Russian CW destruction program has been delayed by environmental, economic, and political concerns. On the other hand, the fear that international criminal organizations such as the Russian *Mafiya* or the Colombian drug cartels might seek to steal or otherwise acquire C/B weapons and sell them to rogue governments appears to be unfounded. Organized-crime groups would tend to avoid such activities because they would almost certainly provoke a harsh crackdown on the part of government officials and the police, on whose tacit or active collusion the mafias rely to stay in business.

Although the news media have exaggerated the ease with which terrorists could produce chemical and biological weapons in basement laboratories, the relevant technology is within the reach of groups that possess sufficient financial resources and technical expertise, such as members with postgraduate education in organic chemistry or microbiology. Leaders of the Aum Shinrikyo cult aggressively recruited university-trained scientists and engineers in Japan and Russia to work on the development of C/B weapons. Many Aum members were young intellectuals in their twenties and thirties who had become disenchanted with mainstream Japanese society (Reid, 1995; Hatsumi, 1995). The cult's chief scientist, for example, was thirty years old and had a master's degree in organic chemistry from a Japanese university (Guest, 1995).

Chemical Ingredients. Aum Shinrikyo reportedly decided to manufacture sarin because of its relative ease of production compared with other nerve agents, its volatility (making it relatively easy to disseminate in an enclosed space—Croddy, 1995), and the fact that the necessary ingredients could be obtained commercially. Chemicals that serve as starting materials in the synthesis of CW agents are known as "precursors." The globalization of the chemical industry has led to large international flows of dual-use precursor chemicals that have legitimate commercial applications but could also be diverted to the production of CW agents. For example, some of the ingredients involved in the production of sarin, such as isopropanol and hydrogen fluoride, are commodity chemicals consumed by commercial industry in millions of tons per year, and hence are difficult to control. (Isopropanol, or rubbing alcohol, is a common industrial chemical, whereas hydrogen fluoride is used in large quantities by oil refineries and can also be derived from phosphate deposits, which usually contain fluorides.) More specialized sarin precursors, such as phosphorus trichloride and trimethyl phosphite, have legitimate industrial applications in the production of pesticides and fire retardants. Although these precursors are manufactured in much smaller volumes, making it somewhat easier to monitor trade flows, phosphorus trichloride has about forty producers worldwide and trimethyl phosphite about twenty (U.S. Department of Commerce, 1991).

Developing countries seeking a CW capability generally lack the ability to manufacture chemical agents from the most basic starting materials, and hence must purchase immediate precursors from foreign sources. Because of this dependency, twenty-nine countries with large chemical industries, including the United States, have sought to slow the proliferation of chemical weapons by establishing a committee—known as the Australia Group—that coordinates national export-control regulations in order to restrict the sale of C/B-relevant materials and production equipment to suspected proliferators (Robinson, 1992). The Australia Group restricts exports to target countries but not to substate actors. Aum Shinrikyo was therefore able to purchase all of the chemical precursors and processing equipment it needed to manufacture sarin by importing them through front companies controlled by the cult, legitimate chemical manufacturers owned by cult members, and overseas shipping agents. Because such illicit transactions often yield extremely high profits, many suppliers and middlemen have been willing to take the risk of violating national export laws. Thus, while export controls are a modest impediment to chemical terrorism, they are far from a definitive solution.

Production of Sarin. Synthetic pathways for the production of sarin involve four basic reaction steps (oxidation, alkylation, chlorination/fluorination, and esterification), which can be carried out in different sequences (Zapf, 1993). Several production pathways have been published in the open literature, all of which begin with the same precursor chemical, phosphorus trichloride (PCl_3). Three steps in the synthesis of sarin are particularly difficult or hazardous and would pose significant technical hurdles to terrorist groups. First, the alkylation reaction requires high temperatures or extremely reactive chemicals and hence is rarely used in the production of commercial pesticides. Second, the fluorination reaction necessitates the use of hydrogen fluoride (HF), a highly corrosive chemical that is difficult to handle and erodes the walls of steel reactor vessels and pipes. Third, if pure sarin with a long shelf-life is desired, the final product must be distilled to remove excess hydrochloric acid, an extremely hazardous operation. Distillation is not necessary if the agent is produced for use within a few weeks (U.S. Congress OTA, 1993). In general, the final stages of sarin production are particularly dangerous because they entail the handling of live agent.

Although it is possible to manufacture sarin without using corrosion-resistant equipment, doing so significantly increases the risk of dangerous leaks. For this reason, a terrorist group intent on producing significant quantities of sarin would probably purchase reaction vessels and pipes lined with glass or teflon, or made of a corrosion-resistant steel alloy containing 40% nickel such as the commercial products Monel and Hastalloy. Other items of specialized equipment that might be used to produce nerve agents include double-walled piping, double-seal or magnetic-drive pumps, diaphragm valves, heat exchangers and condensers, activated-carbon filters and scrubbers capable of purifying large volumes of contaminated air from ventilation systems, and systems for treating and incinerating hazardous chemical wastes (Zapf, 1993). The ease with which Aum was able to purchase such equipment from international suppliers is disturbing, and raises questions about the effectiveness of export controls on dual-use technologies.

Devising and testing an effective CW agent delivery system, such as a bomb or spray device, poses another major technical hurdle—one that caused Aum Shinrikyo particular difficulties. Because of the extreme hazards associated with handling and disseminating chemical agents, terrorists might be attracted to "binary" chemical weapons, which are safer to produce, store, and transport. In a binary system, two relatively nontoxic precursor chemicals are stored in separate containers and mixed immediately before use to produce the lethal agent. Sarin, for example, can be produced in a binary system by reacting isopropanol (rubbing alcohol) with methylphosphonic difluoride (DF).

In advanced binary munitions such as those developed by the U.S. Army in the early 1980s, the two precursors are stored in separate cannisters separated by a metal diaphragm. This barrier ruptures while the shell is in flight to the target, allowing the chemicals to react and form the lethal agent, which is released on impact. Since terrorists would be unlikely to have access to such sophisticated technology, they would probably have to mix the two precursor chemicals manually before use—an exceedingly hazardous operation—or attempt to develop an automatic or remote-controlled device to carry out the mixing and dispersal steps, a task requiring considerable technical expertise.

Sarin Production by Aum Shinrikyo. Aum Shinrikyo's three-story chemical factory near Mount Fuji, known as Satian No. 7, was reportedly "extremely sophisticated" and equipped with computerized process controls. This facility produced thirty kilograms of sarin over a two-year period before an accident in early 1994 caused it to halt operation. Aum members then tested the sarin on sheep at a ranch that the sect had purchased in 1993 in a remote part of Western Australia (U.S. Senate, 1995).

On June 27, 1994, nine months before the Tokyo subway incident, Aum staged a trial poison-gas attack in a quiet residential area of Matsumoto, a town in central Japan about 125 miles northwest of Tokyo. Cult members sprayed a cloud of vaporized sarin from a nozzle device attached to a truck that had been specially modified for that purpose. The motive for the crime was the attempted murder of three judges who were about to reach a guilty verdict in a case involving fraud charges brought against Aum by various landowners in Matsumoto. All three judges were sleeping in a dormitory residence downwind of the sarin release and fell ill as a result of the exposure, delaying the guilty verdict as the cult leaders had planned. The sarin cloud also killed seven people and injured more than 260 others (U.S. Senate, 1995; Morita et al., 1995).

The subsequent March 20 terror attack on the Tokyo subway was prefaced by a curious mixture of careful and haphazard preparation. Aum officials planned the attack to take place simultaneously on three subway trains, which were scheduled to arrive at the central Kasumigaseki Station within four minutes of each other. The sarin used in the attack was of poor quality, however, having been manufactured quickly in a small-scale laboratory inside the Aum compound the day before. Aum chemists also diluted the low-grade sarin with an organic solvent to make it less hazardous to handle by personnel not wearing gas masks (Hadfield, 1995). The sarin solution was then filled into plastic pouches made of three-ply nylon polyethylene, which were sealed with a special laminating machine. The fact that the sarin was low-grade, diluted with solvent, and disseminated as a liquid made it much less hazardous to the terrorists and their victims, so that only those passengers in the immediate vicinity of the releases were killed. As the puddles of dilute agent evaporated, they gave off sarin vapor at relatively low concentrations. Had the Aum terrorists disseminated the sarin as an aerosol of microscopic droplets suspended in the air, delivering much higher concentrations of agent to the lungs, the attack would have caused many more fatalities.

Had the Aum terrorists disseminated the sarin as an aerosol of microscopic droplets suspended in air, delivering much higher concentrations of agent to the lungs than a liquid could, the attack would have caused many more fatalities

For a second chemical attack in the Tokyo subway, Aum Shinrikyo developed a crude binary weapon that fortunately malfunctioned. On May 5, 1995, cult members placed the device in a men's room at Shinjuku subway station, the busiest in Tokyo. The weapon consisted of two plastic pouches, one containing two kilograms of sodium cyanide crystals and the other filled with 1.5 liters of dilute sulfuric acid. A primitive chemical ignition system caused the sodium cyanide pouch to catch fire after a time delay. The two pouches were arranged so that as the flames from the first spread to the second, the cyanide crystals would react with the sulfuric acid to form deadly hydrogen cyanide gas. Fortunately, the jury-rigged device failed to operate as planned. Although four subway workers who doused the flames were overcome by toxic fumes and briefly hospitalized, the station was evacuated before anyone else was hurt (U.S. Senate, 1995).

Aum also sought to develop chemical agents even more lethal than sarin. According to U.S. Senate investigators, Aum chemists synthesized small quantities of VX, a supertoxic nerve agent that can kill both through inhalation and by penetrating the skin. Cult members used syringes filled with a small quantity of VX to assassinate two Aum critics, one in December 1994 and the other in January 1995. The first victim died ten days after the attack, while the second was hospitalized for several weeks after the incident but apparently survived (U.S. Senate, 1995). If future terrorist groups were to use more potent and persistent nerve agents such as VX, or to develop more effective means of delivery—such as remote-controlled binary devices—the risk of mass casualties would increase significantly.

Biological Warfare Agents

Whereas CW agents are man-made poisons, biological warfare (BW) agents are microorganisms and naturally occurring toxins that cause illness or death in people, livestock, and crops. Microbial pathogens considered suitable for military use include the bacteria that cause anthrax, tularemia, and brucellosis; the rickettsia that induce Q fever; and the viruses responsible for Venezuelan equine encephalitis (VEE) and certain hemorrhagic fevers. During the offensive BW program of the 1950s and 1960s, the United States deliberately pursued animal pathogens such as anthrax, tularemia, brucellosis, and VEE that can cause serious infection in humans when inhaled as a concentrated biological aerosol but are not transmitted naturally from one individual to another. Since such agents are not contagious in man, the localized epidemic produced by a BW attack would be self-limiting and unlikely to boomerang against the attacker's own troops or population. Nevertheless, it is conceivable that terrorist groups bent on producing mass casualties might deliberately produce and disseminate disease agents that are contagious in humans, such as pneumonic plague bacteria or various types of hemorrhagic fever viruses, with the aim of triggering widespread epidemics that would undermine social structures.

Anthrax bacteria are not contagious but are considered particularly effective BW agents because of the high lethality of virulent strains, the relative ease of production, and the fact that the bacteria can be induced to form spores—a dormant state in which the microbes form a tough protective coat and thus become considerably more resistant to environmental stresses such as heat, drying, and sunlight. Since even spores are susceptible to ultraviolet radiation, a BW attack would probably be carried out at night, dawn or dusk, or on an overcast day. Inhalation of only about 8,000 anthrax spores—a dose invisible to the naked eye—is sufficient to cause a systemic infection in 50% of the target population that can be fatal within 96 hours (Erlick, 1989). After entering the lungs, the spores travel to the lymph nodes where they germinate, multiply, and give rise to systemic infection; the severity of the illness depends on the dose inhaled and retained by the body. Whereas infections with plague and tularemia respond to intravenous antibiotics if treatment is begun within 24 hours, before the appearance of symptoms, anthrax is unique in that antibiotic therapy can only delay the disease process. When the antibiotics are halted, the clinical disease may appear. Cure of an anthrax infection is only possible if active immunization begins during the antibiotic therapy, and the patient is able to mount a protective immune response (Franz, 1994: 62-63).

Natural toxins are potent poisons synthesized by a wide variety of living organisms, including bacteria (e.g., botulinum toxin, tetanus toxin), fungi (mycotoxins), animals (cobra venom, saxitoxin), and plants (ricin). More than 500 such compounds have been characterized to date. Toxins are nonliving chemicals that range in size from small molecules to large proteins, and they exert their effects with a latency period ranging from a few minutes to several hours. Some natural toxins are lethal in extremely low doses because they act at specific biochemical target sites in the body. A few toxins have been considered in the past for military use, including botulinum toxin, ricin, saxitoxin, and *Staphylococcus* enterotoxin B. Before the 1991 Persian Gulf War, Iraq produced and weaponized large quantities of two toxin agents, botulinum toxin and aflatoxin, and also experimented with ricin and two potent fungal toxins known as trichothecenes (United Nations, 1995).

Weight-for-weight, biological and toxin agents are potentially thousands of times more potent than even the most toxic man-made chemical agents (U.S. Congress OTA, 1993). Because of the ability of pathogenic microorganisms to multiply rapidly within the host, small quantities of a biological agent—if widely disseminated through the air as a respirable aerosol—can inflict casualties over a large area. Under optimal meteorological conditions, producing 50% fatalities over a square-mile area would require about a metric ton of chemical nerve agent but only about 10 grams of anthrax spores (Chester and Zimmerman, 1984). Depending on the type and concentration of agent and the atmospheric conditions, an aerosol cloud of BW agent released from a "point" source would form an elongated plume extending from a few to several tens of kilometers downwind from the site of release. Continous release of agent from a moving "line" source would generate a broader plume covering a much larger surface area.

Production of Biological and Toxin Agents. The cultivation of BW agents does not differ substantially from the production of legitimate biological products. Indeed, nearly all of the materials and items of equipment used to cultivate BW agents have commercial applications in the production of beer, wine, food products, animal feed supplements, biopesticides, vaccines, and pharmaceuticals. Seed cultures of pathogenic bacteria such as anthrax can be purchased from commercial vendors by sending a request letter on the letterhead of a university or research institute. Iraq, for example, purchased bacterial seed stocks that it used to grow anthrax spores and botulinum toxin from biological supply houses in the United States and France (U.S. Senate, 1994). Microbial seed stocks could also be obtained though a third party, stolen from a university or industry laboratory, or extracted from natural sources such as soil or diseased animals. In 1992, the Aum Shinrikyo cult sent a medical mission to Zaire, purportedly to assist in treating the victims of an Ebola virus outbreak. The real objective, however, may have been to obtain a sample of the deadly virus to take back to Japan for BW purposes (U.S. Senate, 1995).

Basic fermentation techniques are widely described in the scientific literature, although the efficient cultivation of pathogenic microorganisms requires practical knowledge and experience in microbiology and fermentation process control. Items of dual-capable equipment that can be used to make BW agents include computer-controlled fermenters, centrifugal separators, freeze- and spray-dryers, high-efficiency particulate air filters and other specialized biocontainment systems, and equipment for microencapsulating microorganisms and toxins to shield them from environmental stresses. According to a report by the Central Intelligence Agency, scores of commercial firms manufacture such equipment (Starr, 1995). A terrorist group might also choose to do without sophisticated equipment by growing small-scale batches of biological or toxin agents in a pilot-scale fermenter or in laboratory glassware. Even using such a low-tech approach, the entire cultivation process—starting with a vial of seed culture and ending with several kilograms of agent (e.g., a concentrated slurry of anthrax spores)—could take as little as 96 hours. As a result, terrorists would not need to stockpile agent for long periods but could produce it to order shortly before a planned attack.

High-containment measures are not required for the production of BW agents, since there is a relatively low risk of generating hazardous aerosols. Adequate protection for personnel during the production phase could be achieved by vaccination against the infectious agent (if a vaccine is available) and through the use of protective masks. The danger of contamination from leaking valves would depend on the infectious agent and its concentration, and might be minimized by applying disinfectant to small leaks. Downstream processing steps—such as concentrating the agent in a continuous-flow centrifuge, drying it in a spray- or freeze-dryer, and milling the dried cake to a fine powder—would have to be effectively contained to reduce the risk of infection. Nevertheless, inspections of dual-capable biological facilities in Iraq by the United Nations Special Commission indicate that the Baghdad government viewed BW production workers as expendable and was prepared to cut corners on safety and biocontainment.

One concern that has often been raised is that technically sophisticated terrorists might employ recombinant-DNA techniques to produce genetically modified pathogens that are more lethal, persistent in the environment, or resistant to existing vaccines and antibiotics. In fact, this scenario appears unlikely. Although recombinant-DNA methods are now widely utilized in science and industry, the techniques are complex and require specialized know-how that would exceed the resources of most terrorist groups. In addition, infectivity or virulence are complex traits controlled by multiple genes, so that simple genetic manipulations would have little effect (Tucker, 1992). It is much more likely that terrorists would grow well-characterized agents such as anthrax or botulinum toxin, although they might seek to develop antibiotic-resistant strains by means of classical selection techniques.

Weaponization and Delivery

Effective delivery of BW agents is considerably more difficult than production. Use of BW agents to contaminate municipal water supplies would probably not be effective because most water-treatment systems employ filtration and chlorination to kill ordinary pathogenic microoganisms present in the water, and would destroy microbial BW agents in the process. The enormous dilution factor would also necessitate using impractically large quantities of agent. To serve as mass-casualty weapons, BW agents would have to be delivered against target populations in the form of a respirable aerosol—a relatively stable cloud of suspended microscopic droplets or particles containing from one to a few thousand bacterial or virus particles. Whereas chemical agents can be disseminated as a vapor or spray, BW agents are nonvolatile solids that, with rare exceptions, do not penetrate the skin. Moreover, only particles between 1 and 5 microns (thousandths of a millimeter) in diameter can remain suspended in the atmosphere for long periods without settling and can also be retained deep in the lungs.

Dry powders of microbial agent or toxin produced by freeze- or spray-drying have the best dissemination characteristics and would be easier to store and handle than liquid slurries, which tend to lose viability and potency over time. Nevertheless, since it would be technically difficult to produce a dry BW agent with the microscopic particle size needed for respiratory infection, a terrorist group would probably prepare the agent in liquid form and store it under refrigeration until use.

It is conceivable, however, that terrorists intent on acquiring sophisticated BW weaponization capabilities, such as the drying and microencapsulation of microbial and toxin agents, might seek technical assistance from a state with an advanced BW program. Indeed, some analysts have expressed concern that Russian President Boris Yeltsin's April 1992 decree to eliminate the massive biological weapons program inherited from the former Soviet Union could lead to a "brain drain" of BW experts. According to congressional testimony by former CIA director Robert Gates, "a

It is conceivable that terrorists intent on acquiring sophisticated BW weaponization capabilities, such as the drying and microencapsulation of microbial and toxin agents, might seek technical assistance from a state with an advanced BW program

few thousand [former Soviet scientists] have the knowledge and marketable skills to develop and produce biological weapons." Gates went on to identify the most serious problem as individuals whose skills have no civilian counterpart, such as engineers specializing in the weaponization of BW agents (Gates, 1992). Given this situation, there is the danger that terrorists might attempt to recruit such individuals for their deadly expertise.

Biological agent in dry or wet form might be dispersed with a commercially available agricultural sprayer or fogger (e.g., for the application of biopesticides) mounted on a small airplane, a helicopter, or a sealed vehicle, or carried by an individual protected from infection by vaccination and/or a surgical mask. The area that can be covered effectively with a given amount of agent depends strongly on the meteorological conditions prevailing at the time of release. Sunny, warm conditions give rise to vertical air currents, causing the agent particles to rise into the atmosphere and dissipate, and living biological agents die fairly quickly in air when exposed to sunlight. For these reasons, an outdoor attack with BW agents would probably occur at dusk, night, dawn, or under overcast skies. Optimal atmospheric conditions for dispersal would occur on a clear, cold night with a gentle breeze, since a stable inversion layer of air would form over the ground and keep the microbes at a low altitude where they can be inhaled. Even under optimal conditions, however, outdoor dissemination of BW agents poses significant uncertainties. Aum Shinrikyo reportedly released anthrax bacteria from a building in central Tokyo at least twice without causing any apparent casualties (U.S. Senate, 1995).

Since biological agents are invisible, odorless, and tasteless, a BW attack would be undetectable by human senses, and no reliable real-time biological detection and warning systems are currently available (Beal, 1995). Moreover, the incubation period that follows upon infection with microbial pathogens means that the effects of exposure would be delayed for several hours or days depending on the type of agent used. Instead of a gradual rise in the number of sick individuals from a small number of precursor cases over several weeks—characteristic of a natural epidemic—there would be an "explosive" outbreak of infectious disease in many hundreds or thousands of people within the span of a few days (Woodall, 1991).

The fact that there is a significant delay before the symptoms of a BW attack manifest themselves represents a major difference between the effects of chemical and biological weapons, and makes the possible terrorist use of BW agents particularly chilling. If the terrorists chose not to provide any advance warning, the appearance of symptoms would be the first indicator of a biological attack. Moreover, if an endemic disease agent were disseminated covertly, it might take several days for public-health officials to determine that the epidemic was the result of a deliberate BW attack and not a natural outbreak of disease. By the time the real cause of the outbreak was determined, the perpetrators could have long since left the country.

Counterterrorism Strategy

The Tokyo subway incident has demonstrated the devastating potential of C/B terrorism. Aum Shinrikyo broke the monopoly that the nation-state has previously held over the most powerful means of organized violence, creating a threat to Japanese and international society disproportionate to its numbers (Gardels, 1995). Indeed, the diffusion of mass destructive power to subnational groups undermines the ability of the nation-state to protect the security of its citizens—the fundamental source of its political legitimacy. Although states are well organized to defend themselves against external enemies, they are much less capable of protecting their populations against terrorist groups operating in their midst.

Chemical/biological terrorism poses a particularly grave threat to the viability of democratic societies. Whereas authoritarian states can crush terrorist groups on their territory through the massive use of surveillance and repression, democratic societies deliberately limit the power of the state and hence are most threatened by the rise of mass-casualty weapons in the hands of extremists. Even so, the potential for C/B terrorism should not cause democratic states to abandon their respect for civil liberties, since such a response would be self-defeating. Democratic societies must instead find the right balance between liberty and regulation. Without banning fringe groups or depriving them of their constitutional rights, government authorities should be prepared to assess and respond promptly to any C/B-related activities that would threaten public health and security.

It is a sobering fact that no simple technical fix can completely eliminate the vulnerability of urban populations to the terrorist use of C/B weapons. Yet this realization does not mean that policymakers should throw up their hands in despair or complacency. An effective C/B counterterrorism strategy would combine two approaches: preemption and civil defense.

Preemption

Preemption, or the ability to prevent terrorist attacks before they occur, presupposes a number of elements. First, it requires good intelligence about terrorist groups and their activities. Before the Tokyo subway attack, intelligence on Aum Shinrikyo was appallingly lacking despite the cult's worldwide efforts to procure C/B agent precursors and production equipment. During U.S. Senate hearings in November 1995 on the threat of C/B terrorism, senior counterterrorism officials from the Federal Bureau of Investigation (FBI), the Central Intelligence Agency (CIA), and the Department of Defense (DOD) admitted that they had focused their intelligence-collection efforts on state-sponsored terrorist groups with a political agenda and thus had been entirely unaware of the existence of the Aum Shinrikyo cult before the Tokyo subway incident (Smith, 1995b).

Since nearly all of the equipment needed to manufacture C/B agents is dual-capable and the agents themselves are fairly easy to conceal and to deliver covertly, there are few distinctive "signatures" associated with such activities. In the case of biological weapons, the delayed appearance of symptoms would also make it difficult to detect an attack in a timely manner. Because of these constraints, national technical means of intelligence collection, such as reconnaissance satellites, are of little help in this area. Instead, good intelligence on terrorism relies heavily on human sources—particularly defectors and infiltrators—supported by communications intercepts and other forms of surveillance.

A second prerequisite for a strategy of preemption is the existence of domestic laws making the development, production, possession, and use of chemical and biological weapons a serious crime. Such domestic legislation provides the legal basis for aggressive law-enforcement activity, including preemptive police raids and arrests when groups are known to have acquired C/B-related materials and equipment for illicit purposes. In particular, the 1972 Biological Weapons Convention (BWC) states in Article IV that each state party shall take "any necessary measures" to make the treaty prohibitions binding on all citizens and businesses on the territories under its jurisdiction or control and on its nationals residing overseas, and to impose punitive sanctions for violations. After a delay of several years, the U.S. Congress finally passed the Biological Weapons Anti-Terrorism Act of 1989, the law under which the federal government successfully prosecuted the defendants in the Minnesota ricin poisoning conspiracy. Several other countries have also passed legislation criminalizing acts prohibited to states under the BWC (including Australia, the Czech Republic, Finland, Germany, The Netherlands, Norway, Russia, Sweden, and Switzerland), but less than 40 of the 135 states parties have done so.

The 1993 Chemical Weapons Convention (CWC), which is still being ratified by the required 65 states and is expected to enter into force in 1997, differs from the BWC in that it includes an explicit requirement for implementing legislation. Article VII of the CWC requires all states parties to enact domestic legislation making it a crime for any persons under their jurisdiction (individuals or businesses) to develop, produce, stockpile, or use chemical warfare agents. According to the proposed legislation submitted to Congress by President Clinton, terrorists convicted of these acts would face up to life imprisonment, fines, and forfeiture of their property, whereas companies that knowingly sold equipment or precursor chemicals to terrorist groups or states that sponsor them would face punitive sanctions. Until such legislation is passed, however, it is not technically illegal for anyone to develop, produce, and stockpile sarin or other chemical weapons—provided there is no conspiracy to use them for criminal purposes.

The CWC further requires states parties to impose export controls on the sale of key precursor chemicals that could be diverted to the production of chemical weapons, either by proliferator-states or subnational groups. After the entry into force of the convention, a new international agency, the Organization for the Prohibition of Chemical Weapons (OPCW), will be established in The Hague (The Netherlands) to monitor the movement of CWC-controlled chemicals around the globe and to conduct on-site inspections of treaty-relevant facilities. Under this regime, any company that manufactures more than a threshold quantity of a chemical that could be diverted to the production of chemical-warfare agents will have to account for it.

A third prerequisite for a strategy of preemption is to control the availability of "cookbook" type information that a layman could use to produce C/B weapons. Over the past several years, detailed instructions on how to produce C/B weapons for terrorist purposes have been disseminated by groups on the extreme left and right of the political spectrum (Stern, 1993). One infamous tract, *The Anarchist's Cookbook*, was published in 1971 as a handbook for left-wing terrorists (Powell, 1971). Two other mail-order primers have been found in the possession of right-wing groups: *The Poisoner's Handbook* describes how to produce poisons (including ricin) in a home laboratory, whereas *Silent Death* informs readers how to deliver such poisons most effectively (Kifner, 1995).

Deadly cookbooks are also available on the Internet. In addition to *The Anarchist's Cookbook*, users of the World Wide Web can access *The Terrorist Handbook*, *The Big Book of Mischief*, and *The Jolly Roger Cookbook*. One web site, titled "Scott's Anarchy Page," includes the following disclaimer: "Through the use of this page you agree to hold me not responsible for any occurrence(s) legal or otherwise that may occur from the misuse of the information contained herin [sic]." Another web site, known as "Candyman's Bomb Page," includes a recipe for the home production of botulinum toxin.

A recent incident demonstrated that such information has more than entertainment value. In February 1996, three thirteen-year-old boys from a town near Syracuse, New York, were arrested and charged with plotting to set off a homemade bomb in their junior high school after obtaining plans for the device on the Internet (Stout, 1996).

Civil Defense

Whereas countries such as Sweden, Switzerland, and Israel have long incorporated civil defense into their overall defense concept, the United States has tended to view the development of effective civil defenses against C/B weapons as belonging in the "too hard" or "unthinkable" category. In the past, the U.S. Department of Defense has tended to focus narrowly on detecting and defending against acute-level exposures to chemical or biological agents on the battlefield, and has developed individual protective gear for use by soldiers but not civilians. Moreover, although the FBI, the Federal Emergency Management Agency (FEMA), and the U.S. Public Health Service have developed an integrated crisis-management plan in the event of a threatened act of C/B terrorism, there has been relatively little emphasis on devising practical measures for protecting public health in the event of such an attack.

There are two possible types of emergency response to threats of C/B terrorism:

- before an incident occurs, assuming that advance warning has been provided; or
- after a toxic agent has been released.

In the former case, federal, state, or local government officials might receive a blackmail threat that a C/B attack will occur in a particular urban area unless some action is carried out, such as the paying of a ransom, the release of a prisoner, or the publication of a political manifesto. Law-enforcement authorities would then have a limited amount of time to track down the perpetrators and/or the toxic material before it is released. Alternatively, as in the case of the Tokyo subway incident, a C/B attack might come without warning. Indeed, this contingency is more likely if the perpetrator is an Aum-like cult that does not wish to promote a political agenda or to extort money or concessions, but merely seeks to inflict large-scale casualties.

According to FEMA, terrorists typically target high-profile locations such as international airports, large buildings, major sporting events, resorts, and famous landmarks because these sites offer relatively easy access, intense media coverage, and large crowds that can enable the perpetrators to avoid detection before and after an attack (FEMA, 1995). If a chemical terrorist incident were to occur at such a location, local emergency officials would have to respond promptly, instructing people to evacuate the area, providing shelter in sealed rooms, and treating immediate casualties.

The public-health consequences of a chemical attack would depend on the location and type of agent employed. Although only 11 people died in the Tokyo sarin attack, more than 5,000 were injured and many hundreds required immediate treatment in hospital emergency rooms with antidotes and medical support. Such a large influx of casualties has the potential to overwhelm emergency medical facilities even in a large city. Another unique characteristic of a CW attack that differentiates it from a conventional terrorist bombing is the potential for post-attack transmission to additional victims from direct contact with liquid contamination, creating a potential multiplier effect. Thus, if persistent chemical agents were used, casualties and buildings would have to be closely monitored and decontaminated to prevent the further exposure of victims and emergency personnel, greatly increasing the number of people needed to manage the disaster (Baker, 1993).

Lessons from Bhopal. Useful lessons about how to respond to a chemical disaster were learned from the tragic leak of the toxic gas methylisocyanate (MIC) from a Union Carbide plant in Bhopal, India. Just after midnight on December 3, 1984, some 50,000 pounds of MIC in vapor and liquid form escaped from a holding tank at the Bhopal plant and formed a cloud that was carried by a light wind over nearby shanty towns. A temperature inversion kept the toxic cloud close to the ground and prevented it from dispersing, allowing the concentrated gas to blanket an area of more than ten square miles. The most vulnerable individuals were small children, the elderly, people with chronic pulmonary disorders, and those who tried to escape by running through the gas cloud. As soon as the severity of the accident was recognized, patients flooded into area hospitals. About 100,000 patients were given some kind of medical care in the first 24 hours. Some 500 died before getting any treatment, almost 2,000 more died within the first week, and roughly 10,000 people in all were seriously injured (Lorin and Kulling, 1986).

Useful lessons about how to respond to a chemical disaster were learned from the tragic leak of the toxic gas methylisocyanate (MIC) from a Union Carbide plant in Bhopal, India

Although the quantity of chemical agent involved in the Bhopal disaster greatly exceeds even the largest plausible terrorist attack, it should be remembered that nerve agents are between 100 and 1,000 times more toxic than MIC. Thus, the Bhopal incident offers some useful insights into managing large-scale toxic exposures. Swedish doctors who visited the city after the disaster drew three main lessons. First, in order to suppress widespread panic and chaos, the government must be ready to provide public information immediately and continuously after a chemical disaster has occurred, both in the immediate area by means of officials equipped with loudspeakers and over a larger area through emergency radio and television broadcasts. Local emergency authorities should be prepared to explain clearly the cause of the disaster, what the victims should do, how long the crisis will last, where to obtain help, and how people can protect themselves from exposure.

Second, the Bhopal incident revealed that organizations taking part in life-saving actions, such as fire-brigade, police, and civil-defense units, do not always know how to treat toxic chemical exposures. Regular training for rescue teams should therefore include first aid for chemical casualties. In disasters involving releases of toxic substances, the injuries are similar for all victims—albeit differing in severity—so that the treatment can be standardized. Indeed, it may be sufficient to have only a few medical specialists on call who can give instructions to other members of the health-care team.

Finally, in large chemical disasters such as Bhopal, all of the injured cannot be brought to hospitals. To avoid chaos and overcrowding, it is important to plan for satellite treatment areas in sports centers, schools, and other buildings that are equipped with central heating, hot and cold running water, and telephones. At these field sites, medical personnel and equipment can be brought in and a large number of patients treated (Lorin and Kulling, 1986).

Lessons from Israel. In developing public-health strategies for coping with the threat of C/B terrorism, U.S. government planners should also consider the case of Israel, which has acquired extensive experience in civil defense against C/B agents. During the three-month period preceding the outbreak of the 1991 Persian Gulf War, Israeli authorities distributed approximately five million gas masks and antidote kits to the general civilian population, at government expense. Households were also instructed through public-service announcements to establish a "sealed room" within the home in which family members could take shelter from Iraqi Scud missiles carrying C/B warheads (Lapidot, 1994).

A sobering lesson of the Israeli experience during the Gulf War is that even when ordinary citizens were equipped with gas masks and other protective equipment, they often failed to use them properly. None of the Iraqi missiles that hit Tel Aviv turned out to have chemical or biological payloads, and only two Israelis were killed directly by Scuds with conventional warheads. Because intense anxiety mimics the signs and symptoms of nerve-agent poisoning, however, many Israeli citizens believed they were being gassed during the missile attacks and were overwhelmed by panic. As a result, ten people died from the indirect effects of protection against chemical weapons—either by suffocating after failing to remove the plug from the gas-mask filter or by injecting themselves with atropine, a nerve-agent antidote that, if not counteracted, can itself cause serious harm.

The United States, of course, does not face the same level of military threat as a country like Israel, which lacks strategic depth and has hostile neighbors armed with C/B weapons and long-range missiles. Moreover, the Israeli population is small enough so that the government could afford to equip all civilians with gas masks free of charge, but that is not a realistic option for a country the size of the United States. In sum, given the problems that Israel experienced with the civilian use of gas masks and the fact that a terrorist C/B attack might occur without warning, it would not be cost-effective to stockpile gas masks for such a contingency. Instead, civil-defense preparations for responding to a C/B terrorist attack should focus on emergency medical responses.

To meet the medical demands associated with a chemical agent attack, initial triage and holding sites would have to be established where patients would be decontaminated and given initial treatment. Within these areas, medical staff would work in full protective clothing. According to Israeli civil-defense specialists, care of chemical casualties should be based on the following principles:

- provision of medical care simultaneously to a large number of victims;
- rapid and logical triage of victims according to severity of injury, followed by matching of seriously ill patients to appropriate tertiary care facilities;
- standardization of delivery of care, including medical equipment and drugs;
  and
- training of paramedical teams to assist in treatment of victims (Shemer and Danon, 1994).

A covert biological attack would be much harder to manage medically because of its delayed effects. Since it would not be feasible to vaccinate civilian populations to putative BW agents prior to an attack, the medical response would have to focus on post-exposure treatment with antibiotics and antisera. Yet the exposed population would not experience the onset of symptoms until after an incubation period of a few days, by which time the affected individuals could have dispersed widely. Effective disease-surveillance mechanisms would therefore need to be in place to detect the onset of the epidemic and differentiate it from a natural disease outbreak. Moreover, given the speed with which pathogens such as anthrax can induce a life-threatening illness, rapid identification of the infectious agent would be essential to save lives with antimicrobial therapy. Finally, if terrorists used a highly contagious pathogen such as pneumonic plague, the victims would have to be quarantined. General hospitals might even refuse to admit BW casualties for fear of infecting the vulnerable patient population.

It should also be noted that BW defense has different detection and masking requirements than CW defense. With only a few rare exceptions, biological agents cannot penetrate intact skin, so that the sole route of exposure is through the lungs. Moreover, since the particles making up a biological aerosol cloud are relatively large, once they settle out they tend to adhere to surfaces and are difficult to reaerosolize. Thus, there is little risk that the downwind settling of biological agent particles would result in a persistent contamination hazard. For these reasons, emergency medical personnel facing a BW threat would not need to wear cumbersome gas masks and full-body protective suits. All that is needed for effective individual protection against biological agents is a relatively low-cost surgical-type mask that forms a tight seal over the mouth and nose and filters out airborne particles in the respirable range (Danzig, 1996). In contrast, persistent chemical agents such as VX can enter the body either as an inhaled vapor or as liquid droplets that penetrate the skin, and may remain toxic in the environment for days or even weeks. Effective protection against chemical agents therefore requires the use of a gas mask with an activated-charcoal filter and a full-body protective suit.

U.S. Policy Options

Since it is very likely that local and state medical resources in the United States would be rapidly overwhelmed in the aftermath of a major C/B terrorist attack, the federal government would have to intervene quickly to manage the disaster. Today the centerpiece of the federal response to both man-made and natural disasters is the National Disaster Medical System (NDMS), which coordinates the emergency medical response activities of FEMA and the Departments of Defense, Health and Human Services, and Veterans Affairs (Brandt et al., 1985; Mahoney and Reutershan, 1987). The NDMS has three major components: pre-hospital treatment, patient evacuation, and in-hospital care. Pre-hospital treatment is provided by Disaster Medical Assistance Teams (DMATs), which are responsible for first aid, casualty clearing, medical staging, and field surgical intervention (Mahoney et al., 1987). There are about 60 DMATs in existence, of which 21 are "level 1" teams that can mobilize within six hours. These teams are self-sufficient with tents, food, and water purification equipment, and have enough medical supplies for 72 continuous hours of operation (Young, 1995).

Nevertheless, while the level-1 DMATs are suitable for natural disasters such as earthquakes and hurricanes, the six hours required to mobilize them would be too long to handle the unique medical emergency that would result from a C/B attack, including—in the case of a chemical but not a biological incident—the need for immediate field treatment of large numbers of stricken victims. Other special requirements associated with an effective medical response to C/B terrorism include:

- rapid identification of the toxic or infectious agent;
- prompt administration of antidotes or antibiotics;
- decontamination of victims, buildings, and equipment; and
- equipping emergency and medical personnel with protective masks and suits so that they can avoid becoming casualties themselves.

Immediately after the Tokyo subway attack, the U.S. National Security Council tasked the Public Health Service (PHS) to develop a plan of operation for the health and medical consequences of a C/B terrorist incident. An inter-agency task force, chaired by the Office of Emergency Preparedness at PHS, was established to draft an interim plan that integrates the immediate health and medical responses of the federal agencies in support of states and local governments. This plan calls for the creation, under NDMS auspices, of special "metropolitan strike teams" in high-risk urban areas—integrated groups of emergency health professionals who would provide pre-hospital patient care, including first aid, triage, decontamination, treatment, and evacuation. These strike teams would receive training in the treatment of C/B agent exposures and would be capable of responding within 30 to 90 minutes of an attack. The interim plan also calls for improved communications systems for use in a terrorist disaster (Young, 1995).

In addition to the interim plan, other policies for dealing with the emerging threat of C/B terrorism should be developed. Such policy options can be divided into two groups: low-cost steps that could be implemented immediately, and longer-term, more resource-intensive options that warrant further consideration. To avoid arousing public anxiety and perhaps even provoking unstable individuals to contemplate acts of C/B terrorism, any steps that the federal government undertakes in this area should remain low-profile.

Short-Term Steps

Short-term steps that might be considered to address the emerging threat of C/B terrorism include the following:

1. *The federal government should better coordinate its C/B counterterrorist planning with state and local authorities.* Although the federal government has established an inter-agency working group on nuclear, biological, and chemical (NBC) terrorism, and major cities such as New York have developed their own contingency plans (Altman, 1995), there has been relatively little communication between them. One problem is that current law authorizes FEMA to advise states and localities on how to do their planning but gives the agency no authority to dictate either planning activities or their content. This lack of coordination at the various levels of government would be a major barrier to effective response in a crisis. To set a national agenda for action, Congress should authorize the FBI, FEMA, and other participating federal agencies to develop a comprehensive national civil-defense plan specifying how emergency-response and public-health resources at the federal, state, and local levels would be mobilized to deal with C/B terrorist incidents. After this plan has been fleshed out, civil-defense officials should conduct annual or semiannual exercises in which they simulate a C/B terrorist attack and test emergency responses under realistic field conditions.

2. *All signatories of the Chemical Weapons Convention (CWC) should work for the prompt entry-into-force of the treaty, urge hold-out states to sign and/or ratify, and pass the domestic implementing legislation required under Article VII.* Although the CWC cannot prevent chemical terrorism, it will reinforce the international norm against the use of chemical weapons and create new obstacles for terrorists by requiring parties to criminalize the acquisition and stockpiling of chemical weapons, allowing law-enforcement agencies to intervene against terrorist groups seeking to acquire chemical weapons before an attack actually occurs. The convention will also require member states to report to the international CWC organization on the activities of companies that produce, process, consume, import, or export certain chemical precursors. Such annual reporting will

oblige both governments and private companies to be more vigilant about suspicious transactions. Similarly, all parties to the Biological Weapons Convention that have not yet passed domestic legislation making the treaty prohibitions binding on their citizens and businesses should be strongly pressured to do so.

3. *The U.S. Department of Commerce (and its counterparts in other countries) should educate domestic chemical companies and biological suppliers about the threat of C/B terrorism and urge them to police themselves more effectively.* A privately based control system in which industry assumes responsibility for preventing the misuse of its own products is much more desirable than adding yet another layer of external government regulation. For example, chemical suppliers would be advised to scrutinize their overseas and domestic customer lists to make sure that dual-purpose precursors and production equipment sold to firms, groups, or individuals for ostensibly legitimate purposes are not diverted to the production of chemical weapons. One way to enforce this system would be to hold chemical and biological suppliers civilly liable for the misuse of their products by terrorists. Companies that undertook reasonable steps to limit the chance of diversion would face a reduced liability in the event of misuse—a provision known in legal circles as a "limited safe-harbor." For example, in the event injuries resulted from the terrorist use of its products, a firm that had made a good-faith effort to screen its customers might be held liable for compensatory damages but not punitive damages.

4. *Commercial laboratories such as American Type Culture Collection (ATCC), which supply seed cultures of pathogenic microorganisms for biomedical and public-health research, should require customers to prove that they have a legitimate need for such materials before being allowed to purchase them.* Demanding that legitimate researchers prove their *bona fides* before being allowed to order dangerous pathogens would make it more difficult for terrorists to obtain them by impersonating biomedical scientists or by submitting orders on stolen or fictitious university letterhead. One approach would be for national or international scientific bodies (such as the American Society for Microbiology, the American Public Health Association, or the International Union of Microbiological Societies) to establish a certification or licensing procedure that would authorize scientific researchers with a legitimate need to purchase seed cultures of dangerous pathogens from biological supply houses. Criteria for such certification might include academic affiliation and publication record, so as to weed out terrorists seeking to impersonate scientists. The list of approved recipients could be stored on diskette and made available to all relevant suppliers.

5. *The U.S. Congress should consider legislation imposing civil liability on any U.S. resident or company that aids and abets terrorists by publishing detailed recipes for the production of C/B weapons, either in book form or on the Internet.* Without infringing on constitutional protections, one can make a compelling case that the publication of cookbooks for the production of C/B agents represents a clear and present danger to the health and security of the nation and thus does not constitute protected speech under the First Amendment. (The constitutional questions surrounding this issue are likely to be clarified by a pending legal case against a book that provides detailed instructions on how to commit assassinations—with a disclaimer that it is strictly for educational purposes—and was allegedly used to commit an actual murder.) Although censoring such materials outright would set a dangerous precedent, publication could be deterred through the threat of legal liability. To this end, Congress might pass legislation imposing treble damages on the author and publisher for any injuries arising from the terrorist use of a C/B primer, and enabling the federal government to recover costs associated with law enforcement. Since the Internet transcends national borders, the United States would have to urge other governments to enact legislation covering content providers operating under other national jurisdictions.

6. *The intelligence community should devote greater resources to tracking attempts to acquire C/B weapons by both domestic and international terrorist groups.* In particular, the CIA and the U.S. Customs Service should improve their ability to detect and interdict foreign trafficking in C/B precursor materials, equipment, and know-how. U.S. intelligence agencies should also expand the sharing of information with friendly countries (including Russia) on international terrorist groups that might be contemplating C/B attacks. Such exchanges could take place through Interpol, the Australia Group, and bilateral intelligence channels. Where there is probable cause to suspect that a domestic group is engaged in the purchase of C/B-related materials, the FBI should obtain a warrant to engage in intensive surveillance, including wiretaps and infiltration by undercover agents. Nevertheless, counterterrorism must not be used as an excuse to curtail the civil liberties of unpopular groups that do not resort to violence.

7. *FEMA and the Public Health Service should develop public-service announcements for emergency radio and television broadcast in the event of a C/B terrorist attack.* These spots would be designed to provide detailed information and instructions to the public, helping to suppress widespread panic.

Longer-Term Steps

At the same time that the immediate measures listed above are being implemented, the following longer-term policies for addressing the threat of C/B terrorism should also be considered.

1. *The U.S. Congress should appropriate funds to expand the epidemiological surveillance programs run by the U.S. Centers for Disease Control and Prevention (CDC) and the World Health Organization (WHO) to monitor background levels of infectious disease around the world.* Beyond the obvious benefits of this surveillance program for international health, it would help differentiate covert BW attacks from unusual outbreaks of disease attributable to natural causes (Wheelis, 1992; Lederberg, Shope, and Oaks, 1992).

2. *FEMA should purchase and stockpile C/B defensive materials at major medical centers in the nation's twenty largest cities.* These stockpiles might include

- chemical and biological agent monitoring devices for identifying contaminated areas and individuals;
- antidotes against chemical nerve agents, such as atropine and PAM; and
- broad-spectrum antibiotics and antisera for treating exposures to known bacterial, viral, and toxin agents.

Enough antidotes and medications should be stockpiled in each city to treat the estimated casualties from a realistic C/B attack scenario, based on population density and other variables.

3. *The U.S. Public Health Service should create a national training program for "first responders" to a C/B terrorist incident, including paramedics, police, firefighters, and other emergency workers.* The curriculum would cover the rapid triage and care of C/B casualties and the use of chemical protective equipment, with the goal of creating a ready reserve of emergency response teams who could be activated promptly in the event of a large-scale C/B terrorist attack.

4. *The FBI should instruct major urban police departments in specialized surveillance and law-enforcement techniques related to the emerging threat of C/B terrorism.* Such a program would require training detectives and officers to recognize criminal behavior on the part of religious cults (along the lines of Aum Shinrikyo), as well as subtle indicators of C/B agent acquisition, development, and production.

5. *The Department of Defense, in cooperation with other federal agencies, should establish specialized detection teams to investigate threats of C/B terrorism prior to an attack, much like the existing Nuclear Emergency Search Teams (NEST) for nuclear terrorist threats* (Waller, 1996). Whereas nuclear weapons are radioactive and emit subatomic particles that can be picked up at a distance by a Geiger counter, a bomb containing a chemical or biological agent would not be detectable unless the agent leaked or was deliberately released. It would therefore be next to impossible to find a device containing a chemical or biological agent hidden somewhere in a large city. Nevertheless, C/B weapon search teams equipped with portable sampling and analysis equipment would be able to identify the agent involved in an attack shortly after it occurred, facilitating the appropriate medical response.

6. *The U.S. Congress should increase government funding for research and development on improved C/B agent detection and identification systems, and encourage joint efforts with other like-minded countries.* Prompt identification of chemical and biological agents is critical to ensure accurate medical diagnosis and effective treatment. Ideally, field detection systems should be capable of identifying C/B agents in close to "real time" with a very low probability of false-negatives or false-positives, yet this goal remains elusive (Starr, 1995). During the 1991 Persian Gulf War, the automatic CW agent detector/alarms deployed with U.S. troops in Saudi Arabia were notoriously unreliable. BW agents could only be detected by taking concentrated air samples at regular intervals and performing an immunoassay, yet because this test takes at least 30 minutes to yield a result, it could only determine in retrospect if troops had been exposed. In the aftermath of the Tokyo sarin attack, the Japanese police were reduced to using caged canaries as crude poison-gas detectors (Van Biema, 1995).

7. *The U.S. Congress should provide incentives for the pharmaceutical industry to develop improved broad-spectrum antibiotic and antiviral drugs capable of treating exposures to a variety of putative BW agents.* New and improved antibiotics are also needed to protect the public health as common disease-causing microorganisms become resistant to existing drugs through natural processes of mutation and selection.

Although another large-scale chemical biological terrorist attack remains unlikely, the Tokyo subway incident has lowered the threshold for future disasters of this type. Given the potential cost in human lives and psychological trauma, the emerging threat warrants a significant U.S. national investment in the preparation of contingency plans, the training of medical personnel, and the stockpiling of relevant medications. Most of the policy recommendations listed above also apply, with appropriate adaptations, to other countries.

References

Altman, L.K. (1995). "Plan Drawn to Help Fight Poison Attack." *New York Times* (March 26):9.

Associated Press (1995). "Biological Weapons Suspect Hangs Himself in Arkansas Jail." *Washington Post* (December 24):A9.

Baker, D. (1993). "Chemical and Biological Warfare Agents—A Fresh Approach." *Jane's Intelligence Review* (January):42-44.

Beal, C. (1995). "An Invisible Enemy." *International Defense Review* 28 (3):36-41.

Brandt, E.N., W.N. Mayer, J.O. Mason, D.E. Brown, Jr., and L.E. Mahoney (1985). "Designing a National Disaster Medical System." *Public Health Reports* 100:455-461.

Chester, C.V. and G.P. Zimmerman (1984). "Civil Defense Implications of Biological Weapons." *Journal of Civil Defense* 18 (6):6-12.

Chevrier, M.I. (1993). "Deliberate Disease: Biological Weapons, Threats, and Policy Responses." *Environment and Planning C: Government and Policy* 11:395-417.

Croddy, E. (1995). "Urban Terrorism—Chemical Warfare in Japan." *Jane's Intelligence Review* (November):520-23.

Crossette, B. (1995). "A Russian Scientist Cautions Chemical Arms Safety Is Lax." *New York Times* (October 1):12.

Danzig, R. (1996). "Biological Warfare: A Nation at Risk—A Time to Act." *INSS Strategic Forum* 58. Washington, DC: National Defense University, Institute for National Strategic Studies (January):3-4.

Erlick, B.J. (1989). Testimony. U.S. Senate, Committee on Governmental Affairs, *Global Spread of Chemical and Biological Weapons: Assessing Challenges and Responses*. 101st Congress, 1st sess., February 9. Washington, DC: U.S. Government Printing Office.

FEMA [Federal Emergency Management Agency] (1995). "Fact Sheet: Terrorism." FEMA homepage, World Wide Web.

Franz, D.R. (1994). "Physical and Medical Countermeasures to Biological Weapons." In K.C. Bailey (ed.), *Director's Series on Proliferation*. Report No. UCRL-LR-114070-4. Livermore, CA: Lawrence Livermore National Laboratory.

Gardels, N. (1995). "Third Wave Terrorism" [interview with Alvin Toffler]. *New Perspectives Quarterly* 12 (June 22):4-6.

Gates, R. (1992). Testimony [as CIA Director] before the Senate Governmental Affairs Committee, "Weapons Proliferation in the New World Order," January 15.

Guest, R. (1995). "Cult Chemist Tells Police He Made Sarin Nerve Gas." *Financial Times* (May 12):14.

GulfLINK (1995). "Iraqis Trained to Use Chemical and Biological Weapons." Document No. 60066.91s. [GulfLINK is a Department of Defense site on the World Wide Web containing declassified intelligence documents from the Persian Gulf War.]

Hadfield, P. (1995). "Tokyo's Deadly Nerve Gas 'Easy to Make.'" *New Scientist* 1970 (March 25):4.

Hatsumi, R. (1995). "What Aum Offered." *New York Times* (May 24):A17.

Herbert, B. (1995). "Militia Madness." *New York Times* (June 7):op-ed page.

Holley, D. (1995). "Japanese Sect Linked to Germ Weapons Plant." *Los Angeles Times* (March 20):A1.

Hurwitz, E. (1982). "Terrorists and Chemical/Biological Weapons." *Naval War College Review* 35 (May-June):36-40.

Keeney, S.M., Jr. (1995). "Tokyo Terror and Chemical Arms Control." *Arms Control Today* 25 (3):2.

Kifner, J. (1995). "Man Is Arrested in a Case Involving Deadly Poison." *New York Times* (December 23):7.

Lait, M. and E. Malnic (1995). "Federal Agents Feared Attack at Disneyland." *Los Angeles Times* (April 22):1.

Lapidot, Y. (1994). "Civil Defense in Israel during the Persian Gulf War: One Year Later." In Y.L. Danon and J. Shemer (eds.), *Chemical Warfare Medicine: Aspects and Perspectives from the Persian Gulf War*. Jerusalem: Gefen Publishing House.

Lederberg, J., R.E. Shope, and S.C. Oaks, Jr., eds. (1992). *Emerging Infections: Microbial Threats to Health in the United States*. Washington, DC: National Academy Press.

Lorin, H.G. and P.E.J. Kulling (1986). "The Bhopal Tragedy—What Has Swedish Disaster Medicine Planning Learned From It?" *Journal of Emergency Medicine* 4:311-16.

Mahoney, L.E. and T.P. Reutershan (1987). "Catastrophic Disasters and the Design of Disaster Medical Care Systems." *Annals of Emergency Medicine* 16 (September 9):1085-91.

Mahoney, L.E., D.F. Whiteside, H.E. Belue, K.P. Mortisugu, and V.H. Esch (1987). "Disaster Medical Assistance Teams." *Annals of Emergency Medicine* 16 (March 3):354-58.

Morita, H. et al. (1995). "Sarin Poisoning in Matsumoto, Japan." *The Lancet* 346 (July 29):290-93.

Nelan, B.W. (1995). "The Price of Fanaticism." *Time* (April 3):38-40.

Post, T. (1995). "Doomsday Cults; 'Only the Beginning.'" *Newsweek* 125 (April 3):40.

Powell, W. (1971). *The Anarchist's Cookbook*. New York: Lyle Stuart.

Purver, R. (1995). "The Threat of Chemical/Biological Terrorism." *Commentary* 60 (August 1995). Ottawa: Canadian Security Intelligence Service.

Reid, T.R. (1995). "New Cults Flourish in a Changed Japan." *Washington Post* (March 27):A1.

Riding, A. (1994). "Swiss Examine Conflicting Signs in Cult Deaths." *New York Times* (October 7):A1.

Robinson, J.P. (1992). "The Australia Group: A Description and Assessment." In H.G. Brauch, H.J. van der Graaf, J. Grin, and W.A. Smit (eds.), *Controlling the Development and Spread of Military Technology: Lessons from the Past and Challenges for the 1990s*. Amsterdam: VU University Press.

Robinson, J.P. (1995). "News Chronology: May through August 1995." *Chemical Weapons Convention Bulletin* 29 (September):19.

Rose, S. (1989). "The Coming Explosion of Silent Weapons." *Naval War College Review* 42 (Summer):6-29.

Shemer, J. and Y.L. Danon (1994). "Eighty Years of the Threat and Use of Chemical Warfare: The Medico-Organizational Challenge." In Y.L. Danon and J. Shemer (eds.), *Chemical Warfare Medicine: Aspects and Perspectives from the Persian Gulf War*. Jerusalem: Gefen Publishing House.

Smith, R.J. (1995a). "Japanese Cult Had Network of Front Companies, Investigators Say." *Washington Post* (November 1):A8.

Smith, R.J. (1995b). "Senators Scold Spy Agencies Over Cult." *Washington Post* (November 2):A15.

Smithson, A. et al. (1995). *Chemical Weapons Disarmament in Russia: Problems and Prospects*, Report No. 17 (October). Washington, DC: Henry L. Stimson Center.

Starr, B. (1994). "NBC Terrorists a 'Most Nightmarish Concern.'" *Jane's Defence Weekly* (December 10):10.

Starr, B. (1995). "CW Detection Is Top of US Shortfall List." *Jane's Defence Weekly* (June 10):26.

Stern, J.E. (1993). "Will Terrorists Turn to Poison?" *Orbis* 37 (Summer):393-410.

Stout, D. (1996). "3 Boys Used Internet to Plot School Bombing, Police Say." *New York Times* (February 2):A1, A12.

Strasser, S. (1995). "A Cloud of Terror—And Suspicion." *Newsweek* 125 (April 3):40-41.

Suzuki, T., H. Morita, K. Ono, K. Maekawa, R. Nagai, and Y. Yazaki (1995). "Sarin Poisoning in Tokyo Subway." *The Lancet* 345 (April 15):980-81.

Tucker, J.B. (1992). "The Future of Biological Warfare." In T.W. Wander and E.H. Arnett (eds.), *The Proliferation of Advanced Weaponry: Technology, Motivations, and Responses*. Washington, DC: American Association for the Advancement of Science.

United Nations (1995). *Report of the Secretary-General on the Status of the Implementation of the Plan for the Ongoing Monitoring and Verification of Iraq's Compliance with Relevant Parts of Section C of Security Council Resolution 687 (1991)*. UN Security Council Document No. S/1995/864 (October 11):6-7.

U.S. Congress OTA [Office of Technology Assessment] (1992). *Technology Against Terrorism: Structuring Security*, OTA-ISC-511. Washington, DC: U.S. Government Printing Office.

U.S. Congress OTA (1993). *Technologies Underlying Weapons of Mass Destruction*, OTA-BP-ISC-115. Washington, DC: U.S. Government Printing Office.

U.S. Department of Commerce (1991). *Foreign Availability Review: 50 CW Precursor Chemicals (II)*. Washington, DC: Department of Commerce.

U.S. Senate (1994). Committee on Banking, Housing, and Urban Affairs, 103rd Congress, 2nd sess., Hearing, *United States Dual-Use Exports to Iraq and Their Impact on the Health of the Persian Gulf War Veterans* [S. Hrg. 103-900] (May 25):264-76.

U.S. Senate (1995). Permanent Subcommittee on Investigations, Committee on Governmental Affairs, "Staff Statement: Hearings on Global Proliferation of Weapons of Mass Destruction: A Case Study on Aum Shinrikyo." Mimeo, October 31.

Van Biema, D. (1995). "Prophet of Poison." *Time* (April 3):27-33.

Waller, D. (1996). "Nuclear Ninjas." *Time* 147 (January 8):38-40.

Wheelis, M.L. (1992). "Strengthening the Biological Weapons Convention Through Global Epidemiological Surveillance." *Politics and the Life Sciences* 11:179-89.

Woodall, J.P. (1991). "WHO Health and Epidemic Information as a Basis for Verification Activities under the Biological Weapons

Convention." In S.J. Lundin (ed.), *Views on Possible Verification Measures for the Biological Weapons Convention*. SIPRI Chemical and Biological Warfare Studies No. 12. Oxford: Oxford University Press.

Young, F.E. (1995). Statement by Dr. Frank E. Young, Director, National Disaster Medical System, before the Permanent Subcommittee on Investigations, Commitee on Governmental Affairs, U.S. Senate, November 1.

Zapf, P. (1993). "Appendix A: The Chemistry of Organophosphate Agents." In B. Morel and K. Olson (eds.), *Shadows and Substance: The Chemical Weapons Convention*. Boulder, CO: Westview Press.

EDITOR'S NOTE

(with thanks to Graham Pearson)

As we go to print, it has become clear that our roundtable on chemical/biological terrorism is indeed timely, as the threat of use of such materials for terrorist purposes was included in the communiqué issued by the Heads of Government of the G7/8, who met in Lyon, France on June 27, 1996. They condemned the attack on Dhahran as a "barbarous and unjustifiable act" and also condemned other recent terrorist acts. They said that these tragedies strengthened them in their conviction that terrorism is "a major challenge to all our societies and states today," and they reaffirmed their "absolute condemnation of terrorism in all its forms and manifestations, regardless of its perpetrators or motives." They also proclaimed their common resolve to unite their efforts and their "determination to fight terrorism by all legal means."

They went on to say that "special attention should be paid to the threat of utilization of nuclear, biological and chemical materials, as well as toxic substances, for terrorist purposes."

The Heads of Government further indicated that they considered the fight against terrorism to be their "absolute priority," and reiterated "the necessity for all states to adhere to the relevant international conventions." They decided that a ministerial meeting should be held in Paris, as early as the month of July, to consider all measures liable to strengthen the capacity of the international community to defeat terrorism and recommend further actions.

This Ministerial Conference on Terrorism, held in Paris on July 30, 1996, issued a Final Declaration which noted that there is a "growing commitment within the international community to condemn terrorism in whatever shape or form, regardless of its motives; to make no concessions to terrorists; and to implement means, consistent with fundamental freedoms and the rule of law, to effectively fight terrorism." The participants affirmed their determination "to work with all states, in full observance of the principles and standards of international law and human rights, in order to achieve the goal of eliminating terrorism, as affirmed in the Declaration adopted by the United Nations General Assembly in December 1994."

The declaration set out a framework of 25 practical measures to be implemented by the G7 countries, and which all states were invited to adopt. Three of these practical measures were concerned with use of chemical and biological materials. First, the parties called on all states to "expand training of personnel connected with counter-terrorism to prevent all forms of terrorist action, including those utilizing radioactive, chemical, biological, or toxic substances." Second, the parties recommended to States "Parties to the Biological Weapons Convention to confirm at the forthcoming Review Conference their commitment to ensure, through the adoption of national measures, the effective fulfillment of their obligations under the convention to take any necessary measures to prohibit and prevent the development, production, stockpiling, acquisition or retention of such weapons within their territory, under their jurisdiction or under their control anywhere, in order, *inter alia,* to exclude use of those weapons for terrorist purposes."

Third, the conference called on all states to "intensify the exchange of operational information, especially as regards," among other things, "the threat of new types of terrorist activities, including those using chemical, biological or nuclear materials and toxic substances."

As the Final Declaration ends by calling on each country's experts on terrorism to meet before the end of 1996 to assess the progress of the work undertaken to implement these measures, *Politics and Life Sciences* is pleased to contribute to one aspect of this initiative through this roundtable on chemical and biological terrorism.

Stalking the Next Epidemic: ProMED Tracks Emerging Diseases

JACK WOODALL, PHD

Ask anyone today what infectious disease they fear the most, and chances are the reply will be not "AIDS" but "Ebola." The publicity given to the recent outbreaks of this disease has made the serpent-shaped virus the poster child for emerging diseases. But HIV and Ebola virus are not alone. We also have to fear hantaviruses, new strains of plague, and a whole host of other emerging or reemerging infections.

Bioterrorism is another perceived threat that has been in the news in recent months. The continuing revelations of Iraq's extensive biowarfare program add to the concern. There have even been suggestions from some quarters in recent years that the dengue hemorrhagic fever epidemics in Cuba and Nicaragua and the 1994 plague outbreak in India were due to biological attacks.

Would the 1995 outbreak of Ebola have come to the attention of the Zairian health authorities—let alone the world—if an Italian nun working at the hospital had not died of it? (Unfortunately, news services pick up the occasional unexplained death of an expatriate rather than the hundreds of similar deaths of local people.) And once word gets out of an outbreak, is there the local expertise to diagnose the cause so that specific countermeasures can be taken? It took months for the first recorded epidemic of yellow fever in Kenya, which occurred in

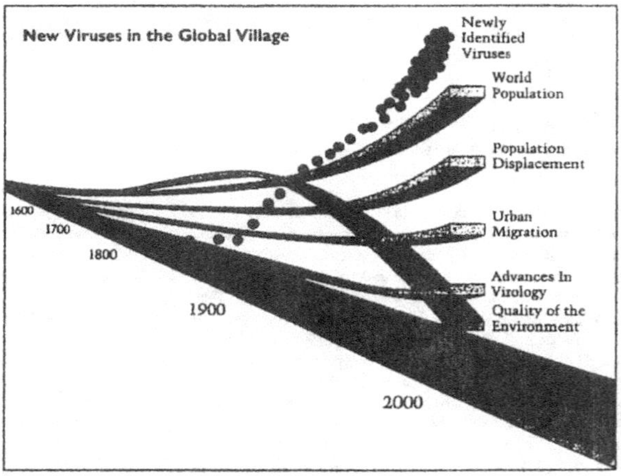

While the world population soars and the quality of the environment plummets, the number of newly identified viruses explodes. These viruses are the causes of emerging diseases in humans, animals, and plants that may have a devastating impact on the world's health.

SOURCE: Mann J, Tarantola DJM, Netter TW. AIDS in the world. Cambridge (MA): Harvard University Press, 1992:827.

1992–1993, to be diagnosed locally. In contrast, the 1994 plague outbreak in India was hastily overdiagnosed, which resulted in needless panic in several neighboring and other countries. What is needed is a global network of reliable disease monitoring centers and a rapid communications system connecting them with health institutions around the world. Newly available technology now puts these lofty ideals within reach.

It has been claimed that if we had only recognized HIV when it first appeared, we would have had several years' start on containing it and on the research we are now doing to identify preventive measures and treatment. If the world community is ever going to be able to nip emerging diseases in the bud, we have to be able to recognize the bud. The same applies to the use of biological agents such as anthrax in war or terrorist attacks or to accidents occurring during the production or transport of a biological weapons agent. The emerging infectious diseases and potential biological weapons agents we should be concerned about today include a new, more virulent, strain of influenza; anthrax; botulinum toxin; cholera; plague; yellow fever and other hemorrhagic fevers; Venezuelan equine encephalitis; bat rabies viruses; karnal bunt disease of wheat; and fungal diseases of potatoes. This list includes for good reason some agents that infect animals and plants; they affect our food security, and large scale outbreaks in livestock or crop plants—whether of natural or artificial origin—could produce economic destabilization in the victimized country. Remember the story of the Irish potato famine 150 years ago?

The U.S. Centers for Disease Control and Prevention's (CDC) world-renowned Epidemic Intelligence Service has gained an enviable reputation for rapid response to reports of epidemics and thorough investigation of every imaginable type of disease or health problem all over the world. The key words here are "response to reports" and "thorough investigation." Before there can be a response, there must be a report. Once there is a report, there should be an investigation.

In January 1996, Joshua Lederberg wrote that concerning world health, "we have never been more vulnerable...."[1] The first need is for "concerted global and domestic surveillance and diagnosis of disease outbreaks and endemic occurrence. This must entail the installation of sophisticated laboratory capabilities at many centers now lacking them."[1] But in spite of the urgency of the situation, "tangible responses by government in the form of budgetary or staffing commitments remain negligible." [1]

Communications

There is one thing that is vital to the functioning of a global network of monitoring centers: rapid communications. It is essential that centers be able to instantly communicate laboratory results and situation updates on outbreak investigations to national and international authorities. Telephone and fax are of course standard equipment, but in this day and age nothing beats full Internet access. Detailed laboratory results, X-rays, EKGs, EEGs, three-dimensional CT scans, and even the sounds of a patient's heartbeat; digital color videos and photographs of external signs such as rashes and bite marks, of internal organs, of pathology slides, or of the shape and color of an infected plant leaf; or computer-enhanced satellite images of croplands showing infected areas in a contrasting color—all can be transmitted across the world for examination by experts, wherever they may be.

Electronic communications can also be used to vastly expand the base of surveillance for unusual outbreaks. The dream is to link clinical and health research facilities around the globe so that newly emerging diseases can be recognized early and dealt with rapidly. This is now achievable through the Internet. What has been achieved so far are a number of partial networks and one global one: the ProMED project and its communications arm, ProMED-mail.

The Federation of American Scientists ProMED Project

The Federation of American Scientists (FAS), sponsored by over 40 American Nobel prize winners, has been a center of policy research, analysis, and education for over 50 years. FAS originally undertook ProMED, a project to promote the establishment of a global Program to Monitor Emerging Diseases, as a basis for the international technological cooperation in the prevention of disease called for under the Biological Weapons Convention. At the project's founding conference in Geneva in 1993, which was cosponsored by FAS and WHO, ProMED was given a mandate by 60 prominent health experts from all parts of the world to assure the design, promotion, and implementation of a global program in consultation with appropriate international, national, and nongovernmental agencies.

Since then, ProMED has been in the vanguard of efforts to monitor the increasingly globalized threat of infectious diseases, with two major achievements to date: the drafting of a detailed proposal for a demonstration network of monitoring centers[2] and the establishment of the first and only publicly accessible global source of timely information on outbreaks, ProMED-mail.

At the 1993 conference, ProMED working groups began to elaborate plans for a global monitoring network; these plans were further developed through subsequent meetings and consultations with more than 300 experts around the world under the guidance of a ProMED Steering Committee. The resulting document proposes a research program to demonstrate the feasibility of a network of centers to monitor emerging diseases directly through clinical surveillance for selected syndromes coupled with effective laboratory back-up. With financial resources in short supply, a small network of strategically located sentinel centers, with capability for surveillance of both endemic and emerging diseases, may be the most effective way, in the near term, not only to test the concept but to begin providing early warning of serious epidemics.

The ProMED project has compiled information on medical centers around the world and identified likely candidate centers for the network. Representatives of some of these centers came together in February 1996 to exchange information at an international conference on Enhancing Infectious Disease Monitoring and Response organized by ProMED members at the request of the Rockefeller Foundation.

Overview of the ProMED Proposal: Outline for a Demonstration Program

Given current financial constraints in the health sector, what can be foreseen is a painfully slow evolution of national and regional surveillance systems toward the distant goal of a unified global system for monitoring emerging diseases. For more rapid progress, significant investment will be needed for coordination and for developing diagnostic and surveillance capabilities in health institutions in those environments where diseases are most likely to emerge. ProMED proposes making a modest start on this track by prioritizing a small number of strategically situated Third World institutions, mainly those least in need of upgrading, for development as sentinel centers. In this way a functional, although limited, network could be rapidly established at minimal cost.

The system would serve as an experimental model for future expansion.

The centers would start by monitoring the emergence of a limited number of defined syndromes through broadly based local clinical outreach from each center. Each center would develop laboratory capabilities for identifying the likely agents for the targeted syndromes as well as for well-known globally and locally endemic diseases. In developing countries, locally endemic diseases will generally overshadow emerging diseases and will therefore be the main focus of concern as well as these centers' incentive for undertaking the program. The goal would be to achieve full competence at each center within, at most, five years and then begin to expand the number of syndromes monitored. If successful, the number of centers could be increased, as resources permit, to cover more areas of the world.

The plan calls for the formation of a network consisting of, roughly, 10 of the most adequately prepared medical facilities in different regions of the developing world. Agreement and cooperation of the government would be essential in each case. Each center would develop its own local/regional network including clinics, hospitals, health care providers, academic centers, government agencies, and voluntary organizations with which it would cooperate and exchange information. The centers would collect clinical data and diagnostic samples with the help of these networks. The centers and their networks would be assisted in developing expertise in recognizing and diagnosing the specified syndromes and would have access to designated specialized reference laboratories.

Concentration on a small number of strategically located medical facilities in developing countries to create comprehensive centers of excellence would establish regional nuclei in areas critical for monitoring emerging diseases. The centers would reach out to other institutions in their regions, providing medical information and training.

The process would be coordinated by a program office, which could be located at one of the centers or at a separate location. The program office, in collaboration with various programs at WHO, would maintain the network's level of competence through a quality assurance program and would provide diagnostic materials and equipment where needed as well as training activities and regular meetings of center heads for coordination and exchange of experience. The program office would also solicit, and help to raise, financial support for individual centers to cover other needs. The centers would be linked to the program office with an electronic communications system, through which surveillance information would be reported in a timely manner and relayed to alert other centers and interested institutions. The network would coordinate with existing networks such as WHONET (a global reporting system for antibiotic resistance) and other WHO electronic reporting systems that may be established, with the goal of forming a unified global communications system on infectious disease surveillance that will incorporate data from existing and future international, regional, national, and local surveillance efforts.

> Through the Internet, we can link clinical and health research facilities around the globe so that newly emerging diseases can be recognized early and dealt with rapidly.

WHO may find it difficult to undertake even a limited trial program such as this in view of its resource limitations. Therefore, a demonstration program could perhaps be established outside WHO as a research project which, if successful, would eventually expand and merge with other surveillance activities at WHO.

Although the initial program must deal primarily with human disease, it could expand later to include veterinary centers and animal diseases, and preliminary feelers are already being put out in that direction. ProMED is developing a separate plan for monitoring emerging plant diseases.

ProMED-mail

Rather than wait until a comprehensive program is funded and implemented by some international agency, the ProMED Steering Committee decided to initiate an e-mail network for rapid reporting and discussion of emerging infectious disease outbreaks. Thus on 19 August 1994 a public e-mail network was born, now known as ProMED-mail. Over the last two years the list has grown to over 7000 direct subscribers from more than 125 countries. Literally thousands of other people receive the information through secondary distribution or visit one of the four sites on the World Wide Web that carry ProMED-mail posts.

The mission of ProMED-mail is fourfold. First and foremost, it is to provide one-stop shopping for early reports of emerging and reemerging infectious disease outbreaks throughout the world. In order to reach the largest possible number of countries, it is based on e-mail because more countries, and more people in many countries, currently have e-mail than have the full Internet access required to reach the Web. ProMED-mail receives WHO's disease bulletins and the reports of the International Office of Epizootics and the European and Mediterranean Plant Protection Organization over the Internet as they are issued. CDC sends regular updates of the hantavirus pulmonary syndrome (HPS) situation in the United States. The State Epidemiologist for Russia has sent regular information on infectious diseases for posting. The Chief Veterinary Officers of Australia and New Zealand have sent us official information on outbreaks by e-mail, and we will shortly be receiving the monthly reports on vesicular diseases of livestock in the Americas from the Pan-American Foot-and-Mouth Disease Center. We have volunteers searching the media and the Internet looking for reports of outbreaks in humans, animals, and plants that are attributed to infectious disease, including those due to antibiotic-resistant organisms. We also have colleagues who subscribe to other Internet discussion groups such as those on virology, BSE ("mad cow disease"), and mosquitoes and forward relevant information.

We encourage first-person reports of unusual cases since an outbreak always starts with a single case. But we impose two conditions. Reports cannot be anonymous, and all are reviewed by a member of our panel of experts in human, animal, and plant diseases to cull irrelevant or dubious reports. Approximately half of our subscribers appear to be interested students or people who are not in the health or biomedical professions but whose wide geographic distribution gives us global coverage that official disease surveillance systems cannot duplicate.

Second, our mission is to permit rapid exchange of information on all aspects of emerging and reemerging infectious diseases. Well over 100 staff members of CDC subscribe along with officials of health departments in many states of the United States, medical staff with U.S. forces worldwide, the U.S. Department of Agriculture, the Food and Drug Administration, and the National Institutes of Health of both the United States and Japan as well as experts at Britain's Public Health Laboratory Service, France's Pasteur Institutes around the world, the state epidemiologists of Russia, Sweden, and Zimbabwe, and universities everywhere. This is an enormous pool of expertise capable of answering practically any query that is raised about a case or outbreak of a rare but emerging disease. Subscribing physicians and public health workers in any country receive a rapid response to their urgent questions with recommendations for prevention, treatment, and control. For example, ProMED-mail has recently elicited responses from subscribers to requests on how to treat conditions as disparate as enterohemorrhagic *E. coli* infection and thallium poisoning.

> With financial resources in short supply, a small network of strategically located sentinel centers may be the most effective way to begin providing early warning of serious epidemics.

Third, we strive to increase intraregional communication and information sharing about emerging diseases within the developing world. Many of the emerging diseases that most concern people today, such as Ebola, plague, and dengue hemorrhagic fever, have arisen in the developing world, where communications are neither rapid nor reliable and where information in the form of paper documentation is scarce. Yet there is a latent, unpublished, and untapped reservoir of information about those diseases and others of potential concern to the industrialized world. An example is the response to a query from South Africa asking if anyone had any experience in using a particular drug to treat a sexually transmitted disease. Back came a reply from Mozambique saying that, indeed, the drug works and giving the dosage. It is this sort of information that is now being exchanged through ProMED-mail and that is filed in archives that are searchable by keyword.

We are also conscious of the need to exchange information in languages other than English. Preliminary contacts are being made to establish regional e-mail networks operating in French, Spanish, and Portuguese.

Fourth, we aim to encourage collaboration among specialists in different fields and in different locations. As mentioned, ProMED-mail reports outbreaks in humans, animals, and plants. We aim to raise consciousness about the fact that our health security is affected by diseases that attack our food animals, crops, and wildlife at least as much as by human diseases. Food shortage leads to malnutrition, leading in turn to a depressed immune system and increased susceptibility to environmental and other microbes that normally do not produce human disease. Developments in techniques for the isolation and identification of viruses and other disease agents in the animal or plant field may have applications in human medicine, and vice versa. The expert's way of looking at epidemic disease in one of those fields could lead to insights that are useful in another field.

It may be questioned what ProMED-mail, which is an unofficial reporting system, can do that is not already being done by international and national disease reporting systems. The fact is that official systems, even WHO's, are not yet fully functional on a global scale, and they are all bound by bureaucratic constraints that require clearances at various levels before publication, leading to delays in warning other countries about a possible problem. There are even countries that forbid WHO to report to the world that an outbreak is occurring on their territory because they are afraid of repercussions on trade or tourism.

SatelLife, HealthNet, and the Outbreak Website

The encumbrances on official reporting and the success of ProMED-mail have demonstrated the value of an independent, nongovernmental rapid reporting system. Therefore, although ProMED-mail was originally conceived as a model and stop-gap measure, it has now been put on a permanent basis, with professional rather than volunteer management. In August 1996, FAS turned over the management and financing of ProMED-mail to SatelLife, a non-profit medical communications organization. FAS continues to host the ProMED-mail Policy Committee, under the chairmanship of the author.

SatelLife is the communications arm of International Physicians for the Prevention of Nuclear War (IPPNW), which has received the Nobel Prize for its work. Several years ago, IPPNW began a unique experiment by launching a low-level satellite into polar orbit—which means that it covers every point on earth, as the Earth rotates below it, two or three times a day, with a transmission window of a few minutes on each pass. SatelLife then installed ultra-low-cost ground stations, consisting of little more than a computer, a sideband radio, and a satellite dish, in key medical schools in developing countries. At each pass of the satellite over the ground station, the medical librarian can upload literature search requests and e-mail messages and download the replies from the previous pass. These are delivered over telephone lines or ground radio links to and from the computers of local subscribers through what is known as HealthNet. HealthNet traffic includes a digest of selected articles from current medical journals, ProMED-mail posts, and posts from similar programs sponsored by SatelLife called ProCAARE, the Program for Collaboration Against AIDS and Related Epidemics, and e-drug, which deals with essential drugs.

The OUTBREAK Website is the brainchild of David Ornstein, a software developer in California. Originally called the Ebola Page, it was designed at the time of the Ebola outbreak in Kikwit, Zaire, to provide links to all the information on the Web about that disease. It became wildly popular—it received one quarter of a million hits during the epidemic—and won several Internet awards. When the Kikwit outbreak died out, many people both within and outside the public health arena urged him to expand the site to provide the answers to frequently asked questions about other emerging diseases. The site, still winning awards, now provides extensive information on a range of diseases for anyone with Web access, including links to the ProMED-mail archives on the relevant diseases. A merger of ProMED-mail and OUTBREAK is under discussion.

Conclusion

Millions of people criss-cross the globe daily by air, and many of them pass through gateway airports in the United States. The speed of air travel means that inevitably some of them become infected in another country and leave it while still healthy only to fall ill and transmit the disease to others on arrival in the United States or while in transit through a gateway. During the 1994 plague outbreak in India, more than 2000 passengers a day arrived at New York City airports from India. Ten of them showed suspicious symptoms on arrival and were quarantined. Fortunately, none of them was a carrier. One traveler fell ill in Chicago with Lassa fever, a hemorrhagic disease, after arriving from Africa some years back; another died of yellow fever in Tennessee in August 1996 after returning from a fishing trip on the Amazon. Dozens of people return to the United States every year infected with dengue fever. Early reporting of, and response to, outbreaks of such diseases at their source will alert physicians in this country and help them treat affected patients and counsel potential travelers about the need for protective vaccinations. The ProMED initiative responds to this need.

It is generally agreed that to safeguard the security of human health, a global surveillance system capable of rapid reporting and investigation of new disease outbreaks is essential. This is true regardless of whether an outbreak is of natural origin or is of artificial origin—as in biowarfare or a bioterrorist attack. The ProMED proposal for a Demonstration Program for Monitoring Emerging Diseases and ProMED-mail, the global public e-mail network for reporting outbreaks, are steps toward implementing such a system.

Dr. Woodall is the Director of FAS ProMED-mail and the Director of the Arbovirus Laboratory, Wadsworth Center, New York State Department of Health.

To subscribe to ProMED-mail, send to <majordomo@usa.healthnet.org> the text: subscribe promed. The Website addresses are: www.healthnet.org/programs/promed.html and www.outbreak.org/.

Address correspondence to Dr. Woodall, Griffin Laboratory, 5668 State Farm Road, Slingerlands NY 12159; tel. 518-869-4524; fax 518-869-4530; e-mail <woodall@wadsworth.org>.

References

1. Lederberg J. Infection emergent. JAMA 1996;275:243–245.
2. Morse SS. Global monitoring of emerging diseases: design for a demonstration program. Health Policy. In press.

REVIEW ARTICLE

Anthrax as a Potential Biological Warfare Agent

James C. Pile, MD; John D. Malone, MD; Edward M. Eitzen, MD, MPH; Arthur M. Friedlander, MD

Anthrax is a zoonotic illness recognized since antiquity. Today, human anthrax has been all but eradicated from the industrialized world, with the vast majority of practitioners in the United States unlikely to have seen a case. Unfortunately, the disease remains endemic in many areas of the world, and anthrax poses a threat as a mass casualty–producing weapon if used in a biological warfare capacity. *Arch Intern Med. 1998;158:429-434*

Anthrax has been described for millennia, beginning with the fifth Egyptian plague (circa 1500 BC). Virgil recorded a lyrical description of anthrax in 25 BC, and the disease became known during the Middle Ages as the "Black Bane."[1,2] In the 1870s, Robert Koch demonstrated for the first time the bacterial origin of a specific disease, with his studies on experimental anthrax, and also discovered the spore stage that allows persistence of the organism in the environment. Shortly afterward, John Bell recognized *Bacillus anthracis* as the cause of woolsorter disease (inhalational anthrax), and was instrumental in establishing wool disinfection procedures. The disinfection measures proved effective in reducing the incidence of woolsorter disease, and they became standard in the British woolen industry.[3,4] William Greenfield's successful immunization of livestock against anthrax soon followed in 1880, although Louis Pasteur's 1881 trial of a heat-cured anthrax vaccine in sheep is usually remembered as the initial use of a live vaccine.[5]

EPIDEMIOLOGY

Livestock

Anthrax is a disease of herbivores, with sheep, goats, cattle, and, to a lesser degree, swine typically infected. Gastrointestinal anthrax with subsequent systemic dissemination is acquired by livestock after grazing on forage plants contaminated by spores. Anthrax may persist in the environment for many years after contamination of a pasture. Environmental persistence appears to be related to a number of factors, including high levels of soil nitrogen and organic content, a pH level higher than 6.0, and ambient temperature higher than 15°C. Drought or heavy rains trigger spore germination and bacterial multiplication, which also appear important in maintaining the organism in potentially infectious quantities.[6] Blowflies and vultures have been implicated in the persistence and spread of anthrax in Africa.[7]

Once prevalent in nearly all areas where livestock were raised, intensive animal vaccination programs have now restricted anthrax mainly to Africa and Asia. Sporadic outbreaks still occur in many other countries including the United States, where an "anthrax belt" extends across the Great Plains.[8] Incidence of the disease has actually increased in Africa in recent years, prompting the World Health Organization to seek to improve surveillance and control efforts. An effective live spore vaccine is marketed by a South African firm for 10 cents per dose (1994 cost), but vaccination in the developing world remains spotty.[9]

This article is also available on our Web site: www.ama-assn.org/internal.

From the Infectious Diseases Division, National Naval Medical Center, Bethesda, Md (Drs Pile and Malone), and the US Army Medical Research Institute of Infectious Diseases, Frederick, Md (Drs Eitzen and Friedlander).

Human

Human cases of anthrax have traditionally fallen into 2 categories, either agricultural or industrial. Agricultural cases consist of laborers in direct contact with infected animals (herders, butchers, and slaughterhouse workers), and industrial cases involve individuals in contact with infected animal products, in particular workers in animal hair processing mills and those handling bonemeal. Not surprisingly, cases in the developed world have tended to be of the industrial variety. Glassman[10] estimated that the worldwide incidence of anthrax in 1958 was between 20 000 and 100 000 cases annually. The incidence may be considerably lower today; however, anthrax is not a reportable disease in more than half of African nations,[9] and the true frequency of the disease is unknown. In the United States, the total annual incidence has fallen from an average of nearly 130 cases in the early part of the 20th century to less than 1 case annually over the past 2 decades. Of the 235 cases reported between 1955 and 1994, 224 were cutaneous and 11 inhalational, and 20 were fatal.[8,11] Most of the US cases in recent decades have resulted from exposure to wool or animal hair.[12]

Human cases are invariably zoonotic in origin, with no convincing data to suggest that human-to-human transmission has ever taken place. Primary disease takes 1 of 3 forms. Cutaneous, the most common, results from contact with an infected animal or animal products. Inhalational is much less common and a result of spore deposition in the lungs, while gastrointestinal is due to ingestion of infected meat. Most literature cites cutaneous disease as constituting 95% of cases, with inhalational disease responsible for 5% and the gastrointestinal form for 0% to 5%; however, the incidence of inhalational anthrax in less industrialized nations is probably lower. Gastrointestinal disease, which has never been reported in the United States, may be more common in the developing world.

Epidemics of human anthrax have been reported, with the 2 most completely described outbreaks from Zimbabwe in 1978 through 1980, and from Sverdlovsk, in the former Soviet Union, in 1979.[13-19] The Zimbabwe epidemic followed on the heels of a cattle outbreak that arose after the breakdown of veterinary care during the Rhodesian civil war. Thousands of human cases resulted, with 1 province alone reporting nearly 6500 infections (virtually all cutaneous), with approximately 100 fatalities.[15-17] The Sverdlovsk (now Yekaterinburg) incident occurred in April 1979 in an industrial city of 1.2 million people just east of the Ural Mountains. Eventually, admissions were made that deaths were due to inhalational anthrax, the result of a mishap at a military microbiology facility, and not to gastrointestinal anthrax as was originally claimed.[18,19] At least 66 deaths occurred in a 4-km swath downwind from the incident, and the details of autopsies performed on 42 patients were eventually published by 2 of the pathologists involved.[14,18] Of interest, the youngest patient known to have been infected in the incident was 24 years old, and a large series of inhalational anthrax cases from southwest Russia earlier this century was also remarkable for a near-total absence of children.[13] Consequently, it has been suggested that the inhalational form of the disease may have a predilection for older patients, although this remains unproven.

MICROBIOLOGY

Bacillus anthracis is a large (1-1.5 ×3-10 μm) gram-positive sporulating rod, with square or concave ends. Growing readily on sheep blood agar, *B anthracis* forms rough gray-white colonies of 4 to 5 mm, with characteristic comma-shaped or "comet-tail" protrusions. Several tests are helpful in differentiating *B anthracis* from other *Bacillus* species. *Bacillus anthracis* is characterized by an absence of the following: hemolysis, motility, growth on phenylethyl alcohol blood agar, gelatin hydrolysis, and salicin fermentation. In the United States, *Bacillus* isolates lacking these characteristics and having morphological features on Gram staining consistent with *B anthracis* should be submitted to the Centers for Disease Control and Prevention via the state laboratory. *Bacillus anthracis* may also be identified by the API-20E and API-50CHB systems used in conjunction with the previously mentioned biochemical tests.[20,21] Definitive identification is based on immunological demonstration of the production of protein toxin components and the poly-D-glutamic acid capsule, susceptibility to a specific bacteriophage, and virulence for mice and guinea pigs.

PATHOGENESIS

The virulence of *B anthracis* is dependent on 2 toxins, lethal toxin and edema toxin, as well as on the bacterial capsule. The importance of a toxin in pathogenesis was demonstrated in the early 1950s, when sterile plasma from anthrax-infected guinea pigs caused disease when injected into other animals.[22] Efforts since have shown the anthrax toxins to be composed of 3 entities, which in concert lead to some of the clinical effects of anthrax.[23,24] The first of these, protective antigen, is an 83-kd protein so named because it is the main protective constituent of anthrax vaccines.[25] The protective antigen binds to target cell receptors and is then proteolytically shorn of a 20-kd fragment. A second binding domain is then exposed, which combines with either edema factor, an 89-kd protein, to form edema toxin, or lethal factor, a 90-kd protein, to form lethal toxin.[26] The respective toxins are then transported across the cell membrane, and the factors are released into the cytosol where they exert their effects. Edema factor, a calmodulin-dependent adenylate cyclase, acts by converting adenosine triphosphate to cyclic adenosine monophosphate. Intracellular cyclic adenosine monophosphate levels are thereby increased, leading to the edema characteristic of the disease.[27] The action of lethal factor, believed to be a metalloprotease, is less understood. Work in recent years has shown edema toxin to inhibit neutrophil phagocytosis.[28] Lethal toxin has been demonstrated at high concentration to lyse macrophages, while inducing the release of tumor necrosis factor and interleukin 1 at lower concentrations.[29,30]

Hanna and colleagues[29] recently showed that a combination of antibodies to interleukin 1 and tumor necrosis factor was protective against a lethal challenge of anthrax toxin in mice, as was the human interleukin 1 receptor antagonist. Macrophage-depleted mice were shown to resist lethal toxin challenge, but to succumb when macrophages were reconstituted. The importance of the poly-D-glutamic acid bacterial capsule, the other major virulence determinant, was demonstrated in experiments early in the 20th century in which an unencapsulated strain resulted in attenuation.[31] Presumably, the capsule enhances virulence by preventing phagocytosis, and perhaps by preventing lysis of the organism by cationic host proteins.[32] The genes for both the toxin and the capsule are known to be encoded by plasmids, designated pXO1[33] and pXO2, respectively.[34,35]

Disease occurs when spores enter the body, germinate to the bacillary form, and multiply. In cutaneous disease spores gain entry through cuts, abrasions, or in some cases through certain species of biting flies.[2,15-17] Germination is thought to take place in macrophages, and toxin release results in edema and tissue necrosis but little or no purulence, probably because of inhibitory effects of the toxins on leukocytes. Generally, cutaneous disease remains localized, although if untreated it may become systemic in 5% to 20% of cases, with dissemination via the lymphatics.[36] In the gastrointestinal form, *B anthracis* is ingested in spore-contaminated meat, and may invade anywhere in the gastrointestinal tract. Transport to mesenteric or other regional lymph nodes and replication occur, resulting in dissemination, bacteremia, and a high mortality rate. Very little pathologic correlation is available for this unusual form of the disease; however, autopsies from Russian cases earlier this century suggest that the initial site of infection is most commonly the terminal ileum or cecum.[13] As in other forms of anthrax, involved nodes show an impressive degree of hemorrhage and necrosis.

The pathogenesis of inhalational anthrax is better studied and understood. Inhaled spores are ingested by pulmonary macrophages and carried to hilar and mediastinal lymph nodes, where they germinate and multiply, elaborating toxins and overwhelming the clearance ability of the regional nodes.[37,38] Bacteremia occurs, and death soon follows. A significant inoculum of spores is necessary for disease to develop; one study in mill workers found that unvaccinated subjects inhaled between 140 and 690 anthrax spores of 5 µm or less (ie, potentially pathogenic) per day without apparent ill effects.[39] Another study of healthy workers in a goat hair processing factory found that 14 of 101 subjects had *B anthracis* isolated from either the nose or the pharynx.[40] The minimum infectious inhaled dose for humans is unknown, and in nonhuman primate studies it has ranged from approximately 4000 to 80 000 spores.[41]

Fritz and colleagues[38] in their autopsy study of inhalational anthrax in rhesus monkeys found hemorrhagic, edematous lymph nodes not only in the mediastinum, but also in the mesenteric, axillary, and inguinal chains, reinforcing the systemic nature of inhalational disease. Some of the monkeys were also found to have hemorrhagic changes in the meninges, lung parenchyma, gastrointestinal tract, pancreas, myocardium, and kidneys. All monkeys tested had heavy loads of *B anthracis* in the blood at the time of death. In an earlier study in rhesus monkeys, intrathoracic nodes were more frequently involved than other lymph nodes.[42] Similar findings were reported in the Sverdlovsk autopsy series.[14] The latter study also shed more light on the inhalational form of the disease, and underscored the systemic nature of the process. Subjects of all 42 autopsies had severe hemorrhagic mediastinitis and lymphadenitis, with 11 showing focal hemorrhagic, necrotizing pneumonia at what was thought likely to be the portal of entry. All but 3 of the cases had evidence of submucosal gastrointestinal tract involvement consistent with hematogenous spread. Hemorrhagic lymphadenitis of the mesenteric nodes was evidenced in 9 of 42 subjects, and the well-recognized propensity of *B anthracis* to cross the blood-brain barrier was emphasized, with fully half demonstrating a hemorrhagic meningitis. The pathologists stressed the remarkable degree of edema seen in their cases, particularly in the leptomeningeal and pulmonary areas, with pleural effusions and a gelatinous mediastinitis commonly found.[14]

CLINICAL MANIFESTATIONS

Cutaneous disease develops an average of 2 to 5 days after exposure (range, 12 hours to 5 days in Gold's series of 117 cases),[43] beginning as a nondescript papule that during the next 24 to 48 hours becomes vesicular, usually 1 to 2 cm in diameter. A striking degree of edema surrounding the lesion is typical, and lesions on the head and neck have a propensity for impressive presentations, on occasion leading to airway compromise.[44] *Bacillus anthracis* is easily isolated from the vesicular fluid and visible on Gram staining at this stage, although neutrophils are conspicuously absent. The lesion, which is sometimes pruritic but not painful, generally ruptures near the end of the first week, leaving an ulcer that progresses to the characteristic black eschar that gave the disease its name (anthrax is derived from the Greek word for coal). The eschar generally sloughs 2 to 3 weeks after appearance. Many patients exhibit fever, headache, malaise, and regional lymphadenopathy. Differential diagnosis includes tularemia, plague, cutaneous diphtheria, staphylococcal disease, rickettsial infection, and orf, a viral disease of livestock. Recovery is the rule, although a fatality rate of 5% to 20% in untreated disease is frequently cited, due to dissemination of disease and resulting septicemia. Mortality in treated patients is less than 1% (1 of 117 patients in Gold's series).[43] Although use of antibiotics prevents dissemination, they do not affect the natural history of the lesion, which progresses through the described sequence despite therapy.

Gastrointestinal anthrax begins 2 to 5 days after ingesting contaminated meat, and has been described in 2 rare forms. One form presents as severe abdominal pain, hematemesis, melena and/or hematochezia, ascites, and on occasion profuse, watery diarrhea.[8,44] Mortality is high, and the disease is difficult to diagnose antemortem except in an epidemic setting. An oropharyngeal variant has also been described, with a 1982 outbreak involving 24 patients in Thailand secondary to eating infected cattle and water buffalo. All had marked neck swelling, most had ulcerative lesions of the oropharynx, and 3 of the 24 died.[45,46]

Inhalational anthrax begins after a 1- to 6-day incubation period following exposure. A nonspecific syndrome consisting of low-grade fever, nonproductive cough, myalgias, and malaise is initially present, with transient improvement in some patients after 2 to 4 days. Abrupt onset of respiratory distress ensues, with shock and death typically following in less than 24 hours. The initial phase is essentially impossible to diagnose in the absence of a known outbreak. Advanced disease may be suspected on the basis of the characteristically widened mediastinum and pleural effusions despite otherwise normal chest x-ray findings. Historically, inhalational anthrax was considered uniformly fatal; however, this was based on case reports prior to the advent of intensive care unit treatment, and there were at least 11 survivors in the Sverdlovsk incident.[18] As in the Sverdlovsk experience, systemic anthrax is complicated by meningitis in up to 50% of cases, is usually bloody, and is sometimes associated with subarachnoid hemorrhage.[47]

TREATMENT

Penicillin remains the drug of choice for treatment of susceptible strains of anthrax, with ciprofloxacin and doxycycline suitable alternatives. Some data in experimental models of infection suggest that the addition of streptomycin to penicillin may be helpful. Penicillin resistance remains extremely rare in naturally occurring strains[48]; however, the possibility of resistance should be suspected in a biological warfare attack. Cutaneous anthrax may be treated orally, while gastrointestinal or inhalational disease should receive high doses of intravenous antibiotics (penicillin G, 4 million units every 4 hours; ciprofloxacin, 400 mg every 12 hours; or doxycycline hyclate, 100 mg every 12 hours). The more severe forms will require intensive supportive care and have a high mortality rate despite optimal therapy. The use of antianthrax serum, while no longer available for human use except in the former Soviet Union, was thought to be of some use in the preantibiotic era, although no controlled studies were performed.[49] Antitoxin was reportedly used in the Sverdlovsk epidemic.[18] Reconsideration of the use of antitoxin in cases of systemic anthrax seems reasonable, along with development of cytokine-modulating agents.[29]

VACCINES

Although anthrax vaccination dates to the early studies of Greenfield and Pasteur, the "modern" era of anthrax vaccine development began with Sterne's work with a toxin-producing, unencapsulated (attenuated) strain in the 1930s. Administered to livestock as a single dose with a yearly booster, the vaccine was highly immunogenic and well tolerated in most species, although somewhat virulent in goats and llamas. This preparation is essentially the same as that administered to livestock around the world today.[50] The first human vaccine was developed in 1943 at the Soviets' Sanitary Technical Institute from nonencapsulated strains. This live spore vaccine, similar to Sterne's product, is administered by scarification with a yearly booster. Soviet studies show a reduced risk of 5- to 15-fold in occupationally exposed workers.[51]

The British and US vaccines were developed in the 1950s and early 1960s, with the US product an aluminum hydroxide–adsorbed cell-free culture filtrate of an unencapsulated strain (V770-NP1-R), and the British an alum-precipitated cell-free filtrate of a Sterne strain culture. The US vaccine has been shown to induce high levels of antibody only to protective antigen, while the British vaccine induces lower levels of antibody to protective antigen but measurable antibodies against lethal factor and edema factor.[52,53] Neither vaccine has been examined in a human clinical efficacy trial, although a study using a vaccine similar to the current US product was carried out in at-risk mill workers in the northeastern United States. The vaccine had an overall efficacy rate against cutaneous anthrax of 92.5%, although it should be noted that the study was not sufficiently statistically powered to assess protection against inhalational anthrax. Thirty-five percent of the recipients reported some type of reaction to vaccination. The preponderance of these events were minor, with 0.7% of recipients reporting systemic and 2.4% experiencing significant local effects with the first dose, rising to 1.3% with systemic and 2.7% with significant local effects with subsequent doses.[54] Manufacturer labeling for the current Michigan Department of Public Health anthrax vaccine adsorbed (AVA) product cites a 30% rate of mild local reactions and a 4% rate of moderate local reactions with a second dose.[55] The current complex dosing schedule for the AVA vaccine, derived from the aforementioned trial in mill workers, consists of 0.5 mL administered subcutaneously at 0, 2, and 4 weeks, and 6, 12, and 18 months, followed by yearly boosters.

Animal studies examining the efficacy of available anthrax vaccines against aerosolized exposure have been performed. While some guinea pig studies question vaccine efficacy,[56,57] primate studies support its role. In recent work, rhesus monkeys immunized with 2 doses of the AVA vaccine were challenged with lethal doses of aerosolized *B anthracis* spores. All monkeys in the control group died 3 to 5 days after exposure, while the vaccinated monkeys were protected up to 2 years after immunization.[58] Another trial used the AVA vaccine in a 2-dose series with a slightly different dosing interval, and again found it to be protective in all rhesus monkeys exposed to lethal aerosol challenge.[59] Thus, available evidence suggests that 2 doses of the current AVA vaccine should be efficacious against an aerosol exposure to anthrax spores. In addition, a highly purified, minimally reactogenic, recombinant protective antigen vaccine has been investigated, using aluminum as well as other adjuvants. Other approaches include cloning the protective antigen gene into a variety of bacteria and viruses, and the development of mutant, avirulent strains of *B anthracis*.[60-63]

BIOLOGICAL WARFARE ASPECTS

Recent incidents, such as the use of sarin in the Tokyo subway system and the bombing of the World Trade Center in New York City and the Oklahoma City Federal Building, as well as concerns over the potential use of biological and chemical weapons during the Persian Gulf War, underscore the threat of biological warfare either on the battlefield or by terrorists. Anthrax has been the focus of much attention as a potential biological warfare agent for at least 6 decades. Modeling studies have shown the potential for use in an offensive capacity. Dispersal experiments with the simulant *Bacillus globigii* in the New York subway system in the 1960s suggested that release of a similar amount of *B anthracis* during rush hour would result in 10 000 deaths.[64] On a larger scale, the World Health Organization estimated that 50 kg of *B anthracis* released upwind of a population center of 500 000 would result in up to 95 000 fatalities, with an additional 125 000 persons incapacitated.[65] Both on the battlefield and in a terrorist strike, *B anthracis* has the attribute of being potentially undetectable until large numbers of seriously ill individuals present with characteristic signs and symptoms of inhalational anthrax.

Given these findings, efforts to prevent disease are of obvious importance. The US military's current M17 and M40 gas masks provide excellent protection against the 1- to 5-μm particulates needed for a successful aerosol attack. Assuming a correct fit, these masks would be highly effective if in use at the time of exposure. Some protection might also be afforded by various forms of shelter. The preexposure use of the current AVA anthrax vaccine, which is approved by the US Food and Drug Administration, appears to be an important adjunct. Results of primate studies also support the concept of postexposure antibiotic prophylaxis. Work by Friedlander et al[66] showed that 7 of 10 monkeys given penicillin, 8 of 9 given ciprofloxacin, 9 of 10 treated with doxycycline, and all 9 receiving doxycycline plus postexposure vaccination survived a lethal aerosol challenge, with all animals receiving antibiotics for 30 days following exposure. Earlier research suggested that short courses of prophylactic antibiotics delayed but did not prevent clinical disease.[67] Accordingly, in the event of documented exposure, prolonged prophylactic antibiotic use, as well as vaccination, would be mandatory. In the biological warfare setting, the differential diagnosis of inhalational anthrax would include plague and tularemia. Fluoroquinolones also have activity against these diseases, supporting the use of ciprofloxacin and perhaps other drugs of this class as either a preexposure or postexposure measure.

CONCLUSION

The inhalational form of anthrax remains a legitimate and perhaps growing military and terrorist threat in the current world situation. Knowledge of inhalational anthrax is necessary for public health officials, as well as the health care providers who would be called on to care for casualties. Important methods of prevention include properly fitting protective masks capable of filtering 1- to 5-μm particles, the use of preexposure and postexposure antibiotics, and the use of preexposure and postexposure vaccination. All these measures would be expected to provide a substantial degree of protection against aerosolized *B anthracis*; not all, however, are easily applicable to a civilian setting. Consequently, the morbidity and mortality of an attack might still be high.

Accepted for publication July 31, 1997.

The views expressed herein are those of the authors and do not necessarily reflect the views of the US Army, US Navy, or the US Department of Defense.

Reprints: James C. Pile, MD, Infectious Diseases Division, National Naval Medical Center, 8901 Wisconsin Ave, Bethesda, MD 20889-5600.

REFERENCES

1. Dirckx JH. Virgil on anthrax. *Am J Dermatopathol.* 1981;3:191-195.
2. Turnbull PCB. *Bacillus.* In: Baron S, ed. *Medical Microbiology.* 3rd ed. New York, NY: Churchill Livingstone Inc; 1991:249-262.
3. Wool disinfection and anthrax: a year's working of the model station. *Lancet.* December 16, 1922:1295-1296.
4. Eurich FW. The history of anthrax in the wool industry of Bradford, and of its control. *Lancet.* January 2, 1926:57-58.
5. Tigertt WD. Anthrax: William Smith Greenfield, MD, FRCP, professor superintendent, the Brown Animal Sanatory Institution (1878-81)—concerning the priority due to him for the production of the first vaccine against anthrax. *J Hyg (Lond).* 1980;85:415-420.
6. Kaufmann AF. Observations on the ocurrence of anthrax as related to soil type and rainfall. *Salisbury Med Bull Suppl.* 1990;68:16-17.
7. De Vos V, Bryden HB. Anthrax in the Kruger National Park: temporal and spatial patterns of disease occurrence. *Salisbury Med Bull Suppl.* 1996;87:26-30.
8. Brachman PS, Friedlander AM. Anthrax. In: Plotkin SA, Mortimer EA, eds. *Vaccines.* 2nd ed. Philadelphia, Pa: WB Saunders Co; 1994:729-739.
9. Anthrax control and research, with special reference to national programme development in Africa: memorandum from a WHO meeting. *Bull World Health Organ.* 1994;72:13-22.
10. Glassman HN. World incidence of anthrax in man. *Public Health Rep.* 1958;73:22-24.
11. Centers for Disease Control and Prevention. Summary of notifiable diseases, 1945-1994. *MMWR Morb Mortal Wkly Rep.* 1994;43:70-78.
12. Whitford HW. Incidence of anthrax in the USA: 1945-1988. *Salisbury Med Bull Suppl.* 1990;68:5-7.
13. Walker DH, Yampolskaya O, Grinberg LM. Death at Sverdlovsk: what have we learned? *Am J Pathol.* 1994;144:1135-1141.
14. Abramova FA, Grinberg LM, Yampolskaya OV, Walker DH. Pathology of inhalational anthrax in 42 cases from the Sverdlovsk outbreak of 1979. *Proc Natl Acad Sci U S A.* 1993;90:2291-2294.
15. Davies JCA. A major epidemic of anthrax in Zimbabwe, part I. *Cent Afr J Med.* 1982;28:291-298.
16. Davies JCA. A major epidemic of anthrax in Zimbabwe, part II. *Cent Afr J Med.* 1983;29:8-12.
17. Davies JCA. A major epidemic of anthrax in Zimbabwe, part III. *Cent Afr J Med.* 1985;31:176-179.
18. Meselson M, Guillemin J, Hugh-Jones M, et al. The Sverdlovsk anthrax outbreak of 1979. *Science.* 1994;266:1202-1208.
19. Wade N. Death at Sverdlovsk: a critical diagnosis. *Science.* 1980;209:1501-1502.

20. Cogne R, Stares NE, Jones MN, Bowen JE, Turnbull PCB, Boeufgras JM. Identification of *Bacillus anthracis* using the 50CHB system. *Salisbury Med Bull Suppl.* 1996;87:34-35.
21. The aerobic gram-positive bacilli. In: Koneman EW, Allen SD, Janda WM, Schreckenberger PC, Winn WC, eds. *Color Atlas and Textbook of Diagnostic Microbiology.* 4th ed. Philadelphia, Pa: JB Lippincott; 1992:467-518.
22. Smith H, Keppie J. Observations on experimental anthrax: demonstration of a specific lethal factor produced in vivo by *Bacillus anthracis. Nature.* 1954;173:869-870.
23. Stanley JL, Smith H. Purification of factor I and recognition of a third factor of the anthrax toxin. *J Gen Microbiol.* 1961;26:49-66.
24. Beall FA, Taylor MJ, Thorne CB. Rapid lethal effect in rats of a third component found upon fractionating the toxin of *Bacillus anthracis. J Bacteriol.* 1962;83:1274-1280.
25. Lincoln RE, Fish DC. Anthrax toxin. In: Montie TC, Kadis S, Ajl SJ, eds. *Microbial Toxins, Volume III: Bacterial Protein Toxins.* New York, NY: Academic Press; 1970:361-414.
26. Leppla SH, Friedlander AM, Singh Y, Cora EM, Bhatnagar R. A model for anthrax toxic action at the cellular level. *Salisbury Med Bull Suppl.* 1990;68:41-43.
27. Leppla SH. Anthrax toxin edema factor: a bacterial adenylate cyclase that increases cyclic AMP concentrations in eukaryotic cells. *Proc Natl Acad Sci U S A.* 1982;79:3162-3166.
28. O'Brien J, Friedlander A, Dreier T, Ezzell J, Leppla S. Effects of anthrax toxin components on human neutrophils. *Infect Immunol.* 1985;47:306-310.
29. Hanna PC, Acosta D, Collier RJ. On the role of macrophages in anthrax. *Proc Natl Acad Sci U S A.* 1993;90:10198-10201.
30. Friedlander AM. Macrophages are sensitive to anthrax lethal toxin through acid-dependent process. *J Biol Chem.* 1986;261:7123-7126.
31. Ball O. Cited by: Sterne M. Anthrax. In: Stableforth AW, Galloway IA, eds. *Infectious Diseases of Animals, Volume I.* London, England: Butterworth Scientific Publications; 1959:22.
32. Keppie J, Harris-Smith PW, Smith H. The chemical basis of the virulence of *Bacillus anthracis*, IX: its aggressins and their mode of action. *Br J Exp Pathol.* 1963;44:446-453.
33. Mikesell P, Ivins BE, Ristroph JD, Dreier TM. Evidence for plasmid-mediated toxin production in *Bacillus anthracis. Infect Immunol.* 1983;39:371-376.
34. Green BD, Battisti L, Koehler TM, Thorne CB, Ivins BE. Demonstration of a capsule plasmid in *Bacillus anthracis. Infect Immunol.* 1985;49:291-297.
35. Uchida I, Sekizaki T, Hashimoto K, Terakado N. Association of the encapsulation of *Bacillus anthracis* with a 60-megadalton plasmid. *J Gen Microbiol.* 1985;131:363-367.
36. Longfield R. Anthrax. In: Strickland GT, ed. *Hunter's Tropical Medicine.* 7th ed. Philadelphia, Pa: WB Saunders Co; 1991:434-438.
37. Ross JM. The pathogenesis of anthrax following the administration of spores by the respiratory route. *J Pathol Bacteriol.* 1957;73:485-494.
38. Fritz DL, Jaax NK, Lawrence WB, et al. Pathology of experimental inhalation anthrax in the rhesus monkey. *Lab Invest.* 1995;73:691-702.
39. Dahlgren CM, Buchanan LM, Decker HM, Freed SW, Phillips CR, Brachman PS. *Bacillus anthracis* aerosols in goat hair processing mills. *Am J Hyg.* 1960;72:24-31.
40. Carr EA, Rew R. Recovery of *Bacillus anthracis* from the nose and throat of apparently healthy workers. *J Infect Dis.* 1957;100:169-171.
41. Watson A, Keir D. Information on which to base assessments of risk from environments contaminated with anthrax spores. *Epidemiol Infect.* 1994;113:479-490.
42. Gleiser CA, Berdjis CC, Hartman HA, Gochenour WS. Pathology of experimental respiratory anthrax in *Macaca mulatta. Br J Exp Pathol.* 1963;44:416-426.
43. Gold H. Anthrax: a report of 117 cases. *Arch Intern Med.* 1955;96:387-396.
44. Brachman PS. Anthrax. In: Hoeprich PD, Jordan MC, Ronald AR, eds. *Infectious Diseases.* 5th ed. Philadelphia, Pa: JB Lippincott Co; 1994:1003-1008.
45. Sirisanthana T, Navachareon N, Tharavichitkul P, Sirisanthana V, Brown AE. Outbreak of oral-oropharyngeal anthrax: an unusual manifestation of human infection with *Bacillus anthracis. Am J Trop Med Hyg.* 1984;33:144-150.
46. Sirisanthana T, Nelson KE, Ezell JW, Abshire TG. Serological studies of patients with cutaneous and oral-oropharyngeal anthrax from northern Thailand. *Am J Trop Med Hyg.* 1988;39:575-581.
47. Levy LM, Baker N, Meyer MP, Crosland P, Hampton J. Anthrax meningitis in Zimbabwe. *Cent Afr J Med.* 1981;27:101-104.
48. Lightfoot NF, Scott RJD, Turnbull BCB. Antimicrobial susceptibility of *Bacillus anthracis. Salisbury Med Bull Suppl.* 1990;68:95-98.
49. Knudson GB. Treatment of anthrax in man: history and current concepts. *Mil Med.* 1986;151:71-77.
50. Turnbull PCB. Anthrax vaccines: past, present, and future. *Vaccine.* 1991;9:533-539.
51. Shlyakhov EN, Rubenstein E. Human live anthrax vaccine in the former USSR. *Vaccine.* 1994;12:727-730.
52. Turnbull PCB, Broster MG, Carman JA, Manchee RJ, Melling J. Development of antibodies to protective antigen and lethal factor components of anthrax toxin in humans and guinea pigs and their relevance to protective immunity. *Infect Immunol.* 1986;52:356-363.
53. Turnbull PCB, Leppla SH, Broster MG, Quinn CP, Melling J. Antibodies to anthrax toxin in humans and guinea pigs and their relevance to protective immunity. *Med Microbiol Immunol.* 1988;177:293-303.
54. Brachman PS, Gold H, Plotkin SA, Fekety FR, Werrin M, Ingraham NR. Field evaluation of a human anthrax vaccine. *Am J Public Health.* 1962;52:632-645.
55. Anthrax vaccine adsorbed [package insert]. Lansing: Michigan Dept of Public Health; 1987.
56. Little SF, Knudson GB. Comparative efficacy of *Bacillus anthracis* live spore vaccine and protective antigen vaccine against anthrax in the guinea pig. *Infect Immunol.* 1986;52:509-512.
57. Broster MG, Hibbs SE. Protective efficacy of anthrax vaccines against aerosol challenge. *Salisbury Med Bull Suppl.* 1990;68:91-92.
58. Ivins BE, Fellows PF, Pitt MLM, et al. Efficacy of a standard human anthrax vaccine against *Bacillus anthracis* aerosol spore challenge in rhesus monkeys. *Salisbury Med Bull Suppl.* 1996;87:125-126.
59. Pitt MLM, Ivins BE, Estep JE, Farchaus J, Friedlander AM. Comparison of the efficacy of purified protective antigen and MDPH to protect nonhuman primates from inhalational anthrax. *Salisbury Med Bull Suppl.* 1996;87:130.
60. Ivins BE, Welkos SL, Little SF, Crumrine MH, Nelson GO. Immunization against anthrax with *Bacillus anthracis* protective antigen combined with adjuvants. *Infect Immunol.* 1992;60:662-668.
61. Iacono-Connors LC, Welkos SL, Ivins BEW, Dalrymple JM. Protection against anthrax with recombinant virus–expressed protective antigen in experimental animals. *Infect Immunol.* 1991;59:1961-1965.
62. Ivins BE, Welkos SL. Cloning and expression of the *Bacillus anthracis* protective antigen gene in *Bacillus subtilis. Infect Immunol.* 1986;54:537-542.
63. Ivins BE, Welkos SL, Knudson GB, Little SF. Immunization against anthrax with aromatic compound-dependent (aro-) mutants of *Bacillus anthracis* and with recombinant strains of *Bacillus subtilis* that produce anthrax protective antigen. *Infect Immunol.* 1990;58:303-308.
64. *Health Aspects of Chemical and Biological Weapons.* Geneva, Switzerland: World Health Organization; 1970.
65. Huxsoll DL, Parrott CD, Patrick WC. Medicine in defense against biological warfare. *JAMA.* 1989;262:677-679.
66. Friedlander AM, Welkos SL, Pitt MLM, et al. Postexposure prophylaxis against experimental inhalation anthrax. *J Infect Dis.* 1993;167:1239-1242.
67. Henderson DW, Peacock S, Belton FC. Observations on the prophylaxis of experimental pulmonary anthrax in the monkey. *J Hyg.* 1956;54:28-36.

ARTICLES

BIOTERRORISM

AMERICA'S NEWEST WAR GAME

by Peter Pringle

"Catastrophic Terrorism" roars the headline over an article in the current *Foreign Affairs*. The three distinguished authors—John Deutch, a former director of Central Intelligence; Ashton Carter, an ex-Pentagon assistant secretary; and Philip Zelikow, a former member of the National Security Council—declare with unswerving certainty that "the danger of weapons of mass destruction being used against America and its allies is greater now than at any time since the Cuban Missile Crisis of 1962." Any act of "catastrophic terrorism," they say, could have the effect of Pearl Harbor; it could divide America into a "before and after."

This is no shot across the bow of a sleeping ship. America is now spending $7 billion a year defending itself against backpack nuclear bombs, canisters of nerve gas and petri dishes of germ weapons planted in crowded cities by an as-yet-unknown adversary. So many different agencies are shoring up the nation's defenses against mega-terrorism, says the government auditor, that it's hard to keep track of where all the money is going, let alone whether it is being spent wisely.

Any new government project tagged with the word "terrorism" goes to the top of the pile in Congress. The Pentagon is ordering devices to sniff out nerve gases and deadly germs. National Guard units that normally deal with floods and hurricanes are being trained as chemical and biological SWAT teams. Under the threat of another war with Iraq, all 2.4 million American troops are being vaccinated against anthrax, and companies are scrambling to provide the vaccines—including, notably, a company founded by Adm. William Crowe Jr., a former chairman of the Joint Chiefs of Staff. The FBI wants to send more agents into embassies abroad and is demanding its own planes to shuttle investigative teams around the world. Local and state governments used to dealing with flu epidemics are preparing for the nightmare gas or microbe attack. And one can only imagine what antiterrorist projects the CIA has been dreaming up with its "black" budget of covert ops. Now the players in this new war game have got a new title for their grim pursuit.

The thrust of "Catastrophic Terrorism" is a grand reorganization of the Pentagon, CIA and FBI bureaucracies to eliminate the perennial agency overlaps and gaps between "foreign" and "domestic" terrorism. The authors want to pool intelligence at the FBI, create new Catastrophic Terrorism Response Offices, already dubbed CTROs, and cut the two dozen agencies with shopping lists for vaccines, gas sniffers and protective clothing down to one—the Defense Department—because, they say, the Pentagon has the expertise when it comes to rapid acquisition. The operation sounds like it's a few steps short of war mobilization.

All but the new title, perhaps, could have been predicted (the original choice, "Grand Terrorism," was rejected on the grounds that there is nothing grand about this method of warfare). Beached by the fall of Communism and the end of the cold war, planners in the Pentagon and military think tanks have been circling a number of new threats: First it was drug wars and then "rogue" states; but international terrorism has an enduring quality in the annals of "threat politics." By dividing the phenomenon into two distinct parts—conventional and catastrophic—Deutch, the quintessential academic/consultant to the Pentagon and the defense industry, and his co-authors have mirrored the old cold war categories of conventional and nuclear weapons.

One must ask whether there is a way of averting chemical or biological catastrophe other than building Fortress America.

Conventional terrorist weapons are truck bombs filled with fertilizer explosive. Catastrophic terrorist weapons are nuclear, chemical and especially biological—the very weapons President Nixon renounced three decades ago in an effort to prevent their spread to other countries. The sixties US arsenal of biological weapons—then the world's largest and most sophisticated—has come back to haunt those now charged with the defense of the nation.

Chemical weapons of mass destruction have been used in state-sponsored warfare—by Iraq against Iran and its own Kurdish population—and fragments of Saddam Hussein's dismantled Scud missiles were alleged by US investigators to have traces of VX, the deadliest of all nerve gases. The worry is that such weapons could also be used by Islamic fundamentalist groups such as the one that President Clinton said he was concerned about when he recently authorized the firing of cruise missiles at a pharmaceutical plant in Sudan—or by groups such as the Japanese cult Aum Shinrikyo, or by homegrown US adherents to survivalism.

No one denies the threat of catastrophic terrorism, but the pace at which it has taken center stage as the prime threat to US security is almost as unnerving as the threat itself. In the media, Russian defectors talk alarmingly of new strains of untreatable anthrax and deadly cocktails of smallpox and Ebola; teenage hackers invade super-secret Pentagon computers; Aum Shinrikyo is said to be back in force, if not in action, after the Tokyo subway nerve gas incident; and three Texans are charged with plotting to assassinate President Clinton with a cactus needle coated with botulin flicked from a cigarette lighter.

Peter Pringle, a British journalist, reported on the end of the cold war from Washington and Moscow for The Independent *of London.*

Outside the calm of the international affairs departments of MIT and Harvard (where Deutch and Carter work), or the offices of the Washington Beltway "bandits" bulging with profits from new contracts related to terrorism, or indeed in the Pentagon itself, where new acronyms bloom, a sense of panic is in the air. Expert after expert says it's not a question of if but when this doomsday will occur. The media cast around for bogymen and find Russia with its rusting biological weapons labs and penniless scientists who could aid and abet the new bioterrorists.

Actually, in most years since 1980 the number of Americans killed by terrorists has been fewer than ten, but the toll can suddenly jump. In 1983, 271 Americans were killed by terrorist attacks, most of them in the bombing of the Marine barracks in Lebanon. Then came bombs at the World Trade Center in 1993 (six dead, 1,000 injured), the Oklahoma City federal building in 1995 (168 dead, 500 injured) and the Khobar Towers Air Force housing complex in Saudi Arabia in 1996 (nineteen dead, 500 injured). The World Trade Center in New York is often taken as a starting point for the new concern. What if the World Trade Center bomb had been nuclear, or had dispersed a deadly pathogen?

In the rush to play a new war game there is always a tendency to hype the threat. Last November Defense Secretary William Cohen appeared on TV holding a bag of sugar claiming the equivalent amount of anthrax spores would be enough to kill half the population of Washington, DC, an illustration that would only be valid if the dispersal were perfect and the wind were always blowing in the right direction. Republican Senator Fred Thompson, chairman of the Senate Governmental Affairs Committee, asked meekly of the terrorist threat, "Is it being overblown?" (The pun was apparently unintended.)

There is, after all, no 100 percent protection against chemical or biological weapons—as there was no 100 percent protection against nuclear weapons. That doesn't prevent the rise of a new threat industry, of course, but one must ask whether there is a way of averting catastrophe other than building Fortress America.

One of the true believers in the need for elaborate defenses against germ weapons is none other than President Clinton. He became a convert, and started pushing for stockpiles of vaccines, after reading—among all the intelligence reports on terrorism and the Iraq crisis—a novel titled *The Cobra Event*, about a fictitious germ attack on Manhattan using a mixture of smallpox and cold viruses. Chemical and biological warfare is great fiction material, of course, but are we in danger of being unable to separate fact from fiction?

The author of the novel, Richard Preston, also wrote a nonfiction account of the rise of "bioterrorism" in a March issue of *The New Yorker*. The article quoted a Russian who was involved in the Soviet biological weapons program named Kanatjan Alibekov, who had been the Number Two in charge of the weapons section of the archipelago of Soviet biological plants known as Biopreparat. He "defected" in 1992, a year after the fall of Communism, and changed his name to Ken Alibek. In *The New Yorker* he said the Soviets had built huge plants for the production of biological weapons.

In the 1972 Nixon-negotiated Biological Weapons Convention, which prohibited the development, production and stockpiling of these weapons, there was a loophole; the treaty did not prevent countries from building a production line for such weapons and keeping it in reserve. This is what the Soviets did—something US intelligence had known about for some time.

But Alibek claims that the Russians had actually used these facilities to produce tons of deadly anthrax, some of which had been genetically engineered so that available vaccines were useless, and some of which may have been put into the warheads of intercontinental ballistic missiles. Alibek also asserted that the Russians had experimented with deadly cocktails of smallpox spiked with the Ebola virus, which causes internal hemorrhaging, and with Venezuelan equine encephalitis, a brain virus.

For almost a dozen breathless pages, *The New Yorker* treated its readers to gruesome details of the power of these pathogens, pausing only when the author, himself out of puff, asked the key question: Does anyone believe Alibek? Or is he, as a defector who has apparently outlived his usefulness to the CIA's covert intelligence world, trying to make a buck in civvy street by exaggerating the importance of his information? Preston consulted an old cold warrior, Bill Patrick, the retired US biological warfare expert who was chief of product development for the US Army's biological warfare laboratories at Fort Detrick, Maryland. Patrick, quite reasonably for an old campaigner, takes the defector on trust; if Alibek doesn't know what the Soviets were doing, then who does? But other scientific experts, not given a hearing until page twelve of the thirteen-page *New Yorker* article, ranged from skeptical to dismissive.

One was Dr. Peter Jahrling, the chief scientist at the US Army medical research Institute of Infectious Diseases. He was one of Alibek's original debriefers. Jahrling told *The New Yorker*, "His [Alibek's] talk about chimeras [mixtures] of Ebola is sheer fantasy, in my opinion." Preston also consulted Joshua Lederberg, the Nobel Prize-winning molecular biologist and a member of a working group at the National Academy of Sciences who advises the government on biological weapons and the potential for terrorism. Lederberg told Preston, "It's not even clear to me that adding Ebola genes to smallpox would make it more deadly." Putting these comments higher up in the article would have been more responsible journalism, clearly, but it would also have spoiled the story.

The week before the *New Yorker* article ran, Alibek was given his first television exposure, on Diane Sawyer's *PrimeTime Live* show. "Biological weapons. They're real, they're here...smallpox, Ebola, anthrax," was how the hourlong show began. Alibek told Sawyer that the Russians had created a deadly genetic merger of smallpox and Ebola. "In this case, [the] mortality rate [is] about 90 percent, up to 100 percent. No treatment techniques," warned Alibek. "How many people could they have killed?" Sawyer asked him. "The entire population of Earth several times," he replied. ABC generously shared Alibek with the *New York Times*, which, in return, promoted Sawyer's show on its front page with an interview with the former Soviet scientist—including a warning (not mentioned by Sawyer) that Alibek was considered by US intelligence to be credible about the "subjects he knows firsthand...[but] less reliable on political and military issues."

Sawyer's search for Soviet malfeasance took her to Ekaterinburg (formerly the Soviet city of Sverdlovsk), where, in 1979, an accidental release of anthrax spores from a Soviet military compound killed more than sixty people. After reports of the accident reached the West through Soviet émigrés, Moscow claimed the deaths were because of anthrax-tainted meat (anthrax is endemic in the region). Matthew Meselson, the Harvard molecular biologist and the scientist who was instrumental in persuading Nixon to outlaw biological weapons in 1969, led a team of investigators to Sverdlovsk. In 1994 Meselson proved in an article in *Science*, the journal of the American Association for the Advancement of Science, that in fact there had been a release of anthrax spores from the military compound, and he confirmed nearly seventy deaths.

The risk in meeting a threat with new entities is that the old art of deterrence through international treaties may take a back seat.

But Sawyer, who spent four months researching the show, never interviewed Meselson or anyone from his team, including Jeanne Guillemin, a sociologist at Boston College who had cross-checked a Russian casualty list with hospital records, local interviews and grave sites. Instead, Sawyer referred to an unnamed director of a Sverdlovsk military hospital as saying there had been 259 victims—but not how many of the victims had died. Sawyer's staff called Professor Meselson the night before the program aired, but merely to ask his help with the pronunciation of a number of drugs used to treat the victims: penicillin, cephalosporin, chloramphenicol and corticosteroids.

In a further effort to suggest that more spookiness was afoot, Sawyer recorded that at the end of 1997 Russian scientists had published a paper in the British medical journal *Vaccine* describing the creation of a genetically engineered anthrax strain that was resistant to standard Russian anthrax vaccine. "Might the Russians be creating germs that can resist vaccines?" asked Sawyer. But was there really anything sinister about the Russian work? Were the Russian experiments threatening a new kind of catastrophic terrorism, or were Russian scientists simply studying the lethality of anthrax, which is endemic in Russia?

Sawyer didn't mention that Western intelligence had known about the new anthrax strains for almost two years—from an unclassified International Workshop on Anthrax held at Winchester, England, in September 1995. The Russian scientists had openly described their experiments at the meeting sponsored by a number of commercial, charitable and professional organizations independent of the US and British governments.

Bioterrorism, biocriminals, bioweaponeers—all good buzzwords for novelists and movie makers who will continue to sound alarms and attract influential followers, no doubt; but the fact is, there have been only two serious uses of biological weapons in this century: one by the Japanese Imperial Army against China, and the other a failed attempt by Aum Shinrikyo to disperse anthrax spores.

So if there are terrorists out there wanting to use biological or chemical or nuclear weapons, how good is our intelligence about them? In hearings before Congress in 1995 the CIA admitted that its terrorism intelligence desk somehow missed the 1994 sarin gas attack by Aum Shinrikyo in Matsumoto, which killed seven people—although the event had been reported in the Japanese and European press and even in the US-owned *International Herald Tribune*. Such revelations suggest that a new, multiagency National Intelligence Center, as proposed by Deutch et al. in *Foreign Affairs*, might not only be a good idea but a necessity.

But why a whole new bureaucracy? Why the Manhattan Project syndrome? The Aum Shinrikyo story suggests that a small band of well-trained researchers who tap into publicly available information could be as useful as national information centers, wiretaps and grand jury investigations.

The risk in rushing to meet the new threat—any new threat—with new departments of counter-espionage and counter-weapons is that the old art of deterrence through international treaties will take a back seat. The United States already has a policy that criminalizes terrorist activity at home, including the post-Oklahoma City Anti-Terrorism Act of 1996. It also supports sanctions against countries promoting terrorism and corporations exporting material that could be used to produce weapons of mass destruction.

In the article on catastrophic terrorism, Deutch et al. mention the proposal of Harvard professor Meselson and his law professor colleague, Philip Heymann, for an international convention making it a crime for individuals to engage in the production of biological or chemical weapons. The existing chemical and biological conventions apply only to states. The idea is to deter national leaders, such as Saddam Hussein, and groups such as Aum Shinrikyo, from seeking to develop chemical or biological weapons, and to discourage corporations from assisting them because the scientist or the CEO could be arrested. If such a treaty had existed and been supported by the United States in the eighties when Iraq was using poison gas and developing biological weapons, the suppliers and advisers on whom Saddam depended could have been brought to trial.

The proposal is being co-promoted by Meselson's longtime ally in the fight to eliminate chemical and biological weapons, Julian Perry Robinson of the University of Sussex in England. The crimes are carefully defined in the precise language of the chemical and biological conventions, now ratified by 120 and 141 countries respectively. Under the proposed law any nation that is party to the existing conventions would be bound either to prosecute or to extradite a violator. Such treaties already in effect are aimed at piracy, genocide, airline hijacking and harming diplomats on active duty. If the proposal becomes law, terrorists would have their support group cut from under them; there is even the suggestion of a reward for anyone who provides information leading to a perpetrator's arrest. Maybe the fiction writers will pick up the idea too. Then, who knows whether the FBI or some adventurer from the plaintiff's bar- -bringing, say, a class action on behalf of aggrieved shareholders of a company caught trading in anthrax -will be the first to be responsible for the arrest of the culprits? The next generation of terror novels should be filled with "biocriminals" and "chemothugs."

For an alternative view, and relief from the drumbeat of the New Threat merchants, one can turn to this quarter's *Foreign Policy*, a rival of *Foreign Affairs*. In an article titled "The Great Superterrorism Scare," Ehud Sprinzak, a professor of political science at Jerusalem's Hebrew University, suggests that the voices of doom are mistaken. Their concept of post-cold war chaos breeding terrorist fanatics is simply not supported by the evidence of three decades. "Despite the lurid rhetoric, a massive terrorist attack with nuclear, chemical, or biological weapons is hardly inevitable. It is not even likely," he writes. "Terrorists wish to convince us that they are capable of striking from anywhere at any time, but there is really no chaos. In fact, terrorism involves predictable behavior, and the vast majority of terrorist organizations can be identified well in advance." Such views tend to go unheard by doomsayers. The Republicans added $9 billion to the military budget, including several additional millions for antiterrorism projects, by emphasizing unpreparedness—sure to be a big issue in Election 2000. ■

Bioterrorism: thinking the unthinkable

Until recently, terrorism has generally involved the use of explosives: the bombings in Northern Ireland, mainland UK, Lockerbie, Oklahoma City, and the World Trade Center in New York are but a few examples. The use of sarin nerve gas in Tokyo 4 years ago changed perspectives. Urban terrorism in the future might involve newer technologies. The potential use of biological weapons adds a further grim dimension.

Picture the following. Over a period of about 1 week, increasing numbers of patients report to their general practitioners and emergency departments with fever, malaise, and myalgia, and other symptoms in keeping with a viral respiratory-tract infection. Increasing numbers of patients become septicaemic and then deaths start to occur. By the time the diagnosis of anthrax is made, each patient will have been in contact with many family members as well as with colleagues and people in the hospitals. The initial exposure of, say several hundred people, to the organism has now spread to many tens of thousands. Panic would ensue and hospitals would be overwhelmed—the clamour for antibiotic prophylaxis and mass vaccination is the stuff of nightmares. In the USA, the Institute of Medicine and the National Research Council have addressed these potential problems and believe that it would be a grave mistake to assume that terrorists will not be able and willing to develop new chemical or biological threats.[1]

Agents that might be used include anthrax, which is simple to produce but more difficult to deliver, brucella, yersinia, and francisella which, if not fatal, may cause a protracted illness. The viral encephalitides and haemorrhagic fevers, although naturally spread by insect vectors, are highly infectious as aerosols, and infection carries a high mortality. Other possible agents include *Coxiella burnetii* (Q fever) and *Burkholderia* sp (melioidosis and glanders), botulinum toxins, and, of course, smallpox.

Anthrax has attracted the most attention as a biological agent, the spore form of the bacterium being stable, especially in an aerosol form. The insidious nature of spread and resulting confusion, as suggested above, might also appeal to terrorists. The US Secretary of Defence, William Cohen, raised a 5 lb bag of sugar on television to demonstrate the amount of anthrax spores that could kill 50% of Washington's population.[2] Treatment with high doses of penicillin, fluoroquinolone, or tetracycline is of limited benefit but a vaccine is available for key personnel. The economic consequences are staggering: US$26·2 billions per 100 000 exposed.[3] Botulinum toxins offer another approach. Symptoms begin more rapidly (12–36 h after ingestion) but there is no secondary spread. The LD_{50} is low (1 ng/kg body weight), hence the threat to water supplies is obvious.

What can be done to prevent these nightmares from becoming reality? 140 countries have signed the Biological Weapons Convention of 1975, but several Middle Eastern states have not. Periodic inspections by United Nations personnel might deter some, but experience with Iraq shows what obstacles there can be. Getting all countries to agree to participate in such a system is probably impractical. Reliance will therefore have to be put upon military and police intelligence, with firm links being developed with the medical community. Tentative links already exist in many countries. Most hospitals have major incident plans designed for natural and man-made disasters—this is a starting point. Foreknowledge will increase the possibility of a better response to threat. New York City has completed an exercise of simulated anthrax attack and other US cities will follow.[4] Increasing the awareness of all concerned is paramount and, again, the USA is taking a lead.[5] Surveillance schemes for detection of covert exposure need to be developed. Rapid diagnosis will be all important, especially after an attack that can spread secondarily. Biosensor technology is available to the military and needs to be made available to civilians.[6] The Biological Integrated Detection System collects air, measures the size of aerosol particles, and detects biological activity by presence of ATP. Flow cytometry and antibody-based tests then can detect anthrax, plague, and botulinum toxin.[1]

The task ahead is great and the USA and Switzerland[1,7] are showing the way. There is a need for planning, communication, and taking financially realistic steps of preparedness. Policies must be developed to prepare for biological attack. The availability of sufficient vaccines, antitoxins, and antibiotics for prophylaxis of key personnel or even the wider public needs to be addressed. Great vigilance is required and politicians will need to be educated. In countries where the approach is less open than that adopted the USA and Switzerland, society could collapse rapidly in the face of a significant threat.

Richard Wise

Department of Clinical Microbiology, City Hospital, Birmingham B8 7QH, UK

1 Improving civilian medical response to chemical or biological terrorist incidents. Washington DC: National Academy Press, 1998.
2 Chevrier MI. The threat that won't disperse. *Washington Post* Dec. 21, 1997, p C1
3 Kaufmann AF, Meltzler MI, Schmid GP. The economic impact of a bioterrorist attack. *Emerging Infectious Dis* 1997; 3: 83–94.
4 Boyce N. Nowhere to hide. *New Scientist* 158: 2127 p4.
5 Eitzen E. Medical preparedness for bioterrorism. International Conference on Emerging Infectious Diseases. March 8–11, 1998, Atlanta. Abstr no p 19.1.
6 Woodall JP. Assessing the risk to civilians after biological attack: the need for international technology transfer. International Conference on Emerging Infectious Diseases. March 8–11, 1998, Atlanta. Abstr no p19.2.
7 Steffen R, Melling J, Woodall JP, et al. Preparation for emergency relief after biological warfare. *J Infect* 1997; 34: 27–32.

Public Law 101-298
101st Congress

An Act

To implement the Convention on the Prohibition of the Development, Production, and Stockpiling of Bacteriological (Biological) and Toxin Weapons and Their Destruction, by prohibiting certain conduct relating to biological weapons, and for other purposes.

May 22, 1990
[S. 993]

Be it enacted by the Senate and House of Representatives of the United States of America in Congress assembled,

Biological Weapons Anti-Terrorism Act of 1989. International agreements. 18 USC 175 note. 18 USC 175 note.

SECTION 1. SHORT TITLE.

This Act may be cited as the "Biological Weapons Anti-Terrorism Act of 1989".

SEC. 2. PURPOSE AND INTENT.

(a) PURPOSE.—The purpose of this Act is to—

(1) implement the Biological Weapons Convention, an international agreement unanimously ratified by the United States Senate in 1974 and signed by more than 100 other nations, including the Soviet Union; and

(2) protect the United States against the threat of biological terrorism.

(b) INTENT OF ACT.—Nothing in this Act is intended to restrain or restrict peaceful scientific research or development.

SEC. 3. TITLE 18 AMENDMENTS.

(a) IN GENERAL.—Title 18, United States Code, is amended by inserting after chapter 9 the following:

"CHAPTER 10—BIOLOGICAL WEAPONS

"Sec.
"175. Prohibitions with respect to biological weapons.
"176. Seizure, forfeiture, and destruction.
"177. Injunctions.
"178. Definitions.

"§ 175. Prohibitions with respect to biological weapons

"(a) IN GENERAL.—Whoever knowingly develops, produces, stockpiles, transfers, acquires, retains, or possesses any biological agent, toxin, or delivery system for use as a weapon, or knowingly assists a foreign state or any organization to do so, shall be fined under this title or imprisoned for life or any term of years, or both. There is extraterritorial Federal jurisdiction over an offense under this section committed by or against a national of the United States.

"(b) DEFINITION.—For purposes of this section, the term 'for use as a weapon' does not include the development, production, transfer, acquisition, retention, or possession of any biological agent, toxin, or delivery system for prophylactic, protective, or other peaceful purposes.

"§ 176. Seizure, forfeiture, and destruction

"(a) IN GENERAL.—(1) Except as provided in paragraph (2), the Attorney General may request the issuance, in the same manner as provided for a search warrant, of a warrant authorizing the seizure of any biological agent, toxin, or delivery system that—

"(A) exists by reason of conduct prohibited under section 175 of this title; or

"(B) is of a type or in a quantity that under the circumstances has no apparent justification for prophylactic, protective, or other peaceful purposes.

"(2) In exigent circumstances, seizure and destruction of any biological agent, toxin, or delivery system described in subparagraphs (A) and (B) of paragraph (1) may be made upon probable cause without the necessity for a warrant.

"(b) PROCEDURE.—Property seized pursuant to subsection (a) shall be forfeited to the United States after notice to potential claimants and an opportunity for a hearing. At such hearing, the government shall bear the burden of persuasion by a preponderance of the evidence. Except as inconsistent herewith, the same procedures and provisions of law relating to a forfeiture under the customs laws shall extend to a seizure or forfeiture under this section. The Attorney General may provide for the destruction or other appropriate disposition of any biological agent, toxin, or delivery system seized and forfeited pursuant to this section.

"(c) AFFIRMATIVE DEFENSE.—It is an affirmative defense against a forfeiture under subsection (a)(1)(B) of this section that—

"(1) such biological agent, toxin, or delivery system is for a prophylactic, protective, or other peaceful purpose; and

"(2) such biological agent, toxin, or delivery system, is of a type and quantity reasonable for that purpose.

"§ 177. Injunctions

"(a) IN GENERAL.—The United States may obtain in a civil action an injunction against—

"(1) the conduct prohibited under section 175 of this title;

"(2) the preparation, solicitation, attempt, or conspiracy to engage in conduct prohibited under section 175 of this title; or

"(3) the development, production, stockpiling, transferring, acquisition, retention, or possession, or the attempted development, production, stockpiling, transferring, acquisition, retention, or possession of any biological agent, toxin, or delivery system of a type or in a quantity that under the circumstances has no apparent justification for prophylactic, protective, or other peaceful purposes.

"(b) AFFIRMATIVE DEFENSE.—It is an affirmative defense against an injunction under subsection (a)(3) of this section that—

"(1) the conduct sought to be enjoined is for a prophylactic, protective, or other peaceful purpose; and

"(2) such biological agent, toxin, or delivery system is of a type and quantity reasonable for that purpose.

"§ 178. Definitions

"As used in this chapter—

"(1) the term 'biological agent' means any micro-organism, virus, or infectious substance, capable of causing—

"(A) death, disease, or other biological malfunction in a human, an animal, a plant, or another living organism;

"(B) deterioration of food, water, equipment, supplies, or material of any kind; or

"(C) deleterious alteration of the environment;

"(2) the term 'toxin' means, whatever its origin or method of production—

"(A) any poisonous substance produced by a living organism; or

"(B) any poisonous isomer, homolog, or derivative of such a substance;

"(3) the term 'delivery system' means—

"(A) any apparatus, equipment, device, or means of delivery specifically designed to deliver or disseminate a biological agent, toxin, or vector; or

"(B) any vector; and

"(4) the term 'vector' means a living organism capable of carrying a biological agent or toxin to a host.".

(b) WIRE INTERCEPTION.—Section 2516(c) of title 18, United States Code, is amended by adding "section 175 (relating to biological weapons)," after "section 33 (relating to destruction of motor vehicles or motor vehicle facilities),".

(c) CLERICAL AMENDMENT.—The table of chapters for part I of title 18, United States Code, is amended by inserting after the item relating to chapter 9 the following new item:

"10. Biological Weapons.......... 175.".

Approved May 22, 1990.

LEGISLATIVE HISTORY—S. 993 (H.R. 237):

HOUSE REPORTS: No. 101-476 accompanying H.R. 237 (Comm. on the Judiciary).
SENATE REPORTS: No. 101-210 (Comm. on the Judiciary).
CONGRESSIONAL RECORD:
Vol. 135 (1989): Nov. 21, considered and passed Senate.
Vol. 136 (1990): May 8, H.R. 237 considered and passed House; proceedings vacated and S. 993 passed in lieu.
WEEKLY COMPILATION OF PRESIDENTIAL DOCUMENTS, Vol. 26 (1990):
May 22, Presidential statement.

Statement on Signing the Biological Weapons Anti-Terrorism Act of 1989

May 22, 1990

I am pleased today to sign S. 993, the ``Biological Weapons Anti-Terrorism Act of 1989." This Act will impose new criminal penalties against those who would employ or contribute to the dangerous proliferation of biological weapons, and it will add teeth to our efforts to eradicate such horrible weapons. I salute the bipartisan consensus in the Congress that has demonstrated its support for this humanitarian objective and the leadership's commitment to our shared goal of destroying forever the evil shadow these weapons have cast around the world.

The United States has renounced these weapons, as have all civilized countries, by joining the Biological Weapons Convention of 1972. Scrupulous compliance with the obligations of that Convention and similar prohibitions against the use of chemical weapons are essential to the security of all mankind. I call upon the leaders of all nations to join us in our drive to rid the world of biological and chemical weapons and to do everything in their power to stop the proliferation of these weapons of mass destruction. We must halt and reverse the threat that comes from such weapons and their proliferation. This Act that I sign today is a measured but important step in that direction.

George Bush

The White House,

May 22, 1990.

Note: S. 993, approved May 22, was assigned Public Law No. 101 - 298.

TERRORISM: THE PROBLEM AND THE SOLUTION—*THE COMPREHENSIVE TERRORISM PREVENTION ACT OF 1995*[1]

I. INTRODUCTION

Recently, the United States has been the target of various terrorist attacks, including the bombing of the Federal Building in Oklahoma City,[2] the bombing of the World Trade Center,[3] the attempted bombing of the United Nations Building in New York City[4] and the bombing of New York-bound Pan Am Flight #103.[5] These deliberate acts of aggression killed innocent bystanders and terrorized countless people in the United States and beyond. It is clear that domestic terrorism is an imminent threat to the national security of the United States and, as a result, the public is exerting pressure on Congress to take action.

Throughout history, national security fears have driven our nation's leaders to take extreme action. During World War II, Japanese-Americans were removed, relocated and placed in internment camps based on wartime suspicions. Then, in the 1960's, the government engaged in widespread infiltration and surveillance of persons and organizations suspected of Communist sympathies during the Cold War.[6] The American public was angry and frustrated. In response, the government quickly acted in the name of national security with absolute intolerance for anyone related in any way to these abhorrent acts. Although seemingly rational in light of the passions of the times, the government's responses injured the rights of many people. Instead of using the deprivation of rights to punish wrongful acts, the government deprived rights based solely on race and suspected political affiliations.

Under the laws of this country, political association and nationality are indeterminate of guilt, innocence, or liability. The principle of legality[7] demands that "the law

---

1. S. 735, 104th Cong., 1st Sess. (1995), reprinted in 141 CONG. REC. S7857 (daily ed. June 7, 1995) (enacted by the United States Senate on June 7, 1995).

2. *See* David Johnston, *Terror in Oklahoma City: The Investigation; at Least 30 are Dead, Scores are Missing After Car Bomb Attack in Oklahoma City Wrecks 9-Story Federal Office Building*, N.Y. TIMES, Apr. 20, 1995, at A1.

3. *See* Robert D. McFadden, *Explosion at the Twin Towers: The Overview; Blast hits Trade Center, Bomb Suspected; 5 Killed, Thousands Flee Smoke in Towers*, N.Y. TIMES, Feb. 27, 1993, at A1.

4. *See* Michael Isikoff & Jim McGee, *8 Foreign Nationals Accused of Plotting to Blow up U.N.*, WASH. POST, June 25, 1993, at A1.

5. *See* Edward Cody, *Bomb Caused Pan Am Crash, British Probers Conclude; Analysis of Debris Suggests Plastic Explosive*, WASH. POST, Dec. 29, 1988, at A1.

6. This surveillance operation, entitled COINTELPRO, was directed at groups opposed to the Vietnam War, particularly Martin Luther King Jr. The FBI, led by J. Edgar Hoover, conducted this extensive operation under the auspices of combating communism. *See, e.g.*, CURT GENTRY, J. EDGAR HOOVER: THE MAN AND THE SECRETS 412, 442, 682-83 (1991).

7. "In a very wide sense, the principle of legality—the 'rule of law'—refers to and requires not only a body of legal precepts but also supporting institutions, procedures, and values . . . [including] legal procedures . . . designed to effect the protection of essential interests of individuals guaranteed by our society through limitations on the authority of the State." (citations omitted) JEROME HALL,

is impartially and regularly administered"[8] through rational procedures which preserve the integrity of the legal process.[9] Alternatively, if the judicial process lacks its essential integrity, its purposes of ascertaining the truth and determining an individual's responsibility are undermined.[10] The result is arbitrary punishment which serves no other purpose than to intimidate, or terrorize. Therefore, procedural safeguards must be provided equally for everyone to preserve the legitimacy of our legal system by providing basic due process rights to everyone,[11] including the politically unpopular. To best determine individual responsibility, a hearing is held in which evidence is presented and refuted on both sides.[12] Such is a minimal due process of law guarantee[13] which is necessary to preserve our system of justice. As Justice Felix Frankfurter aptly observed, "The history of liberty has largely been the history of the observance of procedural safeguards."[14]

Our government deprived many innocent people of their freedom and privacy rights in response to timely national security concerns. But, with hindsight and less reactionary politics, our government eventually recognized these grave injustices. The first official recognition of these wrongs came in 1976, as a response to the widespread infiltration and surveillance practices of the 1960's. The F.B.I. created Domestic Security Guidelines,[15] to establish standards and procedures for investigations, safeguarding against further violations of innocent persons' rights to privacy. Then, in 1988, Congress passed legislation which officially apologized and awarded nominal restitution to Japanese-Americans for the harms inflicted upon their relatives in the internment camps during World War II.[16] An important provision of this legislation anticipates future judgments based upon identities, not actions, of individuals and issues a solemn warning: "[T]o discourage the occurrence of similar injustices and violations of civil liberties in the future."[17]

Within the existing framework of the laws of our country, and in light of lessons learned from history, this note evaluates Congress' most recently proposed solutions to the imminent problem of terrorism: The Comprehensive Terrorism Prevention Act of 1995.[18] This note concedes that national security concerns mandate reasonable limits on rights of anyone suspected of terrorist activities. However, this note takes issue with the extreme action proposed by the United States Senate and House of Representatives, specifically directed at the expedited removal of legal aliens based upon secret allegations.[19] Accordingly, Part II sets forth and analyzes this provision as it was enacted

---

GENERAL PRINCIPLES OF CRIMINAL LAW 27, 27 n.1 (2nd ed.) (1960).

8. JOHN RAWLS, A THEORY OF JUSTICE 241 (1971).

9. *Id.* at 239.

10. *See generally id.* at 235–43.

11. "The 'rule of law' requires some form of due process." *Id.* at 239.

12. For a discussion of the constitutional requirements for a fair hearing, including one's right to know the evidence against them, see Henry J. Friendly, *Some Kind of Hearing*, 123 U. PENN. L. REV. 1264 (1975).

13. U.S. CONST. amend. V.

14. McNabb v. United States, 318 U.S. 332, 347 (1943).

15. *See Excerpts from Attorney General's New Guidelines for F.B.I. Investigations*, N.Y. TIMES, Mar. 8, 1983 at A12 (explaining the original 1973 F.B.I. Domestic Security Guidelines and the 1983 revisions).

16. Public Law 100-383 § 1 (1988), 102 Stat. 903, (codified as amended at 50 U.S.C.A. App. § 1989 (1990)).

17. *Id.* at 6.

18. S. 735, *supra* note 1.

19. Rather than undertake a detailed analysis of the proposed legislation in its entirety, this note

by the United States Senate on June 7, 1995. Next, Part III summarizes the present state of constitutional rights and procedural protections presently afforded to aliens. Based on this foundation, Part IV undertakes a critical evaluation of the secret evidence provisions in light of these rights, concluding with a workable solution.

II. CONGRESS' PROPOSED LEGISLATIVE SOLUTIONS

Originally introduced as part of the Clinton administration's response to the 1993 World Trade Center Bombing,[20] The Comprehensive Terrorism Prevention Act focuses on safeguards against international terrorist threats. Despite the wholly international focus of the legislation, it was an instance of domestic terrorism—the Oklahoma City bombing—which created the intense political pressure on Congress to enact The Comprehensive Terrorism Prevention Act.[21]

The proposed legislation creates a new special removal court to expeditiously remove aliens[22] who are legally present in the United States. An alien qualifies for these new proceedings if he is believed to be part of an organization that has been designated a "terrorist organization" by the Secretary of State. Under the current anti-terrorism laws, the government possesses the power to deport any alien who engages in or supports terrorist activity.[23] Although, under current immigration law,[24] classes of aliens are simply defined as deportable,[25] the proposed legislation focuses on the deportation of a new class of aliens who are considered terrorists according to the

---

focuses on the provisions authorizing secret evidence to be used against an alien at a deportation hearing. ("Alien Terrorist Removal Procedures," S. 735, *supra* note 1, Title V § 503) [hereinafter *Secret Evidence Provision*].

20. The Omnibus Counterterrorism Act of 1995, H.R. 896, S. 390, 104th Cong., 1st Sess. (1995). Most of the provisions of this bill have been adopted by the Comprehensive Terrorism Prevention Act. *S. 735*, *supra* note 1.

21. Shortly after the bombing in Oklahoma City, President Clinton "prodded Congress to act swiftly on the bill, [he said] 'We must not dawdle or delay, Congress must act, and act promptly.'" CONG. Q., May 11, 1995, at 1180. In the same context, Senator Dianne Feinstien said, "I'm going to vote for everything because I think we need to take an unparalleled step in our society to put an end to this." CONG. Q., May 11, 1995, at 1180. Also, during the Senate floor debates on S. 735, Senators Hatch, Dole, Specter, Lieberman, and Daschle each emphasized the need to pass this legislation with urgency in light of the Oklahoma City Bombing. 141 CONG. REC. S7585, S7596, S7599, S7608 (daily ed. May 26, 1995). *Contra* Naftali Rendavid, *Of Primary Concern; Campaign Creeps Up On Senate Crime Bill*, LEGAL TIMES, July 17, 1995 at 1 (Senator Orrin Hatch expressing concerns with the urgency surrounding this legislation: "[W]e'd be better bringing [the bill] up next year . . . where we have some time to really consider it.").

22. "The term 'alien' means any person not a citizen or national of the United States." 8 U.S.C.S. § 1101(a)(3) (1987).

23. "Any alien who has engaged, is engaged, or at any time after entry engages in any terrorist activity . . . is deportable." 8 U.S.C. § 1105(a)(4)(B) (1995). "Terrorist activity" is defined as any activity which is unlawful under the laws of the place where it is committed and involves any of the following, or a threat, attempt or conspiracy to do any of the following: Hijacking; threatening to kill, injure or continue to detain another individual in order to compel another person; violently attacking an internationally protected person; an assassination; using biological agents, chemical agents or nuclear devices; using an explosive or firearm with the intent to endanger the safety of one or more individuals or to cause substantial damage to property. 8 U.S.C. § 1182(a)(3)(B)(ii) (1994). Note, this definition remains intact under the proposed legislation. S. 735, *supra* note 1, § 303(a)(B)(ii).

24. Existing deportation proceedings are governed by 8 C.F.R. § 242 (1995) as authorized by 8 U.S.C.S. § 1252(b) (1987). *See also infra* Part III. B.

25. 8 U.S.C.S. §§ 1251(a)(4)-(7), (11), (12), (14)-(17), (18), and (19)(1987). The classes of deportable aliens include: Anarchists; advocates of opposition to government; affiliates of Communism; narcotic drug addicts and prostitutes, among others. Ironically, this statute authorizes the deportation of an alien who has "ordered, incited, assisted, or otherwise participated in the persecution of any person because of race, religion, national origin, or political opinion." *Id.* § 1251(a)(19).

Secretary of State. Furthermore, unlike current immigration proceedings, the new special removal court allows these aliens to be deported without being informed of the government's evidence against them. This legislation allows the government to use secret evidence against an alien to ultimately deport them from this country.

The secret evidence provision is the result of an attempt to reconcile two competing concerns. First, Congress is concerned with safety risks which may endanger national security, particularly retaliatory action from a terrorist group against confidential informants. Second, however, is the dual recognition that persons accused at hearings have a right to confront the evidence against them. The Comprehensive Terrorism Prevention Act purports to reach a compromise between these competing interests by allowing the government to use secret evidence without exposing confidential information while requiring the government to provide a summary of the classified information to the alien.

A. The Secret Evidence Provisions of The Comprehensive Terrorism Prevention Act

Less than two months after the Oklahoma City bombing, the Senate overwhelmingly approved The Comprehensive Terrorism Prevention Act[26] upon a vote of 91 yeas to 8 nays.[27] Described as "[a] bill to prevent and punish acts of terrorism,"[28] this legislation purports to "add[] important tools to the Government's fight against terrorism . . . in a temperate manner that is protective of civil liberties," thereby attempting to reconcile these competing interests.[29]

The bill creates a new designation, a "terrorist organization," which is defined as "an organization that engages in, or has engaged in, terrorist activity as designated by the Secretary of State, after consultation with the Secretary of the Treasury."[30] Once deemed part of any such terrorist organization, an alien is labeled an "alien terrorist" for the purpose of the newly created "Alien Terrorist Removal Procedures."

Under the proposed Alien Terrorist Removal Procedures, a "Special Removal Hearing" is provided for any alien who, if deported in the present fashion,[31] would "pose a risk to the national security of the United States because such proceedings would disclose classified information."[32] In these hearings, five federal judges, chosen

26. S. 735, *supra* note 1.

27. 141 CONG. REC. S7857 (daily ed. June 7, 1995) [Rollcall Vote No. 242 Leg.].

28. 141 CONG. REC. S7479 (daily ed. May 25, 1995).

29. *Id.* (statement of Senator Hatch).

30. S. 735, *supra* note 1, § 210(2)(iv) (defining terrorist organizations for the explicit purpose of exclusion from the United States). Defining these organizations as excludable, in effect, also defines them as deportable. 8 U.S.C. § 1227 (1995) (Any excludable alien shall be immediately deported).

31. Under current law, the government may introduce classified information at deportation hearings, provided it is relevant. Alternatively, the government may provide an unclassified summary of the information whenever it can do so. Said summary should provide the alien an opportunity to offer opposing evidence. 8 C.F.R. § 242.17(c)(4)(iv) (1995). Further, "[t]he Immigration Judge shall . . . advise the respondent that he will have a reasonable opportunity to examine and object to the evidence against him . . . and to cross-examine witnesses presented by the Government" 8 C.F.R. § 242.16(a). On the other side, the alien has a right to obtain all information compiled against him *except*: 1) matters that are secret by executive order in the interest of national policy, and 2) matters that are "classified pursuant to such an executive order." 5 U.S.C.A. § 552(b)(1) (1977) ("The Freedom of Information Act").

32. S. 735, *supra* note 1, §§ 503(a) & (e).

by the Chief Justice of the United States, hear and decide these cases.[33] The government must prove their case by a clear and convincing evidence standard.[34] The alien is given the right to an attorney at the expense of the government,[35] and illegally obtained evidence is admissible against the alien.[36]

At this special removal hearing, the alien has a "reasonable opportunity to cross-examine any witness"[37] except when the judge determines that to do so would disclose classified information.[38] In such instances, a summary of the classified evidence shall be prepared in a manner sufficient "to provide the alien with substantially the same ability to make his defense as would disclosure of the classified information."[39]

If a summary of classified information does not meet this standard, then the hearing is terminated unless the following three criteria are met:[40] 1) the alien's continued presence in the United States would likely cause serious and irreparable harm to the national security or death or serious bodily injury to any person; 2) any summary prepared according to the standard above,[41] if revealed, would likely cause the same harm or injury; and 3) a summary is provided which is "adequate to allow the alien to prepare a defense."[42]

B. Analysis of The Comprehensive Terrorism Prevention Act

1. *Syntactical Analysis of Secret Evidence Provision*

The Comprehensive Terrorism Prevention Act provides that an alien who is suspected of associating with a terrorist organization, and suspected of being a risk to national security, has a right to see a summary of the government's case against him. But, since the legislation fails to explain the scope of this right, this guarantee is hollow.

Before the new removal procedures are initiated, a group must be declared a "terrorist organization."[43] The importance of this determination cannot be underestimated. The proposed Comprehensive Terrorism Prevention Act defines "terrorist orga-

---

33. S. 735, *supra* note 1, § 503(c)(1).
34. S. 735, *supra* note 1, § 503(f).
35. S. 735, *supra* note 1, § 503(e)(2).
36. S. 735, *supra* note 1, §§ 503(e)(4)(A)(ii) & 503(e)(4)(B). *See also* Immigration & Naturalization Serv. v. Lopez-Mendoza, 468 U.S. 1032, 1040-50 (1984) (exclusionary rule does not apply to current deportation proceedings).
37. S. 735, *supra* note 1, § 503(e)(3).
38. "The judge shall authorize the introduction in camera and ex parte of any evidence for which the Attorney General determines that public disclosure would pose a risk to the national security of the United States because it would disclose classified information." S. 735, *supra* note 1, § 503(e)(C)(5).
39. S. 735, *supra* note 1, § 503(e)(C)(6)(B). The Secret Evidence Provision originated as the Specter-Simon-Kennedy Amendment for the explicit purpose of ensuring due process in deportation proceedings. S. 735, *supra* note 1, §§ 503(e)(C)(6)(B)-(G); 141 CONG. REC. S7761-63, S7765-66, S7773 (daily ed. June 6, 1995).
40. S. 735, *supra* note 1, § 503(e)(6)(E).
41. A summary of the classified evidence shall be prepared in a manner sufficient "to provide the alien with substantially the same ability to make his defense as would disclosure of the classified information." S. 735, *supra* note 1, § 503(e)(B).
42. S. 735, *supra* note 1, § 503(e)(6)(E)(iii).
43. A "terrorist organization" is defined as "an organization that engages in, or has engaged in, terrorist activity as designated by the Secretary of State, after consultation with the Secretary of the Treasury." S. 735, *supra* note 1, § 210(2)(iv).

nization" as whatever organization the Secretary of State determines has threatened, attempted or conspired to commit an unlawful act.[44] In effect, this bill affords broad, unchecked implementation power solely to the Secretary of State, a presidentially-appointed cabinet member.[45] The requisite unlawful act is limited only to a broad range of acts that are specified in a list of "terrorist activities."[46]

Although the bill fails to provide specific requirements of the summary of classified information, the scope of this provision is indicated by the actual language of the bill. By comparing the later description of the guaranteed summary to the earlier mention of the substitute summary, the varying standards surface. The bill initially explains that the summary of the classified information to be used against the alien shall "provide the alien with the same ability to make his defense as would disclosure of the classified information." Later language clarifies that the required summary must only be "adequate to prepare a defense."[47] The initial heightened-standard summary's relevance is unclear in light of the subsequent language which guarantees only the lower-standard summary.

The burden the government must meet before denying an alien a heightened-standard summary, providing him with the same ability to make his defense as would disclosure of the classified information, is ambiguous. The criteria that must be met before the bill permits a lower-standard summary[48] to be acceptable are:[49] 1) the alien's continued presence in the United States would likely cause serious and irreparable harm to the national security or death or serious bodily injury to any person; and 2) any summary prepared according to the heightened standard,[50] if revealed, would likely cause the same harm or injury. Although the language indicates that the lower-standard summary will be substituted only after these specific conditions are fulfilled, a close reading of these two criteria indicates otherwise. This obscurity suggests that these conditions could be quite easily satisfied by even a vague showing of alleged future harm or injury, thereby indicating that the specified criteria are, in fact, quite liberal.

The language of the secret evidence provision is confusing. The question of whether the summary must contain painstaking details or few generalities remains unsettled. Furthermore, the precise procedures for presenting the summary are unan-

---

44. *See supra* note 23 (defining "terrorist activity" which is incorporated as part of the "terrorist organization" definition in S. 735).

45. The Secretary of State is required to consult with the Secretary of the Treasury, another presidentially-appointed cabinet member, before designating a group to be a "terrorist organization." S. 735, *supra* note 1, § 210(2)(iv).

46. The list includes any of the following, or a threat, attempt or conspiracy to do any of the following: Hijacking; threatening to kill, injure or continue to detain another individual in order to compel another person; violently attacking an internationally protected person; an assassination; using biological agents, chemical agents or nuclear devices; using an explosive or firearm with the intent to endanger the safety of one or more individuals or to cause substantial damage to property. 8 U.S.C. § 1182(a)(3)(B) (1994).

47. S. 735, *supra* note 1, §§ 503(e)(C)(6)(B) & 6(E)(iii); *see supra* text accompanying note 40 (explaining the three conditions that must be satisfied before the standard for the requisite summary is adjusted from a heightened standard to a lower standard).

48. A lower-standard summary must only be "adequate to allow the alien to prepare a defense. S. 735, *supra* note 1, § 503(e)(6)(E)(iii).

49. S. 735, *supra* note 1, § 503(e)(6)(E).

50. A heightened-standard summary of the classified evidence shall be prepared in a manner sufficient "to provide the alien with substantially the same ability to make his defense as would disclosure of the classified information." S. 735, *supra* note 1, § 503(e)(6)(B).

swered. Whether the procedures allow oral argument over the summary or whether the document is submitted without question is unspecified by this legislation; these questions are critical to an evaluation of the degree of rights actually afforded to the alien in these new proceedings.

2. *Legislative Intent Analysis*

Although the language of this provision is vague, the Senate's intentions are unambiguous. The Senate's intent behind the language of the new removal procedures was to ensure 1) that aliens are informed of the charges against them, and 2) that aliens are afforded an opportunity to confront the evidence against them. Senator Arlen Specter, a sponsor of the bill, expressed "very grave concerns about the constitutionality of any deportation proceeding in which secret evidence is used and there is not a right of confrontation."[51] To alleviate these concerns, he sponsored an amendment "to ensure due process in deportation proceedings" which was incorporated into The Comprehensive Terrorism Prevention Act.[52] Adding to Senator Specter's concerns, Senator Joseph Biden denounced secret evidence provisions and praised procedural protections while successfully urging members of the Senate to pass this legislation:

> I do not think people fully understand how significant this [provision] is. [T]he dangers posed by secret evidence are neither hypothetical nor are they imagined. Secret evidence runs counter to all the principles underlying due process of law and our judicial system, and it cheapens our system by placing in doubt the accuracy of its decision.[53]

To demonstrate the gravity of his concerns, Senator Biden shared a story with his colleagues in the Senate about an American soldier's German bride. She was excluded from the United States on the grounds she was a national security risk. Initially, the government's evidence against her was not revealed. Ultimately, when the secret evidence was revealed it proved to be wholly unfounded. In fact, the most substantive of the allegations were derived from an estranged lover. Once able to confront and refute this faulty evidence, the bride was admitted to the United States.[54] By telling this story, Senator Biden illustrated the tragic consequences of depriving an accused person the opportunity to prepare a defense through use of secret evidence which may be uncorroborated and unreliable.

Senator Specter and Senator Biden's dissatisfaction with due process inadequacies as described above were raised in objection to an early version of The Comprehensive Terrorism Prevention Act which did not include any provisions for a required summary.[55] In this context, the addition of any form of summary provisions constituted tantamount progress. The Senators' initial constitutional concerns were alleviated upon passage of The Comprehensive Terrorism Prevention Act by the United States

51. 141 CONG. REC. S7760 (daily ed., June 6, 1995) (statement of Senator Specter).
52. *Id.* The Specter-Simon-Kennedy amendment includes the Secret Evidence Provision. *See* S. 735, *supra* note 1, §§ 503(e)(C)(6)(B)-(G).
53. 141 CONG. REC. S7762 (daily ed., June 6, 1995) (statement of Senator Biden).
54. *Id.* For the full version of Senator Biden's true story, see Knauff v. Shaughnessy, 338 U.S. 537 (1950). *See also* Charles D. Weisselberg, *The Exclusion and Detention of Aliens: Lessons from the Lives of Ellen Knauff and Ignatz Mezei*, 143 U. PENN. L. REV. 933 (1995). Although this case involves exclusion, not deportation, the story illustrates the dangers of allowing the government to use secret evidence in immigration proceedings.
55. *See* S. 390, 104th Cong., 1st Sess. (1995) (introduced February 10, 1995).

Senate on June 7, 1995,[56] which guarantees a summary of the classified information to the alien.

3. *Legislative Language that Conflicts with Legislative Intent*

Contrary to the Senators' assurances that due process had, in fact, been satisfied, the language of The Comprehensive Terrorism Prevention Act suggests otherwise. The undefined standards of "injury to any person"[57] and continued presence which "would likely cause irreparable harm,"[58] plus the possibility of conducting a deportation hearing based upon a lower-standard summary[59] which must only meet the unspecified criteria of "adequate to . . . prepare a defense,"[60] create ambiguity and, therefore, dilute any protections set forth in the legislation. Based on this tenuous foundation, the secret evidence provisions seem inadequate to satisfy the protections explicitly set forth by Senator Specter and Senator Biden, should this bill become law.[61] During the Senate floor debate on The Comprehensive Terrorism Prevention Act, Senator Biden explained the injustices inflicted upon an American soldier's wife to illustrate the inherent problems involved when immigration decisions are based upon secret evidence.[62] Ironically, the same uncorroborated statements erroneously relied upon to exclude the soldier's wife could be relied upon to deport legal resident aliens under the secret evidence provision as presently drafted.

III. CONSTITUTIONAL RIGHTS OF ALIENS

Immigration law was structured in light of wartime considerations, therefore these laws antagonistically pitted United States citizens against enemy aliens.[63] Despite changed fears, immigration law is still based on these premises, thereby resulting in modern-day xenophobic laws. Congress granted administration and enforcement responsibilities of immigration law to the Attorney General, who has since delegated authority to the Commissioner of the Immigration and Naturalization Service.[64] In doing so, Congress explicitly left immigration law outside the reach of constitutional protections.[65] Therefore, because immigration law governs aliens' ability to remain in

---

56. S. 735, *supra* note 1.
57. S. 735, *supra* note 1, §§ 503(e)(6)(E)(i)(II) & 503(e)(6)(E)(ii)(II).
58. S. 735, *supra* note 1, §§ 503(e)(6)(E)(i)(I) & 503(e)(6)(E)(ii)(I).
59. *See supra* text accompanying notes 39-42 (explaining the two standards for summaries of classified information as set forth in S. 735, *supra* note 1).
60. S. 735, *supra* note 1, § 503(e)(6)(E)(iii).
61. Perhaps to compensate for this reduction in rights, S. 735 expressly increases the alien's right to counsel by providing a government paid attorney for the alien. S. 735, *supra* note 1, § 503(e)(2). *Compare* 8 C.F.R. § 242.16 (1995) (current deportation procedures afford the alien the right to be represented by counsel at no charge to the government).
62. *Supra* Part II.B.2.
63. *See* Johnson v. Eisentrager, 339 U.S. 763 (1950).
64. United States Government Manual 388, 391 (1994-95).
65. The so-called Plenary Power doctrine granted full power over immigration law to the federal government. This power is not enumerated in the Constitution. *See* Chae Chan Ping v. United States, 130 U.S. 581 (1889) (extending federal control over immigration, specifically exclusion) (often referred to as the Chinese Exclusion case); Fong Yue Ting v United States, 149 U.S. 698 (1889) (extending Chinese Exclusion to deportation proceedings); Hiroshi Motomura, *Immigration Law After a Century of Plenary Power: Phantom Constitutional Norms and Statutory Interpretation*, 100 YALE L. J. 545 (1990) (discussing the Plenary power doctrine's current vitality); Louis Henkin, *The Constitution and United States Sovereignty: A Century of Chinese Exclusion and its Progeny*, 100 HARV. L. REV. 853, 861 (1987) (criticizing the oppressive nature of the Plenary Power doctrine).

this country, protections of aliens' rights are less than citizens' rights under the United States Constitution.[66] Nonetheless, fundamental rights of aliens are recognized by the United States Supreme Court.[67] The following section illustrates the overall scope of constitutional rights afforded to aliens. Then, the superseding section explains rights presently afforded to aliens in deportation hearings under present legislation in conjunction with standards set by the United States Supreme Court.

A. Rights Presently Afforded to Aliens

1. Varying Degrees of Aliens' Rights

In *Johnson v. Eisentrager*, the United States Supreme Court described the overall realm of aliens' rights: "[T]he alien . . . [is] accorded a generous and ascending scale of rights as he increases his identity with our society."[68] The Court explained that permitting an alien to be present in this country implies protection of that alien; this protection does not extend to aliens who have no territorial connection with this country.[69] Based on the Court's reasoning, it follows not only that aliens' rights are acknowledged by the Court, but also that resident aliens are viewed under a heightened standard as compared to non-resident aliens.[70] In general, the Court demands protection of constitutional rights of aliens, not only of resident aliens, but also of non-resident and illegal aliens.[71]

For example, in *United States v. Verdugo-Urquidez*,[72] the Court articulated specific outer boundaries of constitutional protections. The Court held that the Fourth Amendment does not protect property located in a foreign country owned by a nonresident alien.[73] The Court reasoned that because of the alien's lack of voluntary attachment to the United States, and because the property involved was located in a foreign country, the United States Constitution offered him no protection. Other examples are the Insular Cases where the Court held that not every constitutional provision applies to governmental activity even in geographical regions where the United States has sovereign power.[74] "Only 'fundamental' constitutional rights are guaranteed to inhab-

66. *See* Mathews v. Diaz, 426 U.S. 67, 79-80 (1976) ("In the exercise of its broad power over naturalization and immigration, Congress regularly makes rules that would be unacceptable if applied to citizens").

67. This note does not address rights of illegal aliens.

68. *Eisentrager*, 339 U.S. at 770.

69. *Id.* at 777-78.

70. *Id.*

71. United States v. Verdugo-Urquidez, 494 U.S. 259, 270-71 (1990) (listing cases which establish that illegal and legal aliens receive certain constitutional protections).

72. *Verdugo-Urquidez*, 494 U.S. at 259.

73. *Id.* at 274-75; *see also Eisentrager*, 339 U.S. at 763 (rejecting the extraterritorial application of the Fifth Amendment). *But see* Reid v. Covert, 354 U.S. 1, 7 (1957) ("[C]onstitutional protections for the individual were designed to restrict the United States Government when it acts outside of this country, as well as here at home.").

74. The *Insular Cases* as cited in *Verdugo-Urquidez*, 494 U.S. at 268, include Balzac v. Porto Rico, 258 U.S. 298 (1922) (Sixth Amendment right to jury trial inapplicable in Porto Rico); Ocampo v. United States, 234 U.S. 91 (1914) (Fifth Amendment Grand Jury provision inapplicable in Philippines); Dorr v. United States, 195 U.S. 138 (1904) (jury trial provision inapplicable in Philippines); Downes v. Bidwell, 182 U.S. 244 (1901) (Revenue Clauses of Constitution inapplicable to Porto Rico); Hawaii v. Mankichi, 190 U.S. 197 (1903) (provisions on indictment by grand jury and jury trial inapplicable in Hawaii).

itants of those territories."[75]

In *Verdugo-Urquidez* and the *Insular Cases*, the Court articulated two important distinctions: 1) extraterritorial from territorial rights, and 2) nonresident aliens from resident aliens. Although the Court has been reluctant to recognize nonresident aliens' rights in foreign countries, the Court respects the rights of resident aliens in the United States who have demonstrated "voluntary attachment" to the United States: "Mere lawful presence in the country creates an implied assurance of safe conduct and gives him certain rights."[76] Resident aliens seem to demonstrate voluntary attachment to the United States by residing here, thereby satisfying the Fourth Amendment test articulated in *Verdugo-Urquidez*. This level of protection, therefore, should readily be extended to the more general constitutional rights. In fact, as early as 1886, the Court, reinforcing this reasoning, explicitly held that the due process clauses of the Fourteenth Amendment[77] protects resident aliens.[78] The Court describes these provisions of the Fourteenth Amendment as "universal in their application, to all persons within the territorial jurisdiction, without regard to any differences of race, of color, or of nationality."[79] Then, in 1896, the Court declared that aliens are entitled to Fifth and Sixth Amendment rights: "[E]ven aliens shall not be held to answer for a capital or other infamous crime, unless on a presentment or indictment of a grand jury, nor be deprived of life, liberty or property without due process of law."[80] In addition to the Court's consistent recognition of resident aliens' due process protections, the Court acknowledged, in 1945, that resident aliens also have First Amendment rights.[81]

2. *The Hierarchy of Constitutional Rights*

The language of the Constitution describes the beneficiaries of the Fifth and Fourteenth Amendments as "persons."[82] In contrast, those described in the First, Second, Fourth, Ninth and Tenth Amendments are "the people." [83]Although this syntactical ambiguity is by no means conclusive, such distinctions suggest the varying scopes of protections afforded under the Amendments. The Fifth Amendment's "person" category is universal and inclusive, while remaining Amendments, through use of "the people," create a more limited category.[84]

In 1953, the Court used this legislative construction analysis in concluding that a

---

75. *Verdugo-Urquidez*, 494 U.S. at 268 (citing *Dorr*, 195 U.S. at 148).
76. *Eisentrager*, 339 U.S. at 770.
77. U.S. CONST. amend. XIV ("Nor shall any State deprive any person of life, liberty or property without due process of law; nor deny to any person within its jurisdiction the equal protection of the laws.").
78. Yick Wo v. Hopkins, 118 U.S. 356, 369 (1886).
79. *Id.*
80. Wong Wing v. United States, 163 U.S. 228, 238 (1896) (This statement was made in the context of aliens within the territorial jurisdiction of the United States.)
81. Bridges v. Wixon, 326 U.S. 135, 148 (1945).
82. U.S. CONST. amends. V, XIV. The Sixth Amendment uses the language "accused" which has been construed similarly to "person" under the Fifth and Fourteenth Amendments.
83. *Id.* amends. I, II, IV, IX, X.; *see also id.* Art. I, § 2, cl. 1 ("The House of Representatives shall be composed of Members chosen every second Year by *the People of the several States*") (emphasis added).
84. *See, e.g.*, *Verdugo-Urquidez*, 494 U.S. at 265-66, 269; *see also* United States ex rel. Turner v. Williams, 194 U.S. 279, 292 (1904) (The First Amendment does not apply to excludable alien because he is not "one of the *people* to whom these things are secured by our Constitution") (emphasis added); Louis Henkin, *The Constitution as Compact and as Conscience: Individual Rights Abroad and at Our Gates*, 27 WM. & MARY L. REV. 11, 14-15 (1985).

resident alien is a "person" within the meaning of the Fifth Amendment,[85] thereby reinforcing its earlier decisions extending due process to resident aliens. Furthermore, the Court, when refusing to extend the Fourth Amendment's protections in *Verdugo-Urquidez*, noted that "[the Fourth Amendment] operates in a different manner than the Fifth Amendment."[86] In addition, the Court expressly noted that the Fifth Amendment was not at issue in *Verdugo-Urquidez*, thereby distanced its restrictive interpretation of the Fourth Amendment from the Fifth Amendment. These sharp distinctions reinforce the hierarchical distinction between broad due process protections and the other constitutional provisions, as indicated by their language. In sum, the Court has established that resident aliens in the territorial United States are afforded some rights, at the very least. Therefore, aliens must be protected by the most basic procedural shields of due process under present law.

B. Constitutional Rights Presently Afforded to Aliens at Deportation Hearings

Since Congress explicitly left immigration law outside the reach of constitutional protections,[87] the applicability of even the most fundamental constitutional due process protections is less clear. Furthermore, although liberty interests are at stake, deportation proceedings are civil, not criminal;[88] therefore, the guaranteed criminal procedural protections do not apply to deportation hearings.[89]

But, in 1903, the United States Supreme Court acknowledged that due process applies to aliens in the deportation context: "[T]his court has never held . . . that administrative officers, when executing the provisions of a statute involving the liberty of persons, may disregard the fundamental principles that inhere in 'due process of law . . . .'"[90] Then, in 1993, the Court explicitly expanded this principle: "It is well established that the Fifth Amendment entitles aliens to due process of law in deportation proceedings."[91] Although this decision affirmed the extenuation of fundamental procedural rights for aliens in deportation proceedings, the specific application of this due process guarantee has been the subject of much debate.[92]

The United States Supreme Court extends minimal due process requirements, specifically the right of confrontation, not only to criminal procedure, but also to administrative and regulatory hearings.[93] Due process requires an adequate hearing including the opportunity to confront and cross-examine adverse witnesses.[94] Although

85. Kwong Hai Chew v. Colding, 344 U.S. 590, 601 (1953) (An alien's "status as a person within the meaning and protection of the Fifth Amendment cannot be capriciously taken from him.").

86. *Verdugo-Urquidez*, 494 U.S. at 264.

87. *Supra* note 63 (discussing the Plenary Power doctrine).

88. Harisiades v. Shaughnessy, 342 U.S. 580, 594 (1952) (citations omitted).

89. *See, e.g.*, Carlson v. Landon, 342 U.S. 524 (1952) (no bail requirement); Trias-Hernandez v. Immigration & Naturalization Serv., 528 F.2d 366, 368 (9th Cir. 1975) (Miranda warnings are not required).

90. Yamataya v. Fisher, 189 U.S. 86, 100 (1903) (this case is often referred to as The Japanese Immigrant Case). *But see* Fong Yue Ting, 149 U.S. at 707 (equating deportation powers with exclusionary powers, describing both as "absolute and unqualified" rights of the federal government).

91. Reno v. Flores, 113 S. Ct. 1439, 1449 (1993); *accord* Landon v. Plasencia, 459 U.S. 21, 32-34 (1982); *Kwong Hai Chew*, 344 U.S. at 596-97, 602.

92. *See, e.g.*, Jim Rosenfeld, Deportation Proceedings and Due Process of Law, 26 COLUM. HUM. RTS. L. REV. 713 (1995) (tracing this debate from the Alien Acts of 1798 to early versions of Congress's 1995 proposed legislation).

93. Greene v. McElroy, 360 U.S. 474, 496-97 (1959).

94. Goldberg v. Kelly, 397 U.S. 254 (1970) (explaining due process requirements for an adequate

"due process is flexible, subjective, difficult to determine,"[95] the Court explicitly guarantees, at the very least, some degree of procedural protections to aliens in deportation hearings. The minimum basic protection in the context of a hearing is the accused's right to confront the evidence against him or her.[96] Therefore, according to the aforementioned United States Supreme Court decisions, aliens must, *at the very least*, be afforded the right of confrontation.

In accordance with the Court's guarantees, legislation governing present-day deportation hearings explicitly provides the alien with the right to confront opposing evidence.[97] In addition, the alien "shall be given notice . . . of the nature of the charges against him"[98] and the alien "shall have the privilege of being represented (at no expense to the Government) by . . . counsel . . . ."[99] Although not expressly required to do so under the United States Constitution, current deportation legislation provides aliens more than the minimal due process guarantees.

IV. ANALYSIS OF THE COMPREHENSIVE TERRORISM PREVENTION ACT IN LIGHT OF ALIENS' EXISTING RIGHTS

Congress' attempt to reconcile the competing concerns of national security risks with aliens' right to confront evidence resulted in the secret evidence provisions. Without further elaboration, the language of this bill is open to varying interpretations with varying results. Without explicit constitutional guarantees,[100] aliens are susceptible to restrictions on their rights imposed by legislation, limited only by rights explicitly established by the United States Supreme Court. Therefore, the importance of procedural protections afforded to aliens through legislation cannot be underestimated. The secret evidence provisions in The Comprehensive Terrorism Prevention Act constitute an intolerable deprivation of procedural rights. There are two chief concerns with the proposed Act: First, the procedures for determining who is an alien terrorist, and second, the lower-standard summary of classified information provided to the alien to prepare a defense. The following sections explain these concerns and then discuss the long-term ramifications.

A. The Alien Terrorist Determination

The proposed Comprehensive Terrorism Prevention Act gives the Secretary of State, a presidentially-appointed cabinet member, full discretion in defining "terrorist organization."[101] Under the proposed Comprehensive Terrorism Prevention Act, an entire group of people might be officially classified as a "terrorist organization" based upon no more than one unlawful act committed by one of its members. As a result of

---

hearing for the termination of welfare benefits). *But see* Wolff v. McDonnell, 418 U.S. 539, 568-69 (1974) (limiting availability of cross-examination in prison hearings).

95. Morrissey v. Brewer, 408 U.S. 471, 481 (1972).

96. *See* Kenneth Culp Davis, *The Requirement of a Trial-Type Hearing*, 70 HARV. L. REV. 193, 213-14 (1956) (explaining the need for confrontation and the dangers of "faceless" informers).

97. "The Immigration Judge shall . . . advise the respondent that he will have a reasonable opportunity to examine and object to the evidence against him . . . and to cross-examine witnesses presented by the Government . . . ." 8 C.F.R. § 242.16(a) (1995).

98. 8 U.S.C. § 1252(b)(1) (1995).

99. *Id.* § 1252(b)(2); *see also* 8 C.F.R. § 242.16(a) (alien shall be advised of available free legal services programs).

100. *See supra* note 65.

101. S. 735, *supra* note 1, § 210(2)(iv).

this classification, each alien member would be considered an "alien terrorist" for the purposes of the new Alien Terrorist Removal Procedures.[102] In any circumstance where the government has evidence, whether weighty or inadequate, indicating that an alien is a member of an organization which the Secretary of State has declared a "terrorist organization,"[103] the government may initiate Alien Terrorist Removal Procedures against that alien. These procedures provide for the expedited removal of an alien based on the government's secret evidence. Under this legislation, politically unpopular groups may be singled out, and, based upon nothing more than their status as aliens and the Secretary of State's designation of an organization to which they belong, law-abiding resident aliens may be deported.

B. The Substitute Lower-Standard Summary

1. The New Procedure

Although it is not uncommon for some types of hearings to provide less procedural safeguards than a criminal trial, the secret evidence provision, providing that a written summary may be substituted for classified information, contains an even lower level of protection. For example, in bail hearings, the Rules of Evidence do not apply and hearsay evidence is admissible.[104] Although admitting hearsay evidence may limit defendants' opportunities to cross-examine the evidence against them at bail hearings, admitting substitute written summaries *eliminates* the aliens' opportunity to cross-examine evidence against them. The opportunity to call a live witness to testify gives criminal defendants an opportunity to challenge the witness's credibility and explore the issue. In contrast, under the summary provision of The Comprehensive Terrorism Prevention Act, aliens are forced to accept a summary of the evidence against them without dispute. In effect, by allowing the government to present their entire case in a written summary, The Comprehensive Terrorism Prevention Act nullifies the fundamental procedural guarantee of the right to confront opposing evidence outlined by the United States Supreme Court[105] and followed in present-day legislation governing deportation hearings. Although the language of the secret evidence provision requires the lower-standard summary to be adequate to allow the alien to prepare a defense, the procedures deny aliens any opportunity to confront evidence against them.

In the secret evidence provision, not only are the procedural safeguards lower

---

102. *See also* David Cole, *The Politics of Crime Makes for Strange Bedfellows*, CONN. L. TRIB., Nov. 15, 1993, at 25 (discussing early opposition to these and other similar provisions which were later adopted by The Comprehensive Terrorism Prevention Act).

103. This determination, which underlies the alien removal procedures, rests wholly with the Secretary of State, restrained only by a "consultation with the Secretary of the Treasury." This legislation includes no procedures by which an alien terrorist could appeal this determination. S. 735, *supra* note 1, § 210(2)(iv).

104. The Bail Reform Act of 1984, 18 U.S.C. § 3141 (1994). In contrast with The Comprehensive Terrorism Prevention Act, note the increased procedural safeguards provided for defendants in bail hearings, including: detention hearing must be prompt; findings of fact must be in writing; appellate review is expedited; right to counsel at government's expense; and defendant's ability to cross-examine witnesses. *See also* United States v. Salerno, 481 U.S. 739 (1987) (explaining these procedural safeguards).

105. *See* Jay v. Boyd, 351 U.S. 345 (1956) (upholding the use of secret evidence in exclusion case, but expressly stating secret evidence may not be used in deportation proceedings); Joint Anti-Fascist Refugee Comm. v. McGrath, 341 U.S. 123, 171-72 (1951) (Frankfurter, J., concurring) ("Secrecy is not congenial to truth-seeking . . . .").

than those provided for defendants in bail hearings, but the consequences of a deportation hearing are also more severe. Following a bail determination, the defendants are given another opportunity to be heard, with full range of procedural protections, at a criminal trial. In contrast, following the deportation hearing, aliens are not given an opportunity to defend themselves; rather, they must leave the United States.

2. *The Contents of the Substitute Summary*

The language of The Comprehensive Terrorism Prevention Act reads as if openness is the rule and secrecy is the exception, and as if heightened-standard summaries[106] are the rule and lower-standard summaries[107] are the exception. In effect, however, the boundless "exceptions" allow the "rules" to be circumvented with ease. As discussed in Part II.B.1, the prerequisites which must be fulfilled before heightened-standard summaries are bypassed, are ambiguous and provide little protection to the alien.[108] A mere recitation of even the most vague allegations seem to satisfy the ambiguous threshold set forth in the language of this bill. As a result, the purported rules become suggestions, dramatically lowering the standards of protection afforded to aliens, in addition to undermining legislative intent behind this legislation.

A lower-standard summary may, in fact, allow an alien to prepare a defense, but it does not offer the alien substantially the same ability as full disclosure of classified information. By dramatically lowering the standard for the requisite summary, the bill deprives aliens of the right to confront evidence against them, and leaves open the question of whether aliens will be informed of any charges against them when they are subject to deportation proceedings. Although this legislation specifies that the summary presented to the alien must be "adequate to allow the alien to prepare a defense,"[109] this legislation does not explain how, without any indication of the government's accusations, an alien could possibly prepare any defense at all.

C. The Potential Ramifications of The Secret Evidence Provision

Though countless explanations for the passage of the secret evidence provisions are feasible, none are sufficient. Perhaps due to misguided anti-terrorist passions, or perhaps due to politics, the Senate passed a bill which potentially undermines fundamental procedural protections. The assurances of fairness and justice were taken away in the name of national security, for the purposes of combating the modern-day enemy. If history is a fair indicator, the consequences of this legislation, if enacted, will not be widely understood until after substantial damage is done.[110]

Despite political rhetoric to the contrary, this proposed legislation fails to guarantee aliens the most fundamental due process right: The right of confrontation. Without procedural protections, the government is free to unilaterally accuse and administer punishment.[111] The persons whose rights are subject to the newfound vulnerability

---

106. The heightened-standard summary must "provide the alien with substantially the same ability to make his defense as would disclosure of the classified information." S. 735, *supra* note 1, § 503(e)(6)(B).

107. The lower-standard summary must be "adequate to allow the alien to prepare a defense." S. 735, *supra* note 1, § 503(e)(6)(E)(iii).

108. For the list of these prerequisites, see *supra* text accompanying notes 39-42.

109. S. 735, *supra* note 1, § 503(e)(6)(E)(iii).

110. *See supra* Part I.

111. In the context of these provisions, the punishment is deportation.

under The Comprehensive Terrorism Prevention Act include aliens who are legally residing in the United States. Although an argument can be made that such aliens' rights are, and should be, less than rights of citizens, the United States Supreme Court, as discussed earlier, has determined that aliens are afforded fundamental procedural rights, including the right to confront evidence against them. Furthermore, permitting an alleged terrorist to confront evidence does not undermine the government's case against him. Alternatively, procedural protections simply ensure the innocent will not be deported without justification from the United States government.[112]

The legal reasoning behind The Comprehensive Terrorism Prevention Act is an invalid syllogism.[113] The secret evidence provisions are based upon a logical fallacy: Some terrorists are foreigners, therefore all foreigners are terrorists. Such an underlying premise is not only incoherent, but also offensive to the integrity of the principle of legality.[114] Generalizations about what people may do based solely upon their status as an alien intimidates aliens based only upon the belief that foreigners *may* be terrorists.

Terrorism is defined as the "use of violence and threats to intimidate or coerce, esp[ecially] for political purposes."[115] Since no legitimate goals are served by punishing a person who is not culpable and did not act in violation of any laws,[116] it follows that this type of punishment is administered for the purpose of intimidating or coercing. In other words, this legislation proposes a terrorist solution which undermines the impartiality and legitimacy of the rules of law.[117] The Comprehensive Terrorism Prevention Act enables the government to use secret evidence in new deportation proceedings to intimidate and coerce aliens based upon ideological and political fears of foreigners who may be terrorists. Such policy is reminiscent of Japanese-American internment camps and widespread infiltration of organizations suspected of Communist sympathies.[118] In effect, the Senate passed a bill which repeated recognized historic mistakes; the Senate passed a bill which undermined the principle of legality.

V. REDRAFTING THE LEGISLATION

Although supporters of this bill assert its fairness and its effectiveness in both combating terrorism and protecting national security, opponents remain concerned with civil rights abuses.[119] The prevention of terrorist attacks is a goal clearly supported

112. *See supra* notes 7-11 and accompanying text (explaining the importance of procedural protections to preserve the legitimacy of our judicial system).

113. *See generally*, Edwin W. Patterson, *Logic in the Law*, 90 U. PENN. L. REV. 875 (1942) (applying the psychology of problem-solving to legal analysis, including formal and instrumental logic).

114. *See supra* notes 7-11 and accompanying text.

115. THE RANDOM HOUSE DICTIONARY OF THE ENGLISH LANGUAGE 1960 (2nd. ed. 1987).

116. The legitimate goals served by punishment are prevention, restraint, rehabilitation, deterrence, education and retribution. *See* WAYNE R. LAFAVE & AUSTIN W. SCOTT, JR., CRIMINAL LAW 21-25 (1972).

117. *See supra* notes 7-11 and accompanying text (explaining the rules of law).

118. *See supra* Part I (explaining instances of extreme actions taken by the United States government in the name of national security which have since been recognized as wrong).

119. *See, e.g.*, Benjamin Wittes, *Immigrants, Civil Libertarians Unite; Clinton Anti-Terrorism Bill Angers Rights Groups*, LEGAL TIMES, Mar. 13, 1995, at 2; Representative Schumer, *Editorial: Life and Liberty*, N.Y. TIMES, April 28, 1995 at A33; Holly Idelson, *Complaints Slow Panel Action on Anti-Terrorism Bill*, CONG. Q. WK. REP., June 19, 1995 at 1750 (discussing opposition to an earlier House version of these provisions).

unanimously, as are universal civil rights protections. Deportation procedures need to be streamlined to facilitate the expedited removal of aliens who pose a legitimate threat to the safety of the United States. But, as an appeal to fairness and principles of legality, in addition to lessons learned from history, Congress must modify the proposed secret evidence provisions which fail to distinguish between aliens and terrorists. The best solution lies in a synthesis of the competing concerns. In light of the broader principles at stake, the following section focuses on major pitfalls present in the proposed deportation proceedings set forth in The Comprehensive Terrorism Prevention Act: 1) The definition of "terrorist organization;"[120] 2) the secret evidence determination; and 3) the required standard for summaries of secret evidence; and 4) the questionable right of confrontation. Each will be addressed, in turn, along with a workable solution.

A reform of The Comprehensive Terrorism Prevention Act must be founded on basic notions of justice in light of the United States Constitution, lessons learned from history, and the principles of legality.[121] Further, such a proposal must attempt to remedy the imminent threat of terrorism without losing sight of sensitive national security concerns or basic procedural protections. In accordance with these objectives, this following submission attempts to modify the Senate bill to better serve the laudable intentions of the Senators who supported it.

A. Eliminate "Terrorist Organization" Determination

Under the current anti-terrorism laws, the government possesses the power to deport any alien who engages in or supports terrorist activity.[122] Establishing a new class of persons who are defined as deportable does not combat terrorism. Other than facilitating guilt by association, the creation of this new class adds no new powers to the fight against terrorists. In addition, it is important to prevent any one person, namely the Secretary of State, from possessing such a concentration of power to unilaterally declare any group to be a terrorist organization. Eliminating this determination ensures that politically unpopular groups are not singled out under the auspices of security risks. Eliminating this new label also ensures that aliens are not labeled "alien terrorists" unless they personally commit a terrorist act, not because they belong to an organization which is considered a "terrorist organization."

B. Raise the Standard for Secret Evidence Determination

Classified information must remain secret, but the government must be restrained in some way from using it liberally against an alien, without his knowledge, at a deportation hearing. All evidence obtained against an alleged terrorist must be used

---

120. Representative Hyde, a sponsor of this legislation in the House of Representatives, "blamed the bill's broad definition of terrorism for creating problems" passing this legislation. Stephen Labaton, *Bill on Terrorism, Once a Certainty, Derails in House*, N.Y. TIMES, Oct. 3, 1995, at A1.

121. *See supra* notes 7-11 and accompanying text.

122. "Any alien who has engaged, is engaged, or at any time after entry engages in any terrorist activity . . . is deportable." 8 U.S.C. § 1105(a)(4)(B) (1994). "Terrorist activity" is defined as any activity which is unlawful under the laws of the place where it is committed and involves *any* of the following, or a threat, attempt or conspiracy to do any of the following: hijacking; threatening to kill, injure or continue to detain another individual in order to compel another person; violently attacking an internationally protected person; an assassination; using biological agents, chemical agents or nuclear devices; using an explosive or firearm with the intent to endanger the safety of one or more individuals or to cause substantial damage to property. 8 U.S.C. § 1182(a)(3)(B) (1994).

against them to prosecute them effectively. This includes classified information, but it must only be relied upon by the government if it is corroborated and deemed reliable by more than one judge. The problem with the language as drafted[123] can be remedied by instituting a rigorous system of checks and balances. As illustrated earlier, the lower-standard summary, as drafted, potentially deprives the alien of any procedural protections. To avoid this extreme infringement of rights, in all cases purporting to involve classified information, lower-standard summaries should be limited to matters that are 1) secret by executive order in the interest of national policy and 2) classified pursuant to an executive order.[124] Furthermore, harsh sanctions must be imposed on the government if it attempts to withhold evidence from aliens.[125] Such threats will force the government to reveal all that it can, instead of creating incentives for the government to get away with as much as it can. In addition, a detailed definition of the standards "harm to the national security" and "bodily injury to any person" are required before the lower-standard summary may be substituted. Instituting these additional safeguards will guarantee the higher-standard summary to nearly all accused aliens. The vague standard articulated in The Comprehensive Terrorism Prevention Act must be replaced by a heightened standard to curb abuses. By providing the alien with only a heightened summary, the government will no longer be able to avoid the question of confronting witnesses.

C. Redraft the Summary Provisions.

Raising the standards for defining a "terrorist organization," providing the alien with the right to confrontation, and raising the standard of "secret evidence" will improve the application of the Senate bill. Most importantly, the language authorizing the summary provisions must be reformed. As discussed earlier, the Senate's legislation requires the alien to be presented with an unclassified summary, in lieu of mandatory disclosure of classified information. The summary must be sufficient to 1) inform the alien of the nature of the evidence against him, and 2) provide the alien with substantially the same ability to make his defense as would disclosure of the classified information. If the higher-standard summary was the rule and the lower-standard summary was the rare exception, as intended by Senator Specter and Senator Biden, this provision would deprive a smaller group of aliens their rights to confront the evidence against them. The minimal threshold present in The Comprehensive Terrorism Prevention Act, the standard which renders the potential of stripping aliens of all procedural rights, must be resorted to only sparingly.

D. Provide the Alien with the Right of Confrontation.

As discussed in Part III, aliens are protected by the Due Process Clause of the Fifth Amendment. Although the precise scope of this protection remains unclear, the United States Supreme Court has assured them at least a minimal degree of protection.

123. *See supra* Part II.B.3 (explaining the problems with the summary provisions).

124. Institute a definition of classified information similar to the one articulated as an exception to The Freedom of Information Act. *See* 5 U.S.C.A. § 552(b)(1) (1977).

125. For similar sanctions imposed on the government for violations of Classified Information Procedures Act (C.I.P.A), see 18 U.S.C. App. IV § 1 (1995). *Compare* S. 735, *supra* note 1, §§ 503(D)-(E) (giving the government a second chance to draft an acceptable summary, then, upon second failure, proceeding under a lower-standard summary).

The most basic of these protections is the right of confrontation. Affording such a basic procedural safeguard to aliens will not only protect the innocent alien, but will also preserve the integrity of our legal system. In addition to eliminating any temptation to abuse deportation powers, affording procedural safeguards will reinforce public confidence in our system of justice. The alien will be provided this right if the aforementioned proposals are adopted.

VI. CONCLUSION

The bombing of the federal building in Oklahoma City was a horrific tragedy; the perpetrators must be punished to the full extent of the law. However, during the emotional times following such a disaster, we must be cautious to avoid far-reaching legislative remedies which often result in unintended harms inflicted on innocent persons. In a rush to respond to the bombing, the Senate passed legislation which tramples the rights of law-abiding resident aliens. The Comprehensive Terrorism Prevention Act should not be adopted without substantial revisions as discussed above. The government's case against an alleged terrorist will not be undermined if he is permitted to confront the government's evidence against him. Supporters of this legislation are rightfully concerned about the consequences of revealing classified information. But, opponents of this legislation are equally concerned about the far-reaching effects of stripping fundamental rights from an entire group of people. Congress would be unwise to disregard their own codified warning "to discourage the occurrence of similar injustices and violations of civil liberties in the future"[126] based upon popular fears and stereotypes. As discussed above, a workable compromise can be attained without further endangering informants, without facilitating terrorist groups and without violating the principle of legality.

Melissa A. O'Loughlin

126. *See supra* notes 16-17 and accompanying text (statute authorizing nominal reparations to Japanese-Americans for civil liberties violations).

* B.S., Political Science, Santa Clara University, 1993; J.D. Candidate, Notre Dame Law School, 1997.

CQ Weekly

Feb. 2, 2002
Page 329

Provisions of the Anti-Terrorism Bill

By Elizabeth A. Palmer and Keith Perine, CQ Staff

Congress cleared an anti-terrorism bill (PL 107-56▸▸) on Oct. 25, 2001 — a little more than a month after Attorney General John Ashcroft had asked for the additional authority to investigate and prosecute acts of terrorism.

The 131-page law moved quickly through Congress, although it took a tortuous course to the president's desk. The version of the bill approved by the House Judiciary Committee was never considered by the House. That chamber passed a different version negotiated by Republicans leaders and the Bush administration, then passed a final bill worked out between the House and Senate. *(2001 CQ Weekly, p. 2533)*

The Senate Judiciary Committee did not consider the legislation. It went straight to the Senate floor.

Despite concerns from civil liberties advocates on the left and the right, the Bush administration got most of what it sought. The law allows the government to track Internet communications as well as telephone conversations, gives law enforcement greater authority to conduct secret searches of suspects' property, allows authorities to get warrants that are good nationwide and removes the statute of limitations on some terrorism crimes.

The law also includes tougher new money-laundering laws, which the Justice Department already has used to seize several bank accounts it says are related to the September terrorist attacks.

The House passed the bill by a vote of 357-66 on Oct. 24; the Senate cleared the measure for the president on Oct. 25 by a vote of 98-1. President Bush signed it the next day.

Changes in Criminal Law

- **Mass transit.** The law makes it a federal crime to attack a mass transit system, punishable by a fine and as much as 20 years in prison. If the vehicle was carrying a passenger at the time of the attack, or if the attack killed someone, the maximum sentence increases to life.

- **Domestic terrorism.** The law defines "domestic terrorism" as activities that involve acts dangerous to human life that are a violation of federal or state laws and that appeared to be intended to intimidate or coerce a civilian population, change government policy or affect the conduct of government by mass destruction, assassination or kidnaping, and that occurred primarily within the United States.

- **Harboring terrorists.** It is now a federal crime for individuals to harbor a person who they know or should have known was engaged in or would engage in terrorist activities.

- **U.S. criminal jurisdiction.** The law extends U.S. jurisdiction to offenses committed by or against a U.S. national, U.S. diplomatic, consular and military missions, and residences used by U.S. personnel assigned to such missions.

- **Material support for terrorism.** The law adds three terrorism-related offenses to the list of those considered providing material support to a terrorist. These violations may be prosecuted in any federal judicial district in which the offense was committed. It explicitly prohibits providing terrorists with "expert advice or assistance," such as flight training, knowing or intending that it will be used to prepare for or carry out an act of terrorism.

- **U.S. forfeiture authority.** U.S. forfeiture authority is extended to "all assets, foreign or domestic" that are owned or controlled by any person or group planning or carrying out an act of terrorism against the United States, its citizens or residents or their property.

- **Material support for terrorists.** The law clarifies that the provisions of the Trade Sanctions Reform and Export Enhancement Act of 2000 (Title IX of ««PL»» 106-387) do not limit or otherwise affect the criminal prohibitions against providing material support to terrorists or designated terrorist organizations.

- **Crime of terrorism defined.** The law adds the following as a list of offenses under the definition of "federal crime of terrorism": destruction of aircraft or aircraft facilities; violence at international airports; arson within special maritime and territorial jurisdiction; offenses involving biological or chemical weapons; kidnapping or assassination of members of Congress, the Cabinet or the Supreme Court; offenses involving nuclear materials or plastic explosives; arson and bombing of government property risking or causing death; arson and bombing of property used in interstate commerce; killing or attempted killing during an attack on a federal facility with a dangerous weapon; conspiracy to murder, kidnap, or maim persons abroad; offenses against the protection of computers; killing or attempted killing of officers and employees of the United States; murder or manslaughter of foreign officials, official guests, or internationally protected persons; hostage taking; destruction of communication lines, stations, or systems; injury to buildings or property within special maritime and territorial jurisdiction of the United States; destruction of an energy facility; presidential and presidential staff assassination and kidnapping; wrecking trains; terrorist attacks and other acts of violence against mass transportation systems; destruction of national defense materials, premises, or utilities; violence against maritime navigation; violence against maritime fixed platforms; certain homicides and other violence against United States nationals occurring outside of the United States; use of weapons of mass destruction; acts of terrorism transcending national boundaries; harboring terrorists; providing material support to terrorists or terrorist organizations; torture; sabotage of nuclear facilities or fuel; aircraft piracy; assault on a flight crew with a dangerous weapon, explosive o, incendiary devices or endangerment of human life by means of weapons on aircraft.

- **No statute of limitations.** The law eliminates the statute of limitations for certain terrorism-related offenses if they resulted in or created a foreseeable risk of death or serious bodily injury to another person.

- **Increased prison terms.** The law raises the maximum prison terms to 15 to 20 years, or, if death results, life, for the following crimes: arson within the special maritime and territorial jurisdiction of the United States, destruction of an energy facility, destruction of national-defense materials, provision of material support to terrorists and terrorist organizations, sabotage of nuclear facilities or fuel, killings on aircraft, destruction of interstate gas or hazardous liquid pipeline facility.

- **Conspiracy penalties.** The law adds conspiracy provisions to the following criminal statutes: arson within special maritime and territorial jurisdiction of the United States; killings in federal facilities; destruction of communications lines, stations or systems; destruction of property within special maritime and territorial jurisdiction of the United States; wrecking trains; material support to terrorists; torture; sabotage of nuclear facilities or fuel; interference with flight crews; carrying weapons or explosives on aircraft; and destruction of interstate gas or hazardous liquid pipeline facilities.

- **Supervised release.** Once they have served their prison sentence, the law authorizes an extended period of supervised release for people convicted of certain terrorism-related offenses that resulted in, or created a foreseeable risk of, death or serious bodily injury to another person.

- **Terrorism as racketeering.** Certain terrorism-related offenses are included within the definition of "racketeering activity," thus allowing multiple acts of terrorism to be charged as a pattern of racketeering for purposes of the Racketeer Influenced and Corrupt Organizations (RICO) statute, which can triple the damages imposed. The law expands the ability of prosecutors to prosecute members of established, ongoing terrorist organizations.

• **Computer hacking.** The criminal statute prohibiting computer hacking includes computers located outside the United States when used in a manner that affects the interstate commerce or communications of the United States. The law updates the definition of "loss" to ensure that the full costs to victims of hacking offenses are counted.

• **Forensic laboratories.** The attorney general must establish regional computer forensic laboratories and support existing computer forensic laboratories to help combat computer crime.

• **U.S. criminal jurisdiction.** The biological weapons statute's definition of "for use as a weapon" now includes all situations in which it can be proven that the defendant had any purpose not prophylactic, protective, or peaceful. Certain persons, including non-resident foreign nationals of countries that support international terrorism, are forbidden from possessing a listed biological agent or toxin.

Miscellaneous

• **Civil rights oversight.** The Justice Department's inspector general must designate one official to review information and receive complaints alleging abuses of civil rights and civil liberties by employees and officials of the Department of Justice.

• **Condemnation of discrimination.** The law condemns discrimination and acts of violence against Sikh Americans, as well as Arab and Muslim Americans.

• **Denial of admission for money laundering.** Any alien who a consular officer or the attorney general knows, or has reason to believe, is involved in a federal money-laundering offense is barred from the United States.

• **Biometric identifier.** The attorney general must report to Congress on the feasibility of using a "biometric identifier" system, with access to the FBI fingerprint database, at consular offices abroad and at points of entry into the United States. Such devices scan fingerprints or other physical characteristics to check an individual's identity.

• **Suspect lists to airlines.** The FBI must report to Congress on the feasibility of providing airlines with computer access to the names or suspected terrorists.

• **Military installation security.** The Defense Department has temporary authority to enter contracts with a state or local government for the performance of security functions at any military installation or facility in the United States.

• **Charity telemarketing.** Any telemarketer soliciting for charity must disclose to people they call that they are telephoning to solicit charitable contributions, and to make other disclosures that the Federal Trade Commission considers appropriate.

• **Hazardous materials background check.** The Department of Transportation may check the background of any individual applying for a license to transport hazardous materials in interstate commerce.

• **State and local bio-terrorism preparedness.** The law expresses the sense of the Senate that the United States should make a substantial new investment this year toward improving state and local preparedness to respond to potential bio-terrorism attacks.

• **Terrorism grants.** The law authorizes a Justice Department program to provide grants to states to prepare for and respond to terrorist acts including, but not limited to, acts involving weapons of mass destruction and biological, nuclear, radiological, incendiary, chemical and explosive devices. The law revises this grant program to provide additional flexibility to purchase needed equipment.

training and technical assistance to state and local first responders; and a more equitable allocation of funds among the states. It also clarifies that grants under the Crime Identification Technology Act can go for anti-terrorism, and it authorizes grants under that Act at $250 million a year through fiscal year 2007. The law authorizes another $25 million annually from fiscal 2003 through fiscal 2007 for grants to state and local authorities to respond to and prevent acts of terrorism.

CQ Weekly February 1, 2002

Biological Weapons and US Law

During the past 8 years, the US Congress has developed a comprehensive legal framework to prevent the illegitimate use of toxins and infectious agents. As part of this framework, Congress has defined as a federal crime virtually every step in the process of developing or acquiring a biological agent for use as a weapon. At the same time, Congress has vested federal law enforcement agencies with broad civil and investigative powers to enable the government to intervene before such weapons are used or even developed. Finally, Congress has directed the Centers for Disease Control and Prevention to establish a regulatory regime to monitor the location and transfer of hazardous biological agents and to insure that any use of such agents complies with appropriate biosafety requirements.

JAMA. 1997;278:357-360

THE PAST DECADE has witnessed a major shift in the nature and magnitude of the threat posed by biological weapons. For many years, the dangers of such weapons arose solely from the risk of their use in international conflicts. As a result, the class of potential users consisted entirely of a small number of industrialized countries that had developed (or could develop) a biological arsenal for use in warfare.

All this has now changed. In the last 10 years, the class of potential users has expanded to include not only a growing number of developing nations but also a wide range of nonstate actors such as terrorist groups, religious cults, and even individuals.[1,2] Furthermore, many of these new parties now pose a threat of an entirely different kind—the use of biological weapons as agents of terror rather than as instruments of war.[1,2]

The emergence of this threat has carried far-reaching implications for US policy. Where the US government once focused exclusively on preventing other countries from acquiring biological weapons, it now focuses increasingly on the use of such weapons by terrorists and other nonstate actors. Indeed, Congress recently passed 3 major statutes[3-6] in an effort to prevent the use of biological weapons by domestic and international terrorists as well as by nations. In addition, last year, Congress established the framework for a comprehensive regulatory regime to control the domestic use of hazardous toxins and infectious agents. Under this regime, the Centers for Disease Control and Prevention (CDC) regulate the transfer and use of more than 30 toxins, bacteria, and viruses posing significant risks to the public health and safety.

CURBING THE ACQUISITION OF BIOLOGICAL WEAPONS BY OTHER NATIONS: THE BIOLOGICAL WEAPONS CONTROL ACT

To understand the goals of the recent legislation dealing with biological weapons, it is first necessary to trace the history of US bioweapons policy since 1972. Until recently, US policy focused almost exclusively on preventing the acquisition and use of biological weapons by other nations. To this end, the US government relied on 3 major strategies. First, the United States entered into a series of treaties and other international agreements designed to achieve biological disarmament and to prevent the proliferation of biological arms to countries that did not yet possess them. Second, the United States imposed economic and diplomatic sanctions on governments that persisted in their efforts to develop a biological arsenal. Third, the United States created an extensive system of export controls to prevent the transfer to other countries of US goods and technologies that could be used in the development of biological weapons.

Until recently, US policy focused almost exclusively on preventing the acquisition and use of biological weapons by other nations.

These strategies originated in 1972 when the United States and more than 70 other nations entered into an agreement known as the Biological Weapons and Toxin Convention (BWC). In Article I of the BWC, the signatory nations pledged that their respective governments would refrain from developing, producing, stockpiling, or acquiring any biological or toxin weapon. In addition, in Article IV of the BWC, the nations pledged that their governments would take all necessary steps to prevent the development or retention of biological weapons by any party within their respective jurisdictions.

In the wake of the BWC, the United States initiated an aggressive arms-control policy to prevent nations from acquiring biological arms and other weapons of mass destruction. The US effort became increasingly important in the late 1980s, as several medium-sized nations (including regional aggressors such as North Korea, Libya, Syria, Iraq, and Iran)

From Northwestern University School of Law, Northwestern University Medical School, and Sonnenschein Nath & Rosenthal, Chicago, Ill.

Reprints: James R. Ferguson, JD, Sonnenschein Nath & Rosenthal, 6000 Sears Tower, Chicago, IL 60606.

pursued major weapons programs that included chemical and biological arms.[1,2,6,7]

In response to this development, Congress passed the Chemical and Biological Weapons Control Act of 1991.[4] In this act, Congress established an elaborate system of economic sanctions and export controls to curb the proliferation of biological arms. Most notably, Congress created a broad array of economic and diplomatic sanctions to be imposed on any country that used biological weapons in violation of international law. In addition, Congress authorized the imposition of sanctions on international companies that knowingly exported any goods or technologies used in the development of biological weapons to countries designated by the US administration as terrorist states or prohibited nations.

Finally, Congress amended the Export Administration Act of 1979[8]—to prevent US companies and individuals from exporting to certain prohibited countries any goods or technologies that would "directly and substantially assist" a government or group in developing or delivering a biological weapon. By virtue of this amendment, any domestic company or individual who knowingly exported to a prohibited country materials used for biological weapons was subject to civil and criminal penalties, including imprisonment of up to 10 years.

The Biological Weapons Control Act represented a congressional attempt to further the BWC's goal of curbing the transfer of biological weapons to other nations. But for many years after the BWC, the United States had no parallel policy governing the use of biological weapons by groups within its own borders—a parallel policy that had been required by Article IV of the BWC. In fact, until recently, the nation did not have a single law prohibiting the acquisition or use of biological weapons by domestic groups or regulating the domestic sale or transfer of pathogens and toxins.

The need for such legislation became clear in the years following the end of the cold war. During this period, the United States was confronted for the first time by a serious threat of a biological attack on its own soil—a threat that arose not so much from other nations as from subnational groups interested in using biological weapons as instruments of terror.[1,2,7,9,10] These groups included both international terrorists (such as Aun Shinrikyo) and domestic extremists (such as antigovernment groups and right-wing militias).[1,2,6,7]

To address the threat, Congress passed the Biological Weapons Act of 1989[3] and the Anti-Terrorism Act of 1996.[5] In these statutes, Congress attempted to reduce the dangers of bioterrorism in 3 ways. First, the statutes imposed severe criminal penalties on the possession, manufacture, or use of biological weapons. Second, the statutes authorized the federal government to seize any pathogens or other materials used to develop a biological weapon or its delivery system. Third, the statutes created a regulatory system for controlling the use and transfer of hazardous biological agents.

These statutes—and the strategies that underlie them—warrant closer inspection.

CURBING THE DOMESTIC THREAT OF BIOLOGICAL WEAPONS: THE BIOLOGICAL WEAPONS ACT OF 1989

The US Congress passed the Biological Weapons Act of 1989 to implement Article IV of the BWC and to protect the nation against bioterrorist acts.[11] The key provisions of the act define as a federal crime the knowing development, manufacture, transfer, or possession of any "biological agent, toxin, or delivery system" for "use as a weapon."[3] The act broadly defines "biological agent" to include any "microorganism, virus, or infectious substance" capable of (1) causing deleterious changes in the environment; (2) damaging food, water, or equipment supplies; or (3) causing diseases in humans, animals, plants, or other living organisms.[3] Furthermore, the act imposes heavy criminal penalties on those who knowingly violate its prohibitions. Indeed, unlike most other federal criminal statutes (which set forth a maximum period of imprisonment), the act expressly provides that a violator can be imprisoned for any term of years, including life. In addition to its criminal provisions, the act vests the federal government with broad civil and investigative powers to prevent the development, production, or stockpiling of biological weapons. For example, the act authorizes the government to apply for a judicial warrant to seize "any biological agent, toxin, or delivery system" that is "of a type or in a quantity" that has no "apparent justification for... peaceful purposes."[3] This standard enables the government to intervene almost immediately after learning of a potential violation of the criminal provisions of the act. Indeed, to effect a seizure under this standard, the government does not even have to show that the materials to be seized are intended for "use as a weapon." Rather, the government need only show that it has probable cause to believe that the materials have no apparent peaceful justification.

> ... prohibiting any party from attempting to develop or possess a pathogen, toxin, or delivery system having no apparent peaceful justification.

The Biological Weapons Act also authorizes the government to obtain a civil injunction prohibiting any party from attempting to develop or possess a pathogen, toxin, or delivery system having no apparent peaceful justification.[3] This provision enables the government to move quickly to prevent the development or production of biological arms even when the evidence is insufficient to pursue a criminal prosecution. Indeed, to obtain an injunction, the government need only show by a "preponderance of the evidence" that a party is attempting to possess a biological agent or delivery system having no apparent legitimate purpose.[3]

By enacting these provisions, Congress enabled the federal government to intervene swiftly before a potential biological weapon could be used to cause injury or environmental harm. At the same time, however, Congress recognized that these provisions, if applied too broadly, could deter scientists and physicians from pursuing legitimate research involving pathogens and toxins—for example, the use of virulent toxins to target cancer cells or the human immunodeficiency virus.[12]

As a result, in the final version of the act, Congress implemented a 2-part strategy to ensure that the criminal prohibitions would not interfere with legitimate research. First, Congress expressly provided that a criminal violation cannot occur unless an individual acquires a pathogen, toxin, or delivery system with the specific knowledge that the material is intended "for use as a weapon." Congress further provided that the phrase "for use as a weapon" does not apply to any use of a biological agent for "prophylactic, protective, or other peaceful purposes."[3]

By including this language (which applies to all nonhostile uses), Congress incorporated a suggestion repeatedly made by representatives of the biomedical community—to place the burden of proof on the government to establish that an individual intended to use a specific biological agent to cause harm to others.[12] Accordingly, in any prosecution under the act, the government must prove beyond a reasonable doubt that the individual did not intend to use the material for a "peaceful purpose"—a burden of proof that is nearly impossible to carry whenever a scientist, physician, or researcher has a colorable claim of legitimate purpose.

CURBING THE THREAT OF BIOTERRORISM: THE ANTI-TERRORISM ACT OF 1996

In the wake of the Oklahoma City bombing, Congress passed the Anti-Terrorism Act of 1996[5] to provide the federal government with additional tools in the war against domestic terrorism. In this act, Congress conferred on law enforcement agencies a broad range of new investigative, prosecutive, and regulatory powers dealing with biological, chemical, and other weapons.

To begin with, Congress expanded the government's powers under the Biological Weapons Act by amending several key provisions of the earlier legislation. For example, Congress broadened the criminal provisions of the earlier act to reach anyone who "threatens" or "attempts" to develop or use a biological weapon.[5,13] Congress also broadened the same provisions to apply to anyone who uses recombinant technology (or any other biotechnological advance) to create new pathogens or more virulent forms of existing pathogens.[5,13]

The Anti-Terrorism Act also established a new regulatory framework for controlling the use of hazardous biological agents. In particular, Congress directed the CDC to establish a regulatory regime that would identify biological agents posing a threat to public health and regulate the transfer and use of such agents.

To achieve this goal, Congress specified that the CDC should create and maintain a list of biological agents having the "potential to pose a severe threat to public health and safety."[5] Congress further specified that the CDC should select the agents based on several factors, including the effect on human health of exposure to the agent, the contagiousness of the agent, the methods by which the agent is transmitted to humans, and the availability and effectiveness of immunizations and treatments for any resulting illness.[5]

Finally, Congress directed the CDC to establish regulations governing the use and transfer of the restricted agents. Congress specified that the regulations should establish procedures that would protect the public safety and "prevent access to such agents for use in domestic or international terrorism."[4]

In these ways, the Anti-Terrorism Act laid the groundwork for a broad regulatory system governing the acquisition, use, and transfer of biological agents posing a threat to public health and safety. It remained for the CDC to translate this broad statutory command into specific rules and regulations.

THE CDC REGULATORY FRAMEWORK

On April 15, 1997, the CDC's new regulations governing hazardous biological agents went into effect.[14] In drafting the regulations, the CDC sought to accomplish 4 major goals: (1) the identification of biological agents that are potentially hazardous to the public health; (2) the creation of procedures for monitoring the acquisition and transfer of the restricted agents; (3) the establishment of safeguards for the transportation of the restricted agents; and (4) the creation of a system for alerting authorities when an improper attempt is made to acquire a restricted agent.[14]

The Centers for Disease Control and Prevention List of Restricted Agents

Viruses
Crimean-Congo hemorrhagic fever virus
Eastern equine encephalitis virus
Ebola viruses
Equine morbillivirus
Lassa fever virus
Marburg virus
Rift Valley fever virus
South American hemorrhagic fever viruses (Junin, Machupo, Sabia, Flexal, Guanarito)
Tick-borne encephalitis complex viruses
Variola major virus (smallpox virus)
Venezuelan equine encephalitis virus
Viruses causing hantavirus pulmonary syndrome
Yellow fever virus
Exemptions: Vaccine strains of viral agents (Junin virus strain candid #1, Rift Valley fever virus strain MP-12, Venezuelan equine encephalitis virus strain TC-83, and yellow fever virus strain 17-D).
Bacteria
Bacillus anthracis
Brucella abortus, *Brucella melitensis*, *Brucella suis*
Burkholderia (Pseudomonas) mallei
Burkholderia (Pseudomonas) pseudomallei
Clostridium botulinum
Francisella tularensis
Yersinia pestis
Exemptions: vaccine strains as described in Title 9 CFR, 78.1.
Rickettsiae
Coxiella burnetii
Rickettsia prowazekii
Rickettsia rickettsii
Fungi
Coccidioides immitis
Toxins
Abrin
Aflatoxins
Botulinum toxins
Clostridium perfringens epsilon toxin
Conotoxins
Diacetoxyscirpenol
Ricin
Saxitoxin
Shigatoxin
Staphylococcal enterotoxins
Tetrodotoxin
T-2 toxin
Exemptions: Toxins for medical use, inactivated for use as vaccines, or toxin preparations for biomedical research use at a median lethal dose for vertebrates of more than 100 ng/kg; national standard toxins required for biologic potency testing as described in Title 9 CFR Part 113.

To achieve these goals, the CDC regulations first identify 24 infectious agents and 12 toxins that pose a significant risk to public health[14] (Table). The current list includes 12 types of viruses and 7 bacteria as well as recombinant organisms and any genetic elements from any of the listed agents that produce or encode for a factor associated with a disease.

In addition to identifying hazardous agents, the CDC regulations set forth procedures for identifying all facilities possessing such agents and for insuring that the facilities have appropriate safeguards.[14] The regulations provide that any university, research institution, private company or individual that acquires any restricted agent (or that wants to acquire any agent) must register with the federal government. The regulations further provide that, as part of the registration process, each facility must designate a "responsible facility individual" who will certify that the facility and its laboratory operations meet the appropriate biosafety level requirements for working with the specific agent. To ensure compliance, the regulations authorize the government to inspect the facility to determine if it meets the appropriate biosafety level requirements. If the government approves the laboratory, the facility then receives a specific registration number that indicates the facility is authorized to work with the identified agents at the prescribed biosafety level.

The CDC regulations also establish procedures for tracking the transfer of restricted agents from 1 facility to another.[14] The regulations require that, prior to such a transfer, the shipping and receiving facilities must each complete an "official transfer form" that identifies the registration numbers of the shipping and receiving facilities, the name of the relevant restricted agent, and the proposed use and amount of the agent. A copy of the form must then be maintained in a central repository that, while not publicly accessible, is available to both federal and local law enforcement authorities.

The regulations further provide that the responsible facility official at the requesting facility must certify that the requesting researcher is officially affiliated with the facility and that the laboratory meets the appropriate biosafety level requirements.[14] Similarly, the regulations require the responsible facility official at the shipping facility to certify that the receiving facility holds a valid registration number indicating an appropriate biosafety level capability.

The regulations next identify certain clinical uses of restricted agents that are exempt from the regulatory scheme.[14] Under these exemptions, a clinical specimen containing a restricted agent is not subject to regulation if the specimen is intended for diagnostic reference, diagnostic verification, or evaluating the proficiency of diagnostic tests. Any other use, however, is subject to regulation, including any research use.

In addition, the CDC regulations exempt any attenuated strains of restricted agents that have been approved for human vaccination purposes by the Food and Drug Administration. The regulations do apply, however, to all other attenuated, avirulent, or less pathogenic strains of the restricted agents.

Finally, the CDC regulations are enforceable by criminal penalties. In particular, an individual who knowingly makes a false statement on any of the forms required for the registration of facilities or for the transfer of restricted agents is subject to a fine or imprisonment of up to 5 years. In addition, an individual who knowingly violates other provisions of the regulations is subject to a fine of $250 000 and imprisonment of up to 1 year.

CONCLUSION

The effectiveness of recent Congressional legislation enacted to address the threat of biological weapons must remain a matter of intense speculation. But at least 2 features of the recent legislation deserve recognition. First, Congress has erected new barriers to the illicit development and acquisition of biological agents by imposing stringent regulatory controls—including criminal penalties—on the transfer and use of such agents. Second, Congress has enhanced the ability of federal law enforcement agencies to intervene before a biological weapon is used or developed in the United States. In these ways, Congress has reduced the risks of bioterrorism and promoted the public safety in the transfer and use of hazardous biological agents.

James R. Ferguson, JD

References

1. Sopko J. The changing proliferation threat. *Foreign Policy*. 1996;105:6-16.
2. *Global Proliferation of Weapons of Mass Destruction and Domestic Terrorism: Hearings Before the Senate Committee on Governmental Affairs*. 104th Cong, 1st Sess (1995).
3. The Biological Weapons Act of 1989, 18 USC §175 *et seq*.
4. The Chemical and Biological Weapons Control and Warfare Elimination Act of 1991, Pub L No. 102-182 (December 4, 1991).
5. Anti-Terrorism and Effective Death Penalty Act of 1996, Pub L No. 104-132 (April 24, 1996).
6. Cole L. *The Eleventh Plague: The Politics of Biological and Chemical Warfare*. New York: WH Freeman & Co; 1997.
7. Office of Technology Assessment. *Proliferation of Weapons of Mass Destruction: Assessing the Risks*. Washington, DC: Office of Technology Assessment; 1995.
8. 50 USC §§2401-24 (1979).
9. Office of Technology Assessment. *Technology Against Terrorism: Structuring Security*. Washington, DC: Office of Technology Assessment; 1992.
10. Office of Technology Assessment. *Technology Against Terrorism: The Federal Effort*. Washington, DC: Office of Technology Assessment; 1991.
11. Senate Report No. 210, 101st Cong, 1st Sess (1989).
12. *The Biological Weapons Anti-Terrorism Act of 1989: Hearing Before the Senate Committee On the Judiciary*. 101st Cong, 1st Sess (1989).
13. 18 USC §175 *et seq* (1996).
14. US Dept of Health and Human Services, Centers for Disease Control and Prevention. Additional requirements for facilities transferring or receiving select agents: final rule. *Federal Register*. October 24, 1996;61:55190.

BIOLOGICAL TERRORISM: LEGAL MEASURES FOR PREVENTING CATASTROPHE

BARRY KELLMAN*

I. UNDERSTANDING BIO-TERRORISM 425
A. *Why Attack with Biological Weapons?* 426
1. Inflicting Casualties 427
2. Non-Detectability and Manageability 428
3. Panic Potential 429
B. *What Pathogens Might Be Used?* 430
1. Likely Pathogens 430
a. Smallpox 432
b. Anthrax 433
c. The Plague 434
d. Haemorrhagic Fevers 435
e. Tularemia 436
f. Venezuelan Equine Encephalitis 436
g. Ricin 436
2. Choosing the Appropriate Pathogen 437
C. *Devising the Attack* 438
1. Means of Acquisition 439
2. Means of Production 440
3. Means of Dissemination 440
a. Injection or Direct Poisoning 442
b. Contamination of Foodstuffs or Potable Liquids 442
c. Aerosol Delivery 443
d. Animal and Insect Vectors 445

* Professor, DePaul University College of Law; B.A. University of Chicago, 1973; J.D. Yale Law School, 1976. Currently, Professor Kellman is Visiting Scholar at The Center for Nonproliferation Studies, Monterey Institute of International Studies. Gratitude is deeply owed to Michael L. Moodie for reviewing an early draft; to M. Cherif Bassiouni for providing insights relevant to criminal law enforcement; and most especially to Suzanne E. Spaulding for providing the opportunity, in connection with The National Commission on Terrorism, to develop many of the ideas herein.

4. Assessing the Risk 446

II. RESTRICTING ACCESS TO PATHOGENS AND WEAPONIZING EQUIPMENT 446

A. Restriction of Access to Pathogens 448

1. Larry Wayne Harris 449
2. Licensing Possession of Pathogenic Agents 450
   - a. Establishment Licenses 450
   - b. Product Licenses 451
   - c. Registration Controls of Transferring Agents 452
3. Preventing Theft of Pathogens 453
   - a. Facility Regulations 453
   - b. Transfer Regulations 454
   - c. Personnel Regulations 455
4. Stopping Importation of Pathogens 456

B. Regulation of Biological Weaponization Equipment 457

1. Functions of Critical Weaponization Equipment 458
2. Optional Recommendations 460
   - a. Domestic Market 460
     - i. Voluntary Know-Your-Customer Guidelines 461
     - ii. Tagging Capabilities 461
     - iii. Enforceable Know-Your-Customer Guidelines 461
     - iv. Declaration of Transfers 462
     - v. Certification or Licensing of Purchasers 462
   - b. Export Market 462

III. LAW ENFORCEMENT TO COMBAT BIO-TERRORISM 463

A. Criminalizing Bio-terrorism 465

B. Gathering Information and the Detection of Clandestine Bio-terrorism 467

C. Use of Biosensors 469

1. Protection of Air Distribution Systems 470
2. Checkpoint Detectors 471
3. Emissions Detection 472

D. Emergency Authorities for Catastrophic Terrorism Situations 475
1. Defining the Problem........ 476
2. Relevant Fourth Amendment Principles .. 478
   a. Applicable Doctrines........ 478
   b. Relevant Inquiries........ 481
3. Legal Treatment of Searches and Related Measures 483
   a. Cordoning Areas, Preventing Ingress or Egress 483
   b. Compulsory Vaccinations and Other Medical Treatment 483
   c. Lowering the Threshold of Reasonable Suspicion........ 485
   d. Sweep Searches 485
4. Can Anything Be Done To Clarify or Expand Emergency Powers?........ 486

CONCLUSION 488

Biological terrorism is a truly despicable subject, raising nightmares of primal fear. Disease—plague, smallpox, and other decimating maladies—is dire trauma embedded in humanity's collective consciousness. Now, when the threat of thermonuclear holocaust may be ebbing, a few zealots or criminals can kill thousands (or more) and destabilize social order by revealing that no government, even that of superpower America, can protect its citizenry. A biological attack means that everyone is vulnerable. This is terrorism nonpareil.

This Article's agenda is modest: Set forth legal initiatives that might reduce the risks of bioterrorism, recognizing that those initiatives must be combined with nonlegal policies. For example, more money to develop sensors and to train medical personnel could be advantageously spent without proposing or amending legislation or regulations. Legal initiatives should be seen, therefore, as only part of a larger policy response to reduce terrorism opportunities, strengthen detection, focus resources, and deter those terrorists who are averse to harsh penalties.[1]

The agenda here is also overt. Law's contribution to preventing bioterrorism, though limited, is crucial. And time, unfortunately, is not on the side of the angels. This Article, therefore, is a call to action.

Part I of this Article synthesizes the vast literature on bioterrorism,[2] describing various diseases that could be used and how those diseases might fulfill different objectives. Part II and Part III develop this Article's thesis that threats of bioterrorism call for a two-dimensional set of carefully tailored policies to reduce biological threats, but do not justify radical new overtures. Proposed regulatory modifications can restrict the availability of useful materials and equipment and increase the cost and likelihood of detection. Part II advances a regulatory agenda, mindful to not over-burden the bio-

---

1. *See generally Countering the Changing Threat of International Terrorism*, REPORT OF THE NATIONAL COMMISSION ON TERRORISM (2000), *available at* http://www.fas.org/irp/threat/commission.html.

2. *See generally* MARIE I. CHEVRIER ET AL., BIOLOGICAL WEAPONS PROLIFERATION: REASONS FOR CONCERN, COURSES OF ACTION (Henry L. Stimson Ctr., Report No. 24, Jan. 1998) (containing five chapters on the Biological Weapons Convention by various authors) [hereinafter BIOLOGICAL WEAPONS PROLIFERATION], *available at* http://www.stimson.org/pubs/cwc/index.html; RICHARD A. FALKENRATH ET AL., AMERICA'S ACHILLES' HEEL (1998) (describing America's vulnerability to terrorism involving weapons of mass destruction); Ronald M. Atlas, *Combating the Threat of Biowarfare and Bio-terrorism: Defending Against Biological Weapons is Critical to Global Security*, 49 BIOSCIENCE 465 (1999); Jose Vegar, *Terrorism's New Breed*, BULL. ATOMIC SCIENTISTS, Mar.-Apr. 1998, at 50 (discussing the likelihood that today's terrorists will use chemical and biological weapons), *available at* http://www.bullatomsci.org/issues/1998/ma98/ma98vegar.html; Tom Carter, *Biological Terrorism: A Threat Overlooked*, WASH. TIMES, Jan. 16, 2000, at C1; Leonard A. Cole, *The Specter of Biological Weapons*, SCIENTIFIC AMERICAN, Dec. 1996, at 60, *available at* http://www.sciam.com/1296issue/1296cole.html; Thomas V. Inglesby, *The Germs of War: How Biological Weapons Could Threaten Civilian Populations*, WASH. POST, Dec. 9, 1998, at H1; Zachary Selden, *Biological Weapons: Defense Improves, but the Threat Remains*, BUSINESS EX. FOR NAT'L SEC., http://www.bens.org/pubs/bioup.html (last visited January 5, 2001); Dane Jones, *Biological Warfare and the Implications of Biotechnology*, Dep't of Chemistry & Biochemistry, Calif. Polytech. State Univ., *at* http://www.calpoly.edu/~drjones/biowar-e3.html (last visited January 5, 2001); POTOMAC INST. POLICY STUDIES, PROCEEDINGS REPORT PIPS-98-3, SEMINAR ON EMERGING THREATS OF BIOLOGICAL TERRORISM: RECENT DEVELOPMENTS (1998); Ron Purver, *Chemical and Biological Terrorism: The Threat According to the Open Literature*, Canadian Security Intelligence Service, *at* http://www.csis-scrs.gc.ca/eng/miscdocs/purve.html (June 1995) (reporting on the possible terrorist use of chemical or biological agents); *National Symposium on Medical and Public Health Response to Bioterrorism*, EMERGING INFECTIOUS DISEASES, July-August 1999; JAMES H. ANDERSON, MICROBES AND MASS CASUALTIES: DEFENDING AMERICA AGAINST BIOTERRORISM (1998); BIOLOGICAL WEAPONS: WEAPONS OF THE FUTURE? (Brad Roberts ed., 1993).

pharmaceutical industry, that would raise barriers to obtaining pathogens and weaponization technology. Since these regulatory measures are not perfectly prophylactic (i.e. terrorists might still gain deadly agents), modifications of law enforcement policies should detect, investigate, and stop terrorists who overcome the regulatory barriers and prepare weapons. Part III discusses the unique problems that clandestine biological terrorism presents for law enforcement and recommends measures to better identify bioterrorism threats without overstepping civil liberties and privacy rights.

Put simply, the best strategy is two-pronged: Deny access to biological weapons capabilities, and—if capabilities are obtained—apprehend the terrorist before attack. Legal measures offer no guarantee for preventing bioterrorism, but the measures described here might substantially diminish risks when combined with enhanced pathogen-relevant research and development, improved planning and communication among officials, and advanced intelligence capabilities.

Many topics tangentially relevant to biological terrorism are not discussed here, either because law cannot significantly address them or because, even if addressed, law cannot materially diminish the risks of biological terrorism. This Article will not discuss the broad array of issues that span counter-terrorism policy.[3] Neither will it assess the merits of

3. *See, e.g.*, GAO, GAO/NSIAD-99-135, COMBATING TERRORISM: ISSUES TO BE RESOLVED TO IMPROVE COUNTERTERRORISM OPERATIONS (1999) (detailing the array of government counterterrorist operations); *see generally* HENRY H. HAN, TERRORISM & POLITICAL VIOLENCE: LIMITS AND POSSIBILITIES OF LEGAL CONTROL (1993) (providing a broad discussion of measures to combat state-sponsored terrorism); WALTER LAQUEUR, THE NEW TERRORISM, FANATICISM AND THE ARMS OF MASS DESTRUCTION (1999) (discussing motivations of certain new terrorists); LEGAL RESPONSES TO INTERNATIONAL TERRORISM: U.S. PROCEDURAL ASPECTS (M. Cherif Bassiouni ed., 1998) (analyzing modalities of international criminal law useful in combating terrorism); JOHN F. MURPHY, STATE SUPPORT OF INTERNATIONAL TERRORISM (1989) (discussing the extent of state-sponsored terrorism); GLENN SCHWEITZER & CAROLE C. DORSCH, SUPERTERRORISM (1998) (describing links between organized crime, especially in Russia, and terrorism); JESSICA E. STERN, THE ULTIMATE TERRORISTS (1999) (discussing potential biological weapons and their acquisition, uses, and potential users); Beverly Allen, *Talking "Terrorism": Ideologies and Paradigms in a Postmodern World*, 22 SYRACUSE J. INT'L & COM. 7 (1996); Jacqueline Ann Carberry, Comment, *Terrorism: A Global Phenomenon Mandating a Unified International Response*, 6 IND. J. GLOBAL LEG. STUD. 685 (1999) (advocating multilateral terrorism convention); Joseph Dellapenna, *Legal Remedies for Terrorist Acts*, 22 SYRACUSE J. INT'L L. & COM. 13 (1996); Yassin El-Ayouty, *International Terrorism Under the Law*, 5 ILSA J. INT'L & COMP. L. 485 (1999) (discussing terrorism under Islamic and international law); Barry Kellman, *Catastrophic Terrorism—Thinking Fearfully, Acting Legally*, 20 MICH. J. INT'L L. 537

promoting enhanced research on pathogenicity nor consider the appropriate levels of stockpiled vaccines; these questions are better addressed by the medical and pharmaceutical communities.[4] This Article will not discuss the need for enhanced foreign intelligence; crucial information is not publicly available, and legal measures would not make much difference.[5] Nor will this article address preparations to

---

(1999) (discussing private, federal, and international measures to combat terrorism); Neil C. Livingstone, *Terrorism: Conspiracy, Myth and Reality*, 22 FLETCHER F. WORLD AFF. 1 (1998) (questioning extent of terrorist threat); John-Alex Romano, Note, *Combating Terrorism and Weapons of Mass Destruction: Reviving the Doctrine of a State of Necessity*, 87 GEO. L.J. 1023 (1999) (discussing application of laws of war to international terrorism); Yonah Alexander, *Terrorism: Threats and Responses*, WORLD & I, June 1999, at 80 (highlighting trends in government-sponsored terrorism); John F. Sopko, *The Changing Proliferation Threat*, FOREIGN POL'Y, Dec. 1996, at 3 (describing increase of non-ideological terrorism); *Terrorist Threats to the United States: Hearing Before the Special Oversight Panel on Terrorism of the House Comm. on Armed Services*, 106th Cong. (2000); BRAD ROBERTS, HYPE OR REALITY: THE "NEW TERRORISM" AND MASS CASUALTY ATTACKS (Chemical and Biological Arms Control Institute 2000).

4. *See* COMM. ON R&D NEEDS FOR IMPROVING CIVILIAN MEDICAL RESPONSE TO CHEMICAL AND BIOLOGICAL TERRORISM INCIDENTS, INST. OF MEDICINE AND BD. ON ENVT'L STUDIES & TOXICOLOGY, COMM'N ON LIFE SCIENCES, NAT'L RES. COUNCIL, CHEMICAL AND BIOLOGICAL TERRORISM: RESEARCH AND DEVELOPMENT TO IMPROVE CIVILIAN MEDICAL RESPONSE ch. 8 (1999), *available at* http://stills.nap.edu/html/terrorism/ch8.html (discussing the availability, safety, and efficacy of drugs and other therapies) [hereinafter COMM. ON R&D NEEDS]; *see also* Jaclyn Shoshana Levine, *The National Vaccine Injury Compensation Program: Can It Still Protect an Essential Technology*, 4 B.U. J. SCI. & TECH. 9 (1998); David C. Mowery & Violaine Mitchell, *Improving the Reliability of the U.S. Vaccine Supply: An Evaluation of Alternatives*, 20 J. HEALTH POL., POL'Y & L. 973 (1995) (discussing the reliability of U.S. vaccine supplies); Phillip K. Russell, *Development of Vaccines to Meet Public Health Needs: Incentives and Obstacles*, 7 RISK: HEALTH SAFETY & ENV'T 239 (1996) (discussing how politics, lack of a delivery plan, and regulatory costs interfere with global provision of vaccines); Jeff Nesmith, *Target America: Biochemical Warfare—Public Health Sector Ill-equipped for Battle; Poor Funding for Equipment and Training Could Cost Lives in the Event of Bio-terrorism*, ATLANTA J. & CONST., Aug. 2, 1998, at 2E; MICHAEL E. STOUT, COMBATING BIOLOGICAL TERRORISM: IS DEPARTMENT OF DEFENSE PREPARED TO SUPPORT U.S. GOVERNMENT INTERAGENCY QUARANTINE OPERATIONS? (U.S. Army War College 2000) (analyzing military readiness for medical emergencies); MARY J.R. GILCHRIST, LABORATORY SAFETY, MANAGEMENT, AND DIAGNOSIS OF BIOLOGICAL AGENTS ASSOCIATED WITH BIOTERRORISM (American Society for Microbiology 2000) (recommending training epidemiologists to recognize unusual pathogens); Scott Lillibridge, *A Public Health Response to Bioterrorism*, 6 MEDICINE & GLOBAL SURVIVAL 82 (2000) (recommending that the Surgeon General have federal leadership for bioterrorism response); SENATE COMM. ON HEALTH, EDUC., LABOR & PENSIONS, PUBLIC HEALTH THREATS AND EMERGENCIES ACT: REPORT TO ACCOMPANY S. 2731 (2000); Victoria V. Sutton, *A Precious "Hot Zone"—The President's Plan to Combat Bioterrorism*, 164 MIL. L. REV. 135 (2000).

5. *See generally* HOUSE PERMANENT SELECT COMM. ON INTELLIGENCE, 104TH CONG., IC21: INTELLIGENCE COMMUNITY IN THE 21ST CENTURY ch. XIII (1996) (describing intelligence and law enforcement operations); Russell J. Bruemmer, *Intelligence Community Reorganization: Declining the Invitation to Struggle*, 101 YALE L.J. 867 (1992) (discussing intelligence needs); Jonathan M. Fredman, *Intelligence*

respond after an attack happens; those measures are necessary but do not serve to prevent the attack.[6]

A vast set of issues, substantially outside the scope of this Article and meriting separate attention, concerns the international proliferation of biological weapons and negotiated efforts to stanch their spread.[7] Russia had an active biological weapons research program into the early 1990s; many experts believe that the Russian military actively pursued a biological weapons program thereafter and may still be doing so.[8] Even if Russia is not actively pursuing biological weapons capabilities, there is the risk that its facilities are leaking equipment and perhaps even pathogens to other States or terrorist groups.[9] Iraq's biological weapons program was uncovered by United Nations inspectors in 1995.[10] Many

Agencies, Law Enforcement, and the Prosecution Team, 16 YALE L. & POL'Y REV. 331 (1998) (same).

6. Most post-attack efforts will be conducted under the authority of the Stafford Act, 42 U.S.C. § 5121 *et seq.* (2000). For the most thorough and current discussion of response capabilities, see ADVISORY PANEL TO ASSESS DOMESTIC RESPONSE CAPABILITIES FOR TERRORISM INVOLVING WEAPONS OF MASS DESTRUCTION, FIRST ANNUAL REPORT TO THE PRESIDENT AND THE CONGRESS, *Part I: Assessing the Threat*, *available at* http://www.infowar.com/class_3/00/class3_tp-terr.shtml (Dec. 15, 1999); AMY E. SMITHSON & LESLIE-ANNE LEVY, ATAXIA: THE CHEMICAL AND BIOLOGICAL TERRORISM THREAT AND THE U.S. RESPONSE (Henry L. Stimson Ctr., Report No. 35, Oct. 2000), *available at* http://www.stimson.org/pubs/allpubs.htm; PETER E. BARTH, COUNTERING THE BIOLOGICAL WEAPONS THREAT TO THE HOMELAND (U.S. Army War College 2000).

7. *See generally Measures to Eliminate International Terrorism: Report of the Working Group*, G.A. Res. 110, U.N. GAOR, 54th Sess. (1999), *available at* http://www.un.org/documents/ga/res/54/a45r110.pdf; Jonathan B. Tucker & Kathleen M. Vogel, *Preventing the Proliferation of Chemical and Biological Weapon Materials and Know-How*, NONPROLIFERATION REV., Spring 2000, at 88; BRAD ROBERTS & MICHAEL MOODIE, COMBATING NBC TERRORISM: AN AGENDA FOR ENHANCING INTERNATIONAL COOPERATION (Chemical and Biological Arms Control Institute 2000).

8. *See* Atlas, *supra* note 2, at 465; Federation of American Scientists, *Is Russia Prepared for Offensive Biological War?*, *at* http://209.207.236.112/nuke/guide/russia/facility/cbw/ucs980411.htm (April 11, 1998); *see also* Jones, *supra* note 2; GULBARSHYN BOZHEYEVA ET AL., FORMER SOVIET BIOLOGICAL WEAPONS FACILITIES IN KAZAKHSTAN: PAST, PRESENT, AND FUTURE, (Ctr. Nonproliferation Studies, Monterey Inst. Int'l Studies, Occasional Paper No. 1, 1999); C.J. Davis, *Nuclear Blindness: An Overview of the Biological Weapons Programs of the Former Soviet Union and Iraq*, 5 EMERGING INFECTIOUS DISEASES 509 (1999).

9. *See* AMY E. SMITHSON, TOXIC ARCHIPELAGO: PREVENTING PROLIFERATION FROM THE FORMER SOVIET CHEMICAL AND BIOLOGICAL WEAPONS COMPLEXES 19 (Henry L. Stimson Ctr., Report No. 32, December 1999), *available at* http://www.stimson.org/pubs/projpubs.htm.

10. *See id.* Iraqi officials admitted producing anthrax, botulinum toxin, and aflatoxin after years of claiming that they conducted only defensive research. They also admitted preparing—but not using—biological weapons-filled munitions, including twenty-five Scud missile warheads, aerial bombs, and aerial dispensers

experts believe that Iran has a military biological program even if it does not now have an offensive weapons capability.[11] Other countries currently suspected of having programs include: China, Taiwan, North Korea, Syria, Egypt, Cuba, Israel, former Soviet States, the United States, and Japan.[12] According to recently-substantiated allegations, a 500-liter medical fermentation device was sent from the United States to a pharmaceutical plant in China suspected of manufacturing chemical and biological agents for military purposes.[13] Lastly international treaty negotiations are proceeding actively for a new protocol to the Biological Weapons Convention,[14] but that protocol does not explicitly confront threats of terrorism.[15]

---

during the Gulf War. UNSCOM destroyed a range of biological weapons production equipment, seed stocks, and growth media, which Iraq claimed was for use in its biological weapons programs. UNSCOM believed Iraq greatly understated its biological agent production and could have been holding back agents that are easily concealed. Iraq resisted dismantling the Al Hakam biological weapons production facility for nearly one year, claiming that it was a legitimate civilian facility designed to produce single proteins and biopesticides. After discovering in 1995 that Iraq manufactured over 500,000 liters of biological weapons agents at the facility between 1989-90, UNSCOM pressed Iraq to destroy Al Hakam in the summer of 1996. *See* Iraq Weapons of Mass Destruction Programs, U.S. Gov't White Paper (Feb. 13, 1998), *available at* http://www.state.gov/www/regions/nea/iraq_white_paper.html. Iraq has the expertise to quickly resume a small-scale biological weapons program using facilities currently producing vaccines and other pharmaceuticals. Without effective monitoring, Iraq could probably begin production within a few days. For example, Iraq could convert production of biopesticides to anthrax simply by changing seed material. *See* Gregory Koblenz, *Countering Dual-Use Facilities: Lessons from Iraq and Sudan*, JANE'S INTELL. REV., Mar. 1, 1999, at 48; Judith Miller & William J. Broad, *Iraq's Deadliest Arms: Puzzles Breed Fears*, N.Y. TIMES, Feb. 26, 1998, at A1.

11. *Biological Warfare: The Poor Man's Atomic Bomb—Iran*, JANE'S INTELL. REV., Mar. 1, 1999, at 44; Judith Miller & William J. Broad, *Bioweapons in Mind, Iranians Lure Needy Ex-Soviet Scientists*, N.Y. TIMES, Dec. 8, 1998, at A1.

12. *See* William S. Cohen, *Preparing for a Grave New World*, WASH. POST, July 26, 1999, at A19; Cole, *supra* note 2, at 62.

13. *See* Douglas Burton, *Trie's Deadly Deals*, INSIGHT ON THE NEWS, Mar. 20, 2000, at 14.

14. For the text and a discussion of the subsequent development of the 1972 Convention on the Prohibition of the Development, Production and Stockpiling of Bacteriological and Toxin Weapons and on Their Destruction, see http://dosfan.lib.uic.edu/treaties/bwc1.htm (last visited Jan 5, 2001).

15. *See* Amy E. Smithson, *Man Versus Microbe: The Negotiations to Strengthen the BWC*, *in* BIOLOGICAL WEAPONS PROLIFERATION, *supra* note 2, at 107; Jonathon B. Tucker, *Verification Provisions of the Chemical Weapons Convention and Their Relevance to the Biological Weapons Convention*, *in* BIOLOGICAL WEAPONS PROLIFERATION, *supra* note 2, at 77; Gilliam R. Woollett, *Industry's Role, Concerns, & Interests in the Negotiation of a BWC Compliance Protocol*, *in* BIOLOGICAL WEAPONS PROLIFERATION, *supra* note 2, at 39; Scott Keefer, *International Control of Biological Weapons*, 6 ILSA J. INT'L & COMP. L. 107, 131-38 (1999) (discussing the protocol to the Biological Weapons Convention of 1972); Kyle B. Olson, *Aum Shinrikyo: Once*

III. LAW ENFORCEMENT TO COMBAT BIO-TERRORISM

Preventing access to pathogens and critical equipment can diminish risks of bioterrorism, but it would be foolhardy to believe that the regulatory measures previously discussed can eliminate the threat. Pathogens can be imported or cultivated from natural sources, and equipment to propagate those pathogens is widely available. Production of deadly devices is difficult, but domestic or foreign terrorists will be capable of overcoming technical obstacles. Rigorous law enforcement measures must address the threats of bioterrorism; the question is how?

Much of the law enforcement effort is standard; conventional surveillance and investigatory techniques apply to bioterrorism just as they would to more commonplace criminal activity. Arguably, beneficial initiatives could include increasing technological and personnel resources and streamlining cooperation between federal and local law enforcement authorities. But it would be wrong to contend that the current law enforcement effort is insubstantial.[122] While it stands to

120. 15 C.F.R. § 742.2(b)(2).

121. *See* Barry Kellman, *Bridling the International Trade of Catastrophic Weaponry*, 43 AM. U. L. REV. 755 (1994); Gary Milhollin, *Stopping the Indian Bomb*, 81 AM. J. INT'L L. 593 (1987); Jeffrey L. Snyder, *International Operations: Managing the Risks*, N.Y. L.J., May 20, 1996, at S4.

122. *See* HOUSE PERMANENT SELECT COMM. ON INTELLIGENCE, 104TH CONG., IC21: INTELLIGENCE COMMUNITY IN THE 21ST CENTURY ch. XIII (1996).

> Recent claims that the FBI is hamstrung in its efforts to combat domestic terrorism are incorrect. In any given year, the FBI engages in approximately two dozen full domestic terrorism investigations. Nearly

reason that more resources for law enforcement would help to combat bioterrorism, this Part does not grouse about current efforts.

That said, two characteristics distinguish biological terrorism from other crimes. First, the mechanism of the crime is essentially undetectable once it is deployed. Second, the crime has altogether unacceptable consequences. These characteristics mean that post-event law enforcement is of limited value; techniques must be employed before the crime to protect society from decimation. The need to empower law enforcement capabilities *before* the commission of a crime raises issues unique to the threat of biological terrorism that do not fit within typical law enforcement parameters.

This Part discusses four issues. First, is conduct relevant to bioterrorism sufficiently covered by federal criminal law; if not, what modifications should be enacted? Second, what information should be sufficient to stimulate an initial inquiry into the activities of suspected bioterrorists, and how can traditional law enforcement mechanisms of information-gathering be supplemented in order to improve bioterrorism prevention? Third, what are the appropriate uses of biosensors and how can their increased use be reconciled with privacy considerations? Fourth, when threats of emergency arise, how should the power law enforcement has to conduct extraordinary searches and related measures be evaluated in light of the Fourth Amendment and other constitutional strictures?

Underlying the discussion of these issues is a commitment to a meticulous approach to the juncture between law enforcement measures that might be necessary to prevent bioterrorism and a healthy respect for civil liberties. Biological terrorism poses an unprecedented challenge to America's commitments to liberty and justice. Its objective is to demonstrate that, under stress, these commitments are frail and shallow. Thus, terrorism's ultimate target is the Constitution, and its greatest victory would be to see this nation undermine civil liberties in the name of reacting to terrorism. The ends of security from terrorism do not justify means which abrade the

---

> two-thirds of these full investigations are opened before a crime has been committed in order to prevent terrorist crimes before they occur.

Id.

principle that the government derives authority from the rule of law. Indeed, it erodes the foundations of liberty to contend that because terrorists reject legal restraints, adherence to the Bill of Rights should be abdicated in the cause of national security.

The Constitution permits law enforcement officials to perform functions necessary to protect the public safety and preserve order so long as those functions are anticipated and carried out in a manner that is reasonably proportional to a legitimate government interest such as public health, investigation of crimes, or national security.[123] There is no substantial evidence that law enforcement measures in contravention of constitutional rights might actually be effective against terrorism. Nor have experts identified legal inhibitions, restrictions, or prohibitions on law enforcement authority that are applicable in normal circumstances which should be abandoned, mitigated, or suspended in the highly unusual circumstances of counter-terrorism. To the contrary, counter-terrorism measures that unreasonably truncate rights of privacy and due process of law are unwarranted and offensive.

A. *Criminalizing Bio-terrorism*

It is a crime, of course, to create, transfer, or possess pathogens or their delivery systems for use as a weapon[124] unless the accused demonstrates that the development or possession of agents was "for a prophylactic, protective, or other peaceful purpose."[125] Moreover, the prohibition against use of weapons of mass destruction specifically includes weapons involving disease organisms as well as genetically altered products,[126] punishable by up to life imprisonment or, if

123. *See* National Treasury Employees Union v. Von Rabb, 489 U.S. 656 (1989) (upholding suspicionless drug testing of customs officials); *cf.* New Jersey v. T.L.O., 469 U.S. 325 (1985) (upholding search of student's purse). *See also* Scott E. Sundby, *"Everyman"'s Fourth Amendment: Privacy or Mutual Trust Between Government and Citizen*, 94 COLUM. L. REV. 1751 (1994).

124. 18 U.S.C. § 175(a) (2000).

125. 18 U.S.C. § 177(b)(1) (2000).

126. *See* 18 U.S.C. § 2332a (2000) (prohibiting any use, threat, attempt, or conspiracy to use a weapon of mass destruction, including any biological agent, toxin, or vector).

death results, the death penalty.[127] It is unclear whether a hoax constitutes a threat within the meaning of this section.

These prohibitions, applicable in response to a bioterrorist event that may have catastrophic consequences, have limited value. To protect society, rigorous law enforcement techniques must be employed before the bioterrorist crime is committed. Faced with an unaccomplished crime, prosecutors have potential problems in producing evidence to prove a defendant possessed deadly agents for use as a weapon, not for a legally acceptable purpose. Indeed, this hurdle impeded prosecution of Larry Wayne Harris, discussed above, because he claimed that his possession of pathogens was legally protected.[128] The implication here is that someone can legally possess a pathogen without a license, and that it is up to the prosecution to prove intent with evidence other than mere possession. Thus, even someone with acknowledged scientific training in handling and processing pathogens and with a record of anti-social and perhaps criminal conduct can legally possess pathogens and may do so covertly.

It would be preferable simply to prohibit knowing possession of pathogens without a license, simplifying the task of prosecution. Because only licensed facilities could legally develop or possess pathogens, this change would reinforce the primacy of the licensing system by making the regulatory process the proper venue to determine the applicant's purpose and intent; necessarily, any possessor of pathogens who does not successfully obtain a license is subject to prosecution and, at minimum, would face penalties for noncompliance with regulatory reporting requirements. Most important, with a straightforward prohibition against unlicensed possession, law enforcement officials would not have to wait to apprehend the suspect until he demonstrates an intent to use pathogens as a weapon. Someone found to have cultivated pathogens but who has not registered with the CDC or who has submitted false information concerning her activities could be arrested. For these reasons, the Department of Justice has championed making it a federal crime to possess weaponizable agents

127. *See* 18 U.S.C. § 2332a(a)-(b) (2000).
128. *See* Stern, *supra* note 82, at 227. Harris pled guilty to mail fraud. *See id.*

without regulatory approval.[129]

B. Gathering Information and the Detection of Clandestine Bio-terrorism

Undeniably, the best security against biological terrorism is the ability to obtain information about potentially catastrophic activities sufficiently in advance of an attack to be able to prevent it.[130] Just as undeniably, law enforcement officials cannot track every conceivable possibility both because of finite resources and because of civil liberties protections that enable Americans to avoid constant surveillance. It is facile to say that priorities must be set; the important question is what activity should provoke a pre-attack investigation. This Section suggests that, in limited respects, the FBI and their state and local counterparts may be looking in the wrong places and asking the wrong questions.

Counter-terrorism law (which guides application of law enforcement resources) is based on a 1970s conception of terrorism that identifies terrorist activity with groups that have distinct ideological commitments and use terrorism to gain attention to their cause. Revolutionary terrorists, aspiring to overthrow perceived repression, were characterized as seeking to achieve international recognition through overt, stunning events that would mobilize their adherents and coerce their targets into paying attention to their claims. Accordingly, the Secretary of State can designate an organization as a "foreign terrorist organization" upon a showing that the organization is foreign, "the organization engages in terrorist activity," and the terrorist activity of the foreign organization "threatens the security of United States nationals or the national security of the United States."[131] Once a foreign terrorist organization has been designated, it becomes a crime to provide "material support" to it.[132]

---

129. *See* President William Jefferson Clinton, Remarks by the President at 21st Century Crime Bill Unveiling (May 12, 1999), *available at* http://www.clinton.nara.gov/.

130. The Attorney General has authority to search for and seize pathogens that are illegally possessed; action may be taken without a warrant in an emergency. *See* 18 U.S.C. § 176 (2000).

131. 8 U.S.C. § 1189(a)(1) (2000). "Terrorist activity" is defined in 8 U.S.C. § 1182(a)(3)(B)(ii) (2000).

132. 8 U.S.C. § 1182(a)(3)(B)(iii) (2000) (defining and prohibiting material

This perception applied neatly to Hamas, the Irish Republic Army, the Red Brigade, and other prominent terrorist organizations, but terrorists like Ted Kaczynski, Tim McVeigh, and the Aum Shinrikyo group manifest quite different behavior. As discussed above, bioterrorists are likely to be more interested in spreading panic than in advancing a radical political ideology. Even if bioterrorists are sent into this country on behalf of a foreign power, only an absolute fool would employ designated members of a foreign terrorist organization. Indeed, for purposes of initiating an investigation into potential bioterrorism, criteria of suspicion must be formulated for which radical ideology is not central.

It would be more effective to base suspicion on capability rather than ideology. The amount and type of evidence sufficient to constitute a "reasonable suspicion" to investigate in advance of a bioterrorist attack relates to the definition of bioterrorism and whether unlicensed possession of pathogens is a crime. If possession is criminalized, evidence of access to biological agents, expertise in handling and processing those agents, or experience in biological research may be relevant in determining reasonable suspicion. Accordingly, unlicensed acquisition of equipment that would be useful to weaponizing biological agents should prompt an inquiry as to the purposes for that equipment, as part of the system of monitoring domestic transfers of biocritical equipment advocated in Part II.

Perhaps the most useful allocation of law enforcement resources would be to monitor hate groups, especially those that have declared an interest in pathogens. It is currently illegal to teach or demonstrate to any person any "technique capable of causing injury or death to persons, knowing or having reason to know or intending that the same will be unlawfully employed for use in, or in furtherance of, a civil disorder . . . ."[133] There are recurrent proposals to prohibit distribution of information relevant to a destructive device with the intent that the information will be used, or knowledge that it will be used, for or in furtherance of an activity that constitutes a federal crime of violence.[134]

Three noteworthy issues arise from these prohibitions. First,

---

support).

133. 18 U.S.C. §231(a)(1) (2000).

134. *See* 21st Century Justice Act, S. 899, 106th Cong. (1999).

restricting the dissemination of information has obvious First Amendment implications. Second, assuming these restrictions are constitutional, it is difficult to determine whether a person disseminating relevant bioterrorism information has the intent or knowledge that it will be used to create a civil disorder or in an activity that constitutes a violent crime. Third, in view of the fact that Internet sites can easily be located outside the jurisdiction of U.S. law, it is difficult to conceive of how even the most determined effort could prohibit bioterrorists from exchanging information.

It may be appropriate to consider the constitutionality and law enforcement efficacy of prescribing that dissemination of information relevant to bioterrorism will constitute reasonable suspicion to justify investigation and even intrusive surveillance methods. Terrorist web pages, pages discussing biological terrorism, as well as hate group, militia, and other radical information on the Internet could be used to initiate or direct investigations. This proposal somewhat mitigates the First Amendment implications of a prohibition on dissemination (speech would be chilled but not prohibited). However, the proposal also raises Fourth Amendment concerns about the quantity and quality of evidence sufficient to undertake various law enforcement search methods. A related approach is to charge persons disseminating bioterrorism information with aiding and abetting a criminal use or attempt.

C. *Use of Biosensors*

Pathogens are not visually detectable, nor do they send obvious signals comparable to the radiation emitted by nuclear materials. Real-time detection and measurement of biological agents in the environment is further complicated by the number of potential agents to be distinguished, the complex nature of the agents themselves, the myriad of similar microorganisms that are a constant and natural presence in the environment, and the minute quantities of pathogen that can initiate infection. Thus, pre-attack detection of weaponization facilities or transport of pathogens is extremely difficult. Even after a bioterrorist attack, there is little that can be done to trace the movement of pathogens or to identify their dissemination. Technologies capable of detecting the presence of pathogens obviously would be a powerful asset to law-enforcement officials.

Biosensors are miniature devices that convert information about biological material in the environment into an electrical form that can be read by instruments. They have at least three distinct applications that are directly relevant to preventing bioterrorism:[135] (1) to protect air distribution systems; (2) to identify pathogens on persons passing through a portal; and (3) to monitor facilities in order to detect clandestine bioweapons production. These applications of biosensors do not constrain or physically intrude on a person's liberty; furthermore, sensors tend to be exceptionally selective, i.e., they do not uncover broad categories of information in excess of what law enforcement requires. Yet widespread use of biosensors (not technically realistic today but a potential for the near future) should be carefully considered in light of the implications of such use for privacy.

1. Protection of Air Distribution Systems

Sensors could be used to detect the presence of biological agents in air distribution systems where they might be placed by a terrorist intending to harm persons who rely on those distribution systems. In this context, sensors would be entirely passive, lying in wait and functioning analogous to smoke alarms; when stimulated by the presence of certain pathogens, they would either set off a warning or, preferably, shut down the air distribution system. These types of sensors could offer significant protective capabilities but would be essentially irrelevant to law enforcement efforts to detect and stop terrorists, and their use raises no significant legal questions. If such sensors are technologically and economically feasible, they could serve an extremely useful function for some

135. Bio-sensing technology is crucially important in detecting and identifying pathogens in clinical samples. Technologies relevant to this function are advancing rapidly, far beyond the scope of this discussion. Although there are privacy issues attendant to the use of laboratory diagnostics, especially in cases where a sample has been taken from a person without overt consent, those issues are unrelated to the privacy concerns relevant to prevention of bioterrorist attacks and, therefore, are not discussed further. *See, e.g.*, Guido S. Weber, *Unresolved Issues in Controlling the Tuberculosis Epidemic Among the Foreign-Born in the United States*, 22 AM. J. L. & MED. 503 (1996); Andrew S. Krulwich & Bruce L. McDonald, *Evolving Constitutional Privacy Doctrines Affecting Healthcare Enterprises*, 55 FOOD & DRUG L.J. 491 (2000).

facilities, such as enclosed stadia where thousands of people rely on the same air source.

2. *Checkpoint Detectors*

Sensors could be used to detect the presence of trace amounts of pathogens on persons who pass through a portal or checkpoint. These biosensors could perhaps be used at airport checkpoints, in tandem with current metal-detection capabilities. Because pathogens portend less immediate yet more widespread violence than guns, these portal-based sensors would be better used to check disembarking persons. Indeed, this application, if technologically effective, would be virtually the only way to defend against importation of foreign pathogens.

The constitutionality of portal-based sensors is supported by the use of airport checkpoints, which has long been upheld in view of the significant threat of hijacking and bombing to public safety and security.[136] This logic might justify the legality of using portal-based biosensors. However, other modern technologies analagous to biosensors have been criticized. Mechanical canines "sniff" around a person to detect the presence of narcotics. A device named Sentor uses portable vapor phase chromatography to analyze particles on and around individuals.[137] The courts have not yet ruled on the constitutionality of these devices. Concerns have been raised that with these types of sensors—which only detect the presence, but not the source, of contraband in the air—innocent persons may be wrongfully accused or detained.[138] A similar

136. *See, e.g.*, United States v. Doe, 61 F.3d 107, 109-10 (1st Cir. 1995) (stating that "routine security searches at airport checkpoints pass constitutional muster because the compelling public interest in curbing air piracy generally outweighs their limited intrusiveness"); United States v. De Los Santos Ferrer, 999 F.2d 7, 9 (1st Cir.) (describing airport searches as administrative searches conducted for a "limited—and exigent—purpose"), *cert. denied*, 510 U.S. 997 (1993); United States v. $124,570 U.S. Currency, 873 F.2d 1240, 1243-47 (9th Cir. 1989) (describing airport security searches as narrowly limited to their compelling administrative objective of searching for weapons and explosives).

137. *See* Richard S. Julie, Note *High-Tech Surveillance Tools and the Fourth Amendment: Reasonable Expectations of Privacy in the Technological Age*, 37 AM. CRIM. L. REV. 127 (2000); Jason Lazarus, Note, *Vision Impossible? Imaging Devices—The New Police Technology & the Fourth Amendment*, 48 FLA. L. REV. 299 (1996).

138. *See* Peter Joseph Bober, *The "Chemical Signature" of the Fourth Amendment: Gas Chromatography/Mass Spectrometry and the War on Drugs*, 8 SETON HALL CONST. L.J. 75, 108-117 (1997).

objection could be made in regard to bioweapons-sensing technologies.

The analogy to metal detectors is potentially inapt because biosensors reveal information that is potentially more sensitive than what is revealed when one passes through a metal detector. While it is difficult to conceive of how a person could have an intimate privacy interest in metal on one's body, detection of biological substances could reveal the presence of a socially-despised disease or condition, thereby subjecting a person to embarrassment or worse. Even the prospect of having intimate details of one's physiology checked over might be considered offensive regardless of whether there are consequences to that check. Canine sniffers, too, likely provide an inapt analogy. A person's privacy interest in illicit narcotics on his body (if it exists at all) is decidedly less than a person's privacy interests in the intimate details of his own physiology. Ongoing controversies surrounding Millivision and related sensory-enhancing technologies[139] may present better points of reference. The Millivision detectors register the millimeter waves naturally emitted from the human body, enabling an operator to get a fairly detailed outline of a person's body; if the person is carrying a gun, it would show up as an anomaly.[140] As capabilities improve, "a point may be reached where the information provided to the operator about the person's body is of such a personal character that the intrusion is no longer justified—even by the heightened government interest."[141]

3. *Emissions Detection*

By far the most important use of biosensors would be to detect the presence of biological laboratories by analyzing air emissions from those facilities. As discussed above, the most likely bioterrorist strategy involves obtaining a pathogen from an undetectable natural or foreign source and weaponizing that

139. *See* T. Wade McKnight, Comment, *Passive, Sensory-Enhanced Searches: Shifting the Fourth Amendment "Reasonableness" Burden*, 59 LA. L. REV. 1243, 1265 (1999).

140. *See id.*

141. *Id.; see also* Steven Salvador Flores, Note, *Gun Detector Technology and the Special Needs Exception*, 25 RUTGERS COMPUTER & TECH. L.J. 135 (1999); Alyson L. Rosenberg, Note, *Passive Millimeter Wave Imaging: A New Weapon in the Fight Against Crime or a Fourth Amendment Violation?* 9 ALB. L.J. SCI. & TECH. 135, 159 (1998).

pathogen at a clandestine laboratory. A method to detect that laboratory would thus serve a crucial prevention function. This application is analogous to environmental sampling for pollution emissions from industrial sites. Such sensors would enable law enforcement officials to collect information otherwise unavailable without any physical intrusion. The suspect would normally not even be aware of the surveillance because the device "passively" measures the natural emissions from the target.

A practical detection system would have to discriminate between closely related organisms because many pathogens differ little from normal microorganisms. New technology can take advantage of the high affinity and specificity that a pathogen has for its natural receptor.[142] Natural cell receptors for viral pathogens can be used in a biosensor to selectively and sensitively identify the pathogen in a biological warfare agent.

This system will face significant technical hurdles, however. Any closed system capable of containing emissions would escape detection. Even if pathogens are emitted, the sensor would need to distinguish biological weapons agents from normal microorganisms. The sensor would therefore need to be extremely selective. Moreover, this type of sensor can only detect a pathogen it is programmed to detect; terrorist use of another pathogen or a genetically modified pathogen would likely go undetected precisely because a practically useful sensor must not respond to every pathogen in the environment.

"Few, if any, civilian agencies at any level currently have even a rudimentary capability in this area. A number of military units, most notably the Army's Technical Escort Unit, the U.S. Marine Corps Chemical Biological Incident Response Force, and the Army Chemical Corps, presently have some first-generation technology available."[143] The need for faster,

142. Pathogenic bacteria possess novel proteins designed to help them overcome normal host defense mechanisms. Recently, there has been a virtual explosion of information identifying bacterial factors that are needed as accessories to transport virulence factors to the cell surface where they can be detected. *See, e.g.,* Defense Advanced Research Project Agency, Biological Warfare Defense Sensors, *at* http://www.darpa.mil/spo/programs/biowarfaredefensesensors.htm (announcing and describing new program to develop biological warfare defense sensors) (last visited January 10, 2001).

143. *See* COMM. ON R&D NEEDS, *supra* note 4, at 86. For example,

> [T]he Biological Integrated Detection System (BIDS) continuously samples ambient air and determines the background distribution of

more reliable detection of hazardous biological agents has spawned a large and growing number of research programs.[144]

From a Fourth Amendment perspective, the use of sensors to detect emissions from facilities would not appear to raise serious problems. Sampling of air emissions by the EPA in connection with air pollution control has not been successfully challenged, although in those cases the monitored facilities were on notice of being within the scope of the Clean Air Act's regulation and therefore had a diminished expectation of privacy as to their emissions.[145] Greater legal controversy has attended the use of thermal imaging devices used to detect differences in temperature on the surface of a selected target.[146] Current thermal imagers are capable of detecting tiny temperature differences and can locate a human in the dark from over four miles away.[147] These devices are not capable of seeing through an object but can detect heat sources that are hidden from view due to the heat that passes through the intermediate object.[148] Legal challenges to the government's use of thermal imager readings claim that use of an imager is itself a search and should not be conducted without a warrant issued on independent probable cause.[149] The United States circuit courts of appeal are split as to the constitutionality of using thermal imagers and the Supreme Court has granted certiorari to resolve that split this Term.[150]

> aerosol particles. Aerosol particles with diameters in the 2 to 10 micron range are concentrated and analyzed for biological activity . . . . [A]ntibody-based tests are conducted for specific agents. At present, the system includes tests for the bacteria responsible for anthrax, plague, botulinum toxin A, and staphylococcal enterotoxin B.

Id. at 86-87.

144. *See id.* at 78-96.

145. *See* Air Pollution Variance Bd. of Colo. v. Western Alfalfa Corp., 416 U.S. 861 (1974).

146. *See* McKnight, *supra* note 138, at 1249. *See generally* Mark D. Kiser, Comment, *Constitutional Law: Fourth Amendment Search and Seizures and Thermal Imaging*, 51 FLA. L. REV. 723 (1999) (discussing United States v. Kyllo, 140 F.3d 1249 (9th Cir. 1998)).

147. *See* McKnight, *supra* note 138, at 1249.

148. *See id.*

149. *See id.* at 1250-51.

150. *See id.* McKnight notes:

> Four circuits have approved the pre-warrant use of thermal imagers: the Fifth Circuit in *United States v. Ishmael*, [48 F.3d 850 (5th Cir. 1995),] the Seventh Circuit in *United States v. Myers*, [45 F.3d 668 (7th Cir. 1995),] the Eighth Circuit in *United States v. Pinson* [, 24 F.3d 1056 (8th Cir. 1994,] and the Eleventh Circuit in *United States v. Ford* [, 34 F.3d 992 (11th Cir. 1994),] and *United States v. Robinson* [, 62 F.3d 1325 (11th Cir. 1995)]. However,

Notably, biosensors would be less capable of detecting sensitive private information than are thermal imaging devices. For example, area-wide or environmental biosensors could not detect information that most people consider private, such as the presence of numerous people in a building, nor could they detect heat-generating equipment. Yet biosensors raise issues, analogous to the discussion above of what evidence should be required to initiate a search, concerning the basis for focusing biosensors on a particular location. If transfers of sophisticated biological equipment are tracked, as suggested above, is a building containing a regulated fermenter a legitimate target for sensor surveillance? What about a survivalist group's compound? To the extent that biosensing technologies become more prevalent, the interests at stake in their wide-scale application should be carefully weighed.

D. Emergency Authorities for Catastrophic Terrorism Situations

Identification of an imminent threat of biological terrorism, through intelligence sources or other means, should prompt the most rigorous law enforcement efforts to uncover its source and prevent the harm before it materializes.[151] Moreover, in the immediate aftermath of a terrorist event, an equivalent standard of rigor should apply to efforts to apprehend the culprits. In these biological terrorism situations, an important question arises as to whether "emergency authorities" might be necessary or advantageous for law enforcement personnel or for public health officials. Are there legal inhibitions, restrictions, or prohibitions are applicable in normal circumstances that should be abandoned, mitigated, or suspended in the circumstances of biological terrorism? If so,

> two other circuits have issued opinions reaching different conclusions. The Tenth Circuit, in *United States v. Cusumano*, [67 F.3d 1497 (10th Cir. 1995),] ruled that the pre-warrant use of thermal imagers was unconstitutional. Then, on rehearing, the opinion was vacated because the court found independent probable cause. Later, in *United States v. Kyllo*, [140 F.3d 1249 (9th Cir. 1998),] the Ninth Circuit first ruled that the pre-warrant use of thermal imagery was an unreasonable search. Then, on rehearing, the court withdrew its original opinion and, in a 2-1 decision, held that the thermal scan was not a "search" within the meaning of the Fourth Amendment. [United States v. Kyllo, 190 F.3d 1041 (9th Cir. 1999).]

Id. at 1251. The Supreme Court granted certiorari in the *Kyllo* case. *See* Kyllo v. United States, 121 S. Ct. 29 (2000). Oral arguments were held on February 20, 2001.

151. *See* COMM. ON R&D NEEDS, *supra* note 4.

what can Congress do to expand those authorities, in view of the fact that Congress cannot legalize unconstitutional activity?

Law enforcement officials at all levels will have to conduct investigations and implement measures that exceed the standards applicable to calmer situations, measures including quarantines, cordoning off of areas, vehicle searches, compulsory medical measures, and even sweep searches through areas believed to contain terrorists. These responsibilities can be undertaken most effectively and judiciously if all levels and branches of government prepare in advance for the unique, low-probability, high-magnitude threats that terrorism poses to national security. Advance preparation is also necessary to ensure that civil liberties are not undermined in the name of reacting to terrorism. Under unprecedented conditions of mass casualties, panic may overwhelm constitutional protections. When officials are unprepared to address the threat of a biological terrorist event, the risks of an overwrought response are significant.

1. *Defining the Problem*

The problem here is *not* about what measures can be taken in connection with a person suspected of being a terrorist. If there is reason to suspect an individual is a terrorist, then there is no serious legal problem with conducting an investigation. If a warrant can be obtained to conduct that investigation, it should be; if exigent circumstances prevent obtaining a warrant, the requirement is conditionally excused.[152] Depending on his citizenship, the suspected terrorist may have privacy rights, and no court will condone patently unnecessary or abusive law enforcement activity. But the issues pertaining to "emergency authorities" are not, strictly speaking, relevant to what can be done in regard to a suspected terrorist.

The issues pertaining to "emergency authorities" have to do with the privacy rights of everyone who is innocent but caught in the net of the investigation for the actual terrorist. The

152. *See* United States v. Place, 462 U.S. 696, 701 (1983) ("The exigencies of the circumstances" may permit temporary seizure without warrant); *see also* Warden, Md. Penitentiary v. Hayden, 387 U.S. 294, 298-99 (1967) (holding warrantless search for suspect and weapons reasonable where exigent circumstances existed); Schmerber v. California, 384 U.S. 757, 770-71 (1966) (holding warrantless blood test for alcholo reasonable when exigent circumstances were present).

problem is that in investigating or in responding to terrorist activity, law enforcement officials may direct intrusive measures against a much broader group than the actual terrorist. It is the inability to distinguish the terrorist from all the other people in the area, or to distinguish the terrorist's locale from similar locales, that creates the potential for invasions of civil liberties.[153] The following scenarios illustrate the point:

- Intelligence strongly suggests the presence of biological weapons in a six-unit apartment building, and sensor equipment has detected emissions from that building. The difficulty is that there is no evidence as to the specific location of the biological weapons. To prevent the attack, the police will have to search each apartment. If persons in any of the five unrelated apartments deny access, the police will use force, thereby violating those persons' expectations of privacy. Yet until the police enter the apartments, they have no reason to know which apartment houses the terrorist.
- Intelligence strongly suggests that a terrorist is of a certain ethnicity, but further identifying information is unavailable. To pursue the investigation, the police will have to stop everyone who matches that characteristic. Again, the problem is not with investigating the terrorist who is of that ethnicity; the problem is that the police will have to interrogate a large number of persons who have no connection with terrorist activity.

The problem that "emergency powers" must address, therefore, is not what can be done, but rather at whom may the authorities direct their attention. It is not a question of excessive measures but a question of application of appropriate measures to an overbroad group:

> The question arises whether compulsion can be visited upon an individual simply by virtue of her inclusion in a class composed of some dangerous persons absent an individualized assessment of significant risk . . . . Perhaps the most revered principle under antidiscrimination law is the requirement to make individualized determinations of [a] person's qualifications or eligibility . . . . Given the

153. *See* Thomas K. Clancy, *The Role of Individualized Suspicion in Assessing the Reasonableness of Searches and Seizures*, 25 U. MEM. L. REV. 483 (1994).

> unequivocal requirement for individualized assessments of risk, what recourse does the state have when, despite its best efforts, it is not able to reliably separate the perceived from the truly dangerous? This becomes a formidable dilemma when the state is capable of demonstrating that the class as a whole does pose a significant health threat and where the intervention proposed is both effective and non-draconian. . . . The requirement of individualized determinations is also inherent in the doctrine of overbreadth found in the Fourth Amendment and other constitutional jurisprudence.[154]

2. *Relevant Fourth Amendment Principles*

The Fourth Amendment permits only "reasonable" searches.[155] The Supreme Court has held that the "determination of the standard of reasonableness applicable to a particular class of searches requires 'balanc[ing] the nature and quality of the intrusion on the individual's Fourth Amendment interests against the importance of the governmental interests alleged to justify the intrusion.'"[156]

a. *Applicable Doctrines*

The "special needs" doctrine can justify a search, even in the absence of a warrant or probable cause.[157] "[W]here a Fourth Amendment intrusion serves special government needs, beyond the normal need for law enforcement, it is necessary to balance the individual's privacy expectations against the Government's interests to determine whether it is impractical to require a warrant or some level of individualized suspicion

---

154. Lawrence O. Gostin, *Tuberculosis and the Power of the State: Toward the Development of Rational Standards for the Review of Compulsory Public Health Powers*, 2 U. CHI. L. SCH. ROUNDTABLE 219, 257-59 (1995) (citations omitted).

155. U.S. CONST. amend. IV ("The right of the people to be secure in their persons, houses, papers, and effects, against unreasonable searches and seizures, shall not be violated . . . .").

156. O'Connor v. Ortega, 480 U.S. 709, 719 (1987) (quoting United States v. Place, 462 U.S. 696, 703 (1983)).

157. *See* Vernonia Sch. Dist. 47J v. Acton, 515 U.S. 646, 653 (1995). The *Vernonia* Court held:

> [A] warrant is not required to establish the reasonableness of *all* government searches; and when a warrant is not required, . . . probable cause is not invariably required either. A search unsupported by probable cause can be constitutional, we have said, "when special needs, beyond the normal need for law enforcement, make the warrant and probable-cause requirement impracticable."

Id. (quoting Griffin v. Wisconsin, 483 U.S. 868, 873 (1987)).

in the particular context."[158] The Court considers three factors: (1) "the nature of the privacy interest upon which the search . . . at issue intrudes;"[159] (2) "the character of the intrusion;"[160] and (3) "the nature and immediacy of the government's concern . . . and the efficacy of [the search] for meeting it."[161] Cases where courts use this alternative reasonableness formula often involve civil authorities and usually do not involve criminal penalties.[162]

A closely related concept is the "community caretaking" doctrine, based on the notion that police serve to ensure the safety and welfare of the citizenry at large. Certain emergencies require an immediate government response,[163] known as a community caretaking function.[164] When an officer is pursuing a community caretaking function not involving seizure of a person, no particularized and objective justification is required.[165] Traditional constitutional requirements—warrant,

158. Nat'l Treasury Employees Union v. Von Raab, 489 U.S. 656, 665-66 (1989).

159. *Vernonia*, 515 U.S. at 654.

160. *Id.* at 658.

161. *Id.* at 660.

162. *See, e.g.*, *Vernonia*, 515 U.S. at 658 (observing "special needs" student-athlete drug test results were not turned over to law enforcement authorities or used for disciplinary action); *Von Raab*, 489 U.S. at 663 (noting "special needs" search results were not permitted to be given over to the government for prosecution); Skinner v. Railway Labor Executives' Ass'n, 489 U.S. 602, 621 (1989) (noting "special needs" administrative drug test results not sought for criminal prosecution, but rather from adherence to safety regulations). *See generally* Jennifer Y. Buffaloe, Note, *"Special Needs" and the Fourth Amendment: An Exception Poised to Swallow the Warrant Preference Rule*, 32 HARV. C.R.-C.L. L. REV. 529 (1997); Michael Polloway, Comment, *Does the Fourth Amendment Prohibit Suspicionless Searches—or do Individual Rights Succumb to the Government's "So-Called" Special Needs?*, 10 SETON HALL CONST. L.J. 143 (1999). The Supreme Court's most recent pronouncement on the "special needs" doctrine also suggests that the Fourth Amendment standard for biological testing turns, in great part, on whether the information will be used for law enforcement purposes, in which case, the Fourth Amendment standard is rigorous. Ferguson v. Charleston, No. 99-936, — U.S. —, 2001 WL 273220 (Mar. 21, 2001). By implication, where the information is not used for law enforcement purposes, the latitude offered to the government is broader.

163. *See* Camara v. Mun. Court of San Francisco, 387 U.S. 523, 539 (1967) (noting warrantless inspections have been "traditionally upheld in emergency situations"). The Court cited *North American Cold Storage Co. v. Chicago*, 211 U.S. 306 (1908) (seizure of unwholesome food), *Jacobson v. Massachusetts*, 197 U.S. 11 (1905) (compulsory smallpox vaccination), and *Kroplin v. Truax*, 165 N.E. 498 (Ohio 1929) (summary destruction of tubercular cattle). *See Camara*, 387 U.S. at 539.

164. *See* John F. Decker, *Emergency Circumstances, Police Responses, and Fourth Amendment Restrictions*, 89 J. CRIM. L. & CRIMINOLOGY 433, 451 (1999) (discussing *Camara*, 387 U.S. 523 (1967)).

165. *See* Cady v. Dombrowski, 413 U.S. 433, 441 (1973) (concluding community caretaker functions were not within the purview of normal warrant requirements because they are totally divorced from the detection, investigation, or acquisition

probable cause, etc.—do not apply to this form of police-citizen encounter. Government responses to such emergencies need not be judged by normal Fourth Amendment standards because they are not considered searches or seizures within the meaning of the Fourth Amendment.[166]

Courts use a three-prong test to determine whether police actions are justified as caretaking functions: (1) "there must exist an objectively reasonable basis for a belief in an immediate need for police assistance for the protection of life or substantial property interests;"[167] (2) the officer's actions "must be motivated by an intent to aid,"[168] rather than to solve a crime; and (3) "police action must fall within the scope of the emergency."[169]

Accordingly, four principles guide the remainder of this discussion. First, the breadth of discretion afforded to law enforcement authorities should be proportional to the magnitude and proximity of the risk. The more precise the definition of authority for law enforcement officials, and the more that rules of engagement distinguish real security concerns from police caprice, the broader the constitutionally permissible law enforcement authority. Second, counter-terrorism measures must not target persons or groups on the basis of their race or ethnicity or without probable cause. Third, law enforcement measures should be no more intrusive nor entail greater use of force than necessary under specific conditions. Measures likely to raise profound Fourth Amendment concerns, such as intrusion into private dwellings without probable cause, must be justified by an emergency that is both of great magnitude (i.e., the potential level of harm is great) and of great urgency (i.e., the necessity for immediate action outweighs the privacy interest). Measures justified by the necessity of a biological terrorism event may not be used as

---

of evidence relating to the violation of a criminal statute); *see also* Colorado v. Bertine, 479 U.S. 367, 381 (1987) (Marshall, J., dissenting) ("Inventory searches are not subject to the warrant requirement because they are conducted by the government as part of a community caretaking function").

166. *See Cady*, 413 U.S. at 441. *See generally* Mary Elisabeth Naumann, *The Community Caretaker Doctrine: Yet Another Fourth Amendment Exception*, 26 AM J. CRIM. L. 325 (1999); Philip B. Heymann, *The New Policing*, 28 FORDHAM URB. L.J. 407 (2000).

167. Decker, *supra* note 164, at 457.

168. *Id.* at 510.

169. *Id.* at 517.

a pretext to gain unwarranted access for searches nor to conduct other law enforcement activity. Finally, any legal action taken against any individual in connection with counter-terrorism must measure up to the requirements of the Fifth[170] and Sixth Amendments.[171]

b. *Relevant Inquiries*

Where public health and security are at stake, the legal issue is whether searches directly promote a government interest that outweighs the individual's interest in avoiding the intrusion.[172] This issue comprises six subsidiary questions.

First, how weighty or important is the government's interest? Searches may profoundly contribute to a government interest, but that government interest may be relatively insignificant. The more significant the government interest, the greater the scope given to the authority to conduct searches.

Second, how proximate is the relationship between the search and the government interest? If the search is only tangentially related to the interest, or if there are alternative ways of pursuing the interest, then the need for the search is manifestly reduced.

Third, how are persons or sites selected for searches, and does this selection methodology afford due process? An element of this inquiry is whether the method of selection

---

170. U.S. CONST. amend. V.

> No person shall be held to answer for a capital, or otherwise infamous crime, unless on a presentment or indictment of a Grand Jury, except in cases arising in the land or naval forces, or in the Militia, when in actual service in time of War or public danger; nor shall any person be subject for the same offense to be twice put in jeopardy of life or limb; nor shall be compelled in any criminal case to be a witness against himself, nor be deprived of life, liberty, or property, without due process of law; nor shall private property be taken for public use, without just compensation.

Id.

171. U.S. CONST. amend. VI.

> In all criminal prosecutions, the accused shall enjoy the right to a speedy and public trial, by an impartial jury of the State and district wherein the crime shall have been committed, which district shall have been previously ascertained by law, and to be informed of the nature and cause of the accusation; to be confronted with the witnesses against him; to have compulsory process for obtaining witnesses in his favor, and to have the Assistance of Counsel for his defense.

Id.

172. *See generally* David S. Faigaman, *Reconciling Individual Rights and Government Interests: Madisonian Principles Versus Supreme Court Practice*, 78 VA. L. REV. 1521 (1992).

insinuates wrongdoing that might inappropriately diminish the individual's reputation. If the searches are entirely random and apply to virtually everyone within a given sector (e.g., random vehicle checkpoints), the search scheme may be more tolerable. On the other hand, if individuals are selected due to their racial or ethnic groupings, or if a few individuals are targeted for especially demeaning activity, that program of searches is more subject to challenge.[173]

Fourth, where is the search carried out? A search of a vehicle or of an individual in a public place is far more tolerable than searches of homes because of the high expectation of privacy an individual has when in his home.[174]

Fifth, how intrusive is the search—how much force is used, and what is the scope of the search? Protective sweep searches, conducted without a warrant but only superficially and only to determine whether a more intrusive search can be undertaken safely, are more tolerable than extensive searches backed by force.[175] At the opposite extreme, strip searches or body cavity searches are the least tolerable.

Finally, what use is made of evidence obtained in the search? Fewer legal concerns apply to searches to effectuate a government interest that is health-related and non-punitive. Also, a search from which only evidence is used which directly relates to the asserted prosecutorial purpose may be more tolerable than a search for a purpose that is a mere pretext for a wide-ranging prosecutorial investigation. Thus, Fourth Amendment problems are diminished if the law enforcement personnel overlook evidence of wrongdoing that is unrelated

173. *See* Whren v. United States, 517 U.S. 806, 813 (1996) (stating that the Constitution prohibits selective enforcement of the law based on considerations such as race); Brown v. City of Oneonta, 195 F.3d 111, 118-19 (2d Cir. 1999) (stating that an equal protection violation may be premised on police practice of conducting investigations utilizing racially based classifications); United States v. Avery, 137 F.3d 343, 354 (6th Cir. 1997) (holding that race cannot be the sole basis for conducting a search); *see also* Sheri L. Johnson, *Race and the Decision to Detain a Suspect*, 93 YALE L.J. 214 (1983).

174. *Compare* Cardell v. Lewis, 417 U.S. 583, 591 (1974) (holding warrantless search of motor vehicles permissible), *and* Terry v. Ohio, 392 U.S. 1 (1968) (holding warrantless search of person in public permissible given certain conditions), *with* Payton v. New York, 445 U.S. 573, 592 (1980) (prohibiting police from making warrantless and nonconsensual entry into suspects' homes in order to make routine felony arrests).

175. *See* Maryland v. Buie, 494 U.S. 325 (1990) (upholding the constitutionality of warrantless post-arrest protective sweep searches within a limited area).

to the asserted purpose of the search.

3. *Legal Treatment of Searches and Related Measures*

a. *Cordoning Areas, Preventing Ingress or Egress*

Courts have long held that officials may cordon off an area, establish a quarantine, or erect checkpoints for persons and/or vehicles leaving an area.[176] Both the need to prevent escape of suspected criminals[177] (or carriers of contagion[178]) and the individual's diminished right of privacy (on foot or in a vehicle) support this conclusion. Thus, there is no need to establish "emergency powers" to enable officials to cordon off areas.

b. *Compulsory Vaccinations and Other Medical Treatment*

Courts are likely to uphold compulsory medical interventions based upon a reasonable assessment of future harm. The courts have held that compulsory vaccinations during periods of contagious outbreaks do not violate due process.[179] Local, state, and federal government, therefore, may

176. *See* United States v. Martinez-Fuerte, 428 U.S. 543, 566 (1976) (holding stops for brief questioning at checkpoints are consistent with the Fourth Amendment and need not be authorized by a warrant); Jacobson v. Massachusetts, 197 U.S. 11, 25 (1905) (observing quarantine laws are authorized within the police power of the state to provide for public health and safety). The Supreme Court addressed the outer limits of the police power to use checkpoints this Term in *City of Indianapolis v. Edmond,* 121 S. Ct. 447 (2000) (holding that the city's drug interdiction checkpoints were in violation of the Fourth Amendment).

177. *See* Laaman v. U.S., 973 F.2d 107 (2d Cir. 1992) (involving alleged terrorist conspiracy to bomb military offices).

178. *See* Compagnie Française de Navigation à Vapeur v. La. State Bd. of Health, 186 U.S. 380 (1902) (preventing immigrants from a potentially infected area from entering the country).

179. *See, e.g.,* Jacobson, 197 U.S. at 26.

> [T]he liberty secured by the Constitution of the United States to every person within its jurisdiction does not import an absolute right in each person to be, at all times and in all circumstances, wholly freed from restraint. There are manifold restraints to which every person is necessarily subject for the common good.... [A] community has the right to protect itself against an epidemic of disease which threatens the safety of its members. It is to be observed that when the regulation in question was adopted smallpox, according to the recitals in the regulation adopted by the board of health, was prevalent to some extent in the city of Cambridge, and the disease was increasing. If such was the situation,—and nothing is asserted or appears in the record to the contrary, —if we are to attach, any value whatever to the knowledge which, it is safe to affirm, in common to all civilized peoples touching smallpox and the

legally vaccinate those deemed at risk. A more difficult legal question is presented by quarantines of contagious patients. There have been cases of communicable diseases where courts have required persons to be actually infectious to be subject to isolation or quarantine.[180] These cases, however, are distinguishable because the individual was completely deprived of liberty based on scarce evidence of a current or imminent danger to public health. In cases where the state could demonstrate a "rational nexus" between a relatively non-intrusive intervention and the likely reduction in future harm to the public, there has been little judicial inclination to interfere with reasonable medical judgments.

Court precedents from HIV cases, however, weigh heavily in favor of protecting due process rights, thereby strengthening the "rational nexus" requirement. In *Hill v. Evans*,[181] an Alabama statute was held to violate equal protection because it allowed uninformed, non-consensual HIV testing of persons who seek medical services on the basis of a physician's judgment that the person is at high risk for HIV.[182] The court found the absence of a consent requirement unconstitutional because the State "did not establish that the ability of physicians to test without informed consent individuals they consider to be high risk for the HIV virus, for that reason alone, would in any way curb the spread of the disease."[183] The court, however, upheld a medical care exception allowing non-consensual HIV testing where medical treatment might be modified due to the presence or absence of HIV. The court found that "there is a legitimate government interest in a treating physician knowing the HIV status of a patient . . . [and] that governmental interest outweighs the . . . privacy interest of

> methods most usually employed to eradicate that disease, it cannot be adjudged that the present regulation of the board of health was not necessary in order to protect the public health and secure the public safety.

Id. at 26-28.

180. *See, e.g., In re* Halko, 54 Cal. Rptr. 661, 664-65 (1966) (requiring reasonable grounds to believe the person is actually infected (and contagious) in order to justify restraint of personal liberty); People *ex. rel.* Barmore v. Robertson, 134 N.E. 815, 819 (1922) (stating that a person cannot be quarantined upon mere suspicion that he may have a contagious and infectious disease).

181. No. 91-A-626-N, 1993 WL 595676 (M.D. Ala. Oct. 7, 1993).

182. *See id.* at *4-*6.

183. *Id.* at *7.

an individual."[184]

Thus, two issues emerge. First, how are individuals selected for testing or treatment? Second, does the justification for the particular testing or treatment justify the intrusion into the individual's privacy? Legislation can effectively address each of these issues, as discussed below.[185]

c. Lowering the Threshold of Reasonable Suspicion

The suggestion of authorizing searches in the absence of normally sufficient evidence misconstrues the critical issues discussed above. If the search is directed specifically at someone thought to be a terrorist, the typical "reasonable suspicion" standard is appropriate. In view of the low threshold of this standard, officials will not be unreasonably limited in the actions they can undertake. If the search is directed more broadly than at a designated suspect, no lowering of the threshold of reasonable suspicion is relevant. For example, in the apartment hypothetical discussed earlier, there is no reasonable suspicion whatsoever as to the innocent dwellers in five of the six apartments, and no lower threshold could justify individual searches of their dwellings. This problem is the Fourth Amendment rendition of Russian roulette. Only enabling sweep searches, as discussed below, can address this issue.

d. Sweep Searches

Intrusive sweep searches into dwellings have been judicially struck down on a number of occasions, but in each case the State failed to establish the necessity of those searches.[186] Most notably, the Chicago Housing Authority (CHA) attempted to control the rising instances of violence and drug crimes in its public housing by staging a surprise assault on its public housing projects: all entrances and exits were sealed, and every apartment was searched for drugs, weapons, and illegal

184. *Id.* at *12.

185. *See infra* Part III.D.4.

186. *See, e.g.*, Steagald v. United States, 451 U.S. 204 (1981) (holding officers' search unconstitutional without requisite consent of exigent circumstances); Pratt v. Chicago Hous. Auth., 848 F. Supp. 792 (N.D. Ill. 1994) (holding searches conducted in the absence of probable cause or exigent circumstances unconstitutional).

residents.[187] The CHA claimed that the searches were justified by the emergency circumstances of high crime and drug use and were necessary to protect the safety and welfare of tenants. Although the dispute was never litigated to a conclusion, most commentators agree that the CHA confused the meaning of the term "emergency" by substituting a *serious* concern with crime for criteria that focus on the necessity of *urgent* action.[188]

Intrusion into private dwellings without probable cause to believe that there is evidence of a crime inside raises the most profound Fourth Amendment considerations and must, therefore, be justified by an emergency that is both of great magnitude (i.e., the potential level of harm is great) and of great urgency (i.e., the necessity for immediate action outweighs the privacy interest). No case law has been found where this test has been satisfied, but neither has case law been found which has struck down official action in response to mass disaster or contagion.

4. *Can Anything Be Done To Clarify or Expand Emergency Powers?*

Neither Congress nor the Executive Branch can promulgate laws that would contravene or diminish the operative scope of the Fourth Amendment.[189] Manifestly unconstitutional behavior cannot be made legal because Congress so legislates. Yet Congress can address the questions outlined above and, in so doing, both overtly define the need asserted to justify the searches and corral law enforcement to ensure that appropriate boundaries are respected. Accordingly, Congress can take at least six possible steps.

First, Congress can explicitly articulate the government interest at stake in bioterrorism cases and expound on the magnitude of that interest. Legislation to address biological

---

187. *See Pratt*, 848 F. Supp. at 792.

188. *See* Andrew Byers, Note, *The Special Government Needs Exception: Does It Allow for Warrantless Searches of Public Housing?*, 41 WAYNE L. REV. 1469 (1995); Zionne N. Presley, Note, *Privacy or Safety: A Constitutional Analysis of Public Housing Sweep Searches*, 6 B.U. PUB. INT. L.J. 777 (1977); Monica L. Selter, Comment, *Sweeps: An Unwarranted Solution to the Search for Safety in Public Housing*, 44 AM. U. L. REV. 1903 (1995).

189. *See* District of Columbia v. Little, 178 F.2d 13, 19 (D.C. Cir. 1949), *aff'd*, 339 U.S. 1 (1950); *cf.* Dickerson v. United States, 120 S. Ct. 2326, 2329 (2000) (ruling that Congress may not legislatively supersede a "constitutional decision" of the United States Supreme Court).

terrorism obviously can identify the enormous interests to the public and to national security that compel extraordinary preventive and responsive measures. Indeed, the certainty of this identification probably renders congressional action unnecessary.

Second, Congress can specify that a threat of biological terrorism is an "emergency" and can mandate that the President so designate. This designation would satisfy the legal requirement that broader-than-normal law enforcement powers be exercised only during periods of emergency. Moreover, Congress can specify that enumerated measures be undertaken to address this type of emergency.

Third, Congress can authorize and specify the implementation of appropriate medical measures to prevent harm, including vaccination and quarantine programs.

Fourth, Congress can express its view on the relevance of searches to protecting or promoting the articulated government interests. More specifically, Congress can address the difficulty that standard law-enforcement methods might face in detecting easily concealable but highly dangerous items. In connection with presidential identification of explicitly specified cases of biological terrorism, specific powers to conduct limited and necessary sweep searches may be granted.

Fifth, Congress can specify the selectivity, location, and intrusiveness of searches and identify how the characteristics of the search scheme correspond to the interest to be promoted. These specifications would be analogous to those for warrantless searches of commercial sites conducted pursuant to an administrative search scheme.[190] By specifying the regulatory interest and by tailoring the search scheme to that interest, Congress can go far toward establishing that a particular search, if conducted within the scope of that scheme, is reasonable under the Fourth Amendment.[191]

Finally, Congress can implement means to ensure that searches permitted by the necessity of a biological terrorism event may not be used as a subterfuge to gain access to sites

190. *See* Edward A. Tanzman & Barry Kellman, *Legal Implementation of the Multilateral Chemical Weapons Convention: Integrating International Security with the Constitution*, 22 N.Y.U. J. INT'L L. & POL. 475, 506-08 (1990).

191. *See id.* at 508-09.

without a warrant and search for an array of criminal activity.

CONCLUSION

The unique, low probability, high-magnitude risk of bioterrorism confounds the formulation of legal responses. Legal responses, however, are at best a part of the policy picture; other disciplines must contribute their own responses if a coherent and comprehensive strategy is to be implemented. In an even larger sense, the measures that are formulated to respond to the threat of bioterrorism should be part of broader international efforts to control and eliminate weapons of mass destruction. In every conceivable dimension, uncertainty reigns.

Yet this much is certain: with regard to biological terrorism, there is capability and there is motivation. The threat of biological weapons is spreading as technological hurdles diminish and more people in more nations develop the capabilities to produce and use such weapons. The United States cannot ignore the manifestations—both at home and abroad—of the extraordinary hate which motivates such terrorism. If a bioterrorist attack happens, we will all be victims. If we do not do what we can to prevent it, we will all be culprits.

THE DEFENSE THREAT REDUCTION AGENCY: A NOTE ON THE UNITED STATES' APPROACH TO THE THREAT OF CHEMICAL AND BIOLOGICAL WARFARE

Matthew Linkie[*]

INTRODUCTION

On October 1, 1998, the Pentagon merged three cold war agencies into a new $1.9 billion-per-year Defense Threat Reduction Agency (DTRA) to address growing weapons proliferation problems and to meet the threat from weapons of mass destruction in the hands of terrorist and rogue nations.[1] Speaking to DTRA employees in connection with the creation of the new agency, Secretary of Defense, William S. Cohen stated

> Today's harsh reality is too powerful to ignore: at least 25 countries have, or are in the process of developing, nuclear, biological or chemical weapons and the means to deliver them. . . . We must confront these threats in places like Baghdad before they come to our shores. Because America should not rush into the future without being rooted in the proven strengths of the past, we turn to you – the proven professionals.[2]

The DTRA merges, the Defense Technology Security Administration (DTSA),[3] the Defense Special Weapons Agency (DSWA),[4] and

---

* J.D. 1999 Columbus School of Law, The Catholic University of America; B.A. 1994 Villanova University.

1. *See* Walter Pincus, *Pentagon Merges Cold War Units Into 'Threat Reduction' Agency*, WASH. POST, Oct. 2, 1998, at A2.

2. Department of Defense (DOD), *Establishment of the Defense Threat Reduction Agency, Research Intelligence Database*, Oct. 1, 1998, *available in* 1998 WL 674356 (F.D.C.H.) (transcript of the Department of Defense announcement on the establishment of the Defense Threat Reduction Agency).

3. *See DOD News Briefing*, M2 PRESSWIRE, Oct. 2, 1998, *available in* 1998 WL 16525670. The DTSA is headed by Dave Tarbel and was set up during the Cold War to prevent militarily useful technology from leaving the United States and reaching terrorist organizations. *See id.*

4. *See id.* The DSWA, formerly the Defense Nuclear Agency, formed

the On-Site Inspection Agency (OSIA)[5] into one central agency. Its creation sparks a new integrated approach to uncovering chemical and biological stockpiles of weapons and preventing their use.[6]

The establishment of the DTRA is evidence of the nation's dedication to reducing the threat of a chemical or biological attack on the United States.[7] Its establishment, however, also acknowledges America's vulnerability to such a threat[8] and the concern that our nation may be ill-prepared to protect its citizens.[9] In the past, the U.S. relied on geography, international treaties, and international conventions for protection from a possible biological or chemical attack.[10] Most geographic defenses, however, are outdated and the relevant treaties inef-

---

when the Manhattan Project first began. *See id.* It has been the United States' lead agency for dealing with nuclear weapons, deterrence, stockpiling and other nuclear weapons issues. *See id.* The DSWA's field command is at Kirtland Air Force Base and employs an estimated 395 military and civilian personnel. *See Special Weapons Part of New Agency*, ALBUQUERQUE J., Oct. 3, 1998, *available in* 1998 WL 16509805. The Field Command primarily researches and simulates weapon effects at Kirtland and White Sands Missile Range. *See id.* As part of the DTRA, DSWA helps address the proliferation of weapons of mass destruction. *See IG Report Says DSWA Response to Y2K Problem Inadequate*, ARMED FORCES NEWSWIRE SERVICE, Nov. 19, 1998, *available in* 1998 WL 17229092.

5. *See DOD News Briefing*, Oct. 2, 1998, *supra* note 3. Developed towards the end of the Cold War, OSIA was created to oversee inspection programs associated with arms control agreements with the former Soviet Union. *See id.* The OSIA was a key player in developing confidences and reassurances between the two superpowers during the Cold War. *See id.*

6. *See id.*

7. *See id.* (announcing the creation of the DTRA).

8. *New US Agency to Deal with Weapons of Mass Destruction Threat*, AGENCE FRANCE-PRESSE, Oct. 2, 1998, *available in* 1998 WL 16611007. The Director of the DTRA, Jay Davis, stated, "[T]he deterrent capability of the United States is still very effective against national states. It's not so clear that it has the same effect on transnational organizations." *Id.*

9. *See* Bryan Bender, *DOD Seeks Guidance on Threat Reduction*, JANE'S DEFENSE WKLY., July 22, 1998, *available in* 1998 WL 7900819 (discussing the DOD's move to create the DTRA in response to criticism that the Agency is overlooking key issues in countering the proliferation of nuclear, biological and chemical weapons).

10. *See generally United Nations: Convention on the Prohibition of the Development, Production, Stockpiling and Use of Chemical Weapons and on Their Destruction*, 32 INT'L LEGAL MAT'L 800 (1993) [hereinafter *Chemical Weapons Convention*].

fective.[11] For example, because all countries are not parties to these treaties, some countries may disregard them.[12] Compliance by countries that are parties to such treaties is difficult to monitor and "cheating" is not easily detected,[13] as the procedures required to check compliance under current treaties are generally cumbersome.[14] The treaties essentially have failed in their attempt to discover chemical and biological weapons facilities and to stop proliferation.[15] Further, the treaties do not extend to non-statist terrorist organizations. A new approach is necessary.

The unique characteristics of chemical and biological weapons make the establishment of the DTRA a necessity. First, these weapons are easy to produce and do not require large, expensive facilities.[16]

11. *See* Kevin J. Fitzgerald, *The Chemical Weapons Convention: Inadequate Protection from Chemical Warfare*, 20 SUFFOLK TRANSNAT'L L. REV. 425, 446 (1996) (discussing the ineffectiveness of international treaties); *see also* Andrea Stone, *U.S. Encounters Mideast Reluctance to Military Action*, USA TODAY, Nov. 9, 1998, at A12 (discussing Iraq's refusal to permit U.N. inspectors to search for weapons of mass destruction).

12. *See* Fitzgerald, *supra* note 11, at 446 (identifying Libya and other countries not party to U.N. treaties).

13. *See* Richard A. Falk, *Inhibiting Reliance on Biological Weaponry: the Role and Relevance of International Law*, 1 AM. U. J. INT'L L. & POL'Y 17, 18 (1986) (discussing the difficulty of substantiating violations of international law).

14. *See* Chemical Weapons Convention, *supra* note 10, at art. XII(4) (providing, "[t]he Conference shall, in cases of particular gravity, bring the issue, . . . to the attention of the United Nations General Assembly and the United Nations Security Council.") *Id.*

15. *See* Fitzgerald, *supra* note 11, at 429. For example, although the U.S. contends Iraq is building chemical and biological weapons, it has thus far been unable to prevent their proliferation under the U.N. procedures. *See* Stone, *supra* note 11, at A12.

16. *See* David G. Gray, Note, *"Then the Dogs Died": The Fourth Amendment and Verification of the Chemical Weapons Convention*, 94 COLUM. L. REV. 567, 574 (1994) (discussing the characteristics of chemical weapons). "[Y]ou can make the basic compounds [of chemical weapons] in a kitchen sink or a high school lab." *Id.* (citing Robin Wright, *Chemical Arms Race Heating Up*, L.A. TIMES, Oct. 9, 1988, pt. 1, at 1, 6); *see also* W. Edward Montz Jr. and Frank A. Lewis, *The Emerging Threat of Chemical/Biological Terrorism*, 14 ENVTL. COMPLIANCE & LITIG. STRATEGY 6 (1998) (discussing the ease and commercial availability of chemical agents). "A number of chemical agents are commercially available or easy to make with just a basic knowledge of chemistry." *Id.*

They can be developed and produced almost anywhere – in laboratories, basements or small-scale industrial facilities.[17] Mustard gas, for example, can be synthesized by simply mixing two chemicals.[18] In addition, these weapons involve chemicals and biological substances with commercial uses and are readily available throughout the world.[19] Second, chemical weapon facilities are extremely difficult to detect.[20] Because the technologies needed to produce these weapons often have commercial applications, their use as weapons can be easily denied.[21] Third, small quantities of such weapons can be extremely effective[22] and lethal.[23] Fourth, chemical and biological weapons can be delivered by a variety of means and come in a variety of forms.[24] Furthermore, their effects may go undetected for minutes (in the case of chemical agents) or for days (in the case of biological agents),[25] making these weapons particularly attractive to terrorists. Lastly, response tactics vary greatly depending upon the type of chemical or biological

17. *See* Gray, *supra* note 16, at 574 (citing *Chemical Warfare: Ban the World's Machine Guns: Can't Be Done? As Easy as Trying to Get an Effective Global Ban on Chemical Weapons*, THE ECONOMIST, June 4, 1988, at 20).

18. *See* Gray, *supra* note 16, at 574 (citation omitted).

19. *See id.* at 575 (citation omitted).

20. *See id.* (citation omitted).

21. *See id.* (citation omitted) (stating that any production facility could be dual-purpose, readily switching from the manufacture of chemical weapons to the production of aspirin).

22. *See DOD News Briefing*, M2 PRESSWIRE, July 9, 1998, *available in* 1998 WL 14095268. ("Five pounds of anthrax, properly dispersed, would kill over 200,000 in Washington D.C."). *Id.*

23. *See Vaccine Improves Odds Against Anthrax*, REGULATORY INTELLIGENCE DATABASE, Apr. 6, 1998, *available in* 1998 WL 194056 (F.D.C.H.) (discussing the chance of survival after inhaling anthrax used as a biological weapon). "When inhaled, an unvaccinated, unprotected person has about a one percent chance of surviving a concentrated anthrax exposure." *Id.*

24. *See* Montz and Lewis, *supra* note 16, at 6 (discussing the forms of chemical and biological agents). Chemical agents can be solid, liquid or vapor. *See id.* Solids and liquids are put into suspension as aerosols; some liquid aerosols may change to a vapor state. *See id.*

25. *See Vaccine Improves Odds Against Anthrax*, *supra* note 23. "You wouldn't see it, smell it or feel it in the air. But just the same, one deep breath is enough to kill you." *Id.* "One of the hardest things about a chemical and biological event is that unlike a bomb going off, you're not sure what happened and when it happened." *DOD News Briefing*, *supra* note 3.

weapon, making training and defense preparation extremely difficult.[26]

Prior to the establishment of the DTRA, the United States' primary protection from biological and chemical warfare rested with multiple agencies in the intelligence community and the Department of Defense (DOD).[27] These agencies relied on legislation such as the 1996 Defense Against Weapons of Mass Destruction Act[28] and the Chemical and Biological Weapons Threat Reduction Act of 1997;[29] presidential executive orders such as Executive Order No. 12,868;[30] and international treaties including the Geneva Protocol of 1925,[31] the 1972 Biological and Toxin Weapons Convention,[32] and the 1993 Chemical Weapons Convention.[33]

The creation of the DTRA is the result of extensive Congressional

---

26. *See DOD News Briefing*, *supra* note 3. "It takes fundamentally different tactics if its a chemical terrorist weapon or a biological terrorist weapon. . . . If it's a chemical weapon, you want to get people out of the area as soon as possible. If it's a biological weapon, you want to contain people in the area." *Id.*

27. *See id.* (discussing the organizations responsible for reducing key threats to national security).

28. Defense Against Weapons of Mass Destruction Act of 1996, 50 U.S.C. § 2301 *et seq.* (1996).

29. Chemical and Biological Weapons Threat Reduction Act of 1997, S. 495, 105th Cong., 1st Sess. (1997).

30. Exec. Order No. 12,868, 58 Fed. Reg. 51,749 (1993) (repealed).

31. The Geneva Protocol for the Prohibition of the Use in War of Asphyxiating, Poisonous, or Other Gases, and of Bacterial Methods of Warfare, June 17, 1925, 26 U.S.T. 571 [hereinafter Geneva Protocol], *reprinted in United States: Ratification of the 1925 Geneva Protocol for the Prohibition of the Use in War of Asphyxiating, Poisonous, or Other Gases, and of Bacterial Methods of Warfare, 14* INT'L LEGAL MAT'L. *49, 49 (1975).*

32. 1972 Biological and Toxin Weapons Convention, 26 U.S.T. 583 (Apr. 10, 1972). Introduced in 1972 and ratified by the U.S. in 1975, the Biological and Toxin Weapons Convention banned the use of biological weapons by prohibiting the "development, production, stockpiling, acquisition or retention" of biological weapons for offensive purposes. *See* Colonel Guy B. Roberts, *The Counterproliferation Self-Help Paradigm: A Legal Regime for Enforcing the Norm Prohibiting the Proliferation of Weapons of Mass Destruction*, 27 DENV. J. INT'L. L. & POL'Y 483, 499 (1999); *see also Convention on the Prohibition of the Development, Production and Stockpiling of Bacteriological (Biological) and Toxin Weapons and on Their Destruction* (visited Mar. 22, 2000) <http://dosfan.lib.uic.edu/acda/treaties/bwc1.htm> (text of convention).

33. Chemical Weapons Convention, *supra* note 10.

testimony by defense officials,[34] scientists and public health officials,[35] and recent legislation,[36] all demanding a new approach for defending against biological and chemical weapons. In addition, the attacks on the Alfred P. Murrah Federal Building in Oklahoma City, the sarin gas attack in Tokyo,[37] and the events of the Gulf War[38] encouraged officials to reevaluate the nation's chemical and biological weapons defense capabilities.[39]

The push for establishment of the DTRA began with the Defense Reform Initiative of 1997 (DRI).[40] In addition to the cost-saving measures outlined by the DRI, the Secretary of Defense also recognized the current defense infrastructure's inability to prepare and de-

---

34. *See, e.g., Quarterly Readiness Reporting System: Hearing before the Subcomm. on Military Readiness of the House National Security Comm.*, 105th Cong. (1998) (statement of Louis C. Finch, Deputy Undersecretary of Defense for Readiness).

35. *See, e.g., TRICARE Program, 1998: Hearing before the Subcomm. on Military Personnel of the House National Security Comm.*, 105th Cong. (1998) (statement of Edward D. Martin, Acting Assistant Secretary of Defense for Health Affairs).

36. *See generally* 50 U.S.C. § 2301; *see also* Chemical and Biological Weapons Threat Reduction Act of 1997, *supra* note 29.

37. The AUM Shinrikyo nerve gas attack on the Tokyo subway system aimed to kill thousands of people and scare the population away from public transportation. *See* Paul Rogers, *The Next Terror Weapon Will be Biological. And it Could be Used Soon*, THE GUARDIAN (Aug. 18, 1998).

38. *See Fact Sheet on Gulf War Ongoing Initiatives*, Mar. 7, 1997 *available in* 1997 WL 895616 (F.D.C.H.). Since the Gulf War, DOD has increased its attention on biological warfare defense and other force-protection measures. *See Anthrax Vaccination Program Facts,* REGULATORY INTELLIGENCE DATABASE, Department of Defense (Dec. 16, 1997), available in 1997 WL 890912 (F.D.C.H.).

39. *See DOD News Briefing, supra* note 22.

40. *See* William Cohen, Secretary of Defense, *Defense Reform Initiative of 1997*. Primarily, the DRI was meant as a cost-cutting measure. *See* Bradley Graham, *Retired Admiral Pushes Pentagon to Run a Tighter Ship; Cohen Aide Launches Several Reforms*, WASH. POST, Nov. 6, 1998, at A19. The initiative included plans to: (1) eliminate one-third of the 3,000 jobs in the Office of the Secretary of Defense, (2) make substantial reductions in military headquarters staffs and thirteen Defense agencies, (3) switch from reams of paper to electronic networks for issuing regulations, (4) order items and pay bills, (5) privatize utility systems at military bases, and (6) establish a chancellor for education and professional development to oversee the department's thirty civilian schools. *See id.*

fend from an attack such as the one in Tokyo.[41] In particular, the Secretary noted that the agencies currently in charge of countering this new threat were formed to protect the nation from a nuclear attack rather than chemical or biological warfare.[42] Thus, the bureaucracies responsible for monitoring the nation's defense capabilities required restructuring. Testimony noted the proven frailty of existing treaties in protecting the United States against a chemical or biological attack.[43] The DRI and the Secretary's testimony made it clear that, although the threats are by no means new, our methods for combating them must be.

The development of the DTRA to meet these threats, however, presents numerous questions and considerations. The first concern is whether large scale spending to fund the DTRA is necessary or whether spending to educate health officials on how to respond to an attack would be more appropriate. Questions relating to jurisdiction and feasibility, as well as potential infringements upon international treaties and conventions also arise. Another problem is how the DTRA will work with other U.S. government intelligence agencies, federal law enforcement, and state public health officials to enforce its findings. This Note proposes potential answers to these questions.

Part I of this Note presents a history of biological and chemical warfare and describes potential public health effects. This Part examines current law and U.S. capabilities to protect the nation from the threat of weapons of mass destruction. Part II explains the development of the DTRA, its mission, goals, organization, and intended impact on current law. Part III analyzes the need for the DTRA, specifically, how current capabilities to defend against terrorist chemical and biological weapons attacks are insufficient, and considers areas in which the DTRA can succeed where international treaties have failed. In addition, Part III questions whether funds are being spent appropriately on the DTRA, or whether this money could be spent more effectively on public health and readiness programs. This Part discusses the prob-

41. *See* 50 U.S.C. § 2301 (listing congressional findings leading up to the Defense Against Weapons of Mass Destruction Act).

42. *See U.S. DOD: Defense Dept. Makes Progress with Reform Actions*, M2 PRESSWIRE, Oct. 12, 1998, *available in* 1998 WL 16527105 (stating, "Cohen is realigning the Department to better execute its post-Cold War missions. Agencies and offices that were designed to operate in a bi-polar world are now being merged or restructured to meet the realities of today's threats.").

43. *See id.*

lems the DTRA will face in meeting its goals, particularly with regard to jurisdiction, enforcement, and feasibility issues. Part IV concludes that the establishment of the DTRA is necessary for effective reduction of the threat from chemical and biological weapons. Furthermore, Part IV finds that similar efforts must be made to increase the capabilities of the United States' health facilities to respond to a chemical or biological attack in the United States.

I. PREPARING FOR THE THREAT

A. The History and Health Risks of Biological and Chemical Warfare

Biological and chemical weapons historically have played a significant role in military operations.[44] Medieval armies poisoned their enemies' drinking water with the dead bodies of humans and animals.[45] In ancient times, armies burned sulfur and tar, choking their enemies with smoke.[46] In the eighteenth century, the British army spread disease among the Native American tribes by distributing blankets contaminated with smallpox.[47]

Nations recognized the need to regulate the use of such tactics in the late nineteenth and early twentieth centuries however, the Hague Conferences of 1899[48] and 1907[49] and the Geneva Protocol of 1925[50] did not effectively deter their use. The use of chemical and biological weapons by the Germans during World War I,[51] and the

44. *See* ROBIN CLARKE, THE SILENT WEAPONS 12-16 (1968) (discussing the origins of toxic warfare).

45. *See id.* at 14. During the medieval period, poisoning water supplies was a standard military tactic. *See id.*; *see also DOD News Briefing*, *supra* note 22 (discussing how during the middle ages, cadavers were catapulted over besieged city walls to spread death and disease).

46. *See id.* (examining the Spartans' use of noxious fumes from smoldering pitch and sulfur to attack the Athenians).

47. *See* CLARKE, *supra* note 44, at 14-16.

48. *The First International Peace Conference, The Hague*, 1899, *reprinted in* 1 AM. J. INT'L L. 103, 105 (Supp. 1907).

49. *The Second International Peace Conference, The Hague*, 1907, *reprinted in* 2 AM. J. INT'L L. 1, 106 (Supp. 1908).

50. Geneva Protocol, *supra* note 31.

51. *See* Fitzgerald, *supra* note 11, at 429-30 (discussing the German use of chemical weapons in 1915). Germany sidestepped the Hague Conference's

Italians in 1935 against Ethiopia,[52] evidenced this failure and helped usher in the modern era of chemical warfare and abuses of international law.[53]

Since these events, chemical weapons technology has progressed greatly,[54] allowing nations to build up massive stockpiles and conduct intensive research on possible chemical and biological agents. This trend, however, has not been limited to large nations. Developing countries such as Libya began to manufacture chemical weapons as well.[55] In addition, the first large scale use of chemical weapons by a terrorist group[56] was exhibited when the Aum Shinrikyo Cult[57] deployed sarin gas[58] in a Tokyo subway station[59] in 1995. Later, in July

---

ban on chemical warfare by using chlorine filled canisters positioned along a four mile front rather than projectiles during the chemical attack. *See id.* The German Army waited for the wind to blow towards the French positions, then opened the canisters releasing a cloud of chlorine gas over the French troops. *See id.*

52. *See id.* (discussing Italy's use of chemical weapons in 1935). Italy used chemical weapons in its conquest of Ethiopia, despite the Geneva Protocol's ban on their use. *See id.*

53. *See id.* at 430-32. In addition, Japan used poison gas against China (1937-45) as did Iraq against Iran (1982-83). *See* Falk, *supra* note 13, at 23.

54. *See DOD News Briefing*, *supra* note 22 (discussing the use of new technologies as strategic weapons rather than tactical maneuvers).

55. *See* Fitzgerald, *supra* note 11, at 443 (citation omitted).

56. Not until the Aum Shinrikyo cult confessed to the subway attack did analysts discover the same cult was responsible for an attack with VX gas against a twenty-eight year old man in December 1994. *See* David L. Chandler, *Japan Cult May Have Used Agent Found in Sudan*, BOSTON GLOBE, Aug. 26, 1998, at A14. "In that attack, the chemical agent VX was sprayed directly on the victim's skin." *Id.* "The man lost consciousness immediately and died ten days later." *Id.*

57. Founded by Shoko Asahara (whose real name is Chizuo Matsumoto), the Aum Shinrikyo cult is believed to have up to $1 billion in assets and as many as 16,000 members in Russia. *See* Jeff Nesmith, *Target America: Biochemical Warfare*, ATLANTA J. & CONST., Aug. 2, 1998, at E2; *see also* Chris Betros, *Death Sentence Urged for Cult Killer. Former Member First to Face Call for Capital Punishment in Aum Shinri Kyo Trials*, S. CHINA MORNING POST, July 7, 1998, at 12.

58. During the March 20, 1995 Tokyo subway attack, canisters with electric fans placed in three subway lines converging in central Tokyo began dispersing Sarin nerve gas. *See* Fitzgerald, *supra* note 11, at 445. The attack injured 5,000 and killed twelve. *See id.* *See Subcomm. on Labor, Health and Human Services, Education, and Related Agencies of the Senate Comm. on*

1998, more than sixty people were poisoned by cyanide at an outdoor summer festival in Japan.[60] These abuses have not been limited to foreign countries and terrorist organizations. The use of riot control agents and herbicides by the U.S. in Vietnam violated the 1925 Geneva Protocol.[61] In addition, chemical weapons have been used by domestic terrorists in the U.S.[62]

B. U.S. Legislation

In 1996, the U.S. Congress passed the Defense Against Weapons of

---

Appropriations, 105th Cong. (1998) (Statement of Richard Jackson). The cult also attempted to obtain biological agents, such as Ebola, anthrax, and botulin from a United States military base in Japan. *See* Nesmith, *supra* note 57, at E2; *see also S. Subcomm. on Labor, Health and Human Services, Education, and Related Agencies of the Senate Comm. on Appropriations*, 105th Cong. (1998) (Statement of James M. Hughes).

59. *See* Rogers, *supra* note 37, at 14. Although it did not achieve its intended result, "the Tokyo subway attack was the first substantial example of the use of a weapon of mass destruction." *Id.*

60. *See* Willis Witter, *Four Die After Meal at Festival in Japan. Police Suspect Cyanide Was Put in Pot of Curry*, WASH. TIMES, July 28, 1998, at A13.

61. *See* Fitzgerald, *supra* note 11, at 434-35. The actions of the United States, however, "did not technically breach the Geneva Protocol because the United States did not ratify the treaty until after the war, in January 1975." *Id.* (citing Philip Louis Reizenstein, Note, *Chemical and Biological Weapons-Recent Legal Developments May Prove to be a Turning Point in Arms Control*, 12 BROOK. J. INT'L L. 95, 98, n.18 (1986). In addition, the United States interpreted the Geneva protocol not to preclude irritants or herbicides because their effects are not similar to more lethal chemical agents like nerve gas. *See id.*

62. *See U.S. Readies Defense Against Germ Warfare; Terrorism Experts Say Small Scale Attack More Likely*, SALT LAKE TRIB., June 22, 1998, at A6 (stating that "the only real bioterrorism incident in U.S. history occurred in 1984, when members of the Rajneeshee cult in Oregon sprayed salmonella bacteria on 10 local salad bars in an effort to dampen voter turnout and throw an election their way."); *see also* Marie Isabelle Chevrier, *The Threat That Won't Disperse: Why Biological Weapons Have Taken Center Stage*, WASH. POST, Dec. 21, 1997, at C1 (discussing contamination of salad bars in Oregon by a cult and poisoning of lab workers in Texas by food laced with a germ that causes a rare form of dysentery); *see also Reporter's Notebook: Chem-bio, Not As Easy As Pie*, DEFENSE WEEK, Vol. 19 No. 14, April 16, 1998 (discussing how the World Trade Center bombers had attempted to cause an explosion followed by dispersal of a chemical agent, but that the blast from the explosion destroyed the chemical agent).

Mass Destruction Act of 1996[63] to help defend against the threat of nuclear, chemical, and biological (NCB) weapons.[64] The Nunn-Lugar Amendment to the Act included significant Congressional findings supporting the establishment of the DTRA.[65] In particular, Congress found that weapons of mass destruetion[66] in the hands of hostile nations and terrorist groups pose an increasing threat to the U.S.[67] Congress also found that the U.S. lacked adequate planning and countermeasures to address the threat of chemical and biological weapons.[68]

The Nunn-Lugar Amendment proposed an "emergency response assistance program" to aid domestic preparedness by providing civilian personnel and state and local agencies with training and expert advice regarding emergency responses to the use of weapons of mass destruction.[69] In addition, the amendment authorized extensive funding[70] and military assistance[71] to aid in increasing the nation's preparedness.

---

63. Defense Against Weapons of Mass Destruction Act of 1996, 50 U.S.C. §§ 2301 – 66 (1996).

64. *See id.* at § 2311.

65. *See* Nunn-Lugar Amendment No. 4349, S. 1745, 104th Cong. (1996).

66. 50 U.S.C. § 2302(1) defines weapons of mass destruction as "any weapon or device that is intended, or has the capability, to cause death or serious bodily injury to a significant number of people by the release, dissemination, or impact of – (A) toxic or poisonous chemicals or their precursors; (B) a disease organism; or (C) radiation or radioactivity."

67. *See* 50 U.S.C. § 2301(1), (5).

68. *See* 50 U.S.C. § 2301(19). Although Congress noted that the Department of Energy has established a Nuclear Emergency Response Team, no comparable unit exists for emergencies involving biological or chemical weapons. *See* § 2301(20). In addition Congress noted that state and local emergency response personnel are not adequately prepared or trained to handle incidents involving such materials. *See* § 2301(21); *see also U.S. Lags in Biological Warfare Protection Threat Said to Be on the Rise*, NEW ORLEANS TIMES-PICAYUNE, Dec. 27, 1997, at A6 (stating, "the United States is poorly prepared to defend its armed forces from the rising threat of germ warfare attack and lags even more in protecting Americans at home.").

69. *See* 50 U.S.C. § 2311.

70. For example, the Act authorizes $35 million for the emergency response assistance program. *See* 50 U.S.C. § 2312(h). The Act also authorizes $15 million for a nuclear, chemical, and biological emergency response program. *See* 50 U.S.C. § 2313(c).

71. Section 2313 authorizes military assistance to civilian law enforcement in emergency situations involving biological or chemical weapons. *See id.* at § 2313(a).

It urged the United States Sentencing Commission to provide increased criminal penalties for offenses relating to importing and exporting biological and chemical weapons as well as the technology used to create them.[72] Clearly, these provisions placed a new and greater emphasis on identifying the threat of chemical and biological weapons and remedying the lack of U.S. capabilities to respond to such a threat.

A second piece of legislation, the Chemical and Biological Weapons Threat Reduction Act of 1997,[73] gives even greater priority to defending against chemical and biological weapons. For example, the Act provides criminal and civil penalties for "the unlawful acquisition, transfer, or use of any chemical weapon or biological weapon."[74]

Congress recognized that the use of chemical and biological weapons contravenes international law and that their use "is abhorrent and should trigger immediate and effective sanctions."[75] The Act was a response to President Clinton's Executive Order 12,868, declaring a national emergency in response to "the unusual and extraordinary threat to the national security, foreign policy, and economy of the United States" posed by the proliferation of NCB weapons and of the means for delivering such weapons.[76] Congress reviewed the intelligence community's findings that numerous countries possess these weapons and the means to deliver them.[77] Congress also noted that the 1996 Defense Against Weapons of Mass Destruction Act underscored the "urgent need to improve domestic preparedness" to protect against chemical and biological threats.[78] The new Act expanded on the 1996 legislation and aimed to reduce the threat of biological and chemical

72. *See id.* at § 2332.

73. The Chemical and Biological Weapons Threat Reduction Act of 1997, *supra* note 29.

74. *Id.*

75. *Id.* at (2).

76. Exec. Order No. 12,868, 58 Fed. Reg. 51749 (Sept. 30, 1993)(revoked and replaced by Exec. Order 12930).

77. *See* The Chemical and Biological Weapons Threat Reduction Act of 1997, *supra* note 29, Section 2 at (7) (finding that China, Egypt, Iran, Iraq, Libya, North Korea, Syria, and Russia possess chemical and biological weapons and the means to deliver them. Four countries in the Middle East – Iran, Iraq, Libya, and Syria – have also supported international terrorism as a national policy.) *See id.* at § (8).

78. *See id.* at § (11).

warfare by authorizing criminal penalties of imprisonment or death in the case of an action that results in the death of another person.[79] The Act authorizes civil penalties of up to $100,000 for each violation[80] and the forfeiture and destruction of property involved in the offense.[81] Further, other economic sanctions may be imposed.[82]

Congress made significant findings regarding the future threat of chemical and biological weapons.[83] For example, regarding prepared-

---

79. Section 229A (a)(1) states "[a]ny person who violates section 229 of this title shall be fined . . . or imprisoned for any term of years or both." *Id.* Section 229A(a)(2) states "[a]ny person who violates section 229 of this title and by whose action the death of another person is the result shall be punished by death or imprisoned for life." *Id.*

80. Section 229A (b)(1) states

> The Attorney General may bring a civil action in the appropriate United States District Court against any person who violates section 229 of this title and, upon proof of such violation by a preponderance of the evidence, such person shall be subject to pay a civil penalty in an amount not to exceed $100,000 for each such violation.

81. Section 229B(a) states "[a]ny person convicted under section 229A(a) shall forfeit to the United States irrespective of any provision of State law – (1) any property, real or personal, involved in the offense, including any chemical weapon or biological weapon." Section 229B(c) states, "[t]he attorney General shall provide for the destruction or other appropriate disposition of any chemical or biological weapon seized and forfeited pursuant to this section."

82. Title II, § 201 provides "the imposition of sanctions against any foreign government – (A) that has used chemical or biological weapons in violation of international law; or (B) that has used chemical or biological weapons against its own nationals . . . " (amending Title III of the Chemical and Biological Weapons Control and Warfare Elimination Act of 1991).

83. *See id.* at Title II, § 207. In particular, Section 207(a) of the Act states that

> (1) the threats posed by chemical and biological weapons to the United States Armed forces deployed in regions of concern will continue to grow and will undermine United States strategies for the projection of United States military power and the forward deployment of United States Armed Forces; (2) the use of chemical and biological weapons will be a likely condition of future conflicts in regions of concern; (3) it is essential for the United States and key regional allies of the United States to preserve and further develop robust chemical and biological defenses; (4) the United States Armed Forces, both active and nonactive duty, are inadequately equipped, organized, trained and exercised for operations in chemically and biologically contaminated environments; (5) the lack of readiness stems from a deemphasis by the executive branch of government and the United States Armed

ness, Congress found that

> The armed forces of key regional allies and likely coalition partners, as well as civilians necessary to support United States military operations, are inadequately prepared and equipped to carry out essential missions in chemically and biologically contaminated environments; congressional direction contained in the 1997 Defense Against Weapons of Mass Destruction Act is intended to lead to enhanced domestic preparedness to protect against the use of chemical and biological weapons; and the United States Armed Forces should place increased emphasis on potential threats to deployed United States Armed Forces and, in particular should make countering the use of chemical and biological weapons an organizing principle for United States defense strategy and for the development of force structure, doctrine, planning, training, and exercising policies of the United States Armed Forces.[84]

C. The Defense Reform Initiative of 1997

In 1997, Secretary of Defense William Cohen sponsored the Defense Reform Initiative of 1997.[85] The DRI was intended to apply principles from business and industry to make the Department of Defense more effective and productive.[86] During the first year of the DRI, the DOD recognized substantial savings from public-private competition by moving into Internet-based electronic commerce, utilizing ideas from the private sector, consolidating, streamlining, and downsizing.[87] Despite overall reductions in defense costs, the 1996 and 1997 acts assured that defense resources focused on the threat of biological and chemical weapons would continue to increase.[88] One of

Forces on chemical and biological defense . . . .

84. *Id.* at Title II, §§ 207(a)(6)-(8).

85. *See* Frank Wolfe, *Hamre: Possible Restructuring of FMS Process*, DEF. DAILY, Vol. 200, No. 36 (Oct. 9, 1998).

86. *See DOD News Briefing*, *supra* note 42 (containing an interim status report of Deputy Secretary of Defense, John J. Hamre, on the Defense Reform Initiative).

87. *See DOD News Briefing*, *supra* note 42. (Fact Sheet on first year accomplishments of the DRI); *see also*, *DOD News Briefing*, *supra* note 3 (discussing streamlining and downsizing as purposes of the DRI).

88. *See DOD News Briefing*, *supra* note 3 (stating that there is no intention

the stated aims of the DRI is "to strengthen the Department's ability to deal with the proliferation of weapons of mass destruction."[89] Secretary Cohen recognized this stating, "of the challenges facing the Department of Defense in the future, none is greater than the threat posed by the weapons of mass destruction."[90]

The DTRA constituted the DOD's focal point in addressing this complex and comprehensive problem.[91] As a result, the DTRA had a budget of $1.9 billion and employed over 2,000 people in Fiscal Year 1999.[92] The increased spending indicated that reducing the threat of biological and chemical warfare has become a national defense growth industry.[93]

II. The Development of the DTRA

Under Title X of the National Defense Authorization Bill, the Secretary of Defense possesses the authority to create an agency to consolidate DOD functions.[94] Under this authority, Secretary Cohen established the DTRA. Its development[95] began a substantial step toward

to cut capabilities in the area of national security threats from chemical and biological weapons).

89. Department of Defense, *Defense Threat Reduction Agency Director Selected,* REGULATORY INTELLIGENCE DATABASE, May 19, 1998, *available in* 1998 WL 254687 (F.D.C.H.).

90. *DOD News Briefing, supra* note 3 (quoting Secretary of Defense, William Cohen).

91. *See Defense Threat Reduction Agency Director Selected* (released May 19, 1998) <http://www.defenselink.mil/news/May1998/bos/91998_bt248-98.html>; *see also DOD News Briefing, supra* note 3 (discussing the role of the DTRA in stopping the spread of weapons of mass destruction); *DOD News Briefing*, M2 PRESSWIRE, July 9, 1998, *available in* 1998 WL 14095333 (stating the DTRA becomes "the central nervous system for our counter-proliferation plans and preparation.").

92. *See DOD News Briefing, Improvements from Consolidation, supra* note 42.

93. *See DOD News Briefing, supra* note 3 (stating that facing the threat of weapons of mass destruction "is likely to be . . . a growth industry in the Department of Defense.").

94. *See House of Representatives Comm. on National Security Markup: House Comm. on National Security Marks Up H.R. 3616, National Defense Authorization Bill,* 105th Cong. 155-56 (Statement of Rep. Rangel).

95. *See DOD News Briefing, supra* note 3. In response to a question regarding the idea of forming the DTRA, Deputy Secretary of Defense, Dr. John J. Hamre, stated, "[The DTRA] grew very much out of Secretary Cohen's re-

increased protection from the threat of chemical and biological weapons.[96] By combining the expertise of three defense intelligence agencies (DTSA, DSWA, and OSIA) and employing the knowledge of expert scientists in the field of biological and chemical warfare agents, the DTRA appears to have the capability to effectively implement the 1996 and 1997 legislation. In addition, the DTRA's centralized expertise should maximize efforts to discover chemical and biological weapons production and stockpiling programs.

A. The Mission and Goals of the DTRA

The overall goal of the DTRA is to "reduce the present threat [of a chemical or biological attack] and [to] prepare against the future threat . . . ."[97] The DTRA, however, was established with three broad missions in mind:[98] (1) to maintain current U.S. nuclear deterrent capabilities,[99] (2) to reduce the threat from weapons of mass destruction,[100] and (3) to counter threats of weapons of mass destruction.[101] To accomplish its missions, the DTRA needs to learn how to anticipate attacks, speed up response time, work with research and intelligence communities, and protect technology.[102] To satisfy these missions, the DTRA will have to first understand the threat and second, determine who or what constitutes a threat.

---

view last fall, about a year ago at this time . . . .[but] it represents a culmination of a year's worth of change." *Id.*

96. *See id.* (discussing the significance of DTRA's establishment).

97. *Id.*

98. *See DOD News Briefing*, M2 PRESSWIRE, July 9, 1998, *available in* 1998 WL 14095333.

99. *See id.*

100. *See id.* The second mission includes elements such as treaty monitoring and on-going support of confidence building measures. *See id.*

101. *See id.* The third mission involves a combination of responsibilities. The DTRA will develop modeling and simulation skills for biological and chemical weapons, building an intellectual infrastructure for biological and chemical threats, as well as consequence management in its effort to counter weapons of mass destruction threats. *See id.*; *see also DOD News Briefing, supra* note 3 (discussing a variety of approaches such as treaty compliance, cooperative threat reduction, counterproliferation and active deterrence).

102. *See DOD News Briefing*, M2 PRESSWIRE, July 9, 1998, *available in* 1998 WL 14095333.

1. The First Step: Understanding the Threat

The first critical step the DTRA must take to accomplish its goals is to collaborate with intelligence agencies to better understand the threat. To achieve such an understanding, the DTRA proposes to work with U.S. research and intelligence communities to identify evolving threats and the intentions of those who would represent them.[103] Although the formula for determining threats is not new to the DOD, the DTRA's focus on evolution and intent is an untested methodology and therefore is of uncertain value. For example, as stated by the Director of the DTRA

> [I]n the old days with the Soviet Union, you could do the simple exercise that said capability, which was easy to see and photograph; . . . skip over intention because they wouldn't have built [weapons] if they didn't have an intention to use it; and. . . [determine the amount of] threat with some confidence. . . . In the case of the domestic application of a biological weapon, for example, capability sits everywhere [and] you know almost nothing about intent unless you in fact have penetrated a fraternal or nearly religious organization. . . . [T]he multiplication of those two together to get threat is a much more uncertain activity. It makes it much harder to do.[104]

Thus, the first goal of the DTRA is to develop relationships with the intelligence community in an effort to better understand emerging threats of chemical and biological weapons. In response to questions at a DOD news briefing, the Director of the DTRA emphasized the importance of working with the intelligence community, stating

> [T]he intent is to be much more active . . . . We will be working with the intelligence community to come up with an integrated set of threat assessments [by creating] scenarios. . . coupling the intelligence to how you would really act. You produce the best five or six scenarios you can, for example, for domestic events, and then play them out and ask yourself how good was our response, what in anticipation would have made the response better, how do you go back to the intelligence community and tell them to look for [a better

103. *See DOD News Briefing*, M2 PRESSWIRE, July 9, 1998, *available in* 1998 WL 104095333 (statement of Dr. Jay C. Davis, DTRA Director).
104. *Id.*

response].[105]

2. The Second Step: Determining Who or What Is a Threat

Determining the source of the threat and building relationships with countries and groups that might pose a threat constitutes the goals of the DTRA's second step.[106] The first part is admittedly difficult and requires the DTRA's partnership with intelligence agencies. Because the threat is just as likely to stem from transnational, millenarian, or religious groups, as opposed to national states, finding the actor is much more difficult.

The second part, building relationships with countries and groups that might pose a threat, is another daunting task for the DTRA. To accomplish this, the DTRA will rely on the On-Site Inspection Agency and its role in overseeing foreign treaty provisions compliance with disarmament. The DTRA proposes to apply OSIA responsibilities combined with multiple United Nations parties to build relationships with countries that do not currently possess amicable relations with the U.S.[107] As admitted by the DTRA Director, this will involve "a fair amount of politics and policy."[108]

B. Organization of the DTRA

The Director of the DTRA[109] reports directly to the Undersecretary of Defense for Acquisition and Technology.[110] The Director's con-

105. *Id.*

106. *See id.*

107. *See id.*; *see also* Treaty on Open Skies, art. XVI, S. Treaty Doc. No. 102-37 (1992). Ratified by the Senate in 1993, the treaty adopts a principle of territorial openness to areas formerly restricted for national security concerns. *See* Marian Nash, *Contemporary Practice of the United States Relating to International Law*, 88 AM. J. INT'L L. 89, 98 (1994); *see also* Treaty on Open Skies (visited on Mar. 22, 2000) <http://dosfan.lib.uic.edu/acda/treaties/openskie.htm> (for the text of the treaty).

108. *DOD News Briefing, supra* note 3 (response of Dr. Jay C. Davis, DTRA Director).

109. Director Dr. Jay C. Davis is a nuclear physicist and former associate director of the Lawrence Livermore National Laboratory. *See* Pincus, *supra* note 1; Air Force Major General William F. Moore is the Deputy Director. *See DOD Agency Makes Debut*, GOV'T EXECUTIVE, Nov. 1, 1998, *available in* 1998 WL 10315082.

110. *See Defense Threat Reduction Agency Director Selected,*

sulting advisors include senior officials from the Department of State, the Department of Energy, and the Federal Bureau of Investigation, as well as a Threat Reduction Advisory Committee composed of distinguished policy, scientific and defense experts.[111] The DTRA also runs the Advanced Systems and Concepts Office (ASCO), an office responsible for analyzing emerging weapons of mass destruction threats and the technologies and concepts to counter them.[112] Eight directorates within the DTRA carry out these critical mission elements.[113]

The merger of the DTSA, DSWA, and OSIA into the DTRA has not been without criticism. Specifically, employees of the DTSA have criticized the chain of command for the DTRA Director, who reports to the Undersecretary for Acquisition and Technology. Previously, the head of the DTSA – one element merged into DTRA – reported to the Defense Undersecretary for Policy. Critics noted that this creates a conflict of interest because the Undersecretary for Acquisition and Technology seeks to keep the U.S. defense industry profitable through

REGULATORY INTELLIGENCE DATABASE, May 19, 1998, *available in* 1998 WL 254687. The Undersecretary of Defense for Acquisition and Technology is Dr. Jacques Gansler. *See DOD Launches Threat Reduction Advisory Committee*, REGULATORY INTELLIGENCE DATABASE, July 16, 1998, *available in* 1998 WL 403599.

111. *See The Defense Threat Reduction Agency, Organization* (visited Jan. 19, 1999) <http://www.dtra.mil/about/org.html>.

112. One responsibility of ASCO is planning. *See DOD News Briefing*, *supra* note 3.

113. The directorates include: (1) Nuclear Support; (2) On-Site Inspection, which is responsible for conducting on-site inspections and aerial monitoring abroad, gathering information on the accuracy of treaty-related declarations and weapons system reductions and building confidence among treaty members; (3) Cooperative Threat Reduction, responsible for implementing the cooperative threat reduction program and helping the countries of the former Soviet Union destroy nuclear, chemical and biological weapons; (4) Technology Security, which develops and implements policies on international transfers of defense related goods, services and technologies to ensure that such transfers are consistent with U.S. national security interests; (5) Special Weapons Technology; (6) Chem-Bio Defense is the focal point for technical expertise on chemical and biological weapons; (7) Counterproliferation, which aims at responding to proliferation by developing new technologies, training responders, and coordinating response planning for Department of Defense and other agencies; and (8) The Force Protection which is responsible for protecting armed forces and their families from acts of terrorism. *See The Defense Threat Reduction Agency, Organization*, *supra* note 111.

the very sales that it would regulate. Critics contended that national security becomes subordinate to free trade.[114] One DTSA employee, for example, stated that this reorganization "will fatally compromise controls on the export of dangerous technologies."[115]

In response, the DTRA's Deputy Secretary stressed the Defense Undersecretary for Policy would retain overall supervision of export controls and the intent was never to remove Policy's oversight responsibility. The Secretary maintained that the developing fears in Congress regarding the DTRA's role are a result of a misunderstanding of his intent. The agency would do well, however, to better explain its intent with regard to export controls and to formulate a chain of command with distinct reporting responsibilities.

The private sector is concerned about tighter export controls.[116] Since the end of the Cold War, fewer types of exports have been licensed by the U.S. government, making it easier for companies to ship goods to countries once considered off-limits because of national security concerns.[117] Yet, with the emerging threats of biological and chemical warfare, restrictions on shipments of biological and chemical warfare agents and missile technology have increased.

Under the 1949 Export Control Act, the Commerce Department's Bureau of Export Administration (BEA) is authorized to restrict "dual use" goods that have both civilian and military uses.[118] This includes chemicals and biological agents that could be used to produce weapons for attacking the U.S..[119] The increased licensing requirements present a resource problem for the BEA and mandate the involvement

114. *See* Sydney J. Freedberg, Jr., *The Pentagon's Alphabet Warfare*, NAT'L J., Sept. 12, 1998. Congressional Republicans such as Sen. Jon Kyl (R-AZ) support these contentions, stating that the Clinton administration leans toward granting export licenses. *See id.*

115. *Id.* A DTSA export license reviewer testified in Congress that the DOD continually weakened in its ability to keep American technology from leaving the borders. *See id.*

116. *See* Michael Laris, *China Exploits U.S. Computer Advances; American Export Trade Raises National Security Concerns*, WASH. POST, Mar. 9, 1999, at A1.

117. *See Antiterrorism Efforts Threaten Shippers*, AM. SHIPPER, Feb. 1, 1999.

118. *See* Export Control Act, ch. 11, 63 Stat. 7 (1949), replaced by International Emergency Economic Powers Act, 50 U.S.C. § 1701 (1977); *see also Antiterrorism Efforts Threaten Shippers*, AM. SHIPPER, Feb. 1, 1999.

119. *See Antiterrorism Efforts Threaten Shippers*, *supra* note 118.

of other agencies such as the DTRA. The DTRA's role is not to grant licenses, but to monitor the distribution of chemical and biological agents that could be used in weapons.

As we move from the nuclear age to the information age, new threats emerge. It therefore makes perfect sense to strengthen export controls on chemicals and biological agents. Where the U.S. once protected the export of weapons technology, it now must also protect the export of information and scientific technology. The DTRA is organized to assist the BEA in this task.

III. THE DTRA: SOLUTION OR CONFLICT

A. *The Need for the DTRA?*

Before the development of the DTRA, the United States' main defense against national security threats rested with agencies born during the Cold War[120] designed to combat nuclear threats.[121] The DTRA was deemed necessary because the threat from weapons of mass destruction posed significantly different challenges from those posed by nuclear threats, such as the likelihood of a "low-tech" attack by a small group.[122] In discussing this need, Deputy Secretary of Defense John J. Hamre stated

> the new era is a startlingly complicated era, one where national security challenges are far more diverse and far more complex. It no longer has the ease of thinking about it in terms of a communist world and a free world. . . . We needed to have a central organization that was integrated in bringing all of these different

120. *See supra* notes 3-5 and accompanying text.

121. *See* statement of Deputy Secretary of Defense, Dr. John J. Hamre, *DOD News Briefing*, *supra* note 3.

> It has been ten years since the Berlin Wall came down. As with every change in the security history of the United States, there's a period of some transition when you sort out what the last world was like and what is the new world going to be like. In many ways I think this represents one of the very important milestones in this transition.

Id.

122. *See id.* Hamre stated, "The dispersal of weapons of mass destruction capabilities into the hands of small groups that are driven by much more varied motivations than those of the past presents a threat that unfortunately may be obvious to us only after the fact." *Id.*

strands together in one place.[123]

1. The Ineffectiveness of International Treaties and Conventions – The Chemical Weapons Convention

In addition to the organizational issues and ongoing problems of insufficient chemical and biological defense capabilities,[124] the U.S. has voiced concerns that existing international treaties and conventions are insufficient to diminish the threat of the use of weapons of mass destruction.[125] There are numerous reasons for their ineffectiveness.[126] First, since the Chemical Weapons Convention does not extend to terrorist groups, they are left unrestricted in their capacity to produce chemical or biological weapons.[127] Second, the treaties have no direct power over countries that do not ratify them.[128] These countries include Iraq, North Korea, and Libya,[129] all of which are suspected of

---

123. *Id.*

124. *See id.* (discussing tests in Philadelphia and Washington, D.C. showing local law enforcement unpreparedness to handle a chem/bio attack); *see also DOD News Briefing*, M2 PRESSWIRE, July 9, 1998, *available in* 1998 WL 14095333 (stating that the U.S. does not have the intellectual infrastructure for biological and chemical threats the way the U.S. has for nuclear threats).

125. *See* Fitzgerald, *supra* note 11, at 429.

126. For example, when the 1972 Biological and Toxin Weapons Convention (BTWC) was drafted, it did not address the use of biological weapons because they were deemed to be useless by the military. *See* Detlev Vagts and Raymond A. Zilinskas, *The Diplomacy of Biological Disarmament: Vicissitudes of a Treaty in Force, 1975-85*, 84 AM. J. INT'L L. 984 (1990); *see also* Falk, *supra* note 13, at 21 (discussing the shortcomings of the Geneva Protocol). The Geneva Protocol lacks consensus concerning the identity of toxic agents included in the prohibition. *See id.* Parties have interpreted it as merely prohibiting the first use of prohibited weaponry. *See id.* at 22. It prohibits only the use of proscribed substances and does not prohibit research, development, and possession. *See id.* at 23.

127. *See* Fitzgerald, *supra* note 11, at 445-56; *see also* Ronald D. Rotunda, *The Chemical Weapons Convention: Political and Constitutional Issues*, 15 CONST. COMMENTARY 131, 139 (1998) (discussing the difficulty of detecting noncompliance from small groups).

128. *See* Fitzgerald, *supra* note 11, at 446; *see also* Rotunda, *supra* note 127, at 135 (stating one inherent limitation of the CWC is that outlaw countries can simply refuse to ratify it).

129. *See* Fitzgerald, *supra* note 11, at 446; *see also* Rotunda, *supra* note 127, at 135.

producing weapons of mass destruction.[130] While the threat of a direct attack on the U.S. from one of these nations may appear minimal, these nations may sell or convey their weapons to terrorist groups. Such groups pose an even greater threat to the U.S. because they are not easily detected or monitored. Third, the international treaties lack provisions authorizing the use of military force to ensure compliance.[131] Instead, they authorize sanctions for countries in non-compliance.[132] Concerns have been raised that sanctions are an inappropriate response to such circumstances.[133] The Chemical Weapons Convention is illustrative of this.

Iraq's refusal to cooperate with U.N. arms inspectors sent to gather evidence as to whether Baghdad was developing weapons of mass destruction demonstrates the ineffectiveness of the Chemical Weapons Convention.[134] Although Iraq admitted to making VX gas for weapons,[135] it refused to allow U.N. inspectors to investigate its chemical weapons program.[136] Iraqi officials maintained that until the U.N. Security Council lifts the sanctions it imposed after the Gulf War, they would not allow inspections.[137] In return, U.N. officials stated that the sanctions would not be lifted until the U.N. certified

130. *See* The Chemical and Biological Weapons Threat Reduction Act of 1997, 105th Cong., 1st Sess. (1997).

131. *See Chemical Weapons Convention*, *supra* note 10, at art. XII at 819.

132. *See id.* at art. XI.

133. *See* Stone, *supra* note 11, at A12 (discussing the use of sanctions against Iraq, the author states "[m]any believe U.N. sanctions aimed at hurting Saddam's government have instead devastated the Iraqi people. . .").

134. *See* Bill Nichols, *Clinton, Security Team Discuss Iraqi Problem*, USA TODAY, Nov. 9, 1998, at 12A.

135. *See Senate Armed Services Comm. Hearing on Transnational Threats*, 105th Cong. (1998) (statement of the Honorable Walter B. Slocombe, Undersecretary of Defense for Policy) *available in* 1998 WL 11515924.

> During the 1980's, Iraq developed an extensive chemical weapons program and the most advanced biological warfare program in the Middle East. Saddam Hussein used a combination of blister agents, such as mustard, and nerve agents, such as Tabun, against the Iranians and the Kurds. Iraq produced enough precursors for 400 tons of the nerve agent VX per year.

Id.

136. *See* Security Briefs – *Iraqi Nervegas Confirmed on Warheads, Jane's Intelligence Review* – POINTER 7, Nov. 1, 1998 [hereinafter Security Briefs].

137. *See* Nichols, *supra* note 134, at 12A.

that Iraq destroyed its NCB weapons.[138] This stalemate between Iraq and the U.N. led to threatened military action by the United States.[139] Although other Middle East states were less than enthusiastic,[140] the United States began Operation Desert Fox on December 16, 1998. The military operation deployed cruise missiles, which battered Iraqi military targets and intelligence facilities. United States officials believed the intelligence facilities held Iraq's Special Republican Guard that protected Iraq's chemical and biological weapons programs.

In addition, international law has not provided strong guidance in controlling the threat of chemical and biological weapons.[141] The International Court of Justice issued an Advisory Opinion in 1996 which held that the use or threat of weapons of mass destruction "is generally contrary to the rules of international law applicable in armed conflicts except in an extreme circumstance in which a state's very survival would be at stake."[142] Such decision-making contributes little, creating an ineffective international climate for reducing the threat of chemical and biological weapons.

2. How The DTRA Will Make a Difference

By placing increased emphasis on identifying transnational groups that might be developing chemical or biological weapons to carry out terrorist attacks in the United States,[143] the DTRA will help better protect the nation against the threat of biological and chemical warfare. In addition, because the United States' power to respond is limited under the relevant international treaties and conventions, the DTRA will provide a more appropriate response mechanism to the threat of chemical and biological weapon attacks and discourage par-

---

138. *See* Security Briefs, *supra* note 136.

139. *See* Stone, *supra* note 11, at A12. In an effort to get support for a possible military strike, Defense Secretary Cohen visited Jordan, Saudi Arabia, Oman, the United Arab Emirates, Bahrain, Qatar, Kuwait, and Egypt. *See id.*

140. *See id.* Analysts at Washington think tanks, such as the Brookings Institution, state that it is difficult to get the Saudis to agree to the use of military force against Iraq. *See id.*

141. *See* Scott L. Silliman, *Symposium: Contemporary Issues in Controlling Weapons of Mass Destruction*, 8 DUKE J. COMP. & INT'L L. 1, 2 (1997).

142. *Id.*; *see also Legality of the Threat or Use of Nuclear Weapons*, 35 INT'L. LEGAL MATERIALS 809 (1996) (Advisory Opinion of July 8, 1996).

143. *See DOD News Briefing*, *supra* note 3.

ties who do not comply with international treaties and conventions.[144]

The DTRA also intends to be more effective than its predecessors at substantiating allegations of treaty violations. Prior to the establishment of the DTRA, the U.N. relied on medical and technical experts to investigate allegations,[145] often yielding inconclusive results.[146] By dedicating an agency such as the DTRA to investigate treaty compliance and employing the expertise of OSIA officials within the DTRA, conclusive evidence of violations should be more apparent.[147]

For example, in October 1998, the DTRA sent a team of twelve individuals to Kosovo to monitor the Kosovo Liberation Army (KLA) and Serbian army compliance with a U.N. resolution calling for a cease-fire.[148] Although the DTRA members were unarmed observers, they ran at least twenty-five patrols a day, moving in bright orange vehicles.[149] At the end of each day, the patrols reported the day's events to U.S. embassies, the Secretary of State, and the National Security Council. During this period of observation, the DTRA members stated that they worked extremely hard at maintaining their neutrality toward the Serbian authorities, the KLA, and the local populace. One member stated

People would talk to us. Both sides would talk to us.

144. The DTRA's counterproliferation directorate prepares U.S. leaders to respond when weapons of mass destruction are discovered by studying proliferation threats, developing new technologies, training responders and planning across DOD and other agencies. The DTRA also leads the DOD in supporting operational forces. *See Defense Threat Reduction Agency, Counterproliferation* (visited Jan. 19, 1999) <http://www.dtra.mil/counter/counter.html>.

145. *See* Falk, *supra* note 13, at 18-19; *see also* G.A. Res. 144C, 35th Sess., U.N. GAOR Supp. No. 48, at 61, U.N. Doc. A/35/687 (1980) (discussing the General Assembly's request for medical and technical experts to investigate allegations that chemical/biological agents were being used in Southeast Asia).

146. *See Chemical and Biological Weapons: Report of the Secretary-General*, 37th Sess., agenda item 54, U.N. Doc. A/37/259 at 49 (1982).

147. The DTRA's On-Site Inspection directorate is primarily responsible for monitoring activities and developing treaty verification monitoring technologies, conducting on-site inspections and aerial monitoring abroad.

148. *See Threat Reduction Agency Dozen Lead Observer Force*, PERISCOPE-DAILY DEF. NEWS CAPSULES, Feb. 25, 1999, *available in* 1999 WL 8510602. In 1998, fighting between the Kosovo Liberation Army and the Serbian army and police caused an estimated 1,500 deaths and displaced an estimated 230,000 people from their homes. *See id.*

149. *See id.*

> . . . I think the local Albanians were glad we were there. Within our region, there were three shootings – three Albanians were killed. Tensions were always high and we were unarmed. We were always a target. There was a cease-fire in place and violence was limited, but the feeling of being threatened was constant.[150]

The team realized the importance of its presence. As was described by another member, "I had one individual tell me, 'If you leave, we leave.'"[151] The DTRA team members also realized the effect of their presence.[152] More than fifty families returned to one area described as a "ghost town" before the DTRA trucks arrived.[153] Others in the DTRA saw the impact of the mission on a personal level. One member stated, "I was in a shop and an elderly Albanian woman hugged me and kissed me. We ended up talking to her about 30 minutes about how she felt safer since we were there."[154]

Although the DTRA's presence in Kosovo was not to uncover treaty violations with respect to chemical or biological weapons, its accomplishments in Kosovo are representative of the success of the DTRA in international situations. The DTRA Team Leader, U.S. Army Lt. Col. Leonard Blevins stated, "Some people on the mission from outside the DTRA and the DOD had never been faced with this type of situation before. I really believe our folks were the glue that held it together."[155]

The DTRA also indirectly supports Russia's compliance with the Strategic Arms Reduction Treaty.[156] Specifically, the DTRA provides funding to Thiokol Propulsion, a division of Cordant Technologies Inc., to design and construct electrical supply lines, gas lines, product storage tanks, and control systems for the disposal of Russian missile fuel.[157] Funding is supplied as part of the DTRA's Cooperative Threat Reduction program.[158] These efforts are yet another example of the

150. *Id.*

151. *Id.*

152. *See id.*

153. *See Threat Reduction Agency Dozen Lead Observer Force*, *supra* note 148.

154. *Id.*

155. *Id.*

156. *See Thiokol Team Continues Construction of Missile Fuel Disposition Site*, AEROSPACE DAILY, Jan. 8, 1999, at 42, *available in* 1999 WL 9476637.

157. *See id.*

158. *See id.*; *see also* Greg Seigle, *Ukraine Aims to Mirror US Threat Re-*

DTRA's ability to work globally in facilitating treaty compliance.

B. Proper Spending? Should Money be Spent to Improve Public Health Facilities and Educate Doctors Instead of on the DTRA?

Three programs have the unique potential to mitigate the effect of a chemical or biological attack and assist in domestic preparedness. The Centers for Disease Control and Prevention (CDC), the National Network of Electronic Communications, and the National Domestic Preparedness Office can reduce the threats by helping to identify and control outbreaks, providing clear paths of communication, and preparing local and state first responders.

The CDC promotes health and quality of life by preventing and controlling disease. It is the lead domestic agency for disease surveillance and prevention and often collaborates with the United States Agency for International Development (USAID) and the World Health Organization to control infectious disease problems in foreign countries.[159] The CDC has also worked with the Defense Department to develop surveillance mechanisms to monitor outbreaks of infectious diseases.[160] In 1995, representatives from twenty different United States government agencies reviewed the United States' role in detecting and responding to outbreaks of diseases. They made nineteen recommendations to the U.S. government emphasizing that "a global disease surveillance and response network could enable the United States to respond quickly and effectively in the event of an attack involving

duction, JANE'S DEF. WKLY, Jan 20, 1999 (discussing the Cooperative Threat Reduction program and its responsibilities in the former Soviet Union).

159. *See Comm. on the Appropriations, of the Subcomm. on Foreign Operations*, 105th Cong. (1998) (statement of James M. Hughes, Director, National Center for Infectious Diseases, Centers for Disease Control and Prevention.) [hereinafter *Foreign Operations*]. In 1978, the CDC and USAID worked with the WHO to eradicate smallpox. *See id.* CDC also assisted countries that do not host USAID missions, such as China, where CDC supports influenza surveillance sites; Hong Kong, to contain the recent outbreak of avian influenza; and the Sudan, documenting epidemic levels of African trypanosomiasis. *See id.*

160. *See* Air Force, *CDC Agree to Conduct Joint Programs*, REGULATORY INTELLIGENCE DATABASE, Apr. 21, 1997, *available in* 1997 WL 894922.

biological or chemical warfare."[161] Additionally, they noted that "the experience gained in controlling naturally occurring microbes will enhance [the United States'] ability to cope with a biological warfare agent should the need arise."[162]

Collaborative reports such as these strengthen the United States' capacity to detect and respond to the threat of biological terrorism. In addition, initiatives such as the two-year outbreak investigation program, enable the CDC to address the threat of biological warfare.[163] With its expertise in controlling the spread of infectious diseases, the CDC is a logical partner for the DTRA.

Increased spending on the CDC and other U.S. health organizations will aid the fight against the threat of chemical and biological warfare. These organizations have identified a long list of unforeseen infectious disease problems.[164] The experiences of these organizations in identifying diseases, along with their already developed programs could be adapted to detect chemical weapons and biological agents. For example, in 1997, an avian strain of influenza that had never before attacked humans began to kill previously healthy people in Hong Kong.[165] Later that year, CDC learned that vancomycin, a last resort antibiotic, began to lose its power to cure infections caused by staphylococcus aureus, a common bacterium that can cause critical illness.[166] This same expertise that the CDC has demonstrated regarding infectious disease identification and protection could be used to identify the location of biological weapons and reduce the threat of chemical and biological warfare.

The CDC and other public health groups, however, have not received the DTRA's level of funding. For example, in Fiscal Year 1998, USAID received $50 million to strengthen global surveillance and control of infectious diseases,[167] a small amount compared to the DTRA's 1999 budget of approximately $2 billion.

---

161. Senate Comm. on the Judiciary, 105th Cong. (1998) (statement of James M. Hughes, Director, National Center for Infectious Diseases, Centers for Disease Control and Prevention.).

162. *Id.*

163. *See* Air Force, *CDC Agree to Conduct Joint Programs*, *supra* note 160.

164. *See Foreign Operations*, *supra* note 159.

165. *See id.*

166. *See id.*

167. *See id.*

The CDC has a positive relationship with several foreign countries making it an essential partner in confronting the threat of chemical and biological warfare. The CDC historically has played a key role in assisting foreign governments in protecting against infectious disease outbreaks.[168] As a result, collaborative efforts between the DTRA and the CDC on foreign soil could enhance the DTRA's threat reduction efforts.

Furthermore, the CDC has experience dealing with prolonged infectious disease outbreaks. CDC staff have responded to several extraordinarily serious situations requiring numerous personnel over extended periods of time. CDC personnel went to the Democratic Republic of the Congo in 1995 during an Ebola hemorrhagic fever outbreak and to Kenya during an outbreak of Rift Valley Fever in 1998. Thus, the CDC staff could provide extensive knowledge to the DTRA of disease conditions and survivability rates in the event of a biological attack.

A second potentially productive DTRA alliance would be with the recently established National Association of County and City Health Officials (NACCHO). NACCHO represents 3,000 public health departments in the U.S. and is dedicated to increasing nationwide disease surveillance.[169] Because a hospital is often the first entity to recognize public health threats, it is necessary that the hospital be able to communicate quickly and disseminate possible infectious disease outbreaks to other hospitals. In recognition of this, NACCHO proposes increased funding to develop a national network of electronic communications among public health agencies to protect communities from the public health consequences of acts of terrorism.[170] In stark contrast to the funding the DTRA receives,[171] local public health departments

168. *See id.* For example, in 1997, CDC sent personnel to 145 countries for scientific exchange and technical assistance and provided diagnostic support for hundreds of local investigations. *See id.*

169. *See Senate Appropriations Comm., Subcomm. on Labor, Health and Human Services, Education and Related Agencies*, 105th Cong. (1998), *available in* 1998 WL 285767 (discussing the importance of disease surveillance at local, state and federal levels).

170. *See id.* (stating that few of us in public health are familiar with the prevention, diagnosis or treatment of the health effects from agents of biological warfare).

171. *See DOD News Briefing, supra* note 3; *see also DOD News Briefing, supra* note 22. The NATO Workshop on political-military decision-making

are significantly underfunded.[172] Increased funding and better electronic communications for local health departments will clearly aid the DTRA mission. By linking disease surveillance functions of local public health departments with the DTRA's knowledge of chemical and biological threats, the U.S. will be better prepared to answer chemical or biological attacks.

A third area where spending could be increased is the proposed National Domestic Preparedness Office.[173] Increased spending for this entity is important because public health agencies will be the first to respond to, and contend with, the aftermath of a chemical or biological attack. Greater funding will help provide local and state agencies with better training, equipment and resources to deal with this emerging threat.

The National Domestic Preparedness Office is intended to serve as a single point of contact to assist state and local authorities in the event of a chemical or biological attack.[174] The Office's mission is to focus on planning, training, exercises, equipment and research development, information and intelligence sharing, and health and medical issues.[175] An advisory group will compliment the Office and serve as a bridge between federal domestic preparedness programs and the needs and

---

stated, "[w]e will spend over $5 billion on chemical and biological protection and counterproliferation over the next six years. Major emphasis is to develop remote detection systems and non-aqueous diagnostic techniques." *Id.*

172. *See Subcomm. on Labor, Health and Human Services, Education and Related Agencies of the Senate Comm. On Appropriations*, 105th Cong. (1998), *available in* 1998 WL 285767, stating

> About one-half of all local health departments don't have the use of electronic mail. At least one thousand local health departments have no access to any on-line or Internet service. Among those that do, one-third are not even linked to their state health department, and fewer than one-quarter can reach other health departments electronically. In some health departments, up to five employees must share one computer.

Id.

173. *See Subcomm. for the Department of Commerce, Justice, and State, the Judiciary, and Related Agencies of the Senate Comm. On Appropriations*, 105th Cong. (1999) (statement of Louis J. Freeh, Director, Federal Bureau of Investigation) *available in* 1999 WL 8084457. The National Domestic Preparedness office would operate under the auspices of the Federal Bureau of Investigations. *See id.*

174. *See id.*

175. *See id.*

priorities of states and local communities.[176] The Office plans to employ a "coordinator" in each FBI field office who will serve as the primary point of contact for state and local emergency first responders.[177]

C. *Conflicting Duties: Interagency Competition, the Fourth Amendment, and International Agreements*

1. *Interagency Competition*

Senate Hearings in 1975[178] and 1989[179] evidenced the strong role of the CIA in countering the threat of chemical and biological weapons attacks. "It's inherently a law enforcement, an emergency response responsibility of the United States, but . . . [DoD is the only agency] in the entire federal government that . . . [has] mobilization capabilities."[180] Yet, agencies other than the Department of Defense have the lead responsibility in the U.S. when there is an incident involving terrorist activity.[181] Such conflicts of authority between the DOD, law enforcement, and the Federal Emergency Management Agency could generate interagency competition despite the DTRA's statements that it will work with other agencies to combat the threat of biological and chemical warfare.[182]

---

176. *See id.*
177. *See id.*
178. *See Unauthorized Storage of Toxic Agents: Hearings Before the S. Select Comm. to Study Gov't Operations with Respect to Intelligence Activities*, 94th Cong. 1st Sess., at 11 (1975). Then Director of the CIA, William Colby referred to four "functional categories" of CIA activity, including "assessment and maintenance of biological and chemical disseminating systems for operational" use and "providing technical support and consultation on request from offensive and defensive [biological/chemical warfare]." *Id.*; *see also* Falk, *supra* note 13, at 29.
179. *See Senate Comm. on Government Affairs, Hearings on the Global Spread of Chemical Weapons and Biological Weapons*, 101st Cong., 1st Sess., (1989) (Testimony of William H. Webster, Director of the CIA); *see also* Paul Rubenstein, *State Responsibility for Failure to Control the Export of Weapons of Mass Destruction*, 23 CAL. W. INT'L L. J. 319, 323 (1993).
180. *DOD News Briefing*, *supra* note 3.
181. *See id.*
182. *See* Laura Myers, THE MILWAUKEE J. SENTINEL, Oct. 2, 1998, at 5. John Pike, a security analyst for the Federation of American Scientists stated "[t]he CIA, Defense Intelligence Agency and others don't work closely

2. The Fourth Amendment

A large portion of the DTRA's responsibilities falls within the category of domestic weapons' inspection. This has the potential to raise constitutional questions under the Fourth Amendment. Inevitably, situations will arise in which a DTRA authorized search for chemical or biological agents will intrude upon a citizen's right to be free from "unreasonable searches and seizures" as required by the Fourth Amendment.[183] For example, DTRA agents might locate the headquarters of a known anti-government group and want to search for evidence of biological agents. The DTRA might suspect that the group has small amounts of VX gas that it could unleash within the hour at the offices of a nearby multinational corporation. Under the Chemical Weapons Convention, the DTRA could possibly inspect the group's headquarters without a search warrant.[184] Moreover, the DTRA could seize samples, inspect documents and take photographs before a judge made a determination of probable cause.[185] Although authorized by the CDC,[186] DTRA inspections of domestic facilities would surely raise Fourth Amendment challenges. In addition, the DTRA would be held to the same Fourth Amendment standards when inspecting foreign weapons facilities.[187]

3. International Agreements

The establishment of the DTRA may also cause potential conflicts with the endorsement of international agreements. For example, Article 24 of the U.N. Charter gives the Security Council "primary responsibility for the maintenance of international peace and security"[188] and

---

enough." *Id.*

183. U.S. CONST. amend. IV.

184. *See* Rotunda, *supra* note 127, at 149.

185. *See id.*

186. *See Chemical Weapons Convention, supra* note 10, at art. IV. The Chemical Weapons Convention applies to both governments and private individuals and allows inspection of publicly or privately owned places where targeted chemical weapons may be produced. *See id.*

187. *See* Rotunda, *supra* note 127, at 143 (citing *Reid v. Covert*, 354 U.S. 1 (1957) (plurality opinion). "Searches that violate the Fourth Amendment are not cured by the simple expediency of a treaty ratification or an executive agreement." *Id.*

188. Rubenstein, *supra* note 179, at 342.

its resolutions are "absolutely binding on all member states."[189] It is conceivable that the DTRA's primary role in this area will be to ensure that countries are complying with these resolutions. The DTRA however, must play a limited role in the enforcement of treaty violations to comply with the U.N. charter.[190]

IV. CONCLUSION

Establishing the DTRA provides the United States with the capability of dealing with the new era of chemical and biological weapons. History shows that international treaties and conventions have failed to deter terrorist groups and countries from producing and using such weapons. The DTRA provides a means to protect the nation from the unique threat of weapons of mass destruction. However, the DTRA is not sufficient by itself to supply this protection. Additional spending is necessary to fund the civilian health departments and to educate doctors on how to respond to outbreaks caused by these weapons. At the same time, the United States should not rely solely on the DTRA to reduce the overall threat, as every threat cannot be discovered. The health industry must also be adequately prepared in the event that terror strikes.

189. *See id.*

190. Typically, remedies for violation of international law are reparation, in the form of either compensation, restitution or satisfaction. *See id.* at 366.

COMMENTS

BIOTERRORISM: PERFECTLY LEGAL

Heather A. Dagen[+]

The possibility of a large-scale biological weapons[1] attack occurring within the United States is more than merely hypothetical.[2] A number of

[+]J.D. candidate, May 2000, The Catholic University of America, Columbus School of Law.

1. *See* Matthew Meselson et al., *Characteristics of Biological and Toxin Weapons, in* POISON IN THE WIND: THE SPREAD OF CHEMICAL AND BIOLOGICAL WEAPONS 15, 16-18 (Gary E. McCuen ed., 1992) (defining biological weapons). Biological weapons consist of either disease-causing, living microorganisms, or of toxic substances produced by living organisms. *See id.* Biological weapons can kill or harm people, animals, or plants; those containing living microorganisms are particularly dangerous because these living organisms reproduce, spreading the disease throughout populations and ecosystems. *See* Jonathan King, *All Research Programs Are Offensive, in* POISON IN THE WIND: THE SPREAD OF CHEMICAL AND BIOLOGICAL WEAPONS, *supra* at 80, 81. These weapons are thousands of times more lethal per unit than any other type of weapon. *See* James H. Anderson, *Microbes and Mass Casualties: Defending America Against Bioterrorism*, HERITAGE FOUND. BACKGROUNDER (Heritage Found. Wash. D.C.), May 26, 1998, at 1, 6. Bioterrorists can easily elude authorities by disseminating the deadly agents invisibly with aerosol devices. *See id.* at 6. Victims do not show symptoms for hours or days, leaving time for such terrorists to cover their tracks. *See id.* Furthermore, because biological weapons programs can be masked as programs for the production of vaccines, antibiotics, or other legitimate research, bioterrorists can conceal biological weapons programs easily. *See id.* at 8. Scientists have yet to develop effective vaccines against many infectious agents. *See* Meselson, *supra* at 20. Protections for a civilian population against a bioterrorist attack may include: issuing gas masks; constructing shelters; conducting regular education and drills for the entire population; massive medical supplies; and fast-response epidemiological teams. *See id.*

2. *See* Anderson, *supra* note 1, at 1 (discussing the growing threat and likelihood of an attack involving the use of biological weapons against the United States); *see also The Threat of Bioterrorism: Assessing the Adequacy of the Federal Law Relating to Dangerous Biological Agents: Hearings Before the Subcomm. on Oversight and Investigations of the House Commerce Comm.*, 106th Cong. 14 (1999) [hereinafter *House Bioterrorism Hearings*] (statement of James S. Reynolds, Chief, Terrorism and Violent Crime Section, United States Department of Justice). Counterterrorism enforcement officials, numerous academics, and health care professionals agree that "the most serious form of terrorist threat confronting the United States relates to the potential use of a biological weapon." *Id. But see* Daniel S. Greenberg, *The Bioterrorism Panic*, WASH. POST, Mar. 16, 1999, at A21 (criticizing the federal government for increasing the Department of Health and Human Service's budget for "bioterrorism preparedness" by $144 million even though there are no independent assessments of the potential for bioterrorism; noting, however, that skeptics of the current bioterrorism panic have not gone public because of "the real possibility of events proving them horribly wrong").

reasons account for the increasing likelihood of this threat.[3] First, rapid growth in the field of genetic engineering, specifically with cloning technology, has enlarged the number of tools available for biological warfare.[4] The growing number of nations that maintain biological weapons programs has increased the likelihood that terrorists will procure biological weapons expertise, possibly through the sponsorship of bioterrorism by a nation with such capacity.[5] Terrorists, as well as disgruntled or deranged individuals, are showing a growing interest in these weapons and in causing mass fatalities.[6] Finally, Russian scientists who worked exten-

3. *See* Anderson, *supra* note 1, at 2-9 (listing reasons that the threat of bioterrorism on United States soil is increasing); Brad Roberts, *New Challenges and New Policy Priorities for the 1990s*, *in* BIOLOGICAL WEAPONS: WEAPONS OF THE FUTURE? 68, 93 (Brad Roberts ed., 1993) (reviewing past and future issues surrounding biological warfare, and noting that, combined, a number of factors increase the likelihood of an attack involving biological weapons).

4. *See* 142 CONG. REC. 1863 (1996) (testimony of Sen. Orrin G. Hatch (R-Utah)) (introducing the Biological Agents Enhanced Penalties and Control Act, which was later enacted as part of the Antiterrorism and Effective Death Penalty Act of 1996). Senator Hatch urged Congress to pass the Biological Agents Act because new threats, not in existence when Congress and regulatory agencies drafted current laws, have increased the risk of bioterrorist attack. *See id.* An example of these emerging threats is the rapid growth of genetic technology, which allows scientists to alter microorganisms so that the substances are more toxic, or more difficult to treat. *See id.*; *see also* Robert H. Kupperman & David M. Smith, *Coping with Biological Terrorism*, *in* BIOLOGICAL WEAPONS: WEAPONS OF THE FUTURE?, *supra* note 3, at 35, 38 (discussing past threats of biological warfare and terrorism, and evaluating the possible, yet unhelpful defenses to these weapons). Although advances in several fields of science have enhanced human life dramatically, these breakthroughs, particularly in recombinant DNA technology, have introduced new tools for warfare. *See id.*; *see also* Jeremy Rifkin, *Environmental Impact of Biological Weapons Research*, *in* POISON IN THE WIND: THE SPREAD OF CHEMICAL AND BIOLOGICAL WEAPONS *supra* note 1, at 101, 102 (arguing that biological weapons programs pose a threat to the environment and that increasing security at weapons labs, for example, could minimize the damaging effects of these programs). Advances in genetic engineering technology also increased the potential for warfare involving biological weapons. *See id.*

5. *See* Anderson, *supra* note 1, at 1. The likelihood that terrorists could gain possession of biological expertise has increased because approximately 10 nations have biological weapons programs. *See id.* Consequently, these nations may transfer this expertise to terrorists, directly or indirectly. *See id.*; *see also Biological Weapons: The Threat Posed by Terrorists: Hearing on Examining Federal Efforts on Dealing with Chemical and Biological Threats to America Before the Subcomm. on Tech., Terrorism, and Gov't Info. of the Senate Comm. on the Judiciary*, 105th Cong. 10, 12-13 (1998) [hereinafter *Joint Senate Committee Hearings*] (statement of Dr. W. Seth Carus, Visting Defense Fellow, Center for Nonproliferation Research, National Defense University). In addition, the chances that a nation with a biological warfare program will support a terrorist with biological weapons expertise are great. *See id.* at 12-13. For example, the Department of Defense and the Arms Control and Disarmament Agency believe that a number of the nations that have records of supporting terrorist organizations, such as Libya, North Korea, and Iraq, have biological warfare programs. *See id.* at 12.

6. *See House Bioterrorism Hearings*, *supra* note 2, at 13 (statement of James Rey-

sively on the Soviet Union's massive biological weapons program dispersed after that government dissolved, thereby increasing the danger that other nations and terrorist groups will acquire biological weapons expertise.[7]

Threats of biological weapons attacks are increasingly common and response costs are significant.[8] Although many of these threats turn out to be hoaxes,[9] continually having to respond to these threats may eventually desensitize people to the possibility of actual attacks.[10] Furthermore, these threats disrupt the responding community.[11]

Despite the impending dangers of bioterrorism, naturally occurring infectious diseases are still a bigger threat to the American population.[12]

---

nolds). The Five-Year Interagency Counter-Terrorism and Technology Plan, submitted to Congress by Attorney General Janet Reno on December 31, 1998 noted increasing intelligence evidence of terrorist interest in using biological weapons. *See id.* Over the past few years, the FBI has encountered a significant increase in the number of cases involving biological weapons and toxins, which reflects a growing interest in biological agents. *See id.*; *see also* Anderson, *supra* note 1, at 1-2 (stating that most intelligence analysts once agreed that terrorists "want a lot of people watching, not a lot of people dead"). However, recent events, such as the 1995 sarin attack in a Tokyo subway and the 1996 Oklahoma bombing, contradict this view. *See id.*

7. *See* Anderson, *supra* note 1, at 7-9 (stating that Russia maintained the largest offensive biological weapons program during much of this century); *see also House Bioterrorism Hearings*, *supra* note 2, at 97, 133-34 (statement of Richard Preston, expert and author on biological weapons describing the Soviet Union's bioweapons program, called the Biopreparat, and stating that it would be foolish to deny that scientists left Russia without bringing their expertise or master seed strains of biological weapons). *See generally* Richard Preston, *Annals of Warfare: The Bioweaponeers*, THE NEW YORKER, Mar. 9, 1998, at 52 (interviewing scientists who worked on the Soviet Union's biological weapons program and later immigrated to the United States).

8. *See House Bioterrorism Hearings*, *supra* note 2, at 17 (statement of Robert M. Burnham, Section Chief, Domestic Terrorism National Security Division, FBI) (noting that the number of incidents involving weapons of mass destruction, particularly those dealing with biological and chemical weapons, has increased steadily and that the cost of responding to threats of bioterrorism is significant). In the first five months of 1999, the FBI opened 123 cases involving weapons of mass destruction, 100 of which involved biological agents. *See id.* at 19. This is an increase from 37 cases involving weapons of mass destruction in 1996, 74 weapons of mass destruction cases, 22 of which involved biological agents in 1997, and 181 cases involving weapons of mass destruction, 112 of which involved biological agents in 1998. *See id.* The biological agent cited most often in 1998 and 1999 was anthrax and a rash of anthrax-related threats around the country during that period affected businesses, schools, hospitals, and courthouses. *See id.* at 18. Los Angeles estimated that the cost of responding to an onslaught of threats that the city received in the beginning of 1999 was $1.5 million. *See id.*

9. *See id.* Several cases involve "vague or veiled threats, stating only that anthrax has been released." *Id.* Other cases involve callers who stated, "in an apparent[ly] non-threatening manner, that anthrax had been released." *Id.*

10. *See id.* at 20.

11. *See id.*

12. *See id.* at 51 (prepared statement of Dr. Ronald M. Atlas, Co-Chair, Task Force

Research on disease prevention and treatment is necessary for the population's well being.[13] In order to reduce illness and death due to these diseases, microbiologists and other researchers use dangerous pathogens as reference cultures.[14] Researchers also use these agents to increase the nation's medical preparedness against bioterrorism.[15] Extreme control measures that limit the free exchange of microbial cultures may drive microbiologists away from important research and thus, ultimately jeopardize the public's health and safety.[16]

International laws as well as domestic federal laws and regulations, currently pertain to the control of biological weapons in the United States.[17] The applicable international laws, which are the 1925 Geneva Protocol (Protocol)[18] and the 1972 Biological Weapons Convention (BWC),[19] have not prevented nations from creating biological weapons.[20] These treaties do not have verification regimes or effective enforcement mechanisms.[21] Furthermore, the Protocol prohibits use of biological

---

on Biological Weapons Control, American Society for Microbiology). The major cause of death in the world is infectious diseases, which kill approximately 17 million people every year. *See id.*

13. *See id.* at 49.

14. *See id.* at 51.

15. *See id.* at 50.

16. *See id.* at 51.

17. *See infra* Part I.A-B. Practitioners identify the rules of international law by looking to explicit, written agreements and the customary practices of nations, including constitutional, legislative, executive, and judicial promulgations of states. *See* MARK W. JANIS, AN INTRODUCTION TO INTERNATIONAL LAW 4-6 (2d ed. 1993). Part I of this Comment discusses several written agreements between nations. These agreements, whether styled as treaties, conventions, or protocols are "essentially contracts between states." *Id.* at 9. In this Comment, these terms are used interchangeably. For a thorough discussion of the law of treaties, see JANIS, *supra* at 9-39. For an analysis of the relationship between treaties and the municipal law of the United States, see JANIS, *supra* at 84-94.

18. Protocol for the Prohibition of the Use in War of Asphyxiating, Poisonous or Other Gases, and of Bacteriological Methods of Warfare, June 17, 1925, 26 U.S.T. 571, 94 L.N.T.S. 65 [hereinafter Protocol].

19. Convention on the Prohibition of the Development, Production and Stockpiling of Bacteriological (Biological) and Toxin Weapons and on their Destruction, Apr. 10, 1972, 26 U.S.T. 583, 1015 U.N.T.S. 163 [hereinafter BWC].

20. *See The Biological Weapons Anti-Terrorism Act of 1989: Hearing on S.993 Before the Senate Comm. on the Judiciary*, 101st Cong. 28-29 (1989) [hereinafter *Judiciary Hearings*] (statement of Ambassador H. Allen Holmes, Assistant Secretary of State for Politico-Military Affairs, Department of State) (commenting on the general situation with regard to biological weapon proliferation and urging Congress to pass the proposed bill to implement the United States' obligations to the BWC).

21. *See* BWC, *supra* note 19; Protocol, *supra* note 18; *see also* RANDALL FORSBERG ET AL., NONPROLIFERATION PRIMER: PREVENTING THE SPREAD OF NUCLEAR, CHEMICAL, AND BIOLOGICAL WEAPONS 69 (1995) (stating that the Protocol and the BWC do not have verification or effective enforcement provisions).

weapons only during war and only against other Protocol parties.[22] The BWC, unlike the Protocol, includes enforcement provisions.[23] The effectiveness of the BWC's enforcement provisions is questionable, however, because the BWC does not include verification provisions to support allegations of violations.[24]

Congress recently strengthened[25] federal criminal laws and regulations pertaining to bioterrorism[26] but significant gaps remain.[27] For example, merely possessing dangerous pathogens is not a crime unless a prosecutor can prove that the possessor intended to use a pathogen as a weapon.[28] Existing laws also do not address false reports and threats[29] and do not attach criminal penalties to handling pathogens in a reckless

22. *See infra* Part I.A (discussing the Protocol).

23. *See* BWC, *supra* note 19, 26 U.S.T. at 588-89, 1015 U.N.T.S. at 167 (referring to Articles V-VII, which set forth the BWC's enforcement procedures).

24. *See infra* Part I.A.2 (discussing the BWC).

25. *See* Antiterrorism and Effective Death Penalty Act of 1996, Pub. L. No. 104-132, § 511(d)(1)(A), 110 Stat. 1214, 1284 (codified as amended in scattered sections of 42 U.S.C.) (amending several of the provisions enacted by the Biological Weapons Anti-Terrorism Act of 1989, Pub. L. No. 101-298, § 1, 104 Stat. 201 (May 22, 1989), and requiring the Secretary of Health and Human Services to create regulations pertaining to the control of dangerous biological agents).

26. *See* 18 U.S.C. §§ 175-178, 2332a (1994 & Supp. II 1997); Additional Requirements for Facilities Transferring or Receiving Select Agents, 42 C.F.R. § 72.6 (1998); *infra* note 104 and accompanying text (discussing federal laws that prohibit assorted acts pertaining to biological agents).

27. *See House Bioterrorism Hearings*, *supra* note 2, at 16 (statement of Robert M. Burnham) (discussing law enforcement concerns about existing federal laws that criminalize acts pertaining to dangerous biological agents).

28. *See* 18 U.S.C. § 175(a) (1994 & Supp. III 1998) (prohibiting the knowing possession of dangerous agents for use as a weapon); *Joint Senate Committee Hearings*, *supra* note 5, at 62 (statement of Attorney General Janet Reno) (noting that merely possessing biological agents without proving that the possessor intended to use this substance as a weapon is not a federal crime). Current federal criminal laws pertaining to bioterrorism do not take significant factors, such as having a felony record, into account. *See id.* Criminal statutes must balance the need for public safety with the need for legitimate scientific research on these agents. *See id.* A clear public safety concern arises, however, when people who do not have scientific training or who have records of irresponsible conduct possess highly lethal substances, when they do not have a legitimate reason for having such a substance. *See id.*

29. *See* 18 U.S.C. §§ 175, 2332a(a)-(b) (1994 & Supp. III 1998) (prohibiting the knowing attempt or threat to violate the section, but not prohibiting hoaxes pertaining to biological weapons and weapons of mass destruction); *House Bioterrorism Hearings*, *supra* note 2, at 16 (statement of James Reynolds) (stating that existing laws do not address false threats of bioterrorism, which are an increasingly growing type of threat). Current laws do not capture false reports as threats because they require evidence that the terrorists actually intended to use biological weapons or to develop or possess biological pathogens in order to use them eventually as weapons. *See id.*

manner.[30] Although there are biological and toxin agents that can cause widespread and serious illness, current regulations only address lethal agents.[31]

The federal government is currently spending vast sums to prepare for a potential attack involving weapons of mass destruction,[32] but the most efficient as well as most cost-effective way to counter bioterrorism remains to prevent it.[33] To facilitate this objective, the United States Department of Justice is drafting legislation that will strengthen current laws pertaining to bioterrorism.[34] This legislation will establish criminal penalties for the unauthorized possession of biological agents that could be used in biological weapons without a legitimate peaceful purpose, for handling these agents unsafely, and for perpetrating a biological weapons hoax.[35] The Department of Justice worked closely with the Department of Health and Human Services to ensure that this bill maintains the accessibility of dangerous biological agents for legitimate scientific research.[36]

Part I of this Comment reviews current laws pertaining to the control of biological weapons, including the Protocol, the BWC, the Biological Weapons Anti-Terrorism Act of 1989 (1989 Act),[37] and the Antiterrorism

30. *See* 18 U.S.C. §§ 175, 2332a(a)-(b); *House Bioterrorism Hearings*, *supra* note 2, at 15 (statement of James Reynolds) (stating that current federal criminal law does not penalize people who handle dangerous substances in an unsafe manner, thereby consciously disregarding and posing an unreasonable risk to public health and safety).

31. *See House Bioterrorism Hearings*, *supra* note 2, at 15 (statement of James Reynolds). The current list of agents that the Centers for Disease Control and Prevention regulates does not, for example, include Shigella or Salmonella. *See id.* In recent years, however, terrorists have caused hundreds of people to become ill using these agents. *See id.*

32. *See* Greenberg, *supra* note 2. Congress originally allocated $14 million to the Department of Health and Human Services budget for bioterrorism preparedness, but eventually added $144 million for this purpose. *See id.* The White House proposed to provide this agency with $230 million for the next term for bioterrorism preparedness. *See id.*

33. *See House Bioterrorism Hearings*, *supra* note 2, at 14 (statement of James Reynolds) (quoting testimony by Dr. Margaret Hamburg on Mar. 25, 1999, before the House of Representatives, who stated that measures that prevent bioterrorism are the most cost effective ways to counter this type of terrorism).

34. *See id.* at 15 (stating that a crime bill that will improve existing federal statutes pertaining to dangerous biological agents and toxins is currently undergoing finishing touches).

35. *See id.* at 14 (listing the acts that the crime bill will criminalize).

36. *See id.* at 15. The Department of Justice's primary focus in creating the crime bill is to make it easier for law enforcement officials to prevent bioterrorism. *See id.*

37. Pub. L. No. 101-298, § 1, 104 Stat. 201 (1990).

and Effective Death Penalty Act of 1996 (1996 Act).[38] Part I then discusses the legislation that the Attorney General's office is currently drafting to strengthen existing laws. Part II of this Comment argues that existing laws do not sufficiently eliminate the threat of bioterrorism. Part III of this comment asserts that criminalizing the unauthorized possession of dangerous agents, unsafe handling of these agents, and perpetration of hoaxes pertaining to bioterrorism would be more effective than current laws in eliminating the threat of bioterrorism. This Comment concludes by recommending that Congress promptly pass the Attorney General's proposed legislation.

I. CURRENT BIOTERRORISM LAWS AND REGULATIONS

Two international instruments, as well as federal regulations and federal criminal laws, specifically pertain to the control of biological weapons.[39] The Protocol and the BWC are the primary international agreements that specifically restrict the use of biological weapons.[40] The 1989 Act implemented the United States' obligations to the BWC by creating federal criminal laws that prohibit several acts of bioterrorism.[41] Subsequently, Congress enacted the 1996 Act, which strengthened these federal criminal laws.[42] The 1996 Act also required the Secretary of Health and Human Services to promulgate and then to enforce regulations that manage facilities storing and transferring highly lethal substances.[43]

---

38. Pub. L. No. 104-132, § 511, 110 Stat. 1214, 1284 (1996).

39. *See House Bioterrorism Hearings*, *supra* note 2, at 14-16 (statement by James S. Reynolds) (noting that current federal criminal statutes, 18 U.S.C. §§ 175, 2332a, as well as current federal regulations do not protect the United States from bioterrorism sufficiently); *Judiciary Hearings*, *supra* note 20, at 28-29 (statement of Ambassador H. Allen Holmes) (noting the inadequacies of the two international agreements pertaining to biological weapons, the 1925 Geneva Protocol and the 1972 Biological and Toxin Weapons Convention).

40. *See* Elizabeth Smith, Note, *International Regulation of Chemical and Biological Weapons: "Yellow Rain" and Arms Control*, 1984 U. ILL. L. REV. 1011, 1011.

41. *See* 18 U.S.C. § 175 (1994 & Supp. III 1998) (stating that Congress enacted the Biological Weapons Anti-Terrorism Act of 1989 to implement the United States' obligations to the BWC); *Judiciary Hearings*, *supra* note 20, at 5 (statement of Sen. Kohl) (introducing the Biological Weapons Anti-Terrorism Act for several reasons, including implementation the United States' obligations to the BWC, under Article IV).

42. *See* discussion *infra* Part I.B.2.

43. *See* Antiterrorism and Effective Death Penalty Act of 1996, § 511(d)-(e), Pub. L. No. 104-132, 110 Stat. 1284 (requiring the Secretary of Health and Human Services to establish and maintain a list of dangerous biological agents and requiring the Secretary to regulate these substances).

A. International Bioterrorism Laws: The 1925 Geneva Protocol and the 1972 Biological Weapons Convention

1. The 1925 Geneva Protocol: Banning Use of Bacteriological Methods of Warfare

Although people have used biological weapons for centuries,[44] the first international treaty banning the use of these weapons was the 1925 Geneva Protocol.[45] The United States signed the Protocol in 1925,[46] and has generally abided by its terms.[47] However, the United States did not ratify this treaty until 1975.[48] The Protocol merely states a rule of law requiring

---

44. *See* MARTIN VAN CREVELD, TECHNOLOGY AND WAR: FROM 2000 B.C. TO THE PRESENT 72 (1989) (stating that although the use of bacteriological weapons currently is denounced, they have a long and honorable history); *see also Joint Senate Committee Hearings*, *supra* note 5, at 2 (statement of Sen. Shelby (R-Ala.)) (noting that one of the earliest recorded attacks involving a biological weapon occurred in the 15th century, when a Tatar force catapulted the bodies of victims who died from the plague into what is now the Ukraine); Kupperman and Smith, *supra* note 4, at 37-38. More than 2000 years ago, Greeks and Romans contaminated their adversaries' wells with corpses of victims of infectious diseases. *See id.* Combatants also used biological agents during the Crimean War and the American Civil War. *See id.*

45. *See* Alice I. Youmans et al., *Questions and Answers*, 83 L. LIBR. J. 195, 202 (1991) (noting that the Protocol is more comprehensive than previous agreements pertaining to chemical and biological warfare because this treaty specifically prohibits bacteriological, in addition to chemical, asphyxiating, poisonous, or gas weapons). For a historical synopsis on international agreements pertaining to chemical-biological warfare prior to the Protocol, see Youmans et al., *supra* at 199-203 and Smith, *supra* note 40, at 1031-33. The reader can find treaties that existed prior to the Protocol as well as draft treaties of the Protocol in 3 STOCKHOLM INTERNATIONAL PEACE RESEARCH INSTITUTE (SIPRI), CBW AND THE LAW OF WAR: THE PROBLEM OF CHEMICAL AND BIOLOGICAL WARFARE, 151-54.

46. *See* Protocol, *supra* note 18, 26 U.S.T. at 571-72, 94 L.N.T.S. 72 (proclaiming that the United States signed the Protocol at Geneva on June 17, 1925). *See generally* FORSBERG ET AL., *supra* note 21, at 69 (stating that as of January 1, 1994, 130 countries were parties to the Protocol).

47. *See* LEONARD COLE, THE ELEVENTH PLAGUE: THE POLITICS OF BIOLOGICAL AND CHEMICAL WARFARE 9 (1997).

48. *See* Protocol, *supra* note 18, 26 U.S.T. at 571-72, 94 L.N.T.S. 72. On December 16, 1974, the United States Senate consented to ratify the Protocol and on January 22, 1975, the President ratified the Protocol. *See id.* The United States deposited the Protocol on April 10, 1975, whereby this treaty entered into force for the United States. *See id.* The United States originally reserved the right to use prohibited weapons to retaliate against enemies who used these weapons first. *See id.* However, the United States rescinded that reservation in January 1993. *See* FORSBERG ET AL., *supra* note 21, at 69.

Commentators give different reasons for why the United States did not ratify the treaty for almost 50 years after signing the Protocol. *Compare* Hoyt Gimlin, *Chemical-Biological Weaponry*, 23 EDITORIAL RES. REP. 459, 463 (1969) (stating that the Protocol was presented to Congress during a time when the United States was in an "isolationist mood," that Congress did formally vote on the law, and that the treaty was withdrawn when, after humanitarian conduct during war.[49] This instrument is not an arms control agreement, and therefore does not regulate the amount of bacteriological weapons that its signatories produce or stockpile.[50]

The Protocol only applies to allegations of use of biological weapons under certain circumstances.[51] First, the Protocol only applies to confrontations involving its signatories.[52] But the Protocol's rule against use of these weapons may reflect customary international law,[53] and therefore may apply to all nations.[54] Furthermore, some parties reserved the right

---

a lengthy debate, it appeared that defeat was imminent), *with* JEANNE MCDERMOTT, THE KILLING WINDS: THE MENACE OF BIOLOGICAL WARFARE 195-96 (1987) (asserting that Congress did not ratify the Protocol because chemical manufacturing corporations successfully blocked its passage), *and* Youmans et al., *supra* note 45, at 202 (contending that the Senate did not ratify the agreement "because no efforts were made to lobby for the Protocol or to educate the Senators to the terms of the document").

49. *See* Michael D. Diederich, Jr., *"Law of War" and Ecology: A Proposal for a Workable Approach to Protecting the Environment Through the Law of War*, 136 MIL. L. REV. 137, 146 (1992) (stating that various treaties, including the Protocol, prohibit use of weapons that cause unnecessary human suffering and that use of these weapons is considered to be contrary to the laws of humanity, as well as to international law principles, declarations, and binding agreements); Michael J. Matheson, *ASIL International Law Weekend: Panel on Internal Conflicts*, 3 I.L.S.A. J. INT'L & COMP. L. 523, 526 (1997) (observing that commentators often classify the Protocol as an arms control agreement, but that the treaty is actually an important rule prohibiting the use of biological weapons in war); Smith, *supra* note 40, at 1031 & n.134 (reporting that the international community created the Protocol to prohibit use of weapons that inflict or prolong unnecessary suffering).

50. *See* Smith, *supra* note 40, at 1031, n.134 (stating that the Protocol does not try to regulate the number or kinds of biological weapons that nations produce or stockpile).

51. *See id.* at 1040 (concluding that the Protocol only applies to unique circumstances).

52. *See* Protocol, *supra* note 18, 26 U.S.T. at 575, 94 L.N.T.S. at 69 (declaring that the Protocol's parties agree to the Protocol's terms as between themselves); Smith, *supra* note 40 at 1033 (noting that the Protocol applies only when all combatants in a confrontation are signatories).

53. *See* Statute of the International Court of Justice, June 26, 1945, art. 38 (1)(b), 59 Stat. 1055, 1060, T.I.A.S. No. 993 [hereinafter ICJ Statute] (enunciating that one source of international law is international custom, which is evidenced by regular practice that nations accept as the law); DAVID HUNTER ET AL., INTERNATIONAL ENVIRONMENTAL LAW AND POLICY, 223 (1998) (instructing that one form of international law is that which is created from the customary practice of nations when nations practice this rule if these nations believe that this practice is required by law). International customary law is binding on all nations. *See id.* at 224.

54. *See* SIPRI, *supra* note 45, at 15, 23, 26-27 (characterizing the rule prohibiting biological weapons as customary international law). The Protocol states that the civilized world condemns the use of chemical weapons in war, *see* Protocol, *supra* note 18, 26 U.S.T. at 575, 94 L.N.T.S. at 67, but declares that the treaty's ban extends to biological methods of war. *See id.* 26 U.S.T. at 575, 94 L.N.T.S. at 69. Nevertheless, since 1925, nations have generally not used these weapons and nations have expressed commitment to the ban on use of biological weapons. *See* SIPRI, *supra* note 45, at 23, 26-27 (stating that the prohibition against use of biological weapons has become customary international law since its creation); *see also* Matheson, *supra* note 49, at 526 (noting that many nations ac-

to retaliate against enemies that use the prohibited weapons first.[55] Second, the Protocol applies only to the use of biological weapons in war; it does not define the ambiguous term "war."[56] If the Protocol's rule prohibiting use of biological weapons constitutes customary international law, this prohibition may extend beyond international armed conflicts.[57] Thus, the Protocol may also apply when a nation uses biological weapons against another nation, even though the two countries do not recognize each other as belligerents.[58] Third, the Protocol only applies when its parties use agents, including biological weapons, that the treaty prohibits.[59]

The International Court of Justice (ICJ)[60] may determine whether a nation has violated the Protocol[61] and then may fashion an appropriate

---

cept the position that the Protocol's rule against use of biological weapons reflects customary international law); Smith, *supra* note 40, at 1041 (stating that the Protocol's prohibition against use of biological weapons may reflect customary international law).

55. *See* Youmans et al., *supra* note 45, at 202 (arguing that one of the Protocol's weaknesses is that it only operates upon mutuality and that its signatories reserved the right to use biological weapons to retaliate against enemies who use prohibited weapons).

56. *See* Protocol, *supra* note 18, 26 U.S.T. at 575, 94 L.N.T.S. at 69 (declaring that the treaty's signatories agree to prohibit use of biological weapons during war); Matheson, *supra* note 49, at 526 (stating that the Protocol only applies to use of the prohibited weapons during war). *See generally* SIPRI, *supra* note 45, at 28-33 (discussing the meaning of the term "war" in light of other international laws).

57. *See* Matheson, *supra* note 49, at 526 (stating that the Protocol applies solely to use of chemical and biological weapons in war, but that some nations include internal conflicts as well as international wars in this definition); Smith, *supra* note 40, at 1034-35 (stating that the Protocol only applies to wartime situations, but that the treaty may or may not apply to situations other than legally-declared war, such as civil war insurgents); *see also* International Trib. For the Former Yugoslavia, *Decision on the Defence Motion for Interlocutory Appeal on Jurisdiction*, 7 CRIM. L.F. 51, 125-28 (1996) [hereinafter International Tribunal] (explaining that several nations, including Greece, the United Kingdom, Germany, and the United States, declared that Iraq's use of chemical weapons against its civilian population violated the Protocol).

58. *See* SIPRI, *supra* note 45, at 32 (noting that the international rule prohibiting use of biological weapons in war seems to be a minimum standard and thus extends "to conflicts, not of an international character, and perhaps even in cases where the parties do not recognize each other as belligerents.").

59. *See* Protocol, *supra* note 18, 26 U.S.T. at 575, 94 L.N.T.S. at 69 (declaring that the parties will not use bacteriological warfare methods); Smith, *supra* note 40, at 1033, 1035-36 (contending that treaty violations are difficult to identify because there are language differences between the English and French texts).

60. *See* U.N. CHARTER, arts. 92-96; ICJ Statute, arts. 34-36, (stating that all nations that are United Nations parties enjoy full access to the International Court of Justice and must adhere to the court's governing principles); *see also* BARRY E. CARTER & PHILLIP R. TRIMBLE, INTERNATIONAL LAW, 302-03 (3d ed. 1999) (reporting that the International Court of Justice is the primary judicial organ of the United Nations and is comprised of 15 judges who serve nine year terms).

61. *See* ICJ Statute, art. 36(2)(c) (providing that nations may grant the court jurisdiction to resolve whether an action constitutes a breach of an international law obligation).

remedy.[62] A party that alleges that another nation has violated the Protocol has the burden of proving such a violation to the court.[63] The ICJ prefers documentary evidence, but if the alleging nation does not have this type of evidence, the court will scrutinize closely any circumstantial evidence.[64] The Protocol does not, however, include verification or enforcement provisions with which to acquire documentary evidence.[65] Further, nations have not always complied with the ICJ's judgments, and the United Nations Security Council has never enforced an ICJ judgment.[66] Consequently, if the ICJ holds that a nation violated the Protocol, the aggrieved nation may not be able to recover.[67]

Nations may use the international political process and the presence of strong international norms against terrorist use of these weapons.[68] The international community, however, has not always supported the United States' use of sanctions or force.[69] Relying on America's potential adversaries to view offensive use of biological weapons as morally abhorrent may not be realistic, and the fact that Americans view these weapons as morally abhorrent may make bioterrorism more appealing to terrorists.[70]

---

62. *See id.* art. 36(2)(d) (stating that nations may grant the court jurisdiction to determine the type and extent of a reparation for a breach of an international obligation).

63. *See* Smith, *supra* note 40, at 1029 (noting that the ICJ generally requires alleging parties to prove the alleged violation).

64. *See id.* (stating that the court may allow circumstantial evidence of an alleged violation, but that the court scrutinizes this evidence closely).

65. *See* FORSBERG, *supra* note 21, at 69; Smith, *supra* note 40, at 1058 (indicating that the Protocol does not specify the conditions under which parties or the United Nations have authority to investigate alleged Protocol violations).

66. *See* CARTER, *supra* note 60, at 307-08 (citing examples of nations that have not complied with ICJ judgments and noting that the U.N. Security Council has never taken measures to enforce an ICJ judgment); *see also* FORSBERG ET AL., *supra* note 21, at 91 n.10 (stating that the United Nations has never taken official action against parties that have violated the Protocol's prohibitions).

67. *See id.* at 306 (stating that affected parties generally have complied with the ICJ's judgments, but that recently, some affected parties have not complied with these judgments).

68. *See* SIPRI, *supra* note 45, at 18 (comparing sanctions for violations of domestic laws to laws of war and noting that the types of sanctions that apply to the latter are "protests, international condemnation, political isolation, the risk of reprisals, the risk of subsequent trial for war crimes, etc."); Smith, *supra* note 40, at 1058 (concluding that nations rely on world public opinion and the international political process rather than on judicial processes because international laws on biological warfare have extensive interpretational problems).

69. *See* COLE, *supra* note 47, at 197-98 (listing international means of managing biological weapons and observing that the international community has responded inconsistently to the use of sanctions or use of force against international law violations).

70. *See* ANDERSON, *supra* note 1, at 9 (stating that the United States intelligence community did not recognize the growing potential for bioterrorism because that commu-

In 1988, for example, several nations publicly condemned Iraq for violating the Protocol when Iraq allegedly used prohibited weapons against Kurdish nationals.[71] Despite these public condemnations, Iraq merely reaffirmed its commitment to the Protocol without taking any substantive remedial action.[72]

2. *The Biological and Toxin Weapons Convention: Resolving the Protocol's Enforcement Weaknesses, But Not Effectively Curbing Biological Weapons Proliferation*

In the 1950s and 1960s, the Protocol remained the only international agreement that prohibited biological warfare.[73] During this time, a number of nations sought to expand and strengthen the Protocol[74] and proposed draft agreements and resolutions.[75] The Biological and Toxin Weapons Convention (BWC), which complements and expands the Protocol, represents the fruition of these nations' efforts.[76] The BWC bans the development, production, stockpiling, acquisition, or retention of biological weapons or biological agents in types or amounts that are not justified for peaceful purposes.[77]

---

nity assumed that moral norms against offensive use of biological weapons constrains their use by the enemy) ; COLE, *supra* note 47, at 217-25 (noting that, historically, the world community has viewed biological weapons use as repugnant). The United States Army continually faced difficulties in the 1950s and 1960s in trying to establish and maintain a biological weapons program. *See id.* at 217-19. People view biological weapons with repugnance partly because these weapons can kill large numbers of human beings indiscriminately and partly because we constantly face a danger from naturally occurring biological agents. *See id.* at 219. This traditional view, however, does not mean that this sense of abhorrence will continue. *See id.* at 221.

71. *See* International Tribunal, *supra* note 57, at 125-27 (quoting several nations' declarations concerning reports of alleged use of chemical weapons by Iraq in September 1988).

72. *See id.* at 127-28 (stating that when Iraq denied charges of chemical weapons use it also reaffirmed its adherence to the Protocol on September 17, 1988).

73. *See* Youmans et al., *supra* note 45, at 202. In the 1960s, the Soviet Union charged the United States with violating the spirit of the Protocol for using tear gas and herbicides during the Vietnam conflict. *See id.* Although the United States was not a party to the Protocol at the time, Secretary of State Dean Rusk responded to this allegation by arguing that these agents are not prohibited by the Protocol. *See id.*

74. *See id.* at 202.

75. *See* Smith, *supra* note 40, at 1042-43 (providing the history of the BWC).

76. *See id.* at 1041-42 (noting that the BWC resulted from almost twenty years of disagreements between the United States and the Soviet Union over how to avoid some of the Protocol's weaknesses); Diederich, *supra* note 49, at 146 (stating that the BWC expanded the Protocol's restraints on biological warfare).

77. *See* BWC, *supra* note 19, 26 U.S.T. at 587, 1015 U.N.T.S. at 166 (Art. I). *See generally*, Michael Moodie, *Arms Control Programs and Biological Weapons*, *in* BIOLOGICAL WEAPONS: WEAPONS OF THE FUTURE?, *supra* note 3, at 47. There have been three conferences, held in 1979, 1986, and 1991, reviewing the performance of the BWC, and ad-

Unlike the Protocol, the BWC is an arms-control treaty, rather than a mere limitation on wartime acts.[78] Thus, the BWC's provisions apply at all times, rather than in wartime only.[79] Furthermore, the BWC clearly defines which substances, equipment, and means of delivery it prohibits.[80] Notably, however, more nations are developing biological weapons now than before the BWC's creation.[81]

To meet the BWC's goal of halting biological weapons proliferation, the treaty includes provisions that allow its parties to address alleged violations.[82] Parties may consult and cooperate with each other on their own or through help from the United Nations.[83] Parties that believe that other parties are violating the BWC may lodge a detailed complaint stating all possible evidence of alleged violations with the United Nations Security Council.[84] This complaint must request the Security Council to consider investigating the alleged violation.[85] If the Security Council initiates an investigation based on the complaint, the parties must cooperate with this investigation.[86] The Security Council must report investiga-

dressing possible measures to strengthen its provisions. *See id.*

78. *See* Smith, *supra* note 40, at 1042 (comparing the BWC to the Protocol); Youmans et al., *supra* note 45, at 203 (stating that the BWC is basically a disarmament treaty).

79. *See* BWC, *supra* note 19, 26 U.S.T. at 587, 1015 U.N.T.S. at 166. Parties to the BWC agreed, under article I, not to develop, produce, stockpile, procure, or hold dangerous biological agents in any circumstance. *See id.*; *see also* Theodor Meron, *International Criminalization of Internal Atrocities*, 89 AM. J. INT'L L. 554, 574-75 (1995) (observing that the Protocol may only apply to biological weapons' use during international wars and concluding that the BWC is not as limited in its application, and applies against parties in any circumstance).

80. *See* BWC, *supra* note 19, 26 U.S.T. at 587, 1015 U.N.T.S. at 166. Under article I, parties to the BWC agree to not develop or possess "[m]icrobial or other biological agents, or toxins whatever their origin or method of production," as well as weapons, equipment, or means that deliver biological substances or toxins. *Id.*

81. *See id.*, 26 U.S.T. at 585-86, 1015 U.N.T.S. at 164-65 (stating that the BWC parties are determined to achieve progress towards general and complete disarmament and to completely exclude the possibility of use of biological weapons); COLE, *supra* note 47, at 4-5 (maintaining that biological weapons programs are growing as the number of signatories to international agreements prohibiting these weapons increases).

82. *See* BWC, *supra* note 19, 26 U.S.T. at 588-89, 1015 U.N.T.S at 167 (articles V-VII).

83. *See id.*, 26 U.S.T at 588, 1015 U.N.T.S. at 167 (declaring, in article V, that BWC parties must consult with each other and cooperate to solve problems that arise regarding the BWC's objectives or applications).

84. *See id.*, 26 U.S.T. at 588, 1015 U.N.T.S. at 167 (providing, in article VI(1), that BWC parties that find that other parties are breaching their obligations to the BWC may lodge a complaint with the United Nations Security Council).

85. *See id.*

86. *See id.* (stating, in article VI(2), that BWC signatories undertake to cooperate in carrying out the Security Council's BWC investigations).

tion results to all BWC parties.[87]

Critics of the BWC question the effectiveness of these enforcement provisions because the BWC does not provide verification measures to assess potential violations and relies instead on international political pressure.[88] Without sufficient evidence though, parties may be reluctant to report an alleged violation when a nation has harmed its own citizens.[89] Furthermore, the lack of verification provisions permits violating nations to deny other nations access to their lands, delay news of the incident, and destroy evidence, thus thwarting the investigative process.[90] A complaining party may have a particularly difficult time verifying an alleged violation when a nation has taken advantage of biotechnological advances that have decreased the potential for detection.[91]

87. *See id.*

88. *See* Smith, *supra* note 40, at 1046. Although violations of the BWC may be difficult to prove, the BWC does not include mandatory verification requirements. *See id.* The question of allowing for verification measures under the BWC, however, has proven controversial. *See* Moodie, *supra* note 77, at 54 (noting the ongoing debate regarding the potential effectiveness of a verification placed under the BWC). Commentators debate whether verification entails highly intrusive inspections permissible at any time or should merely require a demonstration of compliance. *See id.* at 54; *see also* Roberts, *supra* note 3, at 93 (noting that the various challenges pertaining to biological weapons use have grown more pronounced, and that the proliferation of biological weapons and noncompliance issues have resulted in an erosion of confidence in the BWC).

Commentators note that the BWC is limited in detecting and responding to violations in view of the rising proliferation of biological warfare capabilities, particularly in Iraq and Russia. *See id.* at 78. Iraq managed to evade international detection as it developed an offensive biological weapons program, despite indications that something was amiss in that country. *See id.* Similarly, the United States and its allies alleged that the Soviet Union violated the BWC by providing its allies with biological weapons in the late 1970s, by using these weapons in Afghanistan in the 1980s, and by possessing these weapons after the Soviet Union experienced an anthrax outbreak in 1979. *See id.* at 79. The Soviet Union denied these allegations. *See id.* at 80. In February 1992, however, Russian President Boris Yeltsin acknowledged that past military efforts in the Soviet Union did not comply with international treaties. *See id.* Commentators note that this acknowledgment raises doubts about the BWC as a treaty that relies on international pressure to bring nations in compliance with its provisions. *See id.* at 81. The fact that the international community could not gather the political will to resolve allegations of BWC violations by Iraq and the Soviet Union, or even try to secure compliance when the allegations later proved true, indicts the international community itself. *See id.*

89. *See* Smith, *supra* note 40, at 1046 (noting that parties may be reluctant to report incidents involving another nations' use of biological weapons against its own citizens if the first nation does not have enough evidence to prove this allegation).

90. *See id.* (stating ways that a violating nation can thwart the investigative process).

91. *See* Thomas Dashiell, *A Review of U.S. Biological Warfare Policies*, *in* BIOLOGICAL WEAPONS: WEAPONS OF THE FUTURE?, *supra* note 3, at 1, 5 (noting that biotechnology advances increase the difficulty, and hence decrease the probability, of detecting BWC violations).

Commentators also criticize a BWC loophole[92] that allows its parties to possess dangerous biological agents and toxins for defense research or other peaceful purposes.[93] Critics claim that biological weapons testing and research inherently create a substantial risk that the agents will escape into the environment.[94] Likewise, nations easily could take advantage of this loophole because developing agents for defense purposes is operationally equivalent to developing agents for offensive purposes.[95] On the other hand, a nation that genuinely conducts research on biological agents for defense purposes may have a difficult time convincing others that such research will not be used to develop offensive weapons.[96]

Defenders of the peaceful research exception argue that governments must be allowed to defend against biological warfare.[97] Defensive research reduces the number of casualties from a biological weapons attack

---

92. *See* BWC, *supra* note 19, 26 U.S.T. at 571, 1015 U.N.T.S. at 166 (stating, in article I, that parties to the BWC may not possess substances that could create biological weapons "in quantities that have no justification for prophylactic, protective or other peaceful purposes").

93. *See* Victor W. Sidel, *The History of Biological Warfare and Research*, *in* POISON IN THE WIND: THE SPREAD OF CHEMICAL AND BIOLOGICAL WEAPONS, *supra* note 1, at 9, 13 (arguing that the BWC's exception for defensive or legitimate purposes creates a loophole because the risk of release in the environment and biological weapons research inevitably leads to more biological weapons); Smith, *supra* note 40, at 1046 (stating that BWC commentators have expressed concerns that nations may, under this exception, justify possession of a large amount of these agents as immunizations for their citizens, but then use these agents against their enemies). *See generally* Frank Barnaby, *Chemical and Biological Warfare*, *in* FUTURE WAR: ARMED CONFLICT IN THE NEXT DECADE 106-13 (Frank Barnaby ed., 1984). Under this loophole, the Soviet Union probably did not violate the BWC in 1982, as alleged by the United States, even though an explosion in a biological weapons research laboratory near Sverdlovsk resulted in an anthrax epidemic in that region. *See id.* at 111.

94. *See* Rifkin, *supra* note 4, at 103 (noting that advertent or inadvertent release of dangerous organisms into the environment could come about due to "human error, equipment failure, terrorism, or natural disasters").

95. *See* David L. Huxsoll, *The U.S. Biological Defense Research Program*, *in* BIOLOGICAL WEAPONS: WEAPONS OF THE FUTURE?, *supra* note 3, at 58, 62 (suggesting that it is easy to obscure the line between offensive and defensive research on dangerous biological agents); Smith, *supra* note 40, at 1046 (contending that nations easily could breach the BWC's prohibition against possession of dangerous agents by having research programs).

96. *See* Anthony Robbins, M.D., *The Biological Warfare Program Should Be Abolished*, *in* POISON IN THE WIND: THE THREAT OF CHEMICAL AND BIOLOGICAL WARFARE, *supra* note 1, at 91, 96 (citing reasons that the United States should halt biological warfare testing). Dr. Robinson observes that research on offensive and defensive uses of biological agents are functionally the same, concluding that it is impossible to prove to other nations that the United States conducts this research for legitimate defensive purposes. *See id.*

97. *See* Huxsoll, *supra* note 95, at 61 (stating that biological weapons programs are a legitimate and legal method of preparing a nation for a biological weapons attack).

and prevents technological surprise.[98] Furthermore, many agents that terrorists could use in weapons also occur in nature, and international accords should allow governments to examine and improve their ability to deal with these agents.[99]

B. United States Laws and Regulations that Manage Dangerous Biological Agents

1. The Biological Weapons Anti-Terrorism Act of 1989: Implementing the United States Obligations Under the BWC and the Beginnings of Criminalizing Bioterrorism

Before 1990, federal criminal codes did not regulate private citizens' actions regarding biological weapons specifically.[100] Although the government could have prosecuted bioterrorists for murder for killing people with biological weapons, the manufacture of a biological weapon was not a crime.[101] As a threshold matter, law enforcement authorities could not prevent private citizens from building biological weapons.[102] The Reagan Administration stated that extensive existing legislation prevented private citizens from engaging in conduct prohibited under the BWC.[103] These laws, however, do not cover biological agents and toxins that the BWC describes, and do not implement the BWC's goal of eradicating biological weapons.[104] Consequently, Congress passed the 1989

98. *See id.* at 61-62.

99. *See House Bioterrorism Hearings*, *supra* note 2, at 51 (statement of Dr. Ronald M. Atlas) (noting that microbiologists use the same natural infectious diseases that could be used to create biological weapons to develop means of reducing illness from these agents).

100. *See Judiciary Hearings*, *supra* note 20, at 8 (statement of Rep. Robert Kastenmeier (D-Wis.)). In 1973, the executive branch encouraged Congress to pass legislation that would prohibit and provide penalties for developing and acquiring biological weapons. *See id.* Congress, however, did not consider this legislation because of the delay in ratifying the BWC. *See id.* The 1980 legislative session ended before Congress could enact similar legislation. *See id.*

101. *See id.* at 5 (statement by Sen. Kohl) (citing the reasons that he introduced this bill, one of which was to close the gap in the criminal laws pertaining to use of biological weapons).

102. *See id.*

103. *See id.* at 8 (statement of Rep. Kastenmeier).

104. *See id.* The Reagan Administration stated that "the Arms Export Control Act, the Export Administration Act, Hazardous Material Transportation Act, Toxic Substances Control Act, the Public Health Service Act, [and] the Federal Insecticide, Pesticide and Rodenticide Act" controlled bioterrorism. *Id.* None of these laws, however, effectively prevent this sort of terrorism. *See id.* The Arms Export Control Act, for example, gives the President authority to control the export and import of defense articles, which includes biological agents. *See* 22 U.S.C. § 2778 (1994); 22 C.F.R. § 121.1 (category XIV) (1999). Unfortunately, neither the Act nor its implementing regulations defines

Biological Weapons Anti-Terrorism Act of 1989 (1989 Act) to close the gap in federal legislation controlling bioterrorism, thereby enhancing the nation's safety.[105] This Act also fulfilled the United States' obligations to the BWC.[106]

The 1989 Act created a new chapter in title 18 of the *United States Code* that pertains solely to biological weapons crimes.[107] This chapter contains four sections.[108] The first section mandates fines or imprisonment for anyone in the United States who knowingly creates, transfers, or possesses biological agents, toxins, or delivery systems in order to use these items as biological weapons.[109] The United States has jurisdiction over biological weapons offenses that are committed by or against United States nationals.[110]

The second section of the 1989 Act gives the Attorney General authority to search for and seize biological agents, toxins, or delivery systems that are held to create or transfer biological weapons.[111] The Attorney General may search for and seize agents of the kind or amount that are not justified for peaceful purposes.[112] In emergencies, the Attorney General does not need a warrant to seize and destroy these agents if there is probable cause to believe that violators are using the agents as

---

"biological agents" clearly. *See Judiciary Hearings*, *supra* note 20, at 108 (supplement to the testimony of Francis A. Boyle) (listing legislation that the Reagan Administration held as sufficient to implement the BWC, and explaining why each act is not sufficient to implement the BWC). Furthermore, the Act does not provide the government with adequate regulatory authority over biological agent research and manufacture. *See id.*

105. *See* 135 CONG. REC. 16,501-02 (1989) (testimony of Sen. Kohl); *Judiciary Hearings*, *supra* note 20, at 5 (statement of Sen. Kohl) (stating that one of the reasons he introduced the bill was to close the loophole in the federal criminal laws that prohibits people from killing with biological weapons but does not prohibit people from creating biological weapons).

106. *See* Biological Weapons Anti-Terrorism Act of 1989, Pub. L. No. 101-298, § 2(a), 104 Stat. 201 (1990); 135 CONG. REC. 16,501-02 (1989) (testimony by Sen. Kohl). Before this Act, the United States fulfilled part of its obligations to the BWC by renouncing biological weapons and by destroying the nation's stockpiles of biological weapons. *See id.* However, the United States did not completely fulfill all of its obligations to the BWC because it never took measures to outlaw biological weapons domestically. *See id.*

107. *See* Biological Weapons Anti-Terrorism Act § 3(a), 104 Stat. at 201 (stating that title 18 of the U.S. Code is amended by inserting a new chapter after chapter 9).

108. *See id.*, 104 Stat. at 201-03 (setting forth four sections in chapter 10, titled "Prohibitions with respect to biological weapons," "Seizure, forfeiture, and destruction," "Injunctions," and "Definitions")

109. *See* 18 U.S.C. § 175(a) (Supp. III 1997) (providing that those who violate this section shall be fined, or imprisoned for life or any term of years).

110. *See id.*

111. *See id.* § 176.

112. *See id.* § 176(a).

biological weapons.[113] Alleged violators may defend their biological agent, toxin, or delivery systems against forfeiture by presenting evidence that these items are meant for prophylactic, protective, or peaceful purposes.[114]

The last two sections of the 1989 Act provide for civil injunctions and define several key terms.[115] The 1989 Act gives the United States authority to seek a civil injunction against those who commit actions prohibited by the 1989 Act or against those who prepare, solicit, try, or conspire to violate the 1989 Act.[116] Alleged violators may defend themselves against such civil injunctions if their actions with respect to the dangerous agents are justified for peaceful purposes.[117] Finally, the Act defines four terms: biological agent,[118] toxin,[119] delivery system,[120] and vector.[121]

When Congress introduced the Biological Weapons Anti-Terrorism Act, the biotechnology industry stated that the industry supported the bill, but expressed concern that the 1989 Act would impede legitimate research.[122] Although acknowledging that the 1989 Act provides a defense against the seizure of biological agents,[123] the biotechnology industry argued that legitimate researchers would have the burden of proving this defense.[124] The legislature responded to this concern by clearly stat-

113. *See id.* § 176(a)(2).

114. *See id.* § 176(c). In addition to a peaceful purpose, the alleged violator must show that the agent, toxin, or delivery system "is of a type and quantity reasonable for that purpose." *Id.* § 176 (c)(2).

115. *See id.* §§ 177-178.

116. *See id.* § 177(a).

117. *See id.* § 177(b) (stating that an alleged violator may present an affirmative defense against an injunction by showing a peaceful purpose and that the type and quantity of the material corresponds to such a purpose).

118. *See id.* § 178(1) (defining a biological agent as any microorganism, virus, or infectious substance that can cause other living organisms to die or become ill, cause food, water, equipment or supplies to deteriorate, or deleteriously alter the environment).

119. *See id.* § 178(2) (defining toxins as poisonous substances that living organisms produce or poisonous isomors, homologs, or derivatives of these substances).

120. *See id.* § 178(3). Delivery systems include equipment or apparatus that are designed to deliver or disseminate biological agents, toxins, or vectors. *See id.* § 178(3)(A). A delivery system is also a vector. *See id.* § 178(3)(B); *see also infra* note 121 (defining vector).

121. *See id.* § 178(4). Vectors are living organisms that can carry biological agents or toxins to a host. *See id.*

122. *See Judiciary Hearings*, *supra* note 20, at 70-71 (testimony of Richard Godown, President, Industrial Biotechnology Association).

123. *See id.* at 71 (expressing concerns about the 1989 Act's impact on the research community).

124. *See id.*

ing in the bill's legislative history that the 1989 Act did not intend to prohibit legitimate scientific research.[125]

2. The Antiterrorism and Effective Death Penalty Act of 1996: Responding to United States v. Harris *and Strengthening Biological Weapons Laws*

In 1996, federal laws and regulations were still not sufficient to protect Americans from bioterrorism.[126] On March 12, 1996, Senator Orrin G. Hatch (R-Utah) introduced the Biological Agents Enhanced Penalties and Control Act[127] (Biological Agents Act), which Congress eventually incorporated into the Antiterrorism and Effective Death Penalty Act of 1996 (1996 Act).[128] The Biological Agents Act sought to close gaps in the criminal laws that made it difficult to prosecute people who buy pathogens without legitimate purposes and in the federal regulations that allowed anyone to have dangerous biological agents.[129] Like the 1989 Act, the Biological Agents Act sought to balance citizens' needs to be protected from bioterrorism with researchers' needs to use pathogens without having to meet over-burdensome regulations.[130] The impetus for the creation of the Biological Agents Act was a case involving the

125. *See id.* at 87-88 (statement of Sen. Kohl) (asking Mr. Godown if the biotechnology industry would be more secure if the bill's legislative history clearly stated that the bill did not intend to prevent legitimate research and receiving an affirmative answer); *see also* 135 CONG. REC. 16,501, 16,502 (1989) (statement of Sen. Kohl). Senator Kohl emphasized that the drafters carefully crafted the Biological Weapons Anti-Terrorism Act to ensure that legally valid researchers working with dangerous biological agents or toxins are not targeted for prosecution mistakenly. *See id.*

126. *See* 142 CONG. REC. 1862 (1996) (statement of Sen. Hatch).

127. S. 1606, 104th Cong. (1996); *see also* 142 CONG. REC. 1862 (statement of Sen. Hatch) (introducing the Biological Agents Act, noting the bill's purpose, and acknowledging the bill's cosponsors: Senators Orrin G. Hatch (R-Utah), Diane Feinstein (D-Cal.), Strom Thurmond (R-S.C.), Mike DeWine (R-Ohio), Herb Kohl (D-Wis.), and Joseph R. Biden, Jr. (D-Del)).

128. *See Joint Senate Committee Hearings, supra* note 5, at 6-7 (statement of Sen. Feinstein) (discussing current federal criminal laws pertaining to biological weapons); *id.* at 4-5 (statement by Sen. Kyl, discussing congressional efforts to combat bioterrorism).

129. *See* 142 CONG. REC. 1862 (statement of Sen. Hatch). Senator Hatch also noted that federal regulations pertaining to the interstate transportation of agents that are pathogenic to plants and animals are more strict than those regulating the interstate transportation of human pathogens. *See id.*

130. *See id.* at 1863.

unauthorized possession of dangerous pathogens,[131] *United States v. Harris.*[132]

In 1995, Larry Wayne Harris bought samples of the bacteria that causes bubonic plague for what he claimed was legitimate research "to counteract an imminent invasion from Iraq of super-germ-carrying rats."[133] The court convicted Harris of fraudulently misrepresenting himself to the lab where he faxed his order for the bacteria.[134] When Senator Hatch introduced the Biological Agents Act, he noted that if Mr. Harris had not used fraudulent misrepresentation to buy the substance, the court would not have convicted him of anything because gaps in the laws enabled anyone to obtain dangerous pathogens.[135]

a. Expansion of the Government's Capacity to Prosecute Crimes Involving Biological Weapons

The 1996 Act amended the federal criminal statutes pertaining to biological weapons to update these laws with science and technology and to ensure that bioterrorists will face severe and certain punishment.[136] The 1996 Act accomplished these goals by amending three sections of the 1989 Act.[137] The terms "biological agent," "toxin," and "vector" under

131. *See Joint Senate Committee Hearings, supra* note 5, at 4-5 (statement of Sen. Kyl) (asserting that Congress enacted the Antiterrorism and Effective Death Penalty Act in 1996 as a response to the fact that Larry Wayne Harris acquired the bubonic plague bacteria); 142 CONG. REC. 1862 (statement of Sen. Hatch) (referring to an incident in Las Vegas in May 1995 without specially naming Harris).

132. 961 F. Supp. 1127 (S.D. Ohio 1997).

133. *Id.* at 1129, 1132.

134. *See id.* at 1129. Harris ordered bacteria that causes bubonic plague from American Type Culture Collection (ATCC), a Maryland company. *See id.* He misrepresented to ATCC that he was qualified to order the bacteria by stating that he had an Environmental Protection Agency (EPA) certification number. *See id.* Harris also misinformed ATCC by telling them that he had a small animals laboratory. *See id. See generally* COLE, *supra* note 47, at 3-4. Harris ordered the bacteria a few weeks after the sarin gas attack in a Tokyo subway. *See id.* After a police search in his home revealed racist and anti-Semitic literature, as well as a certificate declaring Harris to be a member of a white supremacist organization, a spokesmember for the Anti-Defamation League of B'nai B'rith expressed concern that Harris intended to use the bacteria for purposes other than against Iraq. *See id.* at 4, 157. Harris entered a guilty plea to a wire fraud charge in exchange for the maximum six-month jail sentence. *See id.*

135. *See* 142 CONG. REC. 1862 (statement of Sen. Hatch).

136. *See id.* at 1862-63 (statement of Sen. Hatch) (noting that existing laws do not reflect current scientific and technological capabilities, and stating that the Biological Agents Act would strengthen these laws by expanding the federal government's jurisdiction to prosecute individuals who might take advantage of these current capacities).

137. *See* Antiterrorism and Effective Death Penalty Act of 1996, Pub. L. No. 104-132, § 511(b), 110 Stat. 1214, 1284 (amending 18 U.S.C. §§ 175, 177-178 (1994)).

the federal criminal code now include genetically altered products.[138] In addition, there are criminal penalties for attempts, threats, or conspiracies to violate federal biological weapons criminal laws.[139] Finally, the federal government now has authority to seek injunctions against those who threaten to violate federal criminal laws involving biological weapons.[140]

b. Criminalizing Genetically Altered Biological Weapons

The 1996 Act also amended the federal statute that criminalizes the use of weapons of mass destruction.[141] Under this section, weapons of mass destruction include poison gas, weapons involving disease organisms, and weapons that release dangerously high levels of radiation.[142] Those who use, try to use, or conspire to use such weapons against United States citizens who are outside of the United States, against people who are within the United States, or against federal property in or outside of the United States will face imprisonment or the death penalty.[143] The 1996 Act expanded this section by including the use of biological agents and toxins as they are defined in 18 U.S.C. § 178 in the general prohibition against use of weapons of mass destruction, thereby including genetically altered products.[144]

c. Tightening Safety and Transfer Regulations

Aside from amending existing federal criminal statutes, the 1996 Act also tightened regulations on transfers and possession of potentially haz-

138. *Compare* 18 U.S.C. § 178 (Supp. III 1998) (including biological products that can be biotechnologically engineered to the provision's definition of biological agent), *with* 18 U.S.C. § 178 (1994) (limiting the definition of biological agent to microorganisms, viruses, or infectious substances).

139. *Compare* 18 U.S.C. § 175(a) (Supp. III 1997) (including attempts, threats, or conspiracies in the section's general prohibitions), *with* 18 U.S.C. § 175(a) (1994) (limiting the section to prohibit the knowing development, production, stockpiling, transfer, acquisition, retention, or possession of the banned substances).

140. *Compare* 18 U.S.C. § 177 (Supp. III 1997) (including threats to engage in prohibited actions pertaining to biological weapons in the list of acts the United States can obtain a civil injunction against), *with* 18 U.S.C. § 177 (1994) (allowing the United States to obtain a civil injunction against those who prepare, solicit, try, or conspire to engage in prohibited actions pertaining to biological weapons).

141. *See* Antiterrorism and Effective Death Penalty Act § 511(c) (amending 18 U.S.C. § 2332a(a), which criminalized use of weapons of mass destruction).

142. *See* 18 U.S.C. § 2332a(c)(2) (Supp. III 1997).

143. *See* 18 U.S.C. § 2332a(a) (1994 & Supp. III 1997).

144. *See* Antiterrorism and Effective Death Penalty Act § 511(c) (codified as amended at 18 U.S.C. § 2332a(a) (Supp. III 1997)).

ardous biological agents.[145] Before the 1996 Act, biological pathogens were available to various legitimate users, yet anyone could legally procure these agents, as long as the sellers of the agents did not impose their own limits.[146] Several federal agencies, such as the Environmental Protection Agency and the Department of Agriculture, regulated the management of these agents.[147] However, the regulations were developed for narrow purposes in an era when most lawmakers did not consider domestic bioterrorism as a realistic possibility.[148] The agencies did not coordinate their biological agents[149] or keep up with advancing science.[150] Therefore, these regulations provided an ineffective response to bioterrorism incidents.[151]

Medical and research facilities must be able to ship infectious agents because these agents are used to further medical research and to diagnose and treat infectious diseases.[152] Communities must have adequate

---

145. *See id.* § 511(d)-(e) (requiring the Secretary of Health and Human Services to promulgate final regulations controlling biological agents within 120 days after the Act passes).

146. *See* 142 CONG. REC. 1862 (1996) (statement of Sen. Hatch). There were three legitimate groups of biological agent users prior to the 1996 Act. *See id.* Clinical laboratories could analyze small amounts of biological agents from patient samples. *See id.* Government and private scientists could use biological agents to conduct legitimate basic and clinical research. *See id.* The Department of Defense could use biological agents to develop protective strategies against the use of biological weapons in war. *See id.*

147. *See id.* (listing the various federal agencies that regulate biological agents, including the Postal Service and the Food and Drug Administration).

148. *See id.* For example, the Centers for Disease Control and Prevention (CDC) grouped biological agents into four classifications, ranging from agents that do not harm humans to agents that are very harmful to humans. *See id.* at 1863. Regulations required laboratories to manage each class of agents in a particular manner. *See id.* The CDC promulgated this classification system to protect laboratory workers and to prevent the accidental release of agents into the environment. *See id.* The regulations did not take theft of the agents into account or attempt to prevent misdirection of dangerous agents to terrorists. *See id.*

149. *See id.* at 1862.

150. *See id.* at 1862-63 (citing, for example, CDC regulations that did not address new strains of organisms or provide an adequate definition of biological agent).

151. *See id.* at 1863 (quoting testimony by Dr. James M. Hughes, the Assistant Surgeon General and Director of the National Center for Infectious Diseases for the CDC, before the Senate Judiciary Committee, in March 1996). Dr. Hughes testified that regulations seeking to safeguard against the acquisition and distribution of agents pathogenic to people are not comprehensive. *See id.* Although these regulations effectively control the packaging, labeling, and transporting of these agents, the number of different departmental regulations do not effectively control the possession and transfer of these substances within the United States. *See id.*

152. *See House Bioterrorism Hearings*, *supra* note 2, at 50 (statement of Dr. Atlas) (noting that combating infectious diseases requires working with the same dangerous agents used by bioterrorists).

protection, however, from those who may steal the agents or intentionally divert the agents to terrorists, who could then use the agents to create biological weapons.[153] Therefore, the 1996 Act sought to ensure that regulations governing the transfer of dangerous biological agents strike a balance between assuring that medical and research communities have access to these materials and preventing non-legitimate users from having such access.[154]

The 1996 Act mandated new responsibilities for the Secretary of Health and Human Services.[155] These responsibilities include establishing and maintaining a list of biological agents that could pose a severe public health and safety threat[156] and creating regulations for transfers of listed biological agents.[157] The 1996 Act specifically states that the Secretary, in promulgating these regulations, must ensure that biological agents remain available for legitimate uses.[158]

d. Whether to Implement the Transfer and Disposal of Biological Agents Requirements: Immediate Criticisms of the Efficacy of the Regulations

In response to the requirements the 1996 Act imposes on the Secretary, the Centers for Disease Control and Prevention (CDC) issued a Notice of Proposed Rulemaking on June 10, 1996.[159] The CDC issued the

153. *See* 142 CONG. REC. 1863 (statement of Sen. Hatch).

154. *See Joint Senate Committee Hearings*, *supra* note 5, at 23 (statement of Dr. Stephen M. Ostroff, Associate Director of Epidemiologic Science, National Center for Infectious Diseases, Centers for Disease Control and Prevention, Atlanta, Georgia).

155. *See* Antiterrorism and Effective Death Penalty Act, Pub. L. No. 104-132, § 511(d)-(f), 110 Stat. 1284, 1285 (amending 18 U.S.C. §§ 175, 177-78) (requiring the Secretary of Health and Human Services to regulate biological agents that could pose severe threats to public health and safety).

156. *See id.* § 511(d), (f) (requiring the Secretary to establish a proposed list of all such agents within three months after the Act's enactment and to promulgate a final version of the list within six months). In creating this list, the Secretary must consider four criteria. *See id.* § 511(d)(1)(B)(i). These criteria include the agent's effect on human health upon exposure, how contagious the agent is, as well as methods by which the agent could be transferred to humans, the availablity and effectiveness of immunizations against infection, and any other appropriate criteria. *See id.* The Secretary must also consult with scientific experts from appropriate professional groups. *See id.* § 511(d)(1)(B)(ii).

157. *See id.* § 511(e). The Act directs the Secretary to create regulations requiring users to have proper training and appropriate skills before handling these agents and directs the Secretary to provide guidelines for containinment and disposal. *See id.* § 511(e)(1)(A)-(B). The regulations must include safeguards preventing access to dangerous biological agents and procedures that protect the public safety in case a listed biological agent is transferred in violation of the safety procedures. *See id.* § 511(e)(2).

158. *See id.* § 511(e)(4) (stating that legitimate purposes include research and education).

159. *See* Additional Requirements for Facilities Transferring or Receiving Select In-

final regulation on October 24, 1996 after a thirty-day comment period and time for the CDC to consider the comments.[160] The final regulation became effective April 15, 1997.[161]

The final regulation has several fundamental components.[162] First, it provides a list of select agents that pose a threat to public health and safety.[163] Commercial suppliers, as well as those agencies, universities, research institutions, individuals, and private companies that transfer or obtain any of the listed agents[164] must now register with the Secretary.[165]

fectious Agents, 61 Fed. Reg. 29,327-28 (proposed June 10, 1996) (suggesting new regulations pertaining to the acquisition and transfer of dangerous biological agents in accordance with the Antiterrorism and Effective Death Penalty Act).

160. *See* Additional Requirements for Facilities Transferring or Receiving Select Agents, 61 Fed. Reg. 55,190 (1996) (codified at 42 C.F.R. pt. 72). The CDC received 67 written responses, many of which contained multiple comments and most of which were favorable. *See id.* These comments focused on specific sections of the regulation, requested clarification of particular provisions, or suggested that agents be added or deleted from the proposed list. *See id.* Some commentaries stated that the regulation would not protect the public against biological terrorism, would impede research, and would simply provide unnecessary additional administrative costs and burdens. *See id.*

161. *See id.*; Additional Requirements for Facilities Transferring or Receiving Select Agents, 42 C.F.R. § 72.6 (1998); Penalties, 42 C.F.R. § 72.7 (1998); Select Agents, 42 C.F.R. app. § 72 (1998).

162. *See Joint Senate Committee Hearings*, *supra* note 5, at 23 (statement of Dr. Ostroff) (noting that the new regulations include six fundamental components, including registration of facilities and verification procedures, as well as a list of select agents that are subject to the rule); 42 C.F.R. § 72.6-7, app.

163. *See* 42 C.F.R. app. § 72; *see also Joint Senate Committee Hearings*, *supra* note 5, at 23 (testimony of Dr. Ostroff). The CDC will supplement or modify this list of 40 select agents as needed. *See id.* CDC based the select agents list on an existing list of infectious agents regulated for export from the United States that can harm the public's health. *See id.* Sen. Feinstein criticized the CDC for not including Salmonella typhimurium on the list because terrorists previously used this agent to harm the public. *See id.* at 37. Dr. Ostroff responded to this criticism by stating that placing this agent on the list "would be an exercise in futility" because Salmonella is ubiquitous, existing naturally in poultry, as well as other types of animals. *See id.* In a persuasive example, he noted that anyone can go to a grocery store, buy several chickens, isolate the Salmonella organism, and then poison several hundred people with it. *See id.* at 37-38. Dr. Ostroff concluded that continually adding agents like Salmonella to the select list would not strengthen the regulations. *See id.*

164. *See* 42 C.F.R. § 72.6(j) (defining the term facility under the regulation).

165. *See id.* § 72.6(a)(1). The registration process involves certifying that facilities meet minimum biosafety levels. *See id.* § 72.6(a)(2)(i). The Secretary may also require facility inspections in order to ensure that facilities meet mandated biosafety levels. *See id.* § 72.6(a)(2)(ii), (g). Once approved, facilities receive unique registration numbers that indicate that the facilities may work with listed agents at specific biosafety levels. *See id.* § 72.6(a)(i), (a)(2)(iii). The Secretary may deny registration to or withdraw registration from a facility if there is evidence that the facility cannot handle these agents safely, that the facility handles the agents unsafely, that the facility intends to use these agents in a manner that could harm people, or that the facility is otherwise not complying with the regulations. *See id.* § 72.6(a)(4). Facilities may appeal denial or withdrawal of registration. *See id.* § 72.6(b).

Transferors and requestors of listed agents must now keep track of these agents[166] and comply with disposal and storage requirements.[167] Certain agents, however, such as the less pathogenic vaccine strains of restricted viral agents, are exempt from the regulations so that legitimate facilities retain the ability to use them for reference, diagnostic, and research studies.[168] In addition, the Clinical Laboratories Improvement Amend-

During federal congressional hearings a year after the CDC promulgated these regulations, Senator Kyl expressed concern that the CDC did not carry out the regulations' mandate by registering facilities quickly enough. *See Joint Senate Committee Hearings*, *supra* note 5, at 33-35 (testimony of Sen. Kyl and Dr. Ostroff). At the same hearing, Sen. Feinstein expressed concern with the registration process, asking Dr. Ostroff whether the CDC may delegate authority to register laboratories to private entities as noted in § 72.6(c). *See id.* at 35 (statement of Sen. Feinstein). Dr. Ostroff stated that the CDC discussed having an outside organization try to implement some aspects of the regulation, but decided that it is most appropriate to keep these responsibilities within the agency. *See id.* at 35.

Senator Feinstein also criticized the regulations for not including a provision requiring that the CDC do a background check on individual employees who work with the select agents. *See id.* at 35-36. She was concerned that another situation similar to the Harris incident, which precipitated these regulations, could recur. *See id.* Dr. Ostroff stated that it would be extraordinarily difficult to prevent people with criminal intentions from obtaining dangerous agents. *See id.* Dr. Ostroff noted, however, that the regulation has safeguards sufficient to prevent another Larry Wayne Harris episode from occurring. *See id.* at 36-37.

166. *See* 42 C.F.R. § 72.6(d)-(f). Transferors and requestors of select agents are required to complete an official transfer form and to provide specific information about the request, such as the purposes for which the agent will be used. *See id.* § 72.6(d). Both parties to the transfer must retain a copy of the transfer form, and the transferor must also send a copy to a designated central repository. *See id.* § 72.6(d)(3), (f)(3). The purpose of the form is to track the whereabouts of select agents, which is helpful in cases of illegitimate access to the agents. *See* Additional Requirements for Facilities Transferring or Receiving Select Agents, 61 Fed. Reg. 55,190, 55,192 (1996). Facilities do not have to follow the regulation's transfer and verification requirements in order to transfer agents within the facility if they maintain adequate records of such transfers. *See* 42 C.F.R. § 72.6(j).

Each registered facility must designate a responsible facility official who is authorized to transfer and receive any of the agents listed, and who is either a safety manager or senior management official of the facility. *See id.* The statute requires the responsible facility official to take an active role in the transfer process. *See id.* § 72.6(d)(1)(iii), (d)(2), (e).

167. *See* 42 C.F.R. § 72.6(i)(1)(i) (stating that select agents must be "stored in accordance with prudent laboratory practices"). The final rule explained that prudent practice includes secure and controlled access to the area and to the equipment where the agents are stored. *See* Additional Requirements for Facilities Transferring or Receiving Select Agents, 61 Fed. Reg. at 55,193. In addition, facility officials must dispose of select agents at the facility, using known effective methods. *See* 42 C.F.R. § 72.6(i)(1)(iii). Facilities must maintain records of disposals and notify the registering agency that the agent was destroyed. *See id.* at (i)(2). The final rule stated that the combination of facility management oversight of the select agents, facility employee responsibilities, and stiff penalties for violations of the regulation will ensure compliance with these regulations. *See* Additional Requirements for Facilities Transferring or Receiving Select Agents, 61 Fed. Reg. at 55,193.

168. *See* 42 C.F.R. app. § 72 (noting exemptions to the list of select agents); Additional

ments of 1988[169] exempt certified laboratories from the regulations if they use listed agents "for diagnostic, reference, verification, or proficiency testing purposes."[170]

Although the CDC promulgated the regulations within the allotted time under the Antiterrorism Act, the agency has not yet completely implemented these regulations due to resource constraints.[171] The CDC requested adequate funding in its 1999 budget, which should have resolved this problem,[172] but to date, many of the facilities managed by the regulations are not registered.[173]

Commentators have criticized the regulations because of this lack of full implementation, and have expressed doubt that the regulations will deter bioterrorists even when fully implemented.[174] The failure to fully implement these regulations means that, for all practical purposes, the United States' ability to control the transfer of dangerous biological agents is no better today than before the 1996 Act.[175] Furthermore, al-

---

Requirements for Transferring or Receiving Select Agents, 61 Fed. Reg. at 55,194 (responding to commentator concerns that this exception provides a loophole in the regulation by explaining that the clinical specimen must be used for diagnostic, reference, or verification purposes to be exempt). Toxins used for medical purposes or biomedical research are also exempt from the select agents list. *See* 42 C.F.R. app. § 72.

169. 42 U.S.C. § 263a (1994).

170. *See* 42 C.F.R. § 72.6(h)(2).

171. *See House Bioterrorism Hearings*, *supra* note 2, at 52 (statement of Dr. Atlas) (stating that, as of May 1999, only half of the 300 institutions that possess listed agents are registered with the CDC because the agency does not have sufficient financial resources to register the additional 150 institutions); *Joint Senate Committee Hearings*, *supra* note 5, at 33-34 (testimony of Dr. Ostroff) (answering questions from Sen. Jon Kyl about the lack of full implementation of the CDC's biological agents regulations). Sen. Kyl noted that, as of March 1998, nearly 25% of the laboratories that should register with the CDC to have select agents were not registered due to a lack of CDC inspectors, and that none of the laboratories had been certified yet. *See id.* at 34. Dr. Ostroff responded that, in order to raise sufficient resources for the CDC to carry out the terms of the regulations, the CDC implemented a user fee, which has deterred some of the approximately 200 facilities required to register with the CDC from doing so. *See id.*

172. *See Joint Senate Committee Hearings*, *supra* note 5, at 34 (testimony of Dr. Ostroff).

173. *See House Bioterrorism Hearings*, *supra* note 2, at 52 (statement of Dr. Atlas) (urging Congress to provide the CDC with additional resources if the legislature expands existing regulations because CDC has not yet fully implemented the current regulations due to the present lack of sufficient resources).

174. *See* Anderson, *supra* note 1, at 14 (commenting that although the 1996 Act established tighter controls over the transfer of biological agents, the CDC has not fully implemented the regulations which would prevent terrorists from procuring lethal agents); *see also Joint Senate Committee Hearings*, *supra* note 5, at 38 (testimony of Dr. Carus) (noting that, once implemented, the regulations may not prevent a determined perpetrator from obtaining dangerous agents from a source other than those which are regulated).

175. *See* Sen. Jon Kyl, Opening Statement submitted to the Subcomm. on Tech., Terrorism, and Gov't Info. of the Senate Comm. on the Judiciary, 105th Cong., 2d Sess., Mar. 4, 1998, (visited Feb. 10, 2000) <http://www.senate.gov/~kyl/sbiowep.htm> ("For all practi-

though limiting access to dangerous agents,[176] the regulations only cover one means of obtaining these agents, which is through medical or research laboratories.[177] Individuals who are not transferors or shippers of these agents can therefore culture these agents in their home.[178] Moreover, regulations cover lethal agents only, leaving nonlethal agents that can harm people and cause widespread illness unregulated.[179] As a consequence, the regulations' restrictions would not deter a dedicated perpetrator from procuring the means with which to create a biological weapon.[180]

C. *Proposed Legislation: Finally Closing the Gaps that Enable Bioterrorism*

On February 19, 1998, enforcement authorities arrested Larry Wayne Harris again, this time in Las Vegas, Nevada.[181] Harris possessed anthrax bacteria, which turned out to be a harmless animal vaccine.[182] Law en-

---

cal purposes, we today appear to be in the same position as we were in 1995 with regard to the lack of controls over transfers of dangerous biological agents within the United States"). The published text of the committee hearing does not contain this language. *See Joint Senate Committee Hearings*, *supra* note 5, at 4-5.

176. *See Joint Senate Committee Hearings, supra* note 5, at 38 (statement of Dr. Ostroff) (responding to questions posed by Sen. Feinstein concerning his level of confidence in the regulations as a means of providing protection against bioterrorism, and noting that the regulations help raise barriers to, and thus limit the acquisition of, dangerous biological agents).

177. *See id.* (noting that obtaining dangerous biological agents legitimately is only one method of obtaining dangerous biological agents); *see also House Bioterrorism Hearings*, *supra* note 2, at 55 (statement of Dorothy B. Preslar, Washington Project Officer, Biological Weapons Verification Project) (urging Congress to require facilities that possess listed agents, rather than those that merely transfer or receive these agents, to register with the CDC, and arguing that the government should impose stricter controls on individuals who fall outside of the confines of registered facilities).

178. *See Joint Senate Committee Hearings, supra* note 5, at 37-38 (testimony of Dr. Ostroff). For example, a person could buy several chickens from a grocery store, isolate the Salmonella organism, and poison hundreds of people with this bacteria. *See id.*

179. *See House Bioterrorism Hearings*, *supra* note 2, at 15 (statement of Mr. Reynolds) (noting that CDC regulations do not cover potentially injurious nonlethal agents).

180. *See Joint Senate Committee Hearings*, *supra* note 5, at 38 (testimony of Dr. Carus) (stating that we should not mislead ourselves by believing that the regulations will prevent bioterrorists from acquiring dangerous biological substances).

181. *See The World Today* (CNN television broadcast, Feb. 19, 1998) (transcript No. 98021901V23), *available in* LEXIS, News Transcripts (interviewing Mr. Harris, noting his recent arrest in Las Vegas, and discussing his history of involvement with deadly agents).

182. *See Joint Senate Committee Hearings*, *supra* note 5, at 1-3 (statement of Sen. Shelby) (noting that information revealed after the Las Vegas anthrax scare showed that the public's safety was never at risk); Roger K. Lowe, *Nation Lags in Protection from Biological Terrorism*, COLUMBUS DISPATCH, Mar. 8, 1998, at 3B (reporting that Mr. Harris boasted in Las Vegas that he possessed anthrax bacteria, but that the substance turned

forcement authorities responded to this threat more quickly than they did to threats concerning weapons of mass destruction a few years ago.[183] Evidentiary requirements, however, delayed positive identification of the strain for three days after authorities seized the agent from Mr. Harris.[184] This delay could have prevented victims from receiving necessary and timely medical treatment and would have caused unnecessary loss of life.[185] This interdiction demonstrated that the United States is not adequately prepared for a bioterrorist attack.[186] To correct this problem, Senator Diane Feinstein (D-CA) stated that Congress should enact legislation that would prohibit citizens from possessing biological agents in the first place.[187]

On April 22, 1998 and on February 4, 1999, Attorney General Janet Reno stated that the Department of Justice is developing a proposal to amend federal criminal statutes pertaining to bioterrorism.[188] The Attorney General stated that under current federal law, it is not a crime to merely possess a substance that could be used as a biological weapon unless a prosecuting attorney can prove that the possessor intended to

---

out to be anthrax vaccine).

183. *See Joint Senate Committee Hearings*, *supra* note 5, at 64-65 (testimony of Louis J. Freeh, Director, Federal Bureau of Investigation) (stating that the government responded more quickly and in a more efficient manner to the 1998 Las Vegas threat then they did to a similar threat in New York in 1995).

184. *See id.* at 32-33 (testimony of Col. David R. Franz, deputy commander, U.S. Army Medical Research and Material Command, Ft. Detrick, MD) (responding to questions from Sen. Kyl about the delayed response in identifying the biological agent from the Las Vegas incident). Col. Franz testified that it takes approximately 30 minutes to identify whether a substance is an infectious disease, but it takes several hours to identify whether the disease is merely a vaccine strain. *See id.* at 32. He also noted that it takes time to work through requirements imposed on laboratories; for example, researchers at the laboratories cannot leave fingerprints on the evidence. *See id.* at 32-33.

185. *See id.* at 32 (statement of Sen. Kyl).

186. *See id.* at 36 (statement of Sen. Feinstein) (expressing concern about the continued availability of dangerous agents under the CDC regulations); *id.* at 41 (statement of Sen. Richard H. Bryan (D-Nev.), noting that federal agencies still lack adequate resources and personnel to respond effectively to bioterrorism); *supra* note 175 and accompanying text.

187. *See Joint Senate Committee Hearings*, *supra* note 5, at 6-7 (statement of Sen. Feinstein).

188. *See id.* at 62 (testimony by Attorney General Janet Reno) (stating that one of the ways that the federal government intends to improve its ability to prevent and respond to bioterrorism is to amend federal criminal statutes that pertain to biological weapons); *Hearing Before the Subcomm. on Counter-terrorism Efforts: Commerce, Justice, and State, the Judiciary, and Related Agencies of Senate Appropriations Comm.*, 106th Cong. (Feb. 2, 1999) [hereinafter *Senate Appropriations Hearing Comm.*] (testimony of Attorney General Janet Reno) (stating that the federal government is reviewing the possibility of amending federal biological weapons criminal laws to clarify the definitions under these laws and to expand these laws to give the government better control over these agents).

use the substance as a weapon.[189] Criminal statutes that control biological agents, the Attorney General explained, must strike a careful balance between the public's need for safety and scientific researchers' need to freely access these agents.[190] She concluded that a clear public safety concern remains when those who do not have the requisite scientific training or have a demonstrated record of irresponsible conduct can legally acquire and retain such dangerous substances.[191]

On May 20, 1999, the Chief of the Terrorism and Violent Crime section of the Criminal Division at the United States Department of Justice, Jim Reynolds, stated that legislation that will criminalize the possession of dangerous biological agents is undergoing finishing touches and will be presented to Congress soon.[192] The model for this crime bill was the Chemical Weapons Implementation Act,[193] which prohibits possession of chemical weapons not justified by legitimate research.[194] The crime bill proposes to keep dangerous biological agents and toxins out of bioterrorists' hands by establishing five new criminal penalties that will prohibit hoaxes pertaining to biological weapons and prohibit unauthorized possession of dangerous biological agents.[195] This crime bill also reflects an attempt to respect legitimate scientific researchers' needs to have access to these dangerous agents.[196] The Department of Justice worked on the bill with representatives from the Department of Health and Human Services to draft a proposal that will intrude minimally on the legitimate research community.[197]

Current law does not address unjustified possession of agents that are not on the CDC's select list, but that are harmful and can cause wide-

---

189. *See Senate Appropriations Hearing Comm.*, *supra* note 188 (statement of Attorney General Janet Reno); *Joint Senate Committee Hearings*, *supra* note 5, at 62 (statement of Attorney General Janet Reno).

190. *See Joint Senate Committee Hearings*, *supra* note 5, at 62 (statement of Attorney General Janet Reno).

191. *See id.*

192. *See House Bioterrorism Hearings*, *supra* note 2, at 14-15 (statement of James Reynolds).

193. Pub. L. No. 105-277, div. I, title II, subtitle A, § 201, 112 Stat. 2681-866 (1998) (codified at 18 U.S.C. §§ 229-229F (Supp. IV 1998)).

194. *See House Bioterrorism Hearings*, *supra* note 2, at 14 (statement by James Reynolds); 18 U.S.C. §§ 229(a)-(b), 229F(7) (Supp. IV) (criminalizing possession and use of chemical weapons but exempting authorized individuals from this law; defining purposes not prohibited by this chapter as peaceful, protective, unrelated military, and law enforcement purposes).

195. *See House Bioterrorism Hearings*, *supra* note 2, at 15 (statement of James Reynolds).

196. *See id.*

197. *See id.*

spread and serious injury.[198] The current list includes only highly lethal agents.[199] The crime bill thus proposes to criminalize the possession of merely harmful agents in addition to listed and lethal biological agents in types or quantities that are not justified by peaceful purpose.[200] For example, neither Shigella nor Salmonella are listed on the CDC select agents list because laboratories handle these agents routinely and because these agents are not highly lethal.[201] Nevertheless, bioterrorists have used these agents to harm hundreds of people.[202]

Current law does not permit law enforcement officers to take action against laboratories that do not have adequate safeguards to prevent bioterrorists from accessing dangerous biological agents, or to take actions against home laboratories[203] that have grossly inadequate or nonexistent safeguards.[204] Hence, the crime bill creates criminal penalties for handling biological agents unsafely and with conscious disregard for the public's health and safety.[205] This provision only attaches criminal penalties when violators consciously disregard the public's health and safety,

198. *See id.* (stating that laws should manage unjustified possession of highly lethal and other harmful agents).

199. *See id. But see supra* note 163 (explaining the consequences of adding ubiquitous agents like Salmonella to the list of select agents).

200. *See House Bioterrorism Hearings*, *supra* note 2, at 15 (statement of James Reynolds); *see also id.* at 53 (testimony of Dr. Atlas) (stating that any laws that propose to manage dangerous pathogens should focus on penalizing possession in types or amounts that are not justified by legitimate research). These biological agents are invisible and undetectable without sophisticated procedures, hence there is a chance that an individual could be in techinical violation of regulations prohibiting possession without knowing it. *See id.* For example, a person could pick up a dead deer mouse that has Hantavirus or a jar of honey with Clostridium botulinum, not knowing that they are in possession of agents included on the select list. *See id.*

201. *See id.*

202. *See id.* at 15 (statement of James Reynolds). Recently, a hospital laboratory technician spread Shigella, a bacteria that causes dysentery, over donuts and made nineteen people sick. *See id.* In 1985, members of a cult in Oregon caused hundreds of people to become seriously ill by spreading Salmonella over restaurant salad bars. *See id.*

203. *See id.* In one instance in 1997, the FBI arrested Thomas Leahy for shooting his son in the face. *See id.* at 19 (statement of Robert M. Burnham). The FBI discovered that the basement in the Leahy home consisted of a makeshift laboratory. *See id.* Field tests on the laboratory indicated that Leahy produced the biological agent ricin. *See id.* As a result, the grand jury indicted Leahy for producing a biological weapon in violation of 18 U.S.C. § 175. *See id.* Further laboratory analysis determined that Leahy tried to cultivate botulism and mixed nicotine sulfate with a solvent, which was in a spray bottle. *See id.* Leahy eventually pleaded guilty for violating biological weapons laws. *See id.* At that time, federal prosecutors did not have sufficient evidence that Leahy intended to use the nitrate sulfate as a weapon. *See id.*

204. *See id.* at 15 (statement of James Reynolds).

205. *See id.*

but does not penalize negligent or accidental conduct.[206]

Existing federal regulations require entities that transfer and receive select agents to register with the CDC,[207] but do not reach individuals who cultivate listed agents without transferring or receiving these agents.[208] The crime bill addresses this concern by requiring those who possess select agents to report this to authorities so that authorities are aware of who has these agents.[209] This additional reporting requirement is still under consideration, however, because the CDC has expressed concerns that this type of a responsibility will conflict with the agency's public health mission.[210]

Current federal criminal laws do not effectively address hoaxes regarding biological agents.[211] Individuals can evade criminal liability by claiming that they never intended to use the reported agents as a weapon thereby stymieing prosecutors, who have the burden of proving intent under current laws.[212] The crime bill would deter hoaxes, which are an increasingly common occurrence,[213] by criminalizing the knowing perpetration of hoaxes pertaining to biological weapons.[214]

Finally, current federal laws do not restrict those who do not have scientific training or those who have a record of irresponsible conduct from possessing dangerous biological agents, even though these individuals do not have legitimate reasons for possessing such agents.[215] Criminalizing

---

206. *See id.* (stating that this complements current regulations that relate to safety and security).

207. *See* Additional Requirements for Facilities Transferring of Receiving Select Agents, 42 C.F.R. § 72.6(a)(1) (1998).

208. *See id.*; *Joint Senate Committee Hearings*, *supra* note 5, at 39 (statement of Sen. Bryan) (questioning Dr. Ostroff about the CDC regulations and confirming that individuals who do not transfer or receive listed agents do not have to apply for registration).

209. *See House Bioterrorism Hearings*, *supra* note 2, at 15-16 (statement of James Reynolds).

210. *See id.* at 16 (noting that the Department of Justice is aware of the CDC's concerns regarding the proposed reporting requirement).

211. *See id.*

212. *See id.* at 14, 16 (referring to the evidentiary requirements imposed by 18 U.S.C. § 175).

213. *See supra* notes 8-11 and accompaying text (discussing the increase in hoaxes pertaining to biological weapons).

214. *See House Bioterrorism Hearings*, *supra* note 2, at 16 (statement of James Reynolds) (stating that the crime bill includes a false reporting provision); *id.* at 20 (statement of Robert Burnham) (stating that legislation that criminalizes threats and false reports pertaining to biological agents is an imperative deterrent to the cost of responding to these false threats).

215. *See id.* at 15 (statement of James Reynolds) (referring to testimony of the Attorney General on April 22, 1998 addressing this concern).

the possession of listed agents by such individuals addresses this problem.[216]

II. CURRENT LAW PERTAINING TO BIOLOGICAL WEAPONS: FAILING TO DETER THE DETERMINED BIOTERRORIST

Existing laws and regulations manage biological agents that can be used to create biological weapons in three different ways.[217] These laws prohibit use of these weapons during war,[218] prohibit possession in amounts or types that cannot be justified by peaceful purposes or for use as weapons,[219] and regulate transferors and shippers of these highly lethal agents.[220] The United States, however, still remains susceptible to bioterrorism.[221]

A. Banning Use of Biological Weapons: Applying the 1925 Geneva Protocol to Bioterrorism

According to the Protocol's terms, this treaty only bans use of biological weapons during wartime situations involving parties to the Protocol.[222] The Protocol's ban may not be so limited, though, as this treaty may reflect customary international law.[223] Thus, the Protocol's rule that pro-

216. *See id.*

217. *See* discussion *supra* Part I (discussing international instruments and federal laws and regulations that manage dangerous biological agents).

218. *See* Protocol, *supra* note 18, 26 U.S.T. at 575, 94 L.N.T.S. at 69 (extending the prohibition against wartime use of prohibited weapons to use of bacteriological methods of war).

219. *See* 18 U.S.C. § 175 (Supp. III 1997) (prohibiting the knowing possession of biological agents, toxins, or delivery systems for use as a weapon); BWC, *supra* note 19, art. I, 26 U.S.T. at 587, 1015 U.N.T.S. at 166 (prohibiting possession in amounts or types that cannot be justified by peaceful or defensive purposes).

220. *See* Additional Requirements for Facilities Transferring or Receiving Select Agents, 42 C.F.R. § 72.6(a)(1) (1998) (requiring facilities that transfer or ship highly lethal agents to register with the CDC).

221. *See House Bioterrorism Hearings*, *supra* note 2, at 12 (testimony of James Reynolds) (noting that numerous law enforcement officials involved with counterterrorism, academics, and health care professionals agree that the potential use of a biological weapon is the most serious form of terrorist threat currently faced by the United States); *see id.* at 16 (testimony of Robert Burnham) (stating that existing laws pertaining to bioterrorism have significant gaps); *see* Anderson, *supra* note 1, at 1 (stating that America remains susceptible to bioterrorism).

222. *See* Protocol, *supra* note 18, 26 U.S.T at 575, 94 L.N.T.S. at 67, 69 (proclaiming that the signatories condemn use of the Protocol's prohibited agents in war and extending its prohibition to bacteriological methods of war).

223. *See supra* notes 53-54, 57-58 and accompanying text (classifying the Protocol's prohibition against use of biological weapons as customary international law, therefore applying at all times rather than merely during international strife, and applying to all na-

hibits use of these weapons may apply against nations that are not at war with the United States, but that attack the United States with biological weapons.[224] Furthermore, the Protocol's prohibition may apply against violating nations that are not parties to the Protocol.[225]

Even if the Protocol's rule against use of biological weapons applies to a bioterrorist attack against the United States, its prohibition will probably not prevent other nations from committing bioterrorist acts against the United States. At the International Court of Justice (ICJ), the United States would bear the burden of proving that another nation committed an act of bioterrorism on United States soil.[226] Yet, biological weapons attacks are difficult to detect,[227] and the Protocol does not give accusing nations the right to verify allegations of violations.[228] Thus, the United States would probably not be able to obtain this preferred documentary evidence.[229] Inevitably, the United States would have to rely on circumstantial evidence, which the ICJ would scrutinize closely.[230] Thus, a nation that commits bioterrorism against the United States would probably prevail against such allegations at the ICJ. Even if the United States manages to prevail against a violating nation at the ICJ, this nation may not comply with the ICJ's resulting judgment.[231] Furthermore, the U.N. Security Council will probably not enforce the ICJ's judgment, because it has never done so before.[232]

The United States cannot protect its citizens from bioterrorist attacks by relying on international law remedies or expecting that other nations will view biological weapons as morally abhorrent.[233] This is because other nations have not always supported the United States' use of sanc-

---

tions rather than only to parties to the Protocol).

224. *See id.*

225. *See id.*

226. *See supra* note 63 and accompanying text (noting that nations that allege that other nations violated international obligations bear the burden of proving these violations before the ICJ).

227. *See* Anderson, *supra* note 1, at 6, 8 (discussing the difficulties of detecting biological weapon attacks).

228. *See* Protocol, *supra* note 18, 26 U.S.T. at 575, 94 L.N.T.S. at 67, 69 (prohibiting use of biological weapons, but not providing enforcement or verification measures).

229. *See supra* text accompanying note 64 (noting that the ICJ prefers documentory evidence).

230. *See id.*

231. *See supra* text accompanying note 66 (noting that, historically, some nations have not complied with ICJ judgments).

232. *See id.* (stating that the U.N. has never enforced ICJ judgments).

233. *See supra* text accompanying notes 69-70 (discussing the unreliability of use of sanctions, force, or overly relying on other nations to view biological weapons with abhorrence).

tions or force in response to violations of international obligations.[234] Unlike the United States, not all nations necessarily view biological weapons with repugnance.[235] Thus, the United States cannot rely on the Protocol's rule against use of biological weapons to protect its citizens from bioterrorism.

B. Prohibiting Possession in Types or Quantities Unjustified by Peaceful Purposes: The Biological Weapons Convention and 18 U.S.C. §§ 175, 2332c

1. The Biological Weapons Convention

The BWC prohibits nations from possessing biological weapons and from transferring biological weapons or biological weapons expertise to other nations or individuals.[236] Nevertheless, the BWC permits nations to possess dangerous biological agents for peaceful or defensive research.[237] Unlike the Protocol, the BWC includes provisions that allow nations to enforce its obligations.[238] Like the Protocol, however, the BWC does not effectively prevent bioterrorism on United States soil. This is because the BWC does not support its enforcement articles with provisions allowing other nations to verify such violations.[239] Furthermore, the BWC's exception for defense or peaceful research, valid or not,[240] creates a loophole that rogue nations can manipulate to create biological weapons.[241] Even if these nations do not intend to use such weapons, increasing the number of biological weapons in the world increases the possibility that the United States will face a bioterrorist attack.[242]

---

234. *See supra* text accompanying note 69.

235. *See* Anderson, *supra* note 1, at 9 (stating that potential United States adversaries may not view biological weapons with the same abhorrence as Americans).

236. *See* BWC, *supra* note 19, 26 U.S.T. at 587, 1015 U.N.T.S. at 166, 167 (stating, in article I, that parties to the BWC agree not to acquire or retain the types or amounts of biological agents or toxins that are not justified for peaceful purposes or biological weapons, equipment or means of delivery, and stating, in article III, that parties to the BWC agree not to transfer these agents or weapons to any recipient).

237. *See id.* 26 U.S.T. at 587, 1015 U.N.T.S. at 166 (art. I).

238. *See id.* 26 U.S.T. at 588-89, 1015 U.N.T.S. at 167 (art. V-VII).

239. *See* FORSBERG ET AL., *supra* note 21.

240. *See supra* text accompanying notes 92-99 (discussing criticisms and defenses of the exception/loophole).

241. *See supra* text accompanying notes 92-95 (noting problems with the loophole in the BWC that allows for peaceful research).

242. *See supra* text accompanying note 5 (stating that the likelihood of bioterrorism rises as the number of nations with biological weapons programs rises).

2. Federal Criminal Laws

The Biological Weapons Anti-Terrorism Act of 1989 created federal criminal laws prohibiting biological weapons and the 1996 Antiterrorism and Effective Death Penalty Act strengthened these laws.[243] These laws implement the United States' obligations to the BWC by creating criminal penalties for violating the treaty's prohibition against possession of biological agents in types or quantities not justified by legitimate research.[244] These laws now extend to possession of genetically altered biological agents and criminalize attempts, threats, or conspiracies to use these weapons.[245] Furthermore, federal criminal laws give the federal government authority to seize biological agents from individuals who create or transfer biological weapons and from individuals who threaten to violate biological weapons laws.[246]

Like the BWC, this type of prohibition does not deter acts of bioterrorism in the United States effectively because there are too many gaps in these laws that permit the determined bioterrorist to commit such acts legally.[247] These laws do not criminalize false reports pertaining to biological weapons attacks.[248] Nor do federal criminal laws prohibit individuals from possessing dangerous pathogens or toxins, even though such individuals may have criminal backgrounds or records of irresponsible conduct.[249] These laws do not penalize individuals who handle these dangerous agents unsafely and with conscious disregard for the public's health and safety.[250] This particular gap prevents law enforcement officials from responding to laboratories and basement operations that do

243. *See* discussion *supra* Parts I.B.1, I.B.2.a-b (discussing the changes that the 1989 and 1996 Acts made to federal criminal laws pertaining to biological weapons).

244. *See* 18 U.S.C. § 175 note (Supp. III 1997) (stating that the law implements international obligations prohibiting possession of biological weapons unjustified by legitimate research).

245. *See id.* §§ 175, 2332a (prohibiting possession of biological weapons and weapons of mass destruction, respectively, and including genetically-altered agents).

246. *See id.* § 177(a).

247. *See House Bioterrorism Hearings*, *supra* note 2, at 14-16 (statement of James Reynolds) (noting the deficiencies of current laws with respect to preventing bioterrorism).

248. *See id.* at 16.

249. *See* 18 U.S.C. § 175 (prohibiting only possession is not justified by legitimate research); *Joint Senate Committee Hearings*, *supra* note 5, at 62 (statement of Attorney General Janet Reno).

250. *See House Bioterrorism Hearings*, *supra* note 2, at 15 (statement of James Reynolds); *Joint Senate Committee Hearings*, *supra* note 5, at 62 (statement of Attorney General Janet Reno).

not have adequate safeguards to prevent bioterrorist access to agents.[251]

C. Regulating Facilities That Transfer and Ship Highly Lethal Substances: CDC Regulations

The 1996 Act required the Secretary of Health and Human Services to create regulations requiring transferors and shippers to register with the CDC, keep track of these agents, and comply with disposal and storage requirements.[252] Aside from the fact that the CDC has not yet fully implemented these regulations,[253] they fall short of protecting the United States from bioterrorism[254] because individuals who do not transfer or ship dangerous agents do not have to comply with them.[255] These regulations do not regulate individuals with home laboratories[256] and thus do not protect the United States from a bioterrorist attack any more than it was protected before the 1996 Act.[257]

III. PROVIDING THE PROPER BALANCE FOR PUBLIC SAFETY WHILE PRESERVING THE RIGHT TO CONDUCT PEACEFUL RESEARCH

Current laws pertaining to the management of dangerous pathogens and toxins do not effectively prevent bioterrorism on United States soil.[258] This is because these laws require prosecutors to show a nexus between possession of biological agents and an attempt to use these agents as weapons.[259] Furthermore, relevant regulations solely govern transfer-

---

251. *See House Bioterrorism Hearings*, *supra* note 2, at 15 (statement of James Reynolds).

252. *See* Antiterrorism and Effective Death Penalty Act of 1996, Pub. L. No. 104-132, § 511 (d)-(f), 110 Stat. 1214, 1284-85.

253. *See supra* notes 171-73 and accompanying text (discussing incomplete implementation of the regulations).

254. *See House Bioterrorism Hearings*, *supra* note 2, at 14-15 (statement of James Reynolds) (listing problems with current regulations pertaining to the management of biological agents).

255. *See* Additional Requirements for Facilities Transferring or Receiving Select Agents, 42 C.F.R. § 72.6(a)(1) (1998) (requiring only facilities that transfer and ship select agents to register with the Secretary of Health and Human Services).

256. *See House Bioterrorism Hearings*, *supra* note 2, at 15 (statement of James Reynolds) (referring to Thomas Leahy).

257. *See* Anderson, *supra* note 1, at 14 (quoting Sen. Kyl).

258. *See House Bioterrorism Hearings*, *supra* note 2, at 14-15 (statement of James Reynolds) (noting that existing laws contain gaps that increase the likelihood of a bioterrorist attack in the United States).

259. *See* 18 U.S.C. § 175 (Supp. III 1997) (prohibiting possession of biological agents for use as a weapon); *Joint Senate Committee Hearings*, *supra* note 5, at 62 (statement of Attorney General Janet Reno).

ors and shippers of these agents.[260] Legislation that prohibits individuals who are not conducting legitimate research from possessing dangerous agents and legislation that criminalizes false reports pertaining to biological weapons, however, would deter bioterrorism.[261]

A. Criminalizing Individual Possession Protects the Public from Bioterrorism

Measures that deter or prevent bioterrorism are the most effective ways to combat bioterrorism.[262] One method of deterring or preventing bioterrorism is to gain better control over who possesses the types of substances that could be used to create these weapons.[263] Thus, federal criminal laws should simply prohibit individuals from possessing these agents absent authority from the CDC, rather than requiring a prosecutor to show that the individual intended to use this agent to harm others.[264]

Another way to deter bioterrorism is to give the federal government better control over the handling of these agents.[265] Unregulated agents in laboratories that do not transfer or receive listed agents could fall into the hands of a bioterrorist, and unsafe handling of these agents could expose populations to disease.[266] Thus, federal laws should criminalize unsafe handling of these agents and require individuals or facilities that possess these agents to report this possession to the appropriate authori-

---

260. *See* 42 C.F.R. § 72.6(a)(1) (1998) (providing that facilities must register with the Secretary of Health and Human Services prior to shipping or receiving select agents).

261. *See House Bioterrorism Hearings*, *supra* note 2, at 14 (statement of James Reynolds) (noting that the best way to prevent bioterrorism is to improve existing federal criminal statutes by criminalizing individual possession of biological agents); *Joint Senate Committee Hearings*, *supra* note 5, at 62 (statement of Attorney General Janet Reno) (stating that the federal government has improved its ability to address bioterrorism since 1995, but that this ability could be improved further by criminalizing individual possession of dangerous substances).

262. *See House Bioterrorim Hearings*, supra note 2, at 14 (statement of James Reynolds).

263. *See id.* at 15-16; *see also id.* at 53 (testimony of Dorothy Preslar) (suggesting ways to prevent bioterrorism, one of which is to strictly control individual possession of dangerous substances); *id.* at 58-59 (statement of Nancy Connell) (suggesting ways to improve current regulations preventing bioterrorism, and stating that individuals should not have access to these substances).

264. *See id.* at 58-59.

265. *See id.* at 15 (statement of James Reynolds) (stating that one way to give the government more control after the handling of biological agents is to impose criminal penalties on individuals or laboratories that handle agents unsafely or do not have sufficient safeguards to protect the United States against bioterrorism).

266. *See id.*

ties.[267]

Another way to prevent bioterrorism in the United States is to close the gap in current federal criminal laws that allow bioterrorists to perpetrate hoaxes pertaining to biological agents without repercussions.[268] Responding to false reports requires vast sums of money and resources, and potentially desensitizes populations to actual attacks.[269] Thus, federal laws should criminalize threats regarding biological agents.[270]

B. Laws Criminalizing Individual Possession in Types or Amounts Unjustified by Legitimate Research Preserves Legitimate Researchers' Ability to Use These Agents

Federal laws that prohibit unauthorized individual possession of dangerous substances of the types or quantities unjustified by legitimate research would not prevent legitimate scientists and researchers from accessing the types of substances they need to improve health care or defenses against bioterrorism.[271] The Secretary of Health and Human Services would register and authorize legitimate laboratories.[272] Furthermore, federal criminal laws would solely criminalize possession of agents in the types or amounts that are not justified by legitimate research.[273]

IV. CONCLUSION

Current laws and regulations governing biological weapons are insufficient to deter bioterrorists from making false reports about biological agents, from buying dangerous pathogens or toxins, and then creating biological weapons. Granted, there are valid reasons for having such agents, and researchers and those in the medical arena who legitimately need these agents should not fear prosecution for such possession. However, the government should not allow individuals who are not qualified to have dangerous biological agents to possess them. Exposure to these agents, purposefully or accidentally, can kill or incapacitate huge popula-

---

267. *See id.*

268. *See id.* at 20 (statement of Robert M. Burnham) (asserting an imperative need for legislation prohibiting false reports regarding biological agents to deter the large amount of resources and money being spent by the government to respond to these hoaxes).

269. *See supra* notes 8-11 and accompanying text (discussing ramifications of the increasing number of hoaxes pertaining to biological agents).

270. *See id.*

271. *See House Bioterrorism Hearings*, *supra* note 2, at 15-16 (statement of James Reynolds).

272. *See id.* at 14.

273. *See id.* at 15.

tions. Furthermore, those who create hoaxes about biological weapons, thereby causing cities to spend vast sums of money to respond, should face criminal prosecution. Congress should criminalize the possession of harmful and lethal pathogens and toxins that could be used as biological weapons in amounts not justified by legitimate purposes and should criminalize hoax perpetration regarding these agents.

A PRECARIOUS "HOT ZONE"— THE PRESIDENT'S PLAN TO COMBAT BIOTERRORISM

VICTORIA V. SUTTON[1]

I. Introduction

The President, since taking office, has "made the fight against terrorism a top national security objective."[2] President Clinton announced on 22 May 1998 that he "is determined that in the coming century, we will be capable of deterring and preventing such terrorist attacks."[3] The President is also convinced that we must also have the ability to limit the damage and manage the consequences should such an attack occur."[4] With this most recent announcement, the President introduced Presidential Decision Directive 62 (PDD 62), which is to "create a new and more systematic approach to fighting the terrorist threat of the next century"[5] and to clarify the roles of agencies and departments to ensure a coordinated approach to planning for such terrorist induced emergencies. However, as yet no formal procedure exists for coordinating federal, state, and local forces should we have a bioterrorism event, or an effective plan for participation of the nation's military forces in response to such an event.

While nuclear, chemical, and biological weaponry all fall within the general classification of WMD; until very recently, nuclear weaponry has dominated planning and discussion. Today, however, it is increasingly recognized that chemical and particularly biological weapons represent much more credible threats in the hands of terrorists than do nuclear ones. This follows for many reasons, for example, ease of maintaining secrecy

---

1. Dr. Sutton is Associate Professor, Texas Tech University School of Law and Adjunct Professor in the Institute of Environmental and Human Health. She received her J.D. degree from American University, Washington College of Law *magna cum laude*, and her Ph.D. degree in Environmental Sciences from The University of Texas at Dallas. The author wishes to acknowledge the comments that were considered in this article from Dr. D. Allan Bromley, former Science Advisor to President Bush; Professor Jamin Raskin, American University; and Dr. Frank Young, member of the Threat Reduction Advisory Committee.

2. The White House, Office of the Press Secretary, Fact Sheet: Combating Terrorism: Presidential Decision Directive 626, Annapolis, Md. (May 22, 1998) [hereinafter Combating Terrorism].

3. *Id.*

4. *Id.*

5. *Id.*

in preparation of the weapons, ease of production and delivery of the weapons, ease of obtaining wide dispersal of the weapons—particularly in the case of biological weapons. It is also true that modern genetic engineering carries with it the specter of modification of familiar weapons species such as anthrax and smallpox into forms against which all our vaccines and other defenses would be worthless.

This current planning is directed against all weapons of mass destruction (WMD), which include technological as well as specifically chemical and biological activities. This article will focus on a plan for biological and chemical weapons that should be distinguished from the approach to a plan for all other technological threats. While the United States skills in planning to combat nuclear weapons and other technological weapons have been practiced throughout the cold war, our skills in beginning to comprehend and meet the threats of chemical and biological warfare on a domestic level have only recently begun to be developed fully.

Although PDD 62 is the most recent formal action, the planning for responses to domestic bioterrorism is shaped by prior presidential directives, statutes, and U.S. constitutional guidance. The planning for the prevention, detection, and actual encounters with bioterrorism now has actually begun, but as separate departmental missions under the auspices of individual agencies and departments. These initial planning and funding activities have been examined through a number of Government Account Office (GAO) investigatory reports at the request of Congress, criticizing the lack of coordination. The implementation of any emergency response capability, fortunately, has not been tested on a major scale as yet, and this article addresses the legal status of the coordination of federal agencies, the military, as well as state and local governments under the constraints of statutes, regulations, case law and the U.S. Constitution.

Richard Preston, a science thriller novelist, produced a response scenario to a bioterrorism event in his 1997 book, *The Cobra Event*.[6] *The New York Times* reported that "Mr. Clinton was so alarmed by . . . *The Cobra Event* . . . that he instructed intelligence experts to evaluate its credibility."[7] More alarming perhaps even than its suggested biological possibility, is the lack of statutory clarity that would be essential for effective implementing of a strategy for the United States in terms of preparedness and emergency responsiveness. This article examines the present status of fed-

6. RICHARD PRESTON, THE COBRA EVENT (1997).

7. *See* Interview by *New York Times* with President Bill Clinton (Jan. 21, 1999).

eral, state, and local preparedness and proposes such changes to statutes and federal regulations and to the implementation of currently applicable statutes to enable our federal, state, and local resources to be effectively used in research, preparedness as well as in emergency responsiveness.

II. Who Is In Charge?

The President's strategy has been to combine threats of all WMD into a single framework for preparation and planned response.[8] The designation of a lead agency or department for coordination appears to fall within the responsibility of the newly created Office of the National Coordinator for Security Infrastructure Protection and Counter-Terrorism, working "within the National Security Council and report[ing] to the Assistant to the President for National Security Affairs."[9] This office is to give "advice on budgets . . . lead in the development of guidelines that might be needed for crisis management, . . . oversee the broad variety of relevant policies and programs included in such areas as counter-terrorism, [and oversee the] protection of critical infrastructure and preparedness and consequence management for [response to] [WMD]" under PDD 62.[10]

The separation of WMD between technological weapons on the one hand and chemical and biological weapons on the other is suggested in the introduction to this article. Moreover, a separation of leadership among preparedness, research, funding, and planning activities and the emergency response activities, matched with respective missions of the departments and agencies would provide the most effective use of our resources. Perhaps a lesson from the Cherokee tribal custom of designating a wartime chief and a peacetime chief, where, "war was decided upon, its conduct was turned over to the town war organization,"[11] should be considered in structuring the leadership for these two activities. That is, preparedness and research are very different activities and require very different skills as compared to the activities and skills of emergency response. Whether the proposed separation is a workable plan is examined in the following sections.

8. *See* Presidential Decision Directive 62 (May 1998).

9. Combating Terrorism, *supra* note 2.

10. *Id.*

11. V. Richard Persico, Jr., *Early Nineteenth-Century Cherokee Political Organization*, *in* THE CHEROKEE INDIAN NATION (Duane H. King ed., 1979).

A. Preparedness, Research, Funding and Planning—Who is in Charge?

Recent GAO testimony before Congress describes the scope of combating foreign-origin as well as domestic terrorism and makes recommendations for crosscutting and coordination management,[12] which repeats many of the same criticisms included in a GAO report issued just over a year earlier.[13]

The second report recommends that the Office of Management and Budget (OMB) conduct a crosscutting review, identify priorities and gaps and identify funding. However, the scope of the responsibility requires the staffer in OMB charged with this duty, to fully understand the scientific merit of programs spanning approximately twenty-two departments and agencies, as well as the legal and interagency constraints. In addition, this OMB staffer must compose a line-item budget for each agency identifying those items which fit into the comprehensive, government-wide program, which will probably be reviewed by dozens of congressional committees and subcommittees that claim departmental jurisdiction—not program jurisdiction.

Before the line-item, crosscutting coordination can be accomplished, as envisioned by the GAO, Congress must also agree to a joint appropriations hearing, with each department's and agency's appropriations committee coming together to receive a joint presentation of the coordinated budget.

This is not an unprecedented achievement. In an historical joint meeting of congressional committees, the Mathematics and Science Education Initiative of the Bush Administration was presented to two congressional committees as a line-item program crosscutting twelve departments' budgets in a comprehensive, coordinated program, which identified priorities and avoided gaps and overlaps in funding and programming.[14] This type of joint hearing would ensure that duplication of terrorism research and

12. *Testimony of Henry L. Hinton, Jr., Assistant Comptroller General, National Security and International Affairs Division, before the Subcomm. on Nat'l Security, Veterans Affairs, and Int'l Relations, Committee on Government Reform,* U.S. House of Representatives, GAO/T-NSIAD/GGD-99-107 (March 11, 1999) [hereinafter Testimony of Henry L. Hinton, Jr.].

13. U.S. GENERAL ACCOUNTING OFFICE, REPORT TO CONGRESSIONAL REQUESTERS, COMBATING TERRORISM: SPENDING ON GOVERNMENT WIDE PROGRAMS REQUIRES BETTER MANAGEMENT AND COORDINATION, GAO/NSIAD-98-39 (Dec. 1997).

14. D. ALLAN BROMLEY, THE PRESIDENT'S SCIENTISTS 84 (1994).

development programs would not occur as they did in one instance identified by the State Department where one congressional committee established a program and approved funds for that program while an identical program already existed and was funded through another congressional committee.[15]

1. Federal Coordination and Leadership

The design of a plan to confront the threats of bioterrorism, with a logical division of leadership between the planning and the emergency response responsibilities could follow previous statutory designs having demonstrated efficacy. Current statutory mechanisms are currently in place that could provide a framework for the recommendations made by the GAO.

The GAO recommendation that these responsibilities be assigned to the OMB represents an overwhelming range of duties. The performance of such crosscutting, coordinated functions was, in fact, performed in a previous Administration by a well-coordinated assemblage of federal employees and appointees, meeting once a month over an annual planning period enabled by the Federal Coordinating Council for Science, Engineering and Technology (FCCSET) statute.[16] During the period from 1989 to 1992, the implementation of this statute required three Ph.D.-level staff from the Office of Science and Technology Policy, one staff member from the OMB, and two levels of coordination among staff and senior policy appointees from twelve or more agencies and departments involved in each of the crosscutting programs.[17]

The GAO has identified twenty-two departments and agencies that should be involved in the crosscutting, coordinated plan to combat terrorism.[18] The use of the statutory FCCSET mechanism fluctuates with the priorities of the Director of the Office of Science and Technology Policy. During the GAO reporting period, the FCCSET mechanism had fallen out of use, otherwise GAO might have identified it as a potential mechanism to implement their recommendations. Such initiatives as biotechnology, advanced computing, global climate change, and math and science educa-

15. GAO Report, GAO/NSIAD-98-39, app. III (Dec. 1997).
16. 42 U.S.C.S. § 6651 (LEXIS 2000).
17. Office of Science and Technology Policy, FCCSET Handbook (March 1991).
18. U.S. General Accounting Office, GAO/NSIAD-98-39, app. I (Dec. 1997).

tion were each coordinated in a crosscutting program such as this between 1989 and 1992. Bioterrorism certainly meets the criteria under the statute and could be identified for this congressionally mandated research and planning mechanism to accomplish the recommendations made by GAO.

With obviously no alternatives, and a vital need to match resources with programmatic goals, the GAO was left to suggest that OMB itself carry out the entire crosscutting, coordination function. On the basis of prior experience with crosscutting budgets, it is apparent that this is an impossible task for OMB acting alone. Without scientific expertise across all agencies working carefully with OMB to prepare a comprehensive research plan matched with specific funding on a line item basis from each participating department or agency, no government-wide plan can be said to be truly crosscutting or coordinated. Such programs in the past were highlighted in the federal budget as separately identified and funded Presidential Initiatives, distinguished by the crosscutting, coordinated line-item approach.[19]

2. *Intergovernmental Planning and Coordination*

The threat of domestic terrorism demands an intergovernmental coordination system as well as a coordinated federal intra-governmental process. This issue was also addressed by the GAO report in its acknowledgment that the Attorney General was in the process of establishing a National Domestic Preparedness Office within the Federal Bureau of Investigation "to reduce state and local confusion over the many federal training and equipment programs necessary to prepare for terrorist incidents involving weapons of mass destruction."[20] This addresses the question of the availability of training resources for state and local governments, but fails to address the more comprehensive issue of ensuring that each state and local government is linked to a process which addresses the legal and public health responsibilities and expectations. The effort to create an accessible laundry list of training programs in the hope of preparing state and local governments is comparable to sending state and local governments out to a grocery store with a grocery list (but without money) to make a specific unique cuisine for which only the federal government has the recipe.

---

19. U.S. Office of Management and Budget, Federal Budget 1990, Federal Budget 1991, Federal Budget 1992.

20. *Testimony of Henry L. Hinton, Jr.*, *supra* note 12, at 2.

B. Emergency Response—Who's in Charge?

1. Federal Coordination and Leadership

Intragovernmental relationships are addressed by Presidential Decision Directive 39 (PDD 39), which identifies the Federal Bureau of Investigation (FBI) as the lead agency for domestic crisis response and the Federal Emergency Management Agency (FEMA) as the lead agency for consequence management. The National Security Council is charged with the lead for interagency terrorism policy coordination.[21] The most recently issued of the directives—PDD 62—designated an office of "National Coordinator for Security Infrastructure Protection and Counter-Terrorism"[22] charged with government-wide responsibility for the broad GAO mandate for accountability, as discussed above. The FBI or FEMA, under the Economy Act of 1932,[23] could then use the broad authority given by Congress to any executive department to place orders with the military (or any other department) for materials, supplies, equipment, work or—from the military—passive services (those not statutorily prohibited).[24]

While the mission of the FBI is reflected in its leadership role in the investigation of terrorism, the expertise required for epidemiological investigations is much more strongly centered in the mission of the Public Health Service. The Centers for Disease Control (CDC) and the U.S. Army Medical Research Institute of Infectious Diseases (USAMRIID) are the world's leading centers for forensic analysis and have been recommended for leadership roles in bioterrorism response.[25] While apprehension of the bioterrorist is clearly within the mission of the FBI,[26] the Public Health Service, the CDC, and the USAMRIID, are more adequately staffed to investigate biological contamination and to provide epidemiological identification of the process and agent being used in any particular bioterrorism event.

21. Presidential Decision Directive 39 (June 1995).
22. Presidential Decision Directive 62 (May 1998).
23. 31 U.S.C.S. § 686 (LEXIS 2000).
24. U.S. v. Jaramillo, 380 F. Supp. 1375, 1379 (D. Neb. 1974).
25. RICHARD A. FALKENRATH ET AL., AMERICAN'S ACHILLES' HEEL—NUCLEAR, BIOLOGICAL, AND CHEMICAL TERRORISM AND COVERT ATTACK 298 (1998).
26. *See* Federal Bureau of Investigations, *FBI Mission Statement* (visited Mar. 22, 2000) <http://www.fbi.gov/contact/fo/kc/mission.htm>.

The shortcomings of the FBI in the context of its leadership of domestic bioterrorism, preparedness, and response have been identified to include its lack of expertise in WMD and its limited experience in counter-intelligence within governmental agencies, and the lack of skills in the investigation and apprehension of extra-governmental counterintelligence agents required in bioterrorism events.[27] The experience in building capacity in interdepartmental bureaucracies in substantive matters is also clearly lacking in the FBI's portfolio of skills, which would make the agency a poor candidate for the leadership role in planning and executing response and preparedness for domestic bioterrorism.[28]

So, too, FEMA, as the lead agency for response to a bioterrorism event, has skill primarily in planning for natural disaster responses. These typically require immediate infrastructure compensation to communities for such natural disasters as earthquakes, flooding, and volcanic eruption and do not address the kinds of responses necessary for the leadership role for bioterrorism response and preparedness.[29]

2. Intergovernmental Coordination and Leadership—Sovereignty Analysis

The authority for the federal government to intervene in state matters such as public health presents an issue of state sovereignty, and must be considered in any intergovernmental plan. Indian reservations, both those held in trust by the Department of Interior or held in fee simple by the tribes, do not have the same sovereignty issues as do states; because although they are separate governments, these reservations apply federal law in areas where states enjoy exclusive jurisdiction. The importance of Indian tribal governments and Indian reservations are critical, however, in

---

26. (continued)

> The mission of the FBI is to uphold the law through the investigation of violations of federal criminal law; to protect the United States from for eign intelligence and terrorist activities; to provide leadership and law enforcement assistance to federal, state, local, and international agencies; and to perform these responsibilities in a manner that is responsive to the Constitution of the United States.

Id.

27. FALKENRATH ET AL., *supra* note 25, at 272-73.
28. *Id.* at 272-73.
29. *Id.* at 273.

part because there are at least nine reservations that have boundaries on international borders or international waters.[30] This requires a federal and tribal relationship focusing on national security against the entry of bioterroristic threats into the U.S. Border-crossing agreements. While the federal government has made agreements with these tribes, special focus is required on the emerging issues of possible bioterrorism.

3. Constitutional Tenth Amendment State Sovereignty

The readiness of state and local governments to respond to domestic terrorism was assessed by RAND Corporation in 1995 through a grant from the U.S. Department of Justice, National Institute of Justice.[31] Although the sponsoring department's mission is the application of law, this effort failed to address or even to identify legal issues for state and local governments as one of import in analyzing readiness.[32]

The first step in the response protocol to bioterrorism must necessarily take place at the state and local levels. The CDC, in collaboration with the Council of State and Territorial Epidemiologists, have developed guidance for public health surveillance which–for the first time–established uniform criteria for state health departments in reporting diseases.[33] This provides for uniform identification of the occurrence of reportable diseases. Laws that mandate the reporting of specific diseases however are state laws which result in variation in multiple lists of varying reportable diseases. A list of nationally reportable diseases however has been identified in the CDC protocol applicable to all states.[34]

Because the myriad of state laws provide no uniformity for federal response, the effort to address public health through the federal level has been lead by associations of state professionals. This reporting protocol was developed in collaboration with the Council of State and Territorial

30. Telephone Interview with Ron Andrade, former-President, National Congress of American Indians (Nov. 30, 1999) (identifying the following international border reservations: Tohona O'Dum, Cocopah, Ft. Huoma, Blackfeet, Red Lake Chippewa, Portage, Sue St. Marie, St. Regis, and Maloceet).

31. KEVIN JACK RILEY ET AL., DOMESTIC TERRORISM—A NATIONAL ASSESSMENT OF STATE AND LOCAL PREPAREDNESS 1-4 (1995).

32. *Id.*

33. Centers for Disease Control, Case Definitions for Public Health Surveillance, MMWR 1997; 46 (No. RR-10): [p.57].

34. *Id.* at 1.

Epidemiologists (CSTE) and approved by a full vote of the CSTE membership. It was also endorsed by the Association of State and Territorial Public Health Laboratory Directors (ASTPHLD). From this, CDC in collaboration with the Council of State and Territorial Epidemiologists have developed a "policy" that requires state health departments nationwide to report cases of the selected diseases to CDC's National Notifiable Diseases Surveillance System (NNDSS).[35] Interestingly, a recommendation was proposed to develop an "NBC Response Center" to respond to nuclear, biological, and chemical attacks as a part of an interagency effort to combine the FBI, FEMA, Department of Defense, Department of Health and Human Services, the EPA, the U.S. Marine Corps, the Chemical and Biological Defense Command and the Department of Energy into a central group, modeled after the existing Counterterrorist Centers, another interagency effort led by the Central Intelligence Agency.[36] Although the NNDSS had been in existence for more than four years, at the time of the recommendation, it was never included in this analysis as a possible national reporting center. While the use of these agencies as the lead intelligence agencies avoids the immediate concern of public health and state sovereignty, it all but ignores the unique agency missions, training, and skills demanded in a public health epidemic crisis.

The responsibilities for developing the reporting protocol of the NNDSS have been set forth in federal regulations promulgated by the CDC, which address the interface between the state associations and the federal agencies.[37] This rather surprising reliance upon non-governmental support for systems to safeguard our nation against presumptively catastrophic biological risks has evolved because of Tenth Amendment[38] constitutional prohibitions against usurping states' authority in the area of public health.

4. Constitutional Non-Delegation of Authority or Ultra Vires Analysis

Further, the broad delegation of authority for rulemaking to these non-governmental organizations suggests that the non-delegation doc-

35. *Id.* at 1-2.

36. FALKENRATH ET AL., *supra* note 25, at 274-76.

37. 64 Fed. Reg. 17,674 (Apr. 12, 1999).

38. U.S. CONST. art. X.

39. The source of the non-delegation doctrine is found in the U.S. Constitution, Article I, § 1, which provides that "[a]ll legislative powers herein granted shall be vested in a

trine[39] may be quietly eroding under the pressure of urgent need for essential national components of our national security considered within a state sovereignty context. If, in fact, this is a delegation of federal legislative powers, what is the legislative source of those powers?

The more obscure *ultra vires* doctrine,[40] which does not permit an agency to go beyond the scope of its delegated authority, may be at the heart of this analysis. Indeed, absent a congressional mandate to carry out a federal public health response system to bioterrorism, the agency has no defined scope to exceed. In fact, the very activity of rulemaking to develop a national public health bioterrorism response system, something that Congress is itself prevented from doing, must be beyond the scope of authority for any agency—*ultra vires.*

5. Federal Laws Applicable to Nationwide Bioterrorism Preparedness and Response

Given these constitutional limitations on congressional and Executive authority to usurp states' sovereignty, the application of existing federal laws must necessarily be considered as a partial solution to the bioterrorism challenge.

Under the Posse Comitatus Act[41] the military cannot be used to enforce any laws against civilians. However, an exception to this use of the military is made where states make a request, or where there is no state request, to suppress any insurrection where it is "impracticable to enforce the laws of the U.S. . . . by the ordinary course of judicial proceedings."[42] The only clear exception (in the absence of insurrection) here is that a state must make a request prior to the use of military enforcement. In addition, to activate this latter exception, the President must issue an order activating the military for that specific exception. Failure to do so can leave in ques-

39. (continued) Congress of the Unites States," and in the Constitution, Article I, § 8 which provides that Congress has the power "[t]o make all laws which shall be necessary and proper for carrying into execution" the other powers in Article I. Therefore, Congress cannot delegate its legislative powers, but can delegate authority to promulgate rules to carry out those legislative powers.

40. 5 U.S.C.S. § 706(2)(C) (LEXIS 2000) (allowing judicial review to determine whether an agency has acted "in excess of statutory jurisdiction, authority, or limitations, or short of statutory right").

41. 18 U.S.C.S. § 1385 (LEXIS 2000).

42. 10 U.S.C.S. § 333 (LEXIS 2000).

tion the authority under which the military might be acting, as was the case in the Wounded Knee incident.[43] Under the Posse Comitatus Act, however, the military can be used for the provision of materials and supplies, and certain other passive activities.[44]

An innovative and clearly viable intergovernmental emergency preparedness statute exists in the area of environmental emergency preparedness. The Emergency Planning and Community Right-to-Know Act of 1986[45] provided for the coordination of local emergency planning committees (LEPCs) with both state and federal emergency planning authorities.[46] By 1989, most states had appointed LEPCs primarily based upon county delineations in compliance with this statute.[47]

> The LEPC has a statutorily prescribed membership which is "to include, at a minimum, representatives from each of the following groups or organizations: elected state and local officials; law enforcement; civil defense; firefighting; first aid; health; local environmental; hospital; and transportation personnel; broadcast and print media; community groups; and owners and operators of facilities subject to the requirements of this subchapter.[48]

The responsibilities of these LEPCs include the collection of release information from local toxic substance emitters, as well as the development of comprehensive emergency response plans.[49]

While there is no mandate for the federal government to avoid duplication of resources at the local level as the result of federal mandates, members of Congress are ultimately accountable for such overlaps.

43. United States v. Jaramillo, 380 F. Supp. 1375, 1379 (1974).

44. United States v. Red Feather, 392 F. Supp. 916 (DCSD 1975). This case sets forth a number of examples of passive activities under the Act to include, reconnaissance missions, but specifically includes advice from the military as participatory and non-passive.

45. 42 U.S.C.S. §§ 11001-11050 (LEXIS 2000).

46. *Id.* § 11001(b).

47. *See generally* Vickie V. Sutton, Perceptions of Local Emergency Planning Committee Members Responsibility for Risk Communication and a Proposed Model Risk Communication Program for Local Emergency Planning Committees Under SARA, Title III (1989) (unpublished Ph.D. dissertation, University of Texas at Dallas) (on file with author) (providing information on the formation of the LEPCs).

48. 42 U.S.C.S. § 11001(c).

49. *Id.* § 11003(a).

Amending the Emergency Planning and Community Right-to-Know Act to provide for the emergency planning for bioterrorism emergencies, using the LEPC resource, would accelerate the development of plans for bioterrorism response by at least one or two years.[50] While the LEPC plans are subject to review and approval by the National Response Team[51] under the National Contingency Plan of the Superfund statute;[52] the bioterrorism component should also be reviewable by the FBI, as well as FEMA under the current leadership designations. The Attorney General's establishment of a National Domestic Preparedness Office within the Federal Bureau of Investigation "to reduce state and local confusion over the many federal training and equipment programs to prepare for terrorist incidents involving weapons of mass destruction"[53] might also be used to review such emergency plans and to identify training needs.

The most important, recent legislation in this area which has been constructed to meet the threat of bioterrorism are the Defense Against Weapons of Mass Destruction Act of 1996[54] and the Combating Proliferation of Weapons of Mass Destruction Act of 1996[55] which finds that "the threat posed to the citizens of the United States by nuclear, radiological, biological and chemical weapons delivered by unconventional means is significant and growing."[56] On its face, the legislation attempts to approach the terrorist threat by combining biological with chemical and radiological—again, biological requiring significantly different personnel, skills and strategies than chemical and radiological threats.

The legislation also recognizes there are shortcomings in the coordination between federal, state, and local governments;[57] however, the legislation finds that the "[s]haring of the expertise and capabilities of the Department of Defense, which traditionally has provided assistance to federal, state, and local officials in neutralizing, dismantling, and disposing of explosive ordnance, as well as radiological, biological, and chemical mate-

50. The appointment of the LEPCs took more than one year, and an additional year to resolve a conflict with the state of Georgia concerning the delineation of planning districts. A similar delay could be anticipated for a bioterrorism planning network for state and local governments.

51. 42 U.S.C.S. § 11003(g).

52. *Id.* § 9605.

53. *Testimony of Henry L. Hinton, Jr.*, *supra* note 12, at 2.

54. 50 U.S.C.S. §§ 2301-2363 (LEXIS 2000) (as amended by the Defense Against Weapons of Mass Destruction Act of 1998).

55. *Id.* §§ 2351, 2366.

56. *Id.* § 2301(13).

57. *Id.* § 2301(19)-(26).

rials"[58] can be a vital contribution against bioterrorism. Although, the Congress may have an expectation that the Department of Defense is coordinating "traditionally" with state and local governments, there is no evidence of such a system or policy. Traditional coordination with states and local governments is more likely to be the result of very long and tedious negotiations, cost allocations, budgetary planning and eventual execution of a coordinated approach to, for example, the disposing of explosive ordnance at a locally closed military base. In fact, the largest appropriation authorized by this legislation for fiscal year 1997 was for $16.4 million to establish a training program for state and local responders, which is the list of courses discussed earlier in this article that fail to present any coordinated effort to link local and state governments with the federal government.

The most significant contribution of this legislation is the money to assist the Public Health Service in establishing Metro Medical Strike Teams in major U.S. cities; however the token $6.6 million appropriated for this effort does not signal serious congressional support for such a plan.[59] Again, there is a "grab-bag" of solutions, under-funded, nestled in the most significant of legislation passed to date on the bioterrorism threat.

6. The Cobra Event *as a Fictional Case Study*

Preston skillfully develops his story in *The Cobra Event* to describe the building of a team which he called the "Reachdeep team,"[60] guided by legal constraints to respond to the unknown bioterrorist. He correctly identified PDD 39 and National Security Directive 7 as the controlling authority[61] and described the FBI (and the head of its National Security Division)[62] convening a meeting and ultimately assembling the "Reachdeep team." A number of "high-level military officers" were included together with a representative from the Office of the Attorney General, Department of Justice.[63] Representatives with no team-leadership, but with supporting roles, were included from the U.S. Public Health Service and the Centers for Disease Control.[64]

---

58. *Id.* § 2301(25).
59. FALKENRATH ET AL., *supra* note 25, at 262.
60. PRESTON, *supra* note 6, at 349.
61. *Id.* at 175.
62. *Id.* at 174.
63. *Id.* at 176.
64. *Id.* at 175.

Intergovernmental coordination included the presence of the "Chief of the Emergency Management Office for the City of New York, representing the mayor,"[65] and dismissed any specific state presence, altogether. In this scenario, the mayor never appeared at any of the meetings and the city police service and firefighting service seemed to willingly take commands from the Reachdeep team without supervision, notification or participation by any local authority. State and local governments are unlikely to respond in this manner and will require a leadership role in any such event. State sovereignty requires constraints by the federal government in the areas of protecting the public health, which is after all a state issue. The passage of the first comprehensive food and drug bill languished for seventeen years in Congress primarily because of the constitutional position of many legislators that this was a matter to be legislated by state and local governments.[66] Federal jurisdiction for this statute and others[67] is the Commerce Clause of the U.S. Constitution and thus applies to interstate sales. But to regulate bioterrorism on the basis of interstate commerce would require that the pertinent biologics be sold in interstate commerce. With the further restriction of *United States v. Lopez*[68] requiring a "substantial effects" standard on commerce further doubt would be raised as to the reliability of a Commerce Clause basis for regulation of bioterrorism in state and local government—hardly making such legislation useful to deal with public health emergencies.

Whether such federal legislation to invoke federal jurisdiction in emergency preparedness and response activities comports with the Tenth Amendment of the U.S. Constitution also poses potential constitutional challenges to any such legislation. Congressional power to determine what should be regulated for states and local governments was articulated by the court in *Garcia v. San Antonio Metropolitan Transit Authority*[69] when the more restrictive test of "traditional governmental functions"[70] was abandoned as "unworkable."[71] However, dissenters find that the Court's reasoning, in the majority opinion, that federal political officials

65. *Id.* at 175.

66. PETER B. HUTT & RICHARD A. MERRILL, FOOD AND DRUG LAW 8 (1991). The Federal Food and Drugs Act of 1906 was enacted after legislation was first introduced in 1879.

67. The Biologics Act of 1902, 32 Stat. 728.

68. 514 U.S. 549 (1995).

69. 469 U.S. 528 (1985).

70. National League of Cities v. Usery, Secretary of Labor, 426 U.S. 833, 852 (1976).

71. *Id.* at 864.

should be "the sole judges of the limits of their own power"[72] runs afoul of the principle that the federal judiciary is the sole determiner concerning the constitutionality of legislation.[73]

However, if the regulation of the intergovernmental process to combat bioterrorism is developed, leaving no state role, then the preemption doctrine could be applied to overcome challenges through state legislation. In one case where nuclear safety for the citizenry was argued by the state to be an issue of state interest, the court found it not to be fully preempted by federal law. But the court did not allow preemption of the federal regulations concerning safety, but on the basis of economic interests of the state, as those would not be preempted by the statute.[74] The Court seems here to find a way to protect the state's jurisdiction over the safety of its citizens, even if through means of an economic test.

The U.S. Supreme Court, in consideration of the Twenty-First Amendment[75] to the U.S. Constitution in *South Dakota v. Dole*, permitted the withholding of highway funds from a state that failed to make unlawful the possession or purchase of alcoholic beverages by a person less that twenty-one years of age.[76] The issue turned on whether this was a condition on a grant or a regulation. Finding a condition on a grant permitted the application of the Spending Power Clause[77] rather than a violation of the Twenty-First Amendment.

A statutory solution to maintaining telecommunications during a disaster, with state and local governments, illustrates another intergovernmental emergency situation; however, the field of telecommunications is traditionally a federal area, not a state and local government issue. The subsequent regulations to implement the statute[78] address an emergency plan for telecommunications in the event of a natural disaster or non-wartime disaster, providing for communications of federal officials with state and local officials. This regulation requires a management structure to include the "legal authority for telecommunications management" and "[a]

---

72. *Id.*

73. *Id.* (referring to *Marbury v. Madison*).

74. Pacific Gas & Elec. Co. v. State Energy Res. Cons. & Devel. Comm'n, 461 U.S. 190 (1983).

75. U.S. CONST. art. XXI.

76. South Dakota v. Dole, 483 U.S. 203 (1987).

77. U.S. CONST. art. XVI.

78. 42 U.S.C.S. § 6611 (LEXIS 2000).

control mechanism to manage the initiation, coordination and restoration of telecommunications services."[79]

Legislation should be structed such as that in *South Dakota v. Dole.* This would mean requiring state coordination with federal governments as a condition for the receipt of grant money related to the objective of preparing and responding to bioterrorism, preempting the field through the principles of *Pacific Gas*, and satisfying the dissenters in *Garcia* by making a narrow delineation of the control of state and local resources at the direction of federal officials, in time of emergency. This would seem to satisfy the constitutional requirements of such legislation.

III. The Current Federal Plan

Current planning, research, and preparedness in the area of potential bioterrorism are accurately reflected in the GAO reports that document an absence of strong leadership and a failure to achieve a crosscutting, coordinated program matched with identified resources in the federal budget. Responses to the GAO report by the various departments identified in the reports were not encouraging and indicated more that the departments and agencies did not fully understand the scope of the problem they were purporting to address.

The Office of Management and Budget identified meetings with representatives of the National Security Council, Departments of State, Defense, Justice and the Public Health Service, for implementing the National Defense Authorization Act,[80] in which they have been establishing methodologies to identify functions in the budgets, which is unfortunate, since there exists a Congressionally mandated methodology for such identification that would address a broader range of resources.[81] Further, the OMB states that it does not concur with the implementation of a formal crosscutting review process based upon its years of experience.[82] Interestingly, the author of this OMB response seems to be unaware of the existing

79. 47 C.F.R. § 202.0 (2000).
80. GAO Report, GAO/NSIAD-98-39, App. III (Dec. 1997).
81. 42 U.S.C.S. § 6651 (LEXIS 2000).
82. GAO Report, GAO/NSIAD-98-39, App. III (Dec. 1997).

statutory, formal, crosscutting review process, which was a major part of the OMB budget review process from 1989 to 1992.

The Department of Defense concurred with the GAO recommendations and expressed concern that the Economy Act prevented its assistance to state and local law enforcement agencies without reimbursement. Such reimbursement requires statutory authority, and since PDD 39 is not a statute, it cannot provide the authorization to waive reimbursement.[83] This is clearly an issue, which must be addressed in any legislation directed toward coordination of federal, state, and local governmental services.

The Department of State sought to establish that the terrorism function was thoroughly coordinated through their Interagency Coordinating Subgroup–although there was no "National Security Council or Office of Management and Budget active participation" in this subgroup.[84]

IV. Recommendations for a Bioterrorism Plan—Congressional Leadership is Essential

Congressional jurisdiction recently has been established by the Committee on Government Reform through its Subcommittee on National Security, Veterans Affairs, and International Relations in the U.S. House of Representatives, in its hearing on terrorism.[85] In the U.S. Senate, the Committee on Health, Education, Labor and Pensions Committee through the Subcommittee on Public Health and Safety, chaired by Senator Frist, have recently held hearings on bioterrorism.[86]

There is an immediate need to propose a statute, with a title such as the Bioterrorism Research, Preparedness and Responsiveness Program, constructed much on the model of the High Performance Computing and Communications Act[87] and the Global Climate Change Research Program[88] to provide for a coordinated, crosscutting effort to avoid gaps in vital areas, to avoid duplication of programs and research and to provide for optimum use of our resources through matching resources with programmatic needs. Further, and as an essential component of this program, a joint appropriations hearing must be agreed among the Congressional

83. *Id.*
84. *Id.*
85. 11 March 1999.
86. 25 March 1999.
87. 15 U.S.C.S. § 5511 (LEXIS 2000).
88. *Id.* §§ 2921-2961.

committees having jurisdiction for appropriations for the participating agencies and departments. While some of these committees may anticipate having small parts of the crosscutting budget, a Joint Appropriations Committee representing all appropriations for this program is essential. Otherwise, each line item identified for the program may be selected for elimination by the respective appropriations committees for those agencies with no regard to the effect upon the comprehensive program placed at risk by these eliminations.

The inclusions of other amendments to existing legislation is essential to the success of such a program. An amendment of the exceptions[89] to the Posse Comitatus Act to include military responses not only for the exceptions of drug enforcement, immigration and tariff laws which were included in amendments of 1981 and 1988, but for bioterrorism-related activities, as well, should be included. An amendment of the Emergency Planning and Community Right-to-Know Act of 1986 to include the preparation of plans in coordination with FEMA and the FBI for bioterrorism prevention, preparedness and response, should also be specifically included to avoid any confusion of interpretation.

Federal leadership in the intragovernmental crosscutting and coordination area for bioterrorism, as distinguished from the broadly defined area of WMD, should be lodged with the Public Health Service, Surgeon General. While other forms of terrorism correspond with the missions of the FBI and FEMA, the mission of the Public Health Service, coupled with the statutory provision for its conversion to a military service,[90] provides the appropriate level of leadership to command both civilian and military resources in response to a bioterrorism event. The Public Health Service, although converted to a military service, is not subject to the Posse Comitatus Act according to the analysis in *United States v. Jaramillo* wherein the special unit of the U.S. Marshall's Office is not found to be subject to the Act[91] and military policy statements,[92] while the Army is regulated by the Posse Comitatus Act, and as a matter of military policy, the Act is also applicable to the Marines and Navy. The use of the Public Health Service in the top leadership role provides the best of both worlds for domestic use of the military, while avoiding the need for any legislative amendment to allow for other branches of the military to take a leadership role.

89. 10 U.S.C.S. §§ 371-380 (LEXIS 2000).
90. 42 U.S.C.S. § 217 (LEXIS 2000).
91. United States v. Jaramillo, 380 F. Supp. 1375 (1974).
92. U.S. DEP'T OF NAVY, SECRETARY OF THE NAVY INSTR. 5820.7 (15 May 1974).

During the NATO visit to Washington, D.C., in May 1999, over seventy museums and all of the Washington Metro stations were closed, and federal government employees were told not to report to work because of fear of a terrorism event. Unfortunately, much of congressional action in the past has been only as a result of a disaster: The Biologics Act of 1906 was a response to the death of several children due to a vaccine infected with tetanus. The Comprehensive Environmental Response, Compensation, and Liability Act of 1980 was a result of the Love Canal environmental disaster; and the Emergency Planning and Community Right-to-Know Act of 1986 was a result of the Bhopal disaster.

The importance of enactment of legislation to address the unique legal, scientific and budgeting problems presented by the issue of bioterrorism is apparent in light of the potential magnitude of the threat to public safety in the United States. As discussed, prior environmental disasters gave rise to major legislative solutions; but a bioterrorism disaster could prove to be greater in magnitude by far, than the previous problems that gave rise to congressional action. The threat of bioterrorism simply cannot be left to languish under the crippled plan of the President. Congressional action should be taken before we as a nation, defenseless, face the disaster of a shattered domestic security, a country in panic, and a national future in jeopardy.

OLR RESEARCH REPORT

November 9, 2001 2001-R-0851

SUMMARY OF FEDERAL "USA PATRIOT ACT"

You asked for a summary of the new federal anti-terrorism act, the "USA PATRIOT Act."

SUMMARY

The "USA PATRIOT Act" (P.L. 107-56) became effective on October 26, 2001. It includes provisions on criminal laws, transporting hazardous materials, money laundering and counterfeiting, investigations and information sharing, federal grants, victims, immigration, and domestic security. It also expands electronic surveillance laws, which are being summarized in a separate report.

Specifically, the act:

1. creates several new crimes, like bulk cash smuggling and attacking mass transportation systems;

2. expands prohibitions involving biological weapons and possession of biological agents and toxins;

3. lifts the statute of limitations on prosecuting some terrorism crimes;

4. increases penalties for some crimes;

5. requires background checks for licenses to transport hazardous materials;

6. expands money laundering laws and places more procedural requirements on banks;

7. promotes information sharing and coordination of intelligence efforts;

8. provides federal grants for terrorism prevention, antiterrorism training, preparation and response to terrorist acts, and criminal history information systems;

9. broadens the grounds for denying aliens admission to the U.S. based on their involvement with terrorism; and

10. alters some domestic security provisions, such as allowing the attorney

general to ask for the military's assistance during an emergency involving weapons of mass destruction and allowing the Department of Defense to contract with state or local governments for temporary security at military facilities.

The act requires the Department of Justice (DOJ) inspector general to receive complaints about civil liberties and civil rights abuses by DOJ and report to Congress.

It requires telemarketers soliciting charitable contributions to disclose the purpose of their call and make other disclosures that the Federal Trade Commissions considers appropriate.

The act also requires various reports which we do not discuss below. These include studies of how certain provisions in the act are working, whether additional legislation is needed, and how technology can assist anti-terrorism efforts.

We have focused on the sections that we believe are of most interest to state legislators. Enclosed is a copy of the act which begins with a table of contents describing all of it's provisions. If you would like more information on any part, please contact us.

CRIMINAL LAWS

Attacks Against Mass Transportation Systems

The act prohibits willfully:

1. wrecking, derailing, setting fire to, or disabling a mass transportation vehicle or ferry;

2. placing a biological agent or toxin for use as a weapon, destructive substance, or destructive device in or near a mass transportation vehicle or ferry to endanger the safety of a passenger or employee or with reckless disregard for safety;

3. setting fire to or placing a biological agent or toxin for use as a weapon, destructive substance, or destructive device in or near a garage, terminal, structure, supply, or facility used to operate or support a mass transportation vehicle or ferry knowing or with reason to know that it would likely derail, disable, or wreck it;

4. removing parts, damaging, or impairing a mass transportation signal system including a train control system, centralized dispatching system, or rail grade crossing warning signal;

5. interfering with, disabling, or incapacitating a person who is dispatching, operating, or maintaining a mass transportation vehicle or ferry, intending to

endanger the safety of a passenger or employee or with reckless disregard for safety; and

6. committing an act (including use of a dangerous weapon) with intent to cause death or serious bodily injury to an employee or passenger of a mass transportation provider or any person, when on the provider's property.

The act also prohibits (1) attempting, threatening, or conspiring to commit one of these prohibited acts and (2) knowingly conveying false information about an attempt or alleged attempt to commit one of these prohibited acts.

The crime is punishable by a fine, up to 20 years in prison, or both if (1) the act is committed against or affects a mass transportation provider engaged in interstate or foreign commerce or (2) the person who committed the crime traveled or communicated across state lines or transported materials across state lines to aid in committing the act. The crime is punishable by up to life in prison if the vehicle or ferry was carrying a passenger at the time of the offense or the offense resulted in death.

Mass transportation is defined as transportation by a conveyance that provides regular and continuing general or special public transportation but also includes a school bus, charter, and sightseeing transportation (§ 801).

Harboring or Concealing Terrorists

The act creates a new crime of harboring or concealing terrorists. A person commits this crime if he harbors or conceals a person he knows or has reasonable grounds to believe has committed or is about to commit certain offenses. These offenses include destruction of aircraft or aircraft facilities; crimes involving biological and chemical weapons and nuclear materials; arson or bombing of government property; destruction of an energy facility; violence against maritime navigation; weapons of mass destruction crimes; acts of terrorism transcending national boundaries; sabotage of nuclear facilities and fuel; and aircraft piracy.

This crime is punishable by a fine, up to 10 years in prison, or both (§ 803).

Material Support for Terrorism

The law prohibits giving material support or resources knowing and intending that it be used to prepare for or carry out certain crimes. It also prohibits concealing or disguising the nature, location, source, or ownership of that support or resources.

The act amends this crime by expanding the definition of "material support or resources" to include monetary instruments and expert advice and assistance. It also adds to the list of crimes that are the object of the support. The act adds crimes involving chemical weapons, terrorist attacks and violence against mass transportation systems, sabotage of nuclear facilities or fuel, and damaging or destroying interstate pipeline facilities (§ 805).

Biological Weapons

The law prohibits developing, producing, acquiring, or possessing biological agents, toxins, or delivery systems for use as a weapon. The act specifies that bona fide research is excluded from the definition of "use as a weapon."

The act prohibits knowing possession of a biological agent, toxin, or delivery system of a type or quantity that is not reasonably justified for prophylactic, protective, bona fide research, or other peaceful purposes. This is punishable by a fine, up to 10 years in prison, or both. A biological agent or toxin is excluded from this provision if it is in its naturally occurring environment and has not been cultivated, collected, or extracted from its natural source.

The act also prohibits certain people from shipping or transporting in interstate or foreign commerce, or possessing in or affecting commerce, a biological agent or toxin. It also prohibits receiving one that has been shipped or transported in interstate or foreign commerce. This crime refers to agents and toxins listed in federal regulations, with certain exemptions. It also excludes agents and toxins in their naturally occurring environment that are not cultivated, collected, or extracted from their natural source.

The prohibition applies to:

1. anyone under indictment or convicted of a crime punishable by more than one year in prison,

2. fugitives from justice,

3. illegal users of controlled substances,

4. aliens illegally or unlawfully in the U.S.,

5. anyone adjudicated mentally defective or committed to a mental institution, and

6. aliens (not one lawfully admitted for permanent residence) who are nationals of a country designated by the secretary of state as repeatedly providing support for international terrorist acts.

The crime is punishable by a fine, up to 10 years in prison, or both. It does not apply to authorized U.S. government activities (§ 817).

In Congress American Civil Liberties Union Freedom Network

USA Patriot Act Boosts Government Powers While Cutting Back on Traditional Checks and Balances

An ACLU Legislative Analysis

When President Bush signed the USA Patriot Act into law last week, he significantly boosted the government's law enforcement powers while continuing a trend to cut back on the checks and balances that Americans have traditionally relied on to protect individual liberty.

"This law is based on the faulty assumption that safety must come at the expense of civil liberties," said Laura W. Murphy, Director of the ACLU's Washington National Office. "The USA Patriot Act gives law enforcement agencies nationwide extraordinary new powers unchecked by meaningful judicial review."

"For immigrants," added Gregory T. Nojeim, Associate Director of the ACLU Washington Office, "the law is a dramatic setback that gives the government the authority to detain - indefinitely in some cases - non-citizens who are not terrorists on the basis of vague allegations of a risk to national security."

Among the USA Patriot Act's most troubling provisions, the ACLU said, are measures that:

Allow for indefinite detention of non-citizens who are not terrorists on minor visa violations if they cannot be deported because they are stateless, their country of origin refuses to accept them or because they would face torture in their country of origin.

Minimize judicial supervision of federal telephone and Internet surveillance by law enforcement authorities.

Expand the ability of the government to conduct secret searches.

Give the Attorney General and the Secretary of State the power to designate domestic groups as terrorist organizations and deport any non-citizen who belongs to them.

Grant the FBI broad access to sensitive business records about individuals without having to show evidence of a crime.

Lead to large-scale investigations of American citizens for "intelligence" purposes.

Following are highlights of the civil liberties implications of the USA Patriot Act, which was signed into law on Friday, October 26, by President Bush.

Immigration

The USA Patriot Act confers new and unprecedented detention authority on the Attorney General based on vague and unspecified predictions of threats to the national security.

Specifically, the new law permits the detention of non-citizens facing deportation based merely on the Attorney General's certification that he has "reasonable grounds to believe" the non-citizen endangers national security. While immigration or criminal charges must be filed within seven days, these charges need not have anything to do with terrorism, but can be minor visa violations of the kind that normally would not result in detention at all. Non-citizens ordered removed on visa violations could be indefinitely detained if they are stateless, their country of origin refuses to accept them, or they are granted relief from deportation because they would be tortured if they were returned to their country of origin.

The ACLU noted that very few countries will agree to take back one of their citizens if the United States has labeled him a terrorist. Even though the Administration said it compromised on indefinite detention, in some circumstances the USA Patriot Act will fulfill the Administration's original goal of being able to imprison indefinitely someone who has never been convicted of a crime.

The ACLU also noted that the bill's expanded definition of terrorism will inevitably ensnare many non-citizens who have done nothing wrong on the basis of their political beliefs and associations. For the first time, domestic groups can be labeled terrorist organizations, making membership or material support a deportable offense. Non-citizens could also be detained or deported for providing assistance to groups that are not designated as terrorist organizations at all, as long as activity of the group satisfies an extraordinarily broad definition of terrorism that covers virtually any violent activity. It would then fall on the non-citizen to prove that his or her assistance was not intended to further terrorism.

Such groups as the World Trade Organization protesters, the Vieques protestors and even People for the Ethical Treatment of Animals (PETA), would, on the basis of minor acts of violence or vandalism, meet this overbroad definition. Non-citizens who provide assistance to such groups -- such as paying membership dues -- will run the risk of detention and deportation.

Wiretapping and Intelligence Surveillance

The wiretapping and intelligence provisions in the USA Patriot Act sound two themes: they minimize the role of a judge in ensuring that law enforcement wiretapping is conducted legally and with proper justification, and they permit use of intelligence investigative authority to by-pass normal criminal procedures that protect privacy. Specifically:

1. The USA Patriot Act allows the government to use its intelligence gathering power to circumvent the standard that must be met for criminal wiretaps. Currently FISA surveillance, which does not contain many of the same checks and balances that govern wiretaps for criminal purposes, can be used only when foreign intelligence gathering is the primary purpose. The new law allows use of FISA surveillance authority even if the primary purpose were a criminal investigation. Intelligence surveillance merely needs to be only a "significant" purpose. This provision authorizes unconstitutional physical searches and wiretaps: though it is searching primarily for evidence of crime, law enforcement conducts a search without probable cause of crime.

2. The USA Patriot Act extends a very low threshold of proof for access to Internet communications that are far more revealing than numbers dialed on a phone. Under current law, a law enforcement agent can get a pen register or trap and trace order requiring the telephone company to reveal the numbers dialed to and from a particular phone. To get such an order, law enforcement must simply certify to a judge - who must grant the order -- that the information to be obtained is "relevant to an ongoing criminal investigation." This is a very low level of proof, far less than probable cause. This provision apparently applies to law enforcement efforts to determine what websites a person had visited, which is like giving law enforcement the power - based only on its own certification -- to require the librarian to report on the books you had perused while visiting the public library. This provision extends a low standard of proof - far less than probable cause -- to actual "content" information.

3. In allowing for "nationwide service" of pen register and trap and trace orders, the law further marginalizes the role of the judiciary. It authorizes what would be the equivalent of a blank warrant in the physical world: the court issues the order, and the law enforcement agent fills in the places to be searched. This is not consistent with the important Fourth Amendment privacy protection of requiring that warrants specify the place to be searched. Under this legislation, a judge is unable to meaningfully monitor the extent to which her order was being used to access information about Internet communications.

4. The Act also grants the FBI broad access in "intelligence" investigations to records about a person

maintained by a business. The FBI need only certify to a court that it is conducting an intelligence investigation and that the records it seeks may be relevant. With this new power, the FBI can force a business to turn over a person's educational, medical, financial, mental health and travel records based on a very low standard of proof and without meaningful judicial oversight.

The ACLU noted that the FBI already had broad authority to monitor telephone and Internet communications. Most of the changes apply not just to surveillance of terrorists, but instead to all surveillance in the United States.

Law enforcement authorities -- even when they are required to obtain court orders - have great leeway under current law to investigate suspects in terrorist attacks. Current law already provided, for example, that wiretaps can be obtained for the crimes involved in terrorist attacks, including destruction of aircraft and aircraft piracy.

The FBI also already had authority to intercept these communications without showing probable cause of crime for "intelligence" purposes under the Foreign Intelligence Surveillance Act. In fact, FISA wiretaps now exceed wiretapping for all domestic criminal investigations. The standards for obtaining a FISA wiretap are lower than the standards for obtaining a criminal wiretap.

Criminal Justice

The law dramatically expands the use of secret searches. Normally, a person is notified when law enforcement conducts a search. In some cases regarding searches for electronic information, law enforcement authorities can get court permission to delay notification of a search. The USA Patriot Act extends the authority of the government to request "secret searches" to every criminal case. This vast expansion of power goes far beyond anything necessary to conduct terrorism investigations.

The Act also allows for the broad sharing of sensitive information in criminal cases with intelligence agencies, including the CIA, the NSA, the INS and the Secret Service. It permits sharing of sensitive grand jury and wiretap information without judicial review or any safeguards regarding the future use or dissemination of such information.

These information sharing authorizations and mandates effectively put the CIA back in the business of spying on Americans: Once the CIA makes clear the kind of information it seeks, law enforcement agencies can use tools like wiretaps and intelligence searches to provide data to the CIA. In fact, the law specifically gives the Director of Central Intelligence - who heads the CIA -- the power to identify domestic intelligence requirements.

The law also creates a new crime of "domestic terrorism." The new offense threatens to transform protestors into terrorists if they engage in conduct that "involves acts dangerous to human life." Members of Operation Rescue, the Environmental Liberation Front and Greenpeace, for example, have all engaged in activities that could subject them to prosecution as terrorists. Then, under this law, the dominos begin to fall. Those who provide lodging or other assistance to these "domestic terrorists" could have their homes wiretapped and could be prosecuted.

Financial Privacy

The USA Patriot Act continues the unfortunate trend of expanding government access to personal financial information rather than safeguarding it against intrusion. While there is certainly a need to shut down the financial resources used to further acts of terrorism, the USA Patriot Act goes beyond its stated goal of combating international terrorism and instead reaches into innocent customers' personal financial transactions.

Under the new law, financial institutions are required to monitor daily financial transactions even more closely and to share information with other federal agencies, including foreign intelligence services such as the CIA. The law also allows law enforcement and intelligence agencies to get easy access to individual credit reports in secret. The law provides for no judicial review and does not mandate that law enforcement give the person whose records are being reviewed any notice.

Student Privacy

The USA Patriot Act allows law enforcement officials to cast an even broader net for student information without any particularized suspicion of wrongdoing. When the changes in federal law dealing with student records privacy are combined with other information-sharing provisions contained in the new law, it becomes clear that highly personal student information will be transmitted to many federal agencies in ways likely to harm innocent students' privacy.

Since September 11, law enforcement agencies from all levels of government have faced few barriers in accessing student information. According to the American Association of Collegiate Registrars and Admissions Officers, about 200 colleges and universities have turned over student information to the FBI, INS and other law enforcement officials.

But law enforcement agencies wanted even easier access to a broad range of student information and the USA Patriot Act gave it to them by allowing them to receive the student data collected for the purpose of statistical research under the National Education Statistics Act. The statistics act requires the government to collect a vast amount of identifiable student information and - until now - has required it to be held in the strictest confidence without exception.

The USA Patriot Act, however, eliminates that protection and - while it requires a court order - allows law enforcement agencies to get access to private student information based on a mere certification that the records are relevant to an investigation. This certification, which a judge cannot challenge, is insufficient to protect the privacy of sensitive information contained in student records.

U.S. Preparations for Biological Terrorism: Legal Limitations and the Need for Planning

Juliette N. Kayyem

ESDP-2001-02
BCSIA-2001-4 **March 2001**

CITATION AND REPRODUCTION

This document appears as Discussion Paper 2001-4 of the Belfer Center for Science and International Affairs and as contribution ESDP-2001-02 of the Executive Session on Domestic Preparedness, a joint project of the Belfer Center and the Taubman Center for State and Local Government. Comments are welcome and may be directed to the author in care of the Executive Session on Domestic Session.

This paper may be cited as Juliette N. Kayyem. "U.S. Preparations for Biological Terrorism: Legal Limitations and the Need for Planning." BCSIA Discussion Paper 2001-4, ESDP Discussion Paper ESDP-2001-02, John F. Kennedy School of Government, Harvard University, March 2001.

ABOUT THE AUTHOR

Juliette N. Kayyem is Executive Director of the Executive Session on Domestic Preparedness at the John F. Kennedy School of Government. She most recently served as Minority Leader Richard Gephardt's appointment to the National Commission on Terrorism. She previously served as a legal advisor to the Attorney General and as Counsel to the Assistant Attorney General for Civil Rights at the United States Department of Justice. She is the author of several articles on the constitutional implications of America's counter-terrorism policies and teaches courses on counter-terrorism at the Kennedy School of Government's Institute of Politics and the Boston University School of Law. Ms. Kayyem is a regular consultant on terrorism for the United States and foreign countries and is a regular contributor on terrorism and national security issues for a number of news agencies, including The NewsHour with Jim Lehrer, NBC News and National Public Radio. She is a 1991 graduate of Harvard College and a 1995 graduate of Harvard Law School.

The Executive Session on Domestic Preparedness is supported by Grant No. 1999-MU-CX-0008 awarded by the Office for State and Local Domestic Preparedness Support, Office of Justice Programs, U.S. Department of Justice. The Assistant Attorney General, Office of Justice Programs, coordinates the activities of the following program offices and bureaus: the Bureau of Justice Assistance, the Bureau of Justice Statistics, the National Institute of Justice, the Office of Juvenile Justice and Delinquency Prevention, and the Office for Victims of Crime. Points of view or opinions in this document are those of the author and do not necessarily represent the official position or policies of the U.S. Department of Justice.

The threat of terrorism has focused the attention of the United States on domestic preparedness. Although the likelihood of a domestic terrorist attack may be relatively low, the country is nonetheless preparing first responders, local, state and federal officials, and the public on what to do and what to expect should one occur. Lawyers have only recently begun to consider the issue of domestic preparedness. Any steps to improve preparedness must, of course, involve an assessment by the proper legal authorities to determine their lawfulness and legitimacy.

This paper addresses two significant legal problems with the U.S. domestic preparedness program. It initially analyzes the doctrinal difficulties inherent in defining a terrorism incident. It then considers – as a distinct subset of terrorism – the particular problem of biological terrorism specifically. Given the nature and impact of biological terrorism, it will likely impact our present legal regime in ways that are unique (as compared to other forms of terrorism) and risky. Two conclusions flow from this analysis. First, deciding which laws apply best is difficult because most laws were created to deal with situations other than terrorism. Second, laws nevertheless do exist that can be applied to domestic preparedness. Claims to the contrary bolster policymakers' calls for more legislating, but they do so at great risk by potentially threatening to dissuade first responders from utilizing existing tools to combat a terrorist attack. Gaps in the law, in particular with regards to biological terrorism, do exist but they do not require the creation of an entirely new legal regime. Instead, in many cases they just need to be deciphered within the vast federal and state legal codes. This paper ultimately argues that the concerns with legal preparedness too often mask the more difficult policy and political considerations that must be evaluated in any counterterrorist policy.

CONVENTIONAL TERRORISM AND EXISTING LAW

Vague and contradictory laws, overlapping jurisdictions, and procedural and professional divides among law enforcement, national security and public health officials have created a confusing set of laws that do not conform easily to the needs of first responders. In a terrorist attack, this confusion could produce at least two unwanted outcomes. First, it could cause institutional inertia, leading ultimately to more deaths and even greater destruction. Second, it could give rise to overreaction and fear, resulting in unnecessary uses of power.

Presently, our law balances government interests against the interests of the public and persons to determine the proper scope of government authority. This is a balancing of public rights, or the expectation that the government provide safety and security to its citizens, against private rights. During a time of crisis, the balance necessarily shifts heavily in favor of the government.

The law may seem confusing because although the necessary authorities often exist, they are not always easily apparent. There is no "law", for example, that applies only to terrorist attacks and there are few analogies that can be studied to determine appropriate and necessary responses to such an attack. Thus, an examination of the doctrines of U.S. law really is only a starting point. The United States' legal regime seeks to balance the often competing needs of defending national security, providing effective law enforcement, and ensuring individual's rights and liberties. For the most part, this regime has been a successful part of the United State's effort to combat conventional forms of terrorism. The balance is often not perfect – as experience and history have shown. At the very least, however, that balance has been the articulated justification for the present state of our legal code.[1]

Lawyers tend to analyze issues in terms of doctrines of law. The law establishes a set of rules and criteria that govern any incident. Table 1 shows the three categories of law currently exist, none a perfect fit for dealing with a terrorist attack. The first category includes laws and regulations that govern governmental conduct and powers during a national security crisis (hereinafter, rules of war), most commonly viewed (and indeed almost always litigated) as powers that exist during wartime. The second grouping includes laws and regulations that apply to criminal conduct and government action (hereinafter rules of personal liberty). These are most commonly understood to include the rights of defendants from government action, for example, the right to due process and a speedy trial. These are also understood to include rights that afford certain actions protection from government intrusion, such as the rights to free speech, expression and equal protection. The third category comprises laws and regulations that establish procedures for dealing with a cataclysmic event (hereinafter rules for disasters). The Federal Emergency Management Agency's (FEMA) Federal Response Plan (FRP), for example, outlines how the U.S. government should assist state and local governments if a major disaster or other emergency overwhelms their ability to respond effectively to save lives, protect public health, safety and property, and restore damaged communities.[2]

A terrorist attack on U.S. soil would not exclusively fall into any one of the three categories just described. Rather, it would fall into all three. A terrorist attack is similar to other types of aggression, but it is not obviously characterized as the kind of event justifying the use of the military and other expansive governmental powers affiliated with international crisis, a civil war or a foreign invasion of troops. An

[1] Dr. Laura Donohue, "The American Counter-terrorism Complex", Forthcoming Discussion Paper (Cambridge, Mass.: Harvard University, John F. Kennedy School of Government, Executive Session on Domestic Preparedness.)
[2] The FRP is authorized by the Robert T. Stafford Disaster Relief and Emergency Assistance Act, as amended. 42 U.S.C. Sect. 5121, et seq.

act of terrorism is like any other heinous crime, but its impact may be too overwhelming to be contained by the traditional rules of personal liberty. Terrorism is similar to other crises, such as an earthquake or hurricane, but it has security and criminal implications not usually seen in a natural disaster.

Cautious and realistic legal planning, in advance, that appreciates both the difficulties that the United States could face in the event of a terrorist attack and the need to be respectful of the rule of law is crucial. Where more authority is deemed necessary, the government should seek it. Explicit authorization of governmental conduct, for example, a broadening of the laws regarding the ability to quarantine, would decrease the likelihood of ad hoc and unauthorized action by the government. Americans live in a democratic society where federal powers are limited and individual rights are protected. Although additional powers may be required to combat a terrorism crisis, the wisdom of engaging such powers must first be fully explored. This is essentially a policy question, but it is guided by the rule of law and U.S. history. Thus, the time for examined reflection, with a proper balancing, should occur well before a terrorism event. An honest assessment of the laws will show which are necessary, which are expendable, and which need clarity. Only then can the even harder political and policy questions be explored (i.e. whether, even if legal, an action is desirable).

TABLE ONE: Categories of Law and Corresponding Authorities

Area of Law	**Authorities**
Rules of War	President as Commander in Chief Congressional authority over troops State authority over the National Guard Suspension of "normal" constitutional protections (i.e. writ of habeas corpus)
Rules of Personal Liberty	Bill of Rights (First, Fourth, Fifth Amendments), including application to states through the Fourteenth Amendment and case law supporting privacy rights Public health laws
Rules for Disasters	FEMA's Federal Response Plan State health, safety, and police laws

An assessment of the laws – which laws are appropriate, which laws need refining, and which laws are missing -- is an essential part of any domestic preparedness program. The cost of ignoring the law, of having an "apologize later" policy, would only further a terrorist's goal of wreaking havoc. To avoid this outcome, the United States needs to establish a legitimate, well-coordinated counterterrorism strategy that can provide the public with a sense of security and a feeling that everything is being done to ensure that there is minimal mass hysteria and blame. The publication of such a document would also underscore the government's responsibility to protect the life, property, and well being of its citizens.

To determine whether new, expanded powers are permissible, two potential legal limitations on the federal government's authority must be addressed. First, under our Constitution, all powers not delegated to the national government under the Tenth Amendment to the Constitution are retained by the states and the people.[3] The war power and the power over foreign affairs, for example, are vested in the national government to the point that state regulation in the same area is essentially precluded. Congress also has the power to regulate commerce, to tax, and to spend. Through the commerce powers, for example, Congress is able to pass legislation affecting a broad spectrum of policies, including race relations, drug policy, and environmental cleanup since all affect interstate commerce. That power, however, is not absolute; recently, the Supreme Court has limited Congress' ability, under the Commerce Clause, to prohibit the knowing possession of firearms in a school zones, holding that Congress needs to show a substantial and commercial effect before it can regulate any activity, especially those where the states have traditionally had control.[4]

Deciding the proper balance of power between the states and the federal government is still, legally speaking, a work in progress. What is clear is that the states retain broad powers in our federal system and the federal government cannot trump the powers reserved to the states. States, for example, maintain police powers to legislate for the health, morals, and well being of their citizens. While the states are subject to the same requirement as the federal government that their laws not violate personal liberties and freedoms, the states also have broad powers to regulate the conduct of their citizens. The federal structure, therefore, places some restrictions on the national government's ability to expand its powers in order to combat biological terrorism.

[3] "The powers not delegated to the United States by the Constitution, nor prohibited by it to the States, are reserved to the States respectively, or to the people." U.S. Constitution, Amendment X [1791].
[4] Lopez v. United States, 514 U.S. 549 (1995).

Second, limited government in the United States is achieved not only through the constitutional allocation of powers but also through the recognition of the personal rights and liberties of its citizens as protected in our Constitution and the Bill of Rights. These protections apply to state governments and state actors as well; thus various fundamental guarantees of the Bill or Rights are, through the Fourteenth Amendment of the Constitution, "incorporated" and made applicable to the states.[5] The continuing vitality of the right to free speech, the right to worship, and the prohibition against unreasonable searches and seizures underscore the notion that governmental authority must be balanced and limited.

Determining the appropriate law within each of the three doctrines outlined earlier is essential so that debates on policy can be decided before an actual terrorist attack. A legitimate legal question, for example, is: whether police officers have sufficient reasonable suspicion to enter an apartment house where it is suspected that one, but not all, of the apartments may contain critical information? As a legal matter, the answer is likely yes.[6] But several policy questions still remain including: Under what circumstances would such a search be permissible? How should the officers behave? How can they best get consent from the apartment owners? These policy matters and others, such as when would the government want to impose a quarantine following a biological attack, should not be ignored because of concerns about legal ambiguity. The law, as most lawyers will say, does not provide all the right answers, but merely offers guidance.

THE SPECIAL CASE OF BIOLOGICAL TERRORISM

A biological terrorism event, specifically, will challenge the explicit balance this country has tried to maintain between conventional terrorism and the law. It is difficult to imagine the extraordinary fear engendered by a tasteless, odorless, invisible enemy. Biological attacks require different responses. Although constitutional and statutory law provide a framework for analysis of the situation and possible responses, they provide very little direct guidance on how much authority, in such an emergency situation, can or should be utilized. The huge number of lives at stake, coupled with the unique nature of biological weapons and their ability to infect entire populations, will place extreme pressures on those designated to prevent the attack, punish the perpetrators or manage the consequences if prevention fails.

---

[5] Mapp v. Ohio, 367 U.S. 643 (1961)(an "incorporated" Bill of Rights guarantee applies against the states to the same extent and in the same manner that it binds the federal government).
[6] See Marlin v. U.S., 620 U.S. 547 (2000).

As a legal matter, the differences between biological terrorism and conventional terrorism are dramatic. The following list provides a comprehensive description of the kinds of operational needs that are often requested by policymakers and first responders in the event of a biological event.[7] First, however, it is important to acknowledge what powers are requested in order to honestly assess whether the law is relevant. If lawyers do not specifically address the needs of policy-makers, then the two will be dialoguing in a vacuum. Second, lawyers are rarely experts on first responders' needs. An analysis of whether these requirements are actually necessary is beyond the scope of this paper. In other words, it is outside the capabilities of legal experts to determine whether quarantine, as a public health matter, might be necessary following a biological agent release. For the purposes of this analysis, then, it is assumed that the powers requested are necessary; the legality of those powers, however, is addressed below.

1. The exigent circumstances of a potential biological terrorism event will require that the President formalize the situation as an emergency so that the necessary powers, such as the power to impose a curfew or federalize the National Guard, can be invoked.

2. Public and private commodities, such as food, water and vehicles, will be necessary in order to provide essential commodities to federal and state emergency workers, as well as ensure that the civilian population has basic necessities. This would also include price controls so that necessary commodities remain accessible to the population.

3. Access to and from infected areas shall be controlled, as will airports, ocean ports and highways.

4. The general prohibition against the use of the military or the Department of Defense for civilian and law enforcement purposes -- the Posse Comitatus rules -- will need to be evaluated where state and local officials may not have sufficient manpower to effect necessary controls.

5. The traditional divide between law enforcement and national security entities -- as well as the divide between federal, state and local intelligence, law enforcement and medical communities -- will need to be bridged to ensure that proper notification is provided to first responders and state officials.

[7] The following list of "necessary" powers during a biological terrorism event was compiled during the December 2, 1999, Executive Session on Domestic Preparedness symposium on "Legal Authorities During a Terrorism Event." Participants of the conference, mostly first responders, described the types of powers that they would want in such an event.

6. Because of their potential to severely damage to efforts to control civilian exodus or mass hysteria, a serious public relations effort must be sustained. This would include restricting media access to threatened geographic areas.

7. Large segments of the population shall likely be forced to restrict their movements and those who may have been exposed to a biological agent may be quarantined. The notion of quarantine includes forms of isolation, such as requiring contaminated individuals to remain in specially designated areas.

8. Present criminal law is both suspect and incident specific: warrants and searches require that the police have a clear sense of the persons and locations under investigation. Despite the potential for devastation and mass casualties in a biological attack, there are no criminal provisions that provide for expansive investigatory powers. This may also limit police from scooping potential terrorist targets or search broad geographic areas.

9. Many European countries permit the detention of individuals for periods of time when they are thought to be planning, or have been involved in, a terrorist attack. The U.S. criminal system has no such provision, though under immigration laws detention rules are much less severe.

10. Many terrorists identify or are affiliated with organized groups, whether ethnic, religious or cultural. Present law prohibits group-based investigations when members are simply asserting their First Amendment Rights. It may be necessary that group-based surveillance or investigations begin to determine any culpability.

11. Privacy and familial rights require that the bodies of the deceased be released and thus they can rarely be examined or held by the state. In a biological terrorist attack, however, the need to protect the general population from infection may outweigh those rights. The state may desire authority to reserve the right to perform autopsies or cremate in the event of a biological terrorist attack.

12. Interstate assistance from health care officials will be necessary to address the threat against the population. Present confidentiality laws generally do not permit the sharing of information about a patient, whether alive or deceased, to law enforcement personnel. Such prohibitions may need to be loosened to provide for the general public safety.

13. Given the likelihood that necessary items, such as foods, vaccines and protective materials, will be in short supply during a biological terrorist incident, the government may require that the private sector produce specific items.

14. Generally the public cannot be compelled to take medications. If a biological agent is released, however, compulsion may be necessary, despite personal or religious objections, to ensure that infected persons do not contaminate others. Three additional requirements will be necessary. First, medicines and medical procedures that have not yet been formally approved may be utilized for purposes of prevention and containment. Second, even approved medical procedures that have not been tested on distinct groups, such as children or pregnant women, may still be required to take the medication. Finally, first responders may need to use force to administer vaccines to individuals refusing them. Force may also need to be used to compel individuals to obey medical instructions, such as agreeing to be quarantined.

Even those not versed in the law will recognize that the procedures and policies as described above would constitute a dramatic reorientation of the United States' present legal order. Table 2 highlights some of the most obvious constitutional and statutory questions that these changes will raise.

TABLE TWO

Desired Power	Potential Constitutional or Statutory Concerns
Declaring a Formal State of Emergency	Article I, Section 8: Congress shall have power "to Provide for calling forth the militia" vs. Article III, Section 2: The President shall be Commander in Chief
Seize Community and Private Assets	Fifth Amendment prohibition on government takings without just compensation
Control Transportation Terminals	Case law recognizes freedom of movement for U.S. citizens; quarantine laws may be too restrictive
Utilize Military for Civil Control Purposes	Posse Comitatus Act
Require Notification of Appropriate Authorities in states and localities	Law enforcement and intelligence rules proscribe sharing of certain information
Control Access to Mass Communication	First Amendment protections
Quarantine: Stay in or Go out	Federal quarantine and public health laws may be too restrictive
Permit More Liberal Interpretation of General Criminal Law Constitutional Standards	Fourth Amendment prohibition on unreasonable searches and seizures
Detention of Individuals for Short Periods of Time	Fourth, Fifth and Sixth Amendment Protections against detention without criminal basis
Investigating Groups Before Required "Reasonable Suspicion" is Met	First Amendment freedoms of association; Fourteenth Amendment equal protection rights
Grant Broad State Authority Over Body of Deceased Individuals	General privacy rights
Loosen Confidentiality and Licensing Laws to Permit Broader Access and Interstate Travel Rights to Health Officials	General privacy rights; state administrative licensing schemes
Order Production of Necessary Goods	Fifth Amendment prohibition on government takings without just compensation
Order Citizens to Take Medicine	General privacy rights

Locating the appropriate authorities will give practitioners a clear sense of where modifications, or full-scale changes, are warranted. In some instances, those changes may not necessarily be desirable, from a policy perspective, and making them lawful would not cure the deficiency. In some cases, however, the rules can be analyzed to determine how they can best be used and what, if any, triggering event is desirable to move it forward. Some of these authorities overlap with others, and they have been combined for purposes of clarity and legal discussion.

Declare a Formal State of Emergency and Utilize Military for Civil Control Purposes

The sorts of authorities that might be needed in a biological terrorism event are in some ways similar to those that a President might exercise during a war or natural disaster. There are, conceivably, three established areas of constitutional authority with regard to the military. At one end is martial law, which basically suspends the Constitution for a period of time. In the middle are the powers of the Executive during wartime; simply put, the President can suspend certain rights and order the deployment of the military. Although the contours of when an emergency exists are somewhat inconsistent, there is no question that the executive possesses broad authorities during such times. The duty to enforce the laws includes a general authority to protect and defend the personnel, property and instrumentalities of the United States from harm.[8] At the other end is the doctrine of Posse Comitatus, which prohibits the use of the military in civilians matters but recognizes exceptions during which the military could be called up – insurrections, civil disturbances, counter-drug operations, and counterterrorism operations. The National Guard has both civilian and military responsibilities and is not bound by Posse Comitatus.[9] The National Guard can also be federalized by the President as an option for homeland defense requirements.

The United States has not prepared itself historically for "homeland defense" – the widespread assumption being that U.S. territory would remain essential safe.[10] A WMD attack on U.S. soil, however, would pose precisely the kind of warlike situation that could threaten the viability of the nation.[11] The United States, however, has prepared for this and, thus, it does not appear that any additional statutory authority is needed to give that the President has the powers to deal with such a threat. The need for prompt, informed, and effective action in domestic and foreign affairs has meant that in times of crisis power has tended to flow to the Executive. While many of the vague, open-ended executive powers provided in the Constitution are technically shared with Congress, presidential initiatives have generally produced only congressional acquiescence and the courts have tended to avoid judicial review of executive actions, especially in the area of foreign affairs and national security.[12] What is of consequence here is that the courts, and history, have provided ample support for an Executive guardian role. What

---

[8] Henry P. Monaghan, "The Protective Power of the Presidency", 93 *Columbia Law Review* 1 (1993).

[9] The Department of Defense recently approved the creation of National Guard Rapid Assessment and Initial Detection (RAID) teams to assist local and state authorities in assessing the conditions surrounding a WMD emergency and to expedite the arrival of additional state and federal military assets, if necessary.

[10] CSIS Report on Military Preparedness for Homeland Defense (1998).

[11] While the Coast Guard and the National Guard have some role in homeland protection, their unique status within the military mission considers their role as auxilliary to any defense mission. Only recently has the National Guard been utilized in homeland defense – domestic preparedness – efforts, with some criticism. See CRS Report: Terrorism: the RAID Teams (1998).

[12] See The Prize Cases, 67 U.S. (2 Bl.) 635 (1863)(upholding President Lincoln's order to blockade certain Southern ports); In re Debs, 158 U.S. 564 (1895)(upholding President Cleveland's power to obtain an injunction against the Pullman Strike during the economic chaos of 1895 and in the absence of any congressional authority since "the wrongs complained of [were] such . . . as affect the public at large").

policymakers need to determine is less is the authority there, but what authority is desired. This is where the military's role is so suspect and why Posse Comitatus is so valued: "Whoever, except in cases and under circumstances expressly authorized by the Constitution or Act of Congress, willfully uses any part of the Army or the Air Force as a posse comitatus or otherwise to execute the laws shall be fined under this title or imprisoned not more than two years, or both."[13] These firm legal limitations imposed by the law inhibit military activities in day-to-day civilian society. Whether the limitations are desirable has been subject to much debate. Presently, the United States has only prepared for a limited role by the Department of Defense in any biological terrorist attack. The Robert T. Stafford Disaster and Emergency Assistance Act of 1974 authorizes the state and local governments to provide direct and primary disaster relief and emergency assistance. Even in the more recent 1996 annex to FEMA's Federal Response Plan (FRP), the government has outlined the appropriate role of the military in any terrorist incident as mere support. The sense, however, that the military may be better utilized in a more than support role animates the literature on biological terrorism.[14] Without explicit authority, the Department of Defense will be unprepared or unwilling to take on a more active role:

> The [Posse Comitatus Act] constraints may have been appropriate in the late 1800s, but in a world where non-state groups have access to weapons of mass destruction . . .. they could prove counterproductive . . . . Outdated and inflexible American legislation has produce a patchwork consisting of constitutional and statutory exceptions so that the realities of domestic operations can be performed. Examples include the [Stafford Act] . . .. contingency planning for U.S. Army assistance in incidents involving use of chemical and biological weapons of mass destruction on U.S. soil, and various methods to facilitate cooperation between the FBI and the U.S. Army in anti-terrorism. The potential consequences of this approach include a convoluted chain of command and control structure, increased response time, and continuity of operations problems; it also leaves the federal response vulnerable to exploitation by the adversary.[15]

Neither concern about the pubic response to such an increased role, nor the Department of Defense's historical reluctance, however, stand as a legal bar to the use of the military. The Posse Comitatus statute contains a number of exceptions to the general ban including provisions for "insurrections and civil disturbances,"[16] "humanitarian assistance,[17] and "counter-terrorism" assistance in the event of a WMD

[13] 18 U.S.C. 1385, sec. 270b.
[14] Lewis Libby, "Legal Authority for a Domestic Military Role in Homeland Defense", CISAC Report (2000).
[15] Maloney, 'Domestic Operations: The Canadian Approach", *Parameters* (Autumn 1997) cited in L.Libby at 270.
[16] 10 U.S.C. 331, et seq.

attack.[18] Given that the law does not bar military involvement in a biological terrorist attack, the question remains: what kind of activities would be appropriate for the Department of Defense to perform?

When in 1996 Congress authorized the military involvement in cases involving weapons of mass destruction, such as agents used for chemical or biological attacks, regulations were required by statute to further delineate the role of the DOD. [19] No such regulations have ever been issued. Yet the law is no bar to the kinds of authorities that may be deemed appropriate in a biological terrorist attack. Whether such authority is desirable is a question that should be answered after the Department of Defense makes clear its plans and intentions. The law already contemplates a vast expansion of the military role in a crisis.

Seize Community and Private Assets

In a biological attack, the federal or state government could choose to assert authority over private entities to marshal resources and ensure public safety. This may include assuming control over scarce hospital facilities, ambulance, or land; private companies with access to antibiotics; and homes and automobiles of private individuals. State and federal governments are generally prohibited from taking private property without just compensation. [20] Historically the ability to marshal such resources has been limited, even in times of national crisis. Thus when President Harry Truman sought to seize and operate steel mills under federal direction to avert a strike during the undeclared Korean War, the Supreme Court ruled his actions unconstitutional absent specific congressional authority.[21] The Court supported the proposition that it was

---

[17] 10 U.S.C. 401, et seq. The President, by proclamation, has invoked this category in several of desegregation cases in the South during the civil rights movement.
[18] 10 U.S.C. 382 and 18 U.S.C. 831, et. seq.
[19] The Secretary of Defense is now permitted to provide materials, expertise and even antidotes to prepare for or respond to emergencies involving nuclear, chemical and biological weapons of mass destruction. Upon request of the Attorney General, and agreement by the Secretary of Defense, DOD may also assist law enforcement during "emergency situations" involving the use of weapons of mass destruction. The statute defines an "emergency situation" as one where there is "(1) a circumstances involving biological or chemical weapons of mass destruction; (2) that poses a serious threat to the interest of the United States; and (3) civilian expertise and capabilities are not readily available to counter the threat immediately posed, special capabilities of DOD are necessary to counter the threat, and enforcement of the criminal statutes would be seriously impaired without DOD assistance." Importantly, "DOD may not make arrests or directly participate in searches and seizures or intelligence collection activities related to enforcement of the statutes unless necessary for the immediate protection of human life and civilian law enforcement officials are not capable of taking action." This last provision will likely provide the necessary authority for the use of the military in a biological terrorist attack.
[20] U.S. Constitution, amend. 5.
[21] Youngstown Sheet & Tube Co. v. Sawyer, 343 U.S. 579 (1952)(Steel Seizure Case).

Congress, not the President, who could assert such authority over private property; stating that, "[t]he branch of government that has the power to pay compensation for a seizure is the only one able to authorize a seizure or make lawful one that the President has effected."[22]

In response to the limitations placed on executive authority over private property and privately produced goods, Congress passed the Defense Production Act of 1950.[23] This Act affords the President an array of authorities to shape defense preparedness programs and to take appropriate steps to maintain and enhance the defense industrial and technological base in order to "reduce the time required for industrial mobilization in the event of an attack on the United States." The Act contemplates that, once the President finds that such material is a scarce and critical ingredient to the national defense, and this need cannot otherwise be met, then the President is authorized to allocate materials, services, and facilities in such manner and to such extent "as he shall deem necessary or appropriate to promote the national defense."[24]

Thus even under present law protecting private property, a properly constructed statute authorizing the taking of necessary materials to combat a biological terrorist attack could likely survive judicial scrutiny.[25] Thus the 1950 Defense Production Act may be a starting point; the difficulty lies, however, in that the Act was never contemplated, or used, to provide presidential authority during a domestic crisis. For example, FEMA's Federal Response Plan does not mention federal authority to marshal resources like that in the Defense Production Act.

Explicitly legislating government authority to allocate resources is an essential tool in any effective consequence management plan. Such action could, of course, have disadvantages. American society values the free market and private property; the authorized taking of private property has been limited to specific situations involving national security and foreign relations. A biological terrorist attack,

---

[22] Id. at 631-632. More recently, however, courts have been willing to hear congressional approval even where there is no clear statutory authority. Dames & Moore v. Regan, 453 U.S. 654 (1981)(President could, in executive orders, nullify private claims against Iranian government in light of general broad congressional delegation of foreign policy power to the executive); Haig v. Agee, 453 U.S. 280 (1981)(Congress' silence is implicit approval of executive power to revoke passports on national security grounds).

[23] 50 U.S.C. 2045, et. seq..

[24] 1950 Defense Production Act, 20 U.S.C. Sec. 220.

[25] See Dames & Moore, supra.

however, likely qualifies for similar consideration. A statute that made clear the conditions under which the President was authorized to seize resources could prove extremely useful in consequence management.

Control Transportation Terminals & Quarantine: Stay in or Go out

Courts have long held that local officials may cordon off an area or establish a quarantine or erect checkpoints for persons and/or vehicles leaving an area. Both the need to prevent escape of suspected criminals[26] or carriers of contagion[27] and the individual's diminished right of privacy when on foot or on a vehicle support these rulings. In addition, U.S. officials are given significant leeway in its control of national borders.

Because of the potential of quarantines to deprive individuals of their personal liberties, federal authority to quarantine outside a declared war is severely limited:

> Special quarantine powers in time of war: To protect the military and naval forces and war workers of the United States, in time of war, against any communicable disease specified in Executive orders . . .. the Surgeon General, on recommendation of the National Advisory Health Council, is authorized to provide by regulations for the apprehension and examination, in time of war, of any individual reasonably believed (1) to be infected with such disease in a communicable stage; and (2) to be a probable source of infection to members of the armed forces . . .. Such regulations may provide that if upon examination any such individual is found to be so infected, he may be detained for such time and in such manner as may be reasonably necessary.[28]

This provision has never been utilized or interpreted to apply to any situation outside World War II, a declared war. The detention of Japanese Americans during World War II was approved by the Supreme Court because of the emergency situation and because Congress had passed a separate statute to authorize such detention. The Court found that this congressional authorization was an essential limitation on the President's authority.

---

[26] Laaman v. U.S., 973 F.2d 107 (1992)(involving alleged terrorists who conspired to bomb military offices).

[27] Compagnie Francaise de Navigation a Vapeur v. Louisiana State Board of Health, 186 U.S. 380 (1902)

[28] 10 U.S.C. 238, et. seq.

The only other example of congressional ability to set up a quarantine by the federal government appears in public health laws. Regulations to control communicable diseases permit the apprehension, detention, or conditional release of individuals only for the purpose of preventing the introduction, transmission or spread of communicable diseases specified in Executive Orders. These regulations, however, also apply only in limited circumstances: when a person is known to be infected and is coming to a state from a foreign country; or when a person is "reasonably believed to be infected with a communicable disease" and is about to move from one state to another state.[29]

The federal government is, therefore, limited in its ability to control the movement of citizens to wartime or when the movement affects interstate travel. Otherwise, pursuant to state law only, state and local officials are authorized to quarantine persons, buildings, and other designated areas in defined and limited ways. Governors and mayors, not the President, may have that statutory authority; that is, of course, assuming full knowledge and cooperation.

To give the federal government broad authority to quarantine, present law would need to be modified and updated. The "special quarantine powers in time of war" would have to state explicitly that "war" includes a biological terrorist attack on American soil. Even if the term "war" were flexible, new legislation would also have to account for the fact that there will be no time for Surgeon General recommendations or advisory panels to convene and write regulations. The statute also contemplates that those not carrying the disease, but who could later be infected, be released; effective consequence management, however, might require that those not yet infected remain detained.

Altering public health laws would also be difficult and expanding the federal law to include the ability to quarantine might not withstand judicial scrutiny. Consistent with limitations on congressional authority under the Tenth Amendment, public health laws only cover persons engaged in foreign or interstate travel. It may be that a President could quarantine a group of people under the reasonable belief that they all are infected with a disease and have the potential to move to another state. Whether that would justify the detention of a city employee who has a home in the suburbs is unclear.

Even if amending the law were possible, it may not be desirable as a policy matter. Expanding federal powers to include the right to quarantine has some advantages. The spread of the contagion could be confined to a limited geographic area and population. Decisive, albeit excessive, action by the federal government would ultimately save lives and resources. But the disadvantages are not only numerous, they

[29] 24 U.S.C. 24, et. seq.

are potentially disastrous. Current U.S. federal law limits the ability of the government to quarantine because it strikes at the core of a citizen's personal liberty and freedom of movement. Policymakers will need to consider the difficult task of predicting when and under what circumstances quarantine might be necessary. Delineating the diseases that should be covered, ensuring fair applications of the law, determining an acceptable time frame, and issuing other protections would first need to occur. Only a carefully tailored statute applying to a biological terrorism outbreak would appropriately limit government authority, yet fit the desired response.

Require Notification of Appropriate Authorities in States and Localities

Present law enforcement rules and historic communication divides between state and federal actors, as well as between law enforcement and national security agencies, hinder timely and effective communication. Federal authorities are not required – indeed, in some cases, they are prohibited from doing so – to notify other federal, state and local officials about potential terrorist attacks. In addition, a culture against information sharing, especially prevalent in U.S. intelligence agencies, is not easily overcome. Concerns regarding national security and the impact that notification could have on law enforcement capabilities tend to favor "close-hold" (few officials notified) situations, whereby the flow of information is tightly controlled.

The states have an essential interest in being well informed as early as possible. Police powers, medical facilities, and other vital services all fall under the jurisdiction of the state. If state actors are not prepared, the effectiveness of consequence management is seriously undermined. There is therefore a serious dilemma between federal and state officials. This tension is mirrored in the rules established by FEMA on how to respond to a terrorist situation: "The Federal Government exercises primary authority to prevent, preempt, and terminate threats or acts of terrorism and to apprehend and prosecute the perpetrators; State and local governments provide assistance as required . . .. State and local governments exercise primary authority to respond to the consequences of terrorism; the Federal Government provides assistance as required."[30] However, crisis and consequence management are not sequential, but simultaneous.

The question, then, is: should state and local actors be notified of prerelease threats? One solution would be to permit narrow exceptions, in the case of biological terrorism threats, to congressional and federal law enforcement guidelines that often prohibit the sharing of criminal investigation information.

[30] Federal Emergency Management Agency, Federal Response Plan, Terrorism Incident Annex, TI-1.

Memorandums of understanding between federal and state law enforcement agencies that would provide for prerelease information flow might curtail unnecessary withholding of information.

This approach does have difficulties, however. For example, at what stage should notification be given? If notification occurs too early, it may compromise U.S. investigatory capabilities. It could also cause public distress, which in turn could harm the ability to control and manage such a situation. If notification occurs too late, it could undermine the consequence management capabilities and use up valuable time when state and local authorities could be preparing for an attack. Nonetheless, a specific triggering event, codified in law, would ensure that proper notification is given.[31]

Control Access to Communication

The government might have an interest in curtailing wide dissemination of a threat or the cause of an outbreak. Such knowledge could create mass fear and hysteria, resulting in civil disorder. In the age of Internet and e-mail, any control of the dissemination of information would be difficult, but perhaps not impossible, especially in the early stages of the crisis. State and federal governments are generally prohibited from censoring materials in advance of publication. This is known as "the doctrine of prior restraint." The doctrine of prior restraint provides that such restraints are highly suspect both substantively and procedurally and are subject to a rebuttable presumption of unconstitutionality. An example of this was the invalidation of a restraint imposed on the publication of a classified study dealing with U.S. policy in the Vietnam War when the federal government failed to meet its burden of proof.[32] In the Pentagon Papers case the Supreme Court implied, however, that the restraint was troubling because there was no federal statute authorizing it. Some of the Justices felt that the presence of a statute might satisfy the heavy burden of justification necessary to authorize a prior restraint.

It is therefore essential to define, beforehand, the characteristics of the government's justification for using a prior restraint.[33] A statute similar to the one the Supreme Court seemed to endorse in the Pentagon Papers case, would need to delineate when and where that restraint was justified. A statute confined to biological terrorism threats involving potential civil disorder might satisfy a court's exacting scrutiny regarding First Amendment guarantees.

[31] See Phil Heymann, "Law Enforcement and National Security: The Problem of Intelligence Collection to Prevent WMD Terrorism" (draft outline), positing a single organization that would track collection, retention, analysis and dissemination of grand terrorism threats. (Original with Author).
[32] New York Times Co. v. United States, 403 U.S. 713 (1971).
[33] Alexander v. United States, 509 U.S. 544 (1993).

Such a statute might be beneficial, in the short term, for controlling information. Whether it could be passed is another question, but not a legal question. The sanctity of the First Amendment is part of the popular belief that the free flow of ideas is beneficial to a democracy; the government is generally prohibited from placing any prior restraint on the publication of materials, during war or a normal domestic crisis, because of First Amendment protections of the right to free speech.

A less stringent alternative would be the adoption of a nonbonding resolution establishing an understanding between the press and the government that would facilitate government action in an emergency situation. This was attempted during the airline hostage situations of the 1980s, but the resolution was adopted by only one major news organization.[34] A similarly cooperative arrangement might be useful during a biological terrorist crisis, but given its nonbinding nature, and the advent of the web as a competitive form of communication, any such resolution would likely have limited benefits.

The desire to exercise some control of the media may be the result of the failure of the current domestic preparedness programs to develop and maintain effective public relations strategies. In other words, this desire may have less to do with the law and more to do with the failure of the United States to consider the policy implications of having a more open counterterrorism strategy.

Permit More Liberal Interpretation of General Criminal Law Constitutional Standards; Detain Individuals for Short Periods of Time; and Investigation of Groups Before Required "Reasonable Suspicion" is Met

This listing of necessary authorities is grouped together because they implicate similar constitutional norms. In a biological terrorism situation, are "emergency authorities" necessary or advantageous for law enforcement personnel or public health officials? This analysis does not implicate a typical criminal law investigation when there is a specific, suspected terrorist. The process for investigation is the same that it would be under normal – i.e. non-biological terrorism event – circumstances. A biological terrorism event, however, will likely (at least, that is what is assumed in the desired authorities section) require that the criminal law's focus on the suspect may have to be expanded. What concerns the legal norm, however, is those situations when there is a broader group of suspects or geographic locale where the specificities of criminal law cannot easily be met.

[34] See "Terrorism, the Press, and the Government," Congressional Research Service Report (1994).

The question is: what lawful authorities can be used against a broad group of persons whose relation to a suspect may be merely based on geography, ethnicity, or simply chance but where – unless action is taken – there may be a demonstrable health or safety threat?[35] U.S. constitutional law requires specific and individual determinations of guilt and risk.[36]

The Fourth Amendment permits only "reasonable" searches. Determining reasonableness requires a detailed assessment of the nature and quality of the intrusion on an individual's privacy interests against the importance of the government interests in the specific action.[37] The current law enforcement system has proved very successful in apprehending terrorists whose crimes, however heinous, were limited in time and impact (the Oklahoma City bombing and World Trade Center bombing). These crimes were not a part of sustained terrorist campaigns; a biological terrorism event, however, might be. The Fourth Amendment's rule that "no Warrants shall issue, but upon probable cause, supported by Oath or Affirmation, and particularly describing the place to be searched, and the persons or things to be seized" is an exceptionally complicated area of law. It applies to both state and federal law enforcement, though the contours of specific state laws may differ slightly. Generally, however, there are many circumstances in which arrests and searches may be made without a warrant.

These warrantless searches must satisfy the dual requirement of "reasonableness" and "probable cause:"[38] "In dealing with probable cause .... we deal with probabilities" ... [probable cause requires] "more than bare suspicion" and "less than evidence which would justify . . .. conviction."[39] In order to justify warrantless searches or arrests, the government is also required to act under a "reasonableness" standard. Courts have generally defined the reasonableness standard viewed in light of the circumstances surrounding the search. Exigent circumstances justifying a warrantless search or arrest might included those in which: (1) a crime of violence was involved; (2) the suspect was reasonably believe to be armed; (3) there was a clear showing of probable cause; (4) there was a strong reason to believe the suspect was within the premises; (5) it appeared likely that the suspect would escape if not swiftly apprehended; and (6) the entry was made peaceably.[40]

[35] For this section, I am indebted to Professor Barry Kellman of DePaul University Law School.
[36] Lawrence O. Gostin, *Tuberculosis and the Power of the States: Toward the Development of Rational Standards for the Review of Compulsory Public Health Powers*, 2 University of Chicago Law School Roundtable 219 (1995).
[37] O'Connor v. Ortega, 480 U.S. 709, 719 (1987).
[38] Arrests and searches which may be made without a warrant must not be "unreasonable" under the Fourth Amendment, and because the requirements in such cases "surely cannot be less stringent" than when a warrant is obtained, probable cause is (also) required in such circumstances. Draper v. United States, 358 U.S. 307, 311 (1959).
[39] Brinegar v. United States, 338 U.S. 160 (1949).
[40] Welsh v. Wisconsin, 466 U.S. 740 (1984).

The Supreme Court has also recognized special circumstances might call for greater discretion by law enforcement officials; this is known as the special needs doctrine and can justify a search, absent a warrant. According to this doctrine: "Where a Fourth Amendment intrusion serves special governmental needs, beyond the normal need for law enforcement, it is necessary to balance the individual's privacy expectations against the Government's interests to determine whether it is impractical to require a warrant or some level of individualized suspicion in the particular context."[41] In such cases, the Court weighs (1) the privacy interest that the search disrupts (i.e. a home is different, legally, than a car); (2) the nature of the intrusion (invasive body searches are truly intrusive); and (3) the immediacy of the governmental interest and the effectiveness of the procedure.[42]

The Fourth Amendment may be, therefore, sufficiently elastic to permit careful and coordinated government action in times of crisis. Practitioners and policymakers should not view domestic preparedness challenges as situations where they need to overcome the Fourth Amendment. Where public health and security is at stake, the Constitution expects there to be consideration of whether police searches directly promote a government interest that outweigh the individual's interest in avoiding the intrusion. Accordingly, the question ought to be about ensuring that the standards for government action provided in the law are effective, and not merely abusive. More simply, policymakers must ask themselves: what is the government interest and how important is it? To satisfy the legal requirements, the government interest in a broad search must be significant, and the means of the search should have a close connection to the government's goals. Random searches, for example that of airport hand-baggage, are more acceptable than those that may stigmatize a specific person; indeed, broad searches are clearly less intrusive than any invasive search, such as a strip search. Searches based on group identity – such as those on religious, ethnic or racial identifications -- are particularly subject to challenge. Searches cannot be a pretext for attempts to hide prosecutorial fishing expeditions. Where health and nonpunitive searches are necessary, evidence of other wrongdoing (such as keeping drugs in the house) should be ignored if not related to the terrorist attacks. Thus, in considering what authorities are necessary, it is essential to keep this realistic legal balancing in mind. By applying it to the desired authorities outlined above, the expectation that new authorities are needed is less likely.

[41] National Treasury Employees Union v. Von Raab, 489 U.S. 656 (1989).
[42] Vernonia School Dist. 47J v. Acton, 115 S.Ct. 2386 (1995).

Mandate Vaccinations and Other Medical Treatment

The courts traditionally have upheld compulsory medical procedures, including vaccination during disease, if there is a reasonable assessment of some societal harm.[43] Local, state and federal governments should face no obstacles to vaccinating those designated at risk. There may be different factors, however, for quarantining contagious individuals. Traditionally, courts have deferred to medical judgment (especially if the treatment was directly observed therapy). But, in the wake of the AIDS epidemic and opposing medical assessments, courts are beginning to take a more critical view of medical necessity. Courts are now more likely to require some showing by the state of some necessity, even if the standard is low.[44] Indeed laws that would apply to the victims or potential victims of a biological terrorist attack should categorically distinguish between communicable and noncommunicable agents. Anthrax, for example, is not communicable; therefore, vaccination or quarantine may not be necessary in such a situation.

Thus public health authorities must consider how individuals are selected for testing or treatment and the justification for such action. This is a difficult enterprise – not merely for legal reasons. Because some biological agents have a two to four week incubation period, discovery may come too late to contain the outbreak. In addition, determining the source of some illnesses can be long and arduous, further hampering treatment. In the case of noncommunicable diseases, the necessity for invasive procedures might be questionable. Hence requirements that public health officials have some rational articulation for limited and effective testing and that it be done because of a potential biological outbreak is entirely appropriate.

---

[43] Another action described in Table One is a desire to loosen confidentiality and licensing laws to permit broader access and interstate travel rights to health officials. Most laws governing confidentiality and the licensing of medical professionals are state laws and do not implicate any federal constitutional concerns. The ability of medical providers to go from state to state, therefore, would merely require a change in state laws providing comity between states during a biological attack.
[44] See Hill v. Evans, 1993 WL 595676 (M.D. Ala.).

Lower the Threshold of "Reasonable Suspicion" and Sweep Searches

There is no Fourth Amendment problem probable cause issue if a terrorist suspect is known by law enforcement agents. "Reasonable suspicion" is a relatively low standard and would not unreasonably limit appropriate actions. If a search is done more broadly, however, then it really is not the Fourth Amendment's prohibition on searches that stands as a bar. Sweep searches are highly suspect and often ruled invalid. Yet, no case has ever questioned the necessity of sweep searches overall – only the necessity in a particular instance. In those cases, state authorities had simply failed to show any law enforcement necessity for performing broad sweep searches.[45] In a recent Supreme Court case, for example, the Court ruled that an informants' statement alone would not alone satisfy probable cause, it explicitly stated that this prohibition would not apply in an instance where the harm (such as a bomb) was so great as to justify a broad search.[46] The law requires what any democratic society would demand: that the emergency is grand and imminent.

Racial and Group Identifications

Few law enforcement mechanisms have engendered as much controversy as the accusation that law enforcement uses racial and ethnic criteria to stop and detain suspects. One of the most recent examples is the possible "profiling" of African Americans by state police. If detention (before the event) or quarantine (after a biological attack) is limited to only certain segments of the population, what standards are permissible?

The Fourteenth Amendment guarantees, "No State shall make or enforce any law which shall deny to any person within its jurisdiction the equal protection of the laws." This rule applies to the states and to the federal government. When the government intentionally acts on the basis of race or national origin, courts will employ strict scrutiny: "[t] he clear and central purpose of the [Equal Protection clause] was to eliminate all official state sources of invidious racial discrimination . . . ."[47] When race is used, the law is suspect and "subject to the most exacting scrutiny."[48] The government has the burden of proving that the

[45] Justified sweep searches might undermine legitimacy of the government in its counterterrorist efforts to the extent that they have critics on both the left and the right of the political spectrum.
[46] Florida v. J.L., 120 U.S. 1375, 1383 (2000) ("The facts of this case do not require us to speculate about the circumstances under which the danger alleged in an anonymous tip might be so great as to justify a search even without a showing of reliability. We do not say, for example, that a report of a person carrying a bomb need bear the indicia of reliability we demand . . . .")
[47] Loving v. Virginia, 388 U.S. 1 (1967).
[48] Palmore v. Sidoti, 466 U.S. 429 (1984).

classification is necessary to a compelling interest: the government must show that the reason for the classification is essential and that there are no other alternatives to the classification. Application of this standard of review generally results in a holding that the law violates equal protection.[49]

Religious liberties and freedom of expression are similarly protected against state and federal deprivations. Direct and indirect burdens on religion are sufficient to invoke strict scrutiny review.[50] Yet, despite the fundamental right of citizens to hold and practice religious beliefs, and to be free to practice them without burden or classification by the state, the Court has held, in Sherbert v. Verner, that "(o) nly those interests of the highest order and those not otherwise served can overbalance legitimate claims to the free exercise of religion."[51]

State and federal governments have reserved some authority to classify persons by race or religion, suggesting that in some cases they believe that it may be permissible for the government to act in a way that classifies persons based on their race or their religious beliefs [e.g., Korematsu talks in terms of "extreme military danger"; Sherbert talks in terms of "a(n) [governmental] interest of the highest order"). However overbroad, or likely to sweep in innocent members of society, the Court has consistently reserved "extreme military danger" as a legitimate basis for racial classifications. The government still must show that there is absolutely no other alternative. The classification must be narrowly tailored; it must be a perfect fit.[52]

Although state and federal governments may have the power to classify persons based on race or religions, exercising such options would likely have harmful consequences. It is difficult to imagine that law enforcement agencies have no better alternative than to classify persons by race or religion. Indeed if a racial or religious classification is not overt, but merely impacts a certain racial segment of society, then government action is given more deference. If, for example, police or federal agents target a restaurant and interview customers, all of whom are Japanese, there is no Fourteenth Amendment problem. In this case, impact alone is not determinative of racial animus. The government can justify the conduct of these law enforcement officers by arguing that there was reasonable suspicion that the restaurant customers may have had some evidence, and it is just a matter of fact that they are all Japanese.

---

[49] In Korematsu v. United States, however, the Court upheld the exclusion of Japanese Americans from certain areas of the West Coast during World War II on the grounds of extreme military danger from sabotage.
[50] Wisonsin v. Yoder, 406 U.S. 205 (1972).
[51] Sherbert v. Verner, 372 U.S. 398 (1963)(striking down state law that denied a Seventh Day Adventist unemployment benefits because she refused to work on Saturdays).
[52] This paper does not address the use of racial classifications for "benign" or affirmative action purposes because one must assume that in the context of a biological terrorism attack such classifications would be for law enforcement purposes.

Nonetheless, racial classifications are anathema to the understanding of permissible government conduct in a democracy. Such classifications are overinclusive and stigmatize an innocent population. Further, they run counter to our notion of equal protection and fairness. Interestingly, no racial classification based on "extreme military danger" has been invoked since Korematsu, a case that has been roundly criticized for its racial bias and extreme deference to the executive and legislative branches.

PLANNING FOR A BIOLOGICAL ATTACK

Manifestly unconstitutional behavior cannot be made legal because Congress so legislates. But some legal planning can be done to ensure proper and effective action. Congress can do much to delineate the implications of a biological terrorism attack and the authorities necessary in such an event. It could also require the Department of Justice to provide a handbook of legal authorities to prepare responders.[53]

Legislation addressing the legal authorities needed in a biological terrorist attack could provide important guidance to policymakers. First, it could set a definite triggering event – whether it be the use of a certain device, the potential for mass casualty, or the President's order – that would automatically trigger certain law enforcement needs. A specific triggering event is essential, even though a number (10,000 casualties) may appear crude. Another standard, such as "very high casualties", is not only inexact, but may leave too much room for interpretation.

Second, the legislative process could provide for open debate and conversation about what kinds of government authorities the public would desire, even in a worse case scenario. Only through such open debate could the public be heard. Counterterrorism legislation in the United States has been a perpetually growing enterprise. In other words, laws in place today are the baseline for determining what is acceptable when the next batch of legislation is proposed.[54] This is an important argument; yet, the alternative may be more risky. Without proper legal authority, the government would act too cautiously or too recklessly. Any effort to curb government power in times of crisis is therefore beneficial. A group of authorities, only to be used in a biological terrorist attacks, would be made exceptional by their temporal specificity and triggering event.

---

[53] The National Commission on Terrorism recommended such a handbook in their June, 2000 Report Countering the Changing Threat of International Terrorism.
[54] Dr. Laura Donohue, "Facing the New Millenium: The Legacy of American Twentieth Century Counterterrorist Policy" (forthcoming, copy with author).

Finally, legislation could allow for temporal specificity in the statute. Providing for a duration is essential to ensure that an emergency state not linger indefinitely. Providing for greater authority during periods of emergency, and providing that they cease when the threat no longer exists, are both essential parts of any legislative scheme.

CONCLUSION

The American legal system has achieved a fragile balance between national security, effective law enforcement, and personal liberties to apply in times of war, peace and national disasters. Terrorism does not fall easily into any of those categories; biological terrorism sometimes does not fit at all. It may be that the "rules of war" are too hard and permit more governmental powers than are desired in a democratic state. It may be that the "rules of personal liberty" are too soft and unduly tie the hands of government actors trying to divert a crisis with no historical antecedent. It may be that the "rules for disasters" are too vague and assume a level of communication and preparation not possible in a biological terrorism situation.

More than a "new" set of rules, though this paper does suggest where Congress and state legislatures can begin to make changes. There needs to be a clearer understanding of what the rules are. The law is not, and should not be, an impediment to protecting life. In the ongoing debate over terrorism, the argument that democratic norms will need to be sacrificed so that democracy can be preserved is often made, or at least intuited. The premise of this argument is that the traditional balance between government powers and personal freedoms will not hold in the event of a catastrophic terrorism event. The balance will undoubtedly shift but to argue that it cannot hold ignores both the comprehensiveness of the U.S. legal structure and the flaw that condemning it in times of crisis entails. The assumption that the Constitution is the problem with domestic preparedness runs counter to our present legal system and constitutional interpretation. With appropriate statutory revisions, a thorough search of authorities, and a clear triggering event providing for broader powers during a biological terrorist attack, legal preparation can be improved.

The Malevolent Use of Microbes and the Rule of Law: Legal Challenges Presented by Bioterrorism

David P. Fidler

Indiana University School of Law, Bloomington, Indiana

Physicians and public health officials would bear the brunt of the health nightmare unleashed by an act of bioterrorism. Mass casualties and the "worried well" would swamp hospitals and health care facilities that barely cope with normal health care needs. Confusion and fear would haunt infectious disease specialists trying to control the aftermath of an attack with biological weapons (hereafter "bioweapons"). Supplies of antibiotics and equipment would likely be quickly used up. Efforts to treat the sick and control the spread of the pathogenic microbe could be hampered by shortages of medical staff and absenteeism. Public order would be imperiled.

What is often neglected in thinking about the threats bioweapons pose to public health is the foundation that law provides for effective public health activities. Focusing on the link between public health and the law reveals that bioterrorism would also constitute a grave threat to the role law plays in regulating public and private behavior in the United States. In this article, I examine 3 significant challenges that the malevolent use of microbes would pose for the rule of law in the United States.

BIOLOGICAL WEAPONS USE AS THREAT TO THE RULE OF LAW

The use of a biological weapon in the United States would trigger a public health and political emergency. Governmental responses to national emergencies in many countries have historically brought the rule of law—the idea that human affairs are governed by law, not the arbitrary exercise of power—under immense pressure, sometimes resulting in the abandonment of fundamental legal protections for populations. The United States' internment of Japanese-Americans after Pearl Harbor stands as a somber reminder that governmental action in an emergency can push commitment to the rule of law to its boundaries and beyond [1].

The use of a biological weapon in the United States would threaten the rule of law because the American legal system is simply not designed to deal with such a complex and insidious act of violence. The 2 areas of the American legal system most immediately affected by a biological weapons attack would be public health law and the law on managing disasters or emergencies (natural or caused by humans). Each of these 2 areas of law has provisions and powers that would be relevant in responding to a biological weapons attack, but those powers were crafted to deal with other kinds of emergencies, not something as unique and terrifying as the intentional use of pathogenic microbes to kill large numbers of people and undermine political and social institutions.

Neither public health law nor the law on emergency management has ever (fortunately) been implemented in a real biological weapons attack. Tabletop exercises and simulated bioterrorism incidents, such as the May 2000 TOPOFF exercise in Denver, Colorado, demonstrate that neither public health law nor emergency management law could currently support an effective response to a major biological weapons incident [2]. The ineffectiveness of existing legal frameworks in a real bioterrorism crisis would exacerbate pressure on governments to take drastic actions that might sweep away the rule of law in the midst of panic or uncertainty.

To analyze the threat of bioterrorism to the rule of law, I examine the structural, substantive, and implementation challenges bioterrorism poses for legal systems in the United States (figure 1). The structural challenge involves how federalism—the constitutional separation of legal authorities into federal and state jurisdictions—affects efforts to prepare for and

Received 7 March 2000; electronically published 30 July 2001.

David P. Fidler is professor of law at the Indiana University School of Law—Bloomington. He is the author of *International Law and Infectious Diseases* (Oxford: Clarendon Press, 1999) and has served as a legal consultant to the US Department of Defense's Defense Science Board on biological weapons defense.

Reprints or correspondence: David P. Fidler, Indiana University School of Law, 211 S. Indiana Ave., Bloomington, IN 47405-1000 (dfidler@indiana.edu).

Clinical Infectious Diseases 2001;33:686–9

1058-4838/2001/3305-0013$03.00

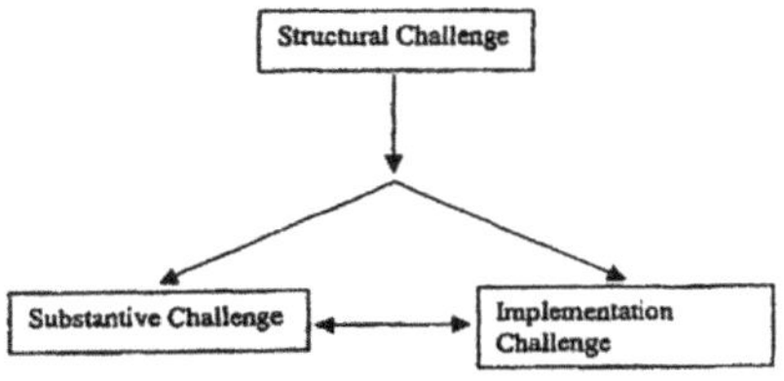

Figure 1. A diagram of the legal challenges posed by bioterrorism

respond to a bioterrorist attack. Beneath the structural challenge, concerns arise about whether the substance of relevant areas of law can support effective responses and state and federal governments can effectively implement legal authorities into the actions needed to respond to a bioterrorist attack. The substantive and implementation challenges are interdependent in that failure to deal effectively with one undermines the ability to deal with the other.

THE STRUCTURAL CHALLENGE

In the United States, political power is divided between state and federal governments. Under the US Constitution, state governments rather than the federal government have primary legal authority and responsibility for public health [3, 4]. Because use of a biological weapon in the United States would trigger a public health emergency, the way the Constitution structures public health powers means that state governments and legal systems are critical in addressing bioterrorism and its aftershocks. On the other hand, the legal authority and power to respond to traditional threats to American national security, such as attacks by foreign nations or terrorists, rest predominantly with the federal government. Bioterrorism's structural challenge to the rule of law means that state governments and public health law are as or more important than are the federal government and federal law. The United States has never developed a legal framework for dealing with a serious national security threat that depends so heavily on the quality of state public health law and institutions.

The division of legal authority between the state and federal governments requires effective and efficient coordination of responses to a bioterrorist attack. Participants in simulated bioterrorist events attest to how difficult cooperation between state and federal government personnel can be in times of emergency [2]. In the TOPOFF exercise, some participants thought the state public health department was in charge, whereas others thought the US Justice Department was in charge [2]. In the context of an epidemic caused by a bioweapon, federal-state turf battles and lack of coordination could be deadly in preventing effective public health responses to the outbreak.

THE SUBSTANTIVE CHALLENGE

Bioterrorism's substantive challenge to the rule of law comprises a number of components. First, use of a bioweapon would implicate many different areas of the law, including public health, emergency management, civil rights, criminal, and national security law. Coordination problems, which federalism already complicates, are exacerbated when bioterrorism engages so many areas of law.

Second, the law must serve numerous complex functions in connection with bioterrorism. They include (1) deterring the development and use of bioweapons; (2) preparing state and federal governments for the possibility of bioterrorism; (3) empowering state and federal governments to respond effectively in the event of an act of bioterrorism; (4) disciplining governmental exercises of power in order to protect individual rights as much as possible; and (5) facilitating identification of and retribution against the bioterrorists [5].

Third, public health law would be on the front lines in the event of a bioterrorist act. Nevertheless, experts in US public health law argue that this body of law is antiquated and in need of serious reform to deal with even ordinary public health problems [6]. Gostin et al. argue that many existing state public health statutes "often do not reflect contemporary scientific understandings of disease, current treatments of choice, or constitutional limits on states' authority to restrict individual liberties" [6, p. 106].

These arguments raise further doubts about whether existing approaches to public health law at the state level in the United States can support effective responses to bioterrorism without special reform efforts being undertaken. A bioweapons event would create a host of legal worries, including the liability of overrun hospitals and health care professionals operating in an emergency environment, the liability of drug and vaccine manufacturers, and the inevitability of lawsuits after the crisis, to name a few.

Fourth, similar concerns exist about federal and state emergency management laws. Both state and federal law deal with emergency management extensively, and some of this law is relevant to managing a public health emergency triggered by bioterrorism. By and large, however, emergency management law supports governmental efforts to deal with natural disasters, such as floods and hurricanes, or industrial accidents, such as chemical spills. Such emergencies briefly threaten human health, with much of the emergency management occurring in the calm aftermath of the event. A bioterrorism emergency does not fit this profile. Emergency management law in the United

States has never been designed to deal with the type of sustained, life-and-death crisis a bioweapon attack would create.

Fifth, the US legal system is highly protective of individual rights. The American conception of government is of a limited government—one that cannot infringe arbitrarily on the rights and freedoms of citizens. Any governmental entity that restricts a civil or political right protected by law has to satisfy strict procedural and substantive criteria. A bioterrorist attack could create enormous pressure on governments at all levels to infringe in drastic ways on individual rights and freedoms without working through the normal procedural and substantive tests for such restrictions. Public health actions to contain an epidemic may require violation of individual rights through such acts as forced quarantine or isolation, compulsory treatment or vaccination, and seizure and destruction of property. Bioterrorism could create a substantive challenge for state and federal governments to balance public health and civil rights in the context of an epidemic—a balancing act of great delicacy in the midst of political confusion and conceivably even social unrest.

Further, the structural and substantive challenges reinforce each other. To correct the substantive deficiencies in existing law and to plan properly for balancing civil rights and effective public health actions, coordinated public health and legal action is needed at state and federal government levels—a Herculean task, even under the best of circumstances. The federal government should take the lead, and the coordination effort should seek to produce harmonized public health and legal strategies for bioterrorism within the individual states.

THE IMPLEMENTATION CHALLENGE

Bioterrorism also presents an implementation challenge because state and federal governments need effective and efficient procedures through which to exercise the public health and emergency powers they possess. In simulated bioterrorist exercises, implementation of legal powers to respond to a public health emergency often failed because the government lacked personnel, resources, strategies, and protocols to carry out the actions required.

In the TOPOFF exercise, Colorado officials issued orders quarantining all persons in Denver in their homes [2]. As Colorado public health officials noted in the aftermath of this exercise, "quarantining two million persons is not simple....[A] one-time, blanket quarantine order is unlikely to be successful and cannot be enforced unless...many...issues are addressed" [7, p. 653]. The implementation challenge deepens when state and federal governments have to coordinate their response procedures, which further illustrates how intertwined the legal challenges posed by bioterrorism can become.

The TOPOFF quarantine experience also demonstrates the interdependence between the substantive and implementation challenges. The State of Colorado had the *legal authority* to quarantine populations in Denver, but the inability to implement the quarantine effectively undermined the *substantive power* to implement quarantine as a public health measure. This interdependence suggests that a great deal of effort has to be focused in legal reform in the bioterrorism context on implementation.

The implementation challenge not only touches on formal legal rules but also engages larger social values and norms, such as fairness and equity, that will influence how public authorities have to ration scarce resources, such as antibiotics, in the event of a bioweapons attack. Forging law in this area will require the government and society to confront difficult ethical conundrums.

THE NEED FOR A LEGAL STRATEGY AGAINST BIOTERRORISM

The 3 legal challenges outlined above point to the need for a legal strategy to cope with the possible problems against bioterrorism. Fortunately, governmental agencies, such as the US Centers for Disease Control and Prevention (CDC), and nongovernmental organizations are raising awareness about the need for people concerned about bioterrorism to include analysis of law in the evaluation of American preparedness. The call for a legal strategy should not surprise anyone familiar with public health. Bioterrorism would predominantly cause a public health emergency. As Frank Grad has argued, "The field of public health is firmly grounded in law and could not long exist in the manner in which we know it today except for its sound legal basis" [8, p. 4]. The same principle applies in the context of public health emergencies and, perhaps more so, in light of the way emergencies tempt governments and populations to abandon fundamental principles of behavior in the name of expediency.

CONCLUSIONS

As a nation dedicated to the rule of law, the United States cannot improve its defenses against bioterrorism without grounding defensive strategies in the law. Much legal analysis and reform needs to be done in connection with preparing for bioterrorism. A great deal of this legal work is not complicated or theoretically difficult but requires lawyers to work through the legal issues with public health officials and other relevant constituencies. The CDC has, for example, encouraged state public health officials to review their statutory authority to ensure they have the powers necessary to deal with a bioweapons event [9]. In addition, lawyers and public health experts can contribute to the bioterrorism defense effort by collaboratively crafting detailed operating protocols and procedures that will make the exercise of public health powers in a time of an emergency epidemic more effective. Working diligently and creatively on the legal strategy for biological weapons defense will help ensure that the rule of law does not become one of the casualties of the malevolent use of microbes against American society.

References

1. *Korematsu v. United States*, 323 US 214 (1944).
2. Ingelsby TV, Grossman R, O'Toole T. A plague on your city: observations from TOPOFF. Clin Infect Dis 2001; 32:436–45.
3. US Constitution, amend. 10.
4. Gostin LO. Public health law: power, restraint, duty. Berkeley: University of California Press, 2000:25–59.
5. Fidler DP. Legal issues surrounding public health emergencies. Pub Health Rep (in press).
6. Gostin LO, Burris S, Lazzarini Z. The law and the public's health: a study of infectious disease law in the United States. Columbia Law Rev 1999; 99:59–128.
7. Hoffman R, Norton JE. Lessons learned from a full-scale bioterrorism exercise. Emerg Infect Dis 2000; 6:652–3.
8. Grad FP. The public health law manual, 2d ed. Washington, DC: American Public Health Association, 1996:3–36.
9. Centers for Disease Control and Prevention (CDC) General Counsel's Office. Public health powers needed in response to a biological weapons event. Atlanta: CDC, May 2000.

CLEAR AND PRESENT DANGER: ENFORCING THE INTERNATIONAL BAN ON BIOLOGICAL AND CHEMICAL WEAPONS THROUGH SANCTIONS, USE OF FORCE, AND CRIMINALIZATION

*Michael P. Scharf**

INTRODUCTION 477

I. THE LETTER OF THE LAW 479
  - A. *The 1907 Hague Convention* 480
  - B. *The 1925 Geneva Protocol* 481
  - C. *The Biological Weapons Convention* 482
  - D. *The Chemical Weapons Convention* 483

II. MEANS OF ENFORCEMENT 485
  - A. *Security Council Enforcement* 485
  - B. *Unilateral Military Action* 488
    1. Anticipatory Self-Defense 488
    2. Assassination 495
  - C. *Criminalization* 500
    1. Prosecution Before International Criminal Tribunals .. 500
    2. Domestic Assertion of Universal Jurisdiction 504

CONCLUSION 508

APPENDIX 511

INTRODUCTION

> *Mr. President, Sir. We've received human intel confirmation. That bastard bin Laden is producing chemical weapons at a facility in the Sudan. Now, the terrorist mastermind who declared jihad on the United States and blew up our embassies in Tanzania and Kenya has the poor man's version of the atom bomb!*

---

* Professor of Law and Director of the Center for International Law and Policy, New England School of Law; formerly Attorney-Adviser, Office of the Legal Adviser, U.S. Department of State, 1989–1993; J.D. Duke University School of Law, 1988; A.B., Duke University, 1985. The author expresses appreciation to Jon Lindeman, Jr. and Jeffrey DiAmico for their research assistance. This article is an expanded and updated version of the lead paper presented on November 18, 1998, at the Hoover Institution Conference on Biological and Chemical Weapons at Stanford University.

[Explicative] . . . General, what are our options?

A conversation like the fictional colloquy set forth above took place between President Clinton and his military advisers on the eve of the U.S. cruise missile attack on the Sudanese chemical weapons plant on August 20, 1998.[1] The purpose of this article is to provide a comprehensive answer to the President's inquiry. First, it analyzes the costs and benefits of the various means of responding to violations of the international ban on chemical and biological weapons, and then suggests alternatives that have not yet been explored.

In spite of the dreadful effects of biological and chemical weapons, nations regularly disregard treaties that forbid the use of such weapons and continue to develop, produce, stockpile, and use threatening quantities of these deadly agents. Chemical and biological weapons have been used in a wide range of conflicts, including Afghanistan, Chechnya, Eritrea, Laos, Myanmar (Burma), Sri Lanka, Yemen, and the former Yugoslavia.[2] By far the best documented cases are Iraq's use in its 1980–88 war against Iran, and subsequently against Kurdish groups in northern Iraq.[3] In the aftermath of the 1990–91 Persian Gulf conflict, inspections by U.N. teams revealed an enormous inventory of chemical weapons.[4] Documents seized from the Iraqi Defense Ministry indicated that Iraq possessed a substantial biological warfare capability at the time of the Gulf War.[5] Some twenty other countries possess or are currently suspected of possessing these weapons.[6]

For a variety of reasons, the proliferation of chemical and biological weapons has recently begun to pose a much greater and more immediate

1. *See infra* notes 78–92 and accompanying text. While the President's advisors provided an analysis of the operational costs and benefits of the possible options, "reliable sources" have acknowledged that the President did not seek an analysis of the international law implications from the Department of State's Office of the Legal Advisor until after the attack was launched. Bruce Zagaris, *Owner of Bombed Sudanese Pharmaceutical Plant Presses the U.S. for Compensation and Release of Frozen Funds*, 15 INT'L LAW REPORTER 97, 98 (1999).

2. BURNS WESTON ET AL., INTERNATIONAL LAW AND WORLD ORDER 462 (3rd ed. 1997); Miriam E. Sapiro, *Investigative Allegations of Chemical or Biological Warfare: The Canadian Contribution*, 80 AM. J. INT'L L. 678 n.3 (1986) (citing reports of U.N. investigators) [hereinafter Sapiro, *Investigative Allegations*].

3. *See* Sapiro, *Investigative Allegations*, *supra* note 2, at n.2.

4. Andrew D. McClintock, *The Law of War: Coalition Attacks on Iraqi Chemical and Biological Weapon Storage and Production Facilities*, 7 EMORY INT'L L. REV. 633 (1993).

5. According to U.S. officials, documents seized from the Iraqi Defense Ministry indicated the production of anthrax, botulinum toxin, and clostridium perfingens (the causative agent of gangrene). *Id.* at 634 n. 2.

6. Jonathan B. Tucker, Director of the Center for Nonproliferation Studies, The Current Status of the BCW Regimes, Paper Delivered at the Hoover Institution Conference on Biological and Chemical Weapons at Stanford University, November 16–18, 1998, at 1 (on file with the author).

threat to international security than in prior years. The globalization of industry has greatly increased access to the technology, expertise, and raw materials required to produce chemical and biological weapons. Unlike nuclear weapons programs, which require sensitive materials that are difficult and expensive to produce and specialized facilities for bomb fabrication, chemical and biological weapons can be developed by most countries and determined terrorist organizations, because they can be produced with readily available dual-use equipment and substances.[7] Thus, chemical and biological weapons can be developed by most countries and even terrorist organizations that are determined to do so. Moreover, if a State can mate chemical and biological weapons to missile delivery systems, it gives that State the ability to attack enemy population centers. For this reason, leaders in the developing world think of chemical and biological weaponry as "the poor man's atom bomb."[8] In addition, chemical and biological weapons have proliferated to states, such as Iraq and North Korea, which have repeatedly flaunted international standards and have been known to sponsor terrorism, increasing the likelihood that these weapons will proliferate still further. Finally, the prohibition on the production and use of these weapons has been weakened by the failure of the international community to respond to Iraq's use of them against Iran and against the Iraqi Kurds.

Currently there are two means of enforcing the international prohibition of chemical and biological weapons. First, the international community can induce compliance through imposition of sanctions, such as trade embargoes, freezing of assets and diplomatic isolation. Second, when sanctions fail, States can individually or collectively respond to the threat of chemical or biological weapons by using military force. After exploring the potential strengths and weaknesses of these approaches, this article examines the desirability of supplementing them with a third approach based on the criminal prosecution of persons responsible for the production, stockpiling, transfer, or use of chemical and biological weapons.

I. The Letter of the Law

Before scrutinizing the means of enforcing the ban on chemical and biological weapons, it is necessary to understand the scope of the prohibition. This section examines the coverage of the law, and demonstrates

7. Anne Q. Connaughton & Steven C. Goldman, *The Chemical Weapons Convention and Department of Commerce Responsibilities*, 760 PLI/COMM 533, 537–538 (1997).

8. Brad Roberts, *Controlling Chemical Weapons*, 2 TRANS. L. & CONTEMP. PROBS. 435 (1992).

that at least part of the problem is due to inadequacies in the existing chemical and biological weapons treaty regimes: the 1907 Hague Convention, the 1925 Geneva Protocol, the 1972 Biological Weapons Convention, and the 1993 Chemical Weapons Convention.

A. *The 1907 Hague Convention*

The laws of war were first comprehensively codified in the 1907 Hague Convention,[9] which constitutes an authoritative source of customary international law.[10] Article 23 of the 1907 Hague Convention prohibits the use of poisonous weapons,[11] as well as the deployment of weapons "calculated to cause unnecessary suffering."[12] Unfortunately, these prohibitions did not deter the use of chemical weapons by both sides in World War I.[13] It is estimated that the use of chlorine and mustard gas during that war caused over a million casualties, including 90,000 deaths.[14]

---

9. Convention (IV) Respecting the Laws and Customs of War on Land, 18 October 1907, *reprinted in* DOCUMENTS ON THE LAWS OF WAR 44 (Adam Roberts & Richard Guelff eds., 2d ed. 1989) [The Hague Convention].

10. The Secretary-General of the United Nations stated in his report on the Statute of the International Criminal Tribunal for the Former Yugoslavia, that "the part of conventional international humanitarian law which has beyond doubt become part of international customary law is the law applicable in armed conflict as embodied in: . . . the Hague Convention (IV) Respecting the Laws and Customs of War on Land and the Regulations annexed thereto of 18 October 1907; . . . ." *See Report of the Secretary-General Pursuant to Paragraph 2 of Security Council Resolution 808 (1993)*, para. 35, U.N. Doc. S/25704, 3 May 1993, *reprinted in* 2 VIRGINIA MORRIS AND MICHAEL P. SCHARF, AN INSIDER'S GUIDE TO THE INTERNATIONAL CRIMINAL TRIBUNAL FOR THE FORMER YUGOSLAVIA 3, 9 (1995). *See also* paras. 609–617 of the judgment of the International Criminal Tribunal in the Tadic case (IT-94-1-T), May 7, 1997, *reprinted in relevant part in* JOHN R.W.D. JONES, THE PRACTICE OF THE INTERNATIONAL CRIMINAL TRIBUNALS FOR THE FORMER YUGOSLAVIA AND RWANDA 40 (1998).

11. *See supra* note 9, art. 23(a).

12. *Id.* art. 23(b). The 1977 Protocol I Additional to the 1949 Geneva Conventions similarly provides:

> 1. In any armed conflict, the right of the Parties to the conflict to choose methods or means of warfare is not unlimited.
> 2. It is prohibited to employ weapons, projectiles and material and methods of warfare of a nature to cause superfluous injury or unnecessary suffering.
> 3. It is prohibited to employ methods or means of warfare which are intended, or may be expected, to cause widespread, long-term and severe damage to the natural environment.

Protocol Additional to the Geneva Conventions of 12 August 1949, and Relating to the Protection of Victims of International Armed Conflicts, 8 June 1977, art. 35, 1125 U.N.T.S. 3, 21.

13. HILARE MCCOUBREY & NIGEL D. WHITE, INTERNATIONAL LAW AND ARMED CONFLICT 245 (1992).

14. *Weston et al.*, *supra* note 2, at 463.

B. *The 1925 Geneva Protocol*

In 1925, the Geneva Protocol (the Protocol) was established to ban the "use in war of asphyxiating, poisonous or other gasses, and of all analogous liquids, materials or devices."[15] The Geneva Protocol was a direct response to the failure of the 1907 Hague Convention to prevent the use of chemical weapons during World War I. Over 145 States have ratified the 1925 Geneva Protocol.[16] The treaty was thought to have prevented the use of chemical weapons by all of the European belligerents in World War II.[17]

However, in subsequent years it became increasingly evident that, because of the many gaping holes in coverage, the Protocol was just as ineffective in preventing the production and use of biological and chemical weapons as its predecessor. First, many States reserved the right to use chemical and biological weapons against non-parties and to retaliate in kind against parties who used chemical or biological weapons first. In addition, the Protocol does not ban the design, testing, production, or stockpiling of biological or chemical weapons or precursors, thereby providing an incentive for countries to continue producing and stockpiling these weapons, and ensuring the short order availability of such weapons for retaliatory purposes. Moreover, the prohibition does not apply to peacetime use of chemical or biological weapons. Nor does it apply to internal use by a government against its own citizens such as the Iraqi government's poison gas attacks on the Iraqi Kurds, which resulted in the deaths of several hundred thousand people. Further, the Protocol contains no verification regime to investigate suspected violations and ensure compliance with the prohibition. Finally, the Protocol has not been enforced. The international community has not imposed sanctions for documented violations of this Protocol, such as the use by Iraq of chemical weapons against Iran.[18] Nor has the international community imposed sanctions on countries which export

15. Protocol for the Prohibition of the Use in War of Asphyxiating, Poisonous or Other Gases, and of Bacteriological Methods of Warfare *done* June 17, 1925, 26 U.S.T. 571, [hereinafter Geneva Protocol of 1925].

16. *See* Theodor Meron, *The Continuing Role of Custom in the Formation of International Humanitarian Law*, 90 AM. J. INT'L L. 238, 246 (1996).

17. *See generally* RICHARD M. PRICE, THE CHEMICAL WEAPONS TABOO (1997). Price argues that the 1925 Geneva Protocol created a "chemical weapons taboo" which was a necessary condition for the avoidance of chemical warfare in World War II. The author acknowledges, however, that the non-use of chemical weapons during the war was largely out of fear that the opposing side would respond by employing chemical weapons against population centers.

18. *See supra* note 7, at 536–37.

chemical weapons precursors.[19] In light of these weaknesses, it became apparent that the Protocol was not an adequate solution to the problems posed by the frequent use of chemical weapons and the growing proliferation and stockpiling of biological weapons.[20]

C. *The Biological Weapons Convention*

Some of the weaknesses of the 1925 Geneva Protocol were eliminated by the 1972 Biological Weapons Convention, which entered into force in 1975.[21] The Biological Weapons Convention was the first treaty to totally outlaw an entire category of weapons.

Under Article I of the 1972 Convention, each State party agrees never to produce, stockpile, or otherwise acquire:

1. [M]icrobial or other biological agents or toxins whatever their origin or method of production of types and in quantities that have no justification for prophylactic, protective or other peaceful purposes; [and]

2. [W]eapons, equipment or means of delivery designed to use such agents or toxins for hostile purposes or in armed conflict.[22]

Article II requires each State Party to destroy existing stockpiles of biological weapons within nine months of the Convention's entry into force.[23]

The 1972 Biological Weapons Convention, which has been widely ratified, reflects a comprehensive repudiation of the development, production, and stockpiling of biological weaponry. Despite its symbolic importance as a norm creating treaty, the absence of verification and enforcement provisions has rendered it "merely a paper agreement that could easily be circumvented."[24] This became apparent when, in 1979,

---

19. *See* Paul Rubenstein, *State Responsibility for Failure to Control the Export of Weapons of Mass Destruction*, 23 CAL. W. INT'L L.J. 319, 322–27 (1993). Rubenstein argues that countries like Germany which allowed the export of chemical precursors, chemical process equipment, and technical expertise to Iraq during the 1980s could be held liable under principles of state responsibility since it was reasonably foreseeable that Iraq would use them to produce chemical weapons for aggressive use.

20. *See* Peter H. Oppenheimer, *A Chemical Weapons Regime for the 1990s: Satisfying Seven Critical Criteria*, 11 WIS. INT'L L.J. 1 (1992).

21. Convention on the Prohibition of the Development, Production and Stockpiling of Bacteriological (Biological) and Toxin Weapons and on their Destruction, *opened for signature* April 10, 1972, 26 U.S.T. 583 [hereinafter Biological Weapons Convention].

22. *Id.* art. I.

23. *Id.* art. II.

24. *See* Susan Wright, *Prospects for Biological Disarmament in the 1990s*, 2 TRANSNAT'L. L. & CONTEMP. PROBS. 453, 454 (1992); *see also* NICHOLAS A. SIMS, THE DIPLOMACY OF BIOLOGICAL DISARMAMENT: VICISSITUDES OF A TREATY IN FORCE, 1975–85

an accident at a covert Soviet biological weapons plant was responsible for the outbreak of an epidemic of anthrax in Sverdilovsk, USSR, which may have killed up to a thousand persons.[25]

Like the Protocol, the Biological Weapons Convention is riddled with gaps and loopholes. First, biological weapons research is not prohibited. Second, the Article I limitation to biological agents or toxins "that have no justification for prophylactic, protective or other peaceful purposes" constitutes an enormous loophole since "protective" and "peaceful" applications cannot reliably be distinguished from hostile military applications. Similarly, the obligation to destroy stockpiles for any biological agent or toxins contained in Article II does not apply to biological agents that are "divert[ed] to peaceful purposes," thereby providing states an alarming degree of discretion.[26]

In 1994, the Parties to the Biological Weapons Convention established an Ad Hoc Group of fifty interested member-States to draft a Compliance Protocol to strengthen the Convention.[27] "The fifth draft of the Compliance Protocol, produced in July 1998, was 251 pages long and consisted of 23 articles, seven annexes, and five appendices. This draft of the treaty also contained more than 3,000 bracketed items indicating points of disagreement."[28] The Ad Hoc Group plans to meet again in 1999 to complete the Protocol.[29]

D. *The Chemical Weapons Convention*

"Given the inherent limitations of the Geneva Protocol, in 1968 the international community began negotiating a comprehensive chemical weapons convention that would ban not only the use, but also the production and stockpiling of chemical weapons, and that would additionally provide the means to verify compliance and to sanction

---

(1988. Sims concludes, "Those who took the British initiative of 1968 [which included strong provisions for verification and complaint investigation] and watered it down into the Convention of 1972 gave the world biological disarmament on the cheap: a disarmament régime of minimal machinery which would cost next to nothing to sustain. It is now painfully evident that these short-term savings have been outweighed by the long-term costs of a régime lacking the means to sustain its credibility in the face of suspicious events which cannot be resolved one way or the other." at 290.

25. Raymond A. Zilinskas, Book Review, 84 AM. J. INT'L L. 984, 984–85 (1990) (reviewing NICHOLAS A. SIMS, THE DIPLOMACY OF BIOLOGICAL DISARMAMENT: VICISSITUDES OF A TREATY IN FORCE, 1975–85 (1988)).

26. Richard A. Falk, *Inhibiting Reliance on Biological Weaponry: The Role and Relevance of International Law*, 1 AM. U. J. INT'L L. & POL'Y 17 (1986).

27. *See supra* note 6, at 8.

28. *Id.* at 9.

29. *See id.* at 11–12.

violations."[30] The objective of the Chemical Weapons Convention (the Convention) was to eliminate an entire class of weapons of mass destruction.

On April 29, 1997, the Convention entered into force.[31] Over 100 states, including the United States, China, India, Iran and Russia, have ratified or acceded to the Convention.[32] The Convention prohibits the development, production, or other acquisition, retention, stockpiling, transfer, and use of chemical weapons and chemical weapons production facilities.[33] It also prohibits State Parties from engaging in any military preparations to use chemical weapons and from assisting or inducing anyone to engage in an activity that is prohibited by the Convention. The Convention requires State Parties to eliminate all chemical weapons and chemical weapons production facilities under their jurisdiction or control within ten years of accession.

Most importantly, the Chemical Weapons Convention establishes a permanent Organization for the Prohibition of Chemical Weapons (the OPCW), whose role is to monitor implementation of the agreement through on-site inspections, including inspections of private, non-military chemical production facilities.[34] In addition, the Convention provides for challenge inspections of any facility or location, public or private, when a State Party suspects that the facility is not in compliance with the Convention. Because of its extensive verification procedures, the Convention is estimated to cost between $33 million and $500 million per year to operate.[35]

While the verification provisions of the Chemical Weapons Convention have been heralded as "among the most intricate and intrusive

30. *Supra* note 7, at 537.

31. *See* John J. Kim & Gregory Gerdes, *International Institutions*, 32 INT'L LAW. 575, 590 (1998).

32. *See id.* The United States Senate gave its advice and consent to the Chemical Weapons Convention on April 24, 1997, subject to twenty-eight conditions. Notably among these is Condition 28, which requires the President to certify that proper search warrants will be obtained for any U.S. facility subject to inspection when consent of the owner was withheld. This condition responded to concerns that U.S. businesses could be subject to unreasonable searches and seizures by the Convention in contravention of their Fourth Amendment rights.

33. Convention on the Prohibition of the Development, Production, Stockpiling and Use of Chemical Weapons and on the Destruction, Jan. 13, 1993, S. TREATY DOC. NO. 21, 103D CONG., 1ST SESS. (1993), *reprinted in* 32 I.L.M. 800 [hereinafter Chemical Weapons Convention]. For an analysis of the Convention's negotiating history, see WALTER KRUTZSCH & RALF TRAPP, A COMMENTARY ON THE CHEMICAL WEAPONS CONVENTION (1994), and THOMAS BERNAUER, THE PROJECTED CHEMICAL WEAPONS CONVENTION: A GUIDE TO THE NEGOTIATIONS IN THE CONFERENCE ON DISARMAMENT (1990).

34. Under Article III of the Chemical Weapons Convention, parties must disclose to the OPCW the location of their production facilities and chemical weapons stockpiles. *See supra* note 33.

35. *See* Zilinskas, *supra* note 25, at 986.

ever designed for a disarmament regime,"[36] the Convention is not without its flaws. In particular, the Convention does not provide mandatory sanctions against violators. Nor does it apply to numerous "hold-out" states which continue to refuse to join[37] or non-State actors, such as terrorist or paramilitary groups. Moreover, it only "regulates chemical weapons and their precursors in terms of *tons*," even though technological developments have produced agents only a few grams of which are lethal.[38] And it permits any State Party to withdraw from the regime in "the supreme interests of the country" on only ninety days notice.

The Convention's most significant weakness is the result of ill-conceived action by the U.S. Congress. In enacting implementing legislation, Congress included three "poison-pill" provisions introduced by treaty opponents that could eviscerate the Chemical Weapons Convention's verification regime.[39] One provision authorizes the president to refuse a challenge inspection on "national security grounds," the second prevents the removal of samples from U.S. territory for analysis, and the third sharply limits the number of U.S. chemical plants subject to inspection. Other countries are likely to treat these as equivalent to reservations and assert them to frustrate verification.[40]

II. MEANS OF ENFORCEMENT

A. *Security Council Enforcement*

None of the treaties on chemical and biological weapons provide for the imposition of mandatory sanctions against violators. The parties to these treaties can individually or collectively impose sanctions,

36. Oppenheimer, *supra* note 20, at 44.

37. Most of the middle eastern countries did not sign and have not ratified or acceded to the Chemical Weapons Convention, citing Israel's refusal to sign the Nuclear non-Proliferation Treaty. *See id.* at 45.

38. *Id.*

39. *See supra* note 6, at 7.

40. The result would be similar to the effect of the U.S. "Connally Reservation" to the compulsory jurisdiction of the International Court of Justice, which provided that the United States acceptance of the World Court's jurisdiction would not apply to "disputes with regard to matters which are essentially within the domestic jurisdiction of the United States of America as determined by the United States of America." BARRY E. CARTER & PHILLIP R. TRIMBLE, INTERNATIONAL LAW 305–06 (2d ed. 1995). One of the reasons given for the U.S. withdrawal from the compulsory jurisdiction of the International Court of Justice in 1986 was that every time the United States attempted to bring a case against a country before the International Court of Justice, the country used the reservation against the United States via reciprocity to successfully defeat the International Court's jurisdiction. *See Statement by the Legal Adviser, Abraham D. Sofaer, to the Senate Foreign Relations Committee* (Dec. 4, 1985), *reprinted in id.* at 324.

but embargoes are ineffective unless they are universally enforced. Thus, the U.N. Security Council may increasingly be called upon to respond to violations of the chemical and biological weapons conventions.

The United Nations Charter charges the Security Council with the responsibility for determining the existence of any threat to, or breach of, the peace. Articles 41 and 42 of the Charter authorize the Security Council to restore international peace and security, by force if necessary. The Security Council may call upon U.N. members to impose sanctions and to use force to ensure compliance, e.g., to interdict vessels violating an embargo. The Security Council can also freeze the assets of responsible leaders[41] and ban their travel.[42] Furthermore, the Security Council can call upon or authorize states to use military force in response to a violation of the international prohibition on biological and chemical weapons. The Security Council can even authorize the capture of persons responsible for serious violations of international law.[43]

In the aftermath of Iraq's invasion of Kuwait, the Security Council adopted a series of resolutions to compel Iraq to destroy its arsenal of chemical and biological weapons. After Iraq invaded Kuwait, the Security Council imposed sweeping sanctions and authorized the use of force against Iraq.[44] At the conclusion of the Persian Gulf conflict, the Security Council adopted Resolution 687 (1991), which specified the conditions which Iraq must satisfy before sanctions would be lifted.[45] To avoid the possibility of a future Iraqi threat using biological or chemical weapons,[46] Resolution 687 required Iraq to "unconditionally accept the

41. *See* S.C. Res. 841, U.N. SCOR, 48th Sess., 3238th mtg. at 3, U.N. Doc. S/RES/841 (1993) (freezing the assets of the de facto military regime in Haiti and their major civilian supporters).

42. *See* S.C. Res. 1137, U.N. SCOR, 52nd Sess., 3831st mtg., U.N. Doc. S/RES/1137 (1997) (imposing travel restrictions on Iraqi leaders).

43. *See* S.C. Res. 837, U.N. SCOR, 48th Sess., 3229th mtg. at 83, U.N. Doc. S/RES/837 (1993) (authorizing the "arrest, and detention for prosecution, trial and punishment," of Somali warlord Mohamed Farrah Aidid, who was responsible for the murder of 24 U.N. Peacekeeping troops in 1993).

44. *See* S.C. Res. 660, U.N. SCOR, 45th Sess., 2932nd mtg., U.N. Doc. S/RES/660 (1990) (demanding withdrawal of Iraqi troops from Kuwait); S.C. Res. 661, U.N. SCOR, 45th Sess., 2933rd mtg., U.N. Doc. S/RES/661 (1990) (imposing economic sanctions); S.C. Res. 665, U.N. SCOR, 45th Sess., 2938th mtg., U.N. Doc. S/RES/665 (1990) (authorizing use of force to enforce the embargo); S.C. Res. 678, U.N. SCOR, 45th Sess., 2963rd mtg., U.N. Doc. S/RES/678 (1990) (authorizing invasion of Iraq by coalition forces).

45. S.C. Res. 687, U.N. SCOR, 46th Sess., 2981st mtg., U.N. Doc. S/RES/687 (1991).

46. In a letter to the leaders of the House and Senate regarding Iraq, President Clinton stated in relevant part:

> Sanctions against Iraq were imposed as a result of Iraq's invasion of Kuwait. It has been necessary to sustain them because of Iraq's failure to comply with relevant UNSC resolutions, including those to ensure Saddam Hussein is not allowed to resume the unrestricted development and production of weapons of mass destruction.

destruction, removal, or rendering harmless, under international supervision, of. . . [a]ll chemical and biological weapons and all stocks of agents and all related subsystems and components and all research, development, support, and manufacturing facilities."[47] The preamble of Resolution 687 invokes *inter alia* the 1925 Geneva Protocol and the 1972 Biological Weapons Convention as the justification for imposing this requirement.

Resolution 687 required Iraq to divulge the locations, amounts, and types of its chemical and biological weapons to the Secretary-General of the United Nations. The destruction of these materials was to be performed under the supervision of the United Nations Special Commission (UNSCOM), which was charged with the responsibility for inspection and investigation of all known or suspected weapon sites. After a series of violations of Resolution 687, culminating in Iraq's refusal to allow the inspection teams access to sites designated by UNSCOM,[48] the United States and Great Britain threatened to use military force to compel Iraqi compliance.[49] The United States and Great Britain asserted that such force was permitted by Resolution 678, which authorized member states to use all necessary means to uphold and implement "all relevant resolutions" subsequent to Resolution 660.[50] Air strikes were temporarily averted when, on February 23, 1998, Iraq's Deputy Prime Minister Tariq Aziz and United Nations Secretary-General Kofi Annon signed a Memorandum of Understanding in which Iraq agreed to accord "immediate, unconditional and unrestricted access" to UNSCOM.[51]

Clinton Letter to the Leaders of House and Senate, Iraq (Dec. 1, 1997) (visited October 1, 1998) <http://www.usis.usemb.se/regional/nea/gulfsec/clnt1201.htm>.

47. *Supra* note 45, at 8.

48. *See Standoff in Iraq: Chronology of Iraqi Violations* (visited Oct. 1, 1998) <http://www.foxnews.com/news/packages/iraq/violations.sml/>.

49. *See Text of Clinton Statement on Iraq; Text of President Clinton's Address to Joint Chiefs of Staff and Pentagon Staff* (Feb. 17, 1998) (visited Oct. 1, 1998) <http://europe.cnn.com/ALLPOLITICS/1998/02/17/transcripts/clinton.iraq/>.

50. *See* Frederic L. Kirgis, *The Legal Background on the Use of Force to Induce Iraq to Comply with Security Council Resolutions*, ASIL FLASH INSIGHT, November 1997. The governments of several other members of the Security Council, including China, France, and Russia, have disputed that Resolution 678 can be used as an ongoing authority to use force. *See id.*

51. *Memorandum of Understanding between the United Nations and the Republic of Iraq* (Feb. 23, 1998) (visited Oct. 1, 1998) <http://www.cnn.com/WORLD/9802/23/un.iraq.agreement/index.html>. The *Memorandum of Understanding* provides in relevant part:

> The United Nations and the government of Iraq agree that the following special procedures shall apply to the initial and subsequent entries for the performance of the tasks mandated at the eight Presidential Sites in Iraq as defined in the annex to the present Memorandum:

Unfortunately, the February 23 Memorandum of Understanding turned out to be a short-lived solution. Notwithstanding President Clinton's warning "that if Saddam failed to cooperate fully [with UNSCOM], we would be prepared to act without delay, diplomacy or warning," on December 16, 1998, UNSCOM head Richard Butler reported to the Security Council that Iraq was once again refusing to turn over key documents and blocking inspections at suspected chemical and biological weapons sites.[52] Within hours of receiving Butler's report, the United States and the United Kingdom launched a massive four-day air campaign against "a wide range of Iraqi weapons facilities and intelligence installations."[53]

From 1991–1998, the UNSCOM inspection regime was the most intrusive and comprehensive ever imposed upon a nation. Notwithstanding Saddam Hussein's intermittent intransigence to permit U.N. inspections,[54] the Security Council's approach to Iraqi chemical and biological weapons convention violations provides a blue print for the future.

B. *Unilateral Military Action*

1. Anticipatory Self-Defense

Prior to the advent of the United Nations Charter, there was a customary right of reprisal, permitting nations to use military force to

(a) A Special Group shall be established for this purpose by the Secretary-General in consultation with the Executive Chairman of UNSCOM and the Director General of IAEA. This Group shall comprise senior diplomats appointed by the Secretary-General and experts drawn from UNSCOM and IAEA. The Group shall be headed by a Commissioner appointed by the Secretary-General.

(b) In carrying out its work, the Special Group shall operate under the established procedures of UNSCOM and IAEA, and specific detailed procedures which will be developed given the special nature of the Presidential Sites, in accordance with the relevant resolutions of the Security Council.

(c) The report of the Special Group on its activities and findings shall be submitted by the Executive Chairman of UNSCOM to the Security Council through the Secretary-General.

52. Gerald Seib and Thomas Ricks, *Attack on Iraq: U.S. Launches Strike as Baghdad Refuses to Comply with U.N.*, WALL ST. J., December 17, 1998, at A1.

53. *Id.*

54. *See* Paul Taylor, *West Found Weakened in Annual Arms Survey*, THE BOSTON GLOBE, Oct. 23, 1998, at A2 ("The study [published by the International Institute for Strategic Studies] noted that although the United States and Britain made a credible threat of force in February to compel Iraq to resume cooperation with U.N. arms inspectors, they had not acted after Baghdad in August effectively ended the searches for weapons of mass destruction.").

enforce international obligations in certain limited circumstances. The specific parameters governing lawful reprisals were set forth in the *Naulilaa Incident Arbitration decision*: (1) the offending state must have committed an act contrary to international law; (2) the injured state must have made a demand on the offending state and that demand have gone unsatisfied; and (3) the force used in the reprisal must be proportionate to the offending act.[55]

If it were still good law, the doctrine of armed reprisal could be used to justify an attack on a chemical or biological weapons facility operating in violation of the chemical and biological weapons conventions. The practice of the United Nations and the opinions of the World Court, however, indicate that the right of armed reprisal is generally contrary to the U.N. Charter. Numerous resolutions condemning armed reprisals as inconsistent with the Charter have been adopted over the years.[56] Most notably, the 1970 Declaration on Principles of International Law Concerning Friendly Relations and Co-operation Among States in Accordance with the Charter of the United Nations, provides that "states have a duty to refrain from acts of reprisal involving the use of force."[57] The International Court of Justice implicitly rejected the right of reprisal in the *Corfu Channel Case*[58] and in the *Case Concerning United States Diplomatic and Consular Staff in Tehran.*[59] While the U.N. Charter generally prohibits armed reprisals, such measures are permissible if they qualify as an exercise of self-defense under Article 51 of the Charter.

Self-defense differs from reprisal, which is punitive in character, in that the purpose of self-defense is to mitigate or prevent harm. But the two concepts overlap in the case of anticipatory self-defense. Hugo

---

55. NAULILAA INCIDENT ARBITRATION, Portuguese-German Arbitral Tribunal, 8 *Rec. des décis. Des trib. Arb. mixtes* 409 (1928), *translated and discussed in* W. BISHOP, INTERNATIONAL LAW: CASES AND MATERIALS 903–04 (3d ed. 1971).

56. *See* Rex J. Zedalis, *On the Lawfulness of Forceful Remedies for Violations of Arms Control Agreements: "Star Wars" and other Glimpses at the Future*, 18 N.Y.U. J. INT'L L. & POL. 73, 123 (1985).

57. *Declaration on Principles of International Law Concerning Friendly Relations and Co-operation Among States in Accordance with the Charter of the United Nations*, G.A. Res. 2625, U.N. GAOR, 25th Sess., Supp. No. 28, at 121, U.N. Doc. A/8028 (1970).

58. Corfu Channel Case, UK. v. Alb., 1949 I.C.J. 4 (rejecting British contention that a mine sweeping operation to clear the waters of mines laid by Albania in contravention of international law constituted a justifiable intervention in self-help to remedy the breach of a general international obligation).

59. Case Concerning United States Diplomatic and Consular Staff in Tehran (U.S. v. Iran), 1980 I.C.J. 3 (expressing concern in regard to the legality of the United States incursion into Iran). Judge Morozov's dissenting opinion expressly characterized the incursion as violative of the Charter because it did not meet the requirements of Article 51. *Id.* at 51, 56–57 (Morozov, J., dissenting).

Grotius, often regarded as the father of international law, first recognized a State's right to use force to forestall an anticipated attack in 1625.[60] The contours of the right of anticipatory self-defense were fleshed out in an exchange of diplomatic notes between the governments of the United States and Great Britain during the *Caroline* incident of 1837.[61] The two countries agreed that international law permitted a military response to a threat, provided that the danger posed was, in the words of U.S. Secretary of State Daniel Webster, "instant, overwhelming, leaving no choice of means and no moment for deliberation."[62] The Webster formulation of self-defense is often cited as authoritative customary law. Following the *Caroline* incident, the imminent threat of armed attack has generally been found to justify defensive military action, provided that the threatened nation has first exhausted all peaceful means of resolution and that the action ultimately taken was proportionate to the threat.

Scholars are divided over whether the specific language contained in Articles 2(4) and 51 of the U.N. Charter has overridden the customary right of anticipatory self-defense as articulated during the *Caroline* incident.[63] Article 2(4) prohibits the use of military force in the territory of another state without its consent.[64] Article 51 provides an exception to that prohibition for the case of self-defense in response to "an armed

60. HUGO GROTIUS, THE LAW OF WAR AND PEACE 169–185 (1646) (Francis W. Kelsey, trans., Clarendon Press, 1925).

61. In 1837, rebels in Upper Canada with American logistical support, unsuccessfully revolted against British rule. The Canadian military identified the American steamboat, *Caroline*, as a vessel running arms to the rebels and sent a military force into the United States to set the ship ablaze, killing an American citizen in the process. Subsequently, American officials arrested a Canadian citizen in New York for the murder which prompted a protest by the British government. *See* Destruction of the "Caroline", 2 John B. Moore. Dig. International Law Digest § 217, at 409–14.

62. *Id.* at 412.

63. Those taking the position that Article 51 prohibits anticipatory self-defense include: LOUIS HENKIN, *How Nations Behave*, LAW AND FOREIGN POLICY (2d ed. 1979)at 141; PHILIP C. JESSUP, A MODERN LAW OF NATIONS 166–67 (3d ed. 1968); IAN BROWNLIE, INTERNATIONAL LAW AND THE USE OF FORCE BY STATES, 275–76 (1963); HANS KELSEN, THE LAW OF THE UNITED NATIONS 797–98 (1950); L OPPENHEIM, INTERNATIONAL LAW 156 (H. Lauterpacht ed. 7th ed. 1948). Those taking the position that Article 51 allows anticipatory self-defense include: Abraham Sofaer, *Terrorism, the Law, and National Defense*, 126 MIL. L. REV. 89 (1989); OSCAR SCHACHTER, INTERNATIONAL LAW IN THEORY AND PRACTICE 150–52 (1991); YORAM DINSTEIN, WAR, AGGRESSION AND SELF DEFENSE, 172–76 (1988); D.W. BOWETT, SELF-DEFENSE IN INTERNATIONAL LAW 188–89 (1958); M. McDougal, *The Soviet-Cuban Quarantine and Self-Defense*, 57 AM. J. INT'L L. 597, 599–600 (1963).

64. Article 2(4) of the U.N. Charter provides: "All Members shall refrain in their international relations from the threat or use of force against the territorial integrity or political independence of any state, or in any other manner inconsistent with the Purposes of the United Nations." U.N. CHARTER, art. 2(4).

attack."[65] Those who favor a restrictive interpretation of self-defense, argue that the original Charter signatories intended to supplant customary self-defense norms and rely on new U.N. enforcement mechanisms for maintaining peace in an effort to minimize the overall use of force.

The modern, though by no means universal, trend is to interpret the U.N. Charter as not requiring a state to absorb a devastating or even lethal first strike before acting to protect itself. International law "is not a suicide pact, especially in an age of uniquely destructive weaponry."[66] It is noteworthy that the equally authentic French version of Article 51 uses the *phrase aggression armee*, meaning "armed aggression," instead of the more restrictive term "armed attack" contained in the English version.[67] The right to respond to armed aggression would include the right to respond to threats, since aggression can exist separate from and prior to an actual attack.[68] Even if that was not the uniform interpretation of the drafters of the U.N. Charter in 1948,[69] interpretation of the Charter must keep pace with technological developments in weaponry that render restrictive interpretations obsolete.

This division among scholars reflects the discordant practice of the United Nations as evidenced in particular by its contrary responses to the Israeli preemptory air strike against Egypt in 1967 and the Israeli bombardment of the Iraqi Osirak nuclear reactor in 1981.[70] The United Nations appeared to recognize the right of anticipatory self-defense when Israel launched a preemptory airstrike against Egypt, precipitating

65. Article 51 of the U.N. Charter provides: "Nothing in the present Charter shall impair the inherent right of individual or collective self-defense if an armed attack occurs against a Member of the United Nations, until the Security Council has taken measures necessary to maintain international peace and security." *Id.*, art. 51.

66. Louis R. Beres, *The Permissibility of State-Sponsored Assassination During Peace and War*, 5 TEMPLE INT'L & COMP. L. J. 231, 239 (1992).

67. Beth M. Polebaum, *National Self-Defense in International Law: An Emerging Standard for a Nuclear Age*, 59 N.Y.U.L. REV. 187, 202 (1984).

68. *Id.* at 202.

69. The meaning of "armed attack" may have appeared self-evident to the drafters of the U.N. Charter who had just experienced a war which began with Hitler's massive blitzkrieg assaults (accompanied by scores of tanks, planes, and soldiers) into Germany's neighboring states.

70. The United Nations has also taken seemingly inconsistent stands on the issue in the context of the 1986 U.S. air raid on Libya and the 1993 cruise missile attack on Iraq. The overwhelming majority of the members of the United Nations rejected the United States' claim that the Libyan raid was justified as anticipatory self-defense as discussed below. In contrast, most members of the United Nations supported the claim by the United States that the 1993 cruise missile attack on Iraq was justified as anticipatory self-defense in light of Iraq's attempts to assassinate former President Bush. *See generally* Stuart G. Baker, Note, *Comparing the 1993 U.S. Airstrike on Iraq to the 1986 Bombing of Libya: The New Interpretation of Article 51*, 24 GA. J. INT'L & COMP. L. 99 (1994).

the 1967 "Six Day War."[71] Many countries supported Israel's right to conduct defensive strikes prior to armed attack and draft resolutions condemning the Israeli action were soundly defeated in the Security Council and the General Assembly.[72]

Fourteen years later, on June 7, 1981, Israeli pilots bombed the Iraqi Osirik nuclear reactor. In a statement released after the air strike, the Israeli government justified its action as an act of self-defense, claiming that "sources of unquestioned reliability told us that [the reactor] was intended . . . for the production of atomic bombs. The goal for these bombs was Israel."[73] This time, the United Nations Security Council and General Assembly responded by condemning Israel for the strike.[74] However, the resolution condemning Israel did not declare that the threat to Israel was not credible, that the Israeli strike was disproportionate to the threat, or that Israel had failed to seek alternative peaceful means to resolve the crisis.[75] Those commentators who agree with the United Nations condemnation generally take the position that the Iraqi threat to Israel was not sufficiently "immediate" within the formula or

71. The Israeli air strike was in response to Egyptian President Nasser having ordered Egypt's armed forces into a state of maximum alert, terminating the presence of the United Nations peacekeeping force in his country, and closing the Gulf of Aqaba and the Strait of Tiran to Israeli shipping. A few days later, the armed forces of Syria, Jordan, and Iraq were placed under unified Egyptian command. Israel pursued alternative means to resolve the conflict by prevailing upon other nations to intercede. But with the Arab leaders issuing increasingly bellicose threats, Israel initiated a preemptory air strike against the Egyptian airfields. *See* Polebaum, *supra* note 67, at 193.

72. A draft resolution submitted by the Soviet Union calling for a condemnation of Israel was not accepted by the Security Council. 22 U.N. SCOR (135th mtg.) at 5, U.N. Doc. S/7951 Rev. 1 (1967). The same resolution was brought to the floor of the General Assembly for a vote and was defeated. U.N. GAOR (5th Emergency Special Session, June 17, 1967–Sept. 18, 1967) (154th mtg.) at 15–17, U.N. Doc. A/L.519 (4 July 1967).

73. Polebaum, *supra* note 67, at 205. Israel's attack on the Iraqi reactor should be viewed within the context of the following factors: (1) Since Israel was created by the United Nations in 1948, Iraq has sought Israel's destruction by participating in all wars against Israel and by rejecting all possibilities for peace. Iraq has remained in an official state of war with Israel throughout its existence. *Id.* at 218. (2) A few months prior to the bombing, the Iraqi government issued public statements suggesting that its nuclear reactor was intended to be used "against the Zionist enemy." *Id.* at 219. (3) Iraq had little need for peaceful nuclear energy in light of its vast oil reserves. *Id.* at 221. (4) Intelligence indicated that the Iraqi reactor would become operational in one to three months, after which time bombardment would endanger civilians by releasing radioactive materials. *Id.* at 222. (5) While an attempt at negotiations with Iraq would have been futile, Israel made repeated unsuccessfully diplomatic efforts to persuade the French and Italian governments to cease shipments of sensitive nuclear material to Iraq. *Id.* at 223.

74. U.N. Doc. S/RES/487 (1981); G.A. Res. A/RES/36/27 (1981).

75. U.N. Res. 487, *supra* note 74; G.A. Res. 27, *supra* note 74; *See also* U.N. Doc. S/PV 2285 (1981).

the spirit of *the Caroline*.[76] Yet, the action of the United Nations, "unaccompanied by clear explanations or analysis, seem[s] to represent a mere political consensus and not a legal one."[77]

Notwithstanding the international community's condemnation of the Israeli attack on the Iraqi nuclear plant, the United States took similar action on August 20, 1998,[78] against a plant in Khartoum, Sudan thought to be producing the lethal nerve agent VX and other chemical weapons components.[79] The U.S. Government justified its cruise missile attack on the Al-Shifa plant by stating that the plant had no commercial uses, was closely guarded, and that its owner had close financial links to Osama bin Laden, a Saudi exile suspected of masterminding the August 1998 bombings of two U.S. embassies in Kenya and Tanzania.[80] In arguing that the attack on the Al Shifa plant was consistent with the right of self defense under Article 51 of the U.N. Charter, Ambassador Bill Richardson informed the Security Council that the attack was necessary to "deter and prevent the repetition of unlawful terrorist attacks on the United States and other countries."[81] But unlike past U.S. assertions of the right of self-defense, Richardson's communication contained no evidentiary support for the U.S. assertion.[82]

---

76. *See* Anthony D'Amato, *Israel's Air Strike Upon the Iraqi Nuclear Reactor*, 77 AM. J. INT'L LAW 584 (1983).

77. Polebaum, *supra* note 67, at 217.

78. This was the second time that the Clinton Administration asserted the doctrine of anticipatory-self defense to justify an attack. Five years earlier, it had relied on the doctrine to justify its June 26, 1993 cruise missile attack on the Iraqi Intelligence Service Headquarters in Baghdad in the aftermath of the failed attempt to assassinate former President Bush during his visit to Kuwait. *See* Statement by Ambassador Madeleine K. Albright, United States Permanent Representative to the United Nations, in the Security Council, on the Iraqi Attempt to Assassinate President Bush (June 27, 1993), USUN PRESS RELEASE 110-(93), June 27, 1993. The majority of States expressed no objections to the 1993 airstrike and seem to have largely accepted the legal justification provided by the United States; the only States that publicly condemned the U.S. action were China, Bangladesh, Yemen, Iran and Sudan. Baker, *supra* note 70, at 99–104.

79. *See generally* Michael Barletta, *Report: Chemical Weapons in the Sudan*, 6 THE NONPROLIFERATION REVIEW (1998).

80. CNN Interactive, *U.S. Missiles Pound Targets in Afghanistan*, Sudan (visited Sept. 16, 1998).

See also, Coordinator for Counterterrorism, U.S. Department of State, *Fact Sheet: U.S. Strike on Facilities in Afghanistan and Sudan*, United States Information Agency, August 21, 1998 (visited April 20, 1999) <http://www.usia.gov/topical/pol/terror/98082112.htm>

81. Letter Dated 20 August 1998 From the Permanent Representative of the United States of America to the United Nations Addressed to the President of the Security Council, U.N. Doc. S/1998/760, 20 August 1998.

82. *See* Statement by Ambassador Madeleine K. Albright, United States Permanent Representative to the United Nations, in the Security Council, on the Iraqi Attempt to Assassinate President Bush, June 27, 1993, USUN Press Release 110-(93), June 27, 1993 (containing photographs and detailed intelligence proving Iraqi involvement in the attempted assassination of former President Bush in Kuwait). *See also*, Milt Bearden, *Explaining Our*

At first, international criticism of the attack on the Sudanese plant was muted, which signaled acceptance of the principle of anticipatory self-defense in the context of the destruction of a chemical weapons facilities in the hands of a known terrorist.[83] However, world opinion, even among America's closest allies, began to coalesce against the United States when it turned out that Osama bin Laden had no financial connection to the Sudanese plant and that the plant actually produced drugs for treating malaria, diabetes, hypertension, ulcers, rheumatism, gonorrhea, and tuberculosis.[84] The American case was further eroded when it was discovered that the Sudanese plant had a contract with the United Nations to provide these medicines—a contract which had been approved by the United State Representative to the United Nations.[85] While the U.S. Government steadfastly refused to provide its intelligence data to dispel doubt, former U.S. President Jimmy Carter, as well as several Arab countries, demanded an independent U.N. investigation to determine whether chemical warfare agents could be detected in the remains of the factory.[86] In contrast with its support for the efforts of UNSCOM to investigate potential chemical weapons sites in Iraq, the United States blocked the Carter initiative, stating: "we don't think an investigation is needed. We don't think anything needs to be put to rest."[87]

It is noteworthy that the international response to the U.S. cruise missile attack on the Sudanese plant focused on the degree of proof required, rather than the underlying legal right to launch anticipatory attacks against chemical weapons facilities. Yet, having failed to suffi-

---

Actions in Sudan, N.Y. TIMES, August 26, 1998, (in justifying the 1986 bombing of Tripoli, the Reagan administration released a decoded message intercepted from the Libyan mission in East Germany, which proved Libyan involvement in the Labelle Disco bombing).

83. This is to be distinguished from the international community's vocal condemnation of the United States' April 1986 air raid against targets in Libya, which were conducted in response to the Libyan bombing of a German discotheque frequented by U.S. serviceman, which is discussed below.

84. Colum Lynch, *Allied Doubts Grow About US Strike on Sudanese Plant*, THE BOSTON GLOBE, September 24, at A2; David L. Marcus, *Frank Criticizes Bombing of Plant in Sudan*, THE BOSTON GLOBE, Sept. 24, 1998, at A9. The Al Shifa plant supplied sixty percent of Sudan's pharmaceutical needs. *See* Barletta, *supra* note 79, at note 34. According to Sudanese doctors and health officials, the Al Shifa plant's destruction could lead to severe drug shortages endangering the lives of thousands of Sudanese. *Id.*

85. In January 1998, the Al Shifa plant had been awarded a $199,000 contract to ship 100,000 cartons of Shifazole veterinary medicine to Iraq, as part of the U.N. oil-for-food program. *See* Barletta, *supra* note 79, at note 37. *See also* Lynch, *supra* note 84, at A2; Marcus, *supra* note 84, at A9.

86. Sudan's head of state, Omar al-Bashir, pledged that the Sudan would cooperate with a United Nations on-site investigation of the remains of the Al Shifa plant to determine whether it had been used to produce chemical weapons or precursor chemicals. *See* Barletta, *supra* note 79, at note 41. *See also* Lynch, *supra* note 84, at A2; Marcus, *supra* note 84, at A9.

87 Barletta, *supra* note 79, at notes 173–178.

ciently prove its case, the action seriously undermined U.S. credibility, making it more difficult to garner international support for such action against biological or chemical weapons facilities in the future. As a congressional critic of the attack against the Sudanese plant pointed out, "Attacking an installation in another country may be justified, but you've got to be very, very sure about the threats before launching the attack. It is important to have self-defense capability, but if you overuse it, you lose it."[88]

The Sudanese bombing incident focused attention on the necessity requirement of the doctrine of self-defense. Because a preemptory attack on a chemical or biological weapons production or storage facility can pose a serious threat to the surrounding civilian population, the issue of proportionality may also become a source of controversy. A direct hit on a conventional ammunition depot will create a massive explosion; any resulting collateral damage will be limited to the immediate vicinity. In contrast, an attack on a chemical or biological weapons facility could result in the release of a deadly cloud of gas.[89] The extent of the contamination of the surrounding area would depend on prevailing environmental conditions and the physical characteristics of the chemical or biological agent.[90] A World War II allied attack on an Italian ship laden with 100 tons of mustard gas, which resulted in the release of a poisonous cloud which drifted over the port town of Bari, killing more than 1,000 civilians, demonstrated the potential for collateral damage.[91] During the Persian Gulf conflict, the U.S. Department of Defense estimated that up to six million Iraqis could have been killed from the dispersion of anthrax and botulism viruses caused by a single attack on a biological weapons facility.[92] Thus, all but the most carefully executed attacks on chemical or biological facilities will likely fail the proportionality requirement of self-defense.

2. Assassination

Consider a situation in which a particular state determines that another state plans to launch a chemical or biological surprise attack upon its population centers. Intelligence assessments reveal that the assassination of selected key figures would prevent this attack altogether. Intelligence further reveals that conventional forms of preemption would generate far greater harm, especially if the attack resulted in

88. Marcus, *supra* note 84, at A9.
89. *See* McClintock, *supra* note 4, at 637–38.
90. *Id.* at 637–38.
91. *Id.* at 637 n.10.
92. *Id.*

releasing the targeted chemical or biological agents. Under this scenario, would a preemptive assassination violate international law?

Just as international law is not a suicide pact, neither is it a license to kill. Assassination has traditionally been viewed as unlawful in both war and peace. Where a condition of war exists between states, international assassination constitutes a war crime. Article 23(B) of the Hague Convention IV of 1907, provides that "it is especially forbidden ... to kill or wound *treacherously*, individuals belonging to the hostile nation or army."[93] The United States Army's field manual on the law of land warfare has incorporated this prohibition in the following terms: "This article ... prohibits *assassination*, proscription or outlawry of an enemy, or putting a price upon an enemy's head, as well as offering a reward for an enemy 'dead or alive.' "[94]

Yet the 1907 Hague Convention's prohibition on assassination is not as broad as it might appear at first blush. Focusing on the "treacherous" requirement of the Hague Convention, a recent military legal analysis of war time assassination concluded that none of the following acts contravened the prohibition: (1) the November 18, 1941 raid by Scottish commandos at Bedda Littoria, Libya whose goal was to kill German Field Marshal Erwin Rommel; (2) the April 18, 1943 downing of a Japanese aircraft known to be carrying Admiral Osoruku Yamamoto by a U.S. Air Force jet fighter; and (3) the October 30, 1951 air strike by the U.S. Navy that killed 500 senior Chinese and North Korean military officers and security forces at a military planning conference at Kapsan, North Korea.[95]

Where agents of one State assassinate the official of another state during peacetime, the action may constitute an internationally prohibited act of terrorism. Article 2(a) of the Convention on Internationally Protected Persons, to which the United States and most other countries are parties, criminalizes "the intentional commission of ... murder, kidnapping or other attack upon the person or liberty of an internationally protected person," which are defined to include heads of state and other high level officials.[96] It is important to note, however, that the Internationally Protected Persons Convention accords a head of state or

93. The Hague Convention, *supra* note 9, art. 23(b) (emphasis added).

94. *Dep't of the Army, The Law of Land Warfare* art. 31 (1956) (Army Field Manual No. 27-10, Washington, D.C.) (emphasis added).

95. W. Hays Parks, Memorandum of Law: *Executive Order 12333 and Assassination*, ARMY LAWYER, Dec. 1989 (Dept. of the Army Pamphlet 27-50-204), at 5.

96. Convention on the Prevention and Punishment of Crimes Against Internationally Protected Persons, Including Diplomatic Agents, *adopted* Dec. 14, 1973, 28 U.S.T. 1975, 1037 U.N.T.S. 167.

state official protected status only when the official is outside his/her own country.[97]

Notwithstanding these international law prohibitions, according to the results of a 1975 Senate investigation, United States presidents have instigated plots to assassinate foreign leaders in Cuba, the Congo, the Dominican Republic, Chile and South Vietnam.[98] In response to these revelations, President Gerald R. Ford promulgated Executive Order 12,333, which provides, "No person employed by or acting on behalf of the United States Government shall engage in, or conspire to engage in, assassination."[99]

Although Executive Order 12,333 has been reissued by Presidents Carter, Reagan, Bush and Clinton,[100] its value is more symbolic than real. A president can circumvent the ban posed by the Executive Order and legally carry out an assassination in four ways: (1) he can declare the existence of hostilities and target persons in command positions as combatants; (2) he can broadly construe Article 51 to mean that certain criminal acts justify the use of assassination as a legitimate means of self-defense; (3) he can narrowly construe Executive Order 12,333, for instance, to prohibit only "treacherous" attacks on foreign leaders; and (4) he can simply repeal or amend the order, or even approve a one time exception to it.[101]

The contours of the Executive Order were tested by the 1986 bombing of Libyan leader Colonel Muammar Qaddafi's personal quarters in Tripoli in response to Libyan involvement in the bombing of the La Belle Disco in West Berlin. According to investigative reporter Seymour M. Hersh, who spent three months interviewing more than seventy current and former officials in the White House, the State Department, the C.I.A., the National Security Agency, and the Pentagon, Qaddafi's assassination was the primary goal of the Libyan bombing.[102] Hersh reported that nine of the eighteen American fighter jets that flew

---

97. The Convention defines "Internationally protected person" as: "Head of State, including any member of a collegial body performing the functions of a Head of State under the constitution of the State concerned, a Head of Government or a Minister for Foreign Affairs, whenever any such person is in a foreign State, as well as members of his family who accompany him." *Id.*, art. 1(1)(a).

98. Select Comm. to Study Governmental Operations, With Respect to Intelligence Activities, Alleged Assassination Plots Involving Foreign Leaders, S. REP. No. 465, 94TH CONG., 1ST SESS. (1975).

99. EXEC. ORDER No. 12,333, 3 C.F.R. 90 (1976).

100. Boyd M. Johnson, III, *Executive Order 12,333: The Permissibility of an American Assassination of a Foreign Leader*, 25 CORNELL INT'L L. J. 401, 403 (1992).

101. *Id.*

102. Seymour M. Hersh, *Target Qaddafi*, N.Y. TIMES MAGAZINES, Feb. 22, 1987, at 17–19.

to Tripoli on April 14, 1986, had a specific mission to target Qaddafi and his family.[103] One well-informed Air Force intelligence officer as stated that "There's no question they were looking for Qaddafi. It was briefed that way. They were going to kill him."[104] The Reagan administration characterized the attack as a legitimate self-defense operation under Article 51 in light of evidence that Libya was planning future terrorist attacks against the United States,[105] an assertion that was rejected by an overwhelming majority of the members of the United Nations.[106] Shortly thereafter, Senior Army lawyers made public a memorandum that concluded that Executive Order 12,333 was not intended to prevent the United States from acting in self-defense against "legitimate threats to national security."[107]

During the Persian Gulf War in 1990, Air Force Chief of Staff Michael J. Dugan publicly stated that the United States might seek to "decapitate" Iraqi leadership by targeting Saddam Hussein, his family and even his mistress.[108] This statement resulted in a great deal of outrage in the United States and abroad, and refocused attention on the permissibility of assassination as an instrument of U.S. policy.[109]

Yet, in the aftermath of the Persian Gulf conflict, an increasing number of scholars have suggested that assassination has become a legitimate preemptive strategy in light of the growing destructiveness of current weapons.[110] By analogy with the domestic criminal law concept

---

103. *Id.*

104. *Id.* at 20.

105. President's Address to the Nation, DEP'T ST. BULL., June 1986, at 1–2 (Apr. 14, 1986).

106. Of America's traditional allies, only Britain, Israel, and South Africa supported the raid. Almost every other State, including many of the United States' allies, resoundingly rejected the legitimacy of the United States' reliance on Article 51 as legal authority for the Libya raid. The United Nations General Assembly adopted a resolution condemning "the armed attack by the United States of America in violation of the Charter of the United Nations and the norms of international law," and the United States had to exercise its veto to prevent a similar resolution from being adopted by the Security Council. Baker, *supra* note 70, at 101, 103–04, 105–06.

107. Parks, *supra* note 95, at 8. The Clinton Administration has recently reconfirmed this position. *Deadly Force Against Terrorists is Legal, White House Officials Assert*, THE BOSTON GLOBE, October 29, 1998, at A29.

108. Robert F. Turner, *Killing Saddam: Would it be a Crime?*, THE WASHINGTON POST, October 7, 1990, at D1.

109. When Secretary of Defense Richard Cheney learned of Dugan's remarks, he immediately fired him, explaining to reporters that Dugan's comments constituted a potential violation of the U.S. ban on assassination. Johnson, *supra* note 100, at 403.

110. *See* Louis R. Beres, *The Permissibility of State-Sponsored Assassination During Peace and War*, 5 TEMPLE INT'L & COMP. L. J. 231, 240 (1992); Michael N. Schmitt, *State-Sponsored Assassination in International and Domestic Law*, 17 YALE J. INT'L L. 609, 646 (1992); Turner, *supra* note 108, at D1.

of "necessity,"[111] these commentators argue that assassination can be justified under a balance of harms analysis, provided that the following conditions are satisfied.

> First, a state must make a good faith effort to circumscribe potential targets to include only those authoritative persons in the prospective attacking state. Second, the assassination must comply with the settled rules of warfare as they concern discrimination, proportionality, and military necessity. Third, state-gathered intelligence must evidence, beyond a reasonable doubt, preparations for unconventional or other forms of highly destructive warfare projected against the acting state. Finally, the state must have decided after careful deliberation that an assassination would in fact prevent the intended aggression, and that it would cause substantially less harm to civilian populations than alternative forms of self-help.[112]

While anticipatory self-defense can be subject to abuse, the risk of unleashing the assassination genie from the bottle is even greater. The prohibition on assassination provides protection to the country's own leaders who would otherwise be vulnerable to assassination plots by other states. A reversal of this customary restraint "could unleash a chain reaction of transnational assassinations and a substantial breakdown of diplomatic relations."[113] In addition to the risk of retaliation, targeting specific individuals may unintentionally strengthen enemy morale and resolve. Finally, the targeted individuals are likely to be replaced by others who will continue their threatening policies or by even less acceptable alternatives. According to Professor Michael Reisman of Yale Law School, "while tyranicide might present a compelling justification for assassination, assassination in any form presents a cascading threat to world order."[114] For this reason, large numbers of other States are likely to oppose the use of assassination as a means of enforcing international law, even if it can be legally justified as a legitimate act of self-defense.

It is noteworthy, however, that there was almost no international opposition to the August 20, 1998, U.S. cruise missile attack against

---

111. See Model Penal Code, Section 3.02 (1985) (providing that conduct believed necessary to avoid some harm is justifiable if "the harm or evil sought to be avoided by such conduct is greater than that sought to be prevented by the law defining the offense charged."); Arnolds & Garland, *The Defense of Necessity in Criminal Law: The Right to Choose the Lesser Evil*, 65 J. CRIM. L. & C. 289 (1974).

112. Beres, *supra* note 110, at 240.

113. *Id.*, at 231, 241.

114. W.M. Reisman, *Covert Action*, 20 YALE J. INT'L L. 419, 424 (1995).

terrorist bases in Khost, Afghanistan in an attempt to eliminate Osama bin Laden and his lieutenants.[115] International outrage has focussed entirely on the attack on the Al-Shifa plant in Sudan, which was launched on the same day.

C. *Criminalization*

The prohibitions embodied in the 1908 Hague Convention, the 1925 Geneva Protocol, the Biological Weapons Convention, and the Chemical Weapons Convention are directed to the actions of states, not individuals. Although the Biological and Chemical Weapons Conventions contain provisions obliging each State party to prohibit persons under their jurisdiction from undertaking activities that are forbidden by the treaties, these provisions fail to deal with the situation in which an offender is present in a state that has not established or otherwise lacks jurisdiction to prosecute, or is complicit with the offender.[116] An approach with great potential, but which has not yet been pursued is to apply international criminal law to prosecute and punish offending leaders before an international tribunal or domestic courts.

1. Prosecution Before International Criminal Tribunals

On May 25, 1993, the U.N. Security Council, acting under Chapter VII of the United Nations Charter, established the International Criminal Tribunal for the Former Yugoslavia (the Tribunal) to prosecute persons responsible for war crimes, genocide, and crimes against humanity during the Balkan conflict.[117] This was the first international war

115. *See* CNN Interactive, *U.S. Missiles Pound Targets in Afghanistan, Sudan*, Aug. 21, 1998, (visited Sept. 16, 1998) <http://www.cnn.com/US/9808/20/us.strikes.02/index.html>.

116. Unlike the Grave Breaches provision of the Geneva Convention, there is no universal jurisdiction or a duty to prosecute persons who violate the 1908 Hague Convention, the 1925 Geneva Protocol, the 1972 Biological Weapons Convention, or the 1992 Chemical Weapons Convention. *See* Michael Scharf, *The Letter of the Law: The Scope of the International Legal Obligation to Prosecute Human Rights Crimes*, 59 LAW & CONTEMP. PROBS. 41 (1996).

117. S.C. Res. 827, U.N. SCOR, 48th Sess., at 29, U.N. Doc. S/INF/49 (1994), *reprinted in* 2 VIRGINIA MORRIS & MICHAEL P. SCHARF, AN INSIDER'S GUIDE TO THE INTERNATIONAL CRIMINAL TRIBUNAL FOR THE FORMER YUGOSLAVIA 177 (1995) [hereinafter MORRIS & SCHARF, INSIDER'S GUIDE]. *See also* the record of the debate leading to the adoption of Resolution 827, U.N. SCOR, 48th Sess., 3217th mtg. at 16, U.N. Doc. S/PV.3217 (1993), *reprinted in* MORRIS & SCHARF, INSIDER'S GUIDE, *supra* at 179, 188. Statute of the International Tribunal for the Prosecution of Persons Responsible for Serious Violations of International Humanitarian Law Committed in the Territory of the Former Yugoslavia since 1991, *annexed to* UNITED NATIONS, REPORT OF THE SECRETARY-GENERAL PURSUANT TO PARAGRAPH 2 OF SECURITY COUNCIL RESOLUTION 808 (1993), U.N. Doc. S/25704 (1993), *reprinted in* MORRIS & SCHARF, INSIDER'S GUIDE, *supra* at 1.

crimes tribunal established since the Nuremberg and Tokyo Tribunals following World War II.

During the next two years, the judges for the Tribunal were elected, Rules of Procedure and Evidence were promulgated, a Headquarters Agreement was entered into, the Tribunal's Prosecutor and Registrar were appointed, courtrooms, offices, and a jail were constructed at The Hague, a staff of over 500 persons was hired, seventy persons were indicted, and trials were commenced.[118] The expenses of the Yugoslavia Tribunal ($60 million in 1998) are covered by a combination of the assessed contributions of the Member States of the United Nations and the voluntary contributions of States, international organizations, and private entities.[119]

A year after the Security Council decided to establish an ad hoc tribunal for the former Yugoslavia, it created a second ad hoc tribunal to prosecute those responsible for the genocidal murder of 800,000 members of the Tutsi Tribe in the small central African country of Rwanda.[120] The creation of the Rwanda Tribunal demonstrated that the international judicial machinery designed for the Yugoslavia Tribunal could be employed for other specific circumstances and offenses, thereby avoiding the need to reinvent the wheel in response to each humanitarian crisis of similar magnitude.

The two ad hoc Tribunals have jurisdiction over *inter alia* violations of the 1908 Hague Convention, which as stated above, prohibits the use of poisonous weapons, as well as the deployment of weapons "calculated to cause unnecessary suffering." In addition to the use of biological and chemical weapons, the Tribunals' jurisdiction also covers planning and preparation which includes production and stockpiling.[121] The Security Council could go even further and expressly endow a new ad hoc tribunal with subject matter jurisdiction over breaches of the Biological Weapons Convention and the Chemical Weapons Convention, in addition to the 1908 Hague Convention.[122]

---

118. *See generally* MORRIS & SCHARF, INSIDER'S GUIDE, *supra* note 117.

119. *Third Annual Report of the International Tribunal for the Prosecution of Persons Responsible for Serious Violations of International Humanitarian Law Committed in the Territory of the Former Yugoslavia since 1991*, at 43–44, U.N. Doc. A/51/292-S/1996/665 (1996).

120. Statute of the International Tribunal for Rwanda, annexed to S.C. Res. 955, U.N. SCOR, 3453rd mtg. at 20, U.N. Doc. S/RES/955 (1994), *reprinted in* 2 VIRGINIA MORRIS AND MICHAEL P. SCHARF, THE INTERNATIONAL CRIMINAL TRIBUNAL FOR RWANDA 3 (1998) [hereinafter MORRIS & SCHARF, TRIBUNAL FOR RWANDA].

121. Yugoslavia Tribunal Statute, art. 7(1), U.N. Doc. S/25704 (1993); Rwanda Tribunal Statute, art. 6(1), U.N. Doc. S/RES/955 (1994).

122. Given the large number of parties, these conventions could be said to reflect customary international law. But even if they do not, it is perfectly fair to use them as the basis

On March 13, 1998, the U.S. Senate passed Concurrent Resolution 78 by a vote of 93 to 0, "call[ing] for the United Nations to form an international criminal tribunal for the purpose of indicting, prosecuting, and imprisoning Saddam Hussein and any other Iraqi officials who may be found responsible for ... violations of international humanitarian law."[123] Iraq, which has produced, stockpiled, and used biological and chemical weapons, would seem to be an ideal candidate for a third Security Council created Tribunal. After all, the Security Council has repeatedly condemned Iraq's violations of international humanitarian law generally and violations of the conventions prohibiting biological and chemical weapons in particular. It has warned Iraq that individuals, as well as the Government of Iraq, would be held liable for such violations. It has called on Member States to submit information about Iraqi violations of international humanitarian law committed during the Gulf War,[124] and it has established a Commission to document subsequent Iraqi violations of the biological and chemical weapons conventions.[125]

It is important to bear in mind that the effectiveness of such a tribunal does not require that the violating State be vanquished and that the victor State(s) have custody of those accused of violating the biological and chemical weapons conventions. There would be utility in obtaining an international indictment of Saddam Hussein, even if, as would undoubtedly be the case, Iraq refused to surrender him to an international tribunal for trial. The indictment would render Hussein a virtual prisoner in his own country, subject to arrest if he ever steps outside its borders.[126]

The procedures for indictment and the issuance of arrest warrants set forth in the Statute and Rules of the ad hoc International Criminal Tribunals may be used to stigmatize and constrain accused persons, even if the accused cannot be arrested and tried immediately. Moreover, the tribunal's process for confirmation of indictments, which has been

---

of an international court's subject matter jurisdiction if the country where the acts were committed is a party to them.

123. *See* 144 CONG. REC. S1907-105.

124. *U.N. Security Council Resolution* 674 (1990) 29 October 1990.

125. *See supra* note 45, at para. 8.

126. Michael Scharf and Valerie Epps, *The International Trial of the Century? A "Cross Fire" Exchange on the First Case Before the Yugoslavia War Crimes Tribunal*, 29 CORNELL INT'L L. J. 635, 661 (1996); Remarks of Dr. Roy S. Lee, Principal Legal Officer at the United Nations, Office of the Legal Counsel, *Symposium on War Crimes Tribunal*, 6 PACE INT'L L. Rev. 93, 101 (1994).

described as akin to a "televised grand jury proceeding,"[127] would go a long way in documenting the international violations.

Yet, the other members of the Security Council have resisted U.S. proposals for the establishment of additional hoc tribunals. There are several reasons why the Security Council has been unwilling or unable to continue with the ad hoc approach to international criminal justice that was employed for Yugoslavia and Rwanda. The first reason, which is sometimes referred to as "tribunal fatigue," is that the process of reaching a consensus on a tribunal's statute, electing judges, selecting a prosecutor, and appropriating funds has turned out to be extremely time-consuming and politically exhausting for the members of the Security Council.[128] One Permanent Member of the Security Council, China, has openly expressed concern about using the Yugoslavia Tribunal as a precedent for the creation of other ad hoc criminal tribunals.[129] Second, the creation of ad hoc tribunals by the Security Council is viewed as inherently unfair by many countries, because the Permanent Members of the Security Council can veto any substantive action by the Security Council and thereby shield themselves and their allies from the jurisdiction of such tribunals, notwithstanding any atrocities that might be committed within their borders. The final reason for the reluctance to create additional ad hoc tribunals is economic. The expense of establishing ad hoc tribunals is seen as too much for an organization whose budget is already stretched thin.

With the overwhelming approval of the Rome Statute for a Permanent International Criminal Court in July 1998,[130] it is unlikely that the members of the Security Council would be willing to support the establishment of an ad hoc tribunal covering violations of the biological and chemical weapons regimes. Instead, they would insist that such persons be prosecuted before the new Permanent International Criminal Court. However, with U.S. opposition to the Permanent International Criminal

---

127. MICHAEL P. SCHARF, BALKAN JUSTICE: THE STORY BEHIND THE FIRST INTERNATIONAL WAR CRIMES TRIAL SINCE NUREMBERG 151 (1997) [hereinafter SCHARF, BALKAN JUSTICE].

128. *See* MORRIS & SCHARF, INSIDER'S GUIDE, *supra* note 117, at 33–34 (explaining compromises necessary to gain support for the statute), 144–145 (describing difficulties in electing judges), 161–163 (discussing controversy in appointing the prosecutor).

129. *Id.* at 344 n.901, quoting statement of Mr. Li Zhaoxing of China at the time of voting on Security Council Resolution 827 (1993), which established the Yugoslavia Tribunal. U.N. Doc. S/PV.3217, 25 May 1993, at 33–34. China later abstained on Security Council Resolution 955 (1994), which established the Rwanda Tribunal.

130. Rome Statute of the International Criminal Court, U.N. Doc. A/CONF.183/9, 17 July 1998. The Statute was approved by a vote of 120 to 7, with 20 abstentions. Of the Permanent Members of the Security Council, the United States and China voted against; France, Russia, and the United Kingdom voted in favor.

Court,[131] the fate of the new tribunal remains in doubt. At a minimum, it will be several years, perhaps as long as a decade, before the Statute for a Permanent International Criminal Court receives the 60 ratifications required for it to enter into force. Even when the Permanent Court is established, its jurisdiction over use of biological and chemical weapons will be largely restricted to cases of an international armed conflict.[132] Further, the jurisdiction of the Permanent Court would not apply to the production, transfer, or stockpiling of such weapons, unless they were ultimately used in combat.[133]

2. Domestic Assertion of Universal Jurisdiction

In the absence of a new ad hoc tribunal or a permanent international criminal court, individual states can accomplish many of the same goals through the exercise of extraterritorial criminal jurisdiction over persons who violate the biological and chemical weapons conventions. The United States recently enacted legislation which takes a step in this direction.[134] Title 18, Section 2332a of the United States Code provides

131. Michael P. Scharf, *Results of the Rome Conference for an International Criminal Court*, ASIL INSIGHT, August 1998; *Prepared Statement of Professor Michael P. Scharf Before the Senate Foreign Relations Committee*, FEDERAL NEWS SERVICE, July 23, 1998; Thomas W. Lippman, *America Avoids the Stand: Why the U.S. Objects to A World Criminal Court*, WASHINGTON POST, July 26, 1998, at C1.

132. The Permanent International Criminal Court would have jurisdiction over "serious violations of the laws and customs applicable in international armed conflict" including:

(xvii) Employing poison or poisoned weapons;

(xviii) Employing asphyxiating, poisonous or other gases, and all analogous liquids, materials or devices;

(xx) Employing weapons, projectiles and material and methods of warfare which are of a nature to cause superfluous injury or unnecessary suffering or which are inherently indiscriminate in violation of the international law of armed conflict, provided that such weapons, projectiles and material and methods of warfare are subject of a comprehensive prohibition . . ."

Supra note 130, at art. 8(2)(b) (xvii), (xviii), and (xx). In the case of an internal armed conflict, the Court has jurisdiction over, inter alia, persons responsible for "intentionally directing attacks against the civilian population as such or against individual civilians not taking direct part in hostilities." *Id.*, at art. 8(2)(e)(i).

133. *Id*, art. 25.

134. The provisions creating U.S. jurisdiction over biological and chemical weapons attacks against U.S. nationals were part of a package of anti-terrorism provisions enacted in the aftermath of the bombing of a federal building on April 19, 1995 in Oklahoma City. *See* Roberta Smith, *America Tries to Come to Terms With Terrorism: The United States Anti-Terrorism and Effective Death Penalty Act of 1996 v. British Anti-Terrorism Law and International Response*, 5 CARDOZO J. INT'L & COMP. L. 249, 260–262 (1997); Thomas C. Martin, Note, *The Comprehensive Terrorism Prevention Act of 1995*, 20 SETON HALL LEGIS. J. 201, 205–06 (1995). There is scant legislative history for the provisions on biological and chemical weapons, which at the time were not viewed as among the more important aspects of the legislation. *See* H.R. CONF. REP. No. 104-518, at 119–27 (1996), *reprinted in* 1996 U.S.C.C.A.N. 924, 952–60.

that any person who, "without lawful authority," person uses or threatens, attempts, or conspires to use a weapon of mass destruction, including any biological agent, toxin, or vector, against a national of the United States shall be punished, whether such national is within the United States or not.[135] Section 2332c of that Title similarly punishes any person who, "without lawful authority," uses, or attempts or conspires to use a chemical weapon against a national of the United States while such national is outside or within the United States.[136] These criminal provisions are based on the "passive personality" theory of jurisdiction, which provides jurisdiction to the United States based on the nationality of the victim.[137]

There are several potential defenses to criminal proceedings under 18 U.S.C. Sections 2332a and 2332c for a person such as Saddam Hussein. First, the law does not cover production or stockpiling; it covers only the *use* of biological or chemical weapons, and then only when such use is against a U.S. citizen.[138] On the other hand, production and stockpiling could be deemed overt acts which are part of a conspiracy to use such weapons, which is covered. Second, as leader of Iraq, Hussein's decision to order the production, stockpiling, or use of biological or chemical weapons would be within the scope of his Presidential authority, thereby falling outside the statute's prohibition. However, since such acts are in violation of international law, a court might conclude that "lawful authority" is absent. Finally, Saddam Hussein could rely on Head of State immunity to quash an indictment brought under this statute while he continues to serve as President of Iraq.[139] However, recent cases involving Ferdinand Marcos of the Philippines, Manuel Noriega of Panama, and Radovan Karadzic of Bosnia[140]

---

135. 18 U.S.C. § 2332(a) (1997).

136. 18 U.S.C. § 2332(c) (1997).

137. *See generally* Geoffrey R. Watson, *The Passive Personality Principle*, 28 TEX. INT'L L.J. 1 (1993).

138. This in part explains why Osama bin Laden has been indicted for his role in the Kenya and Tanzania embassy bombings, but not for producing chemical weapons at the Al Shifa plant. *See* Colum Lynch, *US Indicts Bin Laden in Killings*, THE BOSTON GLOBE, November 5, 1998, at A9.

139. *See generally* Shobha Varughese George, *Head-of-State Immunity in the United States Courts: Still Confused After All These Years*, 64 FORDHAM L. REV. 1051 (1995).

140. *See* In re Doe, 860 F.2d 40, 45 (2d Cir. 1988)("[T]here is respectable authority for denying head-of-state immunity to a former head-of-state for private or criminal acts in violation of American law."); U.S. v. Noriega, 746 F. Supp. 1506, 1519 n.11 (S.D. Fla. 1990) ("[T]here is ample doubt whether head of state immunity extends to private or criminal acts in violation of U.S. law."); *Cf.* Doe v. Karadzic, 866 F. Supp. 734 (S.D.N.Y. 1994) ("[W]e doubt that the acts of even a state official, taken in violation of a nation's fundamental law and wholly unratified by that nation's government, could properly be characterized as an act of state."). *But see* Lafontant v. Aristide, 844 F. Supp. 128, 138 (E.D.N.Y. 1994) (rejecting

suggest that U.S. courts might find the doctrine inapplicable in a criminal case involving flagrant violations of international and U.S. law.[141]

The Harvard Sussex Program on Chemical and Biological Warfare Armament and Arms Limitation has proposed a "Convention on the Prevention and Punishment of the Crime of Developing, Producing, Acquiring, Stockpiling, Retaining, Transferring or Using Biological or Chemical Weapons" (hereinafter Harvard Draft Convention).[142] The Harvard Draft Convention, which is appended at the end of this article, is modeled upon the several anti-terrorism conventions which provide for universal jurisdiction and require States to either prosecute or extradite (*aut dedere aut judicare*) offenders found within their territory.[143]

The Harvard Draft Convention avoids the deficiencies inherent in the current U.S. legislation in three ways. First, the Harvard Draft Convention is based on "universal jurisdiction," which provides State Parties jurisdiction over individual offenders present in their territory irrespective of any nexus to the offense. Like pirates, those who violate the international prohibitions related to chemical and biological weapons would thereby become *hostis humani generis* "an enemy of all humankind." Any State party in which such persons are found would have a duty "without exception whatsoever" to either prosecute or extradite the alleged offender to another State or international tribunal for prosecution. Second, the Harvard Draft Convention explicitly covers the

---

the dicta of In re Doe and finding that such a "theory for circumventing head-of-state immunity is unacceptable.").

141. Head-of-state immunity is based on the doctrine of comity. Thus, U.S. courts traditionally defer to the State Department's view as to whether head-of-state immunity should apply in a particular case. *See* George, *supra* note 139, at 1061, 1067. In contrast to a civil suit brought by a private party, in a criminal matter brought by the United States a court should assume, even without specific State Department guidance, that the U.S. Government has weighed the foreign policy implications and determined that head-of-state immunity would be inappropriate under the circumstances.

142. Draft Convention on the Prevention and Punishment of the Crime of Developing, Producing, Acquiring, Stockpiling, Retaining, Transferring or Using Biological or Chemical Weapons, *drafted* Aug. 15, 1998 (on file with the author).

143. *See* Convention for the Suppression of Unlawful Acts Against the Safety of Maritime Navigation (1988), 27 I.L.M. 672; Convention Against Torture and Other Cruel, Inhuman or Degrading Treatment or Punishment (1984), 23 I.L.M. 1027, 24 I.L.M. 535; Convention on the Physical Protection of Nuclear Material (1980), 18 I.L.M. 1422, T.I.A.S. 11080; International Convention Against the Taking of Hostages, Dec. 4, 1979, 18 I.L.M. 1456, T.I.A.S. 11080; Convention on the Prevention of Crimes Against Internationally Protected Persons, Including Diplomatic Agents, Dec. 14, 1973, 8532 T.I.A.S. 1975, 1035 U.N.T.S. 167; Convention for the Suppression of Unlawful Acts Against the Safety of Civil Aviation, Sept. 23, 1971, 25 U.S.T. 564, 7570 T.I.A.S. 590; Convention for the Suppression of Unlawful Seizure of Aircraft, Dec. 16, 1970, 22 U.S.T. 1641, T.I.A.S. 7192, 860 U.N.T.S. 105. The latest anti-terrorism convention with the prosecute or extradite formula is the International Convention for the Suppression of Terrorist Bombings, which was opened for signature in January, 1998. A/RES/52/164.

development, production, stockpiling, and transfer, as well as actual use, of biological or chemical weapons. Third, it expressly provides that Head of State or diplomatic immunity is inapplicable to these crimes,[144] and denies the defense of superior orders.[145]

While it would certainly help close the gap between the international law prohibiting chemical and biological weapons and the enforcement of that law, the Harvard Draft Convention should not be viewed as a panacea. In light of past politically-motivated, false accusations of violations of the chemical and biological weapons conventions,[146] proceedings before domestic courts exercising universal jurisdiction may not possess the same credibility or carry with them the same international reprobation as proceedings before a neutral international tribunal would. A second weakness inherent in a regime requiring

144. Other international conventions which exempt offenders from claiming diplomatic or head-of-state immunity include: Convention on the Prevention and Punishment of the Crime of Genocide, Dec. 9. 1948, art. 4, 78 U.N.T.S. 277 (1951) ("Persons committing genocide or any of the other acts enumerated . . . shall be punished, whether they are constitutionally responsible rulers, public officials or private individuals."); and International Convention on the Suppression and Punishment of the International Crime of Apartheid (1973), 28 U.N. GAOR, Supp. No. 30, U.N. Doc. A/9030 ("International criminal responsibility shall apply, irrespective of the motive involved, to individuals, members of organizations and institutions and representatives of the State"). The Statutes of the International Criminal Tribunals for the former Yugoslavia and Rwanda similarly provide, "[T]he official position of any accused person, whether as head of State or Government or as a responsible Government official, shall not relieve such person of criminal responsibility nor mitigate punishment." *Statute of the International Tribunal for the Prosecution of Persons Responsible for Serious Violations of International Humanitarian Law Committed in the Territory of the Former Yugoslavia since 1991*, art. 7(2), annexed to UNITED NATIONS, *Report of the Secretary-General Pursuant to Paragraph 2 of Security Council Resolution 808 (1993)*, U.N. Doc. S/25704 (1993), *reprinted in* MORRIS & SCHARF, INSIDER'S GUIDE, *supra* note 117; Statute of the International Tribunal for Rwanda, art. 6(2), *annexed to* S.C. Res. 955, U.N. SCOR, 3453 mtg. At 6, U.N. Doc. S/RES/955 (1994), *reprinted in* MORRIS & SCHARF, TRIBUNAL FOR RWANDA, *supra* note 120.

145. The illegitimacy of the defense of superior orders for international crimes was recognized in the Charter of the Nuremberg Tribunal and has been reaffirmed in the Statutes of the International Criminal Tribunals for the Former Yugoslavia and Rwanda. *See* MORRIS & SCHARF, TRIBUNAL FOR RWANDA, *supra* note 120, at 262–68. Current U.S. law, in contrast, recognizes the defense of superior orders unless the order was manifestly illegal, that is "a man of ordinary sense and understanding" would know the order was illegal. *See* United States v. Calley, No. 26875, 1973 WL 14894 (C.M.A. Dec. 21, 1973); *see also* JORDAN PAUST ET AL., INTERNATIONAL CRIMINAL LAW: CASES AND MATERIALS 1373–76 (1996).

146. For years, the United States government maintained that it had evidence of Soviet responsibility for the use of biological weapons known as "yellow rain" in Indochina from 1982 to 1986. *See* Zilinskas, *supra* note 25, at 984, 986. While many commentators continue to cite the yellow rain episode as a breach of the biological weapons convention, there is reason to believe that the story was fabricated by the United States as part of its cold-war disinformation campaign and as a way to justify further U.S. biowar research and handsome congressional appropriations. Julian Robinson, Jeanne Guillemin & Matthew Meselson, *Yellow Rain in Southeast Asia: The Story Collapses*, *in* PREVENTING A BIOLOGICAL ARMS RACE, Ch. 10 (Susan Wright ed. 1990).

domestic prosecutions concerns protection of sensitive intelligence sources and methods. It is one thing to share satellite surveillance photos, telephone intercepts and information gathered by undercover operatives with other governments in a closed session of the Security Council, which may be necessary to justify use of force or imposition of sanctions; it is quite another to have to divulge such information in open court as would be required in a criminal prosecution.[147] Finally, international adoption of the Harvard Draft Convention would have a significant deterrent effect, but it could no more guarantee an end to all chemical and biological weapons use than the Genocide Convention[148] has prevented outbreaks of genocide in the years since its adoption in 1948.[149]

CONCLUSION

So far there have been three main stages in the evolution of international law governing chemical and biological weapons. First, an international treaty regime prohibiting these weapons was established, a prohibition that is now recognized as customary international law. Second, this treaty regime was expanded and fortified by filling in existing gaps. Third, a verification regime was created, which enabled the international community to detect and publicize non-compliance. To retain vitality, the prohibition on chemical and biological weapons requires that there be an expectation of consequences to its violation. The next stage in the evolution will focus on strengthening the means of enforcement.

The traditional means of enforcement relies on the United Nations Security Council, which may impose a range of sanctions, including the use of force, to enforce the international prohibition on chemical and biological weapons. However, the Security Council's robust response to Iraq's possession of biological and chemical weapons in the aftermath of its invasion of Kuwait has been the exception. More often, the Security Council has been paralyzed by the threat or use of the veto by the

---

147. This prospect may deter governments from making extradition requests or indicting persons for violations of the chemical and biological weapons conventions.

148. *Supra* note 144.

149. The existence of the widely ratified Genocide Convention, with its similar universal jurisdiction regime and extradite or prosecute requirement, did not prevent the extermination of 750,000 Ugandans (1971–1987), the annihilation of 2 million Cambodians (1975–1979), the massacre of 200,000 East Timorans (1971–1987), the gassing of 100,000 Kurds in Iraq (1987–1988), the slaughter of 250,000 Muslims in Bosnia (1992–1995), or the mass murder of 800,000 Tutsis in Rwanda (1994). *See* SCHARF, BALKAN JUSTICE, *supra* note 127, at xiii–xiv.

permanent members, and has taken no action in response to repeated violations of the chemical and biological weapons conventions.

In light of the Security Council's repeated failure to take effective action to eliminate the threat posed by a State's possession of chemical or biological weapons, States may increasingly be tempted to act unilaterally, following the example of the American attack on the Sudanese chemical weapons plant in August 1998. However weak the evidence concerning the Al-Shifa plant turns out to be, the attack sets an important precedent on which States may choose to rely in dealing with terrorist or state-sponsored biological and chemical weapons threats. The danger of abuse created by an expansive interpretation of Article 51 to permit assassination is even greater than it is where it is interpreted to permit attacks on suspected chemical and biological weapons. But at some point, the danger to international stability created by permitting radical leaders such as Saddam Hussein to use biological and chemical weapons with impunity exceeds the danger posed by the potential for nations to abuse an expanded interpretation of Article 51 for their own illegitimate ends.[150]

Deterrence and enforcement of the chemical and biological weapons conventions presently relies on the threat or imposition of sanctions or military force, both of which are blunt instruments which tend to harm the innocent population and infrequently succeed in altering the policies of the responsible rulers. A third means of enforcement, which would supplement rather than replace the traditional approaches, is to apply international criminal law to prosecute and punish offending leaders in domestic courts or international tribunals.

The international criminalization of chemical and biological weapons violations through the establishment of ad hoc international tribunals and/or a regime of universal jurisdiction, using the Harvard Draft Convention as a model, would have many benefits. First, it could potentially strengthen the norm against chemical and biological weapons, enhance deterrence of potential offenders, and facilitate international cooperation in suppressing the prohibited activities. Unlike sanctions and the use of force, criminalization avoids collective punishment by directly targeting those responsible for the international violations. In addition, criminalization can strengthen international political will to maintain sanctions and take more aggressive actions if necessary. A criminal indictment can also serve to isolate offending leaders diplomatically and strengthen the hand of domestic political

150. Baker, *supra* note 70, at 116.

rivals.[151] Just imagine if every time Saddam Hussein's name appeared in the international press, it was followed by the moniker "indicted international criminal."

Ultimately, the success of the anti-chemical and biological weapons regimes requires the reestablishment of what author Richard Price calls the "chemical and biological weapons taboo."[152] The addition of criminalization to the existing means of enforcement will go a long way toward that end.

151. This has proven effective with respect to Radovan Karadzic, the once powerful leader of the Bosnian Serbs who has been forced into hiding and politically marginalized by the international indictment and warrant for his arrest. *See* Interview with General William Nash, former Commander of the U.S. forces in Bosnia (Sept. 29, 1998) (transcript on file with the author).

152. Price, *supra* note 17.

APPENDIX

[Harvard-Sussex Draft, 15 August 1998]

DRAFT CONVENTION ON THE PREVENTION AND PUNISHMENT OF THE CRIME OF DEVELOPING, PRODUCING, ACQUIRING, STOCKPILING, RETAINING, TRANSFERRING OR USING BIOLOGICAL OR CHEMICAL WEAPONS

PREAMBLE

The States Parties to this Convention,

Recalling that States are prohibited by the Geneva Protocol of 1925, the Biological Weapons Convention of 1972 and the Chemical Weapons Convention of 1993, and other international agreements, from developing, producing, stockpiling, acquiring, retaining, transferring or using biological and chemical weapons, and that these prohibitions reflect a worldwide norm against these weapons;

Recognizing that any development, production and use of biological and chemical weapons is the result of the decisions and actions of individual persons, including government officials, and that these activities are now within the capability not only of States but also of other entities and of individuals;

Affirming that all persons and entities should be prohibited from engaging in these activities, and should be subject to effective penal sanctions, thereby ensuring and enhancing the effectiveness of the Geneva Protocol, the Biological Weapons Convention and the Chemical Weapons Convention;

Reaffirming that any use of disease or poison for hostile purposes is repugnant to the conscience of humankind;

Consider that biological and chemical weapons pose a threat to the well-being of all humanity and to future generations;

Resolving that knowledge and achievements in biology, chemistry and medicine should be used exclusively for the health and well-being of humanity;

Desiring. to encourage the peaceful and beneficial advance and application of these sciences by protecting them from adverse consequences that would result from their hostile exploitation;

Determined, for the sake of human beings everywhere and of future generations, to eliminate the threat of biological and chemical weapons;

Have agreed as follows:

ARTICLE I

1. Any person commits an offence who knowingly:

   (a) develops, produces, otherwise acquires, stockpiles or retains any biological or chemical weapon, or transfers, directly or indirectly, to anyone, any biological or chemical weapon;

   (b) uses any biological or chemical weapon;

   (c) engages in preparations to use any biological or chemical weapon;

   (d) assists, encourages or induces, in any way , anyone to engage in any of the above activities;

   (e) orders or directs anyone to engage in any of the above activities;

   (f) attempts to commit any of the above offenses.

ARTICLE II

1. Nothing in this Convention shall be construed as prohibiting activities that are not prohibited under:

   (a) the Convention on the Prohibition of the Development, Production and Stockpiling of Bacteriological (Biological) and Toxin Weapons and on their Destruction, of 10 April 1972, or

   (b) the Convention on the Prohibition of the Development, Production, Stockpiling and Use of Chemical Weapons and on their Destruction, done at Paris on 13 January 1993, or that are directed toward the fulfillment of a State's obligations under either Convention and are conducted in accordance with its provisions.

2. In a prosecution for an offence set forth in Article 1, it shall be a defence that the accused person reasonably believed that the conduct in question was not prohibited under this Convention.

3. It is not a defence that a person charged with an offence set forth in Article I acted in an official capacity, under the orders or instructions of a superior, or otherwise in accordance with internal law.

ARTICLE III

For the purposes of the present Convention:

1. "BIOLOGICAL WEAPONS" means:

(a) microbial or other biological agents, or toxins whatever their origin or method of production, of types and in quantities that have no justification for prophylactic, protective or other peaceful purposes;

(b) weapons, equipment or means of delivery designed to use such agents or toxins for hostile purposes or in armed conflict.

2. "CHEMICAL WEAPONS" means the following, together or separately:

(a) toxic chemicals and their precursors, except where intended for:

(i) industrial, agricultural, research, medical, pharmaceutical or other peaceful purposes;

(ii) protective purposes, namely those purposes directly related to protection against toxic chemicals and to protection against chemical weapons;

(iii) military purposes not connected with the use of chemical weapons and not dependent on the use of the toxic properties of chemicals as a method of warfare;

(iv) law enforcement including domestic riot control purposes. As long as the types and quantities are consistent with such purposes.

(b) munitions and devices, specifically designed to cause death or other harm through the toxic properties of those toxic chemicals specified in subparagraph (a), which would be released as a result of the employment of such munitions and devices;

(c) any equipment specifically designed for use directly in connection with the employment of munitions and devices specified in subparagraph (b).

3. "TOXIC CHEMICAL" means any chemical which through its chemical action on life processes can cause death, temporary incapacitation or permanent harm to humans or animals. This includes all such chemicals, regardless of their origin or of their method of production, and regardless of whether they are produced in facilities, in munitions or elsewhere.

4. "PRECURSOR" means any chemical reactant which takes part at any stage in the production by whatever method of a toxic chemical. This includes any key component of a binary or multi component chemical system, that is to say, the precursor which plays the most important role on determining the toxic properties of the final product and reacts rapidly with other chemicals in the binary or multi component system.

5. "PERSON" means any natural person or, to the extent consistent with internal law as to criminal responsibility, any legal entity.

ARTICLE IV

Each State Party shall adopt such measures as may be necessary:

(a) to establish as criminal offenses under its internal law the offenses set forth in Article 1;

(b) to make those offenses punishable by appropriate penalties which take into account their grave nature.

ARTICLE V

1. Each State Party to this Convention shall take such measures as may be necessary to establish its jurisdiction over the offenses set forth in Article I in the following cases:

(a) when the offence was committed in the territory of that State or on board a ship or aircraft registered in that State;

(b) when the alleged offender is a national of that State;

(c) when, if that State considers it appropriate, the alleged offender is a stateless person whose habitual residence is in its territory;

(d) when the offence was committed with intent to harm that State or its nationals or to compel that State to do or abstain from doing any act;

(e) when the offence involved the use of biological or chemical weapons and victim of the offence was a national of that State.

2. Each State Party shall likewise take such measures as may be necessary to establish its jurisdiction over the offenses set forth in Article I in cases where the alleged offender is present in its territory and it does not extradite such person pursuant to Articles VI and VII.

3. This Convention does not exclude any criminal jurisdiction exercised in accordance with internal law.

4. Jurisdiction with respect to the offenses set forth in Article I may also be exercised by any international criminal court that may have jurisdiction in the matter in accordance with its Statute

ARTICLE VI

1. Upon receiving information that a person who has committed or who is alleged to have committed an offence as set forth in article I may be present in its territory, a State Party shall take such measures as may be necessary under its internal law to investigate the facts contained in the information.

2. If it is satisfied that the circumstances so warrant, a State Party in the territory of which an alleged offender is present shall take that person into custody or shall take such other

measures as are necessary to ensure the presence of that person for the purpose of prosecution or extradition.

3. Any person regarding whom the measures referred to in paragraph 2 are being taken shall be entitled to:

(a) communicate without delay with the nearest appropriate representative of the State of which that person is a national or which is otherwise entitled to protect that person's rights or, if that person is a stateless person, the State in the territory of which that person habitually resides;

(b) be visited by a representative of that State;

(c) be informed of that person's rights under subparagraphs (a) and (b).

The rights referred to in paragraph 3 shall be exercised in conformity with the laws and regulations of the State in the territory of which the offender or alleged offender is present, provided that the said laws and regulations must enable full effect to be given to the purposes for which the rights accorded under paragraph 3 are intended.

When a State Party, pursuant to the present article, has taken a person into custody, it shall promptly notify, directly or through the Secretary-General of the United Nations, the States Parties which have established jurisdiction in accordance with article V, paragraph 1, and, if it considers it advisable, any other interested States Parties, of the fact that person is in custody and of the circumstances which warrant that person's detention. The State which makes the investigation contemplated in paragraph 1 of the present article shall promptly inform those States Parties of its findings and shall indicate whether it intends to exercise jurisdiction.

ARTICLE VII

1. The offenses set forth in Article I shall be deemed to be included as extraditable offenses in any extradition treaty existing between States Parties. States Parties undertake to include those offenses as extraditable offenses in every extradition treaty subsequently concluded between them.

2. If a State Party which makes extradition conditional on the existence of a treaty receives a request for extradition from another State Party with which it has no extradition treaty, it may, if it decides to extradite, consider this Convention as

the legal basis for extradition in respect of the offenses set forth in Article 1. Extradition shall be subject to the other conditions provided by the law of the requested State.

3. States Parties which do not make extradition conditional on the existence of a treaty shall recognize the offenses set forth in Article I as extraditable offenses as between themselves subject to the conditions provided by the law of the requested State.

4. The offenses set forth under Article I shall be treated, for the purpose of extradition between States Parties, as if they had been committed not only in the place in which they occurred but also in the territories of the States required to establish their jurisdiction in accordance with paragraph 1 of Article V.

5. The provisions of all extradition treaties and arrangements between States Parties with regard to offenses set forth in Article I shall be deemed to be modified as between State Parties to the extent that they are incompatible with this Convention.

ARTICLE VIII

The State Party in the territory of which the alleged offender is found shall, if it does not extradite such person, be obliged, without exception whatsoever and whether or not the offence was committed in its territory, to submit the case without delay to competent authorities for the purpose of prosecution, through proceedings in accordance with the laws of that State. Those authorities shall take their decision in the same manner as in the case of any other offence of a grave nature under the law of that State.

ARTICLE IX

1. States Parties shall afford one another the greatest measure of assistance in connection with investigations or criminal or extradition proceedings brought in respect of the offenses set forth in Article 1, including assistance in obtaining evidence at their disposal which is necessary for the proceedings.

2. States Parties shall carry out their obligations under paragraph 1 in conformity with any treaties or other arrangements on mutual legal assistance that may exist between them. In the absence of such treaties or arrangements, States Parties shall afford one another assistance in accordance with their internal law.

ARTICLE X

None of the offenses set forth in Article I shall be regarded, for the purposes of extradition or mutual legal assistance, as a political offence or as an offence connected with a political offence or as an offence inspired by political motives. Accordingly, a request for extradition or for mutual legal assistance based on such an offence may not be refused on the sole ground that it concerns a political offence or an offence connected with a political offence or an offence inspired by political motives.

ARTICLE XI

Nothing in this Convention shall be interpreted as imposing an obligation to extradite or to afford mutual legal assistance, if the requested State Party has substantial grounds for believing that the request for extradition for offenses set forth in Article I or for mutual legal assistance with respect to such offenses has been made for the purpose of prosecuting or punishing a person on account of that person's race, religion, nationality, ethnic origin or political opinion or that compliance with the request would cause prejudice to that person's position for any of these reasons.

ARTICLE XII

States Parties shall cooperate in the prevention of the offenses set forth in Article 1, particularly by:

(a) taking all practicable measures to prevent preparations in their respective territories for the commission of those offenses within or outside their territories;

(b) exchanging information and coordinating the taking of administrative and other measures as appropriate to prevent commission of those offenses.

ARTICLE XIII

1. Each State Party shall inform the Secretary-General of the United Nations of the legislative and administrative measures taken to implement this Convention. In particular, each State Party shall notify the Secretary-General of the United Nations of the jurisdiction it has established under its domestic law in accordance with paragraph 3 of Article V. Should any change take place, the State Party concerned shall immediately notify the Secretary-General.

2. Each State Party shall, in accordance with its national law, promptly provide to the Secretary-General of the United Nations any relevant information in its possession concerning:

   (a) the circumstances of any offence over which it has established its jurisdiction pursuant to paragraph I of Article V;

   (b) the measures taken in relation to the alleged offender, and, in particular, the results of any extradition proceedings or other legal proceedings.

3. The State Party where an alleged offender is prosecuted shall communicate the final outcome of the proceedings to the Secretary-General of the United Nations, who shall transmit the information to the other States Parties.

4. Each State Party shall designate a contact point within its government to which other States Parties may communicate in matters relevant to this Convention. Each State Party shall make such designation known to the Secretary-General. .

ARTICLE XIV

Any dispute between States Parties concerning the interpretation or application of this Convention which is not settled by negotiation shall, at the request of one of them, be submitted to arbitration. If within six months from the date of the request for arbitration the parties are unable to agree on the organization of the arbitration, any one of those parties may refer the dispute to the International Court of justice.

ARTICLE XV

1. Ten years after the entry into force of this Convention, or earlier if it is requested by a majority of Parties to the Convention by submitting a proposal to this effect to the Secretary-General of the United Nations, a Conference of States Parties shall be held at [Geneva, Switzerland], to review the operation of the Convention with a view to assuring that the purposes of the preamble and the provisions of the Convention are being realized.

2. At intervals of seven years thereafter, unless otherwise decided upon, further sessions of the Conference may be convened with the same objective.

ARTICLE XVI

1. This Convention shall be open for signature by all States from [DATE] until [DATE] at United Nations Headquarters in New York.

2 This Convention is subject to ratification, acceptance or approval. The instruments of ratification, acceptance or approval shall be deposited with the Secretary-General of the United Nations.

3. This Convention shall be open to accession by any State. The instruments of accession shall be deposited with the Secretary-General of the United Nations.

ARTICLE XVII

1. This Convention shall enter into force on the thirtieth day following the date of the deposit of the [NUMBER] instrument of ratification, acceptance, approval or accession with the Secretary-General of the United Nations.

2. For each State ratifying, accepting, approving or acceding to the Convention after the deposit of the [NUMBER] instrument of ratification, acceptance, approval or accession, the Convention shall enter into force on the thirtieth day

after deposit by such State of its instrument of ratification, acceptance, approval or accession.

ARTICLE XVIII

The Articles of this Convention shall not be subject to reservation.

ARTICLE XIX

The original of this Convention, of which the Arabic, Chinese, English, French, Russian and Spanish texts are equally authentic, shall be deposited with the Secretary-General of the United Nations, who shall send certified copies thereof to all States.

IN WITNESS WHEREOF, the undersigned, being duly authorized thereto by their respective Governments, have signed this Convention, opened for signature at United Nations Headquarters in New York on [DATE].

The Regime To Prevent Biological Weapons: Opportunities For A Safer, Healthier, More Prosperous World

by Graham S. Pearson

Visiting Professor of International Security, Department of Peace Studies, University of Bradford, Bradford, West Yorkshire BD7 1DP, UK (Previously Director-General and Chief Executive of the Chemical and Biological Defence Establishment, Porton Down, UK.)

Introduction

1. It has been argued that biological weapons -- the deliberate use of disease against humans, animals or plants -- presents the greatest danger of all weapons of mass destruction because the prohibition regime is currently the weakest.[1] In this paper, the prohibition regime for biological and toxin weapons is examined together with the developments over the past decade that have sought to strengthen that regime through the negotiations that are currently nearing completion in Geneva of a Protocol to strengthen the effectiveness and improve the implementation of the Biological and Toxin Weapons Convention.

2. The past decade has seen the States Parties engaged initially in the identification and examination of potential verification measures to strengthen the Convention and then in the negotiation of a Protocol to strengthen the effectiveness and improve the implementation of the Convention. This Protocol is now almost complete with the provision to delegations on 30 March 2001 of a Chairman's composite text . An overview of the Protocol will be presented outlining the central elements in the Protocol regime which include mandatory declarations, declaration follow-up procedures including randomly selected visits, declaration clarification procedures and assistance visits, investigations of alleged use or of non-compliance concerns, provisions to promote technical cooperation in microbiology and biotechnology for peaceful purposes together with an organization to implement the Protocol.

3. The elements of the regime are examined and compared with the comparable provisions in the Chemical Weapons Convention -- the arms control regime that is of the closest relevance to the Biological and Toxin Weapons Convention as both address toxins and both address dual use materials and technology. The paper will demonstrate that all the different elements of the verification regime are inter-related and together will have a considerable synergistic effect that will build confidence in compliance with the Convention, ensure that uncertainties, anomalies and concerns are swiftly investigated and improve the implementation of the Convention. It will also show that the strengthened regime is an important counter to the possible use of biological weapons by terrorist groups. Finally, the Protocol regime will be considered in the wider context of the international initiatives to counter outbreaks of disease, to protect the environment through the Convention on Biological Diversity and the Cartagena Protocol on Biosafety and to harmonise Good Manufacturing Practice around the world for pharmaceutical and biological products. These all share common objectives and together contribute towards a safer, healthier and more prosperous world.

Background

---

[1] Graham S. Pearson, *Why Biological Weapons Present The Greatest Danger*, Seventh International Symposium on Protection Against Chemical and Biological Warfare Agents, Stockholm, Sweden, 15 - 19 June 2001.

4. Following the extensive use of chemical weapons during World War I, there was international agreement in 1925 to prohibit the use in war of asphyxiating, poisonous and other gases, and of bacteriological methods of warfare with the agreement of the Geneva Protocol[2] signed on 17 June, just over 76 years ago. As some of the States Parties entered reservations which stated that (a) the Protocol was only binding on that State Party as regards States that have signed or ratified the Protocol or may accede to it, and (b) the Protocol would cease to be binding on that State Party in regard to any enemy State whose armed forces or whose allies fail to respect the prohibitions laid down in the Protocol, the prohibition was in essence a prohibition of first use as those States Parties which had entered reservations were reserving the right to retaliate in kind should such weapons be used against them. It should, however, be noted that following the entry into force of the Biological and Toxin Weapons Convention (BTWC) in 1975 and the Chemical Weapons Convention (CWC) in 1997, most of the States parties to the Geneva Protocol who entered reservations have today given these reservations up.

5. During World War II there was considerable concern about the possible use of chemical and biological weapons and a number of countries developed retaliatory capabilities so as to be able to retaliate in kind should chemical or biological weapons be used against them.[3] The work on biological weapons during World War II and in the post war years demonstrated that biological weapons would be effective by all means short of actual use. It is evident that in the immediate post war years that biological weapons were seen as a potent weapon of mass destruction capable of being used against humans, animals or plants and consequently considerable priority was given then to national programmes to develop biological weapons.

6. Nuclear weapons were also being urgently developed during the post war period and by the 1950s it was becoming clear that nuclear weapons were perceived as a more attractive ultimate weapon and the national programmes to develop biological weapons were terminated in a number of countries. This led to the negotiation in the late 1960s of the first international treaty to prohibit an entire class of weapons -- the Biological and Toxin Weapons Convention[4] which was opened for signature on 10 April 1972 and entered into force when 22 countries had ratified the Convention on 26 March 1975. As of March 2001, the BTWC has 143 States Parties and 18 Signatory States[5].

The Biological and Toxin Weapons Convention

[2]League of Nations, *Protocol for the Prohibition of the Use in War of Asphyxiating, Poisonous and Other Gases, and of Bacteriological Methods of Warfare*, signed at Geneva, June 17, 1925, Vol. XCIV, 1929, Nos 1,2,3 and 4, p.65

[3]For a history of the developments in biological weapons up to 1945 see Erhard Geissler & John Courtland-Moon (eds), *Biological and Toxin Weapons: Research, Development and Use from the Middle Ages to 1945*, Stockholm International Peace Research Institute, Oxford University Press, 1999.

[4]United Nations, *Convention on the Prohibition of the Development, Production and Stockpiling of Bacteriological (Biological) and Toxin Weapons and on their Destruction*, General Assembly resolution 2826 (XXVI), 16 December 1971.

[5]United Nations, Preparatory Committee for the Fifth Review Conference of the States Parties to the Convention on the Prohibition of the Development, Production and Stockpiling of Bacteriological (Biological) and Toxin Weapons and on their Destruction, *List of States Parties to the Convention on the Prohibition of the Development, Production and Stockpiling of Bacteriological (Biological) and Toxin Weapons and on their Destruction*, BWC/CONF.V/PC/INF.5, 20 April 2001.

7. The basic prohibition is in Article I of the Convention which states that:

Each State Party to this Convention undertakes never in any circumstances to develop, produce, stockpile or otherwise acquire or retain:

(1) Microbial or other biological agents, or toxins, whatever their origin or method of production, ***of types and in quantities that have no justification for prophylactic, protective or other peaceful purposes;***

(2) Weapons, equipment or means of delivery designed to use such agents or toxins for hostile purposes or in armed conflict. [Emphasis added]

This is a comprehensive prohibition which is strengthened by the General Purpose Criterion -- the words emphasised in bold -- which ensures that the prohibition extends to any biological agent or toxin, however produced, that has no justification for peaceful purposes. This General Purpose Criterion ensures that the prohibition covers not only past biological agents but also any future developments. As will be shown later, the extension of the prohibition to cover all developments in microbiology and biotechnology is achieved through reaffirmations to this effect by the successive Review Conferences of the BTWC.

8. Another important obligation arising from the Convention relates to transfers which are addressed in Article III that states that:

Each State Party to this Convention undertakes not to transfer to any recipient whatsoever, directly or indirectly, and not in any way to assist encourage, or induce any State, group of States or international organizations to manufacture or otherwise acquire any of the agents, toxins, weapons, equipment or means of delivery specified in Article I of the Convention.

This effectively places a responsibility on each State Party to satisfy itself that any transfer of agents or equipment will not be used for prohibited purposes.

9. A further requirement in Article IV is for each State Party to take any necessary measures to implement the Convention in its territory or under its jurisdiction or control:

Each State Party to this Convention shall, in accordance with its constitutional processes, take any necessary measures to prohibit and prevent the development, production, stockpiling, acquisition or retention of the agents, toxins, weapons, equipment and means of delivery specified in Article I of the Convention, within the territory of such State, under its jurisdiction or under its control anywhere.

Several States Parties have enacted legislation to meet this requirement. One example is the UK Biological Weapons Act of 1974[6] which states that:

No person shall develop, produce, stockpile, acquire or retain

[6]Her Majesty's Stationery Office, *Biological Weapons Act 1974*, 8 February 1974.

(a) any biological agent or toxin of a type and in a quantity that has no justification for prophylactic, protective or other peaceful purposes; or

(b) any weapon, equipment, means of delivery designed to use biological agents or toxins for hostile purposes or in armed conflict.

and goes on to state that any person contravening this shall be guilty of an offence and shall, on conviction on indictment, be liable to imprisonment for life.

10. A further Article in the BTWC which has attracted much attention in recent years is Article X which addresses the exchange of equipment, materials and scientific and technical information for peaceful purposes:

(1) The States Parties to this Convention undertake to facilitate, and have the right to participate in, the fullest possible exchange of equipment, materials, and scientific and technological information for the use of bacteriological (biological) agents and toxins for peaceful purposes. Parties to the Convention in a position to do so shall also cooperate in contributing individually or together with other States or international organisations to the further development and application of scientific discoveries in the field of bacteriology (biology) for the prevention of disease, or for other peaceful purposes.

(2) This Convention shall be implemented in a manner designed to avoid hampering the economic or technological development of States Parties to the Convention or international cooperation in the field of peaceful bacteriological (biological) activities, including the international exchange of bacteriological (biological) agents and toxins and equipment for the processing, use or production of bacteriological (biological) agents and toxins for peaceful purposes in accordance with the provisions of the Convention.

11. Finally, Article XII sets out the requirement for periodic Review Conferences:

Five years after the entry into force of this Convention.... a conference of States Parties to the Convention shall be held at Geneva, Switzerland, to review the operation of the Convention, with a view to assuring that the purposes of the preamble and provisions of the Convention ... are being realized. Such review shall take into account any new scientific and technological developments relevant to the Convention.

Review Conferences have been held in 1980, 1986, 1991, 1996 and the fifth one is scheduled for 19 November to 7 December 2001. At each Review Conference a Final Declaration is agreed by States Parties by consensus which provide extended understandings of the Convention.

12. The review of the relevant advances in science and technology is of particular importance as this enables the States Parties to reaffirm that all such advances are included in the basic

prohibition. Thus in 1996 at the Fourth Review Conference the Final Declaration[7] stated that:

> *The Conference, conscious of apprehensions arising from relevant scientific and technological developments, inter alia, in* ***the fields of microbiology, biotechnology, molecular biology, genetic engineering and any applications resulting from genome studies,*** *and the possibilities of their use for purposes inconsistent with the objectives and the provisions of the Convention,* ***reaffirms that the undertaking given by the States Parties in Article I applies to all such developments.*** *[Emphasis added]*

This reaffirmation makes it clear that all developments in the fields of microbiology and biotechnology are embraced in the basic prohibition in Article I of the Convention and thus that no such developments are excluded from the scope of the Convention.

13. Also at the Fourth Review Conference the States Parties usefully reaffirmed that the use of biological or toxin weapons is prohibited. There was language in the Final Declaration on both Article I (which addresses the basic prohibition):

> *The Conference reaffirms that the use by States Parties, in any way and under any circumstances, of microbial or other biological agents or toxins, that is not consistent with prophylactic, protective or other peaceful purposes, is effectively a violation of Article I of the Convention.*

as well as on Article IV (which addresses national implementation measures):

> *The Conference reaffirms that under all circumstances the use of biological agents and toxins is effectively prohibited by the Convention.*

These statements effectively extend the understanding by States Parties that use is prohibited, in any way and under any circumstances. The BTWC does not explicitly address use in its text although the Preamble contains the following:

> *Determined for the sake of all mankind, to exclude completely the possibility of bacteriological (biological) agents and toxins being used as weapons,*

which makes it clear that the intention of the Convention is to exclude the possibility of use. The extended understanding at the Fourth Review Convention makes it clear that use would be regarded as a violation of Article I of the Convention and is thus a valuable strengthening of the Convention.

---

[7] United Nations, *The Fourth Review Conference of the States Parties to the Convention on the Prohibition of the Development, Production and Stockpiling of Bacteriological (Biological) and Toxin Weapons and on their Destruction*, Geneva, 25 November – 6 December 1996, BWC/CONF.IV/9, Geneva, 1996.

Analysis of the Composite Protocol Text

47. It is evident from an evaluation[16] of the composite Protocol text that it is in many areas identical to the language in the rolling text and is firmly based on the agreed language out of square brackets in the rolling text. Compromises have been adopted to address those issues where there continued to be a divergence of views. These compromises have emerged from the bilateral informal consultations held by the Chairman and have been explored through the written elements addressing conceptual solutions based on the rolling text which had been circulated by the Chairman for virtually the whole of the Protocol to all delegations by February 2001. Whilst these compromises will not satisfy the aspirations of all the delegations to the Ad Hoc Group, they do successfully ensure that the composite Protocol text achieves its mandate of strengthening the effectiveness and improving the implementation of the Convention. The composite Protocol text has successfully retained all the essential elements for an effective Protocol ranging from definitions and objective criteria, through compliance measures to measures for scientific and technological exchange for peaceful purposes and technical cooperation.

The Value of the Protocol

48. In considering the composite Protocol text, it is important to remember that the BTWC with its basic prohibitions and obligations has been **in force** for over 25 years and that the Protocol is to strengthen the effectiveness and improve the implementation of the Convention. It makes **no** changes to the basic prohibitions and obligations. The Protocol regime is supplementary and additional to the Convention.

49. The key comparison is thus between the BTWC Protocol regime and the BTWC alone, including the procedures devolved from its provisions. A tabulation of the principal measures in the regime, compared with the procedures of the BTWC alone, clearly brings out the significant benefits from the Protocol.

BTWC and its Protocol Regime	BTWC alone
Mandatory declarations -- measures to ensure submission	Confidence-Building Measures -- patchy and variable (if made)
Declaration follow-up procedures -- analysis of declarations -- randomly-selected transparency visits	None -- none -- none
Declaration clarification procedures -- clarification visits	None -- none
Voluntary assistance visits	None
Non-compliance concerns -- Consultations >>> Investigations	Art V consultation procedures Art VI complaint to UN Security Council

[16]Graham S. Pearson, Malcolm R. Dando & Nicholas A. Sims, *The Composite Protocol Text: An Effective Strengthening of the Biological and Toxin Weapons Convention*, University of Bradford, Department of Peace Studies, Evaluation Paper No. 20, April 2001. Available at http://www.brad.ac.uk/acad/sbtwc

Field investigation	Possible UN Secretary-General investigation if invited by State Party concerned
Facility investigation	None
Transfer procedures	None
Assistance -- provisions detailed	Art VII assistance if UN Security Council decides a Party has been exposed to danger
International Cooperation -- elaborated in detail -- Cooperation Committee	Art X provisions -- no implementation procedures -- none
Organization -- CoSP, ExC & Technical Secretariat	None
National implementation -- Penal legislation required -- National Authority	Art IV National implementation -- No penal legislation requirement -- None

50. Taking all of the elements of the BTWC Protocol regime as a whole, it is clear that there are overall three particularly **significant** benefits that will accrue from the BTWC Protocol regime and which are not available with the Convention alone:

BTWC and its Protocol Regime	BTWC alone
Measures to increase transparency and build confidence	Suspicions not addressed -- and over time reduce international confidence in the regime
Procedures to address non-compliance concerns	Art V consultations (no teeth) Art VI complaints to UN SC (not used)
International cooperation and assistance provisions	No action despite aspirations at successive Review Conferences

51. It is evident from the above comparisons that the Protocol regime brings significant and worthwhile benefits to all States Parties -- both developed and developing -- over and above the procedures to uphold the basic prohibitions and obligations of the BTWC, which remain unchanged. In addition, the Protocol will be effective, over time, in building confidence between States Parties that other States Parties are indeed in compliance with the Convention, thereby reinforcing the norm that work on biological weapons, whether directed against humans, animals or plants, is totally prohibited. The Protocol thus brings improved health, safety, security and prosperity to all States Parties.

The Relevance of the CWC to the Protocol

52. It is also appropriate to compare the BTWC Protocol regime with the CWC regime. The CWC regime is of considerable relevance to the BTWC Protocol regime for a number of reasons. First, there is a close relationship between chemical and biological weapons which is shown by the CBW spectrum:

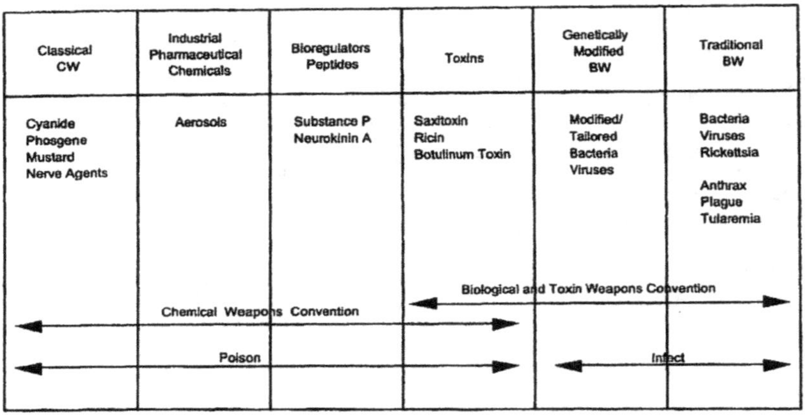

Classical CW
Industrial Pharmaceutical Chemicals
Bioregulators Peptides
Toxins
Genetically Modified BW
Traditional BW
Cyanide
Phosgene
Mustard
Nerve Agents
Aerosols
Substance P
Neurokinin A
Saxitoxin
Ricin
Botulinum Toxin
Modified/
Tailored
Bacteria
Viruses
Bacteria
Viruses
Rickettsia
Anthrax
Plague
Tularemia
Biological and Toxin Weapons Convention
Chemical Weapons Convention
Poison
Infect

This shows that the two Conventions -- the BTWC and the CWC -- rightly overlap in the area of toxins with the CWC listing two toxins -- ricin and saxitoxin in Schedule 1.

53. Both Conventions address dual-use materials and technology, both totally prohibit a class of weapons which cause death or harm to humans primarily through inhalation or ingestion, and both have general purpose criteria in their basic prohibition:

> The BTWC in Article I requiring States Parties to undertake *never in any circumstances to develop, produce, stockpile or otherwise acquire or retain:*
>
> > *(1) Microbial or other biological agents, or toxins, whatever their origin or method of production,* ***of types and in quantities that have no justification for prophylactic, protective or other peaceful purposes;*** [Emphasis added]
>
> The CWC in Article I requiring States Parties to undertake never under any circumstances to develop, produce, otherwise acquire, stockpile or retain chemical weapons... with chemical weapons defined in Article II as meaning:
>
> > *Toxic chemicals and their precursors,* ***except where intended for purposes not prohibited under the Convention, as long as the types and quantities are consistent with such purposes;*** [Emphasis added]

54. In many countries, it is probable that the National Authorities for the CWC and the BTWC Protocol will be colocated. From all these considerations it is evident that the CWC is the regime of greatest relevance to the BTWC Protocol.

A Comparison of the BTWC Protocol and the CWC

55. It is hardly surprising that the BTWC Protocol regime has been largely developed from the CWC regime; it is, however, much more elaborated than the CWC and has been finely tailored to address those biological agents and facilities of greatest relevance to the Convention. There are, however, some particular differences between the CWC regime and the BTWC Protocol regime largely arising from the fact that the CWC came into force in

1997 with a number of States known to be possessors of chemical weapons and chemical weapon production facilities whilst the BTWC came into force over 25 years ago. These differences are summarised in the Table:

Differences

BTWC Protocol Regime	CWC Regime
Biological weapons (BW) not addressed (no declared stockpiles)	Chemical weapons (CW) declared
Biological weapon production facilities (BWPFs) not addressed	Chemical weapons production facilities (CWPFs) declared
Destruction of BW not addressed	CW to be destroyed and verified
Destruction of BWPF not addressed	CWPFs to be destroyed and verified
No tight timelines for declaration and verification	Tight timelines for the declaration and verification of CW, CWPF and their destruction
List of agents and toxins -- No equivalent to SSSF -- Declaration trigger	Scheduled chemicals -- Single Small Scale Facility (SSSF) -- Varying regime for different Schedules

56. If the CW and CWPF elements of the CWC are ignored, then the basic architecture of the BTWC Protocol regime and the CWC regime is the **same.** The differences between the regimes are in the detail with the BTWC Protocol regime having built on the confidence-building measures agreed at the Second Review Conference in 1986 and extended at the Third Review Conference in 1991 as well as being developed from the CWC regime. In respect of the monitoring of dual-purpose materials and facilities, the two regimes are very comparable with the Protocol regime imposing a less onerous but more focussed burden in respect of declarations and visits whilst the international cooperation provisions are much more extensive than those of the CWC. In comparing the BTWC Protocol regime with that of the CWC, the fact that the BTWC is **already** in force has to be remembered.

BTWC and its Protocol Regime	CWC Regime
Mandatory declarations -- range of facilities (BL-4, BL-3, production.. -- requires declaration of biological defence -- measures to ensure submission	Mandatory declarations -- focussed on production of chemicals -- **no** declaration of chemical defence -- **no** measures to ensure submission
Declaration follow-up procedures -- analysis of declarations -- randomly-selected transparency visits	Routine inspections of production facilities for Scheduled chemicals and DOCs (discrete organic chemical)

Declaration clarification procedures -- clarification visits	**No** declaration clarification procedures -- implicit not elaborated
Voluntary assistance visits	**No** provision for voluntary assistance visits -- implicit not elaborated
Non-compliance concerns -- Consultations >>> Investigations	Non-compliance concerns -- Consultations >>> Investigations
Field investigation	Investigation of alleged use
Facility investigation -- team size and duration limited	Challenge inspection -- duration limited
Transfer procedures	Transfer controls
Assistance -- provisions similar to CWC	Assistance
International Cooperation -- elaborated in detail -- Cooperation Committee	International Cooperation -- **not** elaborated in detail -- **no** provision for Cooperation Committee
Organization -- CoSP, ExC & Technical Secretariat	Organization -- CoSP, ExC & Technical Secretariat
National implementation -- Penal legislation required -- National Authority	National implementation -- Penal legislation required -- National Authority

57. The BTWC Protocol regime is much more elaborated throughout with much more constraint on the Organization and its activities than in the CWC. This greater constraint has arisen in part from the reactions of States Parties to their experience and their perceptions during the early stages in the implementation of the CWC and in part from the perception that commercial confidentiality is more important in microbiological and biotechnological facilities. There has frequently been a failure to recognise that under the CWC regime as two toxins -- ricin and saxitoxin -- are included as Schedule 1 chemicals, there could be a challenge inspection under the CWC of a microbiological or biotechnological facility and that the BTWC Protocol regime does not therefore necessarily present a greater challenge to commercial confidentiality in such facilities.

58. The BTWC Protocol regime also contains provisions that have no equivalent in the CWC regime -- examples are the measures to ensure submission of declarations (which clearly reflect the CWC experience where some States Parties were very late in submitting declarations of Scheduled chemical facilities) and the much greater attention given in the Protocol to technical cooperation to peaceful purposes. It is noteworthy that the Director-General of the OPCW has recently been emphasising the importance to the CWC regime of the technical cooperation and assistance aspects when he said[17] that *"The fostering of international cooperation in the peaceful application of chemistry is more than a desirable spin-off of our Organisation's work. It is in fact at one and the same time one of its foundation blocks and one of the Convention's strategic objectives."* He went on to say that *"Enhanced international cooperation is also a powerful tool to attract countries that have yet to join the Convention's regime .... The fostering of international cooperation is thus an important instrument for making the Convention a truly universal and steadfast norm against chemical warfare."* The value of fostering scientific and technical exchange and

[17]Organisation for the Prohibition of Chemical Weapons, *Statement by the Director-General under Agenda Item Seventeen: Fostering International Cooperation for Peaceful Purposes in the Field of Chemical Activities,* . Conference of the States Parties, Fifth Session, 15 -19 May 2000, C-V/DG.13, 18 May 2000.

international cooperation for peaceful purposes -- and its contribution to increasing transparency and enhancing confidence -- has been recognized clearly in the negotiation of the BTWC Protocol regime and has resulted in the much greater elaboration of the Article in the Protocol.

Discussion

59. The BTWC Protocol regime has been crafted to incorporate a range of measures -- mandatory declarations of the activities and facilities of greatest relevance to the BTWC, declaration follow-up procedures including randomly-selected transparency visits, declaration clarification procedures and voluntary assistance visits, measures to ensure submission of declarations, consultation, clarifications and cooperation, field and facility investigations, as well as measures to promote scientific and technical exchange and international cooperation. These elements together increase transparency within a State Party and enhance confidence between States Parties that the activities carried out within States Parties are in compliance with the Convention. There is considerable scope for interaction and synergism between the elements in the different measures and it is evident that the elements are indeed complementary.

60. Insofar as the danger from bioterrorism is concerned, the Protocol provides a useful tool that helps to counter this danger. The requirements in *Article 17 National Implementation Measures* for the enactment of national legislation including penal legislation makes it an offence for any individual within a State Party to develop, produce, acquire, stockpile biological agents or toxins for other than in types and quantities that have justification for peaceful purposes. It is also evident that the obligations in Article III (non-transfer) of the Convention require States Parties to introduce national regulations to control the possession, handling, storage and use of biological agents and toxins -- and such national regulations are also necessary to protect public health and the environment. The overall effect of the Protocol and its implementation nationally is to enhance awareness of the potential dangers from biological agents and toxins and so to increase the attention given to ensuring that such materials are not diverted for prohibited purposes. The provisions in the Protocol for the promotion of scientific and technological exchange will help States Parties develop the necessary national infrastructure to achieve the safe handling, storage and use of biological agents and toxins.

61. The BTWC Protocol regime has been successfully developed from both the previous confidence-building measures agreed by the BTWC States Parties at the Second Review Conference in 1986 and extended and strengthened at the Third Review Conference in 1991 and from the experience and the perceptions of the CWC regime which opened for signature in 1993 and entered into force in 1997. Although there are differences between the BTWC Protocol and the CWC regimes, a quantified and comparative evaluation[18] of the two regimes has shown that an effective and efficient BTWC Protocol regime is being developed. It is clear that the provisions for the two regimes will both be effective in strengthening the norm against biological and chemical weapons -- and the BTWC Protocol regime will achieve its objective of strengthening the effectiveness and improving the implementation of the Convention.

---

[18] Graham S. Pearson & Malcolm R. Dando, *The Emerging Protocol: An Integrated, Reliable and Effective Regime,*, University of Bradford, Department of Peace Studies, Briefing Paper No 25, September 1999. Available at http://www.brad.ac.uk/acad/sbtwc.

Wider Perspectives

62. When considering the regime to prevent biological weapons, it is all too easy to focus exclusively on arms control considerations and to fail to recognise that there are wider perspectives that are relevant to biological agents and toxins and which need to be taken into account in considering how States can increase transparency and build confidence that activities are indeed for peaceful purposes. These wider considerations relate to the international initiatives: to counter outbreaks of disease whether in humans, animals or plants; to protect the environment through the Convention on Biological Diversity and its International Guidelines on Biosafety and, more recently, the Cartagena Protocol on Biosafety; to prevent the illicit use of narcotic drugs and psychotropic chemicals; as well as to harmonize Good Manufacturing Practice for safe and reproducible pharmaceutical and biological products. Each of these is considered briefly:

a. **Countering outbreaks of disease.** It is widely appreciated that an outbreak of disease in one country can in this age of rapid international travel and trade rapidly spread to other countries often before the initial outbreak has been diagnosed. After all, diseases know no frontiers. There is consequently considerable emphasis nationally, regionally and internationally on improving disease surveillance and reporting for diseases in humans, animals and plants. States in which there is effective surveillance and reporting of outbreaks of disease increase transparency within that State and also build confidence that outbreaks are not being concealed for whatever reasons. Over time there is much greater international transparency as to what diseases are endemic in a particular country as well as confidence that outbreaks that appear unusual will be investigated and their causes determined.

b. **Protection of the environment.** The Convention for Biological Diversity[19] opened for signature at the Rio Summit in June 1992 and entered into force in December 1993. This Convention includes in its Article 19 Handling of Biotechnology and Distribution of its Benefits the requirement that the States Parties shall consider the need for and modalities of a protocol setting out appropriate procedures, including, in particular, advance informed agreement, in the field of the safe transfer, handling and use of any living modified organism resulting from biotechnology that may have adverse effect on the conservation and sustainable use of biological diversity. The States Parties decided to adopt a twin-track approach developing International Technical Guidelines on Safety on Biotechnology as well as negotiating a Protocol on Biosafety. The International Guidelines[20] were adopted by a meeting of the Global Consultation of Government-designated Experts held in Cairo, Egypt from 11 to 14 December 1995 and issued by UNEP. The Cartagena Protocol on Biosafety was finalized in January 2000. It is widely appreciated that biological agents, whether genetically modified or not, can cause harm to those working with these agents or, if released, to the surrounding population. Increasingly, States are adopting national regulations for the handling, use and storage of such materials and of genetically modified organisms. These national regulations may be harmonized regionally, as for example in the European Union, and may require the inspection and certification of facilities working with such materials. As more States adopt such

[19]United Nations, *Convention on Biological Diversity,* opened for signature at Rio de Janeiro 5 June 1992, UNEP/CBD/94/1, Geneva, November 1994. Also available as HMSO, Cm 2127, January 1993.

[20]United Nations Environment Programme, *UNEP International Technical Guidelines for Safety in Biotechnology*, UNEP Nairobi, Kenya.

regulations so transparency is increased and confidence gained that such materials are being used for peaceful purposes.

c. **Illicit use of narcotic drugs and psychotropic chemicals.** Many narcotic drugs and psychotropic chemicals are or are produced from naturally occurring materials. They and their precursors also have dual use in that they have significant medicinal purposes as well as illicit use. There are three key drug conventions (the 1961 Single Convention on Narcotic Drugs as amended by the Protocol of 1972, the 1971 Convention on Psychotropic Substances and the 1988 Convention against Illicit Traffic in Narcotic Drugs and Psychotropic Substances) which together control a significant number of narcotic drugs (118), psychotropic substances (111) along with their precursors and essential chemicals (22) used in the illicit manufacture of narcotic drugs and psychotropic substances. The number of States Parties to all three Conventions is close to 160 and it is evident that States continue to accede to them as a result of the efforts of the INCB (International Narcotics Control Board) to further the aims of the treaties and achieve universality. The narcotic drugs, psychotropic substances, precursors and essential chemicals are assigned to Schedules or Tables which are associated with various control measures. The materials controlled are all dual purpose with the Conventions and the INCB seeking to limit the cultivation, production, manufacture and use of drugs to an adequate amount required for medical and scientific purposes whilst preventing illicit cultivation, production and manufacture of, and illicit traffic in and use of drugs. The essential chemicals controlled under the 1988 Convention include materials such as acetic anhydride and potassium permanganate, key chemicals in the manufacture of heroin and cocaine respectively, although the quantities diverted for illicit drug production is very much less than 1 per cent of the permitted use of these chemicals. The control measures include both national monitoring and controls as well as export and import measures.

d. **Good Manufacturing Practice (GMP) .** It is evident that there is considerable harmonization world-wide in respect of the GMP standards to be achieved in facilities producing medicinal products for humans and for animals so as to ensure safe and reproducible products[21]. There is already mutual recognition of inspections and standards between countries within the European Union. MRAs (Mutual Recognition Agreements) have been initialled between the European Community and countries such as the US, Canada, Australia, New Zealand and Switzerland and a start made in the negotiation of MRAs with other countries such as Japan and the candidate states for the expansion of the EU. There are several international harmonization schemes which can usefully be put into context using the schematic relating product and manufacturing licences:

	Requirements for Industry	**Regulatory Authority Action**
Marketing Authorization *Product Licence*	Safety, efficacy & quality data **EU, ICH**	Evaluation, Licensing **EU, PER**

[21]See Graham S. Pearson, *Article X: Pharmaceutical Building Blocks*, University of Bradford, Department of Peace Studies, Briefing Paper No 8, July 1998. Available at http://brad.ac.uk/acad/sbtwc

Manufacturing Authorization ***Manufacturer's Licence***	Good Manufacturing Practice **EU, PIC, WHO**	Inspection, Licensing **EU, PIC, MRAs**

EU = European Union, ICH = International Conference on Harmonization,
PER = Scheme for the Mutual Recognition of Evaluation Reports on Pharmaceutical Products
PIC = Pharmaceutical Inspection Convention, WHO = World Health Organization

Manufacturer's authorizations (product licences) usually have a five year life and the aim generally is to reinspect manufacturers every two years. The purpose of those inspections are to ensure that the facilities being used to manufacture a licensed medicinal product are compliant with GMP and that the processes used are such that cross-contamination of the product will not occur. Consequently, the inspection is limited to those parts of a manufacturing facility used in the production of the licensed product -- this will include everything from receipt and storage of raw materials, through production to packaging together with all aspects of the quality control of the product. Other parts of the facility which are not involved in the product manufacture will not be inspected. Although there is much commercial sensitivity, the existence of both manufacturing and product licences are in the public domain -- although the linkage between a product licence and where that product is manufactured is commercially secret.

Consequently, it is clear that in pharmaceutical and biotechnological production facilities engaged in manufacturing licensed products, these facilities will increasingly be inspected at regular intervals by national regulatory authorities to monitor their compliance with internationally harmonised standards for GMP in order for these facilities to be licensed. Insofar as the Protocol being negotiated by the Ad Hoc Group is concerned, the information as to whether a production facility is licensed to GMP standards should be part of the information to be provided in declarations of such facilities. This information, together with the GMP standard to which it has been inspected, and the date of the last such inspection by the national regulatory authority will help to build confidence that the facility is compliant and is engaged in permitted purposes. It follows that measures to assist developing countries establish a national regulatory system of product and manufacturers' licences to internationally agreed standards would both directly implement Article X of the BTWC and also contribute to building confidence in compliance with the Convention. Such measures would also be in accord with the actions being taken by developed countries following the Rio Summit of 1992 and the emphasis on aiding capacity building in developing countries.

Conclusions

63. When a wider perspective is considered, it is evident that the BTWC Protocol regime to *strengthen the effectiveness and improve the implementation* of the BTWC needs to be considered in the context of an international scene in which there is increasing transparency about the nature of activities and facilities within countries which is facilitated by the information increasingly being made available on the internet and the recognition by more and more countries that they share common goals for a safer, more prosperous world -- a world in which there is greater recognition that the dangers from dual-use materials and

technology in general and biological agents and toxins in particular know no frontiers and that an outbreak in one country can spread all too quickly to its neighbours and, indeed, around the world through international travel and trade. The compliance elements of the Protocol regime -- declarations, visits, investigations -- are complemented by the provisions to promote scientific and technological exchange for peaceful purposes as these provisions help States Parties to develop their infrastructure -- and thereby reap benefits in international trade and commerce as well as increasing transparency and enhancing confidence in compliance. The BTWC Protocol regime will thus enhance international security and counter bioterrorism as well as also contribute directly to achieving a safer, healthier, more prosperous world bringing benefits to all countries, both developed or developing.

Bioterrorism, Public Health, and International Law

David P. Fidler*

I. Introduction

The specter of bioterrorism—long the subject of who-dun-it fiction and well-intentioned but inconclusive policy-making—became a terrifying reality for the United States in October 2001. Less than a month after the worst act of terrorism committed against the United States, and less than two weeks after the United States began waging war against the Taliban in Afghanistan, Americans confronted the malevolent use of microbes to inflict death, illness, fear, and economic damage on the United States. The anthrax crisis developed slowly into a full-blown nightmare as each day seemed to bring new cases, terror, and questions about how ill-prepared the country was for the malignancy of bioterrorism.

The United States is still coming to grips—politically and psychologically—with the perpetration of bioterrorism within its borders. Speculating about the impact of the anthrax attacks on political, economic, or legal areas is, thus, fraught with difficulties. As a veteran of biological weapons and bioterrorism discourse prior to the anthrax attacks, I think it is important, even in this fluid time, to engage in preliminary examination of the possible effects of the recent bioterrorism on the relationship between public health and international law explored in this issue of the *Chicago Journal of International Law*.

In this article, I contemplate the potential impact of the anthrax attacks on various areas of international law that affect public health—namely, the international law on the use of force, arms control, terrorism, global infectious disease control,

Professor of Law and Ira C. Batman Faculty Fellow, Indiana University School of Law—Bloomington. Professor Fidler served as international legal consultant to the US Department of Defense's Defense Science Board Task Force on Defense Against Biological Weapons from April 2000 until May 2001, and he has been a member of the Federation of American Scientists' Working Group on Biological Weapons Verification since 1997. He thanks the members of his course on "Weapons of Mass Destruction and the Rule of Law" and his research assistants Shafiqa Ahmadi and David Wilford for their assistance in the preparation of this article. Professor Fidler also thanks Professor Jack Goldsmith and the staff of the *Chicago Journal of International Law* for inviting him to contribute this article. The article attempts to take into account events up to January 31, 2002.

human rights, trade in goods, and the protection of intellectual property rights. In addition, I make observations about how the recent bioterrorism may affect the direction and content of global public health efforts. In the end, my analysis generates more questions than answers, but the potential impact of the bioterrorist attacks on international law and global public health is so serious that even preliminary consideration of the matter is warranted.

II. Bioterrorism and Public Health: Before and After the Anthrax Attacks

For many Americans, the anthrax attacks were a frightening initiation into a threat that experts in the United States have been analyzing since at least the early 1990s. The attacks also introduced many Americans to "public health"—a discipline distinct from healthcare and largely obscure to the average American.[1] Detailing the discourse on biological weapons and bioterrorism before the anthrax attacks is beyond the scope of this article, but I provide an overview in order to focus on the importance of public health to national and international policy in this area.

A. Proliferation of Biological Weapons by States

In the early 1990s, revelations about the former Soviet Union's and Iraq's biological weapons programs caused many experts to focus new attention on the proliferation of biological weapons in the international system.[2] While US intelligence suspected that the Soviet Union and Iraq had developed biological weapons, no one anticipated the enormous scale and sophistication of the Soviet and Iraqi programs.

Evidence of Soviet and Iraqi bioweaponeering raised fears that biological weapons proliferation had become a serious international problem. Experts worried not only that "rogue" states might possess biological weapons, but also that state proliferation of biological weapons would make it easier for terrorists to gain access to pathogenic microbes.

These fears partly explain the effort, launched in the first half of the 1990s, to negotiate a protocol to the Biological Weapons Convention of 1972 ("BWC")[3] that would establish a verification mechanism for the BWC's prohibition on the

1. For descriptions and definitions of public health, see Institute of Medicine, *The Future of Public Health* 35–55 (National Academy 1988); Lawrence O. Gostin, *Public Health Law: Power, Duty, Restraint* 3–22 (California 2000).
2. George W. Christopher, et al, *Biological Warfare: A Historical Perspective*, 278 JAMA 412, 416 (1997) (discussing biological weapons program of the former Soviet Union); and Raymond A. Zilinskas, *Iraq's Biological Weapons: The Past as Future*, 278 JAMA 418 (1997) (analyzing Iraqi biological weapons program).
3. Convention on the Prohibition of the Development, Production, and Stockpiling of Bacteriological (Biological) and Toxin Weapons and on Their Destruction, 11 ILM 309 (1972).

development, production, and stockpiling of biological weapons. Adding momentum to this effort was the completion in 1993 of the Chemical Weapons Convention ("Convention"), which contained a verification mechanism for improving compliance with the Convention's prohibitions.[4]

B. CATASTROPHIC TERRORISM: PREPARING FOR THE UNTHINKABLE

As the effort to deal with biological weapons proliferation by states got underway, policymakers in the United States and other countries began to confront "catastrophic terrorism"—terrorism conducted with weapons of mass destruction ("WMD").[5] The seminal event that focused attention on catastrophic terrorism in the latter half of the 1990s was the Japanese religious cult Aum Shinriyko's chemical weapon (sarin) attack in Toyko in March 1995. Later, Japanese authorities revealed that Aum Shinriyko had tried unsuccessfully to develop and deploy biological weapons (botulinum toxin and anthrax) as well. Until Aum Shinriyko's development and use of WMD, verified examples of terrorist groups developing or using chemical or biological agents were few and very far between, leading some experts to downplay the likelihood of chemical or biological terrorism.[6] With Aum Shinriyko, terrorism crossed the WMD rubicon in a significant and terrifying way.

The United States reacted to Aum Shinriyko's chemical and attempted biological terrorism by focusing on domestic preparedness for catastrophic terrorism. Previous policy responses to the WMD threat concentrated on counter-proliferation strategies aimed largely at states, not terrorists.[7] Counter-terrorism activities had not, as a general matter, been interested in whether terrorists groups were dabbling with chemical or biological weapons.[8] At the federal level, the Defense Against Weapons

4. Convention for the Prohibition of the Development, Production, Stockpiling and Use of Chemical Weapons and on Their Destruction, 32 ILM 800 (1993).
5. Ashton Carter, John Deutch, and Philip Zelikow, *Catastrophic Terrorism: Tackling the New Danger*, Foreign Aff 80 (Nov–Dec 1998).
6. Jonathan B. Tucker, *Lessons from the Case Studies*, in Jonathan B. Tucker, ed, *Toxic Terror: Assessing Terrorist Use of Chemical and Biological Weapons* 249, 267 (MIT 2000) ("Based on the historical trends identified in this study, however, only a tiny minority of terrorists will seek to inflict indiscriminate casualties [with chemical or biological weapons], and few if any of them will succeed."). For a study of historical cases of bioterrorism, see W. Seth Carus, *Bioterrorism and Biocrimes: The Illicit Use of Biological Agents in the 20th Century* (Center for Counterproliferation Research Working Paper, April 2000 Revision).
7. James R. Ferguson, *Biological Weapons and US Law*, 278 JAMA 357, 358 (1997) (noting that US policy on biological weapons after the BWC focused on preventing other nations from acquiring biological weapons).
8. David E. Kaplan, *Aum Shinriyko (1995)*, in Jonathan B. Tucker, ed, *Toxic Terror at* 224 (cited in note 6) ("Despite the cult's virulent anti-Americanism and international procurement efforts, U.S. intelligence agencies also failed to recognize the threat at hand. As one counterintelligence official told U.S. Senate investigators, 'They simply were not on anybody's radar screen.'").

of Mass Destruction Act of 1996 symbolized this policy shift toward preparedness for catastrophic terrorism.

C. "BIO IS DIFFERENT"—PUBLIC HEALTH AS THE CENTERPIECE FOR INTERNATIONAL AND NATIONAL SECURITY POLICIES

The international efforts to negotiate a BWC verification protocol and US efforts to prepare for catastrophic terrorism eventually confronted the same problem: biological weapons present a fundamentally different challenge from nuclear and chemical weapons. Diplomatic attempts to create a BWC protocol ran into political and technical difficulties that underscored how hard international control of biological weapons was. The BWC protocol negotiations also revealed how important basic public health functions, such as infectious disease surveillance, would be to the successful response to the illegal development and use of biological weapons.

US preparedness for WMD terrorism likewise had to learn that bioterrorism cannot be lumped together with chemical and nuclear terrorism. Responding to bioterrorism would be different from responses to chemical and nuclear terrorism because first responders in bioterrorist cases would be the public health and healthcare systems, not firefighters, law enforcement, and emergency-response personnel. As public health experts concerned about bioterrorism argued, the quality of the nation's public health infrastructure and capabilities had become important for US national security and homeland defense[9]—an argument that traditional national-security thinking inside the Beltway had a hard time grasping.

D. THE ANTHRAX ATTACKS

The anthrax attacks in the United States brought together each strand discussed above in disturbing ways. First, the nation watched as federal, state, and local public health authorities scrambled to deal with the use of anthrax as a weapon of death and terror against civilian populations. As public health experts had predicted, the first line of defense against bioterrorism was the US public health system. Second, the anthrax attacks reinforced the conclusion reached in the mid-1990s that domestic

9. Testimony of Tara O'Toole, Hearing on Terrorism Preparedness: Medical First Response, House of Representatives Committee on Government Reform, Subcommittee on National Security, Veterans Affairs, and International Relations, Sept 22, 1999, available online at <http://www.hopkins-biodefense.org/pages/library/prepare.html> (visited Mar 24, 2002) ("The outcome of a bioterrorist attack on US civilians would be an epidemic. The 'first responders' to such an event would be physicians, nurses, and public health professionals in city and state health departments. A covert bioterrorist attack would likely come to attention gradually, as doctors became aware of an accumulation of inexplicable deaths among previously healthy people. The speed and accuracy with which physicians and laboratories reached correct diagnoses and reported their findings to public health authorities would directly affect the number of deaths, and—if the attack employed a contagious disease—the ability to contain the epidemic.").

preparedness for bioterrorism should be a national priority and revealed that the United States was not sufficiently prepared. Third, analysis and speculation about the source of the anthrax used in the attacks led experts to wonder whether the perpetrators obtained the bacteria from Iraq, providing a possible link between the bioterrorism and a state-sponsored biological weapons program.[10] Finally, in Washington, DC, the legislative and executive branches indicated a new willingness to focus on public health as a national security priority, as evidenced by bioterrorism bills passed by both houses of Congress.[11]

III. BIOTERRORISM AND INTERNATIONAL LAW: WHAT IMPACT WILL THE ANTHRAX ATTACKS HAVE?

The anthrax attacks will affect the United States and the world for years to come and in ways that even the most highly qualified experts would have trouble discerning in the current volatile climate. My focus on the possible impact of these attacks on international law does not imply that this impact is the most important issue on the post-attack agenda. Nevertheless, students and scholars of international law should consider how these acts of bioterrorism may affect international law.

A. THE COMPLEX RELATIONSHIP BETWEEN INFECTIOUS DISEASES AND INTERNATIONAL LAW

As the anthrax attacks demonstrate, bioterrorism involves the malicious use of pathogenic microbes to cause disease, death, and fear in civilian populations. Such use of infectious diseases as weapons of terror implicates a number of areas of international law. The scope of the potential impact is greater still because of the complex, but largely neglected, relationship between international law and infectious diseases. The bioterrorism perpetrated in the United States brings this relationship between infectious diseases and international law to the forefront and underscores why thinking about national and international control of infectious diseases should include consideration of international law.

---

10. The connection between the anthrax attacks and Iraq was prominently drawn by a former director of the Central Intelligence Agency. See R. James Woolsey, *Behind the Terror: The Iraqi Connection*, Wall St J Eur 6 (Oct 19, 2001). As this article was being written, federal authorities were focusing their investigations on domestic terrorism as the source for the anthrax attacks.

11. On January 10, 2002, President Bush signed into law a $2.9 billion bioterrorism appropriations bill. Still pending at the time of this writing was the conference committee reconciliation of the Public Health Security and Bioterrorism Response Act of 2001, passed by the House of Representatives in December 2001, and the Bioterrorism Preparedness Act of 2001, passed by the Senate in December 2001.

B. International Law on the Use of Force: An Anthrax Wrinkle to the Right of Self-Defense?

The US-led "war against terrorism" has produced discussion in international legal circles concerning whether US military attacks against Afghanistan, and the multilateral support such attacks received, affect the scope of the right to use force in self-defense.[12] The UN Security Council, the North Atlantic Treaty Organization ("NATO"), the Organization of American States, and countries in their individual capacities have declared that the September 11th terrorists attacks triggered this right to individual and collective self-defense.[13] Most, if not all, of the statements in support of the United States' right of self-defense were not conditioned on the September 11th terrorism being state-sponsored. Thus, the scope of the right to self-defense in customary international law and the UN Charter—a subject of controversy in international law for decades—may be expanding to provide a legitimate justification for using force against countries that harbor (as opposed to sponsor) international terrorists.

Into this situation came the anthrax attacks. Clearly, if the involvement of a state actor (for example, Iraq) in the anthrax attacks should come to light, then the United States would be justified under the traditional right of self-defense to use military force against Iraq. State-sponsorship of bioterrorism would not, thus, present a radically new context for the use of force in self-defense because the United States has used force against governments that have sponsored terrorism in the past (for example, the 1986 military strikes against Libya). Similarly, if foreign terrorists are linked to the anthrax attacks, the United States will consider military strikes against any state that harbors them, in keeping with the United States' interpretation of the right to self-defense in the context of terrorism.

The anthrax attacks may, however, affect the right to use force in self-defense in other ways. The tolerance of the United States, and perhaps other countries supportive of the war against terrorism, for the possession of WMD programs by "states of concern" may be reduced after the anthrax attacks. This new intolerance may lead the United States and other countries to consider the existence of such programs a serious threat to national and international security, and perhaps to contemplate the use of force to destroy such programs before governments use WMD or such weapons find their way into terrorist hands. In this vein, President Bush, in

12. See analysis posted to ASIL Insights, available online at <http://www.asil.org/insights/insigh77.htm> (visited Mar 24, 2002).

13. Security Council Res No 1368, UN Doc S/RES/1368 (2001); NATO, Statement by the North Atlantic Council, Press Release 124, Sept 12, 2001, available online at <http://www.nato.int/docu/pr/2001/p01-124e.htm> (visited Mar 24, 2002); Organization of American States, Terrorist Threat to the Americas, RC.24/RES.1/01, Sept 21, 2001, available online at <http://www.oas.org/OASpage/crisis/RC.24e.htm> (visited Mar 24, 2002).

his State of the Union address in January 2002, declared that the United States "will not stand by as peril draws closer and closer" and "will not permit the world's most dangerous regimes to threaten us with the world's most destructive weapons."[14]

Historical precedents for this position exist. First, Israel justified its destruction of an Iraqi nuclear facility in 1981 as an act of anticipatory self-defense. While the international community, including the United States, rejected this justification at the time, later revelations of the scale of Iraqi nuclear, chemical, and biological weapons programs have made the Israeli argument look more legitimate. Second, US and British forces attacked alleged Iraqi WMD facilities in 1998 because of Iraq's intransigence toward inspections by the UN Special Commission. While the legal authority for this use of force could be based on Security Council resolutions on disarming Iraq of WMD, the 1998 attacks could also be interpreted as acts of anticipatory self-defense in preventing Iraq from re-developing WMD capabilities.

Third, the Clinton Administration justified the US attack on an alleged chemical-weapons facility in Sudan in 1998 as an act of self-defense after the terrorist bombings of US embassies in Kenya and Tanzania. Neither Sudan nor chemical weapons were involved in the embassy bombings, but the United States argued that the attack was a legitimate exercise of its right of self-defense. The collapse of the evidentiary foundation for this justification does not negate this incident as a possible precedent for widening the right of anticipatory self-defense to deal with the threat of biological weapons and bioterrorism.

C. International Law and Arms Control: Will Bioterrorism Bring the BWC Protocol Back from the Dead?

As Part II mentioned, the latter half of the 1990s witnessed an effort to negotiate a BWC verification protocol. Although the BWC prohibits the development, production, and stockpiling of biological weapons, experts perceived that its Achilles heel was the lack of a verification regime. From 1995 until 2001, the Ad Hoc Group of States worked to draft a verification protocol. In July 2001, the Bush Administration declared that the protocol was not acceptable because it was too weak and posed threats to the confidential business information of US pharmaceutical

14. Michael R. Gordon, *Broadening of 'Doctrine,'* NY Times A1 (Jan 30, 2002). The members of President Bush's now famous "axis of evil" include repressive regimes that sponsor terrorism and that are seeking access to weapons of mass destruction. See President George W. Bush, *State of the Union Address*, available online at <http://www.whitehouse.gov/news/releases/2002/01/20020129-11.html> (visited Mar 24, 2002).

companies.[15] Without US support, the proposed BWC verification protocol was effectively dead.

The anthrax attacks raised the question whether these acts of bioterrorism would change the Bush Administration's hostility toward the proposed BWC protocol. At the end of October 2001, the United States reopened talks with European countries on the BWC protocol.[16] While the Bush Administration claimed that the anthrax attacks were not the stimulus for the new discussions, the timing of the US initiative suggested that the attacks may have softened US opposition to continuing the protocol negotiations.

At the BWC's Fifth Review Conference in late November 2001, the Bush Administration demonstrated that its opposition to the proposed BWC protocol had not, in fact, softened. John Bolton, Undersecretary of State for Arms Control, made clear that the Bush Administration would not support further negotiations on the BWC protocol and offered alternative proposals to improve compliance with the BWC.[17] The US proposals do not constitute an alternative arms-control protocol but stress the immediate adoption of national legal and public health measures by BWC states parties to reduce the threat of biological weapons proliferation and bioterrorism. US proposals involving international cooperation, such as supporting the global disease surveillance and response capabilities of the World Health Organization ("WHO"), do not require the negotiation of a new treaty. The anthrax attacks did not, therefore, resurrect the BWC protocol but rather strengthened the Bush Administration's desire to bury it for good.

D. International Criminal Law: Will International Law Criminalize Bioterrorism?

The anthrax attacks play into another theme in the discourse on biological weapons and bioterrorism—proposals to make the use, development, production, or possession of a biological weapon by any person (including diplomats and heads of state) a crime in international law punishable through the application of universal jurisdiction. The Harvard Sussex Program on Chemical and Biological Warfare Armament and Arms Limitation synthesized this idea in its proposed Convention on the Prevention and Punishment of the Crime of Developing, Producing, Acquiring,

15. Testimony of Ambassador Donald A. Mahley, House Government Reform Committee, Subcommittee On National Security, Veterans Affairs and International Relations, The Biological Weapons Convention: Status and Implications, July 10, 2001, available online at <http://www.fas.org/bwc/news/maht.htm> (visited Mar 24, 2002).

16. *U.S. Eager to Bolster Bioterrorism Treaty*, Intl Herald Trib (Nov 2, 2001).

17. For a summary of the Fifth Review Conference and the position of the Bush Administration at this meeting, see Graham S. Pearson, *Report from Geneva: The Biological and Toxin Weapons Convention*, 54 CBW Conventions Bull 13 (Dec 2001).

Stockpiling, Retaining, Transferring or Using Biological or Chemical Weapons.[18] Making the use, development, or possession of a biological weapon a crime under international law subject to the principle of universal jurisdiction would make the bioweaponeer *hostis humani generis*—an enemy of all humankind.[19] The use of a biological weapon by a state or terrorist organization is, however, already subject to criminal sanctions in international humanitarian law and international law on terrorism. The use by a state (either directly or through state-sponsored terrorism) of a biological weapon against a civilian population would, for example, be a war crime and, depending on the nature of the biological attack, potentially a crime against humanity.[20] The use of a biological weapon by a terrorist is already an offense subject to criminal prosecution by any nation party to the UN Convention on the Suppression of Terrorist Bombings, which entered into force in May 2001. The proposal to criminalize the use of biological weapons by states or terrorist organizations, therefore, would build on existing principles condemning and criminalizing this kind of behavior. What the proponents of this proposal seek is direct and express criminalization of the use of biological weapons and the unauthorized development and possession of such weapons on the part of any person. The anthrax attacks bolster the case for making the unauthorized use, development, and possession of biological weapons expressly a crime in international law.

The larger question is whether such a development in international criminal law will significantly affect state and terrorist calculations about the utility of biological weapons. Experience with international criminal law in areas such as armed conflict and torture suggests that the deterrent effect of criminalizing certain state and individual behavior under international law is not great. Likewise, terrorists might not be deterred, given that their activities are already illegal in most jurisdictions in which they operate. Finally, many people terrorized by the anthrax attacks might wonder why international lawyers focus attention on punishing terrorists or state actors rather than working to prevent attacks from occurring.

---

18. Michael P. Scharf, *Clear and Present Danger: Enforcing the International Ban on Biological and Chemical Weapons Through Sanctions, Use of Force, and Criminalization*, 20 Mich J Intl L 477, 511-21(1999) (draft of the convention is attached as an appendix). See also *International Criminal Law and Sanctions to Reinforce the BWC*, 54 CBW Conventions Bull 1 (Dec 2001).
19. Scharf, *Clear and Present Danger* at 506 (cited in note 18).
20. This result flows from international humanitarian law's principle of the immunity of civilian populations from attack, not from a principle that criminalizes the use of biological weapons. See Rome Statute of the International Criminal Court, art 8.2(b), UN Doc No A/CONF.183/9, (1998) (defining war crimes to include intentionally attacking civilian populations); id at art 7.1 (defining crimes against humanity to include murder committed as part of a widespread or systematic attack directed against any civilian population).

E. International Law and Global Infectious Disease Control: Will Bioterrorism Rescue the Revision of the International Health Regulations?

Outside the contexts of biological weapons proliferation and bioterrorism, the 1990s were also a decade that witnessed concerns about emerging and re-emerging infectious diseases as a global public health problem. In 1996, WHO declared that the world faced a "world crisis" in infectious diseases for which immediate international action was required.[21] Part of the action WHO proposed was revising the International Health Regulations ("IHR"), which constitute the only international agreement on international control of infectious diseases binding on WHO member states.[22] WHO argued that the global crisis in infectious diseases revealed weaknesses and problems with the existing IHR and that the IHR should be reformed to provide a better international legal foundation for global infectious disease control in the twenty-first century.[23]

Prior to the anthrax attacks, the IHR revision process appeared to have made little progress in the years since WHO launched the effort in 1995. I have argued elsewhere that the classical regime on international infectious disease control embodied in the IHR is effectively dead, killed by a combination of technological changes, WHO's indifference, and the jealous guarding of sovereignty by WHO member states.[24]

Will the anthrax attacks breathe new life into the IHR revision process? Critical to the IHR's purpose is the objective of epidemiological surveillance for infectious diseases. Whether a disease outbreak is man-made or naturally occurring, surveillance is vital for public health authorities to understand what is happening and implement appropriate interventions. The IHR were designed to support an international surveillance network for infectious diseases, which—if it functioned—would contribute to handling not only naturally occurring infectious diseases but also bioterrorism.

The perpetration of bioterrorism in the United States may provide a stimulus for states and WHO to pay more attention to the IHR revision and its objectives. The Bush Administration's new proposals for the BWC protocol negotiations include an emphasis on support for WHO's global infectious disease surveillance and response

21. World Health Organization, *World Health Report 1996* 105 (1996).

22. World Health Organization, *Emerging and Other Communicable Diseases Surveillance and Control*, WHO/EMC/96.1 at 3 (1996–2000).

23. World Heath Organization, *Revision and Updating of the International Health Regulations*, WHA Res 48.7 (May 12, 1995).

24. David P. Fidler, *International Law and Global Infectious Disease Control*, Commission on Macroeconomics and Health, Paper No WG2:18, available online at <http://www.cmhealth.org/docs/wg2_paper18.pdf> (visited Mar 24, 2002).

programs,[25] of which the IHR revision is supposed to be a part.[26] The Bush Administration also emphasized the importance of global infectious disease surveillance and response in signing the so-called "Ottawa Plan" in November 2001 with seven other nations and the European Union.[27]

I doubt, however, whether rejuvenated attention to the IHR revision will emerge after the anthrax attacks. First, the substantive approach in the IHR revision may not be worth preserving, even in light of the new reality of bioterrorism.[28] The Bush Administration's emphasis on the need for multilateral support for WHO's disease surveillance network and strategy for disease outbreak containment does not necessarily equal support for the IHR revision process. WHO built and continues to refine its "Global Outbreak Alert and Response Network"[29] without the revised IHR in place. It is not true that, as WHO asserts, the IHR "serve as the legal framework for WHO's alert and response activities"[30] because the existing IHR do not authorize much of the activity WHO is undertaking in its global outbreak alert and response network. Further, the revised IHR are not necessary to make this network operate because it is already operating.[31]

Second, the anthrax attacks highlighted weaknesses in infectious disease surveillance in the United States, which means that the likely response of US policymakers will be on national rather than international infectious disease surveillance capabilities. Other countries watching the ordeal in the United States will also turn first toward national public health problems before worrying about the IHR revision process. This dynamic is revealed in the Ottawa Plan. The anthrax attacks jolted the health ministers of the participating countries into multilateral discussions about protecting their countries from bioterrorism. The IHR revision, however, does not figure into the Ottawa Plan's multilateral cooperation against bioterrorism.

---

25. Federation of American Scientists, *Strengthening the Ban on Germ Weapons*, Press Release, Nov 7, 2001, available online at <http://www.fas.org/bwc/news/FASPressRelease7Nov2001.html> (visited Mar 24, 2002)
26. *Global Health Security*, 76 Weekly Epidemiological Record 166, 168 (2001).
27. US Department of Health and Human Services, *Secretary Thompson Joins Health Ministers in "Ottawa Plan": Countries Forge New Partnership to Strengthen Public Health and National Security*, Press Release, Nov 7, 2001, available online at <http://www.hhs.gov/news/press/2001pres/20011107a.html> (visited Mar 24, 2002). The agreement establishing the Ottawa Plan is not a treaty binding on the signatory states but merely a political agreement setting out objectives for future multilateral cooperation to combat bioterrorism.
28. Fidler, *International Law and Global Infectious Disease Control* at 28–34 (cited in note 24).
29. World Health Organization, *Global Outbreak Alert and Response Network*, available online at <http://www.who.int/emc/pdfs/network.pdf> (visited Mar 24, 2002).
30. *Global Health Security*, 76 Weekly Epidemiological Record at 168 (cited in note 26).
31. Fidler, *International Law and Global Infectious Disease Control* at 30 (cited in note 24).

F. International Law and Human Rights: Homeland Security vs Civil Liberties?

The September 11th terrorist attacks sparked legislative action in the United States for new anti-terrorism measures giving law enforcement officials the power to prevent and punish terrorist activities.[32] These new law enforcement powers created concern about how much civil rights and liberties protected by constitutional and international law would suffer to improve "homeland security." The anthrax attacks exacerbate this tension between homeland security and the protection of civil liberties because they represent a new development in the fight against terrorism. In addition, the anthrax attacks create human rights concerns particular to public health that deserve attention.

Discourse on bioterrorism has addressed the need to balance effective public health responses in emergencies with individual rights and liberties.[33] Public health officials recognize that they may need to infringe on individual rights in order to control effectively an outbreak caused by bioterrorism. The powers public health officials need in the context of bioterrorism range from the moderate (for example, access to private medical records to track an outbreak) to the draconian (for example, quarantine of populations).[34] Potential infringements on individual rights increase if terrorists use a pathogen that is communicable from person to person. Fortunately, anthrax is not communicable in this way, which means that the anthrax attacks did not result in major governmental infringements on individual rights.

The anthrax attacks illustrate, however, the importance of the framework established in international law for infringing on civil and political rights to protect public health. Regional and international treaties on civil and political rights recognized the need for public health to have the power to override individual rights in order to deal with infectious diseases long before bioterrorism concerns emerged.

---

32. Uniting and Strengthening America by Providing Appropriate Tools Required to Intercept and Obstruct Terrorism Act of 2001, Public L No 107-56, 115 Stat 272 (2001); Detention, Treatment, and Trial of Certain Non-Citizens in the War Against Terrorism, Presidential Doc, 66 Fed Reg 57833 (2001).

33. Barry Kellman, *Biological Terrorism: Legal Measures for Preventing Catastrophe*, 24 Harv J L & Pub Pol 417, 475–488 (2001); Juliette N. Kayyem, *U.S. Preparations for Biological Terrorism: Legal Limitations and the Need for Planning*, BCSIA Discussion Paper 2001-4, ESDP Discussion Paper ESDP-2001-02, John F. Kennedy School of Government, Harvard University (Mar 2001); David P. Fidler, *The Malevolent Use of Microbes and the Rule of Law: Legal Challenges Presented by Bioterrorism*, 33 Clinical Infectious Diseases 686, 688 (2001).

34. Centers for Disease Control and Prevention, *List of Powers Public Officials Need to Respond to Bioterrorism* (on file with author) (listing public health powers required for control of persons). See also Center for Law and the Public's Health, Model State Emergency Health Powers Act, Dec 21, 2001, available online at <http://www.publichealthlaw.net/MSEHPA/MSEHPA2.pdf> (visited Mar 24, 2002) (draft model state statute on public health emergency powers prepared for the US Centers for Disease Control and Prevention).

What the treaties on civil and political rights establish, however, is a framework that public health authorities need to follow in order to ensure that individual rights and liberties are infringed only when necessary and in the least restrictive way possible.

International law on civil and political rights disciplines public health power in four ways: (1) the public health authority being exercised must be prescribed by law; (2) the authority must be applied in a non-discriminatory manner; (3) due process of law must be accorded before an individual's rights are infringed, unless an emergency situation exists, and then due process should be accorded as soon as possible after infringement; and (4) the infringement of rights must be necessary from both a scientific and a public health standpoint, and the infringement must be the least restrictive possible under the circumstances.[35]

In the twentieth century, the exercise of public health powers that infringe individual rights faded in developed countries as public health and healthcare systems improved. Bioterrorism raises the possibility that these powers must be dusted off and used in ways that again encroach on individual civil and political rights. The treaty disciplines outlined above have not been prominent in either public health or international human rights law in the last fifty years. The anthrax attacks, and the specter of bioterrorism involving highly communicable pathogens such as smallpox, place the tension between effective public health responses to infectious disease emergencies and civil rights and liberties high on the agenda of public health, constitutional law, and international law.

G. International Law and Trade in Goods: Fear versus Science?

After the anthrax attack in Florida, Russia banned the importation of livestock and meat from Florida out of fear that such products may be infected with anthrax.[36] Florida disapproved of this Russian trade restriction because Florida officials did not think that the restriction was justified scientifically.[37] Russia eventually lifted its ban after meetings between US and Russian agricultural officials.[38]

This episode indicates that bioterrorism may affect international law on trade in goods. In the World Trade Organization ("WTO"), for example, member states have

35. Siracusa Principles on the Limitation and Derogation of Provisions in the International Covenant on Civil and Political Rights, UN Doc E/CN.4/1984/4 (1984); Lawrence O. Gostin and Zita Lazzarini, *Human Rights and Public Health in the AIDS Pandemic* 47 (Oxford 1997) (discussing Siracusa Principles); David P. Fidler, *International Law and Infectious Diseases* 169, 174–175 (Clarendon 1999) (discussing disciplines on public health infringements on civil and political rights).
36. *Florida—Russia Bans Meat From State, Officials Say*, LA Times A22 (Oct 19, 2001).
37. Evan Perez, *Questions of Security: Florida Officials Defend Food Safety After Russian Ban*, Wall St J A9 (Oct 19, 2001).
38. *Russia Lifts Ban on Florida's Meat, Livestock*, 73 Feedstuffs 5 (Oct 29, 2001).

the right to restrict trade in order to protect human, animal, and plant life or health.[39] The exercise of this right is subject, however, to scientific and trade-related disciplines. The scientific disciplines require sufficient scientific evidence and a scientific risk assessment supporting trade-restricting health measures.[40] Further, WTO member states must base trade-restricting health measures on applicable international standards, unless they have scientific evidence that such standards are inadequate.[41] The trade-related disciplines mean that trade-restricting health measures must be non-discriminatory and the least trade restrictive measures possible.[42]

These rules were not designed to deal with the potential adverse trade consequences of bioterrorism. The rules remain relevant in the bioterrorism context, however, because they seek to ensure that trade-restricting health measures protect health, are based on scientific opinion rather than fear, and minimize the impact of *bona fide* measures on flows of international trade. Although Russia has not joined the WTO, the United States addressed Russia's ban against livestock and meat imports from Florida as though the dispute would be handled under the Agreement on the Application of Sanitary and Phytosanitary Measures ("SPS Agreement"). The United States pointed out that Russia's ban exceeded applicable international standards set by the Office International des Epizooties ("OIE") for dealing with anthrax.[43] The SPS Agreement recognizes the OIE as the standard-setting international organization for animal health.[44] In other words, Russia's ban was not justified by the scientific standards internationally recognized as applicable in this context.

This episode reinforces the importance of science and public health as a component of international legal analysis. Bioterrorism is a great producer of fear. International trade law on protecting human, animal, and plant life and health seeks to ensure that science and public health principles drive government decisions rather than fear or protectionism disguised as fear. The anthrax attacks underscore the importance of these disciplines in international trade law.

---

39. General Agreement on Tariffs and Trade, Apr 15, 1994, Marrakesh Agreement Establishing the World Trade Organization, Final Act Embodying the Results of the Uruguay Round, Annex 1A, art XX(b); and Agreement on the Application of Sanitary and Phytosanitary Measures ("SPS Agreement"), Apr 15, 1994, Marrakesh Agreement Establishing the World Trade Organization, Final Act Embodying the Results of the Uruguay Round of Multilateral Trade Negotiations, Annex 1A-4.

40. SPS Agreement at art 2.2 (cited in note 39) (scientific evidence requirement) and art 5.1 (risk assessment requirement).

41. Id at art 3.1 and 3.3.

42. Id at art 2.3, 5.5, and 5.6.

43. *Russia Lifts Ban on Florida's Meat, Livestock*, 73 Feedstuffs 5 (cited in note 38).

44. SPS Agreement at Annex A(1) (cited in note 39).

H. INTERNATIONAL LAW AND INTELLECTUAL PROPERTY RIGHTS: IS BIOTERRORISM BAD FOR PATENTS?

The anthrax attacks generated an enormous increase in demand from federal and state governments and the private sector for ciprofloxacin ("Cipro"), the antibiotic of choice to treat anthrax. Cipro is still under patent protection, and the holder of the patent is Bayer, a German pharmaceutical company. In response to the public health emergency caused by the anthrax attacks, Canada licensed the generic production of Cipro without Bayer's permission, effectively overriding Bayer's patent, and the United States threatened to do the same.[45] The US government was concerned about Bayer's ability to meet demand as well as the prices Bayer charged for its patented antibiotic.

The controversy over whether to use a compulsory license to manufacture generic Cipro fed into an acrimonious global debate about the ability of developing countries to use compulsory licenses to manufacture generic antiretrovirals in the face of growing HIV/AIDS epidemics. Prior to the anthrax attacks, the United States (largely supported by the European Union) fought developing countries and non-governmental organizations tooth-and-nail to prevent developing countries from utilizing compulsory licenses to manufacture generic antiretrovirals and other patented infectious disease drugs. Activists for greater access to HIV/AIDS therapies in developing countries have not missed the hypocrisy revealed by the US willingness to break a patent in the context of bioterrorism at home compared with US opposition to developing countries using compulsory licenses to help deal with diseases ravaging many developing countries on a historically unprecedented scale.

The WTO's Agreement on Trade-Related Aspects of Intellectual Property Rights ("TRIPS") allows WTO member states to use compulsory licenses to deal with public health emergencies.[46] The anthrax attacks demonstrate that bioterrorism can trigger a public health emergency that may require governments to break patents. At the same time, the scale of the public health emergency in the United States caused by anthrax (twenty-two cases with five deaths) pales in comparison to the millions of HIV/AIDS-related deaths developing countries are suffering annually.[47] Surely, if the

---

45. Gardiner Harris, *Questions of Security: Bayer Is Accused of Profiteering on Cipro*, Wall St J A6 (Oct 26, 2001) (reporting Secretary of Health and Human Services Tommy Thompson's "threat to defy Bayer's patent unless the company lowered its price"); Amy Harmon and Robert Pear, *Canada Overrides Patent for Cipro to Treat Anthrax*, NY Times A1 (Oct 19, 2001).

46. WTO Agreement on Trade-Related Aspects of Intellectual Property Rights ("TRIPS"), art 31. On TRIPS and health, see Carlos Correa, *Unfair Competition Under the TRIPS Agreement: Protection of Data Submitted for the Registration of Pharmaceuticals*, 3 Chi J Intl L 69 (2002); Alan O. Sykes, *TRIPS, Pharmaceuticals, Developing Countries, and the Doha "Solution,"* 3 Chi J Intl L 47 (2002).

47. As of November 16, 2001, the anthrax attacks caused twenty-two total cases of anthrax (ten cases of inhalational anthrax with four fatalities and twelve cases of cutaneous anthrax with no fatalities). *Update: Investigation of Bioterrorism-Related Anthrax, 2001*, 50 Morbidity and Mortality Weekly Report

United States can legitimately claim that the anthrax attacks trigger the right to use compulsory licenses under TRIPS, then developing countries can legitimately claim that HIV/AIDS and other infectious disease crises, such as tuberculosis and malaria, are public health emergencies that allow them to use compulsory licenses.

Bioterrorism in the United States, and the US government's threat to break the patent on Cipro, affected the global debate on developing countries' ability to use compulsory licenses under TRIPS. At the WTO Ministerial Meeting in Doha, Qatar in November 2001, WTO member states issued a declaration on TRIPS and public health that supported the position of developing countries and repudiated the previous stance of the United States and the European Union.[48] As the *Wall Street Journal* stated, this declaration constituted a "landmark shift" for the United States and European Union.[49] The anthrax attacks are not the only factor that explains this dramatic development,[50] but the US attitude on patent protection in the bioterrorism context contributed to the political and legal retreat of the United States from its previous hard-line position on patent protection under TRIPS.[51]

1008 (Nov 16, 2001). According to UNAIDS, in 2001 the total number of HIV/AIDS deaths was three million and the number of infections was forty million. UNAIDS, *AIDS Epidemic Update: December 2000* 3 (UNAIDS 2000), available online at <http://www.unaids.org/worldaidsday/2001/Epiupdate2001/EPIupdate2001_en.doc> (visited Mar 24, 2002).

48. World Trade Organization, Declaration on the TRIPS Agreement and Public Health, WT/MIN(01)DEC/W/2, Doc No 01-5770 at para 5(c) (2001) ("Each Member has the right to determine what constitutes a national emergency or other circumstances of extreme urgency, it being understood that public health crises, including those relating to HIV/AIDS, tuberculosis, malaria and other epidemics, can represent a national emergency or other circumstances of extreme urgency.").

49. Helene Cooper and Geoff Winestock, *Tough Talkers: Poor Nations Win Gains in Global Trade Deal, as U.S. Compromises*, Wall St J A1 (Nov 15, 2001).

50. Prominent among the other factors forcing this astonishing retreat of the United States and European Union was the global campaign for access to essential medicines launched by non-governmental organizations, such as Médecins Sans Frontières. See Médecins Sans Frontières, *Campaign for Access to Essential Medicines*, available online at <http://www.accessmed-msf.org> (visited Mar 24, 2002); Ellen 't Hoen, *TRIPS, Pharmaceutical Patents, and Access to Essential Medicines: A Long Way From Seattle to Doha*, 3 Chi J Intl L 27 (2002). Action at the domestic and constitutional legal levels has also played a role in the access debate. See Mary Ann Torres, *The Human Right to Health, National Courts, and Access to HIV/AIDS Treatment: A Case Study from Venezuela*, 3 Chi J Intl L 105 (2002).

51. Geoff Winestock and Helene Cooper, *WTO Envoys Agree to Ease Access to Key Drugs—Public Health Outweighs Patents as Deal Paves Way for Broad Trade Talks*, Wall St J A17 (Nov 13, 2001) (noting importance of US and Canadian threats to break Cipro patent in the global battle over drug patents).

IV. Deeper Concerns: Will Bioterrorism Reshape Global Public Health?

Analyzing the relevance of the anthrax attacks to various international legal areas is important, but such bioterrorism also generates concerns that touch upon the future of national and global public health policy. The anthrax attacks have the potential to affect the direction and content of national and global infectious disease control, and this potential impact may not be for the better.

A. National Public Health and Bioterrorism: Productive Synergy or Faustian Bargain?

In my work on the interface between public health and bioterrorism prior to the anthrax attacks, I noticed tension in the public health community about how to deal with the growing focus on bioterrorism.[52] This tension concerned how bioterrorism preparedness efforts may affect the overall public health mission. On the one hand, public health experts perceived that bioterrorism was a concern and sensed that addressing bioterrorism might bring more attention and resources to a public health system suffering from political and financial neglect. On the other hand, public health experts worried that the bioterrorism bandwagon might misdirect public health priorities and spending and adversely affect the public health system in the long run. The consensus attitude before the anthrax attacks was that public health should support bioterrorism preparedness and build the best public health system possible to deal with any infectious disease outbreak.

The anthrax attacks will profoundly affect the strategy to craft synergy between bioterrorism preparedness and public health capabilities. The acts of bioterrorism demonstrated how the nation's public health system is important for national security. In the aftermath of anthrax, the national security community in Washington, DC may take control of public health by making bioterrorism the most important public health priority. We may witness a shift from a weak national commitment to public health to a strong effort on homeland security, in which public health plays an important part. The bioterrorism agenda, as determined by national and homeland security concerns, will dominate and drive the future direction of US public health. The frenetic activities in Washington, DC in the aftermath of the anthrax attacks to improve US public health for purposes of bioterrorism provide powerful evidence to support this observation.

52. Edward P. Richards, *Bioterrorism and the Use of Fear in Public Health*, presented to ACLME Health Law Teachers Conference, Case Western Reserve School of Law, June 2000, available online at <http://biotech.law.umkc.edu/blaw/bt/epr_bioterror01.pdf> (visited Mar 24, 2002); Elizabeth Fee and Theodore M. Brown, *Preemptive Biopreparedness: Can We Learn Anything from History?*, 91 Am J Pub Health 721 (2001).

Whether the linkage between public health and homeland security produces the synergy public health experts tried to craft before the anthrax attacks remains to be seen. I suspect that public health officials recognize the national security importance of public health *and* worry that bioterrorism will transform US public health in unwelcome and unanticipated ways. Creating the synergy in the post-anthrax environment will require that the national security, homeland security, and public health communities develop a partnership of equals. This partnership requires learning and adjustment by all sides, but public health has more to fear because of its historical weakness and obscurity compared to the power and resources the federal government possesses for national security and the money and political capital being poured into homeland security.

B. Global Public Health and Bioterrorism: Whither the United States?

The global public health debacle of HIV/AIDS and the general global crisis in infectious diseases led experts in the late 1990s and early 2000s to argue that the United States must become more engaged in global public health.[53] Sometimes these arguments connected public health with national security by claiming that both naturally-occurring infectious diseases and bioterrorism constituted a national security threat to the United States.[54] By and large, the arguments that infectious diseases represented a national security threat made little impact in Washington, DC. The only arguments that resonated in Washington related to bioterrorism and biological weapons proliferation, which represented the most traditional form of national security threats.[55] In the wake of the anthrax attacks, the White House and Congress solidified prior spending patterns by preparing to spend billions of dollars for homeland defense against bioterrorism.[56] This mounting national and homeland security effort will dominate US attitudes toward global public health for the

53. See, for example, Jordan S. Kassalow, *Why Health is Important to U.S. Foreign Policy*, Council of Foreign Relations and Milbank Memorial Fund Report (May 2001), available online at <http://www.milbank.org/Foreignpolicy.html> (visited Mar 24, 2002).

54. National Intelligence Council, *The Global Infectious Disease Threat and Its Implications for the United States*, NIE 99-17D (2000).

55. Compare, for example, the sums Congress appropriates annually for WMD defense, see Amy E. Smithson and Leslie-Anne Levy, *Ataxia: The Chemical and Biological Terrorism Threat and the US Response* xix (Henry L. Stimson Center, Report No 35) (October 2000) (stating that the federal budget for defense against WMD terrorism in fiscal 2000 was $1.4 billion), with the US contribution to the UN-brokered Global Fund to Fight HIV/AIDS, Tuberculosis, and Malaria, see Global AIDS and Tuberculosis Relief Act, Pub L 106-264, § 141 (2000), codified at 22 USCA § 6841 (2001) (appropriating $200 million for fiscal years 2001 and 2002 for the Global Fund).

56. For example, President Bush's proposed fiscal year 2003 budget includes $5.9 billion for domestic bioterrorism preparedness, a four-fold increase from previous spending levels. Judith Miller, *Bush to Request A Major Increase in Bioterror Funds*, NY Times A1 (Feb 4, 2002).

foreseeable future. We may witness a shift in the United States from a weak global perspective on naturally occurring infectious diseases that largely affect other countries to a strong national concern about the malevolent use of pathogenic microbes against Americans. US engagement in global public health will, thus, not stray far from the objective of protecting the homeland from bioterrorism, as evidenced by US participation in the Ottawa Plan, even though millions of people in developing countries will continue to suffer and die annually from infectious diseases unrelated to bioterrorism.

As the victim of bioterrorism, the United States understandably needs to focus on homeland defense and the public health contribution to that objective. As people experienced with the bioterrorism debate prior to the anthrax attacks understood, US vulnerability to bioterrorism is enormous. Federal and state governments have almost endless intelligence, law enforcement, and public health work to do to protect Americans from bioterrorism. The combination of the September 11th violence and the anthrax attacks leaves the US government with no choice but to focus energetically on a comprehensive homeland defense.

The focus on homeland defense will filter through to US attitudes toward the role of international law in public health. The United States will attempt to use international law to fight bioterrorism rather than to grapple with the global crisis in naturally occurring infectious diseases. Making sure bioterrorism is criminalized globally will supercede the need to build a global infectious disease surveillance system. Given the fusion of public health and national security in the wake of bioterrorism, the United States will not hesitate to use its power, influence, and resources to make the fight against bioterrorism central to its outlook on the role of international cooperation and international law in global public health.

Infectious disease problems in the developing world will be even less important to the United States in the post-anthrax world than they were previously. The lack of US leadership and engagement with global public health will handicap efforts by other states, international organizations, and non-governmental organizations to advance multilateral cooperation on global public health problems. Even if the 2001 anthrax attacks prove to be an isolated phenomenon, the experience of bioterrorism on US soil will distract US attention from traditional public health challenges around the world. The slow, frustrating, and incomplete progress made in raising US awareness about the global crisis in infectious diseases in the 1990s may now be another victim of bioterrorism in the United States.

V. CONCLUSION

Revolutionary developments have periodically transformed the relationship between international law and public health, especially infectious disease control. The triumph of "germ theory" in the late nineteenth century triggered the establishment of a great body of international law on public health issues. Sanitary-reform movements and the later development of vaccines and antibiotics gave states and international health organizations powerful new weapons in the global battle against infectious diseases.

The latest revolutions have, however, been more sinister for global infectious disease control—the HIV/AIDS pandemic, emerging and re-emerging infectious diseases, and the rise of anti-microbial resistance. As I have argued elsewhere, these and other developments simultaneously raise the profile of international law and create great uncertainty about international law's contribution to global infectious disease control.[57] To this parade of public health horribles we now must add bioterrorism. The prior debates about whether the threat of bioterrorism was real and whether international law should play a role in addressing the threat have vanished in the death, illness, and terror inflicted by the anthrax attacks. Where these acts of bioterrorism take the relationship between public health and international law in the future remains to be seen; but at the moment, the portents are not good.

57. Fidler, *International Law and Global Infectious Disease Control* at 39 (cited in note 24).

Copyright Acknowledgments

John Duffy, "Smallpox and the Indians in the American Colonies," *Bulletin of the History of Medicine* 25 (1951): 324–341. Reprinted with the permission of Johns Hopkins University Press.

George W. Christopher, Theodore J. Cieslak, Julie A. Pavlin and Edward M. Eitzen Jr. "Biological Warfare: A Historical Perspective," *Journal of the American Medical Association* 278 (August 6, 1997): 412–417. Copyright © 1997 The American Medical Association.

Elizabeth Fee and Theodore M. Brown, "Preemptive Biopreparedness: Can We Learn Anything from History?" *American Journal of Public Health* 91 (2001): 721–726. Reprinted with the permission of the American Public Health Association.

Monica Schoch-Spana, "Implications of Pandemic Influenza for Bioterrorism Response," *Clinical Infectious Diseases* 31 (2000): 1409–1413. Reprinted with the permission of University of Chicago Press.

William H. Neinast, "United States Use of Biological Warfare," *Military Law Review* 24 (1964): 1–9, 41–45. Reprinted with the permission of U.S. Army Judge Advocate General's Corps.

Barton J. Bernstein, "The Birth of the U. S. Biological-Warfare Program," *Scientific American* 256 (1987): 116–121. Reprinted with the permission of Scientific America, Inc.

David L. Huxsoll, Cheryl D. Parrot and William C. Patrick III, "Medicine in Defense Against Biological Warfare" *Journal of the American Medical Association* 262 (August 4, 1989): 677–679. Copyright © 1989 The American Medical Association.

Jonathan B. Tucker, "Gene Wars," *Foreign Policy* 57 (Winter 1984–1985): 58–79. Reprinted with the permission of *Foreign Policy*. Copyright © (1984/1985) by the Carnegie Endowment for International Peace.

Eric J. McFadden, "The Second Review Conference of the Biological Weapons Convention: One Step Forward, Many More to Go," *Stanford Journal of International Law* 24 (Fall 1987): 85–109. Reprinted with the permission of the Stanford University School of Law, and the author. Copyright © 1987 by the Board of Trustees of the Leland Stanford Junior University.

Leonard A. Cole, "The Specter of Biological Weapons," *Scientific*

American 275 (December 1996): 60–65. Reprinted with the permission of Scientific American Inc.

Joan Stephenson, "Confronting a Biological Armageddon: Experts Tackle Prospect of Bioterrorism," *Journal of the American Medical Association* 276 (August 7, 1997): 349–351. Copyright © 1997 The American Medical Association.

"Bioterrorism in our Midst?" *Security Management* (November 1, 1997): 12. Reprinted with the permission of American Society for Industrial Security.

Jonathan B. Tucker, "Chemical/Biological Terrorism: Coping with a New Threat," *Politics and the Life Sciences* 15 (September 1996): 167–183. Reprinted with the permission of the Association for Politics and the Life Sciences.

Jack Woodall, "Stalking the Next Epidemic: ProMED Tracks Emerging Diseases,"

Public Health Reports 112 (January/February 1997): 78–82. Reprinted with the permission of the U.S. Public Health Service.

James C. Pile, John D. Malone, Edward M. Eitzen and Arthur M. Friedlander. "Anthrax as a Potential Biological Warfare Agent," *Archives of Internal Medicine* 158 (1998): 429–434. Reprinted with the permission of American Medical Association.

Peter Pringle, "Bioterrorism," *The Nation* 267 (November 9, 1998): 11–17. Reprinted with permission from The Nation Magazine. Copyright © The Nation Company, L.P.

Richard Wise, "Bioterrorism: Thinking the Unthinkable," *The Lancet* 351 (May 9, 1998): 1378. Reprinted with the permission of the Lancet Ltd.

"The Biological Weapons Anti-Terrorism Act of 1989," 104 *Stat.* 201–203

George H. W. Bush, "Statement on Signing the Biological Weapons Anti-Terrorism Act of 1989," May 22, 1989.

Melissa A. O'Loughlin, "Terrorism: The Problem and the Solution—The Comprehensive Prevention Act of 1995," *Journal of Legislation/Notre Dame University Law School*, 22 (1996): 103–120. Reprinted with the permission of the University of Notre Dame.

Elizabeth A. Palmer and Keith Perine, "Provisions of the Anti-Terrorism Bill," *Congressional Quarterly Weekly* (February 2, 2002): 329, 336–338. Reprinted with the permission of Congressional Quarterly Inc.

James R. Ferguson, "Biological Weapons and U.S. Law," *Journal of the American Medical Association* 278 (August 6, 1997): 357–360. Copyright © 1997 The American Medical Association.

Barry Kellman, "Biological Terrorism: Legal Measures for Preventing

Catastrophe," *Harvard Journal of Law & Public Policy* 24 (Spring 2001): 417–424, 463–488 [excerpt]. Reprinted with the permission of the Harvard Journal of Law and Public Policy, Inc.

Matthew Linkie, "The Defense Threat Reduction Agency: A Note on the United States' Approach to the Threat of Chemical and Biological Warfare," *Journal of Contemporary Health, Law & Policy* 16 (Summer 2000): 531–547. Reprinted with the permission of University of Maryland, School of Law.

Heather E. Dagen, "Bioterrorism: Perfectly Legal," *Catholic University Law Review* 49 (Winter 2000): 535–573. Reprinted with the permission of the *Catholic University Law Review.*

Victoria V. Sutton, "A Precarious 'Hot Zone:' The President's Plan to Control Bioterrorism," *Military Law Review* 164 (2000): 135–145. Reprinted with the permission of U.S. Army Judge Advocate General's Corps.

OLR Research Report, "Summary of U.S.A. Patriot Act." (November 9, 2001): 1–4.

"U.S.A. Patriot Act Boosts Government Powers While Cutting Back on Traditional Checks and Balances" of 2001 Enhancing Domestic Security Against Terrorism: An ACLU Legislative Analysis. November 1, 2001: 1–4.

Juliette N. Kayyem, "U. S. Preparations for Biological Terrorism: Legal Limitations and the Need for Planning," *Belfer Center for Science and International Affairs, Harvard University School of Government*, BCSIA Discussion Paper 2001–4, March 2001. Reprinted with the permission of Belfer Center For Science and International Affairs.

David P. Fidler, "The Malevolent Use of Microbes and the Rule of Law: Legal Challenges Presented by Bioterrorism," *Clinical Infectious Diseases* 33 (2001): 686–689. Reprinted with the permission of University of Chicago Press.

Michael P. Scharf, "Clear and Present Danger: Enforcing the International Ban on Biological and Chemical Weapons Through Sanctions, Use of Force, and Criminalization," *Michigan Journal of International Law* 20 (Spring 1999): 477–521. Reprinted with the permission of the *Michigan Journal of International Law.*

Graham S. Pearson, "The Regime to Prevent Biological Weapons: Opportunities for a Safer, Healthier, More Prosperous World" [Biological and Toxin Weapons Convention Paper], 1–4, 21–29. Reprinted with the permission of the Biological and Toxin Weapons Convention Paper.

David P. Fidler, "Bioterrorism, Public Health, and International Law," *Chicago Journal of International Law* 3 (Spring 2002): 7–26. Reprinted with the permission of University of Chicago Law School.

For Product Safety Concerns and Information please contact our EU
representative GPSR@taylorandfrancis.com
Taylor & Francis Verlag GmbH, Kaufingerstraße 24, 80331 München, Germany

www.ingramcontent.com/pod-product-compliance
Lightning Source LLC
Chambersburg PA
CBHW071224290426
44108CB00013B/1279

9780367642464